PC28g

The Ethics of Public Health

The International Library of Medicine, Ethics and Law
Series Editor: Michael Freeman

Titles in the Series:

Death, Dying and the Ending of Life, Volumes I and II
Margaret P. Battin, Leslie P. Francis and Bruce M. Landesman

Abortion
Belinda Bennett

Health, Rights and Globalisation
Belinda Bennett

Health and Human Rights
Rebecca Cook and Charles Ngwena

Children, Medicine and the Law
Michael Freeman

Ethics and Medical Decision-Making
Michael Freeman

The Ethics of Public Health, Volumes I and II
Michael Freeman

Mental Illness, Medicine and Law
Martin Lyon Levine

The Elderly
Martin Lyon Levine

Genetics and Gene Therapy
Sheila A.M. McLean

Rights and Resources
Frances H. Miller

Organ and Tissue Transplantation
David Price

AIDS: Society, Ethics and Law
Udo Schüklenk

Women, Medicine, Ethics and the Law
Susan Sherwin and Barbara Parish

Legal and Ethical Issues in Human Reproduction
Bonnie Steinbock

Medical Practice and Malpractice
Harvey Teff

Human Experimentation and Research
George F. Tomossy and David N. Weisstub

Neuroethics
Paul Root Wolpe

The Ethics of Public Health, Volume II

Edited by

Michael Freeman F.B.A.

University College London, UK

ASHGATE

Published by
Ashgate Publishing Limited
Wey Court East
Union Road
Farnham
Surrey GU9 7PT
England

Ashgate Publishing Company
Suite 420
101 Cherry Street
Burlington, VT 05401-4405
USA

Ashgate website: http://www.ashgate.com

British Library Cataloguing in Publication Data
The ethics of public health.
Volumes 1 and 2. – (The international library of medicine, ethics and law)
1. Public health–Moral and ethical aspects. 2. Medical policy–Moral and ethical aspects.
I. Series II. Freeman, Michael D. A.
174.2'9444-dc22

Library of Congress Control Number: 2009924480

ISBN: 978-0-7546-2605-3

Printed and bound in Great Britain by
TJ International Ltd, Padstow, Cornwall

Contents

Acknowledgements

The editor and publishers wish to thank the following for permission to use copyright material.

British Medical Journal for the essays: Peter A. Singer, Solomon R. Benatar, Mark Bernstein, Abdullah S, Daar, Bernard M. Dickens, Susan K. MacRae, Ross E.G. Upshur, Linda Wright and Randi Zlotnik Shaul (2003), 'Ethics and SARS: Lessons from Toronto', *British Medical Journal*, **327**, pp. 1342–44. Copyright © 2003 British Medical Journal; Ruairí Brugha and Gill Walt (2001), 'A Global Health Fund: A Leap of Faith?', *British Medical Journal*, **323**, pp. 152–54. Copyright © 2001 British Medical Journal.

Case Western Reserve University, School of Law for the essays: George J. Annas (2003), 'Blinded by Bioterrorism: Public Health and Liberty in the 21st Century', *Health Matrix*, **13**, pp. 33–70. Copyright © 2003 Case Western Reserve University, School of Law; Wendy E. Parmet (2003), 'Quarantine Redux: Bioterrorism, AIDS and the Curtailment of Individual Liberty in the Name of Public Health', *Health Matrix*, **13**, pp. 85–116. Copyright © 2003 Case Western Reserve University, School of Law.

Elsevier Limited for the essays: Richard Horton (2001), 'Public Health: A Neglected Counterterrorist Measure', *Lancet*, **358**, pp. 1112–13. Copyright © 2001 Elsevier Ltd; Sarah Macfarlane, Mary Racelis and Florence Muli-Musiime (2000), 'Public Health in Developing Countries', *Lancet*, **356**, pp. 841–46. Copyright © 2000 Elsevier Ltd.

Georgetown Law Journal for the essay: Lisa Heinzerling (2008), 'Climate Change, Human Health, and the Post-Cautionary Principle', *Georgetown Law Journal*, **96**, pp. 445–60. Copyright © 2008 Lisa Heinzerling.

John Wiley and Sons for the essays: David P. Fidler (2003), 'SARS: Political Pathology of the First Post-Westphalian Pathogen', *Journal of Law, Medicine and Ethics*, **31**, pp. 485–505. Copyright © 2003 John Wiley and Sons; Heather H. Horton, James J. Misrahi, Gene W. Matthews and Paula L. Kocher (2002), 'Critical Biological Agents: Disease Reporting as a Tool for Determining Bioterrorism Preparedness', *Journal of Law, Medicine and Ethics*, **30**, pp. 262–66. Copyright © 2002 John Wiley and Sons; James G. Hodge, Jr. (2002), 'Bioterrorism Law and Policy: Critical Choices in Public Health', *Journal of Law, Medicine and Ethics*, **30**, pp. 254–61. Copyright © 2002 John Wiley and Sons; Jonathan D. Moreno (2004), 'Bioethics and the National Security State', *Journal of Law, Medicine and Ethics*, **32**, pp. 198–208. Copyright © 2004 John Wiley and Sons; Lawrence O. Gostin (2004), 'Pandemic Influenza: Public Health Preparedness for the Next Global Health Emergency', *Journal of Law, Medicine and Ethics*, **32**, pp. 565–73. Copyright © 2004 John Wiley and Sons; Jaro Kotalik (2005), 'Preparing for an Influenza Pandemic: Ethical Issues', *Bioethics*, **19**, pp. 422–31. Copyright © 2005 John Wiley and Sons; Stephen Wilkinson (1999), 'Smokers' Rights to Health Care:

Why the "Restoration Argument" is a Moralising Wolf in a Liberal Sheep's Clothing', *Journal of Applied Philosophy*, **16**, pp. 255–69. Copyright © 1999 John Wiley and Sons; Timothy D. Lytton (2004), 'Using Litigation to Make Public Health Policy: Theoretical and Empirical Challenges in Assessing Product Liability, Tobacco, and Gun Litigation', *Journal of Law, Medicine and Ethics*, **32**, pp. 556–64. Copyright © 2004 John Wiley and Sons; Tim Dare (1998), 'Mass Immunisation Programmes: Some Philosophical Issues', *Bioethics*, **12**, pp. 125–49. Copyright © 1998 John Wiley and Sons; Thomas May (2005), 'Public Communication, Risk Perception, and the Viability of Preventive Vaccination against Communicable Diseases', *Bioethics*, **19**, pp. 407–21. Copyright © 2005 John Wiley and Sons; Angus Dawson (2005), 'The Determination of "Best Interests" in Relation to Childhood Vaccinations', *Bioethics*, **19**, pp. 188–205. Copyright © 2005 John Wiley and Sons; Bartha Maria Knoppers (2005), 'Biobanking: International Norms', *Journal of Law, Medicine and Ethics*, **33**, pp. 7–14. Copyright © 2005 John Wiley and Sons; Lori B. Andrews (2005), 'Harnessing the Benefits of Biobanks', *Journal of Law, Medicine and Ethics*, **33**, pp. 22–30. Copyright © 2005 John Wiley and Sons; Fabienne Peter (2001), 'Health Equity and Social Justice', *Journal of Applied Philosophy*, **18**, pp. 159–70. Copyright © 2001 John Wiley and Sons; Paul Farmer and Nicole Gastineau Campos (2004), 'Rethinking Medical Ethics: A View from Below', *Developing World Bioethics*, **4**, pp. 17–41. Copyright © 2004 John Wiley and Sons; Rebecca J. Cook and Bernard M. Dickens (2002), 'The Injustice of Unsafe Motherhood', *Developing World Bioethics*, **2**, pp. 64–81. Copyright © 2002 John Wiley and Sons; Solomon R. Benatar (2001), 'Justice and Medical Research: A Global Perspective', *Bioethics*, **15**, pp. 333–40. Copyright © 2001 John Wiley and Sons; David P. Fidler and Lawrence O. Gostin (2006), 'The New International Health Regulations: An Historic Development for International Law and Public Health', *Journal of Law, Medicine and Ethics*, **34**, pp. 85–94. Copyright © 2006 John Wiley and Sons.

MIT Press for the essay: Ronald Bayer and James Colgrove (2003), 'Rights and Dangers: Bioterrorism and the Ideologies of Public Health', in Jonathan D. Moreno (ed.), *In the Wake of Terror: Medicine and Morality in a Time of Crisis*, MIT Press: Cambridge, MA, pp. 51–74. Copyright © 2003 MIT Press.

Oxford University Press for the essays: Dan W. Brock (2004), 'Ethical Issues in the Use of Cost Effectiveness Analysis for the Prioritisation of Health Care Resources', in Sudhir Anand, Fabienne Peter and Amartya Sen (eds), *Public Health, Ethics and Equity*, Oxford: Oxford University Press, pp. 201–23. Copyright © 2004 Oxford University Press; Simon Szreter and Michael Woolcock (2003), 'Health by Association? Social Capital, Social Theory, and the Political Economy of Public Health', *International Journal of Epidemiology*, **33**, pp. 650–67. Copyright © 2003 Oxford University Press.

Taylor & Francis for the essays: Kelley Lee and Anthony B. Zwi (1996), 'A Global Political Economy Approach to AIDS: Ideology, Interests and Implications', *New Political Economy*, **1**, pp. 355–73. Copyright © 1996 Taylor & Francis; Evan Willis (2002), 'Public Health and the "New" Genetics: Balancing Individual and Collective Outcomes', *Critical Public Health*, **12**, pp. 139–51. Copyright © 2002 Taylor & Francis.

The American Public Health Association for the essay: Muin J. Khoury and the Genetics Working Group (1996), 'From Genes to Public Health: The Applications of Genetic Technology in Disease Prevention', *American Journal of Public Health*, **86**, pp. 1717–22. Copyright © 1996 The American Public Health Association.

The Hastings Center for the essay: Mark A. Rothstein (2005), 'Genetic Exceptionalism and Legislative Pragmatism', *Hastings Center Report*, **35**, pp. 27–33. Copyright © 2005 The Hastings Center.

The University of Chicago Press for the essay: Robert E. Goodin (1989), 'The Ethics of Smoking', *Ethics*, **99**, pp. 574–624. Copyright © 1989 The University of Chicago Press.

Yale University Press for the essay: Scott Burris and Lawrence O. Gostin (1998), 'Genetic Screening from a Public Health Perspective: Some Lessons from the HIV Experience', in Mark A. Rothstein (ed.), *Genetic Secrets: Protecting Privacy and Confidentiality in the Genetic Era*, New Haven: Yale University Press, pp. 137–58. Copyright © 1998 Yale University Press.

Every effort has been made to trace all the copyright holders, but if any have been inadvertently overlooked the publishers will be pleased to make the necessary arrangement at the first opportunity.

Series Preface

Few academic disciplines have developed with such pace in recent years as bioethics. And because the subject crosses so many disciplines, important writing is to be found in a range of books and journals, access to the whole of which is likely to elude all but the most committed of scholars. The International Library of Medicine, Ethics and Law is designed to assist the scholarly endeavour by providing in accessible volumes a compendium of basic materials drawn from the most significant periodical literature. Each volume contains essays of central theoretical importance in its subject area, and each throws light on important bioethical questions in the world today. The series as a whole makes available an extensive range of valuable material (the standard 'classics' and the not-so-standard) and should prove of inestimable value to those involved in the research, teaching and study of medicine, ethics and law. The fifteen volumes together – each with introductions and bibliographies – are a library in themselves – an indispensable resource in a world in which even the best-stocked library is unlikely to cover the range of materials contained within these volumes.

It remains for me to thank the editors who have pursued their task with commitment, insight and enthusiasm, to thank also the hard-working staff at Ashgate – theirs is a mammoth enterprise – and to thank my secretary, Jacqui Bennett, for the enormous assistance she has given me in bringing the series from idea to reality.

MICHAEL FREEMAN
Series Editor
Faculty of Laws
University College London

Introduction

Volume II starts with six case studies. The first of these is the SARS crisis.

The SARS Crisis

SARS (Severe Acute Respiratory Syndrome) appeared in November 2002, was declared contained by the World Health Organization (WHO) on 5 July 2003, and killed 812 people, infecting more than 8,400.[1] It prompted alarm and reaction totally disproportionate to the death and illness it caused (see, for example, Eichelberger, 2007).

As Gostin, Bayer and Fairchild (2003) point out, in an essay not included in this collection, three values involving the ethics of public health were brought into tension: (i) the duty to protect the public; (ii) individual rights of privacy; and (iii) individual rights of liberty. The crisis raised issues of surveillance and privacy (see also Bayer and Fairchild, 2002, reproduced as Chapter 27 in Volume I), of isolation and quarantine (see also Volume I, Part X), and of the ethics of travel advisories and restrictions. The implications of these policies and practices are pinpointed by Gostin, Bayer and Fairchild (2003).

In Chapter 1 David Fidler observes that SARS reintroduced societies to 'long-dormant, large-scale isolation and quarantine practices, raising questions about balancing public health and individual rights' (p. 3). His essay examines 'governance' issues that SARS raises for public health in its post-Westphalian context (see also Volume I, Part VI). Fidler explains Westphalian international politics, and more significantly Westphalian public health. This was premised on the principle that states are the only legitimate actors for governance purposes. This approach, he argues, is bankrupt. What has emerged instead is 'global health governance' (p. 6). This includes states and intergovernmental organizations, but also NGOs and multinational corporations. A second break from Westphalian public health is the pursuit of global public goods for health – that is, public goods or services the benefits of which are 'globally accessible' (p. 7).

The epidemiological profile of SARS means 'it would have presented a crisis even if infectious disease control remained mired in the Westphalian approach' (p. 8). It was, however, the 'first serious challenge to a governance approach that deviates from the traditional model' (p. 8). But China, the epicentre of SARS, 'acted Westphalian in a post-Westphalian world' (p. 8). Although, it seems to have learnt its lesson if its response to the 2008 earthquake – much more open to world scrutiny and help – is to be understood. Fidler examines the Chinese response, and goes on to examine vulnerabilities and problems post-Westphalian public health may face in light of the SARS outbreak.

China's response to SARS is well documented (see also de Lisle, 2004). In Chapter 2 Chinese scholar Ruotao Wang indicates that SARS was a wake-up call for the Chinese government. After SARS, scholars have given 'more in-depth analysis to China's social reform process,

[1] *The Times*, 7 July 2003. The statistics are from WHO.

its health system, and relevant health regulations' (p. 27). And Wang notes the need 'to orient our values and first emphasize humane care' (p. 29). This is not amplified. And, intriguingly, he asks: 'If an individual is sure to die, can this person do whatever he wants before death?' (p. 29).

The final essay on SARS is by Peter Singer *et al.* (Chapter 3). It focuses on Toronto, the Western city most affected by the outbreak. Canadian society was ill-equipped to respond to the ethical questions the outbreak evoked. The essay summarizes the points raised by a working group convened to think through the issues. Ten key ethical values were identified (see p. 31).

HIV and AIDS

The historian Allan Brandt, writing 20 years ago, noted presciently that

> In the years ahead we will, no doubt, learn a great deal more about AIDS and how to control it. We will also learn a great deal about the nature of our society from the manner in which we address the disease. AIDS will be the standard by which we may measure not only our medical and scientific skill but also our capacity for justice and compassion. (1988, p. 168)

The ethical issues relating to HIV/AIDS are found throughout these two volumes, and only one essay, Chapter 4 by Kelley Lee and Anthony B. Zwi, is included under this heading.

The literature on HIV/AIDS – even limiting ourselves to ethical issues in the developing world – is vast, and there is a complete volume in this series on the subject (Schüklenk, 2001) – but it is still worth briefly summarizing the issues. Of course, the ethical issues in developing countries to some extent mirror those in the developed world (on women and AIDS, for example, see Mertz, Sushinsky and Schüklenk, 1996). But the problems are different because resources tend to be much more limited. Parts of the developing world are more enveloped by religious dogma than the more secularized West and, partly as a result, greater stigma attaches to sufferers, and there is more moralizing. In the early 1980s this was, of course, the case in the developed world as well.

But there are problems that affect the developing world more, for example polygamy and also the use of prostitution by workers who spend most of the year away from their wives. Sex work is itself different. This problem cannot be solved without making available alternative careers and sources of income for women, and also empowering women in the sex industry to take steps to prevent themselves from acquiring HIV. This raises more generally the question of sex education. There can be difficulties in preaching safe sex when religious groups prefer to teach abstinence. Health education that promotes the use of condoms is resisted by the Catholic Church and therefore in much of the Catholic-influenced world. This does not, of course, mean that there is no use of contraceptives by Catholics. Perhaps, rather, that their Church is out of touch.

The allocation of medical resources is also a problem. Unfortunately, there is corruption, and there are wars. Too many poor countries spend too much on their military budgets and too little on health care resources. The cost of AIDS drugs is prohibitive for most people in the developing world.

Should the same ethical principles be applied to problems in the developing world, or is this to impose Western concepts? How important is the concept of autonomy (including informed consent) or privacy and confidentiality in an African context? Ankrah and Gostin suggested many years ago that these principles 'are not always fully accepted in Africa and may sometimes even clash with other core African values' (1994, p. 549). However, that these principles are important in Africa is clear from the African Charter on Human and Peoples' Rights 1986. For example, Article 5 states that 'every individual shall have the right to the respect of the dignity inherent in a human being and to the recognition of his legal status'.[2]

In Chapter 4 Lee and Zwi argue that a global political economy approach offers important insights into our understanding of, and therefore our responses to, AIDS. Research can be broadened both spatially and temporally. The authors maintain that policy-making in relation to AIDS has been strongly centred on biomedical and neo-liberal economic discourses. They see the importance of locating the disease with a view that seeks to situate AIDS within 'the broad historical, social, ecological, cultural, and political relationships that mediate humanity, sickness, and the environment' (p. 38, quoting Fortin, 1990, p. 217). There is a need to study the relationship between global economic and political power and the epidemiology of AIDS. There are more than twice as many people in the world infected with HIV than when this essay was published in 1996 (see Table 1, p. 39) but the concentration of cases remain firmly where they were, primarily in sub-Saharan Africa. The problems remain broadly similar, and the analysis offered in this essay remains highly pertinent.

Bioterrorism

Bioterrorism is an act of terrorism using biological agents. But what is terrorism? It has been variously defined. The FBI's definition is 'the unlawful use of force or violence against persons or property to intimidate a government, the civilian population, or any segment thereof, in furtherance of political or social objectives' (quoted in Osterholm and Schwartz, 2001, p. 31; see also Annas, 2002, p. 1337). The modern recognition of bioterrorism as a social problem was brought sharply into focus with the anthrax attacks in the USA in 2001. However, biological weapons were used against populations long before this. The Assyrians poisoned the wells of their enemies in the sixth century BCE. In 184 BCE, Hannibal ordered that earthen pots be filled with snakes to be used in a naval battle. There are many other examples in the ancient and medieval world (see Hagstad, 2000). In the Second World War the Japanese used biological agents against the Chinese.

Biological agents have changed the face of bioterrorism (see Henderson, 1999; Osterholm and Schwartz, 2001, pp. 30–34). Bio-weapons are fundamentally different from other weapons of mass destruction: the release of a bio-agent can be silent and can remain undetected, if the agent is invisible, odourless and tasteless. Bio-agents are also relatively cheap, and the materials are easily available. The NATO handbook dealing with potential bio-agents lists 31 pathogens (see Henderson, 1999, p. 1281). The four top agents are smallpox, anthrax, plague and botulism: smallpox and anthrax are 'top of the list', the others being more difficult

[2] See, further, Jallow and Hunt (1997), who therefore say compulsion with regard to blood tests or quarantine or internment cannot be justified.

to produce and dispense. According to Henderson, 'they can be grown easily and in large quantities and are sturdy organisms that are resistant to destruction' (1999, p. 1281).

The Biological and Toxin Weapons Convention of 1972 was ratified by 140 nations, including the Soviet Union. But the Soviet Union breached the Convention until the early 1990s. The Convention bans the development, production and stockpiling of biological agents for non-peaceful purposes. The possibility that other rogue states (Iran or North Korea, for example) have them (or have recruited them from the former Soviet Union) cannot be discounted (see Osterholm and Schwartz, 2001, p. 107). Iraq ran a bio-weapons programme under Saddam Hussein in the early 1980s and we know he used such weapons against his own people. A Japanese cult released sarin gas in the Tokyo subway system in 1995 (see Osterholm and Schwartz, 2001, pp. 49–52). And, of course, there was the anthrax attack in the USA in October 2001: letters containing anthrax spores were dispersed through the US postal system and five people were killed.

Even before the 2001 attack it was recognized that the USA was ill-prepared (see Gostin 2002a, p. 9; Gostin, 2002b, pp. 80–81). A Model State Emergency Health Powers Act was drafted (see Gostin 2002a and b for discussion). The Act is structured so as to address the five key elements for public health preparedness: preparedness, surveillance, management of property, control of persons, and public information and communication.[3] The preparedness and surveillance functions are to take effect immediately upon the legislation being enacted. The powers over property and persons can only be triggered by a governor declaring a 'state of public health emergency'. This is defined as 'an occurrence or imminent threat of an illness or health condition, caused by bioterrorism, epidemic or pandemic disease, or a novel and highly fatal infectious agent or biological toxin, that poses a substantial risk of a significant number of human fatalities or incidents of permanent or long-term disability' (Section 301 of Article III). Upon such an emergency being declared, authorities have the power to seize private property, and take control of facilities; medically examine and test individuals; and vaccinate and treat individuals. Refusal to undergo any of these constitutes a misdemeanour. Further, if a person poses a danger to public health, they may be subject to isolation or quarantine.

The Model Act has been criticized. George Annas, in Chapter 8, is the most forthright of these critics. He argues that the Act is based on the assumption that physicians and the public are unlikely to cooperate with officials in the event of a bioterrorist attack. But there was a high level of cooperation after the real terrorist attacks in 2001. Alexander comments: 'The terrorist activity may serve to unify and strengthen a society rather than cause it to disintegrate' (2003, p. 126). Annas also believes the definition of a public emergency is far too broad. The compulsory powers can be triggered by 'non-emergency conditions as diverse as annual influenza epidemics and the AIDS epidemic' (Annas, 2002, p. 1339). He is also critical of draconian provisions such as those which provide for quarantine. Annas objects to the sweeping powers which the Model Act confers on public health officials: he sees them as unconstitutional and unethical. But there is precedent supporting such powers,[4] and Gostin argues that trade-offs between civil rights and public health are required. Jacobson objected to being vaccinated. Annas points out that in the early 1900s vaccination was controversial. But medicine is now different – or so it is argued. Annas (2002, p. 1339) claims that trade-

3 On the Act, see Hodge and Gostin (2003).

4 On which see *Jacobson* v. *Massachusetts* 197 US 11 (1905).

offs between civil rights and public health measures are not always required, and, indeed, can be counterproductive. He supports this with two arguments: (i) the experience of the HIV/AIDS epidemic showed that respecting freedoms can promote the public's health (it was soon realized that mandatory screening would drive the epidemic underground); and (ii) the Model Act is likely to undermine public trust in public health. Officials need 'valid reasons for their actions' (Annas, 2002, p. 1340), not just sanctions. The Muncie smallpox epidemic of 1893 illustrates this well: there were armed guards patrolling the streets, and disobedience was swiftly punished. But citizens resisted these measures and violence broke out. Some officials were shot by citizens. In the end the officials caved in: their actions had failed because the public had defied them (Barbera, MacIntyre, Gostin *et al.*, 2001, p. 2713). Of course, trust 'is vital to the success of clinical and public health programs' (Gostin, 2000, p. 233).

But Gostin (2002b, pp. 88–89) maintains there are necessary trade-offs between the collective good and individual interests. The state needs authority to protect the public's health. So, if a person has been exposed to an infectious disease, s/he must be prevented from harming others: there is thus the need for testing vaccination, perhaps isolation. He notes that even the most liberal scholars – a nod in the direction of J.S. Mill[5] – accept the 'harm principle' (Gostin, 2002b, p. 89). Second, not everyone will willingly comply with public health measures: they may resist the loss of liberty even if their behaviour endangers others. The question, as Gostin sees it, is thus not whether compulsory powers should be conferred, but whether they can be hedged with appropriate safeguards. If safeguards exist, citizens should be required to sacrifice their interests in autonomy and liberty for the sake of the community's well-being.

Because of criticisms of the Model Act, it was revised in December 2001. A governor is not allowed to declare a public health emergency for an endemic disease: it may be declared only in the event of bioterrorism or the appearance of infectious agents that pose a high probability of deaths or serious disabilities. Criminal penalties may only be imposed where there is a failure to follow isolation or quarantine rules, and quarantine and isolation can only be imposed by 'the least restrictive means necessary'. There is also greater due process protection for those actually quarantined (Annas, 2002, p. 1340).

For Annas (Chapter 8), all the fundamental problems remain. Gostin, however, defends the Model Act: 'The issue is not whether the Act provides an ideal solution to perennially complex problems. Rather, the issue is whether the Act does a much better job than existing legislation does' (2002b, p. 84). He argues that existing public health legislation is outdated and inadequate. His purpose, he says, is not 'to assert which are the more fundamental interests: personal liberty or health and security. Rather ... to illustrate that both sets of interests are important to human flourishing'. And he maintains the Model Act was 'designed to defend personal as well as collective interests' (Gostin, 2002b, p. 91). He thinks the Act was poorly received because it strengthened governmental authority in a country – the USA – where the orientation was towards 'rights rhetoric'.[6] A number of states (32 by April 2002) have adopted legislation based in whole or part on the Model Act.

It is worth remarking that the UK's legislation does not address the specific threat that emanated from bioterrorism. There is much recent legislation (Terrorism Act 2000, Anti-

[5] *On Liberty*, first published in 1859.

[6] Ronald Dworkin would be flattered: see Dworkin (1977).

Terrorism, Crime and Security Act 2001, Prevention of Terrorism Act 2005 and Terrorism Act 2006), but none is targeted specifically at the threat of biological agents. Nor does it address what is to be done in the aftermath of an attack. Instead, it is focused on giving law enforcement agencies greater powers (and see Richard Horton, Chapter 11).

The issue of quarantine is often raised in discussions of bioterrorism. Different powers need to be distinguished. Quarantine is the compulsory, physical separation (including restriction of movement) of healthy persons who have been exposed to a communicable disease, during its period of communicability, to prevent the disease from being transmitted during the incubation period should infection occur (see Barbera, MacIntyre, Gostin *et al.*, 2001, p. 2712; Gostin, 2000, p. 210). This must be distinguished from 'isolation', which is the separation and confinement, for the period of communicability, of persons known or suspected to be infected, to prevent them from transmitting the infectious agent to others (Gostin, 2000, p. 210). Civil commitment or compulsory hospitalization is the detention of persons with infectious diseases for the purposes of care and treatment, usually in a hospital. Quarantine was abolished in the UK in 1896 (Maglen, 2002). It now exists only for animals to protect the country against the threat of rabies.

Is there a case for instituting quarantine in the context of bioterrorism? Barbera, MacIntyre, Gostin *et al.* (2001) address this. So do Ronald Bayer and James Colgrove in Chapter 5. They offer, in particular, a historical perspective on quarantine (at pp. 59–62). Quarantine is of course an infringement of fundamental rights and therefore needs to be justified. And, as Barbera, MacIntyre, Gostin *et al.* (2001, p. 2714) note, there may be alternatives that are more medically defensible, and more effective in containing the spread of disease. If the disease has a low or no person-to-person transmission, quarantine cannot be justified. It is not, therefore, an option if anthrax is used, since it is not communicable. But, even if smallpox is used in a bioterrorist attack, 'the long incubation period (10–17 days) almost ensures that some persons who were infected in the … attack will have traveled great distances from the site of exposure before the disease is recognized or quarantine could be implemented' (Barbera, MacIntyre, Gostin *et al.*, 2001, p. 2714). Even if quarantine is effective, is its implementation feasible? Which group or area is to be subject to it? Do we have the resources to enforce the confinement? Can the quarantined group be confined for as long as they need to be? If the condition is not susceptible to treatment, are individuals to be confined indefinitely?

Even if these hurdles are overcome, do the potential benefits of quarantine outweigh its possible adverse consequences? History (see Bayer and Colgrove, Chapter 5) points to adverse consequences.

There are legal problems too. In Chapter 9 Wendy Parmet points to some of these (see pp. 143–45, 150–54, 160–65). And she notes out that 'if history teaches us anything about the use of such "traditional powers" it is that they are often, especially in crises, misused, sacrificing the rights of especially vulnerable individuals often for little or no public health benefit' (pp. 153–54). She warns: 'There is no magic bullet for bioterrorism' (p. 160). Is there a case for 'voluntary' quarantine and/or isolation? This may be more tolerable and acceptable to a population. But, as Parmet points out, to obtain voluntary compliance, states may need to move 'beyond a police power model' (p. 164).

Other approaches to bioterrorism preparedness include disease reporting. A good account of this is made by Heather Horton, James Misrahi, Gene Matthews and Paula Kocher in Chapter 6. Disease reporting laws are an educational tool – they highlight what diseases society considers of national importance. They also provide 'incentives for health-care providers to obtain the training and skills to diagnose and respond to those diseases' (p. 86). Because of scarce resources, which will be taxed in any crisis, allocation may become crucial. This is considered by James Hodge in Chapter 7 (see pp. 94–95). Triage may become important. This has its origins in eighteenth-century wars, on the battlefield.[7] Kipnis asks us to 'think of the injured as falling along a horizontal scale, with the most seriously injured toward the right and the walking wounded on the left' (2003, p. 99). Patients at both extremes of the scale are 'lopped away'. Clinicians should focus on the 'middle', on those 'who will live if treated but die otherwise' (Kipnis, 2003, p. 99). There is consensus about the criteria to use to determine priority of medical care among patients. The underlying principle is to save as many lives as possible. This is justified by the principle of utility, by the 'difference principle' of John Rawls (1971) and the so-called 'stewardship' argument. Health care professionals have the duty to ensure that resources are employed efficiently and not wasted (Kipnis, 2003, p. 101).

In Chapter 10 Jonathan Moreno situates the current challenge within a somewhat wider historical timeframe. The concern with bioterrorism and the bioethical questions it raises are not as novel as we may think. It has happened before with the alarm spawned by communism after the Second World War. The communist threat engendered (in the USA) a national security state, as Moreno discusses elsewhere (Moreno, 1999). He sees the issues raised by the events of 9/11 and its aftermath as a continuation of evolving policies from previous years. Of course, others are novel: he cites the application of developments in emerging fields (neuroscience, genetics). Moreno's essay also questions the origins of bioethics, and the part played in this by Henry Beecher (1966), who, according to Moreno, failed 'to connect his interest in [human research ethics] ... with his own Army-sponsored experimental work on hallucinogens, conducted without the subjects' full knowledge or consent' (p. 176; see also Moreno, 2002).

Avian Flu

Avian flu (which must be distinguished from seasonal flu) is a zoonotic disease with outbreaks throughout the world which has the potential to cause a pandemic through the H5N1 strain or one of a number of other viruses.[8] Flu has caused pandemics in the past, most famously in 1918, when it killed more people than died in the First World War (see Kolata, 2000; Barry, 2004).[9]

Lawrence Gostin's essay (Chapter 12) questions our preparedness. Influenza pandemic preparedness requires, Gostin notes, 'careful consideration of the public health strategy as well as the legal and ethical implications' (p. 188). He emphasizes the importance of four ethical values: (i) transparency; (ii) the protection of vulnerable populations; (iii) fair treatment and social justice; and (iv) proportionality.

Jaro Kotalik's concern, in Chapter 13, is also with the ethical issues that confront those planning for an influenza pandemic. First will be scarcity of resources, both human and material (see also Hodge, Chapter 7). Second, mass vaccination is considered important

---

7 On the history, see Childress (2003, pp. 78–79).

8 The annual number of deaths from seasonal influenza is 250,000–500,000 worldwide.

9 It may have killed 50 million people.

(see also Part VII, Vaccination, discussed below), but the existing pandemic plans – the ones Kotalik investigates in the UK, the USA and Canada – do not provide concrete estimates of its benefits and burdens sufficient to assure everyone that the balance is highly favourable. Ethical questions relating to health care workers must also be taken into account. They have a 'strong ethical obligation to serve' but there are also 'strong reciprocal obligations of health care organizations to protect and support their workers' (p. 200; see also Singer *et al.*, Chapter 3). Kotalik also stresses (as does Gostin) transparency and accountability. These require 'that those who are going to be affected, be informed' (p. 201). That it may alarm does not justify not warning the population of the implications of an epidemic for their lives.

Climate Change

This collection contains just one essay on climate change. It is included because it makes the original and provocative claim that climate change can be characterized as a public health threat and not just an environmental threat.

The implications of climate change for human health have been recognized for some time (see Bryson and Murray, 1997). But, on the whole, the projected images of climate change are about glaciers and vineyards in northern Europe, not human beings. Lisa Heinzerling's short essay (Chapter 14) is thus an eye-opening call to something we have missed. As with so many public health issues, it will 'almost certainly be worse for the poorest among us' (p. 210). If climate change is a public health issue, will we take it more seriously? Does it make the moral case for 'aggressive action' on climate change 'unimpeachable' (p. 211)? We are, Heinzerling argues, beyond the 'precautionary' stage (and see Volume I, Part IX) into, what she calls, a post-cautionary world. Her essay concludes with some implications for public policy. Most importantly, she notes, there are serious consequences for the 'moral status of the debate over climate change'. And 'Knowledge that death and suffering will result from our actions leads uncontroversially to a moral obligation to change our behavior' (p. 220; see also Sharpe, 2008).

Tobacco Control

Tobacco smoking was a social necessity in the 1950s: now it is pariah behaviour. The advertising of tobacco products is banned in many countries (though not so subtle forms persist even where banned).[10] Smoking is now unlawful in workplaces in many countries. Cigarette packets contain explicit warnings and, increasingly, graphic pictures that are supposed to deter (though there is no evidence that they do). There is now a Framework Convention on Tobacco Control – the first health treaty regulated under WHO auspices. This came into force in 2005 after ratification by the 40th signatory. Smoking amongst men has declined – at least

[10] Thus, British American Tobacco can sponsor Bizet's *Carmen* at Glyndebourne in 2008 with impunity – though surely not for much longer. And how much longer will Carmen be allowed to smoke on stage?

in the UK, the USA and much of the developed world (see Feldman and Bayer, 2004).[11] The tobacco companies now target Asia to ensure their profits are maintained or enhanced.

Tobacco products cause huge numbers of premature deaths (worldwide over 4 million adults die each year from tobacco-related diseases). It is clearly, therefore, a considerable public health concern. But there exists a strong presumption that individuals should be permitted to engage in risky behaviour so long as their activities cause no harm to others. Smoking is rarely a self-regarding activity, and passive smoking (environmental tobacco smoke) kills.[12] Indoor air pollution is one of the most significant environmental risks to the public's health. There are thus clear arguments for clean indoor air laws. Arno, Brandt, Gostin and Morgan (1996) offer three justifications: risk to public health or safety, risk assumed by children and adolescents, and risk assumed by consenting adults. If we examine these three arguments, the first is straightforward: third parties must be protected and their interest clearly outweighs the individual's right to smoke. The second justification is hardly controversial either: certainly, it is not difficult to justify banning smoking in places children and adolescents are expected to frequent. The third justification is more difficult to substantiate because it is essentially paternalistic. Even so, restrictions can be justified. Banning smoking indoors inconveniences smokers, but it does not stop them smoking; it merely restricts the places where they can smoke. Laws restricting smoking are 'not dictating personal choices', but merely 'limiting the effects of those choices on the public' (Jacobson and Zapawa, 2001, p. 210). Further, the claim of paternalism is undermined by the aggressive polices of the tobacco companies and the addiction of smokers.

As Robert Goodin points out in Chapter 15, traditional Millian precepts have long held sway. But now 'conventional wisdom' is being challenged. Smoking is not just a private-regarding vice: it is other-regarding because of the effect it has on others through passive smoking, and since it is addictive it is difficult for smokers to stop smoking once they have started. The force of the addictive findings is to undercut any claim that there is continuing consent to the risks involved in smoking. Once 'hooked', capacity to consent in any meaningful sense disappears. Further, we 'do not leave it to the discretion of consumers, however well informed, whether or not to drink grossly polluted water, ingest grossly contaminated foods, or inject grossly dangerous drugs. We simply prohibit such things, on grounds of public health, by appeal to utilitarian calculations of one sort or another' (p. 236).

Goodin goes on to discuss the policy alternatives:

- self-regulation
- tort actions against tobacco companies
- taxation
- publicity, for example health warnings
- bans (but we must be alert to the lessons of 'Prohibition' in the USA)
- medicalization (tobacco as a prescription drug).

More significantly, smoking harms non-smokers, and there are policy options again here. Goodin lists them:

---

[11] But there are more than 1 billion smokers in the world today (1 billion men and 215 million women). The majority (925 million) live in poor countries.

[12] On questions of causation, see Parascandola and Weed (2001).

- reduce smoking
- self-regulation/courtesy
- improved ventilation and air filters
- market forces (avoid establishments which permit smoking)
- bans and restriction on smoking in public places.

The fifth of these options is clearly the best way to prevent people from being subjected to environmental tobacco smoke in confined public places, and it is the option most vigorously pursued in an increasing number of countries. It must be virtually impossible today to find an aeroplane in which one can smoke, yet it was not so long ago that non-smokers found themselves sitting only a row away from smokers.

In Chapter 16 Stephen Wilkinson asks a rather different question: do smokers (and others who cause themselves to be ill) forfeit some of their rights to health care? The answer frequently given is that they do, and this answer commands substantial public support. This came out forcibly when it was revealed that the ex-footballer George Best required a liver transplant, his original liver having been destroyed by his 'lifestyle' (very heavy consumption of alcohol). Different arguments are used to reach this conclusion that our actions may cause us to forfeit some rights to health care. Wilkinson examines critically one of these, the 'restoration' argument – that is, we ought to reduce smokers' entitlements to health care because not to do so would mean unfairly making non-smokers pay the price for smokers' unhealthy lifestyles. Wilkinson offers a number of objections to the restoration argument. There is an empirical objection, which is well aired. Smokers are less likely to live into old age. More interestingly, Wilkinson turns the restoration argument on its head. Perhaps, he hypothesizes, the very 'cheapness' of smokers should provide us with a reason for giving their needs a higher priority than those of other people. He constructs a reverse restoration argument. There are, of course, differences between the two restoration arguments, as Wilkinson concedes – most obviously the act/omission difference. He disposes of this, as he does with other arguments, to conclude that the restoration argument is a 'moralising wolf in a liberal sheep's clothing'. And if you accept that rationing decisions should not be based on moral judgements about behaviour or character, you will not penalize smokers for their lifestyles.

Timothy Lytton's essay (Chapter 17) is on the use of litigation to make public health policy. He asks whether the public health benefits of litigation – for example against tobacco companies – outweigh its costs. He also raises questions – which go beyond the scope of this collection – about the proper role of courts within a system of liberal government. On the first question, he points to the lack of empirical evidence, which means that we tend to rely on anecdote. It is Lytton's suspicion that the interest in institutional arguments betrays a desire to avoid having to confront the difficult task of assembling comprehensive empirical data about the benefits and costs of litigation.

Vaccination

Writing in 1998 Tim Dare (Chapter 18) notes 'a rather curious philosophical neglect of immunisation' (p. 304). This certainly was true 10 years ago but there is now substantial literature on the subject, represented in this collection by four essays (see also Menzel, 1995). Vaccination policies have always attracted opposition. They remove autonomy. Some people also doubt their efficacy. Thus, there has been opposition to the MMR vaccine and a rise in measles has been attributed to this. Dare is reluctant to involve himself in this debate, but is happy to conclude that 'so far as the empirical evidence goes, we are entitled to treat certain claims about immunisation as "practically certain" for policy purposes' (p. 309). In looking to the justification of mass immunization policies Dare turns to utilitarianism. He discounts the familiar objection to this. Utilitarian analysis can advance our discussion. It clearly shows the value of immunization, if not compulsory programmes. Dare goes on to compare policies in the USA and New Zealand. Immunization is effectively compulsory in the USA, whereas New Zealand requires evidence not of immunization but of immunization status upon school enrolment. Dare prefers the latter. He is in favour of pro-immunization policies, but not the move to compulsory immunization. It may be thought that this pays over much attention to parental autonomy and too little to the child's best interests.

In Chapter 19 Thomas May addresses risk perception and the viability of vaccination. The more common problem is convincing the public to accept vaccination (for themselves or their children). May, however, addresses the problem that occurs where there is a perceived crisis and a shortage of vaccines, and it is necessary to restrict access to vaccine. The key is public communication. May examines the steps through which better communication can be achieved. The implications of this go wider than the context he addresses, as he acknowledges when referring to the *Schiavo* case. The public is frequently misinformed: education and communication of information is thus vital to public health generally.

The question arises as to what is meant by a child's best interests, a subject much explored by family lawyers and now also by medical ethicists. Angus Dawson addresses this question in Chapter 20. Clearly, as he states, best interests in relation to young children have to be determined by seeking to 'balance the potential harms and benefits of possible actions and inactions' (p. 348). Most importantly, Dawson addresses the role of parental decision-making, in particular the question of whether and when parents' decisions can be overruled. That parents' decisions are sometimes overruled does not dispose of the question. Thus, the Court of Appeal in England sanctioned the separation of conjoined twins in the face of parental opposition in order to allow the stronger twin to live.[13] Many are critical of this decision (for example, see Harris 2001). Just as many are critical of a decision like *Re T*,[14] which allowed parents to prevail on refusing consent to a life-saving liver transplant for a toddler, and which conflated the rights of the child with those of his parents (for example, see Freeman, 2001). In the latter case, the Court of Appeal was influenced by the good faith of the parents (who were coincidentally health care professionals). They believed their child had already suffered enough. The 'good faith' defence is acceptable to Dawson, so that 'where the balance of risk is unclear or finely balanced there is a strong argument for saying that the state should not intervene given ... the risk of harm to the parent–child relationship, linked to such interference by the state' (p. 360). He does, however, accept that the state has a role in protecting children in 'at least some cases'; it has a 'residual power' to step in where best interests are ignored by parents (p. 360). He believes this will happen only rarely.

Jeffrey Ulmer and Margaret Liu's concern in Chapter 21 is that 'inequalities in the distribution and use of vaccines are ... striking' (p. 363). They compare immunization rates

13 See *Re A* [2001] 1 FLR 1.

14 [1997] 2 FLR 502.

in industrialized countries and the developing world. In developing countries one in four children born each year will not be vaccinated. In the developed world the ethical issues about vaccination focus on the rights of individuals. In poorer countries the 'fundamental issue is the lack of access to basic necessities for health' (p. 366), including vaccines. And people in different parts of the world may not necessarily require the same vaccines. For not only are there different diseases (malaria, most obviously), but environmental influences on the immune system might affect the immunological outcome of a particular type of vaccine. Adverse effects of a vaccine may also be specific to one population. The problem, Ulmer and Liu maintain, offers real challenges to 'each economic sector, population and government' to fulfil its responsibility: 'they should treat all of the world's children as their own, rather than denouncing particular groups as causing these inequalities' (p. 367).

Public Health and Genetic Health

Knoppers and Fecteau have written:

> Like the gene pool at the level of the species being considered the common heritage of humanity, so genomic databases, while recognizing the initial contribution of individual participants and of individual researchers or commercial investors, should also account for the needs of present and future generations and foster and promote international collaboration. (2003, p. 27)

We can expect the Human Genome Project (HGP) to provide tools to translate genomic knowledge to clinical diagnosis, and this will have implications for every level of the health care system. Genomics is 'inspiring the development of very large longitudinal cohort studies and even studies of entire populations to establish repositories of biological materials ("biobanks") for discovery and characterization of genes associated with common diseases' (Khoury *et al.*, 2004, p. 936). Knoppers is clear (see also Chapter 25) that 'compiling human genomic databases with databases of pathogens yields the promise of a strengthened scientific basis for the primary and secondary prevention of disease' (2007, p. 144). She is equally insistent that 'norms for the emergence of a new paradigm for public health interventions must be informed by issues beyond the legal and ethical parameters of autonomy and privacy' (Knoppers, 2007, p. 144, quoting Schabas, 2002, p. 98).

Muin J. Khoury, in Chapter 22, discusses the potential applications of genetics in the context of the core functions of public health agencies, as identified by the US Institute of Medicine. These are assessment, policy development and assurance (see Table 1, p. 372). He also offers a succinct analysis of some of the significant ethical issues surrounding genetic testing.

In Chapter 23 Evan Willis offers sociological insights. He considers the main social policy issue, that of maximizing any benefits and minimizing any drawbacks, and provides three case studies: (i) ozone and the melanoma gene; (ii) bladder cancer and chemical workers; (iii) haemochromatosis. Of course, a common theme is 'the tension between individual and collective interests' (p. 383). Of particular value in Willis' essay is his discussion of some of the dangers. For example, the 'overgeneticization of disease' (p. 384): overemphasize the genetic and there is a danger of genetic diagnosis and screening being overemphasized. Another danger is the tendency to 'individualize disease in a form of genetic reductionism; a sort of "Genes-R-Us" approach to the world' (p. 385). As Willis points out, this fits with 'an individualist paradigm of disease that views it as an individual and biological phenomenon' (p. 385). Other changes arise out of the 'globalized nature of the project' (p. 386) and the re-emergence of sociobiological explanations for human behaviour.

Scott Burris and Lawrence Gostin ask, in Chapter 24, what we can learn from the HIV experience. They note that 'Any use of government authority to collect and use sensitive information reflects often controversial assumptions about whose health counts and how. It entails the potential for abuse' (p. 392). Their concern is with balancing authority to promote community health with the need to protect 'those whose health data will be sought in that cause' (p. 392). They offer three principles to assess the costs, benefits and political prospects of screening programmes: (i) they should enhance the health of the population; (ii) they should be an 'efficient and just use of resources' (p. 396); and (iii) the measure adopted must be 'as acceptable as possible to its targets' (p. 397). Burris and Gostin point to the dangers of 'geneticism', 'the pervasive individual and institutional use of genetic information and concepts to disadvantage people whether singly or by creating groups' (p. 404, quoting Wolf, 1995, p. 345).

Biobanks are addressed in the next two essays. As Bartha Knoppers points out in Chapter 25, it is the possibility of combining the power of informatics and microchip technology with the increased knowledge of the probable nature of genetic risk factors in common diseases that has propelled the debate on the ethical, social and legal questions of biobanks. In Chapter 26 Lori Andrews raises a large number of ethical and legal questions. For example, what type of information, if any, should the source of the tissue be given before the tissue is entered on a biobank? Should there be 'one-time general consent' (as advocated by Wendler, 2006)? Mark Rothstein has argued that although some adhere to the view that blanket consent is only permissible when samples are anonymous, 'this position is unnecessarily paternalistic and threatens to impair research. As long as the potential research subjects are clearly apprised of the range of possible future uses of their sample, they should be permitted to give one-time blanket consent to such uses' (2005, p. 93; see also Hansson *et al.*, 2006). Iceland has adopted a presumed consent model (see Gulcher and Stefánsson, 2000). This supposedly has popular support, though it has been successfully challenged for infringing constitutional privacy protections. Iceland apart, the evidence does not suggest that blanket consent policies have popular support.[15]

Andrews also pinpoints cultural values which might be violated if tissue is used without informed consent: she cites the value systems of Jews and Native Americans. There are questions also about how the 'fruits' of biobanks should be distributed. She refers, not surprisingly, to the infamous *Moore* case in California,[16] and also discuses possible legal regimes to govern the emerging biobank economy.

In the final essay in this section Mark Rothstein (Chapter 27) asks whether genetic information should be treated separately from other medical information, whether there should be 'genetic exceptionalism'. He argues that exceptionalism is poor public policy. He sees such laws as having limited value in preventing or redressing harms caused by the uses and

---

15 There is a good summary in Caulfield and Ries (2007, pp. 184–86).

16 793 P. 2d 479 (1990). The case raised the question: if a patient's tissues are used as source material for the commercial development of high technology products, what property rights can the patient assert over his cells and the profit generated from the sale of those products?

disclosures of genetic information. Also, they 'reinforce the stigma of genetic disorders ... and ignore the underlying social problems that genetic privacy and discrimination exemplify' (p. 434). He argues that studying genetics 'forces us to return to first principles' (p. 436), to questions, particularly pertinent in a country like the USA, such as who should have access to health care, the role of insurance and so on (see further Rothstein and Carnahan, 2001).

Public Health and Equity

Sudhir Anand (2002) has posed the questions: why are we concerned with health equity, and what is its relation to equity more generally? Is there any reason why inequalities in health should concern us more than (say) inequalities in income? Should we be more concerned with some types of health inequalities than with others? Should we be less tolerant of inequalities across certain population groups than across others, for example race in South Africa or gender in Bangladesh? He argues that health should be treated as a special good because without it people cannot function as agents. In Amartya Sen's language (1985), health contributes to a person's basic capability to function.

In Chapter 28 Dan Brock discusses methods of prioritizing scarce health care resources. In particular he discusses the ethical problems of using DALYs and QALYs. DALY is a measure adopted by the World Health Organization and the World Bank: it stands for 'disability-adjusted life year'; QALY is 'quality-adjusted life year'. Brock asks 'How should states of health and disability be evaluated?' (p. 443). Those who developed the DALY used the preferences of expert health professionals, not those of the disabled themselves, whose perspectives may well be different. Of the many issues Brock raises (there are nine in all) perhaps the most troubling is whether the use of 'cost-effectiveness analysis' to set health care priorities unjustly discriminates against the disabled. QALYs discriminate because treating the disabled person will produce less benefit than treating the able-bodied.

Fabienne Peter, in Chapter 29, defends what she calls an 'indirect approach'. This is based on the premise that social inequalities in health are wrong 'not simply because actual health outcomes deviate from some pattern of health outcomes that is considered ideal, but rather because, and insofar as, they are the expression and product of unjust economic, social, and political institutions' (p. 466). The pursuit of health equity must then be embedded within the pursuit of social justice generally. Further, if we understand social inequalities in health we may better understand how the institutions of society work, and inform our assessment of the justice of these institutions. The influence of Rawls (1971, 1993) is clear, though Rawls did not address the question of health (but see Daniels, 1985).

Simon Szreter and Michael Woolcock's Chapter 30 is the final essay in Part IX. Their thesis is that 'it is desirable and possible to reconcile the controversies surrounding social capital as it applies to issues in public health, but that doing so requires incorporating empirical and conceptual insights from history and the broader social capital literature' (p. 478).

Public Health and the Developing World

In this final section of this collection attention focuses on the developing world. The subject now has its own journal, *Developing World Bioethics*, in its tenth volume (as at 2010). In a recent essay in this journal Michael Selgelid (2008) has suggested reasons why the developed world should want to improve health care in developing countries. These are:

- to promote equality of opportunity
- to improve the situation of the worst-off
- to promote respect of the human right to have one's most basic needs met
- to reduce undeserved inequalities in well-being
- to promote the greater good of humankind
- to achieve enormous benefits while requiring only small sacrifices
- to amend historical injustices
- to meet the obligation to amend injustices that developed world countries have contributed to
- to reduce the threat of infectious diseases to developed countries
- to promote developed countries' economic interests
- to promote global security.

The first eight of these reasons are moral reasons, the last three self-interested ones. There are egalitarian arguments, utilitarian arguments and libertarian ones. Selgelid believes these reasons 'highlight ordinary values that most of us will share' (2008, p. 124). He is of the view that those who resist change will appeal to the idea that 'coercive taxation for redistributive purposes would violate the right of an individual to keep his hard-earned income' (Selgelid, 2008, p. 125).[17] Selgelid believes those who think this should outweigh the rights and values listed above are expressing a 'morally repugnant, and perhaps imprudent' view (2008, p. 125).

In Chapter 31 Paul Farmer and Nicole Gastineau Campos call for a 'resocialising' of ethics. To resocialize medical ethics means, they say, turning towards disciplines such as 'anthropology, history, and political economy' (p. 513). They believe the sociology of knowledge is 'another field full of promise' (p. 515). The poor 'quite literally *embody* many of the ethical dilemmas stemming from injustices within medicine and public health' and add 'insights that cannot be obtained through reference to philosophy. For ethical reflection is part of everyday life, and when the stakes are high … soliciting these views are central to the quest for understanding' (p. 516).

Rebecca Cook and Bernard Dickens concentrate, in Chapter 32, on one injustice in particular, that of unsafe motherhood (see also Cook, Dickens and Fathalla, 2003). They report that 99 per cent of the 'tragic and often preventable consequences of unsafe motherhood occur in developing countries' (p. 524). The explanation needs to be sought in more than just gender inequity. Cook and Dickens find it in a multiplicity of causes, ranging from health system failures to religious morality (the Catholic Church in particular). Injustices are, of course, exacerbated when women have little or no control over their sexual availability to men, and women in the developing world 'may lack any feasible options in life to early marriage and repeated childbearing' (p. 538). They emphasize, echoing Jonathan Mann (1979, reproduced as Chapter 25 in Volume I), 'how social inequality, economic powerlessness, societal exclusion and denials of human dignity condition preventable disease, disability and premature death' (p. 530).

---

17 A view that has philosophical support in Nozick (1974).

In Chapter 33 Sarah Macfarlane, Mary Racelis and Florence Muli-Musiime further explore public health in developing countries. They make a number of important points including the need to restate the centrality of people in public health and its practice. They argue that 'for public health to succeed, it must be re-crafted in a framework that locates organised and active communities at the centre as initiators and managers of their own health' (p. 545).

Solomon R. Benatar, in Chapter 34, examines the implications of globalization for health-related research. He stresses that the challenge to be faced in international research ethics is 'the development of universal rules for research world wide, at a time when care is being delivered within very different health care systems ... and in a multicultural world in which people live under radically different conditions – ranging from immense luxury to abject poverty' (p. 551). Benatar offers a blueprint for research ethics. Amongst other things he advocates a re-evaulation of the concept of intellectual property rights.

Ruairí Brugha and Gill Walt (Chapter 35) describe the global health fund set up to fight AIDS, tuberculosis and malaria (see also Walt and Buse, 2000).[18] It has a target of raising US$10 billion a year. It is a public-private partnership but has received less from the private sector than was hoped. It is clear that to mobilize these funds it must focus on issues and actions which accord with the perceptions of potential contributors. But, as Lindstrand *et al.* point out: 'Contributors' conceptions may not coincide with the cost-effective and evidence-based actions that are first needed in low-income countries' (2007, p. 305; see further Amery, 2007). The example they cite is the provision of anti-retroviral drugs.

Finally, in Chapter 36 David Fidler and Lawrence Gostin examine the new international health regulations adopted by the World Health Assembly in May 2005. Their purpose is 'to prevent, protect against, control and provide a public response to the international spread of disease in ways that are commensurate with and restricted to public health risks, and which avoid unnecessary interference with international traffic and trade' (as stated in Article 2). As Fidler and Gostin note, there is 'growing consensus on the importance of public health to global governance in the 21st century' (p. 560).[19] Of particular interest is the incorporation within the new Health Regulations of human rights principles (in the Regulations' earlier manifestation in 1995 human rights were overlooked – which says much about changes in our commitment to human rights in the space of a decade). Fidler and Gostin admit the new Regulations do not offer a 'magic bullet' (p. 567) and we must wait to see what impact they have, particularly in the developing world.

References

Alexander, D.A. (2003), 'Bioterrorism: Preparing for the Unthinkable', *Journal of the Royal Army Medical Corps*, **149**, pp. 125–30.

Amery, J. (2007), 'International Development and Public Health', in S. Gillan, J. Yates and P. Badrinath (eds), *Essential Public Health: Theory and Practice*, Cambridge: Cambridge University Press, pp. 285–306.

Anand, S. (2002), 'The Concern for Equity in Health', *Journal of Epidemiology and Community Health*, **56** (7), pp. 485–87.

---

18 In relation to Uganda, see Wendo (2003).

19 They describe it as a 'centerpiece for global health governance in the 21st century' (p. 93).

Ankrah, E.M, and Gostin, L.O. (1994), 'Ethical and Legal Considerations of the HIV Epidemic in Africa', in M. Essex, S. Mboup, P.J. Kanki and M.R. Kalengayi (eds), *AIDS in Africa*, New York: Raven Press, pp. 547–58.

Annas, G. (2002), 'Bioterrorism, Public Health and Civil Liberties', *New England Journal of Medicine*, **346**, pp. 1337–42.

Arno, P.S., Brandt, A.M., Gostin, L.O. and Morgan, J. (1996), 'Tobacco Industry Strategies to Oppose Federal Regulation', *Journal of the American Medical Association*, **275** (16), pp. 1258–62.

Barbera, J., MacIntyre, A., Gostin, L. *et al.* (2001), 'Large-Scale Quarantine following Biological Terrorism in the United States: Scientific Examination, Logistic and Legal Limits, and Possible Consequences', *Journal of the American Medical Association*, **286** (21), pp. 2711–17.

Barry, J.M. (2004), *The Great Influenza: The Epic Story of the Deadliest Plague in History*, New York: Viking.

Bayer, R. and Fairchild, A. (2002), 'The Limits of Privacy: Surveillance and the Control of Disease', *Health Care Analysis*, **10**, pp. 19–35.

Beecher, H. (1966), 'Ethical and Clinical Research', *New England Journal of Medicine*, **274**, pp. 1354–60.

Brandt, A. (1988), 'AIDS: From Social History to Social Policy', in E. Fee and D.T. Fox (eds), *AIDS: The Burdens of History*, Berkeley: University of California Press, pp. 147–71.

Bryson, R.A. and Murray, T.J. (1977), *Climates of Hunger: Mankind and the World's Changing Weather*, Madison: University of Wisconsin Press.

Caulfield, T. and Ries, N.M. (2007), 'Public Opinion, Consent and Population Genetic Biobanks', in B.M. Knoppers (ed.), *Genomics and Public Health – Legal and Socio-Ethical Perspectives*, Leiden: Martinus Nijhoff, pp. 183–96.

Childress, J. (2003), 'Triage in Response to a Bioterrorist Attack', in J. Moreno (ed.), *In the Wake of Terror: Medicine and Morality in a Time of Crisis*, Cambridge, MA: MIT Press, pp. 77–93.

Cook, R.J., Dickens, B.M. and Fathalla, M.F. (2003), *Reproductive Health and Human Rights*, Oxford: Clarendon Press.

Daniels, N. (1985), *Just Health Care*, New York: Cambridge University Press.

de Lisle, J. (2004), 'Atypical Pneumonia and Ambivalent Law and Politics: SARS and the response to SARS in China', *Temple Law Review*, **77**, pp. 193–245.

Dworkin, R. (1977), *Taking Rights Seriously*, London: Duckworth.

Eichelberger, L. (2007), 'SARS and New York's Chinatown: The Politics of Risk and Blame during an Epidemic of Fear', *Social Science and Medicine*, **65**, pp. 1284–95.

Feldman, E.A. and Bayer, R. (2004), *Unfiltered: Conflicts Over Tobacco Policy and Public Health*, Cambridge, MA: Harvard University Press.

Fortin, A. (1990), 'AIDS, Development, and the Limitations of the African State', in B. Misztal and D. Moss (eds), *Action on AIDS: National Policies in Comparative Perspective*, Westport, CT: Greenwood Press.

Freeman, M. (2001), 'Whose Life is it Anyway?', *Medical Law Review*, **9**, pp. 259–80.

Gostin, L. (2000), *Public Health Law: Power, Duty, Restraint*, Berkeley: University of California Press (2nd edn, 2008).

Gostin, L.O. (2002a), 'Law and Ethics in a Public Health Emergency', *Hastings Center Report*, **32** (2), pp. 9–11.

Gostin, L.O. (2002b), 'Public Health Law in an Age of Terrorism: Rethinking Individual Rights and Common Goods', *Health Affairs*, **21**, pp. 79–93.

Gostin, L.O., Bayer, R. and Fairchild, A.L. (2003), 'Ethical and Legal Challenges Posed by Severe Acute Respiratory Syndrome', *Journal of the American Medical Association*, **290**, pp. 3229–37.

Gulcher, J.R. and Stefánsson, K. (2000), 'The Icelandic Healthcare Database and Informed Consent', *New England Journal of Medicine*, **342**, pp. 1827–30.

Hagstad D. (2000), 'Emergency: Bioterrorism', *American Journal of Nursing*, **100** (12), pp. 33–35.

Hansson, M.G., Dillner, J., Bartram, C.R., Carlson, J.A. and Helgesson, G. (2006), 'Should Donors be Allowed to Give Broad Consent to Future Biobank Research?, *Lancet Oncology*, **7**, pp. 266–69.

Harris, J. (2001), 'Human Beings, Persons and Conjoined Twins', *Medical Law Review*, **9**, pp. 221–36.

Henderson, D.A. (1999), 'The Looming Threat of Bioterrorism', *Science*, **283** (5406), pp. 1279–82.

Hodge, J.G., Jr. and Gostin, L.O. (2003), 'Protecting the Public's Health in an Era of Bioterrorism: The Model State Emergency Health Powers Act', in J. Moreno (ed.), *In the Wake of Terror: Medicine and Morality in a Time of Crisis*, Cambridge, MA: MIT Press, pp. 17–32.

Jacobson, P.D. and Zapawa, L.M. (2001), 'Clean Indoor Air Restrictions: Progress and Promise', in R.L. Rabin and S.D. Sugarman (eds), *Regulating Tobacco*, New York: Oxford University Press, pp. 207–44.

Jallow, H.B. and Hunt, P. (1997), *AIDS and the African Charter*, Bangal: African Centre for Democracy and Human Rights Studies.

Khoury, M.J., Milliken, R., Little, J. and Gwinn, M. (2004), 'The Emergence of Epidemiology in the Genomics Age', *International Journal of Epidemiology*, **33**, pp. 936–44.

Kipnis, K. (2003), 'Overwhelming Casualties: Medical Ethics in a Time of Terror', in J. Moreno (ed.), *In the Wake of Terror: Medicine and Morality in a Time of Crisis*, Cambridge, MA: MIT Press, pp. 95–107.

Knoppers, B.M. (2007), 'Of Genomics and Public Health: Building "Public Goods"', in B.M. Knoppers (ed.), *Genomics and Public Health – Legal and Socio-Ethical Perspectives*, Leiden: Martinus Nijhoff, pp. 143–47.

Knoppers, B.M. and Fecteau, C. (2003), 'Human Genomic Databases: A Global Public Good?', *European Journal of Health Law*, **10**, pp. 27–41.

Kolata, G. (2000), *Flu: The Story of the Great Influenza Pandemic of 1918 and the Search for the Virus that Caused It*, Basingstoke: Macmillan.

Lindstrand, A., Bergström, S., Rosling, H., Rubenson, B., Stenson, B. and Tylleskär, T. (2007), *Global Health: An Introductory Textbook*, Lund, Sweden: Studentlitteratur.

Maglen, K. (2002), 'The First Line of Defence: British Quarantine and the Port Sanitary Authorities in the Nineteenth Century', *Social History of Medicine*, **15**, pp. 413–28.

Mann, J.M. (1979), 'Medicine and Public Health, Ethics and Human Rights', *Hastings Center Report*, **27**, pp. 6–13.

Menzel, P. (1995), 'Non-Compliance: Fair or Free-Riding?', *Health Care Analysis*, **3**, pp. 113–15.

Mertz, D., Sushinsky, M.A. and Schüklenk, U. (1996), 'Women and AIDS: The Ethics of Exaggerated Harm', *Bioethics*, **10**, pp. 93–113.

Moreno, J.D. (1999), *Undue Risk: Secret State Experiments on Humans*, New York: W.H. Freeman.

Moreno, J.D. (2002), 'Bioethics after the Terror', *American Journal of Bioethics*, **2**, pp. 60–64.

Nozick, R. (1974), *Anarchy, State and Utopia*, New York: Basil Books.

Osterholm, M. and Schwartz, J. (2001), *Living Terrors: What America Needs to Know to Survive the Coming Bioterrorist Catastrophe*, New York: Delta.

Parascandola, M. and Weed, D.L. (2001), 'Causation in Epidemiology', *Journal of Epidemiology and Community Health*, **55**, pp. 905–12.

Rawls, J. (1971), *A Theory of Justice*, Cambridge, MA: Harvard University Press.

Rawls, J. (1993), *Political Liberalism*, New York: Columbia University Press.

Rothstein, M.A. (2005), 'Expanding the Ethical Analysis of Biobanks', *Journal of Law, Medicine and Ethics*, **33**, pp. 89–101.

Rothstein, M.A. and Carnahan, S. (2001), 'Legal and Policy Issues in Expanding the Scope of Law Enforcement DNA Data Banks', *Brooklyn Law Review*, **67**, pp. 127–78.

Schabas, R. (2002), 'Is Public Health Ethical?', *Canadian Journal of Public Health*, **93**, pp. 98–99.

Schüklenk, U. (2001), *AIDS, Society, Ethics and the Law*, Aldershot: Ashgate.

Selgelid, M.J. (2008), 'Improving Global Health: Counting Reasons Why', *Developing World Bioethics*, **8**, pp. 115–25.

Sen, A. (1985), *Commodities and Capabilities*, Amsterdam: North Holland.

Sharpe, V.A. (2008), '"Clean" Nuclear Energy? Global Warming, Public Health and Justice', *Hastings Center Report*, **38** (4), pp. 16–18.

Walt, G. and Buse, K. (2000), 'Partnerships and Fragmentation in International Health: Threat or Opportunity?, *Tropical Medicine International Health*, **5**, pp. 467–71.

Wendler, D. (2006), 'One-time General Consent for Research on Biological Samples', *British Medical Journal*, **332**, pp. 544–47.

Wendo, C. (2003), 'Uganda Agrees to Increase Health Spending Using Global Fund's Grant', *Lancet*, **360**, pp. 1847–48.

Wolf, S.M. (1995), 'Beyond "Genetic Discrimination": Toward the Broader Harm of Geneticism', *Journal of Law, Medicine and Ethics*, **23**, pp. 345–53.

Further Reading

Articles

Alderman, J., Smith, J.A., Fried, E.J. and Daynard, R.A. (2007), 'Application of Law to Childhood Obesity Epidemic', *Journal of Law, Medicine and Ethics*, **35**, pp. 90–112.

Bailey, D.B., Skinwer, D. and Warren, S.F. (2005), 'Newborn Screening for Developmental Disabilities', *American Journal of Public Health*, **95**, pp. 1889–93.

Baxi, U. (1998), 'Voices of Suffering and the Future of Human Rights', *Transnational Law and Contemporary Problems*, **8**, pp. 125–69.

Bayer, R. (1981), 'Voluntary Health Risks and Public Policy', *Hastings Center Report*, **11** (5), pp. 26–31.

Bayer, R., Dubler, N.N. and Landesmann, S. (1993), 'The Dual Epidemic of Tuberculosis and AIDS: Ethical and Policy Issues in Screening and Treatment', *American Journal of Public Health*, **83**, pp. 649–54.

Bayer, R., Gostin, L., Javitt, G. and Brandt, A. (2002), 'Tobacco Advertising in the United States: A Proposal for a Constitutionally Acceptable Form of Regulation', *Journal of the American Medical Association*, **287**, pp. 2990–95.

Bayer, R. and Moreno, J.D. (1986), 'Health Promotion: Ethical and Social Dilemmas of Government Policy', *Health Affairs*, **5** (2), pp. 72–85.

Beauchamp, D.E. (1980), 'Public Health and Individual Liberty', *Annual Review of Public Health*, **1**, pp. 121–36.

Beauchamp, D.E. (1985), 'Community: The Neglected Tradition of Public Health', *Hastings Center Report*, **15** (6), pp. 28–36.

Beauchamp, T.L., Cook, R.R., Fayerweather, W.E., Raube, G.K., Thar, W.E., Cowles, S.R. and Spivey, G.H. (1991), 'Ethical Guidelines for Epidemiologists', *Journal of Clinical Epidemiology*, **44** (Supplement 1), pp. 151–69.

Boddington, P. (2009), 'Heart Disease and Social Inequality: Ethical Issue in the Aetiology, Prevention and Treatment of Heart Disease', *Bioethics*, **23**, pp. 123–30.

Booy, R., Brown, L.E., Grohmann, G.S. and MacIntyre, C.R. (2006), 'Pandemic Vaccines: Promises and Pitfalls', *Medical Journal of Australia*, **185**, pp. 62–65.

Brock, D. (2001), 'Some Questions about the Moral Responsibilities of Drug Companies in Developing World Countries', *Developing World Bioethics*, **1**, pp. 33–37.

Brody, H. and Avery, E.N. (2009), 'Medicine's Duty to Treat Pandemic Illness', *Hastings Center Report*, **39** (1), pp. 40–48.

Brundtland, G. (2003), 'Global Health and International Security', *Global Governance*, **9**, pp. 417–23.

Burke, W., Coughlin, S.S., Lee, N.C., Weed, D.L. and Khoury, M.J. (2001), 'Application of Population Screening Principles to Genetic Screening for Adult-Onset Conditions', *Genetic Testing*, **5**, pp. 201–11.

Calandrillo, S. (2004), 'Vanishing Vaccination: Why are so Many Americans Opting Out of Vaccinating their Children?', *University of Michigan Journal of Law Reform*, **37**, pp. 353–440.

Cameron, P.A., Rainer, T.H. and Smit, P.D.V. (2003), 'The SARS Epidemic: Lessons for Australia', *Medical Journal of Australia*, 178, pp. 478–79.

Chapman, A. (2009), 'Globalization, Human Rights and the Social Determinants of Health', *Bioethics*, **23**, pp. 97–111.

Childress, J.F. and Bernheim, R.G. (2003), 'Beyond the Liberal and Communitarian Impasse: A Framework and Vision for Public Health', *University of Florida Law Review*, **55**, pp. 1191–219.
Clark, C.C. (2005), 'In Harm's Way: AMA Physicians and the Duty to Treat', *Journal of Medicine and Philosophy*, **30**, pp. 65–87.
Coker, R. (2004), 'Compulsory Screening of Immigrants for Tuberculosis and HIV', *British Medical Journal*, **328** (7435), pp. 298–300.
Coker, R., Thomas, M., Lock, K. and Martin, R. (2007), 'Detention and the Evolving Threat of Tuberculosis', *Journal of Law, Medicine and Ethics*, **35**, pp. 609–15.
Cole, P. (1995), 'The Moral Bases for Public Health Interventions', *Epidemiology*, **6**, pp. 78–83.
Collignon, P.J. and Carnie, J.A. (2006), 'Infection Control and Pandemic Influenza', *Medical Journal of Australia*, **185**, pp. 54–57.
Connolly, M., Gayer, M., Ryan, M.J., Salama, P., Spiegel, P. and Heymann, D.L. (2004), 'Communicable Diseases in Complex Emergencies: Impacts and Challenges', *Lancet*, **364** (9449), pp. 1974–83.
Coughlin, S.S. (2000), 'Ethics and Epidemiology at the End of the Twentieth Century: Ethics, Values and Mission Statements', *Epidemiologic Reviews*, **22**, pp. 169–75.
Courtwright, A.M. (2009), 'Justice, Stigma and the New Epidemiology of Health Disparities', *Bioethics*, **23**, pp. 90–96.
DeAngelis, C. and Flanagin, A. (2004), 'Tuberculosis – A Global Problem Requiring a Global Solution', *Journal of the American Medical Association*, **293**, 2793–94.
Diekema, D.S. (2005), 'Responding to Parental Refusals of Immunization of Children' *Pediatrics*, **115**, pp. 1428–31.
Dowdeswell, E., Daar, A. and Singer, P. (2003), 'Bridging the Genomics Divide', *Global Governance*, **9**, pp. 1–6.
Duncan, P. and Cribb, A. (1996), 'Helping People Change: An Ethical Approach?', *Health Education Research*, **11**, pp. 339–48.
Dworkin, G. (1981), 'Voluntary Health Risks and Public Policy: Taking Risks, Addressing Responsibility', *Hastings Center Report*, **11** (5), pp. 26–31.
Eide, B.L. (1997), '"The Least a Parent Can Do": Prenatal Genetic Testing and the Welcome of Our Children', *Ethics and Medicine*, **13** (3), pp. 59–66.
Elliman, D.A.C., Dezateux, C. and Bedford, H.E. (2002), 'Newborn and Childhood Screening Programmes: Criteria, Evidence and Current Policy', *Archives of Disease in Childhood*, **87** (1), pp. 6–9.
Epstein, C.J. (2000), 'Some Ethical Implications of the Human Genome Project', *Genetics in Medicine*, **2**, pp. 193–97.
Faden, R.R. (1987), 'Ethical Issues in Government Sponsored Public Health Campaigns', *Health Education Quarterly*, **14**, pp. 27–37.
Fidler, D.P. (2005), 'From International Sanitary Conventions to Global Health Security: The New International Health Regulations', *Chinese Journal of International Law*, **4**, pp. 325–92.
Fox, A.M. and Meier, B.M. (2009), 'Health as Freedom: Addressing Social Determinants of Global Health Inequities through the Human Right to Development', *Bioethics*, **23**, pp. 112–22.
Freak, J. and Gómez-Dantés, O. (2002), 'Globalization and Challenges to Health Systems', *British Medical Journal*, **325**, pp. 95–97.
Gable, L. (2007), 'The Proliferation of Human Rights in Global Health Governance', *Journal of Law, Medicine and Ethics*, **35**, pp. 534–44.
Gauthier, C.C. (2000) 'Moral Responsibility and Respect for Autonomy: Meeting the Communitarian Challenge', *Kennedy Institute of Ethics Journal*, **10**, pp. 337–52.
Gordis, L., Gold, E. and Seltser, R. (1977), 'Privacy Protection in Epidemiologic and Medical Research: A Challenge and a Responsibility', *American Journal of Epidemiology*, **105**, pp. 163–68.

Gostin. L.O. (2003), 'When Terrorism Threatens Health: How Far are Limitations on Personal and Economic Liberties Justified?', *University of Florida Law Review*, **55**, pp. 1105–69.
Gostin, L. (2006), 'Medical Countermeasures for Pandemic Influenza: Ethics and the Law', *Journal of the American Medical Association*, **295**, pp. 554–56.
Gray, J.A.M. (2004), 'New Concepts in Screening', *British Journal of General Practice*, **54**, pp. 292–98.
Greenough, P. (1995), 'Intimidation, Coercion and Resistance in the Final Stage of the South Asian Smallpox Eradication Campaign, 1973–1975', *Social Science and Medicine*, **41**, pp. 633–45.
Gruskin, S. and Loff, B. (2002), 'Do Human Rights Have a Role in Public Health Work?', *Lancet*, **359** (9337), p. 1880.
Gudorf, C. (1996), 'Gender and Culture in the Globalization of Bioethics', *St Louis University Public Law Review*, **15**, pp. 331–51.
Guttman, N. and Salmon, C.T. (2004), 'Guilt, Fear, Stigma and Knowledge Gaps: Ethical Issues in Public Health Communication Interventions', *Bioethics*, **18**, pp. 531–52.
Häyry, H. and Häyry, M. (1989), 'Utilitarianism, Human Rights and the Redistribution of Health through Preventive Medical Measures', *Journal of Applied Philosophy*, **6**, pp. 43–51.
Herissone-Kelly, P. (2003), 'Bioethics in the United Kingdom: Genetic Screening, Disability Rights, and the Erosion of Trust', *Cambridge Quarterly of Healthcare Ethics*, **12**, pp. 235–41.
Hobson-West, P. (2003), 'Understanding Vaccination Resistance: Moving Beyond Risk', *Health, Risk, and Society*, **5** (3), pp. 273–83.
Holtzman, N.A. and Andrew, L.B. (1997), 'Ethical and Legal Issues in Genetic Epidemiology', *Epidemiologic Reviews*, **19**, pp. 163–74.
Hubar, S. and Wynia, M.K. (2004), 'When Pestilence Prevails ... Physician Responsibilities in Epidemics', *American Journal of Bioethics*, **4** (1), pp. W5–W11.
Illingworth, P. and Parmet, W.E. (2009), 'The Ethical Implications of the Social Determinants of Health: A Global Renaissance for Bioethics', *Bioethics*, **23**, pp. ii–v.
Isaacs, D., Kilham, H.A. and Marshall, H. (2004), 'Should Routine Childhood Immunizations be Compulsory?', *Journal of Paediatrics and Child Health*, **40**, pp. 392–96.
Isaacs, R. and Nguyen, T. (2005), 'The Global Governance of Infectious Diseases: The World Health Organization and the International Health Regulations', *Alberta Law Review*, **43**, pp. 497–510.
Jacobson, P.D., Wasserman, J. and Anderson, J.R. (1997), 'Historical Overview of Tobacco Legislation and Regulation', *Journal of Social Issues*, **54**, pp. 75–95.
Jennings, B. (2003), 'Framework for Ethics in Public Health', *Acta Bioethica*, **9**, pp. 165–76.
Juss, S. (1997), 'Global Environmental Change: Health and the Challenge for Human Rights', *Indiana Journal of Global Legal Studies*, **5** (1), pp. 121–78.
Kirby, M. (2003), 'Genomics and Democracy: A Global Challenge', *Western Australia Law Review*, **31**, pp. 1–18.
Krieger, N. (1996), 'Questioning Epidemiology: Objectivity, Advocacy and Socially Responsible Science', *American Journal of Public Health*, **89**, pp. 1151–53.
Lachmann, P.J. (1998), 'Public Health and Bioethics', *Journal of Medicine and Philosophy*, **23**, pp. 297–302.
Lappé, M. (1983), 'Values and Public Health: Value Considerations in Setting Health Policy', *Theoretical Medicine and Bioethics*, **4**, pp. 71–92.
Lee, R.G. and Morgan, D. (2001), 'Regulating Risk Society: Stigmata Cases, Scientific Citizenship and Biomedical Diplomacy', *Sydney Law Review*, **23**, pp. 297–318.
Leeder, S.R. (2004), 'Ethics and Public Health', *Internal Medicine Journal*, **34**, pp. 435–39.
Levin, B.W. and Fleischman, A.R. (2002), 'Public Health and Bioethics: The Benefits of Collaboration', *American Journal of Public Health*, **92**, pp. 165–67.
Levine, C. and Bayer, R. (1985), 'Screening Blood: Public Health and Medical Uncertainty', *Hastings Center Report*, **15** (supplement), pp. 8–11.

Lyren, A. and Leonard, E. (2006), 'Vaccine Refusal: Issues for the Primary Care Physician', *Clinical Pediatrics*, **45**, pp. 399–404.
McCormick, J. (1996), 'Medical Hubris and the Public Health', *Journal of Clinical Epidemiology*, **49**, pp. 619–21.
McKeown, R.E. (2000), 'American College of Epidemiology Ethics Guidelines – Filling a Critical Gap in the Profession', *Annals of Epidemiology*, **10**, pp. 485–86.
Mann, J. (1995), 'Human Rights and the New Public Health', *Health and Human Rights*, **1**, pp. 229–33.
Marantz, P.R. (1990), 'Blaming the Victim: The Negative Consequences of Preventive Medicine', *American Journal of Public Health*, **80**, pp. 1186–87.
March, D. and Sasser, E. (2006), 'The Eco- in Eco-Epidemiology', *International Journal of Epidemiology*, **35**, pp. 1379–83.
Murray, C.J.L, Lopez, A.D., Chin, B., Feehan, D. and Hill, K.H. (2006), 'Estimation of Potential Global Pandemic Influenza Mortality on the Basis of Vital Registry Data from the 1918–1920 Pandemic: A Quantitative Analysis', *Lancet*, **368**, pp. 2211–18.
Nelson, M.C. and Rogers, J. (1992), 'The Right to Die? Anti-Vaccination Activity and the 1874 Smallpox Epidemic in Stockholm', *Social History of Medicine*, **5**, pp. 369–88.
Noah, N.D. (1987), 'Immunisation before School Entry: Should there be a Law?', *British Medical Journal*, **294** (6582), pp. 1270–71.
O'Neill, O. (2002), 'Public Health or Clinical Ethics: Thinking Beyond Borders', *Ethics and International Affairs*, **16** (2), pp. 35–45.
Parascandola, M. and Weed, D.L. (2001), 'Causation in Epidemiology', *Journal of Epidemiology and Community Health*, **55**, pp. 905–12.
Parker, L.S. (1995), 'Breast Cancer Genetic Screening and Critical Bioethics' Gaze', *Journal of Medicine and Philosophy*, **20**, pp. 313–37.
Parmet, W. (2003), 'Liberalism, Communitarianism and Public Health', *University of Florida Law Review*, **55**, pp. 1221–40.
Pywell, S. (2000), 'Vaccination and other Altruistic Medical Treatments: Should Autonomy or Communitarianism Prevail?', *Medical Law International*, **4**, pp. 223–43.
Ramsey, J., Richardson, J., Carter, Y.H., Davidson, L.L. and Feder, G. (2002), 'Should Health Professionals Screen Women for Domestic Violence? Systematic Review', *British Medical Journal*, **325** (7539), pp. 314–18.
Reid, L. (2005), 'Diminishing Returns? Risk and the Duty to Care in the SARS Epidemic', *Bioethics*, **19**, pp. 348–61.
Ries, N. (2005), 'Quarantine and the Law: The 2003 SARS Experience in Canada (A New Disease Calls on Old Public Health Tools)', *Alberta Law Review*, **43**, pp. 529–47.
Roberts, M.J.R. and Reich, M.R. (2002), 'Ethical Analysis in Public Health', *Lancet*, **359** (4311), pp. 1055–59.
Rogers, W. (2006), 'Feminism and Public Health Ethics', *Journal of Medical Ethics*, **32**, pp. 351–54.
Rothstein, M.A. (2004), 'Are Traditional Public Health Strategies Consistent with Contemporary American Values?', *Temple Law Review*, **77**, pp. 175–92.
Shapiro, M. (2002), 'Does Technological Enhancement of Human Traits Threaten Human Equality and Democracy?', *San Diego Law Review*, **39**, pp. 769–842.
Shickle, D. and Chadwick, R. (1994), 'The Ethics of Screening: Is "Screeningitis" an Incurable Disease?', *Journal of Medical Ethics*, **20**, pp. 12–18.
Sidel, V.W., Cohen, H.W. and Gould, R.M. (2002), 'Bioterrorism Preparedness: Cooptation of Public Health', *Medicine and Global Survival*, **7**, pp. 82–89.
Skrabanek, P. (1990), 'Why is Preventive Medicine Exempted from Ethical Constrants?, *Journal of Medical Ethics*, **16**, pp. 187–90.

Stone, D. and Stewart, S. (1996), 'Screening and the New Genetics: A Public Health Perspective on the Ethical Debate', *Journal of Public Health and Medicine*, **18**, pp. 3–5.

Tatara, K. (2002), 'Philosophy of Public Health: Lessons from its History in England', *Journal of Public Health Medicine*, **24**, pp. 11–15.

Thomas, J.C., Sage, M., Dillenberg, J. and Guillory, V.J. (2002), 'A Code of Ethics for Public Health', *American Journal of Public Health*, **92**, pp. 1057–59.

Veatch, R.M. (1980), 'Voluntary Risks to Health: The Ethical Issues', *Journal of the American Medical Association*, **243**, pp. 50–55.

Venkatapuram, S. and Marmot, M. (2009), 'Epidemiology and Social Justice in Light of Social Determinates of Health Research', *Bioethics*, **23**, pp. 79–89.

Verweij, M. and Dawson, A. (2004), 'Ethical Principles for Collective Immunisation Programmes', *Vaccine*, **22**, pp. 3122–26.

Weed, D.L. (1999), 'Towards a Philosophy of Public Health', *Journal of Epidemiology and Community Health*, **53**, pp. 99–104.

Weed, D.L. and McKeown, R.E. (1998), 'Epidemiology and Virtue Ethics', *International Journal of Epidemiology*, **27**, pp. 343–49.

Wynia, M.K. (2005), 'Public Health Principlism: The Precautionary Principle and Beyond', *American Journal of Bioethics*, **5** (3), pp. 3–4.

Yeo, M. (1993), 'Toward an Ethic of Empowerment for Health Promotion', *Health Promotion International*, **8**, pp. 225–35.

Books

Bartley, M. (2004), *Health Inequality*, Cambridge: Polity.

Bayer, R., Gostin, L.O., Jennings, B. and Steinbock, B. (2007), *Public Health Ethics*, New York: Oxford University Press.

Beaglehole, R. (2003), *Global Public Health: A New Era*, Oxford: Oxford University Press.

Beaglehole, R. and Bonita, R. (2004), *Public Health at the Crossroads – Achievements and Prospects* (2nd edn), Cambridge: Cambridge University Press.

Beauchamp, D.E. (1988), *The Health of the Republic: Epidemics, Medicine and Moralism as Challenges in Democracy*, Philadelphia: Temple University Press.

Bennett, B. (2008), *Health Law's Kaleidoscope: Health Law Rights in a Global Age*, Aldershot: Ashgate.

Bennett, B. and Tomossy, G.F. (2006), *Globalization and Health: Challenges for Health Law and Bioethics*, Dordrecht: Springer.

BMA (1990), *BMA Guide To Living With Risk*, Harmondsworth: Penguin.

Bowling, A. (1997), *Research Methods in Health*, Buckingham: Open University Press.

Bradley, P. and Burls, A. (2000), *Ethics in Public and Community Health*, New York: Routledge.

Briggs, D., Joffe, M. and Elliott, P. (2003), *Impact of Environmental Pollution on Health*, Oxford: Oxford University Press.

Briggs, D., Stern, R. and Tinker, T.L. (1999), *Environmental Health for All*, Dordrecht: Kluwer.

Brownson, R.C., Baker, E.A., Leet, T.L. and Gillespie, K.N. (2003), *Evidence-Based Public Health*, New York: Oxford University Press.

Callahan, D. (2000), *Promoting Healthy Behavior: How Much Freedom? Whose Responsibility?*, Washington, DC: Georgetown University Press.

Chapman, S. and Lupton, D. (1994), *The Fight for Public Health: Principles and Practice of Media Advocacy*, London: BMJ.

Connelly, J. and Worth, C. (1997), *Making Sense of Public Health Medicine*, Abingdon: Radcliffe Medical Press.

Coughlin, S.S. and Beauchamp, T.L. (1996), *Ethics and Epidemiology*, Oxford: Oxford University Press.

Cranor, C.F. (1993), *Regulating Toxin Substances: A Philosophy of Science and the Law*, New York: Oxford University Press.

Cribb, A. and Duncan, P. (2002), *Health Promotion and Professional Ethics*, Oxford: Blackwell.

Davey, B., Gray, A. and Seale, C. (2001), *Health and Disease: A Reader*, Buckingham: Open University Press.

Detels, R., Holland, W.H., McEwen, J. and Omenn, G.S. (1997), *Oxford Textbook of Public Health* (3rd edn), New York: Oxford University Press.

Donaldson, L.J. and Donaldson, R.J. (2000), *Essential Public Health* (2nd edn), Plymouth: Petroc Press.

Essex, M., Mboup, S., Kanki, P.J. and Kalengayi, M.R. (eds) (1994), *AIDS in Africa*, New York: Raven Press.

Farmer, R. and Lawrenson, R. (2004), *Epidemiology and Public Health Medicine* (5th edn), Oxford: Blackwell.

Fee, E. and Fox, D.M. (1988), *AIDS: The Burdens of History*, Berkeley: University of California Press.

Gillam, S., Yates, J. and Badrinath, P. (2007), *Essential Public Health: Theory and Practice*, Cambridge: Cambridge University Press.

Glynn, I. and Glynn, J. (2004), *The Life and Death of Smallpox*, London: Profile Books.

Held, D., McGrew, A., Goldblatt, D. and Perraton, J. (1999), *Global Transformations: Politics, Economics and Culture*, Cambridge: Polity.

Holland, S. (2007), *Public Health Ethics*, Cambridge: Polity.

Kindhauser, M. (ed.) (2003), *Global Defence against the Infectious Disease Threat*, Geneva: World Health Organization.

Leichter, H.M. (1991), *Free to be Foolish: Politics and Health Promotion in the U.S. and Great Britain*, Princeton: Princeton University Press.

McKibbin, W. and Sidorenko, A. (2006), *Global Macroeconomic Consequences of Pandemic Influenza*, Sydney: Lowy Institute for International Policy.

Marmot, M. (2004), *The Status Syndrome: How Social Standing Affects Our Health and Longevity*, New York: Henry Holt, Times Books.

Marmot, M. and Wilkinson, R.G. (2006), *Social Determinants of Health* (2nd edn), Oxford: Oxford University Press.

Marriott, E. (2002), *The Plague Race: A Tale of Fear, Science and Heroism*, London: Picador.

Mollenkamp, C., Levy, A., Menn, J. and Rothfeder, J. (1998), *The People vs Big Tobacco*, Princeton: Bloomberg Press.

Moreno, J. (2003), *In the Wake of Terror*, Cambridge, MA: MIT Press.

Petchesky, R. (2003), *Global Prescriptions: Gendering Health and Human Rights*, London: Zed Books.

Rabin, R.L. and Sugarman, S.D. (2001), *Regulating Tobacco*, New York: Oxford University Press.

Rawls, J. (1999), *The Law of Peoples*, Cambridge, MA: Harvard University Press.

Reynolds, C. (2004), *Public Health Law and Regulation*, Annandale, NSW: Federation Press.

Rothman, K.J. (2002), *Epidemiology: An Introduction*, Oxford: Oxford University Press.

Scambler, G. (2003), *Sociology as Applied to Medicine* (5th edn), Edinburgh: Saunders.

Steele, J. (2006), *Risks and Legal Theory*, Oxford: Hart.

Veatch, R. and Branson, R. (1976), *Ethics and Health Policy*, Cambridge, MA: Ballinger.

World Health Organization (2006), *World Health Report 2006: Working Together for Health*, Geneva: WHO.

Part I
The SARS Crisis

[1]

SARS: Political Pathology of the First Post-Westphalian Pathogen

David P. Fidler

In March 2003, the world discovered, again, that humanity's battle with infectious diseases continues. The twenty-first century began with infectious diseases, especially HIV/AIDS, being discussed as threats to human rights,[1] economic development,[2] and national security.[3] Bioterrorism in the United States in October 2001 increased concerns about pathogenic microbes. The global outbreak of severe acute respiratory syndrome (SARS) in the spring of 2003 kept the global infectious disease challenge at the forefront of world news for weeks. At its May 2003 annual meeting, the World Health Organization (WHO) asserted that SARS is "the first severe infectious disease to emerge in the twenty-first century" and "poses a serious threat to global health security, the livelihood of populations, the functioning of health systems, and the stability and growth of economies."[4]

As an emerging threat, SARS presents novel problems for public health. SARS challenges scientists to develop diagnostics, treatments, and a vaccine for a virus—the SARS-associated coronavirus (SARS-CoV)—not previously identified in humans. Clinicians struggled to diagnose and treat those infected with the SARS-CoV. SARS forced public health officials to respond to the international spread of a new pathogen amplified by globalization. SARS reintroduced societies to long-dormant, large-scale isolation and quarantine practices, raising questions about balancing public health and individual rights.

With SARS, so much has happened and, at the time of writing, so little time has passed, that attempting a comprehensive analysis of SARS as an emerging public health issue would be misguided. My objective is to probe the political pathology of SARS as the first post-Westphalian pathogen. As WHO stated, SARS is the first severe infectious disease to emerge in the twenty-first century; but SARS is also noteworthy because it is the first pathogen to emerge into a political and governance environment that differs from what existed at the time of earlier outbreaks.

This article examines governance issues that SARS raises for public health in its post-Westphalian context. As explored below, the term "Westphalian" refers to the governance framework that defined international public health activities from the mid-nineteenth century. In the 1990s and early 2000s, literature on globalization's impact on public health described shifts away from Westphalian public health toward new approaches, strategies, and attitudes. Although post-Westphalian public health began to emerge before the SARS outbreak, SARS represents the first pathogen to emerge into this new political and governance context. As such, SARS presents an opportunity to examine the political pathology of a post-Westphalian pathogen. This examination evaluates the strengths and weaknesses of post-Westphalian public health in light of the challenges SARS generated. Not surprisingly, the political pathology of SARS contains good and bad news for public health governance.

My analysis proceeds in three parts. First, I explain "Westphalian" and "post-Westphalian" public health to elucidate how the structure and dynamics of international relations shape public health governance. Second, I examine the political pathology of SARS as a post-Westphalian pathogen. Central to this analysis will be China because the Chinese response to SARS provides insights into why public health has entered a post-Westphalian context. Third, I look at vulnerabilities and problems post-Westphalian public health may face in light of the SARS outbreak. The shift from Westphalian to post-Westphalian public health confirmed by SARS is not without sobering elements that require the attention of public health governance.

WESTPHALIAN AND POST-WESTPHALIAN PUBLIC HEALTH

Of germs and borders

In many respects, what transpired in the SARS outbreak happened frequently in the past—a new pathogenic microbe emerges in humans; spreads through international trade and travel; causes economic, political, and social disruption; and reveals weaknesses in public health systems. The great cliché of infectious disease control—germs do not recognize borders—applies to SARS as it previously applied to earlier outbreaks.

These observations raise the question whether the SARS outbreak really represents something new for public health. Analysis of emerging and re-emerging infectious diseases (EIDs) in the 1990s and early 2000s stressed that the world had not conquered infectious diseases and that microbes were increasingly formidable foes.[5] The global devastation wrought by HIV/AIDS had, by the turn of the century, reached horrifying proportions, making this disease one of the worst in history.[6] SARS joins, thus, a long list of germs that have not recognized borders.

For my purposes, what makes SARS interesting is not its germ; rather, SARS is important because of the context in which SARS-CoV did not recognize borders. Put another way, I am interested in the borders—the political and governance structure—that SARS did not recognize. SARS is the first post-Westphalian pathogen because its non-recognition of borders transpired in a public health governance environment different from what previous border-hopping bugs encountered. So much attention has been placed on the novelty of the SARS germ that we may not fully appreciate the novelty of the borders SARS ignored.

To advance my argument, I distinguish between "Westphalian" and "post-Westphalian" public health. Like all social endeavors, public health governance reflects larger political structures and forces, which shape how societies pursue public health. For example, in the United States, federalism structures public health governance in a particular way.[7] Federalism constructs political borders between federal and state governments. Germs no more recognize these borders than they recognize international borders. Federalism does not, however, disappear as an influence on public health governance simply because germs do not recognize the boundaries it creates.

The same dynamic holds true at the international level—germs do not recognize boundaries between countries; but those boundaries nevertheless structure the political response to infectious disease threats. As explained below, principles for public health governance between countries traditionally derived from the structure for international relations established in 1648 at the Peace of Westphalia. "Westphalian public health" refers, therefore, to public health governance as structured by Westphalian principles. "Post-Westphalian public health" describes public health governance that departs from the Westphalian template. SARS is the first post-Westphalian pathogen because it highlights public health's transition from a Westphalian to a post-Westphalian context.

Before I distinguish Westphalian and post-Westphalian public health, I should acknowledge that the distinctions between them are not, in reality, as crisp as my analysis may project. Concepts that characterize post-Westphalian public health appeared before SARS emerged and have been applied to address existing pathogens. In addition, responses to other recently emerged microbes utilized tools that characterize post-Westphalian public health governance.

Nevertheless, SARS represents the first post-Westphalian pathogen for two reasons. First, the SARS outbreak is the first infectious disease epidemic since HIV/AIDS to pose a truly global threat. Other microbes that emerged in the last thirty years have had limited capacity to threaten international public health because of inefficient human-to-human transmission (such as the avian influenza, Nipah, Hendra, and Hanta viruses), dependence on food or insects as vectors (examples include *Escherichia coli* 0157:H7, variant Creutzfeldt-Jakob disease, West Nile and Rift Valley fevers), or specific geographical locations (e.g., *Neisseria meningitidis* W135, Ebola, Marburg, and Crimean-Congo hemorrhagic fevers).[8] SARS posed a greater threat because of its more efficient person-to-person respiratory transmission and its fatality rate.

Second, because of the nature of the SARS threat, the epidemic severely challenged the emerging post-Westphalian governance system. SARS was a global public health emergency,[9] and the sternest measure of governance systems is their performance in times of crisis. The SARS outbreak provided the first opportunity to evaluate how the new governance approach for infectious diseases would fare under serious microbial attack.

WESTPHALIAN PUBLIC HEALTH

Westphalian international politics

International relations scholars identify the Peace of Westphalia in 1648 as a landmark moment because it ended the Thirty Years' War and established a political structure for international politics that has endured for over three centuries.[10] Independent, territorial states interacting in a condition of anarchy characterize the Westphalian system.[11] States dominate the Westphalian structure and determine the nature of the anarchy in which they interact.[12] In the Westphalian system, anarchy means the absence of a common, supreme authority.[13] Political authority is fragmented among states in the Westphalian structure.

This fragmentation created the need for principles to guide anarchical interaction. The key principle of the Westphalian structure is sovereignty—the state reigns supreme over its territory and people.[14] Sovereignty then generates derivative governance principles. First, because sovereignty means supreme power, the Westphalian system frowned upon one state intervening in the domestic affairs of other states.[15] The principle of non-intervention excluded, thus, a great deal of sovereign behavior from diplomacy. Second, sovereignty meant that rules to govern interaction arose from the states themselves because no supreme, central law-making body existed. In the Westphalian order, a state was free to exercise its sovereignty as it saw fit unless that state had consented to a rule of international law that regulated its behavior.[16]

The combination of sovereignty, non-intervention, and consent-based international law meant that governance in the Westphalian system was horizontal in nature, meaning that (1) only states were involved in governance; (2) governance primarily addressed the mechanics of state interaction (e.g., diplomacy, war, and trade); and (3) governance did not penetrate sovereignty to address how a government treated its people or ruled over its territory. The Westphalian structure exhibited another characteristic—the great powers determined how the system functioned.[17] Great-power management of international relations occurred through warfare and the balance of power.[18] The great powers' role in the Westphalian structure also came to reflect political and cultural prejudices as European power expanded and brought non-European peoples into the Westphalian system.[19]

Like any brief description of complex reality, this overview of the Westphalian structure is simplistic. Nevertheless, it captures basic features of the international governance structure into which public health emerged as an issue in the mid-nineteenth century and under which Westphalian public health governance evolved in subsequent decades.

Westphalian public health

The Westphalian structure for international politics had been in place for two centuries before the cross-border spread of infectious diseases became a subject for international diplomacy in the mid-nineteenth century. International cooperation on infectious diseases conformed to the Westphalian structure and reflected its principles. The international regime constructed to deal with the spread of infectious diseases provides an excellent example of Westphalian public health.

Beginning in 1851, the European great powers began developing diplomatic processes and international legal rules to facilitate cooperation on infectious diseases.[20] These processes and rules formed a horizontal regime between governments that sought to mitigate the friction infectious diseases created for state interactions, primarily trade and travel. In keeping with the principles of sovereignty and non-intervention, international cooperation on infectious diseases did not penetrate the state to require improvements in national public health. For example, the international regime for infectious disease control crafted in the last half of the nineteenth century and the first half of the twentieth century never required states to improve national sanitation and water systems despite knowledge that such improvements would decrease cholera outbreaks and their spread.[21] The regime merely targeted problems caused by infectious diseases moving between states through international trade and travel.

The regime on infectious diseases also reflected the interests of the great powers because disparate national quarantine measures imposed significant costs on growing levels of international trade.[22] Further, the regime addressed only infectious diseases for which trade and travel were considered vectors, such as plague, cholera, and yellow fever. Diseases endemic in Europe, such as tuberculosis, were not included in the regime despite their cross-border transmissibility. The choice of diseases to include in the regime reflected European states' sense of vulnerability to diseases spreading from non-European regions.[23] This fear of disease importation was "not a wish for the general betterment of the health of the world, but the desire to protect certain favored (especially European) nations from contamination by their less-favored (especially Eastern) fellows."[24]

The characteristics of Westphalian public health governance can be seen in WHO's International Health Regulations (IHR).[25] The IHR are the only set of international legal rules binding on WHO members concerning infectious diseases,[26] and the IHR continue the approach to cooperation on infectious diseases begun in the mid-nineteenth century.[27] The IHR are classically Westphalian in their structure and content.

The IHR's objective is to ensure the maximum security against the international spread of disease with minimal interference with world traffic.[28] This objective is horizontal because it focuses on infectious diseases moving between states. The IHR seek maximum security against the international spread of disease by requiring governments to (1) notify WHO of outbreaks of diseases subject to the Regulations;[29] and (2) maintain certain public health capabilities at ports and airports.[30] The IHR seek minimum interference with world traffic by regulating the trade and travel restrictions WHO members can take against countries suffering outbreaks of diseases subject to the Regulations.[31]

In keeping with the Westphalian template, the IHR constitute rules of international law created by states. The rules respect the principle of non-intervention by addressing only aspects of infectious diseases that relate to the intercourse among states. The IHR do not address aspects of public health governance that touch on how a government prevents and controls infectious diseases in its sovereign territory. The IHR's limited governance framework is also clear from the small number of diseases subject to its rules, currently only plague, cholera, and yellow fever.[32]

Another characteristic marked Westphalian public health—infectious disease control ranked low as a foreign policy priority for states. Evidence for this claim comes in many forms. The fact that the existing IHR only deal with the same diseases discussed at the first International Sanitary Conference in 1851[33] suggests the low priority WHO members assigned to international infectious disease control. Widespread violation of the IHR's rules by WHO members also provides an indication of the unimportance of these rules to state behavior.[34] Acknowledgement by WHO personnel in the 1960s and 1970s that the IHR had not achieved their purpose underscores the low priority this governance regime received from WHO members.[35]

Westphalian public health proved ineffective in the form of the IHR. The IHR's irrelevance to the HIV/AIDS epidemic further confirmed that the Westphalian template embedded in the IHR was suspect. Other developments also signaled the demise of Westphalian public health. After its formation, "[i]n a period of great vitality in the scientific understanding of infectious diseases and of progress in medical technology—in vaccines for prevention and drugs for treatment—the WHO added eliminating communicable diseases at their sources to its mandate of containing their spread through its more traditional functions of coordinating international health regulations and serving as an information clearinghouse."[36] Such vertical activities reflected more interest in public health conditions within poor countries than in managing the public health consequences of mechanistic state interaction for the benefit of the great powers' trading interests.

This shift from horizontal to vertical strategies was also apparent in the increasing role human rights played in public health. Comparing the IHR's approach with WHO's Health for All effort and its emphasis on the human right to the highest attainable standard of health[37] illustrates how far Westphalian public health had fallen out of favor by the end of the 1970s. The HIV/AIDS pandemic further highlighted these shifts because international human rights law, not the IHR, provided the norms guiding the fight against this new plague.[38] Human rights law focuses on how a government treats its citizens and governs its territory[39] and, thus, embodies a vertical rather than horizontal strategy that causes dissonance for the Westphalian structure for international relations.[40] The emphasis on human rights in responses to the HIV/AIDS pandemic[41] also stimulated a growing role for non-state actors in public health governance. The human rights strategy made individuals actors in public health and brought non-governmental organizations (NGOs) into public health in new ways.

Post-Westphalian Public Health

In the 1990s and early 2000s, governance strategies different from the IHR's Westphalian approach began to appear in analysis of EIDs. A growing appreciation of globalization's impact on public health informed these strategies.[42] Some themes in literature on the globalization of public health were familiar, such as germs do not recognize borders and infectious disease control requires cooperation. But the discourse on globalization and infectious diseases in the 1990s and early 2000s indicated that the Westphalian approach was bankrupt.

Bankruptcy was apparent in at least five ways. First, the increasing threat from pathogenic microbes challenged the low political priority states accorded to international infectious disease control. Second, the number and variety of EIDs made the focus on traditional epidemic diseases (e.g., cholera, plague, and yellow fever) anachronistic. Third, linking infectious disease policy narrowly to commercial intercourse proved unable to address many social and environmental problems fueling disease spread. Fourth, a state-centric governance framework was inadequate in the face of challenges infectious diseases presented. Fifth, a regime on infectious diseases designed mainly to address the fears and interests of the great powers was no longer appropriate given the disproportionate suffering developing countries experienced from infectious diseases.

The EID threat stimulated new thinking in the 1990s and early 2000s, which began to shape strategies on process and substance different from the Westphalian model. On the process side, "global health governance" (GHG) emerged as a framework distinct from the state-centric approach. On the substance side, experts encouraged the production of "global public goods for health" (GPGH) that differ from the narrower objectives of the Westphalian strategy.

Global health governance

Westphalian public health was premised on the principle that states constituted the only legitimate actors for governance purposes. The IHR reflect this state-centric framework, especially with regard to the flow of epidemiological information. Under the IHR, surveillance information upon which WHO can act comes only from governments.[43] Restricting surveillance and response to government-provided notifications and information proved a debilitating weakness for infectious disease governance under the IHR.[44]

In contrast to the IHR's international governance approach, GHG includes not only states and inter-governmental organizations but also non-state actors, such as NGOs and multinational corporations (MNCs).[45] Non-state actors participate in GHG in two ways. First, participation can be informal in that non-state actors attempt to influence governments and international organizations in policy making. The influence of non-state actors—both MNCs and NGOs—has increased in global public health in the last decade.[46] On some issues, such as access to essential medicines, NGOs have taken the policy initiative, forcing governments and international organizations to respond to NGO agenda-setting.[47]

Second, non-state actors participate in GHG through involvement in formal governance mechanisms. NGOs have long been able to have formal relationships with international health organizations, through which NGOs could provide input, as illustrated by NGOs in "official relations" with WHO.[48] Under GHG, NGO involvement becomes more direct and participatory. Perhaps the best example of formal NGO participation in making global health policy is the Global Fund to Fight AIDS, Tuberculosis, and Malaria (Global Fund), the Board of Directors of which includes NGO representatives.[49] Thus, in contrast to official relations with WHO, NGO participation in the Global Fund involves making policy on an equal footing with governments.

Global public goods for health

The pursuit of GPGH represents the second major break from Westphalian public health that developed in the 1990s and early 2000s.[50] "Public goods" are goods or services the consumption of which is non-excludable and non-rivalrous in nature.[51] "Global public goods" exhibit non-excludability and non-rivalry in consumption across national boundaries.[52] GPGH are health-related public goods or services the benefits of which are globally accessible.[53] Containment and prevention of globally dangerous infectious diseases and health-related information, such as global surveillance information on infectious diseases, are both considered GPGH.[54]

Under the Westphalian model, the regime for infectious disease control sought to reduce problems cross-border microbial traffic caused. The objective was narrowly tailored to the national interests of the great powers, which feared importation of pathogens from poor, developing countries and sought to mitigate the impact of quarantine practices on their trade. The GPGH concept departs from the narrow, state-centric objectives of the Westphalian regime in two ways. First, GPGH envisage policy results that reach beyond the state and its national interests vis-à-vis other states. The ambition is to produce public goods that are accessible globally by governments and peoples. Thus, GPGH encompass more than state interactions and are sought for reasons beyond protecting national public health from exogenous threats and promoting national exports. Finally, the public goods sought promise to be beneficial to not only the great powers but also people in developing countries.

The second way GPGH deviate from the traditional approach involves how the goods are produced. In Westphalian public health, states produced regimes and reacted to their consequences. GPGH differ because they seek the participation of not only governments and international organizations but also non-state actions in their production. "Public-private partnerships" (PPPs) in global public health best illustrate the process innovation in the GPGH concept.[55] PPPs in the infectious disease context "fall into two main categories: to discover new drugs and vaccines for diseases neglected by research and industry, and to vastly improve access by the poor to existing products."[56] In connection with developing new drugs for infectious diseases, PPPs bring together governmental, intergovernmental, and non-governmental resources to produce products designed to improve health globally but especially in the developing world.[57] The deliberate involvement of non-state actors echoes the increased participation of such actors in GHG. WHO describes PPPs for infectious diseases as "reshaping the landscape of public health."[58]

Post-Westphalian public health and the revision of the IHR

Acknowledging the IHR's failure as a governance mechanism, WHO began in 1995 a process of revising the Regulations to make them more effective.[59] The revision process from 1995 to the SARS outbreak identified a number of ideas to improve the IHR's contribution to infectious disease governance,[60] and one of the most important ideas resonates with the GHG and the GPGH concepts—supplement disease reporting by governments with epidemiological information provided by non-governmental sources.[61]

From the earliest stages of the IHR revision process, WHO identified using non-governmental sources of information to improve global surveillance.[62] Two factors encouraged WHO's thinking. First, relying solely on governments to provide outbreak information under formal international legal obligations proved a failure under the IHR.[63] Although WHO still needed governments involved in global surveillance, the Organization wanted to be able to use epidemiological information from non-governmental sources.[64] Second, new information technologies, such as the Internet and e-mail, provided WHO with opportunities to mine non-governmental sources of information in order to enhance global surveillance.[65]

Prior to the IHR revision process, WHO had access to non-governmental sources of information but, in law and policy, was limited in how it could use them. Legally, the IHR operated only on the basis of government-provided information.[66] This legal situation reflected Westphalian limitations on WHO's ability to interfere with sovereignty in connection with infectious diseases. WHO's efforts to establish effective global surveillance suffered from these Westphalian constraints on using epidemiological information. Only once during the IHR's history did WHO report a disease outbreak to the international community based on information not received from the government of the country concerned.[67]

The proposal to allow WHO to use information from non-governmental sources connects with the GHG and GPGH concepts. Giving WHO access to non-governmental information would make non-state actors formal participants in global surveillance. By providing information directly or indirectly to WHO, non-state actors could trigger a process in which governments and inter-governmental organizations would have to respond.[68] Under GHG, the public health initiative would no longer remain the exclusive province of the sovereign state.

The proposal to use non-governmental sources of information also connected with interest in GPGH. The provision of information is a classic public good because information can be consumed in non-excludable and non-rivalrous fashion.[69] As the IHR's history revealed, surveillance information the IHR generated was suspect for two reasons. First, WHO members routinely failed to report outbreaks the IHR required them to report.[70] Second, the short list of diseases subject to the IHR constrained the range of global surveillance information.[71] The quality of global epidemiological information as a public good would improve with WHO able to use sources of information beyond governments. WHO's proposal to expand the IHR's disease coverage would combine with a larger supply of information to improve global surveillance as a public good. Improved surveillance would be a *global* public good because its production would involve non-state actors as providers and consumers of information.

The potential of transforming global surveillance was so substantial that WHO began to harvest it before the IHR revision was completed. WHO began operating its Global Outbreak Alert and Response Network (Global Network) in 1998.[72] According to WHO, "[f]rom January 1998 through March 2002, WHO and its partners investigated 538 outbreaks of international concern in 132 countries."[73] Formal policy recognition of WHO's ability to use information from non-governmental sources came from the World Health Assembly in 2001,[74] before the IHR revision process was even close to being finished. WHO moved into GHG and GPGH production without a specific international legal framework in place—yet another break from the Westphalian model of infectious disease governance.

Post-Westphalian Public Health and Infectious Diseases

Prior to SARS, global public health policy had begun to craft post-Westphalian governance strategies on infectious diseases. These strategies, exemplified by the Global Fund and the campaign for access to essential medicines, owed much to the global disaster that HIV/AIDS had become. The HIV/AIDS pandemic, combined with recognition of the growing threats of tuberculosis and malaria in the developing world, placed the traditional Westphalian approach to infectious diseases under scrutiny; and it was found wanting. With HIV/AIDS, the post-Westphalian strategies represented increasingly desperate attempts to mitigate a public health nightmare of historic proportions. The success of these strategies was, however, very much in doubt before SARS. The Global Fund was nearly bankrupt after operating for less than two years,[75] and WHO's Roll Back Malaria campaign also suffered from inadequate funding.[76] Fears about bioterrorism, especially in the United States, shifted attention and resources away from GHG and GPGH to national defenses against the intentional use of pathogens. If post-Westphalian public health could not handle the strain existing diseases created, what would happen when the next infectious disease crisis broke upon the world?

SARS and Post-Westphalian Public Health

As the first severe infectious disease to emerge in the twenty-first century, SARS is a landmark event in global public health. In SARS, the world confronted a virus never before found in humans that was transmitted from person-to-person, that had a high fatality rate, and against which public health practitioners and physicians had neither adequate diagnostic technologies nor effective treatments or vaccines. The last time the world confronted a virus with this disturbing profile was when HIV emerged in the early 1980s, and HIV triggered one of the worst epidemics in history. As bad as HIV/AIDS became, especially for developing countries, public health experts were thankful that HIV was not transmitted by respiratory means. SARS-CoV is, however, transmitted from person-to-person by such means. Although SARS-CoV is not "airborne HIV" because the fatality rate of SARS is less than untreated HIV, SARS' fatality rate and respiratory route of transmission conjured memories of other global viral killers—the 1918-1919 influenza and smallpox—that wrought havoc upon humankind.

The epidemiological profile of SARS means that it would have presented a crisis even if infectious disease control remained mired in the Westphalian approach. SARS emerged, however, in a policy context that was moving away from the Westphalian framework. The SARS outbreak is, thus, pivotal for global public health because it represents the first serious challenge to a governance approach that deviates from the traditional model. This part examines how SARS reflected and affected the post-Westphalian approach to infectious disease governance. This analysis focuses on the behavior of the country at the epicenter of SARS—the People's Republic of China. The Chinese government's actions during the SARS outbreak cost the country dearly because it acted Westphalian in a post-Westphalian world.

Overview of China's Response to SARS

China's response to SARS divides into three stages. The first stage, which began in November 2002 and lasted until early February 2003, witnessed the Chinese government suppress information about a severe outbreak of a respiratory disease in Guangdong Province. Experts believe that the SARS outbreak started in Foshan, Guangdong Province in mid-November 2002.[77] Despite efforts by China to keep the outbreak from being publicized,[78] news leaked out through the Internet, e-mail, and cell phone text messaging.[79] On February 10, 2003, Pro-MED mail, a non-governmental global electronic reporting system for outbreaks of infectious diseases,[80] posted one such e-mail asking about an epidemic in Guangzhou being linked in Internet chat rooms to hospital closings and fatalities.[81] Also on February 10, WHO staff in Beijing and Geneva received an e-mail from the son of former WHO employee in China asking about a 'strange contagious disease' causing death and panic in southern China.[82]

Although WHO's Global Network had picked up indications of problems in southern China as early as November 2002,[83] WHO's first official approach to the Chinese government about the outbreak information it was receiving from non-governmental sources came on February 10, 2003.[84] The publicly circulating information and WHO's queries led China to make its first official report to WHO about the outbreak on February 11, 2003, when China provided information about an outbreak of an acute respiratory syndrome involving 300 cases and 5 deaths in Guangdong Province.[85]

The second stage of China's response began in mid-February 2003 and lasted until April 17, 2003. In this stage China acknowledged an outbreak but attempted to deny and cover-up the extent of the epidemic. China claimed that the outbreak was under control and declining in Guangdong Province and had not spread to other parts of the country. From mid-February 2003, the Chinese government prohibited state-controlled media from reporting on the outbreak.[86] During this period, the SARS outbreak reached Hong Kong, Vietnam, Singapore, Canada, and other countries, prompting WHO to issue a global alert about cases of atypical pneumonia on March 12, 2003[87] and an emergency travel advisory on March 15, 2003.[88]

Although China requested assistance from WHO in mid-March 2003,[89] the government continued to suppress information about the outbreak. After a February 14, 2003 report to WHO,[90] China did not provide any more information until March 26, 2003.[91] Even then WHO and other experts worried about the data China presented. On April 16, 2003, in a highly unusual move for the Organization, WHO publicly accused the Chinese government of underreporting SARS cases and misleading the public about SARS' spread.[92] On April 18, 2003, *Time* Magazine reported that Chinese government officials deliberately hid SARS patients from WHO personnel investigating the SARS problem in Beijing.[93] China's behavior stood in marked contrast to other countries affected by SARS, which were providing information and cooperating with WHO.[94]

The third stage of China's response began on April 18, 2003, when "China's Communist leaders ... declared a nationwide war on the SARS virus and ordered officials to stop covering up the extent of the epidemic that is spreading throughout China."[95] On April 20, 2003, the Communist Party removed the mayor of Beijing and the Minister of Health from their Party posts because of their failure to address SARS' spread in China, actions that "constituted a political earthquake for the Communist Party, which has rarely acknowledged making mistakes during its 54-year rule."[96] In this third stage of its response, China increased the information it provided, improved its cooperation with WHO and other countries, and heightened the seriousness of its SARS control efforts.[97]

China, SARS, and Westphalian Public Health

The first two stages of China's response conform to patterns of the Westphalian approach to infectious diseases. As analyzed earlier, the central concept of the Westphalian template is sovereignty. States discipline their supreme powers over public health through rules of international law negotiated and accepted by each state. The rules of international law addressed the mechanistic aspects of state interaction by attempting to mitigate the drag public health measures created for international trade. The rules did not penetrate deeply into a state's sovereignty by subjecting its public health system to international scrutiny.

From the perspective of Westphalian public health, China's initial response to SARS was understandable. China was under no international legal obligation to report SARS cases to anyone.[98] If other countries wanted epidemiological information from China, it could handle such requests diplomatically as other issues of interstate concern were handled. China could utilize WHO in such diplomacy if it chose to do so; but China was under no legal obligation to use WHO in handling SARS. Aspects of China's public health system not directly related to the trade-public health nexus of the Westphalian approach would not, unless China consented, be the subject of diplomatic activity. Demands to the contrary would represent intervention into China's domestic affairs and an affront to its sovereignty.

These observations do not mean China's response to SARS was prudent merely because it conforms to Westphalian patterns. Nothing in the Westphalian model prevented China from responding more openly and cooperatively, as other nations did. My point is that the Westphalian approach to infectious diseases did not demand more from China with respect to SARS. Westphalian public health left China's sovereignty unfettered and to be exercised, for better or worse, as China's leadership saw fit.

China Confronts Public Health's "New World Order"

China's response to SARS proved a miscalculation of historic proportions. The miscalculation involves not only the damage China suffered but also China's failure to grasp the post-Westphalian context of infectious disease governance. The unfolding saga of the SARS outbreak in China tells the story of the humbling of the sovereignty of a rising great power. The humbling of Chinese sovereignty occurred in both traditional public health governance areas, such as surveillance and response, and matters of political ideology. As a result of its response to SARS, China suffered extensive and withering international scrutiny and criticism of its attitude toward public health, its health-care system, and the political ideology underlying governance in that country.

Sovereignty versus global health governance

The lack of transparency in China's reporting of SARS cases and uncooperative attitude toward WHO during the first two stages of its response resembled sovereign acts that all too often states adopted during past outbreaks. China feared that openly reporting on the SARS outbreak would damage China's economy and image.[99] This rationale has, in the past, often been the reason states have not reported to WHO outbreaks of diseases subject to the IHR.[100] China was under no international legal obligation to report SARS cases or allow WHO to investigate the SARS outbreak in Chinese territory. Despite exercising its sovereignty in a manner consistent with applicable international law, China eventually engaged in an embarrassing and damaging retreat. Chinese sovereignty could not withstand the forces brought to bear on China by GHG.

China's refusal to provide SARS outbreak information to WHO in a timely, transparent, and verifiable manner ran headlong into the GHG mechanism of WHO's ability to use information from non-governmental sources. Through this mechanism, WHO knew that China was not being forthright and used this knowledge to pressure the Chinese government to cooperate. Unlike past situations of governmental denial and difficult behavior in outbreak situations, on this occasion WHO had a stronger political and epidemiological position because of the World Health Assembly's prior approval of WHO's use of non-governmental information. The SARS outbreak illustrates the power of bringing non-state actors into the process of global surveillance.

The premise of including non-governmental information in global surveillance is that countries can no longer hide outbreaks because of the revolution in information technologies. A WHO consultation on the IHR stated in 1995 that "in this age of wide media coverage, nothing can be hidden."[101] Incentives to cover-up or deny outbreaks disappear when cover-up and denial are doomed to failure. The expanded scope for global surveillance reflects the reality of an increasingly globalized world. As WHO stated in May 2003:

> This is the most important lesson for all nations: in a globalized, electronically connected world, attempts to conceal cases of an infectious disease, for fear of social and economic consequences, must be recognized as a short-term stop-gap measure that carries a very high price—loss of credibility in the eyes of the international community, escalating negative domestic economic impact, damage to health and economies of neighboring countries, and a very real risk that outbreaks within the country's own territory can spiral out of control.[102]

The World Health Assembly's approval in 2001 of using non-governmental information in surveillance represented prior recognition of this reality by most of the international community. Technological transformations altered the context in which states would exercise sovereignty in connection with infectious diseases. The sovereign decision of whether to report disease outbreaks is no longer constrained only by formal rules of international law, as is the case in the Westphalian model. Bringing new information technologies to bear on surveillance has forced sovereignty to transition into a much more demanding environment.

Unfortunately, the SARS outbreak represented China's second mishandling of infectious disease surveillance and reporting in recent years. In 2001, China admitted that the HIV/AIDS problem in its territory was far worse than it previously acknowledged.[103] A UNAIDS assessment of the HIV/AIDS epidemic in China conducted at the end of 2001 argued that China was "witnessing the unfolding of an HIV/AIDS epidemic of proportions beyond belief, an epidemic that calls for an urgent and proper, but currently yet unanswered quintessential response."[104] The same UNAIDS study observed that, in China, "[c]ensorship and restrictions on information concerning HIV/AIDS severely hinders an effective response."[105] Yet, in 2002, China detained a prominent HIV/AIDS activist for distributing by e-mail government information on the true scale of the HIV/AIDS epidemic in Henan Province, the epicenter of HIV transmission through unsanitary blood transfusions at government-run clinics.[106] The *Washington Post* editorialized that a "striking conclusion that emerges from Dr. Wan's disappearance, aside from the atmosphere of secrecy, is how shortsighted are the regime's policies. Facing the risk of an Africa-style AIDS crisis that could decimate its population and economy, any forward-looking government would welcome the efforts of such activists."[107]

As with SARS, China was under no international legal obligation to report HIV/AIDS cases to WHO or to engage in international cooperation; yet the country found itself the subject of intense and withering scrutiny of its governance approach to HIV/AIDS because the international community had information about the growing scale of the Chinese HIV/AIDS epidemic. This incident also reveals the futility of Westphalian concepts of public health sovereignty in a world of globalized information on infectious diseases.

China's handling of SARS demonstrated that it had not grasped the new context for public health governance—epidemiological information about germs does not recognize borders. With SARS, China played the sovereignty card only to retreat when its sovereignty was seen, again, to be a deliberate attempt to hide an outbreak about which the world already knew. In some respects, China's behavior in connection with SARS was more inexplicable than with HIV/AIDS because the SARS virus is more transmissible than HIV and thus more dangerous to a world dependent on global air travel.

Both on its own and in combination with HIV/AIDS, the Chinese approach to SARS raised questions about why China exercised its sovereignty on public health issues in the way it did. In the Westphalian template, the nature of the state's government or ideology is not an issue because the principles of sovereignty and non-intervention mean that a state determines its own political and economic structures. Whether a government is a democracy or a dictatorship does not matter in Westphalian public health.

The post-Westphalian context for public health does not share this agnosticism. GHG contains assumptions about what constitutes good governance. Increasing the quality and quantity of global epidemiological information requires openness, transparency, and wide participation in public health in the collecting, analyzing, and disseminating of public health information. GHG requires political recognition of, and commitment to, an "open public health society" in which (1) citizens have a right to receive and disseminate information important to the protection and promotion of their health; and (2) non-state actors can hold governments accountable for their management of the public's health. In short, GHG requires the exercise of a *certain kind of sovereignty*, which differs from the Westphalian approach to sovereignty.[108]

These deeper implications of GHG help explain why China's mishandling of the SARS outbreak provided commentators with material for critically analyzing China's communist rule. Some claimed that SARS would be "China's Chernobyl"[109] because it could cause a cascade of reforms that might destroy communist control and introduce democratic governance. These arguments assert that communist China cannot exercise the kind of sovereignty required by governance challenges posed by infectious diseases and other globalized phenomena.

National interest versus global public goods for health

The SARS outbreak reveals another aspect of post-Westphalian public health that China failed to grasp. The first two stages of China's response to SARS demonstrated that its leaders pursued a narrowly constructed national interest. These stages of China's response exhibited the government's myopic focus on "social stability" in China, continued flows of trade and investment into China, and the image of the Communist Party. Even in the face of a pathogen bearing all the attributes of an epidemic disease, China behaved as if its national interest could be introverted and non-responsive to the concerns of other countries and of non-state actors, such as MNCs. China's conception of its national interest broke apart in the post-Westphalian atmosphere of SARS.

Expanding global surveillance to include non-governmental sources of information improves the quantity and quality of global surveillance for infectious diseases. Improved surveillance represents a GPGH that benefits governments, NGOs, MNCs, and individuals.[110] China's decision not to contribute to the production of timely and accurate global surveillance on SARS undermined this GPGH and alienated the Chinese government from the global community. Because it initially proved incapable of understanding its role in the production of a GPGH, China's short-sighted approach to its national interest backfired.

As with the confrontation between Chinese sovereignty and GHG, the collapse of China's initial framing of its national interest on SARS has deeper implications. The idea that a country's national interest with respect to infectious diseases can no longer be narrowly tailored and insular is not new. A government can construct its national interest in ways that reflect public health's global realities, and many states affected by SARS took a globalized approach to developing their national interests. China's miscalculation on SARS raises the question whether its communist government is capable of crafting the national interest in a way that recognizes China's public health is intertwined with that of other states and peoples.

For historic and ideological reasons, China has long exhibited sensitivity about outside interests interfering with its sovereignty. The SARS outbreak indicates that China had not grasped how embedded the Middle Kingdom is in global public health. The context of post-Westphalian public health makes China's historical and ideological phobias about threats to its public health sovereignty anachronistic and illegitimate. SARS teaches the lesson that the formulation of the national interest about germs cannot recognize either physical or ideological borders.

SARS and Taiwan

The impact of SARS on China's traditional notions of sovereignty and national interest are also apparent with respect to Taiwan. China fiercely defends its claim to sovereignty over Taiwan, leading experts to worry that China will someday risk war on this issue. This position posed problems for Taiwan's ability to handle its outbreak of SARS. China's attitude toward Taiwan has long plagued Taiwan's efforts to work with WHO on public health concerns because China has opposed any move that suggests Taiwan is an independent country.[111] SARS forced China to bend on its hard-line approach to Taiwan. Beijing approved in May 2003 a WHO team to travel to Taiwan to assist the Taiwanese with their SARS outbreak. As noted in *The Lancet*, this visit "was a historic moment: the first visit by any representatives of a UN-affiliated organization since China took Taiwan's seat on the world body 30 years ago."[112]

This development illustrates the power of post-Westphalian public health to challenge states on deeply and fiercely held political positions. China's refusal to allow WHO or other UN bodies to interact with Taiwan could not withstand the political pressure SARS placed on China. Chinese leaders probably realized that continuing to prohibit WHO assistance for Taiwan would only exacerbate the terrible political situation China had produced in its reaction to SARS. Even China's stance on Taiwan could not stand in the way of the need to incorporate Taiwan into the global effort to bring SARS under control.

Beyond China: SARS and Post-Westphalian Public Health

Although China provides the most dramatic evidence of the post-Westphalian context for public health, the SARS epidemic produced other indications that public health has transitioned into a new governance era. This section analyzes four areas that support the argument that public health governance has entered a post-Westphalian phase.

Strengthening global health governance

The SARS outbreak vindicated WHO's move to include non-governmental sources of information in global surveillance. WHO's efforts in this direction prior to SARS may have encouraged many countries affected by SARS to report information to WHO early, rapidly, and transparently. Countries as diverse as Canada, Singapore, and Vietnam have been praised for their cooperation on SARS, which is an indication that many countries faced with the same decision as China opted for openness, transparency, and cooperation.

The World Health Assembly reaffirmed, in May 2003, the importance of WHO's ability to use information from non-governmental sources when it requested the WHO Director-General "to take into account reports from sources other than official notification."[113] This request marked the second time the World Health Assembly supported this approach to global surveillance; but, coming in the midst of the SARS crisis, this resolution carries more political significance. This most recent action by the World Health Assembly strengthens the GHG strategy pioneered by WHO through its Global Network.

China's behavior during the SARS outbreak elucidates why the World Health Assembly's action is so politically important for GHG. WHO's experience with China's recalcitrance and deception brought home the importance for global public health of WHO having access to non-governmental sources of information. China's behavior put the final nail in the coffin of basing global surveillance only on governmental information. Given the cooperation exhibited by most countries affected by SARS, the World Health Assembly's renewed support for WHO's use of non-governmental information indicates how important such information was to overcoming China's intransigence. In light of the humbling of Chinese sovereignty, the World Health Assembly's action stands as a warning to any government tempted to behave in the future on an infectious disease outbreak as China did on SARS.

The SARS outbreak strengthened GHG in another important way. During the outbreak, WHO issued a global alert and several travel advisories. The global alert issued on March 12, 2003 was designed to alert national public health authorities of the international spread of an atypical pneumonia so that such authorities could heighten awareness within their surveillance and response systems.[114] The March 15, 2003 emergency travel advisory contained "emergency travel recommendations to alert health authorities, physicians, and the traveling public to what was now perceived to be a worldwide threat to health."[115] WHO later issued recommendations that travelers postpone non-essential travel to Hong Kong,[116] Guangdong Province,[117] Beijing,[118] Shanxi Province,[119] Toronto,[120] Tianjin,[121] Inner Mongolia,[122] Taipei,[123] Heibei Province,[124] and Taiwan.[125] Both the global alert and the travel advisories constituted unprecedented actions by WHO[126] and represent further evidence of a transition to post-Westphalian public health.

WHO's authority to issue such alerts and advisories was not a product of the Westphalian template because neither the WHO Constitution nor the IHR invested WHO with this power. The World Health Assembly also had not adopted any decisions or recommendations in this area. Under the Westphalian approach, WHO disseminated government-provided information on areas infected with quarantinable diseases to WHO members, which decided whether to apply measures to persons arriving from or traveling to such areas.[127] During the SARS outbreak, WHO issued alerts and advisories, an indication that the governance context had changed.

WHO's role in the Westphalian model was to act as a conduit for information not to take a strong position on how members should respond to such information. When members took trade-restricting health measures not permitted under the IHR, WHO would sometimes make statements about the appropriate public health response. For example, in 1998, when the European Union banned the importation of fresh fish products from East African countries suffering a cholera outbreak, WHO publicly stated that trade embargoes were "not an appropriate course of action to prevent the international spread of cholera, and can represent an additional burden on the economy of the affected countries."[128] This statement was a recommendation to WHO members about the appropriate way to respond to cholera outbreaks in other countries.

As part of the IHR revision process, WHO argued that it needed authority to issue recommendations for public health emergencies of international concern and proposed that the revised IHR contain a non-exhaustive list of types of potential recommendations.[129] WHO proposed the following process: "During an actual public health emergency of international concern, *WHO and the concerned State(s)* would choose the appropriate measures to be taken from the complete list, and use this as a basis for recommendations for use by Members."[130] Note that the proposal contemplates that WHO and the concerned states would *jointly* issue the recommendations, most likely out of WHO's concern for the affected states' sovereignty. Even though WHO cautioned that its list was non-exhaustive, none of the draft measures listed by WHO involved recommendations to travelers to postpone non-essential travel to disease-affected areas.[131] The measures WHO listed were recommendations to WHO members on how to deal with travelers, goods, and conveyances coming from disease-affected areas.[132]

The SARS outbreak witnessed, however, WHO acting beyond the authority it was proposing to write into the revised IHR. First, WHO's geographically specific travel advisories were directed at travelers, not WHO members. For example, WHO's first geographically specific travel advisory recommended "that persons traveling to Hong Kong Special Administrative Region and Guangdong Province, China consider postponing all but essential travel."[133] Second, WHO issued the March 12 global alert, March 15 emergency travel advisory, and the geographically specific travel advisories without reaching consensus on these actions with the concerned states. The diplomatic uproar that followed WHO's travel advisory concerning Toronto indicates that WHO acted without consulting the Canadian government. Officials at Health Canada "complained that WHO officials did not give them warning" of the travel advisory.[134] Similarly, WHO did not obtain China's consent when it issued advisories to travelers to postpone non-essential travel to many parts of China. In connection with the March 15 emergency travel advisory, WHO officials "agonized over how to limit economic damage but concluded that the conservative course—consulting with national governments—had already failed."[135] This observation captures the abandonment of the Westphalian model by WHO during the SARS crisis.

Through the global alert and travel recommendations, WHO exercised leadership in coordinating a global response to SARS in the absence of an agreed policy and legal framework and without deference to the sovereignty of affected states. An infectious disease specialist at the U.S. Centers for Disease Control and Prevention argued that, through its actions, WHO "has assumed 'police' powers for controlling outbreaks that put it above national governments, the traditional guardians of public health."[136] These bold actions revealed WHO as an autonomous actor influencing events directly rather than just acting as a convenient device for coordinating members' behavior. Without any express policy or legal basis for these actions, WHO took steps with serious political and economic consequences for states affected by SARS.

Further indication of this sea change came in the acquiescence of WHO members affected by the alerts and advisories to their issuance by WHO. Although the WHO travel advisory concerning Toronto became controversial,[137] Canada did not challenge WHO's authority to issue the travel advisory without its consent but only whether the situation in Toronto warranted an advisory. Similarly, China questioned the WHO travel advisory against Guangdong Province but did not publicly challenge WHO's authority to issue the advisory without China's participation.

The World Health Assembly approved WHO's ability to issue alerts when, in May 2003, it requested the WHO Director-General "to alert, when necessary and after informing the government concerned, the international community to the presence of a public health threat that may constitute a serious threat to neighboring countries or to international health on the basis of criteria and procedures jointly developed with Members."[138] In this resolution, the World Health Assembly went beyond the recommendatory powers in WHO's proposals for the revised IHR. The IHR revision proposal sought to create a process where WHO and affected states would jointly choose the appropriate recommendation, but the World Health Assembly resolution empowers WHO to issue alerts after merely informing the governments concerned. The resolution limits joint participation of the members to the development of the criteria and procedures for the exercise of the alert power.[139]

This World Health Assembly's decision is significant for GHG. As the SARS outbreak demonstrated, WHO-issued alerts and advisories could cause a country economic damage by affecting commerce and travel. In contrast to WHO's relative powerlessness in the Westphalian model, post-SARS WHO possesses independent authority that carries real power, which WHO members have approved. Further, the authority to issue global alerts connects with the ability to use information from non-governmental sources. WHO members approved the WHO's ability to issue alerts against sovereign states without their consent based on information collected from governmental and non-governmental sources. Faced with the impossibility of preventing disease information from flowing to the international community, and with the possibility of facing the adverse consequences of a WHO alert based on global surveillance data, a country's incentive to hide an outbreak for fear of the economic consequences has diminished significantly. The argument that WHO alerts will deter countries from reporting outbreak information[140] neglects to recall the effect of WHO's ability to collect such information from non-governmental sources. The powers to use non-governmental information and to issue global alerts create a GHG pincer that squeezes the state's sovereign decision whether to report outbreak information and to cooperate with WHO and other countries.

States structured Westphalian public health through formal agreements under international law, as the IHR illustrate. The strengthening of GHG in the wake of SARS has occurred without any changes in international law on infectious disease control. Although WHO intends to complete the IHR revision process by 2005, the revised IHR will merely reflect changes in policy effected before and during the SARS outbreak without the direct use of international law. This subordinated role for international law is yet another reflection of public health's arrival in post-Westphalian territory.

The SARS outbreak has also produced a new GHG initiative from WHO: the formation of a PPP "to fight SARS and build capacity for surveillance, epidemiology and public health laboratory facilities in China and the surrounding region."[141] WHO plans to collaborate with the Global Health Initiative of the World Economic Forum to raise US $100 million from the global business community, especially enterprises operating in Asia, which monies will fund surveillance and response capabilities at country-level.[142] Nothing equivalent ever appeared under Westphalian public health[143] because the initiative actively seeks participation from non-state actors and addresses national public health capabilities beyond the borders of states. The new PPP effort also connects with GHG because companies, not states or international organizations, took the lead in proposing the idea when "a number of companies approached the WHO offering money or other support toward eradicating the [SARS] virus."[144] The initiative connects, thus, with the interest in vertical governance strategies prevalent in other GHG efforts, such as the Global Fund.

The power of global public goods for health

A second area in which the SARS outbreak supports the argument that public health has entered a post-Westphalian stage involves recognition of the power of producing GPGH. The SARS-related actions taken by WHO and its members to solidify the use of non-governmental information in global surveillance represent recognition that the production of GPGH, such as improved global surveillance information, is important for infectious disease governance. The WHO-proposed PPP on improving country-level surveillance and response capabilities also connects with the desire to produce better global management of infectious diseases.

SARS also triggered unprecedented global scientific cooperation to identify the causative agent for SARS, the formulation of appropriate treatment protocols, and the beginning of efforts to design diagnostic technologies and possible vaccine strategies.[145] Experts hailed these endeavors as a successful global collaboration in the face of an emerging epidemic disease.[146] In this effort, scientific activities on a germ did not recognize borders for the benefit of producing globally useful and needed scientific and clinical knowledge.

The speed with which scientists around the world collaborated to identify a coronavirus as the pathogen responsible for SARS reflected not only rapid advances of microbiology and virology since HIV's emergence but also the strength of collaborative efforts on producing openly available scientific knowledge critical to global SARS responses. Part of these efforts involved strategies to ensure that knowledge and research techniques developed in the SARS investigation remain publicly available and not subject to private appropriation through intellectual property rights.[147] With important scientific information on SARS in the public domain, prospects for the development of effective diagnostic, therapeutic, and prevention technologies as GPGH are enhanced.

Elevating public health as a national political priority

A lament of public health officials for decades has been the neglect of public health by governments. Public health was a low priority of states nationally and internationally in the Westphalian system. Part of the effort to highlight EIDs as a threat was to increase political attention to the inadequacies of national and international public health capabilities. Experts and government officials even tried to elevate the problem by characterizing infectious diseases, especially HIV/AIDS, as a threat to national security.[148]

Before the SARS outbreak, bioterrorism provided more traction for elevating public health as a political priority, particularly after the anthrax attacks in the United States. Public health officials stressed synergies between bioterrorism preparedness efforts and everyday public health capabilities. Conceptually, the synergies worked in two directions: bioterrorism preparedness benefited public health generally, and general public health improvements benefited bioterrorism preparedness. Before SARS, the lion's share of attention focused on how bioterrorism programs would produce positive externalities for public health.

The SARS outbreak has given efforts to elevate public health as a national political priority new momentum. The U.S. National Intelligence Council argued, for example, that "SARS has demonstrated to even skeptical government leaders that health matters in profound social, economic, and political ways."[149] According to WHO, "[o]ne of the most important lessons learned to date is the decisive power of high-level political commitment to contain an outbreak even when sophisticated control tools are lacking."[150] Important in this dynamic is the fact SARS hit economically advanced countries and areas, such as Canada, Hong Kong, Taiwan, and Singapore, hard. Public health experts in the United States also recognized the threat SARS poses for U.S. public health.[151] Although some commentators attributed the low number of SARS cases in the United States to the improvements in public health derived from bioterrorism preparedness, public health officials realized that SARS exposed public health to threats that could strain infrastructure and capabilities severely, as happened in Canada.[152] SARS also elevated public health as a national political priority in many countries because the outbreak caused severe economic damage. SARS-related economic damage to Asian economies has been significant enough to make political leaders realize the economic case for more robust national public health capabilities.[153]

Reinforcing the public health-human rights linkage

SARS has highlighted a fourth area that points toward a post-Westphalian period for public health—the role of human rights in public health. Under Westphalian public health, human rights did not register as a concern. Although the relevance of international human rights law to public health has been apparent from the beginning of the human rights movement, neither national nor international public health paid much attention to human rights until HIV/AIDS exploded on the world. HIV/AIDS caused public health communities to turn to international human rights laws to help guide policy on the epidemic.[154]

This human rights turn brought both civil and political rights (e.g., freedom of movement) and economic, social, and cultural rights (e.g., the right to health) to bear on public health. Civil and political rights became a policy instrument in the fight against stigma and discrimination faced by people living with HIV/AIDS. The right to health became a weapon in advocacy for greater access to essential medicines, including antiretrovirals.[155] As in other areas, HIV/AIDS led public health away from the traditional, state-centric Westphalian approach toward a strategy that placed individuals and not states at the center of concern.

SARS reinforces the public health-human rights linkage but in ways different from what occurred with HIV/AIDS. The widespread resort by countries to isolation and quarantine to control SARS brought to life concerns about public health measures infringing on civil and political rights, such as freedom of movement.[156] The proper balance between public health and individual liberties has been debated in the context of U.S. bioterrorism policy.[157] But, apart from human rights criticisms of isolation and quarantine as responses to HIV/AIDS,[158] striking the proper balance between the protection of population health and respect for civil and political rights has not been a prominent question for public health policy.

SARS makes this question important in global public health policy, which represents yet another deviation from the Westphalian model. The different policy responses of governments affected by SARS indicate that the question of the proper balance between public health and individual rights has received different answers. In some countries, such as Singapore, the government used compulsory and tightly monitored isolation and quarantine, thus producing serious infringements on civil and political rights.[159] Other countries, such as Canada, relied more on voluntary isolation and quarantine strategies than on compulsory powers, creating an approach with less adverse impact on individual rights.[160] And still other nations, such as the United States, did not use voluntary quarantine in cases where other countries have utilized compulsory or voluntary quarantine (e.g., individuals who were in contact with suspect SARS cases).[161]

These varying approaches to balancing public health and human rights mean that SARS creates the need for further examination and application of the criteria international human rights law establishes to evaluate public health measures that infringe on civil and political rights. With public health experts warning that SARS may become endemic, isolation and quarantine will remain key public health instruments until more effective diagnostic technologies, therapies, or a vaccine are developed. More rigorous attention to the human rights implications of SARS is in order as part of the post-Westphalian context of this outbreak.

SARS and the Vulnerabilities of Post-Westphalian Public Health

SARS confirms that public health has moved into a post-Westphalian phase that involves exciting governance possibilities. At the same time, the SARS outbreak contains reminders that post-Westphalian public health faces vulnerabilities that may undermine the new approaches applied in the SARS effort. The vulnerabilities meld into a concern about the sustainability of the post-Westphalian approach to public health.

Public health governance on infectious disease control has experienced innovations in the past, which over time became ineffective. The emergence of public health as a diplomatic issue in the mid-nineteenth century represented a change because diplomacy added an international component to governance. Not long after the elevation of infectious disease control into a foreign policy concern, experts realized that the innovations of ad hoc conferences and the negotiation of international sanitary conventions was an inadequate response to the infectious disease problem. States then reformed the Westphalian approach by creating international health organizations charged with overseeing the international sanitary conventions and/or coordinating cooperation on infectious diseases.[162]

These innovations also proved inadequate. The next reforms involved four changes: (1) the consolidation of the various international health organizations into one organization, WHO; (2) the unification of international law on infectious diseases to provide one set of rules, the IHR; (3) the creation of a different process for crafting international legal rules on infectious diseases in the form of the adoption of international regulations under Articles 21 and 22 of the WHO Constitution; and (4) articulating infectious disease control as part of the individual human right to the highest attainable standard of health.

The EID crisis revealed public health experts dissatisfied with how these four reforms panned out. Casting a pall over the reformed Westphalian approach was, of course, the global HIV/AIDS nightmare. The move from a Westphalian to a post-Westphalian approach merely represents the latest attempt at governance innovation. Believing that public health has reached the "end of history" with respect to infectious diseases in the post-Westphalian period would be naïve in the extreme.

A comprehensive analysis of why previous governance innovations led to dissatisfaction is beyond the scope of this article, but a common theme for all previous reform efforts would be a lack of sustainability. These innovations became unsustainable because (1) the commitment of governments to public health over time waxed and waned, but mainly waned; and (2) political, economic, social, and technological changes created conditions encouraging the emergence and re-emergence of infectious diseases. The lack of political commitment from governments and globalization's stimulation of the resurgence of infectious diseases led to acknowledgement that the Westphalian approach, and all the reforms made to it, did not provide an adequate governance framework.

The sustainability of post-Westphalian public health governance will also be an issue. Whether the elevation of public health as a national and international political priority seen in SARS remains is an open question. Whether the elevation of public health as a political priority because of SARS spills over to affect positively efforts to deal with other infectious disease problems, such as antimicrobial resistance, also is uncertain.[163] SARS may cause governments to shift public health resources away from some existing problems toward SARS-related programs. As WHO indicated in connection with China, "[m]easures may need to be found for sustaining China's present monumental effort to contain SARS, particularly as programmes for responding to other priority diseases, such as HIV/AIDS and TB, may suffer in the long run."[164] The U.S. National Intelligence Council argued that SARS "will not lead to a significant boost in the fight against HIV/AIDS in the coming years. Indeed, many countries are likely to view spending on diseases like SARS and HIV/AIDS as a zero-sum game in the short-term."[165] How much positive spill-over effect, if any, SARS-induced shifts produce for general public health is unknown. If responses to SARS create public health systems only tuned to severe epidemic diseases with high cross-border mobility,[166] then post-Westphalian governance will risk becoming as irrelevant as the IHR became for today's infectious disease problems.

Elevated political commitment to public health in the post-Westphalian period may also have the ironic effect of rejuvenating Westphalian patterns of behavior. If states increase and sustain their national interests in connection with infectious disease control, then they might take firmer control of infectious disease diplomacy. This dynamic may be especially salient for the great powers. In the HIV/AIDS context, the United States' new Emergency Plan for AIDS Relief (Emergency Plan) now overshadows one of the highest profile experiments in GHG, the Global Fund.[167] The United States controls how the vast majority of the Emergency Plan's $15 billion will be spent, with only a small amount being conditionally channeled into the Global Fund.[168] In many ways, the U.S. approach in the Emergency Plan shares more characteristics with Westphalian than post-Westphalian public health.

The SARS outbreak reveals potential vulnerability in post-Westphalian public health when one considers that the 2003 SARS outbreak did not significantly affect developing and least-developed countries, those nations with the least capability to respond to such a disease. For example, as of August 7, 2003, WHO reported only one SARS case from the entire African continent.[169] Even though it does not appear as if people with malaria or HIV/AIDS have greater susceptibility to infection by SARS-CoV, the prospect of SARS becoming a problem in sub-Saharan Africa, with its large population of immune-compromised and immune-challenged people, is nightmarish.[170] If, as public health officials fear, SARS becomes endemic in regions of the world and a seasonal epidemic disease, more developing countries may be affected. Whether post-Westphalian public health can handle SARS becoming endemic and epidemic in more of the developing world is, at this point, uncertain.

The vulnerabilities of the post-Westphalian approach to public health revealed by SARS can also be glimpsed more conceptually. In 1997, I described the pathology of the globalization of public health in connection with EIDs as containing five elements: (1) international trade and travel as effective channels for infectious disease spread; (2) deteriorating or nonexistent public health capabilities, including the declining effectiveness of antimicrobial drugs; (3) the failure of the internationalization of public health; (4) the development of unprecedented levels of deeply rooted social, economic, and environmental problems that provide pathogens with fertile conditions; and (5) the weakening of the state's ability to address public health needs and social, economic, and environmental problems because of the globalization of markets.[171]

SARS underscores this pathology and the challenges it poses for states, international organizations, and non-state actors. SARS reinforces trade and travel as powerful vectors for spreading infectious diseases. SARS also reveals weaknesses and problems in the public health systems of many countries affected. The reliance on GHG mechanisms to address SARS also underscores that traditional internationalization of public health through the Westphalian approach failed to work. SARS' emergence also confirms the fertile conditions pathogens enjoy in the globalized era. The apparent speed with which SARS-CoV jumped from animals to humans and then became an international epidemic is evidence of the potent microbial miasma in which the global village exists.

Finally, SARS also raises concerns about the state's ability to address not only disease emergence but also the underlying economic, social, and environmental causes of such emergence. Post-Westphalian public health has given state and non-state actors new strategies for reacting to disease events. Whether post-Westphalian public health contains a strategy for preventing the emergence of infectious diseases remains murky. Such a prevention strategy would involve more significant interventions into the domestic affairs of sovereign states that post-Westphalian public health, at its present stage, does not contemplate. In addition to the long list of infectious diseases that have emerged or re-emerged in the last three decades, SARS may suggest that the forces of globalization mean that post-Westphalian public health can merely be reactive rather than preventive.

Conclusion

The global containment of SARS by July 2003[172] represents a historic triumph that will enter the annals of public health history as one of the most significant achievements in global infectious disease control since the eradication of smallpox. The world's first post-Westphalian pathogen has not, however, burned itself out like some new diseases that emerged in the recent past. At present, most indications are that SARS will return and remain a public health problem for the foreseeable future.

The political pathology of SARS presented in this article suggests that governance innovations taken to move public health into a post-Westphalian context contributed to the successful global response to a severe infectious disease threat. Commenting on SARS, David L. Heymann, WHO's Executive Director for Communicable Diseases, argued that "[i]n the 21st century there is a new way of working."[173] With the initial outbreak and public health emergency triggered by SARS, the "new way of working" on infectious diseases proved effective, which constitutes a victory for the emerging framework of post-Westphalian public health.

While victory should be savored, all should remember that germs do not recognize victories or defeats. The challenge for post-Westphalian public health is to create the conditions necessary for the governance innovations tested successfully in the SARS outbreak to be refined, improved, expanded, and sustained to meet the on-going threat pathogenic microbes present. The germs will keep coming. The great task for the global community that answered the initial challenge from SARS is to ensure that the "new way of working" continues to work effectively far into the twenty-first century.

Acknowledgements

The author would like to thank Lawrence O. Gostin (Georgetown and Johns Hopkins Universities) for inviting him to write an article on SARS for this issue of the *Journal*. Ideas developed in this article were sharpened in presentations at Southern Illinois University School of Law, McGeorge Law School of the University of the Pacific, and Indiana University School of Law—Bloomington; and I thank all those that participated in these events and helped me refine my ideas and arguments. I would also like to thank Cindy Buys, Leslie Gielow Jacobs, and Mary Kay Kindhauser for their encouragement of my pursuit of this topic. Funding for my research on this article was generously provided by the Indiana University School of Law—Bloomington. This article became the basis for the forthcoming book, David P. Fidler, ***SARS, Governance, and the Globalization of Disease*** (London: Palgrave Macmillan, 2004).

References

1. See, e.g., P. Hunt, The Right of Everyone to the Enjoyment of the Highest Attainable Standard of Physical and Mental Health: Report of the Special Rapporteur, UN Doc. E/CN.4/2003/58, February 13, 2003.

2. See, e.g., Commission on Macroeconomics and Health, *Macroeconomics and Health: Investing in Health for Economic Development* (Geneva: World Health Organization, 2001).

3. See, e.g. J. Brower and P. Chalk, *The Global Threat of New and Reemerging Infectious Diseases: Reconciling U.S. National Security and Public Health Policy* (Santa Monica: RAND, 2003).

4. World Health Assembly, *Severe Acute Respiratory Syndrome (SARS)*, WHA56.29, May 28, 2003.

5. See, e.g., M. S. Smolinski, M. A. Hamburg, and J. Lederberg, eds., *Microbial Threats to Health: Emergence, Detection, and Response* (Washington, D.C.: National Academy Press, 2003); World Health Organization, *World Health Report 1996: Fighting Disease, Fostering Development* (Geneva: World Health Organization, 1996); J. Lederberg, R. E. Shope, S. C. Oaks, eds., *Emerging Infections: Microbial Threats to Health in the United States* (Washington, D.C.: National Academy Press, 1992).

6. For an overview of the HIV/AIDS pandemic, see UNAIDS, *AIDS Epidemic Update: December 2002* (Geneva: UNAIDS, 2002).

7. See L. O. Gostin, *Public Health Law: Power, Duty, Restraint* (Berkeley: University of California Press, 2000): 25–59.

8. World Health Organization, *Severe Acute Respiratory Syndrome (SARS): Status of the Outbreak and Lessons for the Immediate Future* (Geneva: World Health Organization, 2003): 3.

9. World Health Organization, *Severe Acute Respiratory Syndrome (SARS) — Multi-Country Outbreak* (March 15, 2003), *at* <http://www.who.int/csr/don/2003_03_15/en/html> (last visited June 10, 2003).

10. C. Harding and C.L. Lim, "The Significance of Westphalia: An Archaeology of the International Legal Order," in C. Harding and C.L. Lim, eds., *Renegotiating Westphalia: Essays and Commentary on the European and Conceptual Foundations of Modern International Law* (The Hague: M. Nijhoff Publishers, 1999): 1–23.

11. *Id.* at 5–6.

12. J. A. Scholte, "The Globalization of World Politics," in J. Baylis and S. Smith, eds., *The Globalization of World Politics: An Introduction to International Relations*, 2d ed. (Oxford: Oxford University Press, 2001): 12–32, at 20.

13. T. Dunne and B.C. Schmidt, "Realism," in J. Baylis and S. Smith, eds., *The Globalization of World Politics: An Introduction to International Relations*, 2d ed. (Oxford: Oxford University Press, 2001):141–61, at 143.

14. Scholte, *supra* note 12, at 20; I. Brownlie, *Principles of Public International Law*, 5th ed. (Oxford: Oxford University Press, 1998): at 289.

15. R.H. Jackson, "The Evolution of International Society," in J. Baylis and S. Smith, eds., *The Globalization of World Politics: An Introduction to International Relations*, 2d ed. (Oxford: Oxford University Press, 2001): 35–50: at 43; Brownlie, *supra* note 14, at 289, 293–94.

16. Brownlie, *supra* note 14, at 289; *The S. S. Lotus (France v. Turkey)*, P. C. I. J. Series A, No. 10 (1927).

17. H. Bull, *The Anarchical Society: A Study of Order in World Politics* (Basingstoke: Macmillan, 1977): at 200–29.

18. *Id.* at 101–26; 184–99.

19. D.P. Fidler, "The Return of the Standard of Civilization," *Chicago Journal of International Law*, 2 (2001): 137–57; G. Gong, *The "Standard of Civilization" in International Society* (Oxford: Oxford University Press, 1984).

20. On this history, see D. P. Fidler, *International Law and Infectious Diseases* (Oxford: Clarendon Press, 1999): at 21–57; N. Howard-Jones, *The Scientific Background of the International Sanitary Conferences 1851–1938* (Geneva: World Health Organization, 1975) [hereinafter Howard-Jones, *Scientific Background*]; N. M. Goodman, *International Health Organizations and Their Work*, 2d ed. (London: Churchill Livingstone, 1971); N. Howard-Jones, "The Origins of International Health Work," *British Medical Journal*, May 6, 1950: 1032–37 [hereinafter Howard-Jones, "International Health Work"].

21. This situation prompted Robert Koch to argue in 1894 that the negotiation of the international sanitary conventions on cholera was "quite superfluous" because what was needed was for every country "to seize cholera by the throat and stamp it out." Howard-Jones, *Scientific Background*, *supra* note 20, at 76 (quoting Robert Koch).

22. Fidler, *supra* note 20, at 35.

23. *Id.* at 28–35.

24. Howard-Jones, "International Health Work," *supra* note 20, at 1035.

25. World Health Organization, *International Health Regulations*, 3d. ann. ed. (Geneva: World Health Organization, 1983) [hereinafter *IHR*].

26. World Health Organization, *Global Crises — Global Solutions: Managing Public Health Emergencies of International Concern Through the Revised International Health Regulations* (Geneva: World Health Organization, 2002): at 1.

27. D.P. Fidler, "Emerging Trends in International Law Concerning Global Infectious Disease Control," *Emerging Infectious Diseases*, 9 (2003): 285–90, at 285–86.

28. *IHR*, *supra* note 25.

29. *Id.* at Articles 2–13.

30. *Id.* at Articles 14–22.

31. *Id.* at Article 23.

32. *Id.* at Article 1.

33. The first International Sanitary Conference in 1851 addressed maritime quarantine measures against plague, cholera, and yellow fever. Goodman, *supra* note 20, at 46.

34. On such widespread violations, see Fidler, *supra* note 20, at 65–66.

35. P.J. Delon, *The International Health Regulations: A Practical Guide* (Geneva: World Health Organization, 1975); E. Roelsgaard, "Health Regulations and International Travel," *Chronicle of the World Health Organization* 28 (1974): 265–68; P. Dorolle, "Old Plagues in the Jet Age: International Aspects of Present and Future Control of Communicable Diseases," *Chronicle of the World Health Organization* 23 (1969): 103–11.

36. D. Arhin-Tenkorang and P. Conceição, "Beyond Communicable Disease Control: Health in the Age of Globalization, in I. Kaul, P. Conceição, K. Le Goulven, and R. U. Mendoza, eds., *Providing Global Public Goods: Managing Globalization* (Oxford: Oxford University Press, 2003): 484–515, at 487.

37. World Health Organization, Declaration of A lma-Ata, adopted at the International Conference on Primary Health Care, Alma-Ata, USSR, September 12, 1978.

38. J. Mann, "Human Rights and AIDS: The Future of the Pandemic," in J.M. Mann, S. Gruskin, M.A. Grodin, and G.J. Annas, eds., *Health and Human Rights* (London: Routledge, 1999): 216–26.

39. For an overview of international human rights law, see H. Hannum, "Human Rights," in O. Schachter and C.C. Joyner, eds., *United Nations Legal Order* (Cambridge: Cambridge University Press, 1995): 319–48.

40. See generally R.J. Vincent, *Human Rights and International Relations* (Cambridge: Cambridge University Press, 1986).

41. See L.O. Gostin and Z. Lazzarini, *Human Rights and Public Health in the AIDS Pandemic* (Oxford: Oxford University Press, 1997).

42. On globalization and public health, see K. Lee, ed., *Health Impacts of Globalization: Toward Global Governance* (London: Palgrave, 2003); K. Lee, K. Buse, and S. Fustukian, eds., *Health Policy in a Globalizing World* (Cambridge: Cambridge University Press, 2002).

43. *IHR, supra* note 25, at Article 3; World Health Organization, *supra* note 26, at 3; Fidler, *supra* note 20, at 73–74.

44. World Health Organization, *supra* note 26, at 3 (listing dependence on country notification as a major constraint for surveillance and public health protection).

45. On global health governance, see R. Dodgson, K. Lee, and N. Drager, *Global Health Governance: A Conceptual Review* (Key Issues in Global Health Governance Discussion Paper No. 1) (London: World Health Organization and Centre on Global Change and Health, February 2002).

46. R. Loewenson, *Civil Society Influence on Global Health Policy* (April 2003), *at* <http://www.tarsc.org/WHOCSI/pdf/WHOTARSC4.pdf> (last visited June 20, 2003); World Health Organization, *Strategic Alliances— The Role of Civil Society in Health* (2001). *at* <http://www.who.int/civilsociety/documents/alliances_en.pdf> (last visited June 20, 2003).

47. R. Horton, "WHO: The Casualties and Compromises of Renewal," *The Lancet*, 359 (2002): 1605–11.

48. Constitution of the World Health Organization, July 22, 1946, in World Health Organization, *Basic Documents*, 40th ed. (Geneva: World Health Organization, 1994): 1–18, at Article 71; Christopher Lanord, *A Study of WHO's Official Relations System with Nongovernmental Organizations* (June 2002), *at* <http://www.who.int/civilsociety/documents/study.pdf> (last visited June 20, 2003); World Health Organization, *Analysis: NGO Participation in WHO Governing Bodies, 1998–2002* (June 2002), *at* <http://www.who.int/civilsociety/documents/analysis.pdf> (last visited June 20, 2003).

49. *The Global Fund to Fight AIDS, Tuberculosis, and Malaria, at* <http://www.globalfundatm.org/news.html> (last visited June 20, 2003).

50. On global public goods for health generally, see R. Smith, R. Beaglehole, D. Woodward, and N. Drager, eds., *Global Public Goods for Health: Health Economic and Public Health Perspectives* (Oxford: Oxford University Press, 2003).

51. I. Kaul, I. Grunberg, and M.A. Stern, "Defining Global Public Goods," in I. Kaul, I. Grunberg, and M.A. Stern, eds., *Global Public Goods: International Cooperation in the 21st Century* (Oxford: Oxford University Press, 1999): 2–19, at 3; D. Woodward and R.D. Smith, "Global Public Goods and Health: Concepts and Issues," in R. Smith, R. Beaglehole, D. Woodward, and N. Drager, eds., *Global Public Goods for Health: Health Economic and Public Health Perspectives* (Oxford: Oxford University Press, 2003): 3–29, at 4–5.

52. Kaul, Grunberg, and Stern, *supra* note 50, at 10; Woodward and Smith, *supra* note 50, at 8.

53. Woodward and Smith, *supra* note 50, at 10–15.

54. *Id.* at 10–12, 14.

55. On public-private partnerships in global public health, see M. Reich, ed., *Public-Private Partnerships for Public Health* (Cambridge, MA: Harvard University Press, 2002).

56. World Health Organization, *Global Defense Against the Infectious Disease Threat*, (M.K. Kindhauser, ed.) (Geneva: World Health Organization, 2003), at 22.

57. For an example of such a PPP, see *The Global Alliance for TB Drug Development, at* <http://www.tballiance.org/> (last visited June 21, 2003).

58. World Health Organization, *supra* note 56, at 22.

59. World Health Assembly, *Revision and Updating of the International Health Regulations*, WHA48.7, May 12, 1995.

60. For an overview, see World Health Organization, *supra* note 26.

61. *Id.* at 7–8.

62. World Health Organization, *The International Response to Epidemics and Applications of the International*

Health Regulations: Report of a WHO Informal Consultation, WHO/EMC/IHR/96.1, December 11–14, 1995, at 10.

63. World Health Organization, *supra* note 26, at 3.

64. *Id.* at 7–8.

65. *Id.* at 7.

66. *Id.* at 3.

67. D. M. Leive, *International Regulatory Regimes*, Vol. 1 (Lexington, MA: Lexington Books, 1976): at 83–85.

68. World Health Organization, *supra* note 26, at 7–8.

69. Woodward and Smith, *supra* note 51, at 14.

70. Fidler, *supra* note 20, at 65–66.

71. World Health Organization, *supra* note 26, at 3.

72. D.L. Heymann, "The Microbial Threat in Fragile Times: Balancing Known and Unknown Risks," *Bulletin of the World Health Organization* 80 (2002): 179.

73. World Health Organization, *supra* note 8, at 4.

74. World Health Assembly, *Global Health Security: Epidemic Alert and Response*, WHA54.14, May 21, 2001.

75. The Global Fund announced in January 2003 that it did not have sufficient funds to complete a third round of funding and urgently needed more than US$6 billion over the next two years. Global Fund to Fight AIDS, Tuberculosis, and Malaria, *Press Release: Global Fund Awards $866 Million in Grants to Fight AIDS, TB and Malaria; United States Takes Chair of Global Fund Board; Tommy Thompson is Elected* (January 31, 2003), *at* <http://www.globalfundatm.org/journalists/press%20releases/pr_030131b.html> (last visited June 21, 2003).

76. V. Narasimhan and A. Attaran, "Roll Back Malaria? The Scarcity of International Aid for Malaria Control," *Malaria Journal*, *at* <http://www.malariajournal.com/content/2/1/8> (last visited September 7, 2003).

77. World Health Organization, *supra* note 8, at 1.

78. J. Pomfret and P. S. Goodman, "Mysterious Illness Kills 2 in Beijing in Sign of Spread," *Washington Post*, March 22, 2003, at A03 (reporting Chinese government efforts before early February 2003 to suppress media coverage about the outbreak in Guangdong Province).

79. See J. Pomfret, "Outbreak Gave China's Hu an Opening; President Responded to Pressure Inside and Outside Country on SARS," *Washington Post*, May 13, 2003, at A01; H. Hoenig, "Beijing Goes High Tech to Block SARS Messages," *New Zealand Herald* (June 16, 2003), *available at* <http://www.nzherald.co.nz/storydisplay.cfm?thesection=news&thesubsection=&storyID=3507534&reportID=912595>.

80. ProMED, *About ProMed-mail*, *at* <http://www.promedmail.org>.

81. ProMED-mail, Pneumonia — China (Guangdong): RFI, February 10, 2003, Archive Number 20030210.0357.

82. C. Piller, "In SARS Aftermath, WHO's in Charge," *Los Angeles Times*, July 13, 2003, at A1.

83. World Health Organization, *supra* note 8, at 4.

84. D. G. McNeil, Jr. and L. K. Altman, "As SARS Outbreak Took Shape, Health Agency Took Fast Action," *New York Times*, May 4, 2003, at 1.

85. World Health Organization, *Acute Respiratory Syndrome in China* (February 11, 2003), *at* <http://www.who.int/csr/don/2003_02_11/en/> (last visited June 10, 2003).

86. Pomfret and Goodman, *supra* note 78, at A03.

87. World Health Organization, Acute Respiratory Syndrome in Hong Kong Special Administrative Region of China/Viet Nam (March 12, 2003), *at* <http://who.int/csr/don/2003_03_12/en/> (last visited June 10, 2003).

88. World Health Organization, *supra* note 9.

89. World Health Organization, *Severe Acute Respiratory Syndrome (SARS) Multi-Country Outbreak — Update 2* (March 17, 2003), *at* <http://www.who.int/csr/don/2003_03_17/en/> (last visited June 10, 2003).

90. World Health Organization, *Acute Respiratory Syndrome in China — Update 2* (February 14, 2003), *at* <http://www.who.int/csr/don/2003_02_14/en/> (last visited June 10, 2003).

91. World Health Organization, *Severe Acute Respiratory Syndrome (SARS) Multi-Country Outbreak — Update 10* (March 26, 2003), *at* <http://www.who.int/csr/don/2003_03_26/en/> (last visited June 10, 2003).

92. J. Pomfret, "Underreporting, Secrecy Fuel SARS in Beijing, WHO Says," *Washington Post*, April 17, 2003, at A16.

93. S. Jakes, "Beijing Hoodwinks WHO Inspectors," *Time* (April 18, 2003), *available at* <http://www.time.com/time/asia/news/daily/0,9754,444684,00.html>.

94. J. Pomfret, "China Raises Disease's Death Toll; Under Pressure, Officials Admit Spread of Infection to Beijing," *Washington Post*, March 27, 2003, at A16.

95. J. Pomfret, "China Orders End to SARS Coverup; Officials Begin Belated Campaign Against Disease," *Washington Post*, April 19, 2003, at A08.

96. J. Pomfret, "SARS Coverup Spurs a Shake-Up in Beijing," *Washington Post*, April 21, 2003, at A01.

97. World Health Organization, *Update 79 — Situation in China* (June 12, 2003), *at* <http://www.who.int/csr/don/2003_06_12/en/> (last visited July 10, 2003).

98. D.P. Fidler, *SARS and International Law*, American Society of International Law Insight (April 2003), *at* <http://www.asil.org/insights/insigh101.htm> (last visited June 20, 2003).

99. Y. Huang, *Mortal Peril: Public Health in China and Its Security Implications* (Health and Security Series Special Report No. 7) (Washington, D.C.: Chemical and Biological Arms Control Institute, 2003): 65–77.

100. Fidler, *supra* note 20, at 66.

101. World Health Organization, *supra* note 62, at 10.

102. World Health Organization, *supra* note 8, at 8.

103. P.P. Pan, "China Admits AIDS 'Epidemic'; Disease May be Spreading Twice as Fast as Reported," *Washington Post*, August 24, 2001, at A01.

104. UNAIDS, *HIV/AIDS: China's Titanic Peril— 2001 Update of the AIDS Situation and Needs Assessment Report* (Geneva: UNAIDS, June 2002): 7.

105. *Id.* at 70. On China's violation of freedom of speech, association, and assembly in connection with HIV/AIDS, see Human Rights Watch, *Locked Doors: The Human Rights of People Living with HIV/AIDS in China* (Washington, D.C.: Human Rights Watch, 2003): 28–33.

106. E. Rosenthal, "China's Top AIDS Activist Missing; Arrest Suspected," *New York Times*, August 29, 2002, at A3; P. P. Pan, "China Detaining Prominent AIDS Activist," *Washington Post*, September 7, 2002, at A14.

107. "China Under Cover," *Washington Post*, September 2, 2002, at A22.

108. Arguments about the direct connection between the quality of the public's health and the nature of a state's government have been around since at least the eighteenth century. Thomas Jefferson asserted, for example, "that sick populations were the result of sick political systems .... According to Jefferson, despotism produced disease, democracy liberated health." D. Porter, *Health, Civilization, and the State: A History of Public Health from Ancient to Modern Times* (London: Routledge, 1999): 57.

109. See, e.g., "China's Chernobyl," *Washington Post*, April 22, 2003, at A18; J.M. Goldgeier, "Will SARS Be the Chinese Chernobyl?," *Los Angeles Times*, April 23, 2003, at 13; "China's Chernobyl?," *The Economist*, April 26, 2003, at 9–10.

110. M. W. Zacher, "Global Epidemiological Surveillance: International Cooperation to Monitor Infectious Diseases," in I. Kaul, I. Grunberg, and M.A. Stern, eds., *Global Public Goods: International Cooperation in the 21st Century* (New York: Oxford University Press, 1999): 266–83.

111. See generally, E. Ting-Lun Huang, "The Modern Concept of Sovereignty, Statehood and Recognition: A Case Study of Taiwan," *New York International Law Review* 16 (2003): 99–190.

112. J. Watts, "China Takes Drastic Action Over SARS Threat," *The Lancet*, 361 (2003): 1708–09, at 1709.

113. World Health Assembly, *Revision of the International Health Regulations*, WHA56.28, May 28, 2003, at ¶4(1).

114. World Health Organization, *supra* note 87.

115. World Health Organization, *supra* note 9.

116. World Health Organization, *Severe Acute Respiratory Syndrome (SARS) Multi-Country Outbreak — Update 17* (April 2, 2003), *at* <http://www.who.int/csr/don/2003_04_02/en/> (last visited June 10, 2003).

117. *Id.*

118. World Health Organization, *Severe Acute Respiratory Syndrome (SARS) Multi-Country Outbreak — Update 37* (April 23, 2003), *at* <http://www.who.int/csr/don/2003_04_23/en/> (last visited June 10, 2003).

119. *Id.*

120. *Id.*

121. World Health Organization, *Severe Acute Respiratory Syndrome (SARS) Multi-Country Outbreak — Update 50* (May 8, 2003), *at* <http://www.who.int/csr/don/2003_05_08/en/> (last visited June 10, 2003).

122. *Id.*

123. *Id.*

124. World Health Organization, *Severe Acute Respiratory Syndrome (SARS) Multi-Country Outbreak — Update 58* (May 17, 2003), *at* <http://www.who.int/csr/don/2003_05_17/en/> (last visited June 10, 2003).

125. World Health Organization, *Severe Acute Respiratory Syndrome (SARS) Multi-Country Outbreak — Update 61* (May 21, 2003), *at* <http://www.who.int/csr/don/2003_05_21/en/> (last visited June 10, 2003).

126. WHO has described the emergency travel advisory issued on March 15, 2003 as "rare," World Health Organization, *supra* note 8, at 4, and "unprecedented," World Health Organization, *Severe Acute Respiratory Syndrome (SARS) Multi-Country Outbreak— Update 27* (April 11, 2003), *at* <http://www.who.int/csr/don/2003_04_11/en/> (last visited June 10, 2003) [hereinafter World Health Organization, *Update 27*]. WHO reported that, prior to SARS, the Organization had never issued travel advice for specific geographical locations because of an outbreak of infectious diseases. World Health Organization, *Severe Acute Respiratory Syndrome (SARS) Multi-Country Outbreak — Update 19* (April 2, 2003), *at* <http://www.who.int/csr/don/2003_04_02/en/> (last visited June 10, 2003) [hereinafter World Health Organization, *Update 19*].

127. World Health Organization, *Update 19, supra note 126.*

128. World Health Organization, *Director-General Says Food Import Bans are Inappropriate for Fighting Cholera*, Press Release WHO/24, February 16, 1998.

129. World Health Organization, *supra* note 26, at 8–10.

130. *Id.* at 10 (emphasis added).

131. *Id.* at 9–10.

132. *Id.*

133. World Health Organization, *Severe Acute Respiratory Syndrome (SARS) Multi-Country Outbreak — Update 18* (April 2, 2003), *at* <http://www.who.int/csr/don/2003_04_02/en/> (last visited June 10, 2003).

134. D. L. Brown, "Virus Worry Fades in Toronto, but Concern Lingers; Residents Begin to Pick Up Their Old Routines; Officials Call WHO Travel Advisory Unnecessary," *Washington Post*, April 24, 2003, at A20.

135. Piller, *supra* note 82, at A1.

136. *Id.*

137. On the controversy over the Toronto travel advisory, see S. Frank, "Suddenly, All Smiles," *Time* (Canadian Edition), May 12, 2003, *available at* 2003 WL 11985677.

138. World Health Assembly, *supra* note 113, at paragraph 4(2).

139. *Id.*

140. National Intelligence Council, *SARS: Down But Still a Threat* (Intelligence Community Assessment 2003-09) (Washington, D.C.: National Intelligence Council, 2003): 23.

141. World Health Organization, *World Health Organization Announces New Public-Private Initiative on Disease Surveillance*, (Press Release) (May 22, 2003), *at* <http://www.who,int/mediacentre/releases/2003/prwha3/en/> (last visited May 22, 2003).

142. *Id.*

143. Commenting on the PPP initiative, David L. Heymann, Executive Director of Communicable Diseases at WHO, observed that "[t]here have been no resources for this in the past." Quoted in V. Fuhrmans and G. Naik, "The WHO Wants Company Money to Battle SARS," *Wall Street Journal*, May 22, 2003, at D3.

144. *Id.*

145. World Health Organization, *Update 27*, *supra* note 126; R. Stein, "Mystery Illness Mortality Rate 4%, WHO Officials Say," *Washington Post*, March 27, 2003, at A15.

146. The Director of the U.S. Centers for Disease Control and Prevention noted: "Speed of scientific discovery and speed of communication are hallmarks of the response to SARS and reflect amazing achievements in science, technology, and international collaboration." J. Gerberding, "Faster ... but Fast Enough? Responding to the Epidemic of Severe Acute Respiratory Syndrome," *New England Journal of Medicine*, 348 (2003): 2030–31, at 2030.

147. "SARS: Race to Patent Virus Renews Debate Over 'Patents on Life,'" *Medical Letter on the CDC & FDA*, June 1, 2003, *available at* 2003 WL 8982543 (reporting on efforts of the CDC's patent strategy on the SARS virus to prevent others from monopolizing it through intellectual property rights).

148. See sources cited in note 3 *supra*.

149. National Intelligence Council, *supra* note 140, at 29.

150. World Health Organization, *Update 83 — One Hundred Days into the Outbreak* (June 18, 2003), *at* <http://www.who.int/csr/don/2003_06_18/en/> (last visited June 20, 2003).

151. "*SARS: How Effective is the State and Local Response?": Hearing Before the Permanent Subcommittee on Investigations of the U.S. Senate Governmental Affairs Committee*, 108th Cong., at 10-24 (May 21, 2003) (testimony of J.L. Gerberding, A.S. Fauci, and M.T. Osterholm).

152. The General Accounting Office argued, for example, that "while the efforts of public health agencies and health care organizations to increase their preparedness for major public health threats such as influenza pandemics and bioterrorism have improved the nation's capacity to respond to SARS and other emerging infectious disease outbreaks, gaps in preparedness remain." General Accounting Office, SARS Outbreak: Improvements to Public Health Capacity Are Needed for Responding to Bioterrorism and Emerging Infectious Diseases, GAO-03-769T, May 7, 2003.

153. See, e.g., S. McBride, "China and ASEAN Make Overtures to Calm Public; National Leaders Agree on Measures to Combat Illness, Protect Economies," *Asian Wall Street Journal*, April 30, 2002, at A1.

154. See generally Gostin and Lazzarini, *supra* note 41.

155. WHO argues that "[a]ccess to essential drugs is part of the human right to health." World Health Organization, Globalization, *TRIPS and Access to Pharmaceuticals* (WHO Policy Perspectives on Medicines No. 3, March 2001), at 5.

156. D.G. McNeil, Jr., "Health Official Wield a Big Stick, Carefully, Against SARS," *New York Times*, April 20, 2003, at A12; Fidler, *supra* note 98.

157. See, e.g., G.J. Annas, "Bioterrorism, Public Health, and Civil Liberties," *New England Journal of Medicine*, 346 (2002): 1337–42.

158. For discussion, see Fidler, *supra* note 20, at 200–03.

159. M. Pottinger, "The SARS Outbreak: In Some Nations SARS Appears to Have Peaked," *Wall Street Journal*, April 29, 2003, at A2 ("Singapore adopted even stricter measures, imposing 10-day home quarantines on thousands of people who might have come in contact with SARS patients, and threatening stiff penalties for people who violated the orders.").

160. McNeil, *supra* note 156, at A12 (noting use of voluntary isolation and quarantine by Canadian health officials).

161. U.S. Centers for Disease Control and Prevention, *Questions and Answers: Travel and Quarantine, at* <http://www.cdc.gov/ncidod/sars/qa/travel.htm> (last visited June 21, 2003) ("CDC is requesting locating information from travelers who are on flights with people suspected of having SARS. CDC, with the help of state and local health authorities, is attempting to follow-up with these travelers for 14 days to make sure no one develops symptoms consistent with SARS.").

162. See Fidler, *supra* note 20, at 47–52.

163. With respect to China, "[b]oth WHO and the Chinese Ministry of Health regard the emergency response to SARS as an excellent opportunity to strengthen, throughout the mainland, systems for directing and responding to all emerging and epidemic-prone infectious diseases." World Health Organization, *Update 77 — WHO Officials to Visit China* (June 10, 2003), *at* <http://www.who.int/csr/don/2003_06_10/en/> (last visited June 10, 2003).

164. *Id.*

165. National Intelligence Council, *supra* note 140, at 31.

166. See criticism of Medecins Sans Frontieres that "[t]he only section of the [G8] Action Plan [on Health issued in June 2003] that shows determination is for SARS. Diseases that primarily affect poor people and occur in places of little consequence to the global economy are not treated with the same urgency." Medecins Sans Frontieres, *G8*

Offers World an "Inaction Plan" on Health (June 3, 2003), *at* <http://www.accessmed-msf.org/prod/publications.asp?scntid=3620031159124&contenttype=PARA&> (last visited June 21, 2003). The G8 Action Plan on Health can be found at <http://www.g7.utoronto.ca/summit/2003evian/health_en.html> (last visited June 21, 2003).

167. For an overview, see *Fact Sheet: The President's Emergency Plan for AIDS Relief, at* <http://www.whitehouse.gov/news/releases/2003/01/20030129-1.html> (last visited June 21, 2003). Congress passed legislation to implement this plan in May 2003. See United States Leadership Against HIV/AIDS, Tuberculosis, and Malaria Act of 2003, Pub. L. No. 108-25.

168. United States Leadership Against HIV/AIDS, Tuberculosis, and Malaria Act of 2003, *supra* note 167 at §202(d).

169. World Health Organization, *Cumulative Number of Reported Probable Cases* (August 7, 2003), *at* <http://www.who.int/csr/sars/country/2003_08_07/en/> (last visited September 7, 2003).

170. National Intelligence Council, *supra* note 140, at 24.

171. D. P. Fidler, "The Globalization of Public Health: Emerging Infectious Diseases and International Relations," *Indiana Journal of Global Legal Studies* 5 (1997): 11–51, at 33–34.

172. World Health Organization, *SARS Outbreak Contained Worldwide: Threat Remains and More Research Needed, Says WHO* (July 5, 2003), *at* <http://www.who.int/mediacentre/releases/2003/pr56/en/> (last visited September 7, 2003).

173. *Severe Acute Respiratory Syndrome Threat (SARS): Hearing Before the Senate Comm. on Health, Education, Labor and Pensions*, 108th Cong., at 15. (April 7, 2003) (testimony of David L. Heymann, Executive Director, Communicable Diseases, World Health Organization).

[2]

CHINA'S RESPONSE TO SARS*

*Ruotao Wang***

I. OVERVIEW OF THE SARS EPIDEMIC IN CHINA

On January 2, 2003, a local city hospital sent a report to the Health Bureau of Guangdong Province about an outbreak (eight cases) of an unknown-caused pneumonia among health workers and relatives of patients of the hospital and asked for the help of the provincial health authority. Preliminary investigation carried out by a provincial task force team failed to identify the cause of the pneumonia outbreak in the hospital, but the team highly suspected that it might be a communicable disease caused by a virus. The team also carried out a retrospective survey that suggested that on Nov. 16, 2002, a similar outbreak (four cases) happened within a family in this region. Subsequently, several outbreaks clustered in families or hospitals happened in Zhongshan city and Guangzhou city of Guangdong province; later this outbreak spread to the whole province. This epidemic reached its peak by the end of February 2003 in Guangdong province, and then the number of new cases started to decrease. However, in March 2003, this kind of unknown pneumonia (now called severe acute respiratory syndrome ("SARS")) was also discovered and reported in Beijing, Shanxi province, and Inner Mongolia. By June 12, 2003, there was a total of 5,327 probable SARS cases reported, with 343 deaths in 26 provinces of China. The SARS epidemic reached a peak in late April 2003, and from the middle of May, this epidemic began to decrease and finally stopped in mainland China as a whole.

* This article is based on a presentation at the March 2004 "SARS, Public Health, and Global Governance" Symposium at Temple University James E. Beasley School of Law. Several sources were consulted by the author in the development of his presentation, including: CHINESE CENTER FOR DISEASE CONTROL AND PREVENTION, OVERVIEW OF EPIDEMICS AND RESPONSES TO THE SEVERE ACUTE RESPIRATORY SYNDROME (SARS) IN THE PEOPLE'S REPUBIC OF CHINA (2003); TSINGSHUA UNIVERSITY CENTER FOR THE STUDY OF CONTEMPORARY CHINA, SARS AND AIDS: THE CHINESE CASE IN THE CONTEXT OF GLOBALIZATION (2003); CAO KANGTAI, EXPLANATION OF THE EMERGENCY REGULATION ON SUDDEN PUBLIC HEALTH (China Fazhi Press 2003); CHINA MINISTRY OF HEALTH, DOCUMENTS AND MATERIALS FROM THE 2002 NATIONAL MEETING ON HEALTH (2002).

** Professor of Epidemiology and Public Health, Union School of Public Health, Chinese Academy of Preventive Medicine, Beijing, China.

II. CHINA'S RESPONSE DURING THE PERIOD OF THE 2003 SARS EPIDEMIC

Before April 24, 2003, China's response to the SARS epidemic followed its traditional approach to handling epidemics. Health authorities silently tried to control the epidemic without upsetting social stability. Although the first report of SARS reached the national health authority on January 2, 2003, China failed to report to WHO about a possible outbreak of a new communicable disease. Rather, it was Dr. Carl Urbani, a doctor working outside of China, who was credited with giving a report to WHO and naming this unknown disease "SARS," in March of 2003. By contrast, the health authorities in China named SARS "atypical pneumonia," which was a name that was misleading and confusing to the public as well as to doctors at the early stage of the epidemic.

On April 24, 2003, however, Beijing started to take unusually strong steps to control the epidemic, and a few days later, the mayor of Beijing and the minister of the national health department were both removed from their official positions because of their failure to control the epidemic. It caused a panic nationwide in China. Many excessively severe measures were imposed, such as unnecessary disinfections and community quarantines. Controlling the SARS epidemic became the top political issue for administrative leaders at all levels in the whole of China.

On June 16, 2003, the Chinese Center for Diseases Control and Prevention ("CDC") summarized nine strategies that were successful in controlling the SARS epidemic and that should be consistently taken in the future. This reflects the health approach in response to the SARS epidemic:

1) Establish multi-sector cooperation and coordination mechanisms at all levels.
2) Establish and improve a SARS surveillance system.
3) Adopt comprehensive control and prevention measures with identification and management of infection resources as the key element, and prevent transmission occurring within the hospitals and outbreaks in communities.
4) Strengthen treatment and care services to reduce the fatality rate.
5) Develop technical guidelines for prevention and control, and conduct training for professionals.
6) Conduct inspection and supervision in the field.
7) Strengthen community-based prevention and health education.
8) Strengthen scientific research on SARS.
9) Strengthen information exchange and cooperation.

Soon after the SARS epidemic, health authorities emphasized the urgency of enhancing the public health system, in part through the establishment and improvement of the disease surveillance system in China. Now health workers at all levels in China are discussing the improvement of public health emergency systems. An effort to integrate various surveillance and reporting systems is currently being tested. A comprehensive training program for grassroots health workers is under implementation. Building up a health management information system is one of the most important objectives.

III. REEXAMINING THE EXPERIENCES OF CHINA: RESPONSE AFTER THE 2003 SARS EPIDEMIC—SOCIAL APPROACH

After 30 years of isolation, China reopened to the world in the 1980s. Since 1989, China has been going through great social transition. The outbreak of SARS in 2003 might be an isolated incident, but China did not prepare for it at all. After SARS, many social scholars have given a more in-depth analysis to China's social reform process, its health system, and relevant health regulations.

A. What Kind of Health Law Do We Really Need?

During the SARS epidemic, health authorities repeatedly cited the Communicable Diseases Control and Prevention Law, issued in 1989, as their source of power. The health authorities asserted that health laws are tools and powerful weapons to carry out tasks of the state. The health administrative organs were citing health laws only to justify their authority, and during the SARS epidemic the health administrative agencies hoped to expand their power without mention of power-checking and accountability.

It is the Communicable Diseases and Prevention Law that provides that the health administration departments of government at various levels shall exercise uniform supervision over and control of the work of preventing and treating infectious diseases. The Criminal Law of the Peoples Republic of China, as revised in 1997, has more punitive provisions:

Article 409 of the Criminal Law provides that any functionary of an administrative department for public health who is engaged in prevention and treatment of infectious diseases, who through his gross neglect of duty, causes the spread or epidemic of an infectious disease, if the circumstances are serious, shall be sentenced to fixed-term imprisonment of not more than three years of criminal detention. But up to the present, no government official has ever been prosecuted for violation of this provision.

The new Emergency Regulations on Sudden Public Health Incidents, an administrative document, is inferior to a law, but nonetheless grants great power to the health administrative agencies. Article 44 of the regulation stipulates that, in an unexpected incident, if competent health authorities or relevant departments take medical measures against a patient, who needs to receive isolated treatment or medical observations, the person must cooperate; if the person refuses to cooperate, the public security department assists medical care institutions in taking measures to enforce the treatment in isolation according to law. Should health law address possible compensation mechanisms for damages to citizens caused by negligence or intention of administrative agencies in exercising their authority? Should health law provide strict legal procedures that must be followed when health administrative agencies exercise their power in decision-making, infringing upon a person's right?

In China, health authorities control the release of information on epidemics and statistics on communicable diseases. The health authorities used to believe that news reports should be controlled tightly. Reports must be reviewed by the Ministry of Health. The reporting standards must be set high to prevent setting a bad influence and causing unnecessary alarm. Should health law set up a procedure and standard for health information collection and release?

Most specialized (such as infectious diseases hospitals) and comprehensive hospitals in China are subordinate to health administrative agencies, and all of them are becoming more and more profit-seekers. On the one hand, most of the grassroots hospitals or clinics are independent, private institutions. However, during the SARS epidemic, health administrative agencies merely issued policies, without being responsible for the profits of all kinds of hospitals. Should health law provide clear definitions of duties and responsibilities of the health authority as one branch of the government, the agencies of public health institutes, and doctors and nurses working in various kinds of hospitals or other medical care institutions?

B. Economic Development vs. Human Development

SARS requires China to rethink the relationship between economic development and human development. Human development implies that people are free to employ their talents as they choose. Reaching the goal of human development requires not only that people are able to live healthily and educate themselves fully, but also that society provides them with sufficient space for full participation in its social, economic, and political life. Specifically, the most important points of human development are: to recognize and protect individual rights, including the right to health; to let people participate in decisions that will affect their lives, such as government policies relevant to income distribution, medical care, public measurements, education, and environmental protection; and to follow procedural fairness and equitable principles against any forms of human discrimination, such as towards gender and ethnic minorities.

China signed the International Covenant on Economic, Social, and Cultural Rights in 1997 and the National People's Congress Standing Committee ratified it in 2001. States that have signed the covenant recognize the right of everyone to the enjoyment of the highest attainable standard of physical and mental health. China has made a commitment to take certain steps, including: to reduce the stillbirth rate and infant mortality and to promote healthy child development; to improve all aspects of environmental and industrial hygiene; to prevent, treat, and control epidemic, endemic, occupational, and other diseases; and to create conditions that will assure universal medical service and medical attention in the event of sickness. After the SARS epidemic China now should seriously rethink how to honor this commitment.

C. Science and Technology vs. Humanities and Ethics

The trend of globalization and urbanization and the experiences of the SARS epidemic made China realize that a new communicable disease may happen at any time and anywhere within China. China must now fully prepare for it. But how should China prepare? During and after the SARS epidemic many people emphasized the importance of science and technology. However, some social scholars have been arguing that science and technology and not always good for human development. They argue that humanities and ethics are equally, if not more, important to us. In selecting policies, making laws, and setting up systems, what we need is to orient our values and first emphasize human care. Should we value people over things? Should we work absolutely for our own interests, or should we put ourselves in the place of another? Should we require others to adopt our own values and standards, or advocate diversity and pluralism?

In the SARS epidemic, some health workers alleged that SARS was preventable and curable in an attempt to prevent social panic. However, social scholars pose the question that if SARS was not preventable and not curable, should we have panicked? If an individual is sure to die, can this person do whatever he wants before death? Now more and more social scholars are calling for a rebuilding of trust in the science and technology approach to social transition.

[3]

Ethics and SARS: lessons from Toronto

Peter A Singer, Solomon R Benatar, Mark Bernstein, Abdallah S Daar, Bernard M Dickens, Susan K MacRae, Ross E G Upshur, Linda Wright, Randi Zlotnik Shaul

The SARS epidemic showed how easy it is for infectious diseases to spread round the world. Ethical as well as clinical issues need to be resolved to improve the response to the next epidemic

The outbreak of severe acute respiratory syndrome (SARS) in the Toronto area earlier this year forced medical and government workers to make hard choices, often with limited information and short deadlines. Healthcare providers were on the firing line, and were the people most affected by the disease.[1] Decision makers had to balance individual freedoms against the common good, fear for personal safety against the duty to treat sick people, and economic losses against the need to contain the spread of a deadly disease. Such decisions have to be guided by both scientific knowledge and ethical considerations. The SARS outbreak showed that Canadian society was not fully prepared to deal with the ethical issues.

Evaluating ethical issues

We formed a working group to identify the key ethical issues and values most important for an analysis of ethical dimensions of the SARS epidemic. The final list of issues and values was agreed by a consensus process and found to have face validity and credibility. We then developed a framework for looking at the ethical implications of the SARS outbreak, identifying 10 key ethical values relevant to SARS (box), and five major ethical issues faced by decision makers.

We examined the underlying ethical values for the five major issues and drew lessons from how each was tackled. The following case studies illustrate the issues and are an amalgam of our experiences.

Ethics of quarantine

A medical clerk is asked by public health officials to remain at home in quarantine for 10 days because of possible exposure to SARS. She wants to comply but fears this could cost both her job and her apartment.

Five ethical values were associated with this issue, starting with individual liberty. Even the most highly valued individual liberties have to be balanced against

CP/KEVIN FRAYER/AP

a second value—that of protecting the public from harm caused by the uncontrolled movements of people who may be infectious.[2] Under the value of proportionality, authorities exercising public health powers should do so in a way that is relevant, legitimate, and necessary. They should use the least restrictive methods that are reasonably available to limit individual liberties and should apply restrictions without discrimination.

The value of transparency requires stakeholders to be fully informed about issues, including the risks and benefits, particularly if they affect their health, wellbeing, and personal liberty. Finally, the value of reciprocity requires society to ensure that those quarantined receive adequate care and do not suffer unfair economic penalties.[3]

Privacy of personal information and public need to know

A nurse at a hospital affected by SARS feels unwell and has a fever. After weighing the risk of having the disease against losing income and placing a burden of extra work on her colleagues, the nurse takes a commuter train to work. She is later found to have SARS. Medical officials choose not to name the nurse but use the media to warn people who may have been on her train that they should be tested for SARS.

Although the individual has a right to privacy, the state can over-ride this right if it would greatly help protect the public from serious harm. As a general rule, the privacy and confidentiality of individuals should be protected unless a well defined public health goal can be achieved by making personal information public.

In the initial stages of the outbreak, authorities named the woman who carried SARS to Canada from China, and her son, with the family's consent, because they believed it would provide additional public health benefit. Although public health officials took great pains to avoid linking ethnicity and illness, the linking of SARS with someone who had travelled from China,

Ten key ethical values

- Individual liberty
- Protection of the public from harm
- Proportionality
- Reciprocity
- Transparency
- Privacy
- Protection of communities from undue stigmatisation
- Duty to provide care
- Equity
- Solidarity

University of Toronto Joint Centre for Bioethics, 88 College St, Toronto, Canada M5G 1L4
Peter A Singer *Sun Life financial chair and director*
Abdallah S Daar *director, programme in applied ethics and biotechnology*
Susan K MacRae *deputy director*
Linda Wright *bioethicist*
Randi Zlotnik Shaul *bioethicist*
Department of Public Health Sciences, University of Toronto
Solomon R Benatar *visiting professor*
Division of Neurosurgery, University of Toronto
Mark Bernstein *professor*
Faculty of Law, University of Toronto
Bernard M Dickens *Dr William M Scholl professor of health law and policy*
Sunnybrook and Women's College Health Sciences Centre, Toronto
Ross E G Upshur *director, primary care research unit*
Correspondence to: P A Singer peter.singer@utoronto.ca

BMJ 2003;327:1342–44

The decision making tool is available on bmj.com

combined with the public's limited understanding of transmission, resulted in many people unnecessarily avoiding Chinese businesses.

Proportionality requires that private information be released only if there are no less intrusive means to protect the public health. For example, naming an individual or releasing a photograph could be justified if that person violates a quarantine order. Transparency can be achieved without naming individuals or communities. Indeed, the need to protect communities from undue stigma is an important lesson for future epidemics.

Duty of care

An intensive care nurse is afraid of contracting SARS at work and infecting her husband and three small children. She feels torn between the potential danger posed to her family and her professional duties.

For the first time in more than a generation, Canadian healthcare workers faced a deadly infectious disease for which there was no known effective treatment. Dozens of healthcare workers, many of them nurses, were infected with SARS because of their work. Some infected their families, and two died. Many others had to wear cumbersome equipment to protect themselves, causing appreciable discomfort, reducing their ability to work, and reducing contact with their patients.

Healthcare workers were forced to weigh serious and imminent health risks to themselves and their families against their duty to care for the sick. This duty is mainly determined by professional ethics. By analogy, firefighters do not have the freedom to choose whether to face a particularly bad fire and police officers do not get to select which dark alleys they walk down.

Nonetheless, these professional duties do have limits. For example, healthcare workers also have a professional obligation to maintain their own health and ability to provide care for patients.[4] However, the nature of such limits is contested. Some believe that under dire circumstances professionals should have minimal self regard and pursue their duties at potential cost to their own lives. Others claim that it is unreasonable to demand extreme heroism as the norm, and even more unreasonable to demand that the lives of children and families should be held hostage to professional duties. How these two positions are balanced is intensely personal but has vital implications for handling pandemics.

The value of reciprocity requires healthcare institutions to support and protect healthcare workers, to help them cope with very stressful situations, to acknowledge their work in dangerous and difficult conditions, and to have workable plans for emergency situations. Ontario's minister of health acknowledged the heroic work of healthcare workers, and this was an important act of reciprocity. In addition, measures such as an insurance fund to cover healthcare workers who become sick or die through work should be considered for future epidemics. Although many doctors and nurses have supplemental insurance, other healthcare workers, such as technicians and clerks, do not.

We could not reach consensus on the issue of duty to care, particularly regarding the extent to which healthcare workers are obligated to risk their lives in delivering clinical care. This issue requires urgent attention from researchers, regulatory bodies, and the public.

Collateral damage

Surgery for a patient with breast cancer is postponed during the SARS outbreak, increasing the anxiety of the woman and her family about the spread of her disease.

Severe restrictions on entry to hospitals affected by SARS in the Toronto area meant that thousands of people were denied medical care, sometimes for severe illnesses such as cancer and heart disease. Some of these patients died before receiving treatment. Those who were admitted, with or without SARS, suffered loss of contact and emotional support from family and friends as hospitals closed their doors to visitors.[5]

Strong measures taken to contain the spread of a deadly disease will inevitably cause considerable collateral damage. Authorities in the Toronto region had to make hard choices about which medical services to maintain and which to place on hold. They had to weigh risks, benefits, and opportunity costs. How such decisions can best be made needs thorough re-evaluation. Clearly, they should be made in a fair manner, preserving as much equity as possible between the interests of patients with SARS and those who need urgent treatment for other diseases. Procedural fairness should also be ensured in making such decisions.

The collateral damage of the SARS outbreak has yet to be fully quantified and may be substantial. Health systems need to have plans for setting priorities in place for future epidemics.

SARS in a globalised world

In Guangdong province in rural China a farmer develops a severe respiratory infection. Normally, the disease would have stayed in the community, but family travels begin a chain of events that takes SARS around the world. The World Health Organization issues travel warnings for areas with large numbers of cases.

The SARS outbreak sounded a dramatic wakeup call about global interdependence and the increasing risk to global human security from the emergence and rapid spread of infectious diseases. SARS leapt the Pacific Ocean to Toronto on an aeroplane. This shows the urgent need for people around the world to adopt the value of solidarity as much for self interest as altruistic reasons. Infectious diseases can spread in either direction between poor rural areas and rich urban areas, anywhere in the world.

The SARS epidemic also showed the urgent need to strengthen the way the world deals with emerging infectious diseases. This will require new visions of global solidarity and cooperation.[6]

Transparency, honesty and good communications on health issues also need emphasis. It took months for China to acknowledge that it was the source of the outbreak. It is no longer acceptable for countries to hide health information that can protect others. Sharing public health information is part of maintaining the global public good of health protection, and should be encouraged and admired.

Next steps

The lessons learnt from the ethical choices in the Toronto SARS crisis can inform efforts to control the disease elsewhere and guide our responses to future epidemics. The approach outlined here is provisional and derived from reflection on recent experiences. Nevertheless, the values identified are a useful starting point for evaluating the ethical dimensions of outbreaks of communicable disease. Our evaluation points towards a broader, public health focused approach based on a more comprehensive set of guiding values than usually considered in the ethics of interpersonal relationships.

Further research, both conceptual and empirical, is needed. As a first step we have created a decision tool derived from the values identified above (see bmj.com). Further work is required to examine how the values identified relate to moral theory. A review of professional codes and communicable disease legislation would help to clarify professional duties and define the acceptable extent of professional obligation and public health power. Additionally, public discussion about the acceptable limits to individual liberty in public health emergencies and the expected scope of healthcare workers' duty to care would help to harmonise the actions of the health community and public expectation.

We thank Sheela Basrur for comments on an earlier version of this paper.

Contributors and sources: The authors formed the working group and are scholars in bioethics who come from various disciplines, including medicine, surgery, health law, social work, teaching, nursing, and epidemiology. Several of the team members worked in directly affected hospitals and some were involved in decision making regarding the outbreak. Michael Keating drafted the report on the basis of the discussions of the working group, and it was then reviewed and revised by all authors.

Summary points

The response to the SARS epidemic by public health, governmental, and healthcare workers raised new ethical issues

Analysis of decision making in Toronto provides lessons for dealing with a global public health threat

Five key ethical issues were identified and 10 underlying values

Public discussion is required to resolve issues surrounding acceptable limits to individual liberty and healthcare workers' duty of care in an epidemic

Funding: PAS is a distinguished investigator and REGU is a new investigator of the Canadian Institutes of Health Research.

Competing interests: None declared.

1 Booth CM, Matukas LM, Tomlinson GA, et al. Clinical features and short-term outcomes of 144 patients with SARS in the greater Toronto area. *JAMA* (in press). http://jama.ama-assn.org/cgi/content/full/289.21.JOC30885v1 (accessed 26 Oct 2003).

2 Upshur RE. Principles for the justification of public health intervention. *Can J Public Health* 2002;93:101-3.

3 Barbera J, Macintyre A, Gostin L, Inglesby T, O'Toole T, DeAtley C, et al. Large-scale quarantine following biological terrorism in the United States: scientific examination, logistic and legal limits, and possible consequences. *JAMA* 2001;286:2711-7.

4 Maunder R, Hunter J, Vincent L, Bennett J, Peladeau N, Leszcz M, et al. The immediate psychological and occupational impact of the 2003 SARS outbreak in a teaching hospital. *CMAJ* 2003;168:1245-51.

5 Bernstein M, Hawryluck L. Challenging beliefs and ethical concepts: the collateral damage of SARS. *Crit Care* 2003;7:269-71.

6 Benatar SR, Daar AS, Singer PA. Global health ethics: a rationale for mutual caring. *Int Affairs* 2003;79:107-38.

(Accepted 15 September 2003)

Q&A

Alcohol and the genitourinary tract

Question

Is there such a phenomenon as alcohol induced kidney pain?

Fergus J Dignan, *Lyneham*

Answer

Intermittent pelvi-uretereic junction obstruction (PUJO) is a reasonably common condition, and it often presents (usually in young men) as severe loin pain after drinking alcohol. The partially obstructed pelvi-ureteric junction, where the kidney drains into the upper ureter (the tube that conveys urine into the bladder), can handle the normal fluid load given to it. When the subject takes alcohol, however, the amount of urine produced suddenly and dramatically increases (a commonly observed event). The partially obstructed junction then cannot take the volume produced, and expands, causing pain—usually severe, like that caused by a kidney stone. In fact, PUJO is a differential diagnosis in stone disease.

Diagnosis requires an x ray examination (intravenous urography), but often a radioisotope scan is needed to show the obstruction. There are several causes of PUJO, but usually it is just a functional inability of that part of the ureter to carry the normal peristaltic wave. Treatment is surgical if the symptoms are severe and frequent enough to warrant an operation—that is, not just every time the patient goes on a bender. There's an easier solution, then.

John F Bolton *clinical fellow in urology, Bristol Royal Infirmary, Bristol*

http://bmj.com/cgi/qa-display/short/bmj_el;40367

This exchange was posted on the Q&A section of bmj.com. If you want to respond to the question, or ask a new question of your own, follow the link above or go to: http://bmj.com/q&a

Part II
HIV and AIDS

[4]

A Global Political Economy Approach to AIDS: Ideology, Interests and Implications

KELLEY LEE & ANTHONY B. ZWI

The AIDS (Acquired Immune Deficiency Syndrome) pandemic has been, in many respects, unprecedented. The rapid emergence of a new disease and the mobilisation of significant financial and human resources for research, treatment and control strategies has seen no parallel.[1] Given the global spread of infection, and the global nature of the response, AIDS is of clear relevance to scholars of international relations (IR) and international political economy (IPE). Yet little attention has been devoted to health in the IR field, and even less to AIDS.

The bulk of initial research on AIDS in the early 1980s was devoted to understanding its occurrence and presentation within and across populations. In the past 10 years there has been a growing body of research in the medical and social sciences focused at the national or subnational level. These studies have contributed much to exploring transmission of the human immunodeficiency virus (HIV) among particular groups (notably the homosexual community and intravenous drug users in the USA and Europe, and commercial sex workers in sub-Saharan Africa, Asia and Latin America), the historical and cultural factors which have facilitated transmission of the HIV virus, and the economic impact of AIDS on health systems and labour markets. Other studies have examined individuals in terms of their sexual behaviour and awareness of HIV and AIDS. Analyses in recent years have broadened to include women and youth, gender, human rights, the impact of prevention strategies, and the costs of treating HIV/AIDS.

As part of this broadening perspective on AIDS, this article argues that a global political economy (GPE) approach offers further insights for understanding and responding to the disease.[2] First, widening the spatial dimension of AIDS research to the global level is apt, given the spread of the disease across national boundaries and the attempts to tackle it as a global phenomenon. Second, a GPE approach enables us to extend our analysis temporally by locating AIDS within a particular world order of 'transnational neoliberalism' defined below by material, institutional and ideological forces distinct to inter-

Kelley Lee & Anthony B. Zwi, Health Policy Unit, London School of Hygiene and Tropical Medicine, Keppel Street, London WC1E 7HT, UK.

national relations since the late 1960s. After describing the global spread of AIDS, the article suggests that there is growing evidence that this world order has created fertile conditions within which AIDS has spread, particularly among peripheral interests in the GPE. Importantly, this includes 'the way in which ideas about what constitutes the *political* and the *economic* have emerged historically',[3] and it will be shown that policy making on AIDS has been strongly centred on biomedical and neoliberal economic discourses.

The article concludes by arguing for a more critical awareness of the theoretical and practical lineage of existing knowledge of AIDS. Given that the limitations of this knowledge have been part of the conditions within which the disease has thrived, an expanded research agenda is put forth for the study of IPE and AIDS. It is in locating the disease within what Fortin calls a 'longer view', which seeks 'to situate the present disease within the broad historical, social, ecological, cultural, and political relationships that mediate humanity, sickness, and the environment',[4] that the beginnings of a truly global response to AIDS can be built.

The global spread of AIDS

AIDS is a complex of symptoms and signs in infected individuals, ultimately culminating in the fatal depression of the immune response system. The disease was first identified in 1981 among male homosexuals in the USA. Within a remarkably short period the responsible infectious agent, HIV, was identified and the routes of transmission clarified. These were unprotected penetrative sexual intercourse, transfusion with infected blood products, injection using infected equipment, and from an infected mother to her child either during pregnancy, the birthing process or breastfeeding. There are two recognised serotypes of the virus, HIV-1 and HIV-2. HIV-1 predominates worldwide, while HIV-2 has spread since the mid-1980s, notably in west Africa, but by no means confined to that area.

HIV infection has spread rapidly across the globe. In North America, western Europe, Australia, New Zealand and many urban areas of Latin America, it is believed that HIV began to spread from the mid- to late-1970s and early 1980s. This spread occurred initially among homosexual and bisexual men through unprotected sexual intercourse; among intravenous drug users (IVDU); and among the recipients of contaminated blood products. In sub-Saharan Africa, Latin America and the Caribbean, the heterosexual spread of HIV was recognised as a key means of transmission by the second half of the 1980s. Subsequent spread through infected blood products, given a high prevalence among the general population and limited access to technologies for screening and testing, is also likely. The estimated prevalence of HIV infection in these regions is sobering. In Africa, around 10 million adults are believed to have been infected to date, with over three million cases of AIDS. Those at particular risk, such as commercial sex workers without access to condoms, have been found to have HIV prevalence rates as high as 90 per cent.[5] In eastern and central Europe, the Middle East, north Africa, Asia and the Pacific, future increases in HIV infection are likely to be most dramatic, with the number of new cases of HIV

TABLE I. Estimated cases of HIV and AIDS by mid-1994

Region	Estimated total adult HIV infections[1]	Estimated total adult AIDS cases[2]	Cumulative reported AIDS cases (adult and paediatric)[3]	Ratio of HIV infections in men to those in women[4]
Australasia	>25,000	>5,000	5,158	5–6:1
North America	>1,000,000	>450,000	421,418	5–6:1
Western Europe	>500,000	>150,000	111,877	5–6:1
Latin America and the Caribbean	2,000,000	>400,000	102,359	4:1
Sub-Saharan Africa	>10,000,000	2,000,000	330,805	0.8–0.9:1
South and Southeast Asia	>2,500,000	250,000	7,195	2–3:1
East Asia and Pacific	50,000	>2,000	1,073	5–6:1
Eastern Europe and Central Asia	>50,000	>7,000	3,932	5–6:1
North Africa and the Middle East	100,000	>15,000	1,302	4:1
Global total	> 16 million	>3 million	985,119	1.5:1

Source: WHO, *The HIV/AIDS Pandemic: 1994 Overview* (Global Programme on AIDS, 1994).
Notes:
[1]Figures represent cases of HIV infection recorded from the late 1970s to mid-1994.
[2]Figures represent estimated HIV infection which has progressed to AIDS.
[3]Figures represent reported cases of AIDS which, in some regions, are a fraction of estimated cases.
[4]Ratio of male to female infections provides insights into the nature of spread and general impact on a society.

infection in Asia soon likely to surpass those in Africa. Initial cases in Asia have occurred primarily among commercial sex workers and drug injectors. However, this pattern is rapidly changing and alarming increases in transmission and disease have occurred among the general population of both Thailand and India.[6] This looming epidemic is expected to 'ultimately dwarf all others in scope and impact'.[7]

Table 1 shows that there was an estimated 16 million adults infected with HIV worldwide by mid-1994. In some parts of North America, western Europe, Australia and high-prevalence areas of east and central Africa, there is emerging evidence that the spread is stabilising.[8] The number of heterosexual people infected with HIV in industrialised countries is expected to remain stable or increase more slowly as those currently infected die and new cases are averted.[9] In other regions, however, the rate of increase will remain alarmingly high. Table 2 shows the projected number of HIV-infected people in broad continental areas for 1994 to the year 2000. Most notable is the expected increase in Asia, from 2.5 million to between 12 and 45.5 million cumulative cases.

TABLE II. Projection of cumulative adult HIV infections by geographic area to the year 2000

GAA	Low estimate	High estimate
North America	1,811,000	8,150,000
Western Europe	1,188,000	2,331,000
Oceania	22,000	45,000
Latin America	1,599,000	8,554,000
Sub-Saharan Africa	20,778,000	33,609,000
Caribbean	536,000	6,962,000
Eastern Europe	>2,000	20,000
South East Mediterranean	893,000	3,532,000
North East Asia	>6,000	486,000
Southeast Asia	11,277,000	45,059,000
Total	>38,112,000	108,748,000

Source: Jonathan Mann, Daniel Tarantola & T. Netter (Eds), *AIDS in the World: A Global Report* (Harvard University Press 1992), p. 107.

AIDS and the global political economy: an emerging transnational neoliberal order

There are no simple answers to how and why HIV infection has spread in the manner it has. Billions of US dollars have been spent on understanding the HIV virus, the pathogenesis of HIV disease, its epidemiology and clinical manifestations. Between 1982–91, about US$5.63 billion was spent on AIDS-related research worldwide, the vast majority by the governments of the 10 largest industrialised countries and almost all since 1985.[10] In order to broaden our understanding of the AIDS pandemic, this article examines how the study of the global political economy can enhance our understanding of HIV and AIDS. In turn, it is argued that HIV and AIDS can reveal new empirical applications for IPE scholars. Traditionally, the realist—liberal orthodoxy which has dominated the study of international relations has neglected the study of health. As Thomas writes, 'disease is a transnational phenomenon which pays no heed to territorial state boundaries; yet it rarely features in the discussion of International Relations'.[11] Critical or post-positivist approaches, which have emerged in recent years, seek to widen the intellectual boundaries of IR, extending the disciplinary agenda to include gender, the environment and social policy.[12]

Briefly, the GPE approach taken in this article is based on the writings of critical theorists in IR. Critical theorists share the aim of challenging positivist approaches to social science and proposing alternatives. Applied to the GPE, Gill writes that, first, 'there is a relativity in the claim to truth'; and second, that 'social conditions interact with and influence the survival, scientific status and consequences of rival social theories: knowledge is also a process of social struggle, again between hegemonic and counter-hegemonic perspectives and principles'. Given that all 'thought processes and knowledge systems' are at variance with reality, the aim is not to determine which truth is a true reflection of reality, but 'how and why and with what consequences' these particular 'truths' hold within a given historical period.[13] In this sense, the approach goes beyond the economic determinism found in the early political economy of health literature.[14]

This dialectic between the realms of ideas and material conditions is central to the ontology and theory of GPE put forth in critical theory. Drawing on the writings of Antonio Gramsci, Gill writes that the global political economy 'implies an integrated system of knowledge, production and exchange, and includes the dialectical relations between capital and non-capitalist systems and states, and ecological, ethical and other aspects of the whole'.[15] Central to such relations is the Gramscian concept of *hegemony* which is achieved by core interests (individuals, classes, states or transnational actors) through a mixture of coercive and consensual means. The use of coercion or force to assert leadership is domination. In contrast, the mobilisation of the consent of peripheral groups to a given order is achieved through intellectual, moral and political leadership. This suggests a complex concept of power which can be structurally embedded in historical social constructs (i.e. historic blocs) as well as vested in individual actors.[16]

Applying this GPE approach to the study of AIDS, it is argued that the disease can be located within a particular world order characterised by transnational neoliberalism. Briefly, this world order is defined by unprecedented growth of capital, production and exchange relations across state boundaries, with the effects of this process of globalisation[17] far from uniform. The material basis of this world order is 'a global economic system dominated by large institutional investors and transnational firms which control the bulk of the world's productive assets and are the principal influences in world trade and financial markets'. Its institutional nucleus is comprised of 'elements of the G-7 state apparatuses and transnational capital (in manufacturing, finance, and services)' which have created an 'internationalisation of authority and governance that not only involves international organisations ... and transnational firms, but also private consultancies and private bondrating agencies'.[18] Global governance is thus led by what Cox calls a 'transnational managerial class' and their institutional homes (e.g. ministries of finance, trade and industry, the World Bank and IMF, the Organisation of Economic Cooperation and Development) who increasingly shape policy making on a global scale.[19] Intellectual, moral and political leadership of this transnational managerial class is centred on consent to the ideas of political and economic neoliberalism, an ideology which is 'largely consistent with the world view and political priorities of large-scale, internationally-mobile forms of capital'.

It is within this world order that a fuller understanding of the global spread of AIDS can be achieved. First, the spread of AIDS has been facilitated by resultant changes in the spatial dimension of human relations. Globalisation, as described above, has led to an unprecedented increase in the worldwide movement of people (within and across national borders) in the form of migration and migrant labour,[20] tourism, displacement, occupying military forces,[21] and rapid urbanisation. Where development strategies have been adopted which seek to integrate a country into the global economy through liberalised markets and rapid industrialisation, pressures of transience on populations have increased at the same time as weakening systems of social support and the increased prices of many products and services. These changes have led to fundamental changes to social structures in both lower and higher income countries which have provided fertile conditions within which HIV has appeared and spread. For example, in Senegal and Uganda, it was found that 'mobility is an independent risk factor for acquiring HIV', noting that 'it is not the origin, or the destination of migration, but the social disruption which characterises certain types of migration, which determines vulnerability to HIV'.[22] Similarly, a study in the USA found that 'the disintegration of minority community physical or social structures has created such turmoil that AIDS spread rapidly to intravenous drug users and their sex partners, and rapidly followed commuting patterns into the suburbs'.[23]

Second, the ability of individuals, societies and countries to adapt to the process of globalisation is unequal, with those less able to adapt engaging in risk behaviours under conditions of poor access to health care that have made them more susceptible to HIV infection. For many low-income countries, the period since the late 1970s has brought rising levels of foreign debt, negative economic growth and declining terms of trade and levels of foreign aid. The introduction of structural adjustment programmes (SAPs) by the World Bank during the 1980s as a response to these macroeconomic problems has, as Asthana writes, 'contributed to an unprecedented decline in the health and living standards of the Third World poor'.[24] The main cause has been reduced public spending on the social sectors which much recent evidence shows has led to a decline in health status among the poorest communities. In Zambia, real expenditure on health fell between 1982–85 by 22 per cent, while in Bolivia per capita expenditure on health by the government declined by 30 per cent.[25] The introduction in many countries of cost-recovery mechanisms, such as user charges for health services, has been found to reduce utilisation despite exemption mechanisms for the poor.[26] It is now widely recognised by the development community, including the World Bank, that, in the mid-1990s, insufficient emphasis on 'poverty alleviation' by SAPs has had detrimental effects on the health status of poor communities.[27]

It has been within communities worst affected by these declining health conditions that HIV infection has gained the biggest foothold. The fastest growing epidemics have been among the most socioeconomically disadvantaged populations within and across countries. In low-income countries, greater human insecurity and social inequities have led many individuals to resort to coping strategies (e.g. migrant labour, commercial sex) under conditions which have placed them at greater risk of HIV infection. In Tanzania, it was found that 70 per cent of commercial sex workers engage in prostitution for economic survival.[28] In west Africa, large numbers of men migrate seasonally to work in neighbouring countries because of poor employment opportunities at home. In a study of Côte d'Ivoire, it was found that an agricultural enterprise provides accommodation for 2000 young male migrant workers in a camp which is visited after each payday by sex workers. Each sex worker 'services' a 'mean of 25 workers each over a period of two nights'. The study found that it is 'this pattern of mixing, and not the actual number of partners, which is responsible for the extensive spread of HIV among migrant workers'.[29] In India, research by the World Health Organisation (WHO) found that poverty is a key factor contributing to AIDS because financial hardship has forced men to leave their families to find employment. The use of drugs and/or sex workers has often followed suit.[30] An exacerbating factor in the spread of HIV infection among these low-income groups is the inadequate treatment of sexually transmitted diseases (STDs). Conditions such as genital ulceration increase the vulnerability to HIV infection, yet treatment for such conditions has not been forthcoming given limited access to health services. A study in Nairobi showed declines in clinic attendance for sexually transmitted diseases following the introduction of user charges.[31]

It has not only been in low-income countries that deteriorating political economies have increased vulnerability of populations to HIV infection. In the 'economies in transition' of central and eastern Europe, the end of the Cold War, and subsequent pressures to integrate rapidly with the emerging transnational neoliberal order, have brought upheaval to political and economic infrastructures. Health systems have been particularly badly affected, accompanied by sudden rises in such health indicators as infant mortality rate, incidence of infectious diseases and substance abuse. In relation to AIDS, the incidence of high-risk behaviours within unsafe conditions has increased.[32] In Albania, described as the 'bargain-basement brothel of the West', 'sex tourism' has become one of the main sources of income for many women.[33]

Finally, in many Western industrialised countries, globalisation has led to the rise of a disenfranchised, disempowered and impoverished 'underclass'. Individuals and groups within this class are those most adversely affected by globalised economic and political relations: the under- or unemployed thanks to monetarist economic policies; low-skilled labour because of the international mobility of production; small businesses because of the globalised scale of production of goods and services; and women and ethnic minorities who make up the majority of part-time and temporary workers. In the UK this class has emerged amid the widest social inequalities since the 1930s.[34] Similarly, Singer found that urban poverty and socially devalued ethnicity have been contributing factors to the spread of HIV/AIDS in the USA.[35]

In summary, there is much evidence that the emergence of a transnational neoliberal order has widened the health gap between haves and have-nots within and across countries. Within both lower and higher income countries, individuals and groups have had variable capacity to respond to rapidly changing global political and economic relations. Across countries, Figure 1 shows that a small number of countries continue to control the vast majority of global wealth. Over 80 per cent of people estimated to be infected with HIV live in low-income countries.[36] While some have gained access to employment, education and quality health care, others have faced limited employment and educational prospects, social dislocation and limited access to health care. It is within conditions of poverty that low-income groups have been more likely to engage in risk behaviours that heighten their exposure to HIV infection.

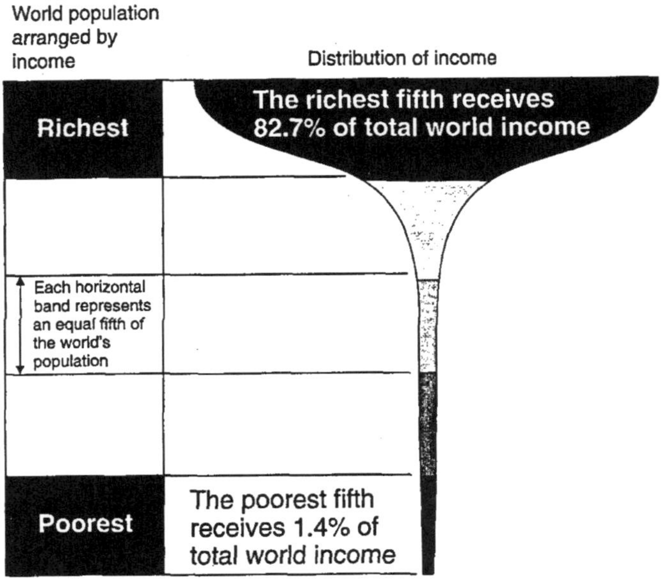

Source: N. Alexander, 'Remarks to the Banking Subcommittee on Domestic and International Monetary Affairs, U.S. House of Representatives on the World Bank and Poverty,' Bread for the World Institute, 27 March 1995.

FIGURE 1. Champagne glass of inequality in global wealth.

Orthodoxy and ideology: the discourse of AIDS

It is within the context of the global inequities described above that a critical analysis of the discourse on AIDS can be located. As well as changes in the structural conditions in which AIDS has emerged and spread, a key aspect of the GPE of AIDS is the way in which the disease has been understood by both scholars and practitioners. How AIDS has been theorised has had profound implications, not only for how we understand the disease, but for our responses to it. At the global level two main discourses, biomedical and neoliberal, have dominated.[37]

The *biomedical discourse* has focused on the clinical and epidemiological characteristics of the disease, modes of transmission, strategies emphasising individual risk behaviours, and developing methods of prevention, treatment and care. The proponents of this biomedical discourse have been scientists and medical professionals, trained within the Western medical tradition, who see the origins of disease primarily in terms of individual agents (i.e. viruses, people) and seek solutions through the medical sciences directed at the agents of infection. This tradition, as Doyal writes, is 'hospital-centred, highly technological, and is dispensed on an individual curative basis'.[38] For AIDS, the problem is seen to be a lack of knowledge and its application. It is held that, with sufficient amounts of the 'right' information, AIDS can be 'solved'. So far, the search for this 'magic bullet' to treat and cure AIDS has been unsuccessful.[39] Policy makers in the meantime have turned to promoting preventive measures, such as education and information campaigns, directed at changing individual behaviours.

Critiques of the biomedical approach to health are not new. Of particular note has been Lesley Doyal's *The Political Economy of Health* (1979) in which she argues that the legacies of early capital accumulation, social inequalities, colonialism and racism laid the foundations for ill-health in both developed and developing countries. Other writers, such as Vincent Navarro, David Sanders and Meredith Turshen,[40] have raised similarly important questions for social scientists seeking to understand the relationship between medicine, health and society. These ideas have increasingly been applied to HIV/AIDS, albeit with emphasis on the national and subnational levels.[41]

In relation to AIDS, there are three main shortfalls to the biomedical discourse. First, by focusing on the biology of the individual, it neglects potential explanations of disease and its treatment within wider social, economic and political contexts which create conditions of risk. Second, the discourse conceives the major response to health problems in terms of medical care, and thus fails to recognise the key importance of power in shaping policy responses to AIDS. Third, because medicine is seen as essentially 'good', the problem is perceived in terms of insufficient amounts of medical knowledge rather than any shortfalls in the knowledge itself.

A second, and increasingly powerful, AIDS discourse since the mid-1980s has been based on the principles of *neoliberal economics*. The ascendance of neoliberalism within the health sector has been part of the wider global shift in ideology, interests and institutions described above. Neoliberalism argues that the causes of ill-health are allocative and technical inefficiencies, and that health can be improved through, for example, reducing corruption and waste, supporting cost-effective interventions and increasing the operation of market forces in health-service delivery and financing.[42] Like the biomedical discourse, it implicitly assumes that ill-health is primarily a resource issue, in this case making better use of health resources. Applied to AIDS, this discourse has focused on the financial implications of the disease for national economies, with direct costs estimated at US$11 billion worldwide in 1993.[43] Costing studies have thus been carried out, for example, on the impact of AIDS on patterns of health care expenditure, and the cost-effectiveness of different control strategies.[44] Other studies have examined the effect of the disease on local labour markets, given that, in many countries, AIDS has affected people in their most economically productive years.[45]

The main shortfall of the neoliberal discourse has been the legitimation of economic above other criteria (e.g. moral, ethical, clinical) in the allocation of resources for AIDS. Within the context of seeking greater 'value-for money', an increasing number of national and international policy makers have placed financial considerations foremost in the selection of control and treatment strategies. The promotion of equity, human rights and gender issues have received lower priority. This is perhaps best illustrated by the World Bank's *World Development Report 1993: Investing in Health*, which puts forth the concept of the 'global burden of disease' measured by 'disability-adjusted life years' (DALY). A DALY is calculated by 'the present value of the future years of disability-free life that are lost as a result of the premature deaths or cases of disability occurring in a particular year' (p. x). Importantly, this formula is based on the normative assumption that individuals in economically productive age and socioeconomic groups are of higher value. AIDS is calculated to cause a heavy burden of disease and, hence, should be given high priority by policy makers, because it has 'powerful negative economic effects on households, productive enterprises, and countries' (p. 100).

Together, both the biomedical and neoliberal discourses have framed the AIDS debate in apolitical terms, legitimised by the claim that they are confined to non-normative issues. Little discussion has taken place within these discourses of the role of power, and particularly how AIDS can be located within changing structures of global political and economic power. Furthermore, the dominance of these discourses has not been limited to an intellectual exercise, but has directly shaped the global response to AIDS.

The global response to AIDS: policy making and the biomedical discourse

National and international policy makers were initially slow to respond to AIDS as a public health issue. In high-income countries this was largely the result of its characterisation by the medical community as being limited to, and controllable within, particular 'risk groups' (i.e. homosexuals, IVDUs, certain geographical regions). Between 1981–85, researchers focused on gathering clinical, albeit vital, information on the disease. This slow response by public health officials was exacerbated by distrust within affected communities. Within the Afro-American community, which has suffered disproportionately from HIV infection in the past decade, efforts by public health officials were looked upon with suspicion because of historical experiences of unethical medical research practices. Most notorious was the Tuskegee study on syphilis in which researchers left people untreated to allow for observation of longer-term effects.[46] In sub-Saharan Africa, apparent Western preoccupation with the alleged link between Africa and AIDS was seen by many as racist and delayed recognition and public acknowledgement of the importance of HIV infection in some regions.[47]

It was not until 1985 that the first International AIDS Conference was held, after which there occurred a mobilisation of expertise and other resources with unprecedented speed. Soon afterwards the international community began to discuss AIDS as a serious global issue and, in February 1987, the World Health Organisation's Global Programme on AIDS (GPA) was created as the main multilateral channel for Western aid.[48] This was followed by a high-level consultative meeting on AIDS and Development held in Talloires, France, whose attendance included the heads of WHO and the UN Children's Fund (Unicef), senior aid officials, and the Minister of Health for Uganda, a country where AIDS was already well established. In 1987 AIDS became the first disease to be discussed at the UN General Assembly, which prompted Resolution 42/8 to mobilise the entire UN system in a worldwide campaign to control the disease. A World Summit of Health Ministers on AIDS was held soon after in January 1988 and put forth the London Declaration on AIDS.

Financial resources for AIDS have reflected this rapid growth in international attention. In 1987 US$30 million was allocated by GPA; by 1990 this had grown to $109 million. Total external aid flows for AIDS and STD reached $185 million in 1990, more than 10 times that for tuberculosis and 20 times that for intentional injuries, conditions responsible for a similar 'burden of disease'.[49] By 1991 global spending on AIDS reached 10 per cent of total investments in health and population, with development agencies contributing some $250 million annually.[50] Notably, 95 per cent of annual global AIDS budgets has been spent within high-income countries.[51]

Bilaterally, the USA has spent the largest sums on AIDS. By the end of 1993, the US government had spent over $17 billion, with nearly $1 billion on basic scientific research by the Public Health Service in 1993 alone.[52] Abroad, the US Agency for International Development (USAID) has made the highest financial contributions to HIV prevention activities in low-income countries. Initially officers were advised to minimise their involvement in HIV/AIDS, given limited available resources and sensitivity over the distribution of condoms. It was only after recognition of the impact of AIDS on other development efforts (e.g. child survival) that the USA played a more active role in the creation of GPA, providing $88.5 million of funding from 1986–91. This was in addition to $79.5 million allocated by USAID for bilateral projects, and another $68 million worth of other USAID activities supporting HIV prevention.[53]

From a GPE perspective, this growth of international effort to control AIDS from the early to mid-1980s was firmly located within the biomedical discourse. Internationally, GPA was designated as the lead organisation to mobilise resources and promote the development of national AIDS control programmes. Nationally, governments worked closely with GPA to initiate and implement their own strategies. These strategies were centred on the screening of blood products, clinical care for those affected, education and information campaigns, social marketing of condoms, and peer education among commercial sex workers. The screening of blood products was particularly emphasised during the early years, despite being the least common route of infection.[54] As a technical intervention, it was seen as less controversial than, for instance, the promotion of condom use. Improving the safety of blood supplies also had other potential benefits, such as safety from other blood-borne infections. By no means insignificant were the concerns among travellers from high-income countries to the developing world.[55] Information and education campaigns warning of 'risk behaviours' have also been an important component of prevention strategies. In these campaigns, emphasis is placed on informed individuals taking responsibility for not engaging in such behaviours. AIDS was seen, in this context, as a disease of poor technical capacity, clinical practice or personal knowledge, and less a disease of broader structural features within and across countries.

As national AIDS control programmes became widely adopted by governments, and resources began to flow to support their implementation, many policy makers turned to the development of appropriate drugs to treat the disease—and a vaccine to prevent HIV infection—as key components of a global AIDS policy. With the prominent success of WHO's Intensified Smallpox Eradication Programme still in recent memory, and other campaigns such as the Polio Eradication Initiative underway, many believed that the AIDS pandemic could also be defeated if the right technologies were available. Thus the race to develop such technologies has led to a massive effort by researchers worldwide. In a survey of 'leading [vaccine] researchers, public health officials, and manufacturers' carried out by the magazine *Science* in 1994, a vaccine for HIV infection was ranked first as the 'most urgently needed vaccine' in both high and low-income countries.[56]

While biomedical research has, and will continue to contribute, vital knowledge in the treatment and control of AIDS, social scientists have played a prominent role in pointing to the need to take account of broader political, economic and social factors behind the AIDS pandemic. In the mid-1990s, there is much concern that biomedical interventions alone have failed to halt the alarming spread of the disease. Policy makers have responded by reassessing the global AIDS strategy. In January 1996 GPA was replaced by UNAIDS, a joint and cosponsored programme of the WHO, Unicef, UN Population Fund (UNFPA), UN Development Programme (UNDP), UN Educational, Scientific and Cultural Organisation (UNESCO) and the World Bank. Foremost among the new programme's goals is to develop a multisectoral and multidisciplinary approach to HIV/AIDS, drawing from a broader range of knowledge and expertise. How this will be achieved, amid uncertainty and rivalry among UN organisations, is unclear. Yet it reflects a recognition that the biomedical discourse alone cannot provide a complete global policy response to AIDS.

The global response to AIDS: policy making and the neoliberal discourse

As well as the biomedical discourse, the global response to AIDS has been strongly shaped by neoliberalism. As described above, neoliberal economic principles such as market-driven resource allocation, privatisation, deregulation and free trade have influenced national and international health sector reform since the 1980s. In relation to AIDS, it is argued that the neoliberal discourse has legitimised certain institutions, interests and ideas in the setting and evaluation of policies according to economic criteria. First, the rise of neoliberalism within the health sector during the 1980s was accompanied by the increased prominence of the World Bank in international health policy. Since 1980, when the Bank began to lend specifically for health projects, it has become the largest source of external health financing for low-income countries. This financial clout has been followed by a greater voice in policy development, with Bank publications having widespread influence on the international health policy agenda.[57]

World Bank lending for AIDS projects began in 1986, and by 1993 it had loaned a cumulative total of US$500 million.[58] One of the key activities supported by the Bank has been research on the economic effects of HIV and the cost-effectiveness of alternative interventions. Lending policies for AIDS programmes, in turn, have been based on the argument that prevention among 'high-risk groups' is one of the most cost-effective health interventions in the 'global burden of disease'.[59] For example, in India the Bank has worked with the government to study the cost of health care and the indirect national income loss from AIDS. As part of a US$84 million 'multi-pronged prevention strategy', the Bank has combined this research with biomedical interventions emphasising 'behavioural change and condom use, control [of] STDs, strengthen[ing] blood safety, rais[ing] surveillance and clinical management capacity, enhanc[ing] national and provincial capacity for managing HIV/AIDS control activities, and ensur[ing] humane treatment of people with AIDS or HIV infection'.[60] Similar studies have been carried out in the worst affected countries in sub-Saharan Africa, and in Thailand. Overall, the World Bank's lending policy on AIDS has been strongly informed by the neoliberal discourse. Neoliberal economic principles have been foremost in the allocation of resources for AIDS over other health needs, and for the selection of specific interventions. These criteria have been backed by large amounts of financing by the Bank.

Second, the neoliberal discourse has led to an increased emphasis on non-state health care financing and service delivery as viable alternatives to nonexistent or weakened government institutions. As part of a broad shift in the 'public—private mix' within the health sector of many countries, there has been a marked increase in the role of both 'for-profit' (e.g. transnational corporations) and 'not-for-profit' institutions (e.g. non-governmental organisations) in health since the mid-1970s. In low-income countries, this trend has been partly fuelled by an increase in health sector aid through NGOs. Between 1975–85, total official development assistance (ODA) grew by 115 per cent with the amount channelled through NGOs increasing by 1400 per cent. By 1990 NGOs accounted for 17 per cent of the US$4800 million disbursed as external assistance,[61] and about 13 per cent of health sector aid.[62] The rationale for this support includes the belief that NGOs can enhance political and economic pluralism (i.e. civil society), work more closely with local communities and marginalised groups, and fill gaps in service provision. NGOs are also seen to encourage greater cost-effectiveness by offering alternatives to inefficient public health care, and even creating a competitive market where greater choice and competition will improve services.[63] There is no doubt that NGOs are playing a vital and, in many cases, ground-breaking role in the field of AIDS. NGOs have, for example, been at the forefront in drawing attention to human rights issues. The effective implementation of community-based strategies will also depend in large part on NGOs. However, questions have also been raised about the lack of accountability of these organisations and their financial links with traditional donor agencies. There are also concerns of duplication or the establishment of parallel structures, some of which undermine the central role of government.[64]

Third, the neoliberal discourse has strongly defined the race for biomedical technologies to treat and prevent AIDS. The key players in this race have been large pharmaceutical and biotechnology companies, such as the US companies Repligen Corporation, Merck & Company and MicroGeneSys Incorporated, which have spent billions of dollars since the 1980s on research and development. While public subsidies helped to motivate companies into establishing research programmes,[65] the main spur has been the prospect of a profitable payoff should an effective treatment or vaccine be found. A similarly lucrative market for blood-testing equipment and storage has already emerged.

Leaving the development, and presumably the eventual allocation, of potential treatments and vaccines to the private sector raises several concerns, including the question of access. Private companies have clearly identified their key markets to be in high-income countries where individuals and governments can afford to pay the expected price. An estimate put forth in 1990 of the potential market for vaccines in the USA and Europe was 67 million people. It was calculated that, if 15–20 per cent of these people paid US$150, this would create a market of over US$1.6 billion.[66] From the companies' perspective, it would require such a large return to pay for the huge sums that pharmaceutical companies invest in the research and development of new products. As argued by the Vice President for Scientific Affairs of the International Federation of Pharmaceutical Manufacturers Associations (IFPMA), Margaret Cone, 'if companies are going to invest enormous sums to develop a vaccine, they have got to get a good return on their investment. And an AIDS vaccine is not going to be cheap. The manufacturing procedure is likely to be long, complicated and expensive'.[67] In low-income countries, however, where more than 80 per cent of people infected with HIV currently live, and where 90 per cent of new infections currently occur, this 'market price' lies beyond the reach of the vast majority of people. For example, Uganda is among the countries so far worst affected by HIV and AIDS. An estimated 1–1.5 million people are HIV-infected and GNP per capita is US$170.[68] For many Africans, a vaccine costing US$150 will clearly be economically inaccessible.

A related concern is the danger of overreliance on market-driven research should the perceived market prove unprofitable. Indeed, in the mid-1990s, some private companies have begun to reassess the investment potential of AIDS vaccine research in the light of new estimates of market potential in high-income countries. Recent evidence has shown that rates of HIV infection have stabilised in some high-income countries,[69] while they continue to rise in many low-income countries. In July 1994 the US biotechnology company Repligen Corporation announced the cancellation of its AIDS vaccine programme for financial reasons. Many are concerned that public health priorities, rather than profits, need to be behind decision making over research.

A further concern lies in the clinical appropriateness of the research being carried out in meeting the needs of countries worst affected by HIV and AIDS. In the report of a meeting on HIV vaccines held by the Rockefeller Foundation at Bellagio, Italy, in 1994, concerns were expressed that companies are 'catering to the needs of the developed world' by focusing on 'a small number of the potential vaccine approaches.'[70] This has included an emphasis on the HIV strain, the B subtype, which predominates in Europe and the USA but not in low-income countries. One notable example has been trials in China and Thailand beginning in June 1993 of a potential HIV-B vaccine. In China the trials have been carried out by the US company United Biomedical with the agreement of the Chinese government, while in Thailand it has been a joint project between the US and Thai armies. Grady writes that governments and private companies have been under pressure to 'do something ... do anything' in the development of an AIDS vaccine.[71] However, both projects have been criticised on the grounds that the HIV-B virus generally does not occur in Asia.

In summary, the global policy response to AIDS from the mid 1980s has been strongly informed by a neoliberal discourse. As well as conceptualising the problem of AIDS in economic terms, neoliberalism has privileged the needs of certain interest groups, including private companies, and has defined the criteria by which policy responses have been evaluated and implemented.

Towards an expanded understanding of AIDS: a global political economy research agenda

The purpose of this article has been to bring the study of the GPE and AIDS closer together and to show how each can be more fully understood through the other. We argue that, while social sciences have made vital contributions to the study of AIDS over the past decade, scholars of IR have largely neglected global health issues. This is beginning to be addressed,[72] but there are several avenues of research to be explored that would enrich our understanding of both the emerging GPE and the AIDS pandemic.[73]

First, there is a need to explore more fully the relationship between the emerging structure of global economic and political power, and the epidemiology of AIDS. As Porter writes, 'the profile of the epidemic is increasingly one of poorer people in developing countries ... [yet] resource allocations are declining in many quarters'.[74] The link between structures of national political economy and health has been increasingly explored, for example, in relation to the debt crisis, urban decay and perceptions of personal responsibility for health.[75] These analyses must now be extended to the global level by pulling together existing studies, as well as studying AIDS as a transnational and global phenomenon. What has been the relationship between the spread of AIDS and levels of foreign debt in low-income countries? Has there been a link between the employment practices of transnational corporations and the global pattern of AIDS? What impact has the movement of armed forces had on the spread of HIV infection? What aspects of globalisation must international organisations, like the World Health Organisation and the World Bank, recognise as contributing factors to the spread of AIDS? Are existing AIDS policies focused at the national level, sufficiently taking account of global factors? What can AIDS tell us about the winners and losers of globalisation? Have changes in international relations since the end of the Cold War, such as a potential growth in global civil society, and the rise of ethnic and territorial tensions, influenced policy making on AIDS? How has the transformation of production relations, including the reorganisation of labour and technological change, affected the health status of workers worldwide?

Second, more detailed and critical analysis of the epistemological and ontological lineage of policy responses to AIDS so far is clearly needed. This article has begun to show how the biomedical and neoliberal discourses have strongly informed the AIDS debate within key institutions since the early 1980s. Further study of the GPE of AIDS would show more precisely how these discourses have been located within, and disseminated by, the many other individuals and institutions that have become involved in AIDS research, treatment and control, education and policy making. This includes the impact of global telecommunications and the mass media on how we think about and respond to AIDS. Identifying emerging contradictions between such thought, and actions intended to prevent and control the disease, forms a key part of this critical analysis. Furthermore, there is a need to consider what other discourses, from the rich history of political and social thought, can be explored to broaden the AIDS debate methodologically, theoretically and conceptually. Accompanying the existing orthodoxy has been limited recognition of the structural and historical roots of the pandemic, and hence the more fundamental social and political changes needed to address it effectively. AIDS, in short, teaches us about the current limitations in thinking about health, development and international relations.

Third, there is an urgent need to apply an expanded understanding of the GPE to develop ethical and practical approaches to AIDS. National and international policy makers are presently seeking to widen the AIDS agenda in recognition that biomedical and economistic responses alone are insufficient. As Mann and Tarantola write, 'it is now clear that HIV/AIDS is as much about society as it is about a virus. This new understanding of the societal basis for vulnerability to HIV/AIDS has the potential to provide a strategic coherence to efforts in HIV/AIDS prevention and control'.[76] Public health experts are looking to social scientists to contribute to a new policy agenda,[77] with hopes that there will be a move in focus 'away from science to issues of sociology and sexual behaviour, organization and management of programs, NGOs, and Government relations and the epidemic's economics'.[78] A key part of this new agenda must be the impact of globalisation on health. It is on this subject that scholars of the global political economy can offer much. As part of our efforts to redefine the concept of security in a post-Cold War world, issues concerning global human security (e.g. health, environment, migration) need to be given far greater and urgent attention.

Notes

An earlier version of this paper was presented to the Health and International Relations Panel, British International Studies Association Annual Conference, University of York, December 1994. The International Health Policy Programme is funded in part by the UK Economic and Social Research Council, and Social Sciences and Humanities Research Council of Canada. The Health Economics and Financing Programme is funded by the UK Overseas Development Administration. The views presented here are those of the authors only. Thanks are offered to Charlotte Watts who provided useful comments on the penultimate draft of this paper.

1. The other notable global effort to control or eradicate a specific disease is the World Health Organisation's Intensified Smallpox Eradication Programme (1967–80). The total cost of this programme was US$81 million. In comparison, the budget for WHO's Global Programme on AIDS was about US$100 million in 1989 alone.
2. This article uses the term '*global*' rather than '*international*' political economy because, as Gill & Law argue, 'political economy analysis should not be narrowly limited to relations between nation-states and their governments. It needs to be global as well as international in character'. Stephen Gill & David Law, *The Global Political Economy: Perspectives, Problems and Policies* (Harvester Wheatsheaf, 1988), p. xxii.

3. *Ibid.*, p. xviii. Emphasis in original.
4. A. Fortin, 'AIDS, development, and the limitations of the African state', in: B. Misztal & D. Moss (Eds), *Action on AIDS: National Policies in Comparative Perspective* (Greenwood Press, 1990), p. 217.
5. S. Hawkes & Keith McAdam, 'AIDS in the Developing World', *Medicine International*, Vol. 21, No. 2 (1993), pp. 69–72.
6. N. Ford & S. Koetsawang, 'The Socio-Cultural Context of the Transmission of HIV in Thailand', *Social Science and Medicine*, Vol. 33, No. 4 (1991), pp. 405–14; and 'AIDS: The Third Wave', *Lancet*, Vol. 343 (1994), pp. 186–88.
7. Michael Merson, 'Slowing the Spread of HIV: Agenda for the 1990s', *Science*, Vol. 260 (1993), pp. 1266–68.
8. Stabilisation is defined as the number of deaths from AIDS over the past year being roughly equal to the number of new cases of HIV infection. However, it is important to note that this measure may hide disproportionate increases in certain groups within a national population. World Health Organisation, *The HIV/AIDS Pandemic: 1994 Overview* (Global Programme on AIDS, 1994), p. 4.
9. John Caldwell, 'Understanding the AIDS Epidemic and Reacting Sensibly to it', *Social Science and Medicine*, Vol. 41, No. 3 (1995), p. 301.
10. Figures of amounts spent by pharmaceutical companies are not readily available. Jonathan Mann, Daniel Tarantola & T. Netter (Eds), *AIDS in the World: A Global Report* (Harvard University Press, 1992), p. 263.
11. Caroline Thomas, 'On the Health of International Relations and the International Relations of Health', *Review of International Studies*, Vol. 15, No. 3 (1989), p. 273.
12. Craig Murphy & Roger Tooze, *The New International Political Economy* (Lynne Rienner, 1991).
13. Stephen Gill, *Gramsci, Historical Materialism and International Relations* (Cambridge University Press, 1993), p. 45.
14. Lesley Doyal, *The Political Economy of Health* (Pluto Press, 1979); and Vincent Navarro, *Imperialism, Health and Medicine* (Baywood, 1981).
15. Gill, *Gramsci*, p. 45.
16. Kelley Lee, 'A neo-Gramscian approach to international organization: an expanded analysis of current reform to UN development activities', in: John MacMillan & Andrew Linklater (Eds), *Boundaries in Question: New Directions in International Relations* (Pinter, 1995), pp. 144–62.
17. It is recognised that the concept of globalisation has been applied with 'casual abandon' by scholars and policy makers. It is defined here as a process of intensified social, political and economic relations on a global scale. For a fuller conceptual discussion, see R.J. Barry Jones, *Globalisation and Interdependence in the International Political Economy: Rhetoric and Reality* (Pinter, 1995).
18. Stephen Gill, 'Globalisation, Market Civilisation, and Disciplinary Neoliberalism', *Millennium*, Vol. 24, No. 3 (1995), pp. 399–423.
19. Robert W. Cox, *Production, Power, and World Order: Social Forces in the Making of History* (Columbia University Press, 1987), p. 359.
20. Mary Bassett & M. Mhloyi, 'Women and AIDS in Zimbabwe: The Making of an Epidemic', *International Journal of Health Services*, Vol. 21 (1991), pp. 143–56.
21. The Civil—Military Alliance to Combat HIV and AIDS was established in November 1994 in recognition that the military tends to have sexually transmitted disease rates of two to three times that of civilian age group counterparts. This rate multiplies even further in wartime. Sven Groennings, 'Civil—Military Alliance to Combat HIV and AIDS', *AIDS in Asia*, No. 4 (1995), p. 8.
22. J. Decosas, F. Kane, J. Anarfi, K. Sodji & H. Wagner, 'Migration and AIDS', *Lancet*, Vol. 346 (1995), p. 826; and F. Kane, M. Alary & I. N'Doye, 'Temporary Expatriation is Related to HIV-1 Infection in Rural Senegal', *AIDS*, Vol. 7 (1993), pp. 1261–65.
23. R. Wallace & D. Wallace, 'US Apartheid and the Spread of AIDS to the Suburbs: A Multi-City Analysis of the Political Economy of Spatial Epidemic Threshold', *Social Science and Medicine*, Vol. 41, No. 3 (1995), pp. 333–45.
24. Sheena Asthana, 'Economic crisis, adjustment and the impact on health', in: D. Phillips & Y. Verhasselt (Eds), *Health and Development* (Routledge, 1994), p. 51.
25. Asthana, 'Economic crisis,' p. 59; and Frances Stewart, 'Can adjustment programmes incorporate the interests of women?', in: H. Afshar & C. Dennis (Eds), *Women and Adjustment Policies in the Third World* (Macmillan, 1992).
26. Lucy Gilson, Steven Russell & Kent Buse, 'The Political Economy of User Fees with Targeting: Developing Equitable Health Financing Policy', *Journal of International Development*, Vol. 7, No. 3 (1995), pp. 369–401.

27. Anthony Ugalde & Jeffrey Jackson, 'The World Bank and International Health Policy: A Critical Review', *Journal of International Development*, Vol. 7, No. 3 (1995), pp. 525–42.
28. Panos Institute, *AIDS and the Third World* (Panos Institute/Norwegian Red Cross, 1988), p. 88.
29. Decosas *et al.*, 'Migration and AIDS', p. 827.
30. Shiv Lal, 'The HIV/AIDS Situation in India', *AIDS in Asia*, No. 4 (1995), p. 6.
31. F. Moses, F. Manji & J. Bradley, 'Impact of User Fees on Attendance at a Referral Center for Sexually Transmitted Diseases in Kenya', *Lancet*, Vol. 340 (1992), pp. 463–66.
32. See, for example, Renee Danziger, 'HIV/AIDS in the former Soviet Union', unpublished paper, London School of Hygiene and Tropical Medicine, February 1996; and M. Field, 'The Health Crisis in the Former Soviet Union: A Report from the "Post War" Zone', *Social Science and Medicine*, Vol. 41, No. 11 (1994), pp. 1469–78.
33. B. Einhorn, *Cinderella Goes to Market: Citizenship, Gender and Women's Movements in East Central Europe* (Verso, 1993), p. 136.
34. N. Timmons, 'Inequality is worst for 50 years', *The Independent*, 10 February 1995; and Will Hutton, *The State We're In* (Jonathan Cape, 1995).
35. Singer found that almost half of people in the USA who have been diagnosed with AIDS are African-Americans and Latinos from impoverished urban neighbourhoods, M. Singer, 'AIDS and the Health Crisis of the US Urban Poor: The Perspective of Critical Medical Sociology', *Social Science and Medicine*, Vol. 39, No. 7 (1994), pp. 931–48.
36. World Bank, *World Development Report: Investing in Health* (IBRD, 1993), p. 99.
37. For a discussion of how the biomedical and economistic discourses have shaped policy making at the national level, see G. Seidel, 'The Competing Discourses of HIV/AIDS in Sub-Saharan Africa: Discourses of Rights and Empowerment vs Discourses of Control and Exclusion', *Social Science and Medicine*, Vol. 36 (1993), pp. 175–94.
38. Doyal, *The Political Economy of Health*, p. 255. See also Ivan Illich, *Limits to Medicine* (Penguin, 1976) and G. Moon & R. Gillespie (Eds), *Society and Health: An Introduction to Social Science for Health Professionals* (Routledge, 1995).
39. Lesley Doyal, Jennie Naidoo & T. Wilton (Eds), *AIDS: Setting a Feminist Agenda* (Taylor & Francis, 1994).
40. Navarro, *Imperialism, Health and Medicine*; David Sanders, *The Struggle for Health: Medicine and the Politics of Under-development* (Macmillan, 1985); and Meredith Turshen, *The Politics of Public Health* (Zed Books, 1989).
41. David Sanders & A. Sambo, 'AIDS in Africa: The Implications of Economic Recession and Structural Adjustment', *Health Policy and Planning*, Vol. 6, No. 2 (1991), pp. 157–65; Anthony Zwi and A. Cabral, 'Identifying "High Risk Situations" for Preventing AIDS', *British Medical Journal*, Vol. 303 (1991), pp. 1527–29; John Caldwell, 'African Families and AIDS: Context, Reactions and Potential Interventions', *Health Transition Review*, Vol. 3 (1993), pp. 1–16; and C. Evian, 'AIDS and the Socio-economic Determinants of the Epidemic in Southern Africa—A Cycle of Poverty', *Journal of Tropical Pediatrics*, Vol. 40 (1994), pp. 61–2.
42. The seminal publication is the World Bank, *Financing Health Services in Developing Countries: An Agenda for Reform* (IBRD, 1987).
43. Jonathan Mann & Daniel Tarantola, 'Preventive Medicine: A Broader Approach to the AIDS Crisis', *Harvard International Review*, Vol. 17, No. 4 (1995), pp. 46–9, 87.
44. Margaret Ainsworth & Mead Over, *The Economic Impact of AIDS: Shocks, Responses, and Outcomes*, World Bank Technical Working Paper 1, Africa Technical Department, Washington DC, 1992; J. Cuddington, 'Modeling the Macroeconomic Effects of AIDS, with an Application to Tanzania', *World Bank Economic Review* (1993), pp. 173–89; and Susan Foster & Anne Buve, 'Benefits of HIV Screening of Blood Transfusions in Zambia', *Lancet*, Vol. 346 (1995), pp. 225–27.
45. World Bank, *World Development Report: Investing in Health*, p. 100.
46. S. Thomas & S. Quinn, 'The Tuskegee Syphilis Study, 1932–1972: Implications for HIV Education and AIDS Risk Education Programs in the Black Community', *American Journal of Public Health*, Vol. 81 (1991), pp. 1498–1504.
47. Richard Chirimuuta & Rosalind Chirimuuta, *AIDS, Africa and Racism* (Free Association, 1989).
48. Jonathan Mann, 'The Global Picture of AIDS', address to the Fourth International Conference on AIDS, Stockholm, 12 June 1988, pp. 4–5.
49. C. Michaud & C. Murray, 'External Assistance to the Health Sector in Developing Countries: A Detailed Analysis 1972–90', *Bulletin of the World Health Organization*, Vol. 72 (1994), pp. 639–51.

50. J. Decosas & J. Finlay, 'International AIDS Aid: The Response of Development Aid Agencies to the HIV/AIDS Pandemic', *AIDS*, Vol. 7, No. 1 (1993), pp. 282–83.
51. 'AIDS: The Third Wave', *Lancet*, Vol. 343 (1994), pp. 186–88.
52. US Agency for International Development, 'Building partnerships to stop AIDS', mimeo, Washington DC, n.d.
53. US General Accounting Office, *Foreign Assistance: Combating HIV/AIDS in Developing Countries* (National Security and International Affairs Division, 1992).
54. Deutsche Gessellschaft für Technische Zusammenarbeit, *Responding to AIDS in the Developing World: The GTZ Contribution* (Health, Population and Nutrition Division, 1995).
55. S. Buchanan, 'Lack of AIDS blood screening in some nations raises concerns', *International Herald Tribune*, 29 September 1987; and M. Potts & W. Carswell, 'AIDS: Losing the Battle and the War?', *Lancet*, Vol. 341 (1993), pp. 1442–43.
56. 'Bumps on the Vaccine Road', *Science*, Vol. 265 (1994), pp. 1371–73.
57. Kent Buse, 'Spotlight on International Organisations: The World Bank', *Health Policy and Planning* Vol. 9 (1994), pp. 95–9.
58. World Bank, *World Bank HIV/AIDS Activities* (Population, Health and Nutrition Department, 1994), p. 2.
59. World Bank, *Investing in Health*, Table 4.7.
60. World Bank, *World Bank HIV/AIDS Activities*, p. 5.
61. Michaud & Murray, 'External Assistance to the Health Sector'.
62. Julian Lob-Levyt, 'Compassion, Economics, Politics ... What are the Motives behind Health-sector Aid?', *Health Policy and Planning*, Vol. 5. No. 1 (1990), pp. 82–7.
63. S. Crane & J. Carswell, 'A Review and Assessment of Non-governmental Organization-based STD/AIDS Education and Prevention Projects for Marginalized Groups', *Health Education Research*, Vol. 7 (1992), pp. 175–94; and Michael Bratton, 'The Politics of Government—NGO Relations in Africa', *World Development*, Vol. 17, No. 4 (1989), pp. 569–87.
64. Andrew Green & Ann Matthias, 'NGOs—A Policy Panacea for the Next Millennium?', *Journal of International Development*, Vol. 7, No. 3 (1995), pp. 565–73; and P. Godwin, 'Strengthening the Role of NGOs in Responding to the HIV Epidemic in Asia and the Pacific: A UNDP Initiative', *AIDS in Asia Newsletter*, Vol. 4 (1995), pp. 1, 3.
65. For example, the US government spent US$111 million out of US$160 million spent worldwide on HIV/AIDS vaccine research and development. See Jon Cohen, 'AIDS Vaccines: Are Researchers Racing Toward Success, or Crawling?', *Science*, Vol. 265 (1994), pp. 1373–5.
66. *Ibid.*, p. 1373.
67. As quoted in World Health Organisation, 'AIDS: A Challenge to Science and Industry', *World AIDS Day Features*, No. 4 (1992).
68. World Bank, *Investing in Health*, p. 99.
69. Michael McCarthy, 'New US Head of HIV/AIDS Policy Appointed', *Lancet*, Vol. 346 (1995), p. 692.
70. Rockefeller Foundation, *Accelerating the Development of Preventive HIV Vaccines for the World* (Rockefeller Foundation, 1994).
71. Christine Grady, *The Search for an AIDS Vaccine: Ethical Issues in the Development and Testing of a Preventive HIV Vaccine* (Indiana University Press, 1995).
72. Leon Gordenker, Roger Coate, Christer Jonsson & Peter Soderholm, *International Cooperation in Response to AIDS* (Pinter, 1995).
73. This proposed research agenda is partly based on the new historical materialist research agenda for the study of global politics put forth in Gill, *Gramsci*, pp. 16–7.
74. Michael Porter, 'From Yokohama to Vancouver—Towards the 11th International AIDS Conference', *AIDS in Asia*, No. 4 (1995), p. 5.
75. For example, S. Ogoh Alubo, 'Debt Crisis, Health and Health Services in Africa', *Social Science and Medicine*, Vol. 31, No. 6 (1990), pp. 639–48; and J. Donahue & M. McGuire, 'The Political Economy of Responsibility in Health and Illness', *Social Science and Medicine*, Vol. 40, No. 1 (1995), pp. 47–53.
76. Mann & Tarantola, 'Preventive Medicine', p. 46.
77. B. Walker, 'A New Agenda for AIDS Research', *British Medical Journal*, Vol. 311 (1995), pp. 1448–9.
78. Porter, 'From Yokohama', p. 5.

Part III
Bioterrorism

[5]

Rights and Dangers: Bioterrorism and the Ideologies of Public Health

Ronald Bayer and James Colgrove

The history of American public health is punctuated by controversies over the extent to which the state may legitimately impose restrictions on liberty in the name of the common good, and over the extent to which protection of the public's welfare has served as a pretext for erosion of fundamental rights. Such conflicts were animated by deep-rooted mistrust of overreaching, by concerns about arbitrary exercises of power, and by the antiauthoritarian ethos that is such a prominent feature of American politics and civic culture. Periods of divisive controversy alternated with times of consensus during which dissident ideologies and underlying tensions largely disappeared from view. Extraordinary events, however, forced into the open assumptions underlying the dominant views of public health and revealed the existence of unresolved tensions, kindling anew debates over matters long thought to be settled. The shattering of the illusion of American continental impregnability by the events of September 11, 2001, and by the subsequent anthrax scare provided the occasion for a debate over the ideologies of public health. A controversy was sparked by proposals to enact a model emergency health powers act that would radically enhance the power of the state to respond to threats to the public health.

Looking Backward

In the nineteenth and early twentieth centuries public health officials who sought to institute mandatory vaccination programs, quarantines, and surveillance repeatedly faced resistance. Control of smallpox through government authority to compel vaccination and isolation of the infected served as a rallying point for groups and individuals motivated not only by antigovernment ideology but by concrete fears of physical harms that sometimes resulted from the procedure. Many state laws during this period were repealed or modified in response to pressure from opponents, especially in the second half of the nineteenth century when antivaccination societies gained strength (Kaufman 1967). In Milwaukee, for example, forceful application of the state's mandatory vaccination law sparked riots among the city's large German immigrant population in the 1890s (Leavitt 1982). Health officers who went into neighborhoods seeking to vaccinate residents and remove sick individuals to quarantine hospitals were greeted by angry mobs throwing rocks. In Massachusetts, a smallpox epidemic in 1901–1902 was the occasion for a court challenge to the state's compulsory vaccination law that ultimately led to a landmark Supreme Court ruling establishing the right of the government to use its "police powers" to control epidemic disease (Albert, Ostheimer, and Breman 2001). In its seven to two decision the Court affirmed the right of the people, through their elected representatives, to enact "health laws of every description to protect the common good" (Jacobson v. Commonwealth of Massachusetts 1905).

The history of efforts to impose quarantines on those viewed as threats to public health involved the exercise of authority that from the perspective of less threatening moments looks excessive and profoundly unfair (Fox 1988). On occasion the association of diseases with disfavored minority groups led to harsh measures supported by large segments of the population. In New York City, for example, arriving immigrants in 1892 could be isolated under squalid conditions to prevent the spread of cholera and typhus. At a moment of massive immigration and concomitant nativist sentiment, health officials encountered little popular opposition to their efforts (Markel 1997).

Finally, popular as well as professional opposition characterized early efforts to initiate case reporting by name to public health registries for purposes of disease control. Physicians opposed such requirements as an intrusion on their autonomy and as a violation of the confidentiality of the doctor-patient relationship (Fox 1988). Reflecting on controversies that greeted his efforts to mandate the reporting of tuberculosis cases as he moved forward to begin surveillance of sexually transmitted diseases, Herman Biggs, Commissioner of Health in New York, remarked early in the twentieth century, "The ten year long opposition to the reporting of tuberculosis will doubtless appear a mild breeze compared with the stormy protest against the sanitary surveillance of the venereal diseases" (Winslow 1929). Despite the existence of such opposition, reporting of cases by name to local and state health departments and to special confidential registries ultimately became part of the tradition and practice of public health (Thacker and Berkleman 1988). The same was true for mandatory vaccination.

The courts almost always deferred to public health authorities who deprived individuals of their liberty in the name of public health. Thus one state high court declared at the beginning of the twentieth century, "It is unquestionable that the legislature can confer police powers upon public officers for the protection of the public health. The maxim *Salus populi supreme lex* is the law of all courts in all countries. The individual right sinks in the necessity to provide for the public good" (Parmet 1985, 61). Perhaps most remarkable, such a plenary grant of authority could still be found to be constitutional in the seventh decade of the twentieth century. In upholding the detention of a person with tuberculosis pursuant to statute that provided virtually no procedural protections, a California appellate court in 1966 declared, "Health regulations enacted by the state under its police power and providing even drastic measures for the elimination of disease . . . in a general way are not affected by constitutional provisions, either of the state or national government" (In re Halko 1966).

The breadth of public health powers that were virtually unchallenged through most of the twentieth century increasingly became subject to scrutiny in the century's last decades. And when that occurred, the roles of mandatory screening and examination, reporting names those who were sick or infected to public health registries, and imposition of quarantine once again became the subject of dispute. Development of a robust jurisprudence of privacy (Karst 1980), and the "due process revolution" that extended rights to prisoners, mental patients, and others under the authority of the state (Tribe 1978) ultimately brought into question assumptions that protected public health from searching constitutional scrutiny. But whereas the groundwork was prepared in the transformations of American politics, law, and culture in the 1960s and 1970s, it was the AIDS epidemic that forced a fundamental rethinking of the dominant ideology of public health.

The controversies that raged during the 1980s, when the HIV epidemic emerged in the United States, reveal the profound effects that political and historical context have had on the enforcement of health. In the epidemic's early years a broad coalition of gay rights activists and civil libertarians were largely successful in their efforts to place the protection of privacy and individual rights at the forefront of the public health agenda (Bayer 1988). Fierce battles occurred when proposals were made to mandate reporting of people with HIV infection, and it was not until many years later that such reporting became possible. Intense controversy also surrounded efforts to preserve the right of individuals to determine whether they would be tested for the infection. Policies were adopted requiring exacting and specific informed consent for testing, and only in the 1990s did significant public support emerge for relaxing these standards. Finally, every attempt to use the power of quarantine to control those whose behavior placed their sexual partners at risk provoked extensive debate about the counterproductive impact of recourse to coercion.

Paralleling the development of a rights-based perspective on public health, and drawing on some of the same broad cultural changes, was the emergence of visible antivaccination movement in United States. During the late 1970s and 1980s heterogeneous collections of groups and individuals representing various goals, ideologies, and strategies came together to question the safety and efficacy of vaccines and the ethics of compulsory policies. A common thread of the movement is the argument that public health officials have willfully denied the dangers of immunization, which render any attempt to compel the procedure ethically unjustifiable (Freed, Katz, and Clark 1996). An antistatist, antiauthoritarian outlook characterizes many of the groups in the movement. The libertarian Association of American Physicians and Surgeons (2002) thus declared in a position paper, "It's obscene to threaten to seize a child just because his parents refuse medical treatment that is obviously unnecessary and perhaps even dangerous. [We believe] that parents with the advice of their doctors should make decisions about their children's medical care—not government bureaucrats."

Bioterrorism

In the late 1990s the threat of bioterrorism surfaced as a concern of a few public health officials and experts. Alarmed by reports that Iraq had invested in a bioweapons program, the lethal gas attack by a Japanese cult, and information regarding activities of the former Soviet Union, advocates sought to jar America into coming to grips with the danger of and its utter lack of preparedness for a potential attack. That the efforts were spearheaded by D.A. Henderson, who had gained worldwide recognition for his work in the global smallpox-eradication campaign, lent credibility to these efforts (Bor 1999). For him, the prospect of the use of biological weapons was "more likely than ever before" (Henderson 2001, 1918). In early 1999 President Clinton announced that he was allocating $158 million to the Department of Health and Human Services for research into and preparation for bioterrorism. Additional sums would be requested for the next year (Garrett 1999).

The mounting concern had its antagonists, especially among those identified with the public health left. Victor Sidel and his colleagues thus wrote in the *American Journal of Public Health*, "Should we be guided by a perspective that focuses on a hypothetical bioterrorism as a main concern while relegating to the background the monumental issues of infectious disease, food borne illness, and chemical accidents, not to mention the daily problems that are inadequately attended? The road to bioterrorism preparedness may be paved with good intentions [but] traveling down that road may be a disastrous course for public health" (Sidel, Cohen, and Gould 2001, 717). But such opposition could not stem the growing sense of concern.

On April 26–27, 2001, a meeting to address the public health threat posed by bioterrorism was convened by the Centers for Disease Control and Prevention (CDC), the American Bar Association's Standing Committee on Law and National Security, and the National Strategy Forum. Held outside Chicago, the Cantigny Conference brought together federal, state, and local public health and law enforcement officials, representatives of the Departments of Defense and Justice, as well as university-based researchers. The goal of the meeting, which strikingly did not include representatives of civil rights and liberties organizations, was to consider the extent to which states had the legal capacity to invoke emergency powers in the face of an act of bioterrorism, and whether current public health law would be adequate to the challenge posed by such an event. A premise of the meeting was that law was a central component of the public health infrastructure, that there could be no preparedness that did not include the statutory authority that would govern efforts of officials faced with a terrorist-created emergency.

From the outset officials at the CDC underscored the necessity of a legal framework that would govern access to medical and other records, permit the control over private property, allow procurement and rationing of medicines and vaccines, and provide for control over individuals who were thought to pose a risk. Such control would include the possibility of mandatory examinations and implementation of quarantines when deemed necessary to prevent spread of disease. Whereas conference participants appeared to acknowledge that in the face of a bioterrorist attack public health authorities would be able to count on voluntary cooperation of the population, they noted that "statutory mechanisms needed to be in place for dealing with uncooperative people." Although public health officials had experience in the exercise of compulsory powers, the extent to which coercion might be called upon in a bioterrorist event would be much greater.

It was the specific dimensions posed by the threat of bioterrorism that suggested the need to confront the adequacy of public health laws, many of which were enacted in the early twentieth century and had not been updated in decades. Conference participants expressed concern about ways in which some recent modifications in the law were designed to impose due process limits on the exercise of public health powers, and that some privacy protections might serve as impediments to action in the face of an emergency. Thomas Gillespie of the Johns Hopkins Center for Civilian Biodefense Studies, directed by D.A. Henderson, thus noted that it might be necessary to change the health care system, "which currently treats the individual patient with the highest regard and is less concerned with the public good." Most important, given the leadership role he ultimately assumed in drafting the model public health act, Larry Gostin noted that the rights-centered transformation of recent decades had created a situation in which "laws that protect individual rights appear to have superseded those preserving the common good." It was, of course, no small irony that Gostin, director of the Georgetown–Johns Hopkins Center for Law and the Public's Health, had himself been a forceful advocate for civil liberties during the 1980s and 1990s and as such had been instrumental in the very transformation he now viewed with some concern.

Emerging from the Cantigny Conference was a consensus on the powers that would be required by public health officials faced with a bioterrorist event. They mirrored the conventional strategies of infectious disease control that emerged at the end of the nineteenth century and in the first decades of the twentieth century: reporting of cases by medical personnel; mandatory medical examinations; contact investigation; and imposition of isolation and quarantine. In addition, the importance of having authority to seize, confiscate, and make use of private property, including hospitals, was noted.

The Cantigny Conference participants were committed to drafting a model act that would help states clarify and strengthen their existing public health laws. But the time frame for such an undertaking remained unspecified. In part, this was so because an ambitious effort, funded by the Robert Wood Johnson Foundation, to redraft public health laws was already very far along. It took the assaults of September 11 to create the context within which a sense of urgency would take hold.

Ideology, Politics, and the Model State Emergency Health Powers Act

Soon after the events of September 11, Gene Matthews, legal advisor to the CDC, called on Larry Gostin quickly to prepare a model public health emergency act. "It wasn't," said Matthews, "in anyone's interest to have 50 states running off in different directions on this" (Matthews 2002). On October 30, a model act that had been speedily drafted was released to the public. In every way the proposed statute bore the marks of an initiative with powerful and broad-based official backing. A press release by Secretary of Health and Human Services Tommy Thompson noted that the Act was the outgrowth of a "CDC-led process" (U.S. Department of Health and Human Services 2001). The CDC's director Jeffrey Koplan commented that adoption of the emergency act would facilitate his agency's efforts. "Many of the current laws don't make sense anymore . . . This will update the public health laws to fit the world we live in" (McKenna 2001). An official at the National Governors' Association said that the Act "goes a long way to helping governors improve their public health infrastructure to respond to today's health emergencies" (Center for Law and the Public's Health 2001b). It is thus not surprising that press reports saw in the proposed act a government initiative.

The *Atlanta Constitution* headlined "CDC Pushes Bill Boosting State's Powers" (McKenna 2001). For Gostin and his colleagues the draft, while open to refinement, was "polished and strong" (Darraj 2001), nearly ready for consideration by state legislatures (Center for Law and the Public's Health 2001b).

Those who drafted the Act were haunted by the specter of a catastrophic threat to the public health, and although the impetus for the proposed legislation was the prospect of bioterrorism, concern extended much more broadly (Center for Law and the Public's Health 2001a). Indeed the Act referred to dangers associated with "emergent and resurgent infectious diseases" as well as "epidemics and pandemic threats." In the face of challenges that posed a "substantial risk of a significant number of human fatalities or incidents of permanent or long term disability," the governor was to be given authority to declare a public health emergency. If the situation warranted, and when prompt action was necessary, such a declaration could be issued without consultation with public health officials. It would also allow the governor to mobilize the state's militia and initiate a range of extraordinary measures that would last for thirty days, at which point it could be renewed. The legislature could intervene to override the executive decision only after sixty days and only by a two-thirds vote of both chambers.

Although its preamble noted the importance of balancing the "common good with individual liberties" and asserted that it was designed to grant authority to prevent and manage emergency health threats without unduly interfering with civil rights and liberties, the Act allowed for coercive interventions bearing on privacy, bodily integrity, and liberty backed by the threat of criminal sanction. Health care providers and medical examiners would be required to report to public health authorities within twenty-four hours the name, date of birth, gender, race, and current address of individuals with conditions that could be related to bioterrorism or other highly fatal or dangerous infectious agents. In a marked departure from convention, pharmacists were to be included among those required to report unusual increases in prescriptions for conditions that could be linked to public health emergencies. Based on such reports, public health officials were to engage in the time-tested process of contact investigation designed to trace the origin and track the potential spread of disease.

Far more striking were the powers enumerated under Article 13 dealing with "control of persons" and the extent to which those powers were to be enforced through the threat of criminal sanction and potential deprivation of liberty. The public health authority was granted the right to "compel" individuals to undergo medical examination and medical testing, and those who refused would be liable for misdemeanors. When authorities were uncertain if individuals who refused to undergo examination or testing had been exposed to an infectious agent or otherwise posed a threat to public health, they could impose isolation or quarantine. When it was determined that public health required either treatment of those who were sick or vaccination of those who were at risk for infection, such interventions could be mandated under threat of a misdemeanor charge. Furthermore, "if by reason of refusal of vaccination or treatment" the individual was thought to pose a danger to public health, he or she might be subject isolation or quarantine. Health care providers who refused to be party to such interventions would be subject to criminal prosecution.

Recognizing that much had occurred since quarantine laws of an earlier era were enacted, the model legislation sought to balance due process considerations with exigencies imposed by public health emergencies. In general, quarantines and isolation were to be imposed only after courts had issued a written *ex parte* order, based on a showing that probable cause existed that such measures were necessitated by a threat to public health. When urgency dictated immediate action, however, deprivation of liberty could occur without a court order being obtained first. Those quarantined or isolated could request a court hearing and representation by counsel. Such hearings were to be held within seventy-two hours of the request. The court's determination regarding both initial and continued isolation or quarantine was to be based on presentation of clear and convincing evidence.

In all, the Act was a stark expression of the view that grave threats to public health might necessitate abrogation of privacy rights, imposition of medical interventions, and deprivation of freedom itself.

Release of the Act was the occasion of considerable media attention, much of which was subtly supportive of the drafters' analyses of public health infrastructural inadequacies and limits of the prevailing legal regime (Copeland 2001). An editorial in the *New Republic*, for example, concluded, "Here's hoping we won't have to experience a real outbreak before we realize that when it comes to public health, temporarily sacrificing liberty may be the price of staying alive" (Brownlee 2001).

That was the perspective shared by sympathetic public health officials and by legislators who moved swiftly in a number of states to introduce legislation that largely mirrored the model act. "In tough times you have to make tough decisions," said an assistant commissioner of public health in Massachusetts (Lasalandra 2001). In Minnesota, Thomas Huntley, a Democratic Farm Labor Party representative, announced plans to introduce his public health emergency legislation in January 2002. Noting the existence of quarantine laws the state had relied on in the 1950s, he declared that in the earlier period "the minuscule trade-off in individual liberties was clearly understood in light of the consequences of letting these diseases run rampant. We must be prepared and empowered to take the same course of action if necessary to prevent similar epidemics, particularly since bioterrorists have engaged our country in this kind of warfare" (deFiebre 2001). In California, Republican Assemblyman Keith Richman acknowledged that his proposed legislation, which was virtually identical to the model act, would raise questions about civil liberties. But given the risks of smallpox, from which one-third of the infected could die, "we should have a public health law in place that could minimize the situation as much as possible" (Tansey 2001). Finally, in New York, Democratic Assemblyman Robin Schimminger also asserted that civil liberties concerns paled by comparison to what would be necessary in "extraordinary circumstances." "We're dealing with a bona fide public health emergency declared by the governor and confirmed by the legislature in which the hazard to the public is contagious and insidious" (Ernst 2001).

In striking contrast to those who endorsed the model act's provisions, many policy makers and health advocates viewed the proposal as a grave threat rather than as a necessary tool in the struggle against bioterrorism. These critics came from the left as well as the right, and shared deep suspicion of the state's authority, even when exercised in the name of public health. Where architects of the Act and their allies believed it was possible to delegate extensive authority to officials faced with emergencies, opponents saw only prospects of the abuse of power. Whereas the nightmare that informed the world view of the Act's advocates involved tens of thousands of imperiled individuals, the true threat, according to opponents, was arrogation of unlimited executive authority to confront dangers that could instead be managed by measures that were respectful of privacy and individual rights.

Among the broadest challenges was an open letter to the Secretary of Health and Human Services by the New England Coalition for Law and Public Health, an ad hoc group of law professors and others concerned with public health policy led by Boston University's George Annas. The coalition asserted that it was not necessary to enhance public health emergency powers. Indeed, what modification was required would entail imposition of constitutional limits on older public health statutes. Whereas the Act forcefully asserted the need to engage coercive authority of the state during emergencies, the coalition saw such "undue reliance" on power as a diversion from the central problem: failure adequately to fund public health departments and hospital emergency services, or to provide preventive care and treatment to those in need. Recourse to threats and coercion treated the people as if they, rather than pathogens, posed a problem. "In other words this statute limits individual rights without providing individuals with any substantial assurance of protection against bioterrorist attacks or other more ordinary threats to public health."

Finally, the coalition denounced the breadth of statutory language that would permit declaration of a state of emergency when less drastic efforts might suffice. "Individual civil liberties and property rights may be disregarded even when more benign measures might achieve a comparable results" (New England Coalition for Law and Public Health 2001, 2). The Act was described as a replica of statutes from the early twentieth century, an era of therapeutic limits, "when officials had to rely on quarantining sick people because they have little else at hand" (Parmet and Mariner 2001). Annas (2001) described it as "the old Soviet model of public health (lots of power and no standards for applying it), hardly a 'new' American model."

Like the New England Coalition, groups with special concern about privacy expressed alarm at the way in which the model act treated medical information. The Health Privacy Project at Georgetown University's Law Center noted that the "breathtakingly expansive scope of the definition" of public health emergencies could open the way to name-based reporting of cases of HIV and hepatitis, "a controversial proposition indeed" (Health Privacy Project 2001, 1–2). Furthermore, the Act was denounced for the inadequacy of protections afforded medical information on identifiable individuals. Crafted to highlight problematic features of the Act's specific provisions, the Project's challenge was embedded in a perspective radically distinct from that which animated the work of the drafters. Giving voice to an understanding that had taken hold in the first years of the AIDS epidemic, the critique concluded by asserting that gaps in public health capacity to respond to emergencies could be resolved by "fully" respecting civil liberties and privacy rights. "These ends are not mutually exclusive; rather they are integrally linked" (Health Privacy Project 2001, 5).

To the Lambda Legal Defense and Education Fund—a gay and lesbian civil rights organization that had been involved for more than a decade in combating policies such as reporting names of HIV-infected individuals—the Act was anathema. With its recourse to compulsory measures, threats of quarantine and criminalization, and reliance on collaboration between public health and law enforcement agencies, it represented a regressive step that could have dire effects on those the AIDS advocacy group had so fiercely sought to protect (Lambda Legal Defense and Education Fund 2001).

But from whatever vantage point they challenged the Act, informing the liberal opposition's position was the unmistakable sense that, wittingly or not, the drafters permitted themselves to bring forth the public health equivalent of policies emanating from John Ashcroft's Justice Department. As the threat of war and terrorism provided a warrant for cabining civil liberties, the danger of bioterrorism provided justification for yet one more perilous threat to fundamental rights.

But broad and thoroughgoing challenges came not only from those who embraced liberal political values and a progressive social agenda. Conservative libertarians also saw in the Act exemplification of an appalling philosophical outlook. It represented "an unprecedented assault on the constitutional rights of the American people [and] on our fundamental principles of limited government and separation of powers" (Schlafly 2001). Like critics on the left, groups such as the Association of American Physicians and Surgeons denounced intrusions on privacy that would occur as the result of disease-reporting requirements, imposition of medical interventions and vaccinations, and criminalization of refusals to undergo such treatment. Invocation of a broad power to quarantine was viewed as especially egregious. In short, said the physicians' group, the model act "turns governors into dictators," permitting them to "create a police state by fiat" (Association of American Physicians and Surgeons 2001).

Ironically, as liberal civil libertarians responded with dismay to what they took to be Larry Gostin's betrayal of his libertarian past, conservative opponents characterized Gostin as the embodiment of left-wing values. Jennifer King, an official with the American Legislative Exchange Council, portrayed Gostin as a "very strong public health, police state type." Nothing more tellingly revealed his commitments than the work he had done as one of more than 500 consultants assisting the Clintons during the ill-fated effort at health care reform (Betsch 2001).

Finally, with its authorization of mandatory vaccinations on penalty of criminalization and quarantine, and with its invocation of a much-hated century-old Supreme Court decision upholding imposed immunization, it was inevitable that the Act would draw the ire of antivaccination advocates. These groups typically, although not always, shared the antistatist perspectives of the broader conservative libertarian movement. In one such on-line denunciation (Richardson 2002), which was especially harsh in its reference to Gostin because of his "long history of trying to brainwash people into sacrificing individuals' rights for society," the Act was described as "horrifying." It would impose immunizations on adults and children and would enhance the "powers of public health bureaucrats." The legislation offered the false promise of security in exchange for the freedom to make one's own medical decisions. This was all too predictable given the history of coercive childhood vaccinations. It was time for the "extortion" to stop.

Denunciations from groups that believed that the exercise state authority, even the name of public health, had to be carefully circumscribed, and from those who had a visceral antagonism to state authority, were not unexpected. Perhaps more striking was the response of constituencies that, according to first reports, had enthusiastically participated in the legislative initiative. Indeed, in the weeks after the late-October public release of the Act, the very organizations that had been listed as collaborators in its development sought to distance themselves from it.

The same official at the National Governors' Association (NGA) who at first described the Act as "extremely useful" later was compelled to acknowledge that the NGA had not taken a full position on the Act, that a number of states had indicated "we don't need this," and "governors don't like models, they like options" (Thomasian 2002). The Association of State and Territorial Health Officials (ASTHO) noted that "at the request of the CDC" it circulated the document for review and comment, and many respondents expressed discomfort with overreliance on criminalization, recourse to mandatory treatment and vaccination, and reliance on quarantines. Most significant, ASTHO noted that the model act would best serve as a "tool" for states as they considered the necessity of new or amended authority; in no way was it to be viewed as a template for a radical revision of extant public health laws. States should "retain the flexibility to adopt all or part of the model act as they deem appropriate for their jurisdictions" (Association of State and Territorial Health Officials 2001). A similar stance was adopted by the National Association of County and City Health Officials (Brown 2002). Although the National Association of Local Boards of Health did not immediately take a position on the Act, its director for governmental relations cautioned about the dangers of thoroughgoing legislative reform. "It has been my experience that the more comprehensive legislation becomes, the greater the effect of the law of unintended consequences. State and legislating jurisdictions within them should be encouraged to adopt as little new law as possible and to focus on amendments of existing statutes only as much as necessary" (Pratt 2001). Finally, the National Council of State Legislatures (NCSL) indicated that it did not typically indorse model acts. An observer sympathetic to the project of reform recounted that the NCSL had "gone ballistic" on being listed as a collaborator on the draft (Fox 2002). One account of meetings convened by the Council suggested that most attendees saw the model as "bad" legislation. At least two legislators underscored the extent to which it appeared like a "governmental takeover" (Guiden 2001). In lieu of wholesale reform, many groups suggested using the Act as a checklist for thinking about the adequacy of extant legislative provisions.

This then was the context in which those who crafted the model act were compelled to undertake the redrafting. It was a process that would seek to preserve core elements of the Act while modifying aspects—language and substance—that provoked criticism from those alarmed by the breadth of the statutory formulations and the impact they could have on the rights of those who might become subjects of the Act's compulsory dimensions. In undertaking the refinement, drafters could not ignore the fact that even among many who thought legislative reform to meet the challenge of bioterrorism was necessary, there appeared to be no great enthusiasm for the grand recodification foreseen when the Act was first released. Thus whatever was done would have to be understood as providing states with a checklist of matters with which they would have to deal. Thus said Maryland's Health Secretary Georges Benjamin, "States should look at [the Act] as a menu . . . I think the most important thing is that people not take any model act and simply try to push it through Willy Nilly" (Gillis 2001).

Nevertheless, in light of the fact that the CDC was to be distributing approximately $1 billion to states for emergency preparedness, and that in making its determination the CDC would look for evidence that efforts had been made to provide the legal infrastructure for confronting public health threats, it was inevitable that action at the state level would be forthcoming. Whether CDC funding was viewed as an inducement or a bludgeon depended very much on how one saw the effort to craft a legislative bulwark against bioterrorism.

At the end of December 2001 a new draft was made public. Changes, both cosmetic and substantive, were evident (Center for Law and the Public's Health 2001c). The amended Act reflected the political lessons of the previous six weeks. Perhaps most striking was the characterization of the relationship between the legislative proposal and constituencies that had been portrayed as "collaborators" in crafting the earlier effort. Now the Act was described as serving to "assist" those very organizations. Indeed the National Association of Attorneys General was simply listed as having provided "input and suggestions." To dispel the illusion that the Act represented CDC-endorsed legislation, a disclaimer asserted that the emergency measure did not "represent the official policy, endorsement or views" of the federal agency. Oddly, the disclaimer was extended to the CDC-funded Center for Law and the Public's Health that had itself drafted the model act! In all, a distinct effort was made to avoid the suggestion that states had before them a legislative measure that had the full backing of powerful national public health and law enforcement bodies.

The new draft also underwent significant linguistic transformation. Whereas the earlier version unabashedly employed terms that reflected the necessity of coercive measures, the new draft sought to soften the harsh tone. Thus, for example, the subsection dealing with property—which evoked such concern on the part of those who viewed it as an invitation to unwarranted seizures—was now denominated "management" rather than "control" of property. The subsection dealing with compulsory powers over individuals, which drew the ire of those committed to civil liberties, was no longer termed "control of persons"; now it was called "protection of persons." Finally, the new draft subtly acknowledged that the original version had, by emphasizing the importance of coercive measures, inadequately underscored the centrality of a well-financed and organized public health system. The preamble now declared, "although modernizing public health is an important part of protecting the population during public health emergencies, the public health system itself needs improvement."

More important were substantive changes, all of which sought to prevent exercise of authority from becoming an occasion for abuse of power. First, responding to the alarm evoked by the very breadth of the definition of threats that could occasion the declaration of an emergency, the new draft eliminated references to "epidemic and pandemic diseases" (critics asserted that the flu and AIDS could trigger a declaration). In so doing the drafters sought to demonstrate that their understanding of what constituted an emergency was similar to that of their antagonists, who asserted that there were, of course, situations that might require the exercise of extraordinary public health powers. What had been the sweeping authority of the governor to impose a state of emergency with very limited legislative oversight was now to be subject to the possibility of an override by a simple majority of both legislative houses. Concerns that the October version would have permitted gross violations of privacy was similarly given credence. Mandatory reporting by name remained a central element of the Act, but steps were taken to ensure that the data would be protected from unwarranted disclosure and misuse. Criminalization of refusals to undergo treatment and vaccinations by those deemed a potential threat to public health were gone, although those who declined such interventions would still be subject to isolation and quarantine. Gone too were criminal sanctions for physicians and other health care providers who refused to impose treatment or vaccination, although their licensure could be endangered. The capacity to move swiftly to impose isolation and quarantine, so central to the original Act, remained untouched. The revised legislative proposal did, however, provide a much more extensive elaboration of due process procedures that would surround such deprivations of liberty.

Some of those who expressed fierce opposition to the October draft acknowledged that the proposed substantive changes had improved the legislation. Core concerns remained, however, revealing a deep philosophical divide. Thus, for example, the Health Privacy Project noted improvements represented by the narrower definition of public health emergencies but continued to voice objections to the way in which the Act would violate the privacy of medical information. Bluntly it said, "The necessary changes . . . have not been made" (Health Privacy Project 2002). George Annas revealed the gulf that separated those who saw limitations on liberty as central to the response to public health threats and those who were profoundly skeptical of this assumption. "We do not have to trade off civil liberties for public health to effectively respond to a bioterrorist attack" (Annas 2002). Indeed, he viewed the constitutional premise on which the act was predicated—the 1905 Jacobson v. Massachusetts decision—as part of a bygone era. Invoking the lessons of the AIDS epidemic he concluded, "The promotion of human rights can be essential to deal effectively with an epidemic" (Annas 2002).

The New York Civil Liberties Union (2002), in testimony before a state legislative committee, gave voice to the fundamental opposition that no cosmetic changes or limited adjustments could address. The Act was an "anachronism" and failed to "fully anticipate the ways in which [it] would empower the state to violate fundamental rights and liberties." Giving credence to the need to respond to real incidents of bioterrorism, it believed it crucial to recognize the history of abuse by the state. "Government acting in the name of public safety, has demonstrated bad judgment and worse using state police powers in a discriminatory manner to suspend freedoms based upon race or national origin." Given such a perspective it is not surprising that the group challenged even the revised version of the Act in every detail: the definition of public health emergency was still too broad; the requirement that names be used for reporting purposes ignored the principle that without demonstration of an overriding interest such a privacy-violating measure was unacceptable; the "protection of persons" clauses presumptively overrode the individual's right to refuse medical treatment; the Act failed to incorporate procedural protections already available in some states, including New York. Finally, the limited scope of judicial review on matters of treatment, testing, isolation and quarantine "constituted a fundamental and "fatal" flaw in the act (New York Civil Liberties Union 2002).

The arguments of the libertarian right were not very different, although they were informed by a characteristic stridency. The Association of American Physicians and Surgeons denounced the new draft as a "disingenuous effort to mute criticism." Limitations on liberty for ordinary citizens were less severe, but the draft still imperiled clinicians and those who owned medical facilities. "Their property can be commandeered and their skills usurped to perform duties that might well violate their oath to serve patients to the best of their own judgment and ability." In short, the revision was "still a prescription for tyranny" (Association of American Physicians and Surgeons 2002). The American Legislative Exchange Council (2002) also acknowledged that changes had been made in the October draft but asserted that "the release of a revised draft [did] not mask the original intent of the authors." Finally, Georgia Republican congressional representative Bob Barr described the act as a "fearsome power grab" by the CDC and the nation's governors. Barr drew a parallel between the proposed legislation and the Clinton administration's effort at health care reform. The earlier attempt was a "federal takeover" of the health care industry. Now there was an effort "to hijack not only the health care industry, but also the constitutional freedoms of [Americans]." The entire enterprise was "unprecedented," at least in "non-dictatorial regimes" (Barr 2002).

Although some antivaccine advocates found in the modification an acceptable compromise—quarantine for refusal to undergo immunization rather than criminalization (Reiss 2002)—the most redoubtable voice of the movement continued to denounce the proposal. Terming the CDC-funded drafting effort as one that "Treats us like runaway slaves in need of subjugation," Barbara Loe Fisher, head of the National Vaccine Advisory Center, attacked the Act's continued use of compulsion as a choice between freedom and vaccination. Linking her struggle to a broad liberty-preserving agenda she declared, "I've said many times during the past decade that if the state can tag, track down and force citizens to be injected with biologicals of unknown toxicity, then there will be no limit on what individual freedoms the state can take away in the name of the greater good tomorrow. Now tomorrow is here" (Fisher 2002).

It was against a backdrop of such fervid attacks and more sober critiques that the work of state legislatures took place. Some states considered legislation based on the revised version, whereas others moved to adopt even more scaled-back versions that would be acceptable to those concerned about overreaching. Thus, for example, in Wisconsin adaptations from the Act were characterized as "pretty minor" by a state senator (Rosenzweig 2002). In Ohio the health department cautiously reconsidered its options given the need to face a legislature "very leery of big government" (Govern 2002). The California state health department remained skeptical of the need for wholesale legislative action even though a bill closely following the October version of the model act was introduced into the legislature (Reilly 2002). In Minnesota, the need to accommodate those opposed to the Act resulted in a legislative proposal that was "barely adequate," according to the state's epidemiologist, who had been among the proponents of a more expansive version (Hull 2002).

But despite such resistance it was clear by March 2002, five months after the model act was first proposed, that significant legislative activity was inspired by the proposal to create a legal infrastructure responsive to the threat of bioterrorism. Indicative of the state of affairs was the enthusiastic involvement of Richard Gottfried, chair of the New York State Assembly's health committee (Gottfried 2002). Long an advocate of both public health and privacy rights, an architect of the state's extensive AIDS confidentiality act, Gottfried assisted the Milbank Memorial Fund in convening two meetings in early 2002 for state legislators and their staff members. At those sessions the concept of creating a legal infrastructure for responding to bioterrorism received an enthusiastic response. As of April 2002 the Center for Law and the Public's Health reported that legislation had been introduced in thirty-two states based wholly or in part on the model act (Hodge 2002). In many states, bills were being sponsored by legislators with considerable political influence, in contrast to the first round of bills in the fall of 2001, some of which were introduced by less well-connected lawmakers. Nevertheless, despite such extensive activity, only two states, Utah and South Dakota, had by the spring of 2002 enacted emergency health powers legislation. Only in the case of the former did the model act serve as a template.

Conclusion

Whatever the ultimate legislative outcome, the debate inspired by the MEHPA illuminated the enduring ideological tensions that inform the world of public health. In the 1980s the AIDS epidemic provided the occasion for articulation of a new paradigm of public health. Given biological, epidemiological, and political factors that shaped the public policy discussion, it became possible to assert that no tension existed between public health and civil liberties, that policies that protected the latter would foster the former, and that policies that intruded on rights would subvert the public health. And what was true AIDS was true for public health more generally. Indeed, the experience of AIDS provided the opportunity to rethink the very foundations of public health with its legacy of compulsory state powers. Even when some elements of the privacy- and rights-based approaches to AIDS were subject to modification in the 1990s as the epidemic was "normalized," the core values that had taken hold remained largely undisturbed.

The effort to articulate a new public health ideology masked a conflict that, however dormant, remained prime for exacerbation under appropriate conditions. At one pole were those who, like health and human rights activist Jonathan Mann, had come to believe that "it may be useful to adopt the maxim that health policies and programs should be considered discriminatory and burdensome on human rights until proven otherwise" (Mann, Gostin, and Gruskin 1994, 16). Very different was the view that respect for individual rights, however important, could and should be subordinated to the common good when threats to public health emerged. From this perspective the compulsory vaccination decision of the Supreme Court in 1905 rested on sound moral as well as constitutional assumptions.

It was possible, given the nature of HIV as a behaviorally transmitted virus, to avoid confronting tensions between these ideologies of public health because of the strategic importance of engaging those most at risk in the work of prevention. But with a threat that involved virulent communicable viral or bacteriological agents, such strategic constraints would not inform the discussion. It was inevitable, then, that in the shadow of September 11 the conflict over rights and dangers would resurface, shattering for the time being the illusion of a single guiding vision for public health.

References

Albert, Michael R., Kristen G. Ostheimer, and Joel G. Bremen. 2001. "The Last Smallpox Epidemic in Boston and the Vaccination Controversy, 1901–1903." *New England Journal of Medicine*. 344(5): 375–379.

American Legislative Exchange Council. 2002. "ALEC Opposes the Model State Emergency Health Powers Act." American Legislative Exchange Council web site. Available at www.alec.org/viewpage.cfm?phname=5.103 (visited March 4, 2002).

Annas, George. 2001. Letter to James Hodge. November 1.

Annas, George. 2002. "Bioterrorism, Public Health, and Civil Liberties." *New England Journal of Medicine*. 346: 1337–1342.

Association of American Physicians and Surgeons. 2001. "Model Emergency Health Powers Act (MSEHPA) Turns Governors into Dictators." Association of American Physicians and Surgeons web site. Available at www.aapsonline.org/testimony/emerpower.htm (visited February 4, 2002).

Association of American Physicians and Surgeons. 2002. "Revised Draft of Model State Emergency Health powers Act (Dec. 21) Still a Prescription for Tyranny." Association of American Physicians and Surgeons web site. Available at www.aapsonline.org/testimony/emerpower2.htm (visited February 4, 2002).

Association of State and Territorial Health Officials. 2001. Summary of Comments on October 23, 2001, Draft of Model State Emergency Health Powers Act, November 5. Washington, DC: Association of State and Territorial Health Officials.

Barr, Bob. 2002. "A Fearsome Power Grab by the CDC and State Governors." Congressman Bob Barr web site. Available at hillsource.house.gov/barr/newsdescr.asp?N=20020215170247 (visited March 13, 2002).

Bayer, Ronald. 1988. *Private Acts, Social Consequences: AIDS and the Politics of Public Health*. New York: Basic Books.

Betsch, Michael. 2001. "Bio-terror Response Plan Would Invade Civil Liberties." CNSNews web site. Available at www.cnsnews.com/Nation/Archive/200112/NAT20011211a.html (visited April 15, 2002).

Brown, Donna. 2002. Personal communication to James Colgrove. January 29.

Brownlee, Shannon. 2001. "Why America Isn't Ready for Bioterrorism." The New Republic Online. Available at www.thenewrepublic.com/102901/brownlee102901.html (visited January 23, 2002).

Bor, Jonathan. 1999. "Spreading the Word About Bioterrorism." The Baltimore Sun. December 27, A1.

Center for Law and the Public's Health. 2001a. *The Model State Emergency Health Powers Act (Draft as of October 23, 2001)*. Washington, DC: Center for Law and the Public's Health.

Center for Law and the Public's Health. 2001b. "Model Emergency Health Powers Act in Repsonse to Bioterrorism Written for the CDC and Governors." News release. October 30.

Center for Law and the Public's Health. 2001c. *The Model State Emergency Health Powers Act (Draft as of December 21, 2001)*. Washington, DC: Center for Law and the Public's Health.

Copeland, Larry. 2001. "CDC Proposes Bioterrorism Laws." *USA Today*. November 8, A3.

Durraji Susan Muaddi. 2001. "Model Legislation: Balancing Civil Rights and Public Health." *Johns Hogkins Public Health Magazine*, Special Edition, late Fall 2001. Available at www.jhsph.edu/magazine/model.htm (accessed February 5, 2002).

deFiebre, Conrad. 2001. "More Power Sought to Fight Bioterror." *Star Tribune* (Minneapolis). November 6, B1.

Ernst, Tom. 2001. "Bill Proposes Quarantine Powers During Crisis." *Buffalo News*. November 21, B3.

Fisher, Barbara Loe. 2002. "Editorial: Vaccinating America at Gunpoint." National Vaccine Information Center Web site. Available at www.909shot.com/smallpoxspecialrpt.htm (visited March 13, 2002).

Fox, Daniel. 1988. "From TB to AIDS: Value Conflicts in Reporting Disease." *Hastings Center Report*. 16 (December): 11–17.

Fox, Daniel. 2002. Interview with Ronald Bayer. March 7.

Freed, G.L., S.L. Katz, and S.J. Clark. 1996. "Safety of Vaccinations. Miss America, the Media, and Public Health." *Journal of the American Medical Association*. 276(23): 1869–1872.

Garrett, Laurie. 1999. "Wake-Up Call on Germ Warfare." *Newsday*. February 21, A4.

Gillis, Justin. 2001. "States Weighing Laws to Fight Bioterrorism." *Washington Post*. November 19, A1.

Gottfried, Richard. 2002. Interview with Ronald Bayer. March 14.

Govern, Jodi. 2002. Interview with James Colgrove. March 18.

Guiden, Mary. 2001. "Lawmakers Not Keen on 'Model' Public Health Law." Available at www1.stateline.org/print_story.do;jsessionid=gi6uwx9ld1?storyId=212079 (visited March 4, 2001).

Health Privacy Project, Institute for Health Care Research and Policy, Georgetown University. 2001. Letter to Lawrence O. Gostin. November 7.

Health Privacy Project, Institute for Health Care Research and Policy, Georgetown University. 2002. "Health Privacy Project Comments on Model State Emergency Health Powers Act, January 18, 2002." Washington, DC: Institute for Health Care Research and Policy.

Henderson, D.A. 2001. "Biopreparedness and Public Health." *American Journal of Public Health*. 91(12): 1917–1918.

Hodge, James. 2002. Personal communication to Ronald Bayer.

Hull, Henry. 2002. Interview with Ronald Bayer. March 7.

In re Halko. 1966. 54 Cal. Report. 661.

Jacobson v. Commonwealth of Massachusetts. 1905. 197 U.S. 11.

Karst, K.L. 1980. "The Freedom of Intimate Association." *Yale Law Journal*. 99: 624–692.

Kaufman, Martin. 1967. "The American Anti-Vaccinationists and Their Arguments." *Bulletin of the History of Medicine*. 41.5: 463–478.

Lambda Legal Defense and Education Fund. 2001. Letter to Lawrence O. Gostin. December 20.

Lasalandra, Michael. 2001. "Smallpox Attack Preparedness Plan Would Give Officials Sweeping Powers." *Boston Herald*. November 8, 16.

Leavitt, Judith Walzer. 1982. *The Healthiest City: Milwaukee and the Politics of Health Reform*. Princeton, NJ: Princeton University Press.

Mann, Jonathan M., Lawrence Gostin, and Sofia Gruskin. 1994. "Health and Human Rights." *Health and Human Rights*. 1: 7–23.

Markel, Howard. 1997. *Quarantine! East European Jewish Immigrants and the New York City Epidemics of 1892*. Baltimore: Johns Hopkins University Press.

Matthews, Gene. 2002. Interview with Ronald Bayer. March 6.

McKenna, M.A.J. 2001. "CDC Pushes Bill Boosting States' Powers." *Atlanta Journal and Constitution*. October 30, A8.

New England Coalition for Law and Public Health. 2001. Letter to Health and Human Services Secretary Tommy Thompson. November 13.

New York Civil Liberties Union. 2002. Testimony of Robert Perry on behalf of the New York Civil Liberties Union before the Assembly Standing Committee on Health and the Assembly Standing Committee on Codes Concerning the Model State Emergency Health Powers Act. March 14.

Parmet, Wendy. 1985. "AIDS and Quarantine: The Revival of an Archaic Doctrine." *Hofstra Law Review*. 14: 53–90.

Parmet, Wendy E. and Wendy K. Mariner. 2001. "A Health Act that Jeopardizes Public Health." *Boston Globe*. December 1, A15.

Pratt, Ted. 2001. Memorandum to Lawrence Gostin, James Hodge, and Richard Goodman. November 8.

Reilly, Kevin. 2002. Interview with James Colgrove. March 6.

Reiss, Lisa. 2002. Testimony on behalf of Connecticut Vaccine Information Alliance before Public Health Committee of Connecticut State Assembly. February 19.

Richardson, Dawn. 2002. Posting to groups.yahoo.com/group/i-v-y/message/5971 (visited March 18, 2002).

Rosenzweig, Peggy. 2002. Interview with James Colgrove. March 15.

Schlafly, Phyllis. 2001. "Where Do Politicians Go in Their Afterlife?" *Toogood Reports*. December 20. www.toogoodreports.com/column/general/schlafly/122001.htm (visited March 4, 2002).

Sidel, Victor W., Hillel W. Cohen, and Robert M. Gould. 2001. "Good Intentions and the Road to Bioterrorism Preparedness." *American Journal of Public Health*. 91.5: 716–718.

Tansey, Bernadette. 2001. "Health Bill Endangers Civil Rights." *San Francisco Chronicle*. November 25, A1.

Thacker, S.B. and R.L. Berkleman. 1988. "Public Health Surveillance in the United States." *Epidemiologic Reviews*. 10: 164–190.

Thomasian, John. 2002. Interview with James Colgrove. March 8.

Tribe, Lawrence. 1978. *American Constitutional Law*. Mineola: New York Foundation Press.

U.S. Department of Health and Human Services. 2001. "Statement by HHS Secretary Tommy G. Thompson regarding the Model Emergency Health Powers Act." News release. October 30.

Winslow, C.-E.A. 1929. *The Life of Hermann Biggs*. Philadelphia: Lea & Febiger.

[6]

Critical Biological Agents: Disease Reporting as a Tool for Determining Bioterrorism Preparedness

Heather H. Horton, James J. Misrahi, Gene W. Matthews, and Paula L. Kocher

Before September 11, 2001, a mass-casualty terrorist attack on American soil was generally considered a remote possibility. Similarly, before October 4, 2001 — the first confirmed case of anthrax caused by intentional release — widespread bioterrorism seemed implausible.[1] Among the arguments that such a biological attack was unlikely included: the lack of a historical precedent; the technological and organizational challenges to acquiring and weaponizing a biological agent; and the almost universal moral opprobrium that would certainly accompany the use by terrorists of such a weapon.[2] In the wake of September 11th and October 4th, however, many are reconsidering the likelihood of a large-scale bioterrorist attack against civilians.

The Centers for Disease Control and Prevention (CDC) defines "bioterrorism" as the intentional release of viruses, bacteria, or toxins for the purpose of harming or killing civilians.[3] One measurement of the public health system's level of bioterrorism preparedness is the quality and distribution of laws mandating the reporting of diseases caused by certain biological agents. In fact, the timely and accurate reporting of such diseases would likely be the triggering event for investigating and responding to a bioterrorism event.

In order to assess the nation's bioterrorism preparedness, as measured by its disease reporting laws, CDC's Bioterrorism Preparedness and Response Program commissioned a study of state and local laws requiring the reporting of diseases caused by specific biological agents. This article discusses the background, methods, and results of the study and suggests that states and localities would benefit from examining their existing disease reporting laws in light of bioterrorism concerns.

The CDC's strategic plan for bioterrorism has focused on the following five areas: preparedness and prevention; detection and surveillance; diagnosis and characterization of biological and chemical agents; response; and communication.[4] The strategic plan has included, among other things: distance learning programs for health-care workers; the creation of a multilevel laboratory response network for bioterrorism; a national pharmaceutical stockpile of medical supplies to be used in an emergency; and a national electronic infrastructure to improve the exchange of emergency health information.[5] While these efforts are an essential part of a coordinated federal response to a bioterrorist event, they are necessarily dependent on a strong and flexible public health system at the state and local level. Advanced laboratory tests and caches of medical supplies are useful only if public health officials are aware that a suspected release of a biological agent has occurred. It is therefore important not only that health-care providers be able to identify unusual patterns of disease or injury, but also that they report such unusual occurrences to appropriate public health officials to ensure a timely response.

CDC's study of disease reporting laws examined the reporting requirements for twenty-four biological agents (or the diseases caused by these agents): anthrax; botulism;[6] brucellosis; cholera; *Cryptosporidium*; *E. coli*;[7] glanders; hantavirus; melioidosis; mycotoxins; plague; psittacosis; Q fever; ricin poisoning; *Salmonella*; *Shigella*; smallpox; staphylococcal enterotoxin B; toxic syndromes;[8] tularemia; typhus fever; *Vibrio cholerae*;[9] viral encephalitis; and viral hemorrhagic fevers. These particular agents are regarded as "critical biological agents" because of their potential to harm the public health if used in a terrorist act. In determining which biological agents were most critical, CDC sought the counsel of federal agencies, infectious disease experts, national public health experts, civilian and military experts, and law enforcement officials.[10] The following factors were considered in developing the list of agents:

- morbidity and mortality;
- potential for distributing the agent population-wide based on the stability of the agent, ability to mass produce and distribute a virulent agent, and the possibility for person-to-person transmission of the agent;
- potential for public fear and potential civil disruption; and
- special public health preparedness needs based on stockpile requirements, enhanced surveillance, or diagnostic needs.[11]

The resulting list of critical biological agents was divided into three categories (Category A, B, and C), based on the level of public health importance.[12] Terrorism experts are most concerned with Category A agents because they have the greatest potential for harm if used in a bioterrorist attack. These agents can be easily disseminated or transmitted person-to-person; cause high mortality; severely affect

Table 1. Symptoms and Treatment for Category A Diseases.

Category A Diseases	Common Symptoms	Treatment/Prevention
Anthrax[1]	Initially resembles common cold; progresses to severe breathing problems and shock.	Treatable if antibiotics taken very soon after exposure; limited supply of investigational vaccine exists.
Botulism[2]	Blurred vision, difficulty swallowing and speaking, and muscle paralysis.	Treatable if assistance with breathing is provided; antitoxin is effective if administered early in course of disease.
Plague (pneumonic)[3]	Fever, headache, weakness, and cough; may cause shock.	Early treatment with antibiotics can be effective; there is currently no vaccine available for use in the United States.
Smallpox[4]	Fever, headache, nausea, and rash leading to hard blisters.	Routine vaccinations ended in the United States by 1972; no proven treatment.
Tularemia[5]	Fever, chills, body aches, and weakness; inflammation and hemorrhaging of airways.	Vaccine is under review by the Food and Drug Administration; early treatment with antibiotics can be effective.
Viral Hemorrhagic Fevers[6]	Fever, fatigue, dizziness, muscle aches, exhaustion, and diarrhea; severe cases include bleeding under the skin, in internal organs, or from body orifices.	With few exceptions, there is no cure or established drug treatment; care is supportive in nature.

1. *Centers for Disease Control and Prevention, U.S. Department of Health and Human Services,* Facts about Anthrax, at *<http://www.bt.cdc.gov/DocumentsApp/FactSheet/Anthrax/about.asp> (last visited March 20, 2002).*

2. *Centers for Disease Control and Prevention, U.S. Department of Health and Human Services,* Facts about Botulism, at *<http://www.bt.cdc.gov/DocumentsApp/FactSheet/Botulism/about.asp> (last visited March 20, 2002).*

3. *Centers for Disease Control and Prevention, U.S. Department of Health and Human Services,* Facts about Pneumonic Plague, at *<http://www.bt.cdc.gov/DocumentsApp/FactSheet/Plague/About.asp> (last visited March 20, 2002).*

4. *Centers for Disease Control and Prevention, U.S. Department of Health and Human Services,* Facts about Smallpox, at *<http://www.bt.cdc.gov/DocumentsApp/FactSheet/SmallPox/About.asp> (last visited March 20, 2002).*

5. *The Working Group on Civilian Biodefense, "Tularemia as a Biological Weapon,"* JAMA, *285, no. 21 (2001): 2763–73.*

6. *Centers for Disease Control and Prevention, U.S. Department of Health and Human Services,* Viral Hemorrhagic Fevers: Fact Sheets, at *<http://www.cdc.gov/ncidod/dvrd/spb/mnpages/dispages/vhf.htm> (last visited March 20, 2002).*

the public health; might cause public panic and social disruption; and require special action for public health preparedness. Six diseases are caused by Category A agents: anthrax; botulism; plague; smallpox; tularemia; and viral hemorrhagic fevers.[13] Each of these are analyzed in terms of their symptoms and known treatment in Table 1.

Category B agents are less of an immediate bioterrorism concern because they are only moderately easy to disseminate and cause moderate morbidity and low mortality.[14] Nonetheless, there are recent examples of terrorists using Category B agents in the United States. In 1984, the Rajneeshee religious cult used *Salmonella* to contaminate restaurant salad bars, which sickened hundreds of people in Oregon.[15] Similarly, in the 1990s, members of an anti-government group (the Patriots Council) reportedly used ricin in an attempt to assassinate law enforcement agents in Minnesota.[16] Accordingly, Category B agents are important for bioterrorism preparedness and require enhancements of diagnostic capacity and disease surveillance.[17]

Category C agents include emerging pathogens that could be engineered for mass dissemination in the future, but are not presently likely to be used as a bioterrorist weapon.[18] These agents result in such diseases as hantavirus, typhus fever, and viral encephalitis.[19] Preparedness for Category C agents includes continued research to enhance disease surveillance, diagnosis, and treatment.[20]

Methods

The CDC study's primary purpose was to determine for fifty-four participating jurisdictions which of twenty-four critical biological agents (or the diseases caused by those agents) are explicitly reportable by law and the timeframe for reporting these agents or diseases. Additionally, the study ascertained for each jurisdiction the persons or institutions mandated to report; to whom disease reports should be made; and the sources of disease reporting laws (i.e., statute or administrative code). The participating jurisdictions included the fifty states, Chicago, Los Angeles County, New York City, and Washington, D.C. These jurisdictions were chosen because they had agreed, in cooperation with CDC, to develop preparedness and response plans specifically related to bioterrorism.[21]

To obtain preliminary results, CDC searched electronic legal databases for laws mandating that diseases caused by specific critical biological agents be reported. While electronic databases provided the necessary information for many of the jurisdictions, information for the remaining jurisdictions was obtained from health department websites or by directly contacting state or local health departments. Preliminary results were presented in fifty-four charts, representing each of the jurisdictions surveyed. The chief epidemiologist or other health department representative from each jurisdiction reviewed, verified, amended, or updated these preliminary findings. The fifty-four charts were then finalized; they reflect the status of disease reporting laws as of March 31, 2001, when the study was completed.

Findings

Table 2 indicates the number and percentage of the fifty-four jurisdictions surveyed that require (as of March 31, 2001) the reporting of particular diseases caused by critical biological agents.

The study found that three of the six Category A agents — anthrax, botulism, and plague — are "reportable immediately" in the vast majority (89 percent, 96 percent, and 89 percent, respectively) of jurisdictions surveyed. Conversely, the other three Category A agents — smallpox, tularemia, and viral hemorrhagic fevers — are "reportable immediately" in less than half (39 percent, 46 percent, and 26 percent, respectively) of these jurisdictions.

The Category B agents cholera, *Salmonella*, and *Shigella* are "reportable immediately" or "explicitly reportable" in 100 percent of the jurisdictions surveyed. In contrast, glanders, melioidosis, mycotoxins, ricin poisoning, and staphylococcal enterotoxin B are "reportable immediately" or "explicitly reportable" in only a small percentage (6 percent, 4 percent, 4 percent, 9 percent, and 20 percent, respectively) of jurisdictions. The remaining Category B agents (brucellosis, *Cryptosporidium*, *E. coli*, psittacosis, Q Fever, toxic syndromes, and *Vibrio cholerae*) and all Category C agents (hantavirus, typhus fever, and viral encephalitis) are "reportable immediately" or "explicitly reportable" in a majority of the jurisdictions surveyed.

The study further showed that persons who have a mandatory duty to report diseases caused by critical biological agents usually are physicians and other health-care providers, laboratory directors, and hospital administrators. In addition, some jurisdictions mandate reporting by school principals (e.g., New Mexico), child care centers (e.g., South Dakota), nursing home administrators (e.g., Alabama), heads of families (e.g., Kentucky), personnel of food establishments (e.g., North Carolina), or anyone with knowledge of a case of a reportable disease (e.g., Montana). The entities to which persons must report are generally state, county, or local health agencies or other health authorities.

Disease reporting requirements, in most cases, can be found in state administrative codes, but may also be located in state statutes, rules and regulations of local boards of health, and municipal regulations. Furthermore, laws requiring the reporting of diseases caused by critical biological agents tend to be scattered among other disease-specific reporting laws, such as those requiring the reporting of measles or tuberculosis. Although this study did not systematically review penalty provisions, it was noted in a number of jurisdictions that non-compliance with disease reporting laws constitutes a misdemeanor punishable by fine or imprisonment.[22]

TABLE 2. SUMMARY OF DISEASE REPORTING REQUIREMENTS OF THE 50 STATES, THE DISTRICT OF COLUMBIA, CHICAGO, NEW YORK CITY, AND LOS ANGELES COUNTY AS OF MARCH 31, 2001.

CRITICAL BIOLOGICAL AGENT OR COMMUNICABLE DISEASE ASSOCIATED WITH BIOTERRORISM	REPORTABLE IMMEDIATELY*	EXPLICITLY REPORTABLE**	NOT EXPLICITLY REPORTABLE***
Category A			
Anthrax	48 (89%)	5 (9%)	1 (2%)
Botulism	52 (96%)	2 (4%)	0 (0%)
Plague	48 (89%)	4 (7%)	2 (4%)
Smallpox	21 (39%)	1 (2%)	32 (59%)
Tularemia	25 (46%)	22 (41%)	7 (13%)
Viral Hemorrhagic Fevers	14 (26%)	1 (2%)	39 (72%)
Category B			
Brucellosis	23 (42%)	29 (54%)	2 (4%)
Cholera	49 (91%)	5 (9%)	0 (0%)
Cryptosporidium	12 (22%)	40 (74%)	2 (4%)
E. Coli	28 (52%)	24 (44%)	2 (4%)
Glanders	3 (6%)	0 (0%)	51 (94%)
Melioidosis	2 (4%)	0 (0%)	52 (96%)
Mycotoxins	2 (4%)	0 (0%)	52 (96%)
Psittacosis	13 (24%)	37 (69%)	4 (7%)
Q Fever	17 (31.5%)	20 (37%)	17 (31.5%)
Ricin Poisoning	5 (9%)	0 (0%)	49 (91%)
Salmonella	15 (28%)	39 (72%)	0 (0%)
Shigella	15 (28%)	39 (72%)	0 (0%)
Staphylococcal Enterotoxin B	8 (15%)	3 (5%)	43 (80%)
Toxic Syndromes	8 (15%)	30 (55%)	16 (30%)
Vibrio Cholerae	30 (56%)	11 (20%)	13 (24%)
Category C			
Hantavirus	25 (46%)	19 (35%)	10 (19%)
Typhus Fever	15 (28%)	19 (35%)	20 (37%)
Viral Encephalitis	20 (37%)	31 (57%)	3 (6%)

**Must be reported immediately or within 24 hours. **Must be reported either within a timeframe beyond 24 hours (i.e., within 48 hours, within 72 hours, or within 7 days) or within no specified timeframe. ***Law does not specifically provide that the particular disease must be reported.*

DISCUSSION

Disease reporting laws may not only serve as an educational tool in highlighting what diseases society considers of national importance, but may also provide incentives for health-care providers to obtain the training and skills to diagnose and respond to those diseases. This study yielded important information about the status (as of March 31, 2001) of laws mandating the reporting of specific diseases associated with bioterrorism.

Because such laws, however, may raise practical and legal concerns for the public, patient, and physician, further research may be required in the following areas:

- the administrative burden in reporting diseases;
- penalties for non-compliance with the law;
- privacy rights affected by disease; and
- procedures for effective implementation of disease reporting requirements.

Since the study's completion, and especially in response to the 2001 anthrax attacks, some jurisdictions may have revised their disease reporting laws to include critical biological agents. Nonetheless, considering the study's findings, jurisdictions that have not already done so may wish to review their disease reporting laws in light of bioterrorism concerns. If existing laws do not require the reporting of diseases caused by critical biological agents, states may choose to revise or expand their disease reporting requirements to include such bioterrorism-associated diseases. In particular, states may decide to require the immediate reporting of diseases caused by Category A critical biological agents because of the extreme risk to public health that these agents pose if used as a bioterrorist weapon.

States considering revising their disease reporting laws may find useful the draft Model State Emergency Health Powers Act, a legislative template developed in 2001 by the Center for Law and the Public's Health at Georgetown and Johns Hopkins Universities.[23] This draft model law, among other things, provides one example of a method to address which diseases or health conditions should be reported; who should be legally obligated to report; the manner and timeframe in which a disease should be reported; and the enforcement of disease reporting laws.[24]

Conclusion

The events of September 11 and the subsequent anthrax mailings have elevated protecting the public's health to the status of a national security issue. Thus, this study of laws mandating the reporting of specific diseases caused by critical biological agents may be considered one measurement of the nation's level of bioterrorism preparedness. In preparing the nation to respond to a potential bioterrorist event, disease reporting is a key element. Inadequate disease reporting requirements may lead to such harmful consequences as delayed recognition of a possible bioterrorism event, confusion over whether a particular disease is reportable, and an untimely and ineffective response to bioterrorism or other public health emergency. Accordingly, disease reporting laws are a crucial element in an overall plan for bioterrorism preparedness.

Acknowledgments

The authors would like to thank Jennifer Pritzker (Emory University School of Law) and Kristin Cunningham (Saint Louis University School of Law) for their important and thorough research of state disease reporting laws. The opinions and findings in this article are those of the authors and should not be construed as official policies or positions of the Office of the General Counsel for the U.S. Department of Health and Human Services.

References

1. J.A. Jernigan et al., "Bioterrorism-Related Inhalational Anthrax: The First 10 Cases Reported in the United States," *Emerging Infectious Diseases*, 7, no. 6 (2001), *available at* <http://www.cdc.gov/ncidod/eid/vol7no6/jernigan.htm>.

2. J. Tucker, *Toxic Terror: Assessing Terrorist Use of Chemical and Biological Weapons* (Cambridge: MIT Press, 2000): at 116–37.

3. Centers for Disease Control and Prevention, U.S. Department of Health and Human Services, *The Public Health Response to Biological and Chemical Terrorism, Interim Planning Guidance for State Public Health Officials* (July 2001), *available at* <http://www.bt.cdc.gov/Documents/Planning/PlanningGuidance.PDF>.

4. Centers for Disease Control and Prevention, U.S. Department of Health and Human Services, "Biological and Chemical Terrorism: Strategic Plan for Preparedness and Response," *Morbidity and Mortality Weekly Report, Recommendations and Reports*, 49, no. 4 (Apr. 21, 2000): 1–14, at 8.

5. *Id.* at 12–13.

6. The study did not specify *foodborne* botulism (as opposed to infant or non-foodborne botulism), but jurisdictions appear to have assumed, correctly, that the study was most interested in foodborne botulism since it is the type most associated with bioterrorism.

7. Although the study did not specify *E. coli* O157:H7, it appears that jurisdictions assumed, correctly, that the study was interested in the harmful *E. coli* O157:H7 and not in the benign varieties of *E. coli*.

8. Some jurisdictions assumed that "toxic syndromes" referred to toxic shock syndrome only, which is often reportable but not associated with bioterrorism. The survey attempted to gather information on the reporting requirements for toxic syndromes generally (e.g., Epsilon) associated with bioterrorism.

9. The study listed both cholera and *Vibrio cholerae*. *Vibrio cholerae* is the agent that causes the disease cholera. While the study intended that cholera and *Vibrio cholerae* be treated the same for disease-reporting purposes, some jurisdictions assumed that *Vibrio cholerae* represented vibrio infections generally, which are often not reportable.

10. L.D. Rotz et al., "Public Health Assessment of Potential Biological Terrorism Agent," *Emerging Infectious Diseases*, 8, no. 2 (2002), *available at* <http://www.cdc.gov/ncidod/eid/vol8no2/01-0164.htm>.

11. *Id.*

12. *Id.*

13. *Id.*

14. Centers for Disease Control and Prevention, *supra* note 4, at 6.

15. Tucker, *supra* note 2, at 181.

16. *Id.* at 115.

17. Centers for Disease Control and Prevention, *supra* note 4, at 6.

18. *Id.*

19. *Id.*

20. *Id.*

21. Centers for Disease Control and Prevention, U.S. Department of Health and Human Services, *National Bioterrorism Preparedness and Response Initiative*, *at* <http://www.bt.cdc.gov/documents/RegMeetingSlides/Overview.pdf> (updated May 8, 2000).

22. See, e.g., Conn. Gen. Stat. Ann. § 19a-215(e) (West 2001) ("Any person who violates any reporting … provision of this section shall be fined not more than five hundred dollars.").

23. Model State Emergency Health Powers Act (December 21, 2001), *available at* <http://www.publichealthlaw.net/MSEHPA/MSEHPA2.pdf>.

24. *Id.*

[7]

Bioterrorism Law and Policy: Critical Choices in Public Health

James G. Hodge, Jr.

There is perhaps no duty more fundamental to American government than the protection of the public's health, safety, and welfare.[1] On September 11, 2001, this governmental duty was severely tested through a series of terrorist acts. The destruction of the World Trade Towers in New York City and a portion of the Pentagon in Washington, D.C., presented many Americans with a new, visible reality of the potential harms that terrorists can cause. The staggering loss of lives (estimated from 2,600 to 2,900)[2] damaged the national psyche in ways far exceeding the physical scars to American institutions.

As horrific as the images of destruction and loss of human lives may be, events that unfolded after September 11 revealed another dreaded, and potentially more catastrophic, threat to Americans' sense of security and public health: *bioterrorism*. Unlike terrorists that use bombs, explosives, or other tools for mass destruction, a bioterrorist's weapon is an infectious agent. Bioterrorism involves the intentional use of an infectious agent (e.g., microorganism, virus, infectious substance, or biological product) to cause death or disease in humans or other organisms in order to negatively influence the conduct of government or intimidate a population.[3]

In the weeks that followed the terrorist attacks on September 11, public health and law enforcement officials discovered that some person or group had intentionally contaminated letters with potentially deadly anthrax spores. These letters were mailed to a variety of individuals in government and the media in three states and the District of Columbia. Dozens of persons that handled or received the tainted letters tested positive for anthrax exposure. To date, at least five persons have died. Many government officials predict the potential for additional bioterrorism attacks as the "war on terrorism" continues in Afghanistan and surrounding territories.

For state and local public health agencies that may find themselves on the frontline of defense to a bioterrorism event, prevention through preparation is essential.[4] Prior training exercises have demonstrated that preventing mass causalities or infections resulting from bioterrorism is difficult.[5] Public health authorities, medical practitioners, and hospitals[6] may lack the infrastructure,[7] resources, knowledge, or tools to effectively respond to mass exposure to diseases for which there are potentially inadequate detection[8] or tests,[9] no (or insufficient) vaccines, few treatments, or no cures. Prior to September 11, federal and state public health authorities had already allocated some resources and engaged in efforts to prevent a major bioterrorism event.[10] Congress authorized the spending of over $500 million in 2001 for bioterrorism preparedness through the Public Health Threats and Emergencies Act.[11] Additional commitments to improve surveillance of unusual diseases or clusters, train health-care workers, improve existing vaccination[12] and treatment supplies through increases of national stockpiles, and collaborate across jurisdictions are needed to improve the public health infrastructure.[13]

Public health authorities must also be legally empowered with the authority to respond to potential or actual bioterrorist threats.[14] Some states have legislatively (e.g., Colorado[15]) or administratively (e.g., Rhode Island[16]) developed public health response plans for a bioterrorism event. However, in many states, existing legal standards for response are absent, antiquated, or insufficient. Prior to September 11, many state health departments did not address bioterrorism in their emergency response plans.[17] Recently, public health lawyers and scholars at the Center for Law and the Public's Health at Georgetown and Johns Hopkins Universities were asked by the Centers for Disease Control and Prevention and a series of national partners (i.e., the National Governors Association, the National Conference of State Legislatures, the Association of State and Territorial Health Officials, the National Association of City and County Health Officers, the National Association of Attorneys General, and the Turning Point Public Health Statute Modernization National Collaborative) to develop a model act for states to respond to public health emergencies. The Model State Emergency Health Powers Act[18] gives state and local public health authorities a modern series of powers to track, prevent, and control disease threats resulting from bioterrorism or other public health emergencies. These powers include measures (e.g., isolation, quarantine, treatment, and vaccination requirements) that may temporarily compromise individual civil liberties (e.g., rights to due process, speech, assembly, travel, and privacy) to protect the public's health. To date, thirty-two states have introduced legislative bills based on the Model Act.[19]

Vesting state and local public health authorities with a modern series of public health powers is an important component of a national legal strategy to respond to bioterrorism events.[20] The Model Act, existing state laws, and other planning tools suggest the need for broad cooperation among all levels of government and the private sector. The consequences of a public health emergency, like many other emergencies, cannot be handled through the efforts of a single state or local agency. To ensure cooperation and better prepare for and respond to existing and future domestic bioterrorism attacks, federal, state, and local public health authorities must make a series of critical choices in law or policy based on the following questions:

- What is the extent of government's duty to protect the public's health in response to a bioterrorism event?
- When does a bioterrorism event justify the declaration of a "public health emergency"?
- What are the respective roles of federal, state, and local public health authorities?
- How should public health authorities coordinate with other governmental actors, specifically law enforcement authorities, to address criminal components of bioterrorism events?
- How can restrictive public health powers (e.g., isolation, quarantine, mandatory treatment, or vaccination) be balanced with individual civil liberties in responding to a public health emergency?
- How should scarce resources (e.g., vaccines, treatments, hospital beds, health-care personnel) be allocated during a public health emergency?

The section below presents an overview of the population-wide threats of bioterrorism to provide a context for addressing these questions. Making choices now about questions of governmental power, particularly from the perspective of state and local public health agencies that may be the nation's first source of detection, may improve coordination and accountability among the various levels and branches of governments in their efforts to prevent or respond to a future bioterrorism event.

Bioterrorism: Past and Present

Recent developments concerning the intentional spread of anthrax through the U.S. mails provide a modern example of bioterrorism activity in the United States. However, bioterrorism has long been a part of the nation's past. Numerous examples of attempted and actual bioterrorist activity (with varying degrees of success and impact) have been documented in American and world history. The Chemical and Biological Weapons Nonproliferation Project of the Monterrey Institute's Center for Nonproliferation Studies has catalogued more than 400 incidents of known bioterrorist activity worldwide between 1900 and 1999. In the United States, British and French troops exchanged dry goods intentionally contaminated with smallpox with Native American populations.[21] In 1972, several persons were arrested for possessing kilograms of Typhoid bacteria intended for the contamination of the water supply of several Midwestern cities.[22] In 1984, members of the Rajneeshee cult contaminated restaurant salad bars in Oregon with a form of salmonella, resulting in more than 700 cases of non-fatal food poisoning.[23] Each of the past several years, the Federal Bureau of Investigation (FBI) has investigated hundreds of claims of bioterrorism threats.

Historical accounts and modern risk assessments of bioterrorism activities provide the nation with some experience in handling future events. Public health and other authorities have also conducted numerous hypothetical and table-top exercises to better prepare for a modern bioterrorism event. The subject of many of these exercises became reality immediately following the tragedy of September 11. In late September, the media reported that an individual in a Florida office building was potentially exposed to anthrax, a biological agent that can be deadly when inhaled and left untreated. Within a month, numerous additional cases of exposure and infection were tracked by public health authorities in Connecticut, Florida, New York, Maryland, Nevada, New Jersey, and Washington, D.C. Law enforcement and public health officials determined that most exposures resulted from intentional efforts to spread the pathogen through contaminated letters delivered through the U.S. postal service. Some of the anthrax strains were the product of sophisticated manufacturing techniques designed to make the agent more virulent.[24]

Authorities quickly began warning the public through broadcasts and printed sources to be cautious about suspicious packages or powdery substances in the mail, although government warnings were mixed in their accuracy and tone.[25] Media coverage was dominated by images of people lining up for testing and health officials clad in plastic, biodefense suits collecting samples of anthrax from mailrooms, elevators, and trucks. Mail service in some places was suspended or significantly delayed. Federal institutions, including some members of Congress and the Supreme Court, were forced to temporarily relocate. At least five people died from exposure to anthrax. Dozens of others, including aids to prominent members of Congress and news anchors, tested positive.[26]

The anthrax attacks fueled apprehension among government officials[27] and the public about future bioterrorism attacks.[28] A recent national poll suggests that 70 percent of the public believes a subsequent biological or chemical attack on the United States will occur in the next year.[29] These fears of bioterrorism may be justified. A broad range of groups or individuals may have access to and use biological agents as weapons to inflict harm on a population-wide basis.[30] Multiple infectious agents, including genetically enhanced agents, may be used.[31] Diseases such as smallpox,[32] tularemia (a.k.a. rabbit fever),[33] plague,[34] and viral hemorrhagic fever may present far more serious dangers to the public's health than the non-contagious and largely treatable anthrax.

Bioterrorists may infect individuals through multiple routes: (1) intentional spread of contagious diseases through individual contact; (2) airborne dissemination of some infectious agents; or (3) contamination of water, food, controlled substances, or other widely distributed products. The equipment needed to manufacture biological weapons is easy to obtain and conceal. Prior doubts about the potential or ability for an individual or group to intentionally unleash these agents on an innocent population have been nullified by the brazenness of recent terrorist events.[35]

Bioterrorism and Public Health Law: The Critical Choices

Given the nation's current level of preparedness for bioterrorism, a large-scale bioterrorist attack would be unprecedented in its impact on morbidity and mortality in the U.S. population. The limited, intentional spread of anthrax has shown that public health (and other) authorities are not fully prepared to handle a large-scale bioterrorism event.[36] Preparing for a bioterrorism event should become a central mission of federal, state, and local public health, law enforcement, and emergency authorities. As part of this mission, the public health community, law- and policymakers, and society in general must address a series of critical choices.

Understanding the duty of government to protect the public health

Perhaps the most important choice is also the most difficult to make: What is the government's duty to protect the public health in response to a bioterrorism event? Few discount the responsibility of government to respond to a bioterrorism event, but what is the extent of this response? Consistent with the traditional police powers of state governments to protect the health, safety, and general welfare, government's duty to protect the public's health may be viewed as comprehensive and extensive.[37] This includes virtually any governmental action needed to control the threat in the population. Thus, to fulfill its responsibility to ensure the public's health, state public health authorities could (as they have in the past) temporarily constrain certain civil liberties, require private sector participation in public health objectives, shut down potentially harmful industries, destroy contaminated property, deport or prevent the entry of individuals who may infect others, ration supplies, and control the flow of information.

Do governmental duties to protect the public's health allow public health authorities to go further? Bioterrorism experts suggest that the intentional release of smallpox through just a few outlets could quickly spread the disease and leave hundreds of thousands of unvaccinated Americans dead in a few months.[38] At the apex of this type of human tragedy, can authorities temporarily ignore constitutional principles that respect individual liberties (e.g., rights to due process, travel, assembly, or privacy) or maintain the structure of government (e.g., federalism or separation of powers)? Concerning the latter powers, for example, can federal health authorities, who lack broad police powers, command state public health authorities to participate in a federal, national response to a bioterrorism event that is limited to one state (and thus not seen as an interstate matter or a threat to national security)? The federal government may lack the constitutional power to do this under existing interpretations of federal commerce powers consistent with principles of federalism.[39] Can we choose to ignore such legal interpretations to accomplish public health objectives? In reality, it is unlikely that any bioterrorism event, even one that it initially localized to one state, would be viewed solely as a state matter when it is highly predictable that the bioterrorism agent will spread to other states.

Declaring a public health emergency

Responding to a bioterrorism event may require public health authorities to exercise broader powers than they traditionally employ. Who should choose when to declare a public health emergency and under what criteria? Many state legislatures presently fail to specify whether a bioterrorism event may justify a state of emergency status, leaving this decision to executive authorities. Though state executive authorities need some discretion, statutory laws must better define the conditions for declaring public health emergencies. Otherwise, a state of emergency may be called unjustifiably.

The Model State Emergency Health Powers Act gives public health authorities the ability to exercise enhanced powers to protect individuals and manage property upon the declaration of a public health emergency by the state governor. The Model Act broadly defines a "public health emergency" as:

> an occurrence or imminent threat of an illness or health condition that: (1) is believed to be caused by bioterrorism or the appearance of a novel or previously controlled or eradicated infectious agent or biological toxin; and (2) poses a high probability of any of the following harms: (a) a large number of deaths in the affected population; (b) a large number of incidents of serious permanent or long-term disability in the affected population; or (c) widespread exposure to an infectious or toxic agent that poses a significant risk of substantial future harm to a large number of people in the affected population.[40]

Thus, under this definition, the declaration of a public health emergency may follow (1) the occurrence or imminent threat of an illness or health condition, (2) caused by bioterrorism or the appearance of novel or previously controlled diseases through any means, (3) that poses a high probability of a significant number of current or future deaths or disabilities. These criteria serve as guides, but may allow for the declaration of a public health emergency for bioterrorism events that do not justify restrictive public health controls. Consider, for example, the definition of "bioterrorism" used in the Model Act:

> the intentional use of any microorganism, virus, infectious substance, or biological product that may be engineered as a result of biotechnology, or any naturally occurring or bioengineered component of any such microorganism, virus, infectious substance, or biological product, to cause death, disease, or other biological malfunction in a human, an animal, a plant, or another living organism in order to influence the conduct of government or to intimidate or coerce a civilian population.[41]

On its face, this definition might include the actions of persons who have recently attempted to infect others with anthrax through the mail. This may be unlikely, however, because their actions may not pose "a high probability" of a large number of human deaths or incidents of serious permanent or long-term disability, as defined under "public health emergency." From a public health perspective, this limited interpretation of the criteria for declaring a public health emergency may be preferable. It would be unwise to declare a public health emergency for an event that involves an infectious agent, but does not otherwise pose a significant risk to the public's health.

Consider, for example, an individual with HIV who intentionally tries to spread the virus to dozens of others through his own risky behavior (e.g., unprotected sex, unsafe sharing of needles for injecting drugs). Numerous individuals have attempted to intentionally infect others with HIV in documented cases across the United States.[42] Their activities probably were not motivated by an intent to "influence the conduct of government." Yet, depending on how a governor, or a court reviewing the governor's authority, may define what it means to "intimidate" or "coerce," or what constitutes a "population" (is it the population of a state, a county, a city, or a neighborhood?), the individual with HIV may be said to be engaging in bioterrorism. Depending on whether there is a high probability of a large number of human deaths or disabilities as a result, a governor could declare a state of public health emergency pursuant to the Model Act. This is problematic because (1) public health and law enforcement authorities have not traditionally viewed such persons as bioterrorists, but rather as mere criminals; and (2) declaring a public health emergency in these cases is an extreme response to a limited public health threat.

Additional refinement of the criteria for responding to a bioterrorism event through the declaration of a public health emergency is important where infringements of civil liberties and the legitimacy of public health activities are at stake. The criteria may be strengthened by employing more restrictive measures during a public health emergency depending on the severity of the disease threat.

Defining the roles of federal, state, and local public health authorities

There is no central public health system in the United States. Instead, a collaborative workforce of federal, state, and local authorities work in conjunction with other inter-level agencies (e.g., environmental protection agencies; departments of housing, labor, or civil rights) to accomplish public health outcomes. In this system, public health roles and responsibilities of the federal, state, and local levels of government are complex and unclear. As stated above, state public health authorities act pursuant to broad police powers that authorize the government to act in the interests of protecting or promoting the health, safety, or general welfare of the population. Some public health functions are delegated by states to local governments. A federal agency's power to act in the interest of public health is, comparably, more limited in the use of authorized powers. It must rely on its delegated authority pursuant to Congress's powers to protect national security, regulate interstate commerce, tax and spend, or promote the constitutional principles of the Fourteenth Amendment (e.g., due process, equal protection).[43]

A large-scale bioterrorism event will accentuate existing uncertainties in the distribution of public health powers.[44] It may also prove to be a catalyst for redefining roles for the future. The critical choice for public health authorities is not to decide where the power to protect the public health lies or which level of government has the primary power to act, but rather where the leadership to respond to a bioterrorism event will derive. If leadership capacity is properly developed, public health authorities can use their respective powers to bring about desired goals.

Through agencies such as the Department of Health and Human Services (DHHS), its subsidiary Centers for Disease Control and Prevention (CDC), and the newly created Office of Homeland Security, the federal government has taken a leadership role in response to existing and future bioterrorism threats.[45] There are many reasons state and local public health authorities might defer to this leadership initiative. First, the federal government has greater financial resources at its disposal to respond to a bioterrorism threat.[46] Second, it may be in a better position to negotiate the price of needed vaccines, drugs, or supplies, or to suspend the patent rights of high-demand medications. These techniques were recently used by President George Bush and DHHS in negotiations with the German drug company Bayer, concerning the sale of Cipro, the antibiotic used to treat anthrax.[47] Third, most significant bioterrorism threats will exceed the boundaries of any single state, thus requiring a national, coordinated response. Fourth, the federal government may be better able to rapidly develop personnel and institutional expertise in monitoring and identifying the existence of new or emerging infectious pathogens. Fifth, bioterrorism may also constitute a threat to national security (the protection of which is specifically a federal responsibility).[48] Finally, imminent warnings of bioterrorism activity may come through national intelligence or federal law enforcement agencies that can coordinate public health responses through federal agencies.

Choosing to assign a primary leadership role to the federal government for responding to bioterrorism threats does have its drawbacks. Federal public health authorities may be slowed by inter-organizational or bureaucratic problems.[49] As well, they are not well-positioned to serve on the frontline of defense to a bioterrorist attack. State and local public health authorities, in conjunction with private sector healthcare workers, will in most cases be the first to detect potential bioterrorism activity through effective surveillance. Federal authorities may facilitate detection by sharing resources or intelligence data. However, detection of a potential bioterrorism threat through state and local public health authorities is distinct from the response functions of the federal government. Clarifying these roles will improve response capabilities and public accountability over time.

Investigating bioterrorism from the public health or criminal perspectives

Beyond setting roles and responsibilities among the various levels of government is the need for public health authorities to choose how to coordinate with law enforcement and national security authorities. Unlike the spread of naturally occurring diseases that can be monitored and controlled exclusively through public health authorities, a bioterrorism event always features an unlawful element. Bioterrorism, by definition, is the product of criminal activity. Existing and newly passed federal antiterrorism laws, for example, criminalize the mere possession of certain biological agents.[50] Every bioterrorism event thus involves a criminal investigation that is outside the purview of public health authorities. How should public health and criminal authorities choose to collaborate? Should they collaborate at all?

From either side's perspective, clearly they should collaborate. Public health and criminal authorities need to know of potential or actual health threats to the population in order to take steps to prevent or mitigate threats. Each can learn from the other about these threats without jeopardizing their differing central missions, provided that the exchange of information is confidential, accomplished through high-ranking personnel, and consistent with existing federal intelligence laws and federal or state privacy laws that may limit the sharing of some data.

Second, after a bioterrorism event has materialized, should public health authorities assist criminal investigators at the federal, state, or local level? Prevailing public health practice suggests they should not. Public health authorities resist participating in criminal investigations primarily because there is the potential that public health authorities could be seen by community members as health police. Yet, prevailing public health practice does not typically involve the spread of disease through criminal activity. In some cases where criminal activity has been at the source of potential infection (e.g., intentional spread of HIV, intentional contamination or pollution of air or water), public health authorities have worked with criminal investigators in limited ways to stymie a public health threat.[51] Bioterrorism events may justify a greater working relationship between criminal and public health authorities that the public may not only understand, but support.

If public health and criminal authorities must work in collaboration to control a bioterrorism event, who takes primary jurisdiction over an investigation, given an outbreak? In many of the places where anthrax exposures recently occurred, criminal authorities quickly asserted their jurisdiction over exposure sites to gather evidence and any other facts needed for their investigations. The potential for public health and criminal authorities to clash in executing their responsibilities is evident, especially where the primary criminal or intelligence authorities may be federal (e.g., the FBI, the Central Intelligence Agency), and the responding public health officials are primarily state or local. The only choice for public health officials in these circumstances may be to defer to law enforcement or intelligence authorities for a period of time as the investigation proceeds, but to encourage collaborative sharing of data to allow both sets of authorities to accomplish their respective goals.

Restricting individuals for the sake of public health

During a bioterrorism attack that involves the potential for mass casualties or disabilities, public health authorities may need to employ powers that restrict individual activities and behaviors. The Model Act, for example, allows public health authorities to quarantine or isolate persons believed to be exposed to or infected with a contagious disease during a public health emergency.[52] In addition, authorities can encourage persons to be vaccinated or treated where necessary to prevent the spread of a contagious disease. Persons who refuse to be vaccinated or treated may, if needed, be quarantined or isolated.[53]

Such measures have traditionally been used by public health authorities to control the spread of contagious disease. Few question their potential value in accomplishing the same, despite their potential to infringe on human rights. The critical choice for public health authorities during a bioterrorism emergency is how to balance these restrictive measures with civil liberties.[54] There may be strong legislative and public support for the use of highly restrictive powers during a bioterrorism crisis. Yet, constitutional principles and public health practices emphasizing an ethic of voluntarism intimate that not every restrictive measure can be taken. Professor Lawrence O. Gostin has summarized the modern constitutional criteria for exercising confining public health powers:[55]

- *A compelling state interest in confinement.* Public health authorities must have a compelling interest that is substantially furthered by civil confinement. Only persons who are truly dangerous (i.e., pose a significant risk of transmission) can be confined.
- *A "well-targeted" intervention.* Interventions that confine individuals must be well-targeted to accomplishing public health objectives. Thus, interventions that are over- or underinclusive may be constitutionally impermissible if they deprive individuals of liberty or equal protection without justification. For example, the quarantine of every person within a geographic area is overinclusive if some members would not transmit infection. Underinclusive interventions would restrain some, but not all, potentially contagious persons, and thus be open to criticisms of being arbitrary or purposefully discriminatory.
- *The least restrictive alternative.* Public health authorities should not resort to civil confinement if they can achieve their objectives through less drastic means (although it is not likely that they have to use extreme or unduly expensive means to avoid confinement).
- *Procedural due process.* Persons subject to confinement for public health purposes are entitled to some form of procedural due process depending on the nature and duration of the restraint. The Model Act requires a court order prior to the isolation or quarantine of any individual, unless emergency circumstances demand otherwise. In all cases, individuals have the right to a hearing and counsel to contest their confinement.[56]

Allocating scarce resources

In virtually any widespread and rapidly developing bioterrorism event, available public health resources will quickly be taxed. Scarce resources may include physical goods (e.g., vaccines, medical treatments and supplies, hospital beds, isolation or quarantine facilities), personnel (e.g., physicians, nurses, other health-care workers, epidemiologists, lab technicians), and services (e.g., laboratory testing, mental health counseling). Attempts to hoard existing supplies or personnel by competing governmental units or private sector groups may be expected. The private sector may be disinclined to donate its facilities for public health goals, or participate in the vaccination, treatment, or confinement of exposed or infected individuals. Concerning these issues, the Model Act allows state executive authorities to confiscate hoarded supplies, take possession of facilities or other property for public health purposes, and seek the assistance of medical personnel during a public health emergency.

A critical and unresolved choice for public health authorities is how to allocate scarce resources. There is no uniform, central proposal governing the distribution of limited resources during a public health emergency. In fact, such a proposal may be ill-advised. Public health authorities may need the discretion, depending on the circumstances of the specific bioterrorism event, to decide how best to allocate limited resources. *Ad hoc* allocation decisions, of course, leave open the possibility of egregious, unfair, or discriminatory distributions of limited resources. Is it predictable that: (1) wealthier individuals (or nations) will have access to potentially life-saving treatments over persons of lesser wealth; (2) persons in the military will be vaccinated before civilians; or (3) public health investigators will attend to health threats to legislators over other governmental workers?[57] Each of these choices, which are based on actual decisions made during the recent anthrax exposures in the United States, may be supported or contested on various legal, political, and ethical grounds.

Public health and other governmental authorities must be guided by a fair set of principles in making their allocation decisions. These principles include:

- *Promoting the public's health.* Any decision relating to allocating scarce resources during a public health emergency should be principally motivated by the need to promote the public's health to the highest extent possible, and not by outside political or social pressures.

- *Providing incentives to help.* To provide incentives to individuals to participate in public health efforts, certain resources may be allocated to protect the health of public health personnel or health-care workers (and their families) working to control the spread of disease or treat infected individuals.
- *Respecting each individual.* Distribution of limited resources may naturally tend to favor persons in government or those with sufficient wealth or stature in the community. Public health authorities need to determine a method of distributing resources evenly across at-risk populations to protect the public's health. Specific care should be taken to avoid making decisions that discriminate against equally situated individuals.
- *Prioritizing immediacy over potential.* The distribution of limited vaccines or treatments should be made with consideration of the immediate health consequences to affected populations rather than the potential impact on unaffected groups. Thus, for example, if a particular group of individuals living in one county of a state is presently susceptible to smallpox infection due to a localized outbreak, those persons should be vaccinated to the exclusion of other state residents who may be vulnerable in the future, provided such vaccinations are consistent with controlling the epidemic.

These principles will not resolve every difficult question, but they may provide some guidance as public health authorities struggle to decide how to allocate dwindling resources during an emergency.

Conclusion

Bioterrorism is a catalyst for change in public health practice. Preparing for existing and future bioterrorism events in the United States requires federal, state, and local public health authorities to collaborate in new ways with law enforcement, intelligence, and emergency personnel to strengthen the existing public health infrastructure. Working to improve public health detection, prevention, and response capabilities requires effective training, additional resources, use of existing and new technologies, and public health law reform. These and other tools for responding to existing and future bioterrorism events call for public health authorities, law- and policymakers, and society to make a series of critical choices.

The duty of government to protect the public's health must be understood within political, legal, and realistic limits. A central legal objective of the Model State Emergency Health Powers Act is to better define the criteria, powers, roles, and limits of governmental actions during a public health emergency. The leadership roles of federal, state, and local public health authorities must be distinguished between detection and response. Public health and law enforcement authorities need to share information and resources in the interest of protecting the public. Civil liberties must be respected, when possible, in the exercise of restrictive state public health powers. And limited resources must be allocated fairly according to a pre-determined set of principles. Addressing these critical choices may facilitate government's ability to effectively protect the public's health during the next, inevitable bioterrorism event.

References

1. L.O. Gostin, *Public Health Law: Power, Duty, Restraint* (Berkeley: University of California Press, 2000): at 16.

2. E. Lipton, "Hard to Figure: A Difference in the Numbers," *New York Times*, October 25, 2001, at B1.

3. Model State Emergency Health Powers Act § 1-104(a) (December 21, 2001), *available at* <http://www.publichealthlaw.net/MSEHPA/MSEHPA2.pdf>. The Act can also be found on pages 324–348 of this issue.

4. D.E. Shalala, "Bioterrorism: How Prepared Are We?," *Emerging Infectious Diseases*, 5, no. 4 (1999): 492–93, *available at* <http://www.cdc.gov/ncidod/EID/vol5no4/shalala.htm>.

5. T. Inglesby, R. Grossman, and T. O'Toole, "A Plague on Your City: Observations from TOPOFF," *Biodefense Quarterly*, 2 (2000): 1–10.

6. M. Freudenheim, "Few Hospitals Are Ready for a Surge of Bioterror Victims," *New York Times*, October 26, 2001, at B8.

7. S. Khan and D.A. Ashford, "Ready or Not — Preparedness for Bioterrorism," *N. Engl. J. Med.*, 345 (2001): 287–89.

8. D.E. Rosenbaum and S.G. Stolberg, "New Battlefield: Questions on Adequacy of Health System and Public Protection," *New York Times*, October 23, 2001, at A1.

9. R. Weiss, "Anthrax Testing Shaky," *Pittsburgh Post-Gazette*, October 16, 2001, at A4.

10. J. Fialka et al., "Are We Prepared for the Unthinkable?," *Wall Street Journal*, September 18, 2001, at B1.

11. Public Health Threats and Emergencies Act, Pub. L. No. 106-505, 114 Stat. 2314 (2000).

12. J. Miller and S.G. Stolberg, "Sept. 11 Attacks Led to Push for More Smallpox Vaccine," *New York Times*, October 22, 2001, at A1.

13. Shalala, *supra* note 4.

14. D.P. Fidler, "Legal Issues Surrounding Public Health Emergencies." Paper presented at the *Second Annual Symposium on Medical and Public Health Response to Bioterrorism*, Baltimore, November 28–29, 2000.

15. Colo. Rev. Stat. Ann. § 24-32-2103 (West 2001).

16. T. Bertrand et al., *The Emergence of Bioterrorism as a Public Health Concern in the 21st Century: Epidemiology and Surveillance, at* <http://www.healthri.org/environment/biot/article.htm> (last updated October 15, 2001).

17. Khan and Ashford, *supra* note 7.

18. Model State Emergency Health Powers Act (December 21, 2001).

19. These thirty-two states are Arizona, California, Connecticut, Delaware, Florida, Georgia, Hawaii, Idaho, Illinois, Kansas, Kentucky, Maine, Maryland, Massachusetts, Minnesota, Mississippi, Missouri, Nebraska, New Hampshire, New Jersey, New Mexico, New York, Oklahoma, Pennsylvania, Rhode Island, South

Dakota, Tennessee, Utah, Vermont, Washington, Wisconsin, and Wyoming. Center for Law and the Public's Health, *Model State Emergency Health Powers Act State Legislative Activity* (April 8, 2002), *available at* <http://www.publichealthlaw.net/MSEHPA/MSEHPA_Legis_Act.pdf>.

20. B. Kellman, "Biological Terrorism: Legal Measures for Preventing Catastrophe," *Harvard Journal of Law and Public Policy*, 24 (2001): 417–88.

21. R.S. Root-Bernstein, "Infectious Terrorism," *The Atlantic Monthly*, 267 (1991): 44–50.

22. Y. Alexander, "Terrorism in the Twenty-First Century: Threats and Responses," *DePaul Business Law Journal*, 12 (2000): 59–81.

23. J.B. Tucker, "Historical Trends Related to Bioterrorism: An Empirical Analysis," *Emerging Infectious Diseases*, 5, no. 4 (1999): 498–504, at 503, *available at* <http://www.cdc.gov/ncidod/eid/vol5no4/tucker.htm>.

24. C. Haberman, "New Legal Powers, Fresh Anthrax Worries, Resilient Taliban," *New York Times*, October 26, 2001, at B1.

25. J. Miller and S.G. Stolberg, "Wider Anthrax Monitoring; U.S. Officials Acknowledge Underestimating Mail Risks," *New York Times*, October 25, 2001, at A1.

26. J. Lancaster and S. Schmidt, "31 Exposed to Anthrax on Capitol Hill," *Washington Post*, October 18, 2001, at A1.

27. Fialka et al., *supra* note 10.

28. L. Parker, T. Watson, and K. Johnson, "Anthrax Incidents Create Growing Sense of Anxiety," *USA Today*, October 15, 2001, at A1.

29. "Snapshot," *USA Today*, October 25, 2001, at 1A.

30. M.G. Kortepeter and G.W. Parker, "Potential Biological Weapons Threats," *Emerging Infectious Diseases*, 5 (1999): 523–27.

31. *Id.*

32. D.A. Henderson, "Smallpox: Clinical and Epidemiologic Features," *Emerging Infectious Diseases*, 5, no. 4 (1999): 537–39, *available at* <http://www.cdc.gov/ncidod/EID/vol5no4/henderson.htm>.

33. D.T. Dennis et al., "Tularemia as a Biological Weapon," *JAMA*, 285 (2001): 2763–73.

34. T. Inglesby et al., "Plague as a Biological Weapon," *JAMA*, 283 (2000): 2281–90.

35. Fialka et al., *supra* note 10.

36. L.K. Altman, "On Many Fronts, Experts Plan for the Unthinkable: Biowarfare," *New York Times*, October 23, 2001, at D4.

37. J.G. Hodge, "The Role of New Federalism and Public Health Law," *Journal of Law & Health*, 12 (1998): 309–57.

38. "Dark Winter," available online at <http://www.homelandsecurity.org/darkwinter/index.cfm>.

39. Hodge, *supra* note 37.

40. Model State Emergency Health Powers Act § 1-104(m) (December 21, 2001).

41. *Id.* § 1-104(a).

42. J.G. Hodge and L.O. Gostin, "Handling Cases of Willful Exposure Through HIV Partner Counseling and Referral Services," *Rutger's Women's Rights Law Reporter*, 22 (forthcoming 2002).

43. Gostin, *supra* note 1, at 34–46.

44. Letter from John J. Hamre, president and chief executive officer of the Center for Strategic and International Studies, dated July 26, 2001 (referring to findings from "Dark Winter" exercise in June, 2001).

45. Shalala, *supra* note 4.

46. C. Connolly and S. Gray, "Thompson Seeks $1.2 Billion to Expand Stockpile of Drugs," *Washington Post*, October 18, 2001, at A19.

47. E.L. Andrews, "Bayer Is a Bit Taken Aback by the Frenzy to Get Its Drug," *New York Times*, October 26, 2001, at B8.

48. V. Sutton, "Bioterrorism Preparation and Response Legislation — The Struggle to Protect States' Sovereignty While Preserving National Security," *Georgetown Public Policy Review*, 6 (2001): 92–103.

49. J. Lancaster and S. Schmidt, "31 Exposed to Anthrax on Capitol Hill," *Washington Post*, October 18, 2001, at A1.

50. R. Willing, "Anti-Terror Bill Extends Government's Reach," *USA Today*, October 25, 2001, at 7A.

51. Hodge and Gostin, *supra* note 42.

52. Model State Emergency Health Powers Act § 604 (December 21, 2001).

53. *Id.* § 603.

54. *Jacobson v. Massachusetts*, 197 U.S. 11 (1905).

55. Gostin, *supra* note 1, at 213–16.

56. Model State Emergency Health Powers Act § 604 (December 21, 2001).

57. Rosenbaum and Stolberg, *supra* note 8.

[8]

BLINDED BY BIOTERRORISM: PUBLIC HEALTH AND LIBERTY IN THE 21ST CENTURY

George J. Annas†

Ah yes, the quarantine, it didn't do any good.

José Saramago, Blindness

In *Blindness*, Nobel Prize laureate José Saramago chronicles the quarantining of the first victims of a plague of blindness.[1] We meet many people who become blind in Saramago's novel, including an opthamologist, a one-eyed man with an eye patch, and a man born blind. Saramago reminds us that we are all blind in one way or another, and that there are many things about ourselves and our society that we can't or won't see. The quarantine itself turns out to be isolating, inhumane, and degrading; the interred blind being portrayed by themselves and others as pigs, dogs, and "lame crabs." Soldiers stand guard, and shoot anyone trying to escape, mostly out of fear that they themselves might become infected by the blindness virus.

Of course many Americans were temporarily blinded on September 11 by the smoke and debris in the terror attacks on the World Trade Center and the Pentagon. And even after the smoke cleared, fear and anger fueled a desire for revenge and a quest for security. The security quest seemed even more urgent following the anthrax attacks through the mail. Fear generated responses that in retrospect appear overzealous, potentially counterproductive, and unnecessarily destructive of human rights. This is easier to see after almost two years have elapsed since 9/11, especially in the area of bioterrorism.

---

† George J. Annas is the Edward R. Utley Professor and Chair of the Health Law Department, Boston University School of Public Health, Professor of Socio-Medical Sciences and Community Medicine, Boston University School of Medicine, Professor of Law, Boston University School of Law, and cofounder of Global Lawyers and Physicians. A.B., Harvard College (1967); J.D., Harvard Law School (1970); M.P.H., Harvard School of Public Health (1972).

[1] José Saramago, Blindness (Giovanni Pontiero trans., Harcourt Brace & Co., 1998) (1995).

In this article I examine two specific public health responses to 9/11, the treatment of those exposed in the anthrax by mail attacks, and the proposal for new state antibioterrorism legislation. I suggest that our "new kind of war" on terror requires us to abandon our 19th century vision of public health as essentially a coercion-based state and local activity, and to accept the fact that in the 21st century public health is properly and primarily a national and international activity that should be based on human rights. It is simply not true that we must always sacrifice individual rights and liberty to take effective public health action against contagious diseases: modern public health measures must put human rights first to be effective. Finally, I will briefly examine the severe acute respiratory syndrome (SARS) epidemic of 2003 and the attempt to vaccinate some health care providers against smallpox as of way of testing the reasonableness of the conclusions drawn from our experiences with anthrax and state anti-bioterrorism legislation as they relate to modern public health.

I. THE ANTHRAX ATTACKS

In emergency situations, including war, bioterrorism, and epidemics, all sorts of decisions may be made and justified in a free society that would in normal circumstances be seen as repulsive and contrary to the constitutional foundations of the society itself. Immediately after September 11, for example, the civil liberties of suspected terrorists were suspended, secret military tribunals were proposed to try terrorists, and torture was proposed to obtain information from terrorists.[2] Although we have a tendency to opt for safety over liberty, this is often a false choice that produces neither.[3] In this regard the public health reaction to America's first major bioterrorist attack involving

[2] *See, e.g.*, *President Bush's Order on the Trial of Terrorists by Military Commission*, N.Y. TIMES, Nov. 14, 2001, at B8 (authorizing secretive military tribunals); Elisabeth Bumiller & David Johnston, *Bush Sets Option of Military Trials in Terrorist Cases*, N.Y. TIMES, Nov. 14, 2001, at Al (indicating the creation of military tribunals & the loss of rights); Robin Toner, *Civil Liberty vs. Security: Finding a Wartime Balance*, N.Y. TIMES, Nov. 18, 2001, at Al (discussing reduced civil liberties and the creation of military tribunals as a result of the September 11, 2001 attacks); Alan M. Dershowitz, *Yes, It Should be "On the Books,"* BOSTON GLOBE, Feb. 16, 2002, at A15 (expressing his opinion against torture without legislative and judicial approval); Jeffrey Rosen, *The Difficult Balance Between Liberty and Security*, N.Y. TIMES, Oct. 6, 2002, § 4 (Late Edition), at 13 (discussing the constitutionality of laws enacted after September 11, 2001 that allow investigation of all Americans).

[3] *See, e.g.*, BENJAMIN FRANKLIN, AN HISTORICAL REVIEW OF THE CONSTITUTION AND GOVERNMENT OF PENNSYLVANIA (1759) (containing the oft-quoted statement: "Those who exchange liberty for security deserve neither").

multiple locations in the United States, which used anthrax delivered through the mail, holds lessons for emergencies.[4]

Twenty-two people developed anthrax (about half inhalation and half cutaneous) from the attacks, and five died.[5] More than 10,000 people were advised to take antibiotics on the presumption that they were at risk for inhalation anthrax.[6] In late December, the Food and Drug Administration (FDA), the Department of Defense (DOD), and the Centers for Disease Control and Prevention (CDC) together released the anthrax vaccine, previously only available to the military, and approved by the FDA only to prevent cutaneous anthrax, for use by those exposed to anthrax in the attacks.[7] Of the 10,000 people eligible to take the vaccine, only 152 did.[8] In the face of continuing high anxiety about the possible health effects of anthrax exposure, this less than 2 percent positive response to the federal government's invitation to take the vaccine is extraordinary. CDC officials wanted to know why so few chose to take the vaccine, but reportedly decided not to survey them to find out why they refused to consent to take this investigational vaccine because the survey itself would have necessitated obtaining consent.[9]

We can take some comfort in the small number of casualties in the anthrax attacks. Nonetheless, the anthrax bioterrorist was extremely effective in meeting his or her goal: not mass killing (the goal in biowarfare), but terrorizing the civilian population. Since we cannot be sure that similar attacks will not occur in the future, it is impor-

[4] Julie Louise Gerberding et al., *Bioterrorism Preparedness and Response: Clinicians and Public Health Agencies as Essential Partners*, 287 JAMA 898, 898 (2002).

[5] *Id.*

[6] *Id.*

[7] *See Thomas* V. Inglesby et. al., *Anthrax as a Biological Weapon, 2002: Updated Recommendations for Management*, 287 JAMA 2236, 2243-44 (2002) (discussing the history, benefits, and limitations of the anthrax vaccine).

[8] *See* Steve Twomey, *Vaccine Offer Draws Few Postal Workers*, WASH. POST, Dec. 28, 2001, at A6 (detailing the limited acceptance of the vaccine offer); *see also* Sheryl Gay Stolberg, *Civilians Are Reluctant to Join U.S. Test of Anthrax Vaccine*, N.Y. TIMES, Jan. 8, 2002 at A13 (confirming that less than two percent of the 10,000 workers received the vaccine); Gerberding et al., *supra* note 4 at 899.

[9] *See* Stolberg, *supra* note 8 (noting the irony of a consent requirement for a survey of why individuals chose not to receive the vaccine). *See also* Lawrence Altman & Gina Kolata, *Anthrax Missteps Offer Guide to Fight Next Bioterror Battle*, N.Y. TIMES, Jan. 6, 2002, at A1 (suggesting the steps to be taken in the event of another bioterror attack). It was later learned that only 44% of those exposed who were told to take antibiotics for 60 days actually did. Approximately 13% took no medication at all. Lawrence K. Altman, *Many Workers Ignored Anthrax Pill Regimen*, N.Y. TIMES, Oct. 30, 2002, at A18.

tant to understand the belated response of the federal government in making the anthrax vaccine available, and why the public rejected its use, in order to be better prepared for the next bioterrorist attack or similar public health emergency. The basic rules regarding the use of investigational drugs in biowarfare, and arguably in bioterrorism, go back to the 1991 Gulf War.

II. INVESTIGATIONAL DRUGS IN WAR AND BIOWAR

Just prior to the Gulf War, the Pentagon sought an FDA waiver of informed consent requirements for the use of specific investigational drugs and vaccines on U.S. troops in the Gulf.[10] Informed consent is, of course, required for all human experiments, including the use of investigational drugs and vaccines. Specifically, the DOD sought waivers of informed consent under FDA rules so DOD could use an investigational drug (pyridostigmine bromide to be used as a pre-treatment against an attack by the nerve gas soman), and an investigational vaccine (botulinum toxoid, a protective against clostridium botulinum) without obtaining informed consent from the soldiers.[11]

There is provision in the FDA regulations for waiver of informed consent when consent is not "feasible," but this exception had never before been applied to competent adults. The basis of the DOD waiver request was that informed consent was not feasible because the military mission could be compromised if individual soldiers could opt out of taking these agents.[12] The FDA adopted a new regulation permitting waiver of consent for military operations, and approved the requested waivers under the provisions of the new regulation.[13] The FDA did, however, require the military to make information sheets on the agents available to the troops, and to collect, review and report on adverse experiences.[14]

Because it was an approved drug, the military use of pyridostigmine bromide as a "pretreatment" for a gas attack could have alternatively been justified as use of an approved drug for an unapproved indication based on the argument that it was a safe drug, even if not

---

[10] For a more detailed discussion of the Gulf War waiver, see George J. Annas, *Protecting Soldiers from Friendly Fire: The Consent Requirement for Using Investigational Drugs and Vaccines in Combat*, 24 AM. J.L. & MED. 245 (1998).

[11] *Id.* at 247.

[12] 21 C.F.R. § 50.23 (1999).

[13] *Id.*

[14] Human Drugs and Biologics; Determination that Informed Consent is NOT Feasible or is Contrary to the Best Interests of Recipients; Revocation of 1990 Interim Final Rule; Establishment of New Interim Final Rule, 64 Fed. Reg. 54,180, 54,184 et. seq. (Oct. 5, 1999).

proven effective for this particular use.[15] Moreover, the military command ultimately decided to make botulinum toxoid vaccination voluntary.[16] Nonetheless, the FDA's 1990 waiver-of-consent rule itself cannot be justified on the facts. Obtaining consent was feasible in the field, and failure to obtain it in the case of investigational drugs and vaccines is a direct violation of the consent requirements of the Nuremberg Code that the military had adopted as their own in 1953.[17] The FDA policy also turned out to be counterproductive and dangerous. It led to a situation in which the troops were put in much more jeopardy by taking pyridostigmine bromide than they would have been by not taking it. This is because while the drug may protect against soman, the agent US intelligence thought Iraq had, the nerve gas the Iraqis were actually prepared to use was sarin – and pyridostigmine can make sarin more deadly to humans.[18]

Although the FDA and DOD defended their waiver of consent actions after the Gulf War, almost no one else did. Ultimately, Congress passed a law that repealed the FDA's military combat exception to informed consent, and put sole power to grant any future wartime exception to informed consent in the hands of the president.[19] The new law provides that only the president can authorize the military to use an unapproved or investigational drug or vaccine in wartime without consent, and to do so the president must find, in writing, that obtaining consent is not feasible, is contrary to the best interests of the military, or is not in the interests of national security.[20] The FDA has also adopted regulations to help the president and his advisers make this decision.[21]

A more basic question regarding drugs and vaccines designed for emergency use in events like biowarfare and bioterrorism remains, however: Assuming that it is impossible to ethically test the efficacy

---

[15] Annas, *supra* note 10, at 250. The use of other drugs during the first Gulf War was apparently justified on this basis.

[16] *Supra* note 14.

[17] C.E. WILSON, MEMORANDUM FOR THE SECRETARY OF THE ARMY, SECRETARY OF THE NAVY, SECRETARY OF THE AIR FORCE (Feb. 26, 1953), *reprinted in* THE NAZI DOCTORS AND THE NUREMBERG CODE: HUMAN RIGHTS IN HUMAN EXPERIMENTATION, 343-45 (George J. Annas & Michael A. Grodin eds., Oxford Univ. Press, 1992).

[18] Robert W. Haley & Thomas L. Kurt, *Self-reported Exposure to Neurotoxic Chemical Combinations in the Gulf War*, 277 JAMA 231, 232 (1997); I Koplovitz et al., *Reduction by Pyridostigmine Pretreatment of the Efficacy of Atropine and 2-PAM Treatment of Sarin and VX Poisoning in Rodents*, 18 FUNDAMENTAL & APPLIED TOXICOLOGY 102, 103-105 (1992).

[19] 10 U.S.C. § 1107(f) (2000).

[20] *Id.*

[21] *Supra* note 14.

of a drug or vaccine designed for a bioterrorist or biowarfare agent (because it would be unethical to expose human volunteers to a potentially lethal agent), should there be an alternative way for the FDA to approve such agents for use in a war or other national emergency?

In 1999 the FDA proposed a set of new rules to permit the approval of such agents upon demonstration of safety in human subjects, and efficacy in appropriate multiple animal studies, and these rules were finalized in mid-2002.[22] Using multiple animal models for efficacy testing seems reasonable in this context, since the FDA is right to conclude it would be unethical to expose human subjects to toxins which could be lethal to them (this would, for example, violate another provision of the Nuremberg Code). But the ethical rule requiring the informed consent of competent adults before they are subjected to drugs or vaccines that have not been demonstrated effective in human populations is equally applicable. No soldier or civilian should be required to take any such drug or vaccine (which would be offered on the basis that it could be effective) where the only scientific support for efficacy is the result of animal studies.

III. INFORMED CONSENT TO THE ANTHRAX VACCINE

Anthrax vaccine has been approved for use to prevent cutaneous anthrax and was mandatorily given to the troops in the Gulf War on the basis that it was an approved agent that could be given for an unapproved but closely-related use (inhalation anthrax).[23] This vaccine was developed in 1970. After the Gulf War, DOD signed a sole source contract with a new company, Bioport, to produce anthrax vaccine.[24] In 1998 Secretary of Defense William Cohen ordered that all active duty troops be given the anthrax vaccine, which was to be de-

---

[22] *See* New Drug and Biological Drug Products; Evidence Needed to Demonstrate Efficacy of New Drugs for Use Against Lethal or Permanently Disabling Toxic Substances When Efficacy Studies in Humans Ethically Cannot Be Conducted, 64 Fed. Reg. 53,960 (proposed Oct. 5, 1999) (to be codified at 21 C.F.R. pts. 314 and 601) (seeking to approve drugs without human efficacy trials if they treat or prevent life-threatening conditions). *See also* New Drug and Biological Drug Products; Evidence Needed to Demonstrate Effectiveness of New Drugs When Human Efficacy Studies Are Not Ethical or Feasible; Final Rule, 67 Fed. Reg. 37,988, 37,989 (May 31, 2002) (to be codified at 21 C.F.R. pts. 314 and 601) (finalizing the approval of marketing of drugs for life-threatening illnesses based only on animal models).

[23] The vaccine has been shown to protect rhesus monkeys from inhalation anthrax. *See* Terry C. Dixon et al., *Medical Progress: Anthrax*, 341 NEW ENG. J. MED. 815, 822 (1999).

[24] Thomas V. Inglesby et al., *Anthrax as a Biological Weapon: Medical and Public Health Management*, 281 JAMA 1735, 1740 (1999).

livered in a series of six injections over an 18 month period.[25] Some soldiers refused, and challenged the orders, arguing that the vaccine was experimental and thus could not be given without informed consent. Many of them were court-martialed.[26] Anthrax vaccination was halted in 2001 when supplies ran out and the sole-source company was shut down by the FDA for failure to maintain proper manufacturing standards.[27] Production and military vaccination resumed in 2002.[28] There is no evidence of any military personnel or installation ever being attacked by anthrax anywhere in the world.

The bioterrorist anthrax attacks in the U.S. were on civilians, none of whom had been vaccinated. The recommended course of treatment for exposure to anthrax is 60 days of antibiotics, and antibiotics were made available to the 10,000 people potentially exposed.[29] The anthrax vaccine was not available to civilians in October or November. In late December, 2001, however, DOD agreed to supply sufficient vaccine to vaccinate the 10,000 exposed civilians. Since the anthrax vaccine was an investigational drug when used for postexposure inhalation anthrax, it could only be used in the context of a clinical trial, and then only with the informed consent of the subjects.[30]

The FDA and CDC designed a consent form, together with a counseling process, for use in obtaining the consent of the exposed civilians to participate in the research project. Unlike the case of the military in the Gulf War, or even the peacetime military with the anthrax vaccine, in which the government required soldiers to be vaccinated, the choice was left entirely to individuals. Government officials did not even make a recommendation as to what they thought

---

[25] Steven Lee Myers, *U.S. Army Forces to be Vaccinated Against Anthrax*, N.Y. TIMES, Dec. 16, 1997, at A1.

[26] Kelly Morris, *U.S. Military Face Punishment for Refusing Anthrax Vaccine*, 353 LANCET 130 (1999). *See also* Laura Johannes & Mark Maremont, *Injecting Doubt: Worries about Safety of its Anthrax Vaccine Put the Army in a Bind*, WALL ST. J., Oct. 12, 2002, at A1 (explaining that as of Oct. 12, 2002, 102 service men and women were court-martialed for refusing to take the vaccine).

[27] Jon Cohen & Eliot Marshall, *Vaccines for Biodefense: A System in Distress*, 294 SCI. 498, 500 (2001).

[28] Wade-Hahn Chan, *What Are You Taking for That?*, INSIGHT ON THE NEWS, Oct. 23, 2002, at 23.

[29] Altman, *supra* note 9.

[30] *See* Lawrence K. Altman, *In Offering Anthrax Vaccines, Officials Admit to Unknowns*, N.Y. TIMES, Dec. 25, 2001, at F5 (noting that "[r]ecipients must sign a five-page form that explains the experimental nature of the use and states that they should not consider the vaccine a treatment for anthrax"). BioPort's contract with the Pentagon may also permit it to sell up to 20% of its annual production to others. Judith Miller, *Anthrax Vaccine Maker Calls Finances Shaky*, N.Y. TIMES, Aug. 5, 2002, at A10.

any individual should do. D.A. Henderson, the chief bioterrorist adviser to the Secretary of Health and Human Services (HHS), justified this failure to recommend for or against taking the anthrax vaccine by saying that there was insufficient information available to make a recommendation.[31] But on what basis could individuals make a decision if those with the most experience with the anthrax vaccine refused even to advise them about what action was medically reasonable?

Although no survey of the exposed civilians has been conducted, it seems likely that the potential subjects mostly decided for themselves that their 60 days (or less) of antibiotics was sufficient protection. It is also unlikely that anyone who actually read and understood the information in the consent forms provided (for adults, adolescents, and children) would have chosen to take the vaccine. Specifically, the consent forms (which are essentially identical) are five-page, single-spaced documents. Designed for a clinical trial, the forms are nonetheless captioned "Anthrax Vaccine and Drugs Availability Program for Persons Possibly Exposed to Inhaled Spores." Most of the form is in regular typeface, but the following information is in bold:

> **Before you decide to take part in this program, there are several important things that you should know...**
>
> · **Anthrax vaccine has not been shown to prevent infection when given to people after exposure to anthrax spores . . .**
> · **The vaccine that you will receive in this program has not been approved by the Food and Drug Administration (FDA) for this use and is considered investigational . . .**
> · **FDA has not approved this lot of vaccine (Lot FAV-063) because the company's license to produce the vaccine is under review...**
> · **You should not consider the vaccine as a treatment for anthrax. The vaccine given in this program has not been shown to give long term protection against anthrax.**
> · **You may have undesirable side effects from taking the vaccine.**

[31] *Id.* and Sheryl Gay Stolberg & David E. Rosenbaum, *U.S. Will Offer Anthrax Shots for Thousands*, N.Y. TIMES, Dec. 19, 2001, at A1.

> **. . . DHHS is <u>not</u> making any recommendation whether you should or should not take this vaccine. DHHS is making the vaccine available to you to allow you to decide whether or not you wish to use the vaccine.**[32]

The form also tells potential subjects that the vaccine is to be given in three injections, once every two weeks, and is to be supplemented by 40 days of additional antibiotics, although taking antibiotics is not required to obtain the vaccine. A two-year follow up is planned. The remainder of the form is in relatively standard language, with the exception of the phrases, "Although unconfirmed, a recent preliminary study suggests that the vaccine may be linked with an increase in the number of birth defects when given during pregnancy. At this time no one knows for sure whether this vaccine can cause fetal harm." The adolescent and pediatric forms also note that the vaccine has not been studied in anyone under the age of 18.[33]

The fact that it is unethical to expose human subjects to potentially lethal toxic agents does not, of course, mean that studies cannot be undertaken with individuals who have been exposed by a terrorist and who may need an investigational drug or vaccine that has not been approved. The FDA's new regulations make provisions for such research, and appropriately so.[34] Of course, informed consent must be an integral part of any such research project, even if advanced with the hope of possible therapeutic benefit. The FDA reasonably recognized this when it made the investigational anthrax vaccine available to exposed civilians only with their informed consent.[35] Informed

---

[32] CDC, *Anthrax Vaccine and Drugs Availability Program for Persons Possibly Exposed to Inhaled Spores, available at* http://www.cdc.gov/od/oc/meida/adolescent.pdf; http://www.cdc.gov/od/oc/media/adult.pdf; http://www.cdc.gov/od/oc/media/parental.pdf (last visited Jan. 21, 2003).

[33] *Id.*

[34] *See* New Drug and Biological Drug Products, Evidence Needed to Demonstrate Effectiveness of New Drugs When Human Efficacy Studies Are Not Ethical or Feasible, 67 Fed. Reg. 37,988, 37,990 (May 31, 2002) (to be codified at 21 C.F.R. pts. 314 and 601) (noting that therapeutic benefits need not be established). The FDA approved pyridostigmine bromide under this rule in February 2003, just prior to the Iraq war. Donald G. McNeil, *Drug Tested in Gulf War is Approved for Troops*, N.Y. TIMES, Feb. 6, 2003, at A19. This approval was not without controversy. Jennifer Cohen, *New Rule Triggers Debate Over Best Way to Test Drugs*, 299 SCIENCE 1651 (2003).

[35] Shankar Vedantam & Mary Pat Flaherty, *CDC Pushed Paperwork for Anthrax Vaccinations: 48 Congressional Aides Received Inoculations*, WASH. POST, Dec. 22, 2001, at A10.

consent is not a form, nonetheless, the forms are worth reviewing for what their content reveals about the proposed study.

One of the most striking provisions is that the FDA was willing to enroll both children and pregnant women at the outset, even though the vaccine has never been used in children, and even though there is some evidence that it might be teratogenic. There is no ethical justification for putting children or fetuses at risk at this time (there is no evidence that any parent enrolled their child, or that any pregnant woman enrolled), since the 60 days of antibiotic use has always been a successful prophilaxis in humans. This seems to be another example of FDA/National Institutes of Health (NIH) policy to try to do research on children and women, without making distinctions about the type of research and the likelihood of harm to the children and women (as well as their fetuses) involved.[36]

The FDA does seem to have learned from its experience in the Gulf War, and did seem to understand that there could be no justification for waiving informed consent for competent adults, even in the face of a bioterrorist attack and uncertainty about the usefulness of the anthrax vaccine. Informed consent for research on competent adults is always feasible and is always ethically required. Informed consent is also required for treating competent adult civilians – only military personnel agree to accept reasonable and necessary approved medical procedures without specific consent.[37] That is only one reason why it is dangerous to civilians to argue that after 9/11 "we are all soldiers now."

The anthrax attacks convinced Congress and the public that the U.S. does not have sufficient safe and effective drugs and vaccines available to respond to a bioterrorist or biowarfare attack on civilians. The primary reason for the drastic increases in NIH funding, for example, are to do research in areas that might lead to better bioterrorist-

[36] *See, e.g.*, Ass'n. of Am. Physicians and Surgeons v. FDA, 226 F. Supp. 2d 204 (D.D.C. 2002) (containing a challenge to FDA regulation requiring drug tests on children). Almost a year later controversy erupted over a plan to test a diluted vaccinia vaccine (Dryvax) on children. Solicitation of Public Review and Comment on Research Protocol: A Multicenter Randomized Dose Response Study of the Safety, Clinical and Immune Response of Dryvax Administered to Children 2 to 5 Years of Age, 67 Fed. Reg. 66,403 (Oct. 31, 2002). The plan to test the smallpox vaccine on children was ultimately dropped.

[37] And it is probably time to re-examine this policy, at least in peacetime, as well. Moreover, the anthrax vaccine seems to be used currently in the military as a protection against cutaneous anthrax (which it is licensed for, but which is no real risk to soldiers) rather than as a protection against inhalation anthrax (which it is not licensed for, but which is a combat risk).

related drugs and vaccines.[38] Congress agrees with the FDA that these new agents should be approvable on the basis of animal studies of efficacy.[39] There may, however, be indirect ways to test for human efficacy (such as antibody levels and tests like those used to determine the efficacy of diluted smallpox vaccine), and when such indirect human efficacy measures exist, their use should be required for FDA approval.

A related question is whether there should be a new narrower category of FDA approval for products that cannot be tested for efficacy, and whose use would be limited to certain populations in specific circumstances. Although there is no precedent for this, teratogenic drugs like accutane and thalidomide have labeling that attempts to limit their prescription to people taking effective birth control measures.[40] This is reasonable. Similarly, when drugs and vaccines are developed for the use of soldiers in war it seems reasonable to restrict their use to competent adults, and to exclude children. It also seems reasonable to limit the use of the agent to military personnel – at least if combat and the military mission are the rationales used to approve the use – and to require that the product be labeled "For Military Use Only."[41] If such a restriction is not made, there is at least the potential for the drug to be used for other reasons (since once the drug or vaccine is approved for one purpose, physicians can lawfully prescribe it for others if it is available to civilians) although the primary reason short cuts were taken in its testing was military necessity.

The labeling of bioterrorist drugs and vaccines is more complicated because the consumers are primarily civilians. A label like, "For Use Only in the Event of a National Emergency or Bioterrorist Attack," might not be sufficient, although that will be the primary reason the drug or vaccine has been approved without the usual re-

---

[38] *NIH Breaks Down How It Will Spend Bioterrorism Funds*, WALL ST. J., Feb. 19, 2002, at A4.

[39] Congress required the FDA to adopt the regulation cited in note 22 by legislation; see Public Health Security and Bioterrorism Preparedness Response Act of 2002, H.R. 3448, 107th Cong. §§ 122-23 (2002); Bioterrorism Preparedness Act of 2001, S. 1765, 107th Cong. §§ 405-06 (2001); both of which contained this language which became law in 2002.

[40] *See, e.g.*, George J. Annas & Sherman Elias, *Thalidomide and the Titanic: Reconstructing the Technology Tragedies of the Twentieth Century*, 89 AM. J. PUB. HEALTH 98 (1999) (describing the FDA's most stringent postmarking monitoring ever used for reintroduction of thalidomide, which caused serious birth defects in the 1950s and 1960s).

[41] During the Gulf War pyridostigmine bromide (as a pretreatment for a poison gas attack) was labeled "For military use and evaluation" instead of the usual IND label, "Caution: New Drug-Limited by Federal Law to Investigational Use." It was approved for use by the troops just prior to the Iraq war. *See supra* note 34.

quired human efficacy studies. To permit it to be used by physicians for other purposes is not justified.

In reality, however, it is probably not the labeling as much as the physical control of these new drugs and vaccines that will matter. For example, if the products are all manufactured under military or HHS contract, and the entire supply is controlled either by DOD or HHS, their availability and use will be governed by these agencies, and the drugs and vaccines will not be available to private physicians or the general public (except in times of national emergency) in any event. This, for example, is the current situation with the anthrax vaccine that is wholly supplied by a single manufacturer who is under contract only to manufacture it for DOD. That is why only DOD can authorize its supply to others, as it did in December, 2001.[42] Anthrax research continues on a number of fronts: can fewer than six shots of the current vaccine provide immunity?, can a test for antibodies in the blood measure immunity?, what side effects have been experienced by the military personnel who have taken the vaccine?, and, of course, can a better vaccine be developed to replace the current one that is "old, inefficient and the cause of many complaints."[43]

There is a tendency to jettison fundamental rules that protect citizens against arbitrary government action, especially those like informed consent, in times of war or crises like bioterrorism. Reflection has caused us to regret our haste in waiving informed consent in the Gulf War and this mistake was not repeated during the Iraq War. Not only was informed consent feasible with the troops, but the use of pyridostigmine bromide as a pretreatment to a soman attack is contraindicated for the primary chemical agent the Iraqis actually had in their arsenal, sarin. When confronted with this fact by U.S. Senator Jay Rockefeller in a Senate hearing in 1997 General Norman Schwarzkopf admitted that the military was responding primarily out of fear rather than knowledge, saying: ". . . we were scared to death of the Iraqi chemical weapons . . . what you are probably recounting, is a reaction, perhaps an overreaction to coming up with any kind of antidote that they could come up with to prevent our troops from being killed by chemical weapons."[44] At a later 1997 hearing before the same panel, General Colin Powell testified that he approved the drugs and vaccines used "with the full assurance from the FDA that they

---

[42] *But see* Judith Miller, *supra* note 30.

[43] Eliot Marshall, *Anthrax Vaccine Begins a New Round of Tests*, 295 SCIENCE 427, 427 (2002).

[44] *Persian Gulf War Illnesses, Part II: Hearing Before the Comm. on Veterans' Affairs United States Senate*, 105th Cong. 26 (1997) (testimony of General Norman H. Schwarzkopf, U.S. Army Retired).

were safe for human use and that they were effective."[45] In other words, the federal agencies were wrongly relying on the expertise of each other rather than exercising their own independent judgment: FDA granted DOD's request for a combat waiver of consent because it believed that its use was a military decision for DOD to make, and DOD used the drugs and vaccines it did because it thought a drug safety decision had been made by the FDA.

There is no reason for civilians (or soldiers) to have to trade safety for liberty in an emergency in which unapproved or partially-tested drugs or vaccines are made available. The choice to use them should continue to be an individual's choice, as it properly was for civilians in the case of the anthrax vaccine. The public health or military authorities that make these drugs and vaccines available, however, should only do so if they are prepared to recommend their use. Otherwise the decision to make them available becomes purely a political one, made to cover the behinds of government officials, not a medical or public health one.[46]

IV. THE "MODEL" STATE EMERGENCY HEALTH POWERS ACT

In the immediate aftermath of 9/11 and the subsequent anthrax attacks, hospitals, cities, states, and federal officials began developing or revisiting plans for future biological attacks. The federal response almost immediately emphasized stockpiling drugs and vaccines that could be used to respond to a future attack, especially one involving smallpox.[47] Other initiatives have proposed enhancing the public health infrastructure of the country (especially its ability to monitor emergency department diagnoses and pharmacy sales of relevant drugs), and the training of first responders to recognize and treat the diseases most likely to be caused by a bioterrorist attack (such as anthrax, smallpox, and plague). Major efforts are also underway to im-

---

[45] *Persian Gulf War Illnesses, Part III: Hearing Before the Comm. on Veterans' Affairs United States Senate*, 105th Cong. 14 (1997) (testimony of General Colin Powell, Former Chairman of the Joint Chiefs of Staff).

[46] In this regard there are many lessons to be learned from the 1976 attempt to vaccinate all Americans against swine flu. *See, e.g.*, RICHARD E. NEUSTADT & HARVEY V. FINEBERG, THE SWINE FLU AFFAIR: DECISION-MAKING ON A SLIPPERY DISEASE (U.S. Dept. HEW, 1978). *See also* GINA KOLATA, FLU: THE STORY OF THE GREAT INFLUENZA PANDEMIC OF 1918 AND THE SEARCH FOR THE VIRUS THAT CAUSED IT 129-95 (1999).

[47] *See* William Broad, *U.S. Acts to Make Vaccines and Drugs Against Smallpox*, N.Y. TIMES, Oct. 9, 2001, at F1 (discussing U.S. response to the threat of smallpox).

prove coordination and communication among local, state, and federal officials responsible for emergencies, and to more clearly delineate lines of authority involving "homeland security." All of these are reasonable and responsible steps our government should take.

On the other hand, planning for mass quarantine and forced vaccination – likely with investigational vaccines – are unreasonable steps that are more likely to foster public panic and distrust than to be effective in a real emergency. Mass quarantine was a staple of public health from the 14th century to the early 20th century, and its implementation has been historically justified by labeling those groups quarantined as not only dangerous but almost diabolical.[48] As historian-physician Howard Markel has put it:

> History teaches us that society has no shortage of means available to dehumanize and minimize so-called undesirable groups of people. The grave risks of this minimization process are magnified when combined with the threat of contagious disease. It is at this moment that rhetorical scapegoating may be transformed into a mentality of quarantine. Not only does the infectious disease become the 'enemy' but, so, do the human beings (and their contacts) who have encountered the microbe in question. A common symptom of the quarantine mentality is to do everything possible to prevent the spread of an epidemic, often at the neglect of the human or medical needs of those labeled contagious.[49]

Properly worried that many state public health laws are outdated and perhaps inadequate to permit state officials from effectively containing an epidemic caused by a bioterrorist attack, in the wake of 9/11 the CDC advised all states to review the adequacies of their laws with special attention to quarantining people in the event of a smallpox attack.[50] In addition, the CDC released a proposed model law for the states, entitled the "Model State Emergency Health Powers

[48] HOWARD MARKEL, QUARANTINE!: EAST EUROPEAN JEWISH IMMIGRANTS AND THE NEW YORK CITY EPIDEMICS OF 1892 185-86 (1997).

[49] *Id.*

[50] *See* CDC Smallpox Response Plan and Guidelines, *available at* http://www.bt.cdc.gov/agent/smallpox/response-plan/index.asp (laying out state and local guidelines for vaccination). *See also* Justin Gillis & Ceci Connolly, *U.S. Details Response to Smallpox: Cities Could be Quarantined and Public Events Banned*, WASH. POST, Nov. 27, 2001, at Al (suggesting increased awareness by public officials in detecting smallpox outbreak and a possibility of quarantine should control measures fail).

Act"(model act) on October 23, 2001.[51] The act was written under extreme time pressure and in the state of high emotion. Co-drafter

[51] This model was released on October 23, 2001 to great fanfare, but has since been removed from the sponsor's website. A copy is on file with the author. I first saw the model act on October 31 when it was emailed to me by project director James G. Hodge, Jr. On November 1, I emailed him and the distribution list the following response:

> Dear Mr. Hodge: Thanks for bringing your draft model law to my attention. There certainly is a need to improve our public health infrastructure and to find new and effective drugs and vaccines to deal with the threat of bioterrorism. I think uniform state laws can be a useful tool for state legislatures and that some good could come out of this exercise. I do not however think your current proposal is helpful, since it treats both American citizens and American physicians and hospitals as the enemy, and grants unnamed and unaccountable "public health officials" unprecedented (and I think unconstitutional) power to compel both citizens and their physicians to undergo testing and treatment and perhaps quarantine with no standards as to how these powers are to be applied or reviewed. This is, of course, the old Soviet model of public health (lots of power and no standards for applying it), hardly a "new" American model. The problem RIGHT NOW is not the lack of public health power, but a lack of public health honesty (about how little is known about anthrax, for example) and the lack of vaccines and drugs to deal with various risks. It is NOT the case that Americans are resisting being tested or treated (what makes you think this is the problem?); rather it is the CDC and other public health officials who are urging Americans who are lining up to be screened for anthrax in New York City, for example, to go home and not worry about it, and people who want to begin antibiotic treatment immediately not to do so. Also, I have not witnessed any physicians or hospitals around the country that have failed to offer full voluntary cooperation with public health and even law enforcement officials.
>
> In short, this seems to be an overreaction to a crisis that significantly misses the mark. I urge you not to stick to an unrealistic November 7 rewrite deadline, but to take the time to do a more thoughtful job on this. Such a rewrite would require, among other things, much more careful attention to definitions (including limiting mandatory actions to communicable diseases), taking the constitutional rights of American more seriously (and not trying to rely so heavily on *Jacobson*, a case that is almost 100 years old and that reflects both old public health practice and outdated constitutional law), treat Americans as the beneficiaries and friends of public health, not as your enemies; treat private physicians and hospitals as allies, not enemies; and develop explicit and understandable standards under which power over individuals and private institutions can be exercised; and eliminate the immunity provisions.
>
> I hope these comments are helpful, and would be happy to discuss any or all of them with you. Sincerely, George J. Annas (copy of email on file with the author; there was no response from the authors of the Model Act).

Shortly thereafter, on Nov. 7, 2001, Janlori Goldman and Joanne L. Hustead of Georgetown University's Institute for Health Care Research and Policy, wrote Larry Gostin a much longer letter, saying among other things:

Steve Teret, for example, explained that he had just finished reading José Saramago's *Blindness* when asked to help on this project. He

---

Given the current political climate and the intense desire of policymakers and the public to be fully prepared for similar attacks and acts of bioterrorism, we believe it is critical for proponents of any proposed model legislation to be especially vigilant in protecting civil liberties and privacy rights.
As an initial matter, we are extremely concerned with the breathtakingly expansive scope of the definition of "public health emergency" – a definition that is central to the invocation of the extraordinary powers granted to state authorities. Most alarming is the inclusion of "epidemic" and "pandemic" in this definition (terms which themselves are not defined). We approached this model with the understanding that it was intended to combat new, emerging threats, specifically the outbreak of disease caused by bioterrorism, but the model act, as drafted, appears to allow the existence of any epidemic, whatever the cause, to trigger the emergency powers vested in state authorities – powers that include the ability to quarantine individuals and compel treatment . . .
We do not argue that quarantine, isolation, or forced treatment – with the obvious attendant loss of liberty and autonomy – are never an appropriate exercise of government power. There may be circumstances where such action is the only and last resort. We do question, however, the breadth of situations in which state authorities would have these powers under the model act, and we urge you to more precisely define and limit the circumstances under which such extraordinary powers could be invoked . . .
We have several concerns about the draft's approach to protecting the privacy of medical information.
The draft does not consistently restrict access to protected health information (PHI) to those within the public health authority (or the public safety authority) with a need to know, or put explicit limits on disclosure of such PHI by state authorities. Several sections, notably section 201 (which creates a mandatory reporting system), section 202 (which requires public health authorities to identify, interview, and counsel exposed individuals and track other potentially exposed individuals), and section 203 (which requires public health and public safety authorities to share information about reportable illnesses) will result in the accumulation of PHI by public health and safety authorities. We believe it is essential for this model law to state explicitly that all PHI collected or received by state public health or public safety authorities will be available only to those within the authorities with a need to know. (Section 2043(c)'s reference to exchanges between "authorized personnel" is a start.) It also is essential for this model law to prohibit disclosures of PHI by state authorities, with stated exceptions that are limited to the reasons why the information was collected in the first place.
(letter on file with the author)

In retrospect such comments were inevitable. As two sympathetic commentators put it, "In their understandable haste, the Georgetown-Hopkins drafting group also produced a confusing document, posted first and discussed afterwards." John M. Colmers & Daniel M. Fox, *The Politics of Emergency Health Powers and the Isolation of Public Health*, 93 AM. J. PUB. HEALTH 397, 398 (2003). *And see generally*, Ronald Bayer & James Colgrove, *Rights and Dangers: Bioterrorism and the Ideologies of Public Health*, *in* IN THE WAKE OF TERROR 51-74 (Jonathan D. Moreno ed., 2003).

told an interviewer that the horrific quarantine described in this fictional epidemic of blindness was something he could not get out of his mind. In his words, "It was the most disturbing book I've ever read."[52]

The draft act permits the Governor to declare a public health emergency, after which the state's public health officials are given extraordinary power to essentially take over all of the health care facilities in the state, order physicians to act in certain ways, and order citizens to submit to examinations and treatment on the threat of being quarantined or criminally punished for refusing. Under the act, public health officials, and those working under their authority, are immune from liability for their actions (except for gross negligence and willful misconduct), including those which cause permanent injury or death. Specifically, the act defines a public health emergency (the condition that permits the Governor to declare a state of public health emergency), as "an occurrence or imminent threat of an illness or health condition, caused by bioterrorism, epidemic or pandemic disease, or novel and highly fatal infections agent or biological toxin, that poses a substantial risk of a significant number of human fatalities or incidents of permanent or long-term disability."[53]

An emergency declaration permits the Governor to suspend state regulations, transfer personnel, and mobilize the militia. All public health personnel will be issued special identification badges, which they shall wear "in plain view" that "shall indicate the authority of the bearer to exercise public health functions and emergency powers . . ." In regard to health care facilities, public health personnel may "compel a health care facility to provide services or the use of its facility if such services or use are reasonable and necessary for emergency response . . . includ[ing] transferring the management and supervision of the health care facility to the public health authority . . . ."[54]

Public health personnel are given exceptionally broad powers, and failure of physicians and citizens to follow their orders is a crime:

> Sec. 502(a)(4) **Individual examination or testing**. Any person refusing to submit to the medical examination and/or testing is liable for a misdemeanor. If the public health authority

[52] Susan Muaddi Darraj, *Model Legislation: Balancing Civil Rights and Public Policy*, JOHNS HOPKINS PUB. HEALTH MAG., Late Fall 2001, at 18. In the same article Gostin is quoted as saying that the model act is "polished and strong because we had a brain trust of the best public health minds at Hopkins and the best legal minds at Georgetown, thus ensuring the best dividends for our nation." *Id.*

[53] Model Act, Sec. 104(f) at p. 11, *supra* note 51.

[54] *Id.*, sec. 402(b), at 20, *supra* note 51.

> is uncertain whether a person who refuses to undergo medical examination and/or testing may have been exposed to an infectious disease or otherwise poses a danger to public health, the public health authority may subject the individual to isolation or quarantine.
> Sec. 502(b) **Health care provider assistance**. To require any physician or other health care provider to perform the medical examination and/or testing. Any person refusing to perform a medical examination or test as authorized herein shall be liable for a misdemeanor . . . An order of the public health authority given to effectuate the purposes of this subsection shall be immediately enforceable by any peace officer.
> Sec. 504(b) **Vaccination and treatment.** Individuals refusing to be vaccinated or treated shall be liable for a misdemeanor. If, by reason of refusal of vaccination or treatment, the person poses a danger to the public health, he or she may be subject to isolation or quarantine . . . (c) An order of the public health authority . . . shall be immediately enforceable by any peace officer.[55]

Of course, state public health, police, fire, and emergency planners should be clear about their authority, and to the extent the model act encourages states to review their emergency laws this is constructive. On the other hand, many of the provisions of this model act, especially those giving authority of public health officials over physicians and hospitals, and authority to quarantine without meaningful standards, seem to be based on the assumption that neither physicians nor the public are likely to cooperate with public health officials in the aftermath of a bioterrorist attack, and that panic is likely. This assumption itself seems to be based on the results of tabletop exercises involving simulated bioterrorist attacks, including TOPOFF and Dark Winter. TOPOFF involved a simulated bioterrorist attack on Denver by using aerosolized *Yersinia pestis*, the bacteria that causes plague.[56]

---

[55] *Id.* at 25-29.

[56] TopOff (Top Officials) was a Congressionally mandated exercise to simulate three simultaneous attacks: chemical in New Hampshire, nuclear in Washington, D.C., and biological in Denver. The most dramatic was the scenario involving the aerosol release of pneumonic plague at the Denver Performing Arts Center and the four-day sequel played out in May 2000 which included the closing of Colorado's borders on day three. Among the questions raised by Denver TopOff were: who is in charge, how to handle drug supply, how to avoid a hospital crisis, whether and how to quarantine those infected, and whether to close city and state borders to contain the disease. BIOHAZARD NEWS, TOPOFF: A PLAGUE EXERCISE, *at* http://www.biohazardnews.net/scen_plague.htm (May 2000).

Dark Winter was a tabletop exercise that simulated a smallpox attack on Oklahoma City.[57] Using these simulated cases as a basis for legislation, however, is unreasonable given the overwhelming voluntary cooperation of the public, physicians, and hospitals to both 9/11 and the anthrax attacks.

Selective blindness was perhaps inevitable, and led to three major objections to the initial version of the model act. First, it is far too broad, applying as it does not just to a smallpox attack, but to non-emergency conditions as diverse as our annual flu epidemic and the HIV epidemic.[58] Second, although it may make sense to put public health officials in charge of responding to a smallpox attack, it may

---

[57] Dark Winter, played out June 22 and 23, 2001, was a simulated smallpox attack on Oklahoma City. The exercise resulted in five major "learning points," including that biological weapons could threaten vital national security interests, current organizational structures are not well suited to managing a biological attack, there is no surge capacity in our health system, dealing with the media is critical, and finally, "Should a contagious bioweapon pathogen be used, containing the spread of disease will present significant ethical, political, cultural, operational and legal challenges. THE ANSER INSTITUTE FOR HOMELAND SECURITY, DARK WINTER, *at* http://www.homelandsecurity.org/darkwinter/index.cfm (last visited Jan. 19, 2003).

[58] *See* Wendy Parmet & Wendy K. Mariner, *A Health Act that Jeopardizes Public Health*, BOSTON GLOBE, Dec. 1, 2001, at A15 (noting that the definition of "emergency" in the Model Act is too broad and without review). *See also* letter of the New England Coalition for Law & Public Health to Secretary Tommy Thompson, dated Nov. 13, 2001 which reads in part:

> It is especially important today that public health retain the trust of the American public. The Model Act risks jeopardizing the public's confidence in both state and federal public health agencies by viewing public health as an arm of law enforcement rather than as an independent health protection profession. The Act treats the American public, rather than a chemical, biologic, disease (or even terrorist) as the source of the problem. It relies on coercion to the exclusion of identifying and reducing risks, distributing medicines, and educating the public about prevention and treatment. This approach will neither protect the public health nor support the efforts of public health officials. To sustain public support for public health measures, both now and in the long run, public health officials must be viewed as acting in the interest of the population. This cannot happen if they are seen as seeking extreme, unnecessary powers that can be used arbitrarily, against individuals who have committed no crime but becoming ill.
>
> We firmly believe that there is no need for model legislation enhancing public health's *emergency* powers. If there is any value in changing some state laws affecting public health, it lies in placing constitutional limits on the use of emergency powers to make the text of old statutes consistent with modern practices and amending statutes to provide and facilitate true commitments to public health . . . Signed by George J. Annas, Leonard H. Glantz, Wendy K. Mariner, Frances H. Miller, Patricia A. Roche, Richard A. Daynard, Wendy E. Parmet, Anthony Robbins, Eileen O'Neil, and Nicholas A. Ashford (on file with author).

not make sense to put them in charge of responding to every type of a bioterrorism event. This is because although the state public health department has a major role to play in limiting the public's exposure to a bioterrorist agent, contact identification, information gathering and dissemination, most of the actual treatment of affected individuals and preventive actions at the level of identifiable patients will be done by physicians, nurses, emergency medical personnel, and hospitals.[59] The primary role of public health authorities will usually be, as it was after the anthrax attacks, to provide guidance to the public and other government officials about how to identify and deal with the disease, and to provide laboratory facilities to assess exposure and definitively establish diagnoses.

The third objection to the act is that there is no evidence from either 9/11 or the anthrax attacks that physicians, nurses, or members of the public panic, are reluctant to cooperate in responding to a bioterrorist attack, or are reluctant to take drugs or vaccines recommended by public health or medical officials. Quite the opposite, physicians and hospitals in the areas affected, universally volunteered their time, space, and expertise to respond to 9/11, and the public lined up to be tested for anthrax and stockpiled ciprofloxacin. Instead of resisting treatment or testing, the public actually wanted treatment and testing so much that the CDC had to publicly recommend against both.[60] The major problem in a bioterror attack or epidemic will be delivering drugs to a public that is demanding them, not forcing treatment. Another important lesson learned from 9/11 was that Americans are primarily concerned about the safety of their families – and it will not be possible to separate them from their families if they do not believe separation is in their family's best interests.

---

[59] *See* Donald A. Henderson, *Public Health Preparedness*, *in* SCIENCE AND TECHNOLOGY IN A VULNERABLE WORLD: SUPPLEMENT TO AAAS SCIENCE AND TECHNOLOGY POLICY YEARBOOK 2003 37 (Albert H. Teich et al. eds., 2002), *available at* http://www.aaas.org/spp/yearbook/2003/yrbk03.htm (expressing need to prepare physicians at local level to respond to bioterrorism). And as bioterrorist expert Margaret Hamberg has noted, "A strong and robust public health system requires effective working partnerships with the medical care community." Margaret A. Hamburg *Addressing Bioterrorist Threats: Where Do We Go from Here?* 5 EMERGING INFECTIOUS DISEASES 564, 564 (1999).

[60] Jonathan Bor, *Americans are Taking Antibiotics into own Hands, in Case of Anthrax: Officials Vainly Caution Against Stockpiling, Random Self-medication*, BALT. SUN, Oct. 13, 2001, at 5A; *see also Postal Service Security: Hearing on Postal Service Security Before the Senate Comm. on Government Affairs*, 106th Cong. (Oct. 31, 2001) (providing testimony of Tara O'Toole, Deputy Director of Center for Civilian Biodefense).

Of course anthrax is not spread from person-to-person like smallpox. The response could have been different in a Dark Winter-type smallpox attack, or if thousands or tens of thousands of people had become infected with anthrax. Nonetheless, there is no empirical evidence to suggest that a draconian state criminal quarantine law of the type authorized in the act is necessary or desirable. Individuals with smallpox, for example, are most infectious only after they develop fever and a rash; and then they are usually so sick and immobile that they will likely accept whatever care is available.[61] Moreover, the "long incubation period (10-17 days before a rash develops) almost ensures that some persons who are infected in the [smallpox] attack will have traveled great distances from the site of exposure before the disease is recognized or quarantine could be implemented."[62] The key to an effective public health response is making voluntary treatment available. Without a sufficient supply of smallpox vaccine, for example, even police-supported quarantine would not likely be effective. People will come to centers for treatment; they will obviously flee if they do not want treatment and all that is offered is confinement and separation from their families.

Finally, even if it is concluded that a quarantine law might be useful to respond to a bioterrorist-induced emergency (e.g., by permitting the few unwilling Americans, if there are any, to be treated, vaccinated, or quarantined), such a law should be a federal law, not a state law. This is because bioterrorism is a matter of national security, not just state police powers. Existing federal quarantine law based on the commerce clause (and which has special provisions for tuberculosis, cholera, plague, smallpox, viral hemorrhagic fever and yellow fever) could usefully be examined and updated to deal with bioterrorism.[63] Moreover, to the extent that the federal government funds "dual use" public health infrastructure, federal public health officials will be able to dictate its use. The Governors of the states involved in actual anthrax attacks all realized that bioterrorism is fundamentally a federal

---

[61] *E.g.*, Donald A. Henderson et al., *Smallpox as a Biological Weapon: Medical and Public Health Management*, 281 JAMA 2127, 2129 (1999).

[62] Joseph Barbera et al., *Large-Scale Quarantine Following Biological Terrorism in the United States: Scientific Examination, Logistic and Legal Limits, and Possible Consequences*, 286 JAMA 2711, 2714 (2001).

[63] *See* Public Health Service, 42 U.S.C. § 264 (2001) (noting use of authority by the Surgeon General to control communicable disease outbreak); Quarantine, inspection, licensing: interstate quarantine, 42 C.F.R. 70 (2000). Of course bioterrorism is fundamentally a global issue as well. *See* Wendy Mariner, *The Wrong Response*, NAT'L L.J., Dec. 17, 2001, at A20, *and* David F. Fidler, *Bioterrorism, Public Health, and International Law*, 3 CHI. J. INT'L L. 7 (2002).

issue, and quickly called for action by both the FBI and the CDC to deal with the attacks.[64]

V. CIVIL LIBERTIES AND PUBLIC HEALTH EMERGENCIES

The act is premised on a not uncommon belief that in public health emergencies there must be a tradeoff between protecting civil rights and effective public health interventions.[65] There is, of course, precedent for this belief, and the preamble to the model act cites the 1905 case of *Jacobson v. Massachusetts* for the proposition that "the whole people covenants with each citizen, and each citizen with the whole people, that all shall be governed by certain laws for the 'common good.'"[66] *Jacobson* involved a Massachusetts statute that permitted local boards of health to require vaccinations when they deemed it "necessary for the public health or safety." There were no quarantine provisions in that law, and refusal was punishable by a $5 fine. Vaccination refusals at the beginning of the last century – before the Flexner report – were anticipated because vaccination itself remained controversial, there were no antibiotics, physicians were not universally trusted, science and medicine was in its infancy, and hospitals were seen primarily as "pest houses."[67] Trade offs between civil liberties (the right to refuse treatment) and public health (mandatory vaccinations) seemed necessary in such circumstances. There was no FDA, no such thing as an investigational drug or vaccine, and the doctrine of informed consent wouldn't be articulated for more than half a century.

The U.S. Supreme Court cited the military draft as precedent for upholding the Massachusetts law.[68] The point is not that the constitu-

---

[64] *See, e.g.*, Eric Lipton, *On a Day of Jitters, City and F.B.I. Differ Over Anthrax Sweep at ABC*, N.Y. TIMES, Oct. 17, 2001, at B6 (discussing the combination of local police and federal agents during the anthrax outbreak at ABC).

[65] James G. Hodge, Jr., *Bioterrorism Law and Policy: Critical Choice's for Public Health*, 30 J. L. MED. & ETHICS 254 (2002). The drafters knew quarantine and restricting civil liberties would be controversial. As James Hodge put it in November, 2001, "They [vaccination and quarantine] are the central issues of this act, and they will probably be the most controversial." Quoted by Deidre Davidson, *Health Center's Quarantine Proposal Sparks Debate*, Boston Law Tribune, Nov. 12, 2001 at 1, 2. More recently Hodge has said: "These are not going to be popular measures, but necessary ones." Quoted by Marcia Coyle, *Bioterror Law Gains Ground*, NAT'L L.J., Sept., 23, 2001, A1, A8, *available at* http://www.nlj.com/archive/0923.shtml.

[66] Jacobson v. Massachusetts, 197 U.S. 11, 27 (1905).

[67] CHARLES ROSENBERG, THE CARE OF STRANGERS: THE RISE OF AMERICA'S HOSPITAL SYSTEM 15-32, 209-11 (1987).

[68] *Jacobson*, *supra* note 66, at 29.

tion does not give the government wide latitude to respond in times of war and public health emergencies – it does; the point is that civil rights tradeoffs are not always required for effective public health response. Just as we have been able to abolish the draft and go to an all volunteer armed forces, so it seems reasonable to think that we can predictably rely on well-informed Americans – who are not the enemy in a bioterrorist attack – to follow the reasonable instructions of government officials they trust for their own protection.

Almost one hundred years after *Jacobson*, neither medicine nor constitutional law is what it was. We now take constitutional rights much more seriously, including the constitutional right of a competent adult to refuse any medical treatment, even lifesaving treatment.[69] Of course, we still would permit public health officials to quarantine individuals who have a serious communicable disease who either cannot or will not accept treatment for it or agree to stay in their home, and who threaten to infect others with it, such as active tuberculosis. Even then, however, we require public officials to use the "least restrictive alternative" and resort to quarantine only after other interventions, such as directly observed therapy, have failed.[70] Involuntary confinement almost always represents a failure of modern public health. It also must be accompanied by procedural due process protections, including the right to legal representation and to a judicial hearing.[71]

The act seems to have been drafted for a different age, and would be more at home in the U.S. of the 19th century rather than the 21st. Today, all adults have the constitutional right to refuse examination and treatment, and such a refusal should not result in involuntary confinement simply on the simple say so of a public health official. At the very least, the individual with a contagious disease should have

---

[69] *See* George J. Annas, *The Bell Tolls for a Constitutional Right to Physician-Assisted Suicide*, 337 NEW ENG. J. MED. 1098 (1997) (discussing *Washington v. Glucksberg*, 521 U.S. 702 (1997) and *Vacco v. Quill*, 521 U.S. 793 (1997)). *See also Sell v. U.S.*, 2003 U.S. LEXIS 4594 (June 16, 2003) (prisoner awaiting trial may not be medicated against his will to make him competent to stand trial without a judicial hearing and a finding that the medication is both necessary to further essential governmental interests and is in the patient's best medical interest in light of his medical condition).

[70] *See, e.g.*, Greene v. Edwards, 263 S.E.2d 661, 663 (W.Va. 1980) (stating specific procedural safeguards that must be followed before committing individuals for tuberculosis treatment); City of Newark v. J.S., 652 A.2d 265, 272 (N.J. Super. L. 1993); George J. Annas, *Control of Tuberculosis: The Law and the Public's Health*, 328 NEW ENG. J. MED. 585 (1993). The analogy modern courts have adopted is to the due process protection now constitutionally-required to confine a person to an institution because they are mentally ill and dangerous.

[71] *Id. See generally*, Wendy Parmet, *AIDS and Quarantine: The Revival of an Archaic Doctrine*, 14 HOFSTRA L. REV. 53 (1985).

the option of identifying a qualified examining physician of their own, and if isolation is necessary, isolating him or herself in their own home. Requiring physicians to treat patients against their will and against their medical judgment under penalty of criminal law has no precedent at all, makes no ethical or legal sense, and can only produce destructive conflict. Governors already have broad emergency powers; there is no compelling reason to expand them.[72]

Constitutional rights need not be compromised for effective public health intervention. But even if policy makers were unconcerned with restricting civil liberties, such a strategy as that outlined in the model act would be counterproductive. This is because the proposal is likely to undermine public trust in public health, trust that is absolutely essential to containing panic in a bioterrorist-induced epidemic. Unlike 1900, for example, we now have 24 hour a day news television, the internet, cell phones, and automobiles. These make effective large-scale quarantine impossible unless the public is convinced that it is absolutely necessary to prevent the spread of fatal disease and is fairly and safely administered. Making it a crime to disobey a public health officer, for example, will only increase public distrust in that it proclaims that public officials cannot provide valid reasons for their actions. Former Senator Sam Nunn, who played the president in the Dark Winter exercise, accurately observed after it was over: "There is no force on earth strong enough to get 250 million Americans to do something they do not believe is in their own best interests or that of their families."[73]

The necessity for maintaining public trust and confidence also means that the argument that in a public health emergency there must be a tradeoff between effective public health and protecting civil rights is simply wrong. As the AIDS epidemic has demonstrated, the promotion of human rights can be essential to deal effectively with an epidemic. Public health officials recognized early that draconian mandatory HIV screening measures, for example, would simply help drive the epidemic underground where it would spread faster and wider.[74] Likewise, draconian quarantine measures seem most likely to create public panic that will encourage people to avoid public health officials and physicians rather than seek them out. In this regard, pro-

---

[72] See *supra* note 58.

[73] Quoted by Tara O'Toole, oral presentation, Boston University School of Public Health, October 18, 2002.

[74] *See, e.g.*, Lawrence Gostin & Jonathan Mann, *Toward the Development of a Human Rights Impact Assessment for Formulation and Evaluation of Public Health Policies, in* HEALTH AND HUMAN RIGHTS: A READER 54 (Jonathan Mann et al., eds., 1999).

tection of civil liberties is a core ingredient to successfully responding to a bioterrorist attack. Treating our fellow citizens as the enemy, and using police tactics or martial law to force treatment and isolate them, is much more likely to cost lives than to save them. This is one reason why there has not been a large-scale quarantine in the U.S. since World War I, and why bioterrorism experts doubt that a mass quarantine could be effective.[75]

VI. THE REVISED MODEL ACT

On December 21, 2001, in response to criticisms of the model act, including those I have summarized, a revised version was released. No one any longer considers the act a "model." Instead, the December version is labeled simply a "draft for discussion." The December version does "not represent the official policy, endorsement, or views" of anyone, including the authors themselves and the CDC.[76] As then

---

[75] *See* Barbera, *supra* note 62, at 2713-14 (noting that quarantines that were undertaken in the past century primarily involved recent immigrants and ethnic minorities).

[76] *See* The Center for Law and the Public's Health at Georgetown and Johns Hopkins Universities, The Model State Emergency Health Powers Act, Draft (Dec. 21, 2001) [hereinafter MSEHPA Draft] *at* http://www.publichealthlaws.net/MSEHPA/MSEHPA2.pdf.

> A comparison of the cover pages of the two versions of "The Model State Emergency Health Powers Act" is both instructive and deeply disturbing. The **October 23, 2001 version** contains the following language immediately under the act's title and the date: "Prepared by The Center for Law and the Public's Health at Georgetown and Johns Hopkins Universities For the Centers for Disease Control and Prevention In collaboration with the: National Governors Association, National Conference of State Legislatures, Association of State and Territorial Health Officials, National Association of City and County Health Officers, and National Association of Attorneys General."
>
> The cover page of the **December 21, 2001 version** (apparently the final one) reads as follows after the title of the Act: "The Model State Emergency health Powers Act: As of December 21, 2001. A Draft for Discussion Prepared by: *The Center for Law and the Public's Health at Georgetown and Johns Hopkins Universities* For the Centers for Disease Control and Prevention [CDC] To Assist: National Governors Association [NGA], National Conference of State Legislatures [NCSL], Association of State and Territorial Health Officials [ASTHO], and National Association of County and City Health Officials [NACCHO].
>
> The cover page also contains a footnote to the title of the Act which reads: "Members of the National Association of Attorneys General (NAAG) also provided input and suggestions to the drafters of the Model Act. The language and content of this draft Model State Emergency Health Powers Act do not represent the official policy, endorsement, or views of the *Center for Law and the Public's Health*, the CDC, NGA, NCSL, ASTHO, NACCHO,

Director of the CDC, Jeffrey Koplan, wrote me on December 28, 2001: "The draft model act does not represent any official or unofficial CDC position."[77]

Although the revised act is a modest improvement (some suggestions were taken by the authors), all the fundamental problems remain. Failure to comply with the orders of public health officials for examination or treatment is no longer a crime but results in isolation or quarantine. Criminal penalties continue to apply for failure to follow isolation or quarantine "rules" that will be written at a future time. Physicians and other health care providers can still be required "to assist" public health officials, but cooperation is now coerced as "a condition of licensure" instead of a legal requirement with criminal penalties for noncompliance. The quarantine provisions have been improved, with a new requirement that quarantine or isolation be imposed by "the least restrictive means necessary" and stronger due-process protection, including hearings and legal representation for

---

or NAAG, or other governmental or private agencies, departments, institutions, or organizations which have provided funding or guidance to the *Center for Law and the Public's Health*. This draft is prepared to facilitate and encourage communication among the various interested parties and stakeholders about the complex issues pertaining to the use of state emergency health powers."

Assuming the second cover page is accurate, the first, which claims far more support and authority for the model act than it actually had, is unprofessional and misleading in the extreme. This may be acceptable behavior for a lawyer-advocate, but is not acceptable from an academic or scholar. Nonetheless, the authors continue to overstate the extent of support for their product, writing in the summer of 2002, for example, that "16 states and the District of Columbia already have enacted a version of the act (as of June 26, 2002, states enacting or expected shortly to enact legislation influenced by the Model Act were Arizona, Florida, Georgia, Hawaii, Maine, Maryland, Minnesota, Missouri, New Hampshire, New Mexico, Oklahoma, South Carolina, South Dakota, Tennessee, Utah, and Virginia)." Lawrence Gostin et al. *The Model State Emergency Health Powers Act: Planning for and Response to Bioterrorism and Naturally Occurring Infectious Diseases*, 288 JAMA 622, 622 (2002). What some of these states actually did is summarized in notes 85 and 86 *infra*.

The most supportive organization, the National Conference of State Legislatures, set forth its views in June 2002: "NCSL does not endorse or recommend passage of the Model State Emergency Health Powers Act. This document [the Act] and the checklist questions are provided as a service to legislators and their staff who are considering changes to state statutes regarding public health emergencies." LISA SPEISSEGGER & CHERYL RUNYON, THE MODEL STATE EMERGENCY HEALTH POWERS ACT: A CHECKLIST OF ISSUES 1 (NCSL, Washington, D.C., 2002).

[77] Letter on file with the author, responding to the letter quoted in note 58, *supra*.

those actually quarantined. Nonetheless, on the basis of a written directive by a public health official, a person can still be quarantined for 15 days before a hearing must be held, and the hearing itself can be for groups of quarantined persons rather than individuals.[78] Nothing in the revised act distinguishes between approved drugs and vaccines and investigational agents, even though the latter are the most likely to be used, and even though state law cannot override federal drug laws that govern their use and informed consent requirements.[79]

Some of the revised quarantine provisions seem even more arbitrary. A major criticism of the original version of the act was the extreme vagueness of its standard for quarantine, which invited the arbitrary use of force. According to the original version, reproduced above, public health officials could order a person quarantined if they were "*uncertain* . . . [whether a person who refuses to be examined or tested has] been exposed to an infectious disease or otherwise poses a danger to public health."[80] In the revised version the standard is made even more vague. Quarantine can be ordered when the person's refusal to be examined or tested "*results in uncertainty* regarding whether he or she has been exposed to or is infected with a contagious or possibly contagious disease or otherwise poses a danger to public health."[81] This is no standard at all, and simply permits public health authorities to quarantine anyone who refuses to be examined or treated, for whatever reason, since all refusals will result in uncertainty – if you were already certain, you wouldn't order the test. At the hearing, if requested, it seems like the standard for continued quarantine is that the individual would significantly jeopardize the public health authority's ability "to prevent or limit the transmission of a contagious or possibly contagious disease to others."[82] This standard also makes no sense because the public health focus, I think, should be on the person's condition and on the determination of whether the person poses a danger to others, not on the public health authority's ability to function.

These vague standards are especially troublesome because the act's incredible immunity provision remains unchanged. Thus, all state public health officials and all private companies and persons operating under their authority are granted immunity from liability for their actions (except for gross negligence or willful misconduct), even in the case of death or permanent injury. Out-of-state emergency

[78] *Id.*, sections 605(a) and (b) at pp. 28-29.

[79] *Supra* notes 19 to 46 and accompanying text.

[80] *Supra* note 53 and accompanying text.

[81] *See* MSEHPA Draft, *supra* note 76, at 26 (emphasis supplied).

[82] *See* MSEHPA Draft, *supra* note 76, at 30.

health care providers have even greater protection; they are given immunity from liability for everything but manslaughter. In my opinion, such immunity is something public health authorities should not want (even though it may have superficial appeal), because it means that they are not accountable for their actions, no matter how arbitrary. The immunity provision thus serves only to undermine the public's trust in public health authorities. Citizens are not soldiers, and should never be treated against their will by their government. But if they ever are, they should be fully compensated for injuries suffered as a result.[83]

VII. A MODEL FOR DISASTER?

There is no chance that every, or even many, states will adopt the suggested act as written, so if uniformity is seen as necessary or desirable, only a federal statute can provide it. Obviously, it is also much more important what states like New York and California (large states that are likely bioterror targets) do than what states like Montana, Wyoming or Arkansas do. So far, only a few states, like Delaware, Oklahoma, and South Carolina, have adopted the suggested act wholesale. More typically states have ignored it, or like California, have considered it and rejected it outright. Other states, like Minnesota, have modified their quarantine laws, but have updated them to be consistent with contemporary medical ethics and constitutional rights, rather than making them more arbitrary.

The drafters, nonetheless, continue to grossly overstate their support. In their August 7, 2002 JAMA article, for example, the act's drafters state: "Legislative bills based on the MSEHPA have been introduced in 34 states and the District of Columbia; 16 states and the District of Columbia have enacted a version of the act (as of June 26, 2002, states enacting or expected shortly to enact legislation influenced by the Model Act were Arizona, Florida, Georgia, Hawaii, Maine, Maryland, Minnesota, Missouri, New Hampshire, New Mexico, Oklahoma, South Carolina, South Dakota, Tennessee, Utah, and

---

[83] *See, e.g.*, George J. Annas, *The Nuremberg Code in U.S. Courts: Ethics Versus. Expediency*, *in* THE NAZI DOCTORS AND NUREMBERG CODE 201, 212-19 (George J. Annas & Michael A. Grodin, eds., Oxford U. Press, 1992) (arguing that U.S. policy on human experimentation places human rights and ethics behind national security & expediency). A good example of how arbitrary power tends to be used in emergencies is the use of potentially lethal gas by Russian commandos to "rescue" hostages held by Chechen nationals in October 2002. *See* Steven Lee Myers, *From Anxiety, Fear and Hope, The Deadly Rescue in Moscow*, N.Y. TIMES, Nov. 1, 2002, at A1 (stating that the gas killed at least 118 of the hostages).

Virginia)."[84] This is the language of salespeople, not legal scholars. It is incorrect to state that "16 states . . . have enacted a version of the act;" it is justifiable, but misleading, to state that this group of states has (or will) "enact legislation influenced by the Model Act." In fact, of the list, the following states (and the District of Columbia) rejected all or most of the language of the Act, and none of them adopted the most controversial items regarding treatment and quarantine as proposed: Georgia, Missouri, New Hampshire, New Mexico, South Dakota, Tennessee, Utah, and Virginia.[85] In the cases of these bills, for the drafters of the model act to take credit for them is a bit like the old story of the rooster taking credit for the sun rising in the morning. Some states, including Florida, Maine, Maryland, New Hampshire, Hawaii, Minnesota and Arizona did adopt quarantine laws affected by the model act, but none are substantially identical to it.[86] Of their list,

---

[84] *See* Gostin et al., *supra* note 76, at 622-23.

[85] A detailed state-by-state comparison of the laws so far enacted is well beyond the scope or purpose of this article, and would serve little purpose. It is also difficult to generalize about this group of state statutes (except to say that they are all substantially different from the model act). Nonetheless, a few examples illustrate the range and content of these laws. Georgia provides in relevant part that the department of health shall "promulgate appropriate rules and regulations" for vaccination and isolation and quarantine "in the case of a public health emergency." S.B. 385, 146th Gen. Assem., Reg. Sess. (Ga. 2001) enacted May, 2002 and codified in GA. CODE ANN. §§ 31-12-3 and 4; and § 38-3-51(i)(2)(Supp. 2002). New Mexico's entire act is only two pages long and provides for a petition to the court in case a person refuses voluntary treatment, detention or observation, and an evidentiary hearing based on clear and convincing evidence. Moreover, "The provisions of this section do not permit the forcible administration of medications." H.B. 195, 45th Leg., 2d Sess. (N.M. 2002) codified in N.M. STAT. ANN. § 24-1-15(I.) (Michie Supp. 2002). South Dakota passed two 2 page laws dealing with emergencies; no quarantine or treatment provisions are included, but the Governor may "provide for the examination and safe disposal of any dead body as may be reasonable and necessary to respond to the disaster, emergency, or act of terrorism." H.B. 1303, 77th Legis. Assem., Reg. Sess. (S.D. 2002) codified in S.D. CODIFIED LAWS ANN. § 33-15-8 (8) (LexisNexis Supp. 2002). Missouri's act is mostly devoted to wiretapping and communications interception, and various types of terrorism, issues not even addressed in the model act (the only provision of the model act is disaster planning and temporary licensure). S.B. 712, 91st Gen. Assem., 2d Reg. Sess. (Mo. 2002).

[86] This group of laws is all over the place, ranging in anticipated coercive actions from Florida to Minnesota. Florida is perhaps the most draconian of these laws, providing that "If the individual [who refuses to be examined or treated] poses a danger to the public health, the state health officer may subject the individual to quarantine. If there is no practical method to quarantine the individual, the state health officer may use any means necessary to vaccinate or treat the individual. Any order of the state health officer given to effectuate this paragraph shall be immediately enforceable by a law enforcement officer." Florida S.B. 1262 (2002). New Hampshire, the "live free or die" state, has provisions for treatment and quarantine, but provides that "Nothing in this chapter shall be construed to require the medical ex-

only Oklahoma and South Carolina can accurately be described as having "enacted a version of the act," and in no case is it an identical version.

Notably, under the new Minnesota law, even in a public health emergency, "individuals have a fundamental right to refuse medical treatment, testing, physical or mental examination, vaccination, participation in experimental procedures and protocols, collection of specimens, and preventive treatment programs."[87] The law further requires a health care provider "where feasible" to "notify the individual of the right to refuse."[88] Of course there are extreme circumstances under which isolation or quarantine can be employed. But the Minnesota legislature permits such measures only under very limited conditions, the right to refuse all interventions continues in isolation and quarantine, and family members are specifically given the right to choose to enter the isolation or quarantine area to visit. Most of the other provisions of the suggested act, including the immunity provisions, were referred to the Minnesota commissioner of health who was instructed to study them and report back to the legislature, after having solicited public comment on any recommendations.[89] The Minnesota legislature properly recognized that human rights and health are not inherently conflicting goals that must be traded off against each other. They are, as Jonathan Mann first articulated in the context of the international HIV/AIDS epidemic, "inextricably linked."[90]

The suggested act was drafted under extreme albeit self-imposed time constraints in the immediate aftermath of 9/11 and the anthrax

---

amination, medical treatment, or immunization of a person who objects, and no criminal penalties shall be imposed as a result." Moreover, should quarantine be ordered, it shall be at the place of the individual's own choosing "unless the Commissioner determines such place to be impractical or unlikely to adequately protect the public health." 2002 NH H.B. 1478 (enacted May 17, 2002). Minnesota also, and even more explicitly, protects an individual's right to refuse treatment: "Notwithstanding laws, rules, or orders made or promulgated in response to a national security emergency, peacetime emergency, or public health emergency, individuals have a fundamental right to refuse medical treatment, testing, physical or mental examination, vaccination, participation in experimental procedures and protocols, collection of specimens, and preventive treatment programs." MINN. STAT. ANN. § 12.39 (West Supp. 2003).

[87] *Id.*

[88] *Id.*

[89] *Id.*

[90] Model act drafter Lawrence Gostin used to share this belief as well. *See, e.g.*, Jonathan M. Mann et al., *Health and Human Rights*, 1 HEALTH AND HUMAN RIGHTS 6 (1994) (explaining collaboration among health and human rights programs). Gostin & Mann, *supra* note 74.

attacks when fear ruled reason. This is a predictable prescription for disaster. Sensible public health and bioterrorism legislation must be drafted in a calm atmosphere, in a transparent, public process. Perhaps most importantly, as Ken Wing has noted, "statute drafting is a technical and instrumental job – one that should follow, not precede the more fundamental task of deciding what the statute ought to say."[91] Public health must ultimately rely not on force but on persuasion, and never on blind trust. Trust itself must be based on transparency, accountability, democracy and human rights.

There is plenty of time to draft and debate a 21st century federal public health law that takes constitutional rights seriously, unites the public with its medical caretakers, treats medicine and public health as true partners, and moves us in the direction of global cooperation. The revised act could be useful as a checklist for reviewing existing law, but only if it is continuously subject to scrutiny and improvement, and is rewritten to be consistent with federal statutory, regulatory and constitutional law.

VIII. FEDERAL (AND GLOBAL) PUBLIC HEALTH

A bioterrorist attack on the US is inherently a matter of national security, making it a federal, not a state, matter. Epidemics arising from outside the US are also matters of national concern. Public health policy should be national, and the addition of national security to national financing and interstate commerce, provides constitutional authority for Congress to enact legislation giving the federal government the leadership role in public health in the 21st century. To re-

---

[91] Kenneth Wing, *The Model Act: Is It the Best Way to Prepare for the Next Public Health Emergency?*, 19 NW. PUB. HEALTH 10 (2002). Epidemiologic models for responding to a smallpox attack did not begin to appear in the literature until almost a year after the model act was drafted. Controversy continues about which model is most likely to mirror reality, and all are based on assumptions about the number of people each person with smallpox is likely to affect. As one commentator put it, "Without appropriate data, models cannot indicate whether we should target contacts for quarantine or vaccination when those contacts have been made in households, schools, workplaces, at public events, or under other circumstances." Jim Koopman, *Controlling Smallpox*, 298 SCIENCE 1342, 1343 (2002). *See also* M. Elizabeth Halloran et al., *Containing Bioterrorist Smallpox*, 298 SCIENCE 1428 (2002). Of course, developing an effective legal strategy is dependent upon reasonable epidemiology, and without it legal plans are likely to be unresponsive or irrelevant to real world epidemics – whether naturally-occurring or terrorist-created.
The authors are currently working on yet another "model" public health act under the Turning Point Project for the Robert Wood Johnson Foundation. Speissegger & Runyon, *supra* note 76. The credibility of their new act could, of course, be severely undermined by their zealous attempts to sell this one.

spond effectively to bioterrorism and epidemics, it is imperative that the federal government develop a national plan that individual states can help implement, and that the federal government supply the states with the badly needed financial and other resources to improve public health infrastructure, training, and coordination.

At the outset of the 21st century, bioterrorism, although only one threat to public health, can be the catalyst to effectively federalize and integrate much of what is now uncoordinated and piecemeal state and local public health programs. This should include a renewed effort for national health insurance, national licensure for physicians, nurses, and allied health professionals, and national patient safety standards.[92] Federal public health leadership will also encourage us to look outward, and to recognize that prevention of future bioterrorist attacks and even ordinary epidemics will require international cooperation.[93] It is time to not only federalize public health, but to globalize it as well.

The sudden appearance of SARS (Severe Acute Respiratory Syndrome) on the world stage in February 2003 illustrates all of these points. It is a useful illustration because SARS is like a 19th century epidemic in that there is no diagnostic test, no effective treatment, and no vaccine. Although it is far too early in this new viral epidemic to predict its outcome, a few observations can be made. First, SARS is a global epidemic. It began in China, and quickly spread throughout Asia and to North America, often by infected persons traveling by air.[94] No individual country, let alone a state within a country can effectively deal with a global epidemic alone. The World Health Organization quickly (and appropriately) took the lead in responding to

---

[92] *See* George J. Annas, *Bioterrorism, Public Health, and Human Rights*, 21HEALTH AFFAIRS 94, 96 (2002) (arguing for a more federalized and global public health system, protection of basic human and constitutional rights, and modernization of public health system).

[93] Although I have argued in this piece that modern public health will from now on be considered primarily a federal rather than a state responsibility, it would be even better if it were treated as a global issue, since epidemic diseases know no geographic boundaries and effective public health measures demand international action. *See generally*, LAURIE GARRETT, BETRAYAL OF TRUST: THE COLLAPSE OF GLOBAL PUBLIC HEALTH (Hyperion, 2000) (discussing the global impact of disease); *see generally* INSTITUTE OF MEDICINE, EMERGING INFECTIONS: MICROBIAL THREATS TO HEALTH IN THE UNITED STATES (Joshua Lederberg et al. eds., 1992) (noting the need for a "comprehensive global infectious disease surveillance system"); Lauren Z. Asher, *Confronting Disease in a Global Arena*, 9 CARDOZO J. INT'L & COMPARATIVE L. 135 (2001) (noting the importance of international health regulations).

[94] Julie Louise Gerberding, *Faster . . . but Fast Enough? Responding to the Epidemic of Severe Acute Respiratory Syndrome*, 348 NEW ENG. J. MED. 2030 (2003).

the epidemic by, among other things, initiating travel advisories.[95] Second, sick people and their health care providers almost universally acted appropriately. Those who were diagnosed with SARS, for example, agreed to voluntary treatment and isolation, and physicians and nurses did not try to avoid their duties (even though they were the individuals who turned out to be most at risk to contract SARS). As two U.S. public health experts put it, "praise is due to the hundreds of health care workers throughout the world who come to work every day to assist patients with SARS despite some risks to their own health."[96] Public health and medicine have been partners, not enemies, in responding to SARS.

Third, mass involuntary quarantine is generally unnecessary and almost always ineffective because it leads to mistrust of the government. In one three day period, for example, after a rumor that Beijing itself might be quarantined or put under martial law, almost a quarter of a million migrant workers fled to rural Henan province; and in a small rural town, Chagugang, thousands rioted and destroyed a building that was being finished to quarantine SARS patients.[97] Mistrust of the Chinese government generally made it more difficult for China to deal with its epidemic effectively.[98] A more effective strategy, employed in every affected democratic country, was to ask those people possibly infected with SARS to voluntarily stay at home for ten days and monitor their temperatures. In the United States, this method was used almost exclusively, with the exception of two tourists in New York City, and one in Dallas, who were quarantined involuntarily in hospitals because they had no home to stay in.[99] No governor declared a state of emergency – so no emergency public health law was

---

[95] Margot Cohen, Gautam Naik & Matt Pottinger, *Inside the WHO as it Mobilized for War on SARS*, WALL ST. J., May 2, 2003, at A1; Matt Pottinger, Elena Cherney, Gautam Naik & Michael Waldholz, *How Global Effort Found SARS Virus in Matter of Weeks*, WALL ST. J., April 16, 2003, at Al; Lawrence K. Altman, *W.H.O. Expected to Gain Broader Powers*, N.Y. TIMES, May 28, 2003, at A10.

[96] Richard P. Wenzel & Michael B. Edmond, *Managing SARS amidst Uncertainty*, 348 NEW ENG. J. MED. 1947, 1948 (2003).

[97] Charles Hutzler, *China Reverts to Top-Down Rule with Heavy Hand to Fight SARS*, WALL ST. J., May 8, 2003, at A8; Leslie Chang & Peter Wonacott, *SARS Measures in China Add to Air of Panic*, WALL ST. J., April 25, 2003, at B7; Erik Eckholm, *SARS is the Spark for a Riot in China*, N.Y. TIMES, April 29, 2003, at A1.

[98] John Pomfret, *A Mistrust of Government Undercuts China's Effort*, WASH. POST, April 29, 2003, at Al. A small authoritarian state, like Singapore, ruthlessly (and effectively) enforced quarantines. Wayne Harold, *In Singapore, 1970's Law Becomes Weapon Against SARS*, N.Y. TIMES, June 10, 2003, at D5.

[99] Lawrence K. Altman, *Public Health Fears Cause Officials to Detain Foreign Tourist*, N.Y. TIMES, April 28, 2003, at A15, and Marci Layton, N.Y.C. Health Dept. (personal communication, June 18, 2003).

triggered. Finally, response to major epidemics must be federal. The only legal change in the United States in response to SARS was made by the federal government, and applies primarily to individuals arriving to the United States from areas in which SARS is present. SARS was added to the list of federal "quarantinable communicable diseases" on April 4, 2003.[100]

Similar lessons about the appropriate level of government for public health planning for bioterrorism can be drawn from the preparations for a smallpox attack. The need for trust in public officials is also illustrated, since in this case (like the case of offering anthrax vaccine to those potentially exposed to anthrax) it seems to be primarily distrust of government that led the vast majority of those eligible for smallpox vaccination to refuse it. No one can quantify the risk of a smallpox bioterrorism attack; it is very low, but its potential for harm is so great should it happen that it cannot be ignored by government.[101] All major discussions and planning for such an attack have been done at the federal level, especially at the CDC.[102] Stockpiles of existing smallpox vaccine have been created by the federal government, tests to dilute the vaccine have been sponsored by the federal government, and the development of new smallpox vaccines is being financed by the federal government.[103] All of the existing and proposed supply of smallpox vaccine will be owned and controlled by the federal government.[104] Not only will the individual states have no say as to whether or not smallpox vaccine will be available to them, decisions about whom the vaccine will be available to (such as military personnel, emergency department nurses, physicians and other employees, first responders), etc., will be made by federal officials, not by governors or other state officials. The most difficult decision,

[100] *Executive Order 13295, Revised List of Quarantinable Communicable Diseases*, April 4, 2003. *See also*, DHHS, *Control of Communicable Diseases*, 68 FED. REG. 17559 (April 10, 2003).

[101] *See, e.g.*, Gina Kolata, *A Nation Challenged: Vaccinations; With Vaccine Available, Smallpox Debate Shifts*, N.Y. TIMES, March 30, 2002, at A8 (stating potential harm of smallpox attack but also stating that the potential for such an attack is low).

[102] *E.g.*, CDC Smallpox Response Plan and Guidelines, Draft 3.0 (Sept. 21, 2002), *at* http://www.bt.cdc.gov/agent/smallpox/repsonse-plan/index.asp. *See also*, *e.g.*, *supra* notes 37-43 and accompanying text for FDA regulation of drugs and vaccines related to a bioterrorist attack.

[103] Robert Pear, *Frozen Smallpox Vaccine is Still Potent, Officials Say*, N.Y. TIMES, March 30, 2002, at A8.

[104] Lawrence Altman, William Broad & Denise Grady, *White House Debate on Smallpox Slows Plan for Wide Vaccination*, N.Y. TIMES, Oct. 13, 2002, at 10.

whether to make smallpox vaccine available to members of the public prior to an attack, will be made by the president.[105]

Two points about smallpox preparation merit emphasis: first, this is a federal public health activity;[106] and second, smallpox vaccination is likely to remain an entirely voluntary decision. Troops slated to go to Iraq were involuntarily vaccinated, but even this military exception was put in place only after the vaccine itself was properly licensed by the FDA, and screening was performed so that military personnel at risk of an adverse reaction were excluded.[107] The military smallpox vaccination program went essentially as planned, although more than

---

[105] *Id. See also* Marilyn Chase and Greg Hitt, *Ugly Side Effects of Smallpox Vaccine Color Terror Plans*, WALL ST. J., Oct. 21, 2002, at A1 (noting health and liability risks associated with the vaccine). Homeland Security Director Tom Ridge has also been quoted as saying, "The president on down-everyone-recognizes in this life-and-death decision that the president has to make, there will be some families that endure losses and others that endure permanent injury. There has to be some way to compensate them." *Id. See also* The Homeland Security Act, which provides that all lawsuits involving the smallpox vaccine must be filed against the federal government. H.R. 5710, 107th Cong. § 304(c)(p)(2)(B) (2002).

[106] The new Homeland Security Act, H.R. 5710, 107th Cong. § 304(c)(p)(1)-(2)(A)(i), (c)(p)(7)(B)-(C) (2002), made special provisions for the administration of "any substance used to prevent or treat smallpox" to civilians. Specifically, if the Secretary of Health and Human Services issues a declaration "concluding that an actual or potential bioterrorist incident or other actual or potential public health emergency makes advisable the administration" [of smallpox vaccine or treatment] a "covered person shall be deemed to be an employee of the Public Health Service with respect to liability arising out of administration of a covered countermeasure against smallpox." Covered person is defined to mean not only the "qualified person" who administers the drug or vaccine, but also the manufacturer, the health care entity under whose auspices the smallpox vaccine or treatment is administered, and any "official, agent or employee" of the manufacturer, health care entity, or person administering the treatment or vaccine. A "qualified person" (i.e., the one administering the vaccine or treatment) "means a licensed health professional or other individual who is authorized to administer such countermeasure under the law of the State in which the countermeasure was administered." All lawsuits for injury would have to be filed against the U.S. (Sec. 304)
Of course what this means for a state that adopts the provisions of the "model act" is that recovery for negligence of the individuals administering smallpox vaccine and treatment will be available (albeit, only by suing the federal government, as was the case in the 1976 swine flu vaccination program). It also means, however, that the qualifications of the people administering the treatment will be determined by state law; under the model act, whoever the public health authority designates to fill the vaccinator and/or treatment role. Congress could, of course, make different rules for agents other than those designed for smallpox, and could amend these rules as well.

[107] Altman et al., *supra* note 98, and Denise Grady, *Pentagon Faces Difficulties in Smallpox Shots for Troops*, N.Y. TIMES, Dec. 17, 2002, at A16. *See also* Lawrence K. Altman & Sheryl Gay Stolberg, *Smallpox Vaccine Backed for Public*, N.Y. TIMES, Oct. 5, 2002, at A1 (noting that when the vaccine is publicly available it will be offered on an optional basis).

100 women who were pregnant were vaccinated who should have been excluded.[108] The plan to vaccinate up to 500,000 health care workers who would be responsible to vaccinate the public in the event of a smallpox attack, however, faltered badly, and by June, 2003 was officially "paused."[109] Many explanations have been provided for a response rate of less than 10% of eligible physicians and nurses. The most reasonable one seems to be that both the risks and the benefits of the smallpox vaccine were exaggerated, and physicians and nurses concluded (reasonably I think) that notwithstanding the government's position, the risk of the vaccine was not worth the benefit.[110]

After the conclusion of the Iraq War, the public relations disaster of recommending that all Americans get a supply of duct tape and plastic sheeting, and the growing public cynicism with repeated "orange alerts," few health care workers could take the prospect of a smallpox attack seriously.[111] Thus, even though the risk of the vaccine was relatively low, the benefits appeared to be even lower. In this regard, trust in what the government said was very low – I think because if the government has information about a country or group that has weaponized smallpox, it has an obligation to share this information with the American public. It is terrorists who would want to keep this information a secret, not the potential targets of an attack. Thus the federal government's failure to make their intelligence available to the public led, I think, to the reasonable conclusion that the government actually possessed no credible information – and could even have been using the smallpox scare to build support for the Iraq

108 Donald McNeil, 2 Programs to Vaccinate for Smallpox are 'Paused,' N.Y. TIMES, June 19, 2003 at A13; Denise Grady, Despite Warnings, Pregnant Women Got Smallpox Vaccine, N.Y. TIMES, May 2, 2003 at A18.

109 *Id.*, and Richard W. Stevenson & Sheryl Gay Stolberg, *Bush Lays Out Plan on Smallpox Shots; Military is First*, N.Y. TIMES, Dec. 14, 2002, at 1A. *See also*, Jon Cohen & Martin Enserink, *Rough-and-Tumble Behind Bush's Smallpox Policy*, 298 SCIENCE 2312 (2002), and Ceci Connolly, *Panel Urges Caution on Smallpox Innoculation,* Washington Post, June 20, 2003, at A9.

110 *See generally* George J. Annas, *Smallpox Vaccine: Not Worth the Risk*, HASTINGS CENTER REPORT, March-April 2003, at 6 (arguing that the federal government's statement that "there is not a zero risk of a smallpox attack" was "useless information" and "counterproductive" without disclosing the basis of the information because "[s]ecrecy makes sense only for the attacker, not the defenders."); Joan Stephenson, *Smallpox Vaccine Program Launched Amid Concerns Raised by Expert Panel, Unions*, 289 JAMA 685 (2003).

111 *Id. See* William J. Broad, Bush Signals He Thinks Possibility of Smallpox Attack is Rising, N.Y. TIMES, Dec. 14, 2002 at A10; Judith Miller, C.I.A. Hunts Iraq Tie to Soviet Smallpox, N.Y. TIMES, Dec. 3, 2002, at A20; Anita Manning, How Prepared are we Against Smallpox?, USA TODAY, March 6, 2003, at 1D.

War.[112] Nonetheless, the conclusions regarding federal authority over public health policy related to bioterrorism, support for voluntary public health programs, and the necessity of public trust for effective public health interventions are all illustrated by our experience to date with smallpox vaccination. Reducing the risk of a smallpox attack will also require global action. Specifically, the US should take a leadership role in strengthening international treaties to prevent the manufacture, storage, and use of biological toxins.[113]

IX. CONCLUSION

Our new kind of war against bioterrorism should be built on a goal of protecting liberty, not depriving Americans of it. As the American Civil Liberties Union has put it after 9/11, we should keep America "safe and free" (although I'd reverse the order). There is a knee jerk tendency in times of war and national emergencies to restrict civil liberties as the most effective way to counteract the threat. But history has taught us that such restrictions are almost always useless and often counterproductive, and we usually wind up with deep regrets for our action.[114] The tendency to return to the days before liberty and informed consent were taken seriously was evident both in the Gulf War and in the immediate aftermath of 9/11. In neither instance did these responses help make Americans safer or more secure, and in both they threatened the very liberties that make our country worth protecting.

The planned use of arbitrary force by Americans against Americans is un-American, even if done in the name of public health. No American physician should be forced to do anything to a patient that the physician does not believe is in the patient's best interests, and even then only with the patient's consent. No American soldier should be forced to take experimental drugs and vaccines; and no American citizen should be forced to take any drug or vaccine, or to be quarantined against their will, when any other less restrictive alter-

---

[112] *E.g.*, Marie McCullough & Marian Uhlman, *National Campaign Against Smallpox Falters*, PHILADELPHIA INQUIRER, April 3, 2003 at B1; Martin Ensherink, *Smallpox Vaccination Campaign in the Doldrums*, 300 SCIENCE 880 (2003).

[113] *See, e.g.*, Bruce Alberts & Robert M. May, *Scientist Support for Biological Weapons Control*, 298 SCIENCE 1135 (2002).

[114] The interment of Japanese Americans during World War II is only the most spectacular of these "emergency" civil rights violations – not only did it unfairly and unjustly impact on the Japanese involved, but its legacy made it impossible to engage in any sort of rational airport screening in the wake of 9/11. *But see*, Eric Lichtblau, *Bush Issues Racial Profiling Ban but Exempts Security Inquiries*, N.Y. TIMES, June 18, 2003 at 1A.

native is available. America is strong because its people are free, and to be both moral and effective public planning for war and public health emergencies must be based on respecting freedom and trusting our fellow citizens. Rather than adopt the tactics of repressive totalitarian regimes, the United States should lead the world in proclaiming a new, global public health, based on transparency, trust, and science, and most importantly, based on respect for human rights.

[9]

QUARANTINE REDUX: BIOTERRORISM, AIDS AND THE CURTAILMENT OF INDIVIDUAL LIBERTY IN THE NAME OF PUBLIC HEALTH

Wendy E. Parmet[†‡]

Novel sources of death are especially frightening. In the early 1980s, the emergence of the AIDS epidemic was the source not only of suffering and loss, but also of fear, hysteria, and irrationality. It was in that heated climate that public debate turned to the questions of when and whether government may infringe upon individual liberties in order to protect public health.[1]

Although AIDS is still with us, and indeed it causes more suffering each year,[2] in the United States it is no longer the public health threat that induces the greatest fears. Bioterrorism may now claim that honor. And so *it* now provokes the old debate pitting individual liberties against the state.

The confluence of the terrorist attacks on the United States last September and the anthrax mail attacks in the subsequent weeks focused attention and fear on the use of pathogens as weapons of mass

---

† Professor of Law, Northeastern University School of Law. Many thanks to Anthony Robbins, M.D. and Anthony Moulton, Ph.D., for their comments on an earlier version of the paper, to Daniel McCabe, Jennifer Hoenig, Jamie Quigley, Kevin Pechulis, David Roberts and Jason Smith for their wonderful help researching this paper, and to Jan McNew for her terrific secretarial assistance. All opinions and errors are my own.

‡ This paper was written in September 2002 and does not discuss developments in the field subsequent to that date.

1 The literature from that time is extensive. For a few examples, *see* RONALD BAYER, PRIVATE ACTS, SOCIAL CONSEQUENCES: AIDS AND THE POLITICS OF PUBLIC HEALTH (1989); *see also* Scott Burris, *Fear Itself: AIDS, Herpes, and Public Health Decisions*, 3 YALE L. & POL'Y REV. 479 (1985) (discussing the role of health law as related to individual rights against the public good).

2 *The Report on the Global HIV/AIDS Epidemic: The Barcelona Report*, UNAIDS, XIV International Conference on AIDS (July 2002) (reporting the latest global HIV/AIDS statistics and putting forth new suggestions on how to better deal with the crisis), *available at* http://www.unaids.org/barcelona/presskit/report.html.

destruction. In response, the Centers for Disease Control and Prevention ("CDC"), in collaboration with the National Governors Association, the National Conference on State Legislatures, the Association of State and Territorial Health Officials and the National Association of County and City Health Officials commissioned the center for Law and the Public's Health at Georgetown and Johns Hopkins Universities ("the Center") to develop a model act for states to consider enacting in preparation for bioterrorism. In November 2001, the Center released a draft version of the "Model State Emergency Health Powers Act" ("Model Act") which was revised in December.[3] Many states are now considering legislation based upon the Model Act.[4]

Although the two versions of the Model Act differ significantly in many ways, both would grant governors the ability to declare a public health emergency which would then permit the imposition of isolation, quarantine, mandatory medical examinations, and other coercive measures.[5] In effect, both versions of the Model Act grant states coercive powers in order to meet the threat of bioterrorism. At the same time, the Model Act's authors attempt to mediate the perceived clash between the use of the coercive powers and individual rights. The preamble states that

> the Act recognizes that a state's ability to respond to a public health emergency must respect the dignity and rights of persons . . . . The Act thus provides that, in the event of the exercise of emergency powers, the civil rights, liberties, and needs of infected or exposed persons will be protected to the fullest extent possible consistent with the primary goal of controlling serious health threats.[6]

As Yogi Berra has been quoted as saying, "It's déjà vu all over again!" As in the early years of the HIV epidemic, public health appears to be in conflict with the rights of the individual. In the case of HIV, many have argued that "exceptional" policies prevailed and that

---

[3] THE MODEL STATE EMERGENCY HEALTH POWERS ACT (Center for Law and the Public Health at Georgetown and John Hopkins Universities, Draft for Discussion 2001), *at* http://www.publichealthlaw.net/msehpa/msehpa2.pdf (Dec. 21, 2001) [hereinafter MODEL ACT].

[4] *See* The Model State Emergency Health Powers Act: State Legislative Activity (as of Oct. 1, 2002) (compiling all 50 states activity relating to the Model State Emergency Health Powers Act), *available at* http://www.pubichealthlaw.net/MSEHPA_Leg_Activity_050102.pdf.

[5] *See* text accompanying notes 27-54, *infra.*

[6] MODEL ACT, *supra* note 3, at Preamble.

protection of the public health gave way to individual rights.[7] This time around, with a new, perhaps even scarier threat, the outcome should be different, or so the proponents of the Model Act would proclaim. But have we learned the right lessons?

In this Article, I review a revised version of the Model Act in light of public health law's encounter with HIV. I begin in Part I by reviewing the Model Act and other legal responses that have been adopted or proposed with respect to bioterrorism. In Part II, I discuss the debates that emerged in the 1980s and early 1990s about individual rights in the wake of HIV. I suggest that although the government did not by and large adopt coercive policies with respect to HIV, a consensus developed, at least among policymakers and influential public health theorists, that HIV was treated exceptionally, and that the "normal" approach to public health threats is to invoke "traditional police powers" that allow for placing restraints upon individual liberty.[8] In Part III, I question that consensus, arguing that "traditional police powers" are far more varied than is often appreciated. In particular, I discuss the important role that social and structural reforms, as well as education, have long played in the protection of public health. Restraint on individual liberty, I contend, has been a far less critical part of public health's legal palate than is commonly assumed. In Part IV, I turn to the role of law and legal procedures in mediating the rights of the individual and the interests of the state in the face of public health threats. Here I caution against excessive confidence in modern statutes and judicial review as arbiters of the tensions that exist between individuals and public health. Although courts played a vital role in protecting individual rights during the AIDS epidemic, I question whether they can or will do so during the next public health emergency. Finally in Part VI return to bioterrorism I also suggest that our legal preparations for bioterrorism should not rely too heavily on laws pertaining to individual restraints and rights. Such an approach may lull political leaders and others into thinking they have solved a problem when they have not. Rather than rely unduly on constraints upon individuals, we must look to other more complex and perhaps more expensive legal approaches that may help not only to

---

[7] *See* Ronald Bayer, *Public Health Policy and the AIDS Epidemic: An End to HIV Exceptionalism?* 324 NEW. ENG. J. MED. 1500 (1991) (arguing that the public health response to AIDS has differed from responses to other diseases, but that this different response is deteriorating).

[8] More coercive policies have been adopted than is commonly appreciated. *See* Scott Burris, *Public Health, "AIDS Exceptionalism," and the Law,* 27 J. MARSHALL L. REV. 251, 253 (1994) (noting the governmental activity designed to curb the spread of HIV). See also text accompanying notes 62-67 *infra.*

prevent and contain bioterrorism, but to preserve individual interests in the event of a misuse of governmental powers.

I. LEGAL RESPONSES TO BIOTERRORISM

Since ancient times, human beings have been known to use disease to injure their enemies.[9] During the middle ages, soldiers threw the bodies of plague victims over the walls of enemy cities.[10] During the French and Indian Wars, the English gave blankets exposed to smallpox to enemy Indian troops.[11]

Legal responses to biological warfare and bioterrorism are more recent.[12] In 1925 the Geneva Protocol banned the use of biological weapons in war by its signatories[13] (although the United States signed the Protocol in 1925, it did not ratify the treaty until 1975).[14] In 1972 the Biological and Toxin Weapons Convention banned the development, production and stockpiling of biological weapons.[15] As part of its implementation of the Convention, in 1989 Congress passed the Biological Weapons Anti-Terrorism Act,[16] which criminalized the possession or use of biological weapons. In 1996 the Antiterrorism and Effective Death Penalty Act filled some of the gaps left by the 1989 Act by strengthening its criminal provisions and tightening the regulation of the transfer and shipment of potentially hazardous biological material.[17] In addition, Congress turned its attention to bioterrorism once again in 2000, empowering the Secretary of Health and Human Services to make grants and enter into contracts to respond to

---

[9] *See* JUDITH MILLER ET AL., GERMS: BIOLOGICAL WEAPONS AND AMERICA'S SECRET WAR, 37-38 (2001) (explaining several uses of disease to harm opponents during warfare throughout history).

[10] *Id.*

[11] *Id.* at 38.

[12] For the purposes of this article, I will rely upon the term "bioterrorism" to refer to any intentional use of a pathogen or biological toxin to harm or kill a human being. The distinction between biological warfare, use of biological weapons to commit an "ordinary crime," and bioterrorism, are subject to debate and not relevant for this purposes of this discussion.

[13] Protocol for the Prohibition of the Use in War of Asphyxiating Poisonous or Other Gases, and of Bacteriological Methods of Warfare, June 17, 1925, 26 U.S.T. 571, 94 L.N.T.S. 65, 67 [hereinafter Geneva Protocol.]

[14] Geneva Protocol, *supra* note 13, at 26 U.S.T. at 571-72.

[15] Convention on the Prohibition of the Development, Production and Stockpiling of Bacteriological (Biological) and Toxin Weapons and on their Destruction, Apr. 10, 1972, 26 U.S.T. 583, 1015 U.N.T.S. 163.

[16] 18 U.S.C. §§ 175-78 (2002).

[17] *Id.* at § 175(b).

a public health emergency and establishing a workgroup on bioterrorism.[18]

Nevertheless as concerns about terrorism and bioterrorism intensified in the 1990s,[19] commentators increasingly pointed to deficiencies in U.S. law as part of the problem. For example, in March 2001, Juliette N. Kayyem, Executive Director of the Executive Session on Domestic preparedness at the John F. Kennedy School of Government, surveyed U.S. laws that applied to bioterrorism and concluded that "[t]here needs to be a clearer understanding of what the rules are. The law is not, and should not be, an impediment to protecting life."[20] Likewise in a September 2001 article, undoubtedly written before the September 11 attacks, Professor David P. Fidler wrote that "the American legal system is simply not designed to deal with such a complex and insidious act of violence."[21]

It was in response to the urgency created by September 11 and the anthrax attacks, as well as the perception that inadequate laws undermined the nation's ability to respond to bioterrorism that the CDC commissioned the Center to draft the Model Act. According to Secretary of Health and Human Services Tommy Tompson, "[w]e need[ed] not only a strong health infrastructure and a full stockpile of medical resources, but also the legal and emergency tools to help our citizens quickly."[22] The Model Act's chief drafter, Professor Lawrence O. Gostin concurred saying that the act was needed because "[c]urrent public health laws are too highly antiquated and inadequate to ensure

---

[18] *See* Public Health Threats and Emergencies Act of 2000, 42 U.S.C. § 247(a) (2000) (referring to the powers of the Secretary of Health and Human Services in an emergency).

[19] Many factors help explain the increasing salience of bioterrorism in the 1990s. These include the 1993 bombing of the World Trade Center, the discovery of the massive bioweapons program run by the Soviet Union, as well as the program run by Iraq, and the discovery that the Japanese cult, Aum Shunrikyo experimented with biological weapons before using sarin gas to attack to the Tokyo subway system. For a full discussion of these and other events, *see* MILLER ET AL., *supra* note 9.

[20] Juliette N. Kayyem, *U.S. Preparation for Biological Terrorism: Legal Limitations and the Need for Planning*, BCSIA Discussion Paper 2001-4, ESDP Discussion Paper ESDP-2000-02, John F. Kennedy School of Government, Harvard University, March 2001 (analyzing current laws and their ability to also cover terroristic acts), *available at* http://ksgnotes1.harvard.edu/BCSIA/Library.nsf/pubs/2001ESDP2.

[21] David P. Fidler, *The Malevolent Use of Microbes and the Rule of Law: Legal Challenges Presented by Bioterrorism*, 33 CLINICAL INFECTIOUS DISEASES 686 (2001) (explaining how bioterrorism could have a negative effect on the rule of law in the United States), *.pdf file available at* http://www.journals.uchicago.edu/CID/journal/contents/v33n5.text.htm.

[22] Justin Gillis, *States Weighing Laws to Fight Bioterrorism*, WASH. POST, Nov. 19, 2001, *at* A-1.

a strong and effective response to bioterrorism . . . [Public health laws] tend to be highly inadequate, confusing and contradictory – even within states there's an inconsistent response."[23]

In response to this perceived need, the Model Act seeks first and foremost to clarify and rationalize public health law. In the tradition of the uniform law movement,[24] the drafters and their sponsors sought to provide states with a model act that would put in one place all state laws pertaining to public health emergencies.[25] And, the Act sought to ensure that states would have sufficient "authority" to deal with the threat of bioterrorism. As the Model Act's findings state, "government must do more to protect the health, safety, and general well being of its citizens."[26]

The key provisions in the Act for providing the state with the authority to "do more" are found in Articles III, IV, and V, which enable the Governor to declare a "state of public health emergency"[27] thereby triggering "special powers."[28] Under the Model Act, the Governor

---

[23] Matt Mientka, *CDC Releases Model Bioterroism Law*, U.S. MEDICINE INFORMATION CENTER (Dec. 2001), *at* http://www.usmedicine.com/article.cfm?articleID=314&issueID=33 (last visited Oct. 24, 2002).

[24] *See generally*, James G. Hodge, Jr., *Bioterrorism Law and Policy: Critical Choices in Public Health*, 30 J.L. MED. & ETHICS 254 (2002) (explaining need for uniform collaborative effort between state, local and federal government organizations to protect the public from bioterrorism); Lorena Matei, *Quarantine Revision and the Model State Emergency Health Powers Act: "Laws for the Common Good,"* 18 SANTA CLARA COMPUTER & HIGH TECH. L.J. 433 (2002) (arguing for implementation of a comprehensive law to protect citizens from bioterrorism).

[25] *See* Lawrence O. Gostin et al., *The Model State Emergency Health Powers Act: Planning for and Response to Bioterrorism and Naturally Occurring Infectious Diseases*, 288 JAMA 622, 625-26 (2002). The sponsors of the Act did note that the Model Act was just a model, that each state should use it as a template for discussion and review of their own laws, and that it was appropriate for states to make individual adjustments. Nevertheless, the sponsors have pointed to the advantages of consistency across state boundaries. *See also* George J. Annas, *Bioterrorism, Public Health, and Civil Liberties*, 346 NEW ENG. J. MED. 1337, 1341 (Apr. 25, 2002) (explaining the need for new public health legislation relating to bioterrorism and how the Model State Emergency Health Act will not suffice). Given the ability of bioterrorism to cross state boundaries, the viability of relying upon state as opposed to federal laws is questionable.

[26] MODEL ACT, *supra*, note 3, at § 102(a).

[27] *Id.* at § 401.

[28] *Id.* at § 403(a), Article V. The Model Act also has provisions that apply prior to an emergency. For example, Article II of the Act requires the Governor to appoint a commission charged with developing a "public health emergency plan." *Id.* at §§ 201, 202 (emphasis omitted). The Act, however, does not require the state to actually implement any elements of the plan. In addition, Article II of the Act requires health care providers, coroners, and medical examiners to report "any illness or

may declare a "state of public health emergency" upon the occurrence of an

> imminent threat of an illness or health condition that:
> (1) is believed to be caused by any of the following:
>
> > (i) bioterrorism;
> > (ii) the appearance of a novel or previously controlled or eradicated infectious agent or biological toxin;
> > (iii) [a natural disaster;]
> > (iv)[a chemical attack or accidental release; or]
> > (v) [a nuclear attack or accident]; and
>
> (2) poses a high probability of any of the following harms:
>
> > (i) a large number of deaths in the affected population;
> > (ii) a large number of serious or long-term disabilities in the affected population; or
> > (iii) widespread exposure to an infectious or toxic agent that poses a significant risk of substantial future harm to a large number of people in the affected population.[29]

Importantly, the Governor may declare such a state even "without consulting with the public health authority or other experts when the situation calls for prompt and timely action."[30] Once declared the state of emergency may continue for thirty days, whereupon the Governor (presumably again without consulting with anyone) may renew the declaration for another thirty days.[31] This process apparently can continue ad infinitum although at any time the legislature may termi-

---

health condition that may be potential causes of a public health emergency." *Id.* at § 301(a). Pharmacists are also required to "report any unusual or increased prescription rates, unusual types of prescriptions, or unusual trends in pharmacy visits that may be potential causes of a public health emergency." *Id.* at § 301(b). *But see* Annas, *supra* note 25, at 1340 (criticizing what the Model Act actually requires and the potential privacy implications of the requirement). The uncertainty as to what that actually requires, and the potential privacy implications of the requirement, have elicited significant criticism.

[29] MODEL ACT, *supra* note 3, at § 104(m) (emphasis omitted). The sections in brackets are meant to offer states the choice to expand the category of public health emergencies beyond bioterrorism, if they desire. *See* Letter of Lawrence O. Gostin, December 21, 2001 (on file with author).

[30] MODEL ACT, *supra* note 3, at § 401.

[31] *Id.* at § 405(b).

nate the declaration if it finds that the "illness or health condition that caused the emergency does not or no longer poses a high probability of a large number of deaths in the affected population, a large number of incidents of serious permanent or long-term disability in the affected population, or a significant risk of substantial future harm to a large number of people in the affected population."[32] Hence a state of emergency can continue without any legislative affirmation indefinitely unless a majority of the legislature votes to repeal it.[33]

Once a declaration is made, the Model Act gives the Governor and the public health agency extraordinary powers.[34] Briefly, the declaration gives the Governor authority to "[s]uspend the provisions of any regulatory statute prescribing procedures for conducting State business, or the orders, rules and regulations of any State agency, to the extent that strict compliance with the same would prevent, hinder, or delay necessary action . . . by the public health authority."[35] It would also permit the Governor to mobilize the militia into service.[36] In addition, the public health authority would be authorized to close or decontaminate facilities,[37] to require health care facilities to provide services,[38] and to require other facilities (the nature of which is undefined) to provide a wide variety of services to the state.[39]

---

[32] *Id.* at §§ 405(b), (c). It is an interesting question whether such a legislative veto is constitutional under all state constitutions. *Cf.*, INS v. Chadha, 462 U.S. 919 (1983) (holding that federal legislative veto violates U.S. Constitution).

[33] The Model Act is unclear as to whether the declaration or its repeal is reviewable by a court. Although the Act provides for immunity for the state and its officials for injuries or damages caused by the declaration (except when there is gross negligence or willful misconduct), it says absolutely nothing about reviewability and the possibility of prospective injunctive relief. Presumably many state courts would find that they have the power to review such orders. Indeed, they may find that the denial of any possibility of review raises grave questions under the due process clause of the 14th amendment as well as state constitutional provisions guaranteeing access to the courts. *See, e.g.*, Heather Brann, *Utah's Medical Malpractice Prelitigation Panel: Exploring State Constitutional Arguments Against a Nonbinding Inadmissible Procedure*, 2000 UTAH L. REV. 359, 365-67 (2001) (applying due process clause and state open courts provision to pre-litigation panels in medical malpractice cases).

[34] *See* Annas, *supra* note 25, at 1338, 1340. *See also* Jennifer King, *Power Grab: The States in a State of Emergency. The Model Emergency Health Powers Act,* American Legislative Exchange Council Issue Analysis (Jan. 2002) (discussing the key points of the Model Emergency Health Powers Act), *at* http://www.alec.org/meSWFiles/pdf/0202.pdf.

[35] MODEL ACT, *supra* note 3, at § 403(a)(1).

[36] *Id.* at § 403(a)(4).

[37] *Id.* at § 501(a).

[38] *Id.* at § 502(b).

[39] *See id.* at §§ 503(b), (c) (noting that the services must be "reasonable and necessary to respond to the public health emergency").

The most interesting provisions, however, authorize the state to exert broad coercive powers over individuals, once a declaration of emergency has been made. First, the public health authority may perform physical examinations and/or tests "necessary for the diagnosis or treatment of individuals."[40] Because the Model Act does not specify what types of tests may be performed, or whether the examinations need to have anything to do with the health threat instigating the declaration, a state of emergency would presumably authorize the public health authority to perform almost any diagnostic test on anyone. Thus a public health authority acting in bad faith would have the lawful authority to use a public health threat as an excuse to perform mandatory HIV tests! Under the Act, an individual's refusal to permit this examination might justify isolation if the authority was uncertain if the individual was infected.[41]

Once a public health emergency has been declared, the public health authority would also have the power to vaccinate and treat individuals.[42] Individuals who are "unable or unwilling" to submit to these procedures "for reasons of health, religion, or conscience" may be subject to isolation and quarantine.[43] What happens to people who refuse to submit for other reasons (such as suspicion of public authorities) is not made clear.

The isolation and quarantine provisions are undoubtedly among the most central in the act.[44] Under the Model Act, isolation and/or

---

[40] MODEL ACT, *supra* note 3, at § 602.

[41] *Id.* at § 602(c). Although the Act would seem to permit the public health authority to conduct almost any kind of diagnostic test or examination, quarantine or isolation is only permitted if there is uncertainty as to whether the individual has been exposed to a contagious disease. *Id.* Generally, a contagious disease is one that can be transmitted by casual contact. *See* MERRIAM-WEBSTER'S COLLEGIATE DICTIONARY 249 (10th ed. 1998). However, the Act defines a contagious disease more broadly to include any "infectious disease that can be transmitted from person to person." MODEL ACT, *supra* note 3, at § 104 (c). Hence while HIV is not typically considered a "contagious disease," it would appear to be so within the literal meaning of the Act.

[42] *Id.* at § 603.

[43] *Id.* §§ 603(a)(3), (b)(3).

[44] Isolation, as the term is defined by the Model Act

> [I]s the physical separation and confinement of an individual or groups of individuals who are Infected or reasonably believed to be infected with a contagious or possibly contagious disease from non-isolated individuals, to prevent or limit the transmission of the disease to non-isolated individuals.

Id. at § 104(h).

Furthermore, the Model Act defines "quarantine" as:

> The physical separation and confinement of an individual or groups of individuals, who are or may have been exposed to a contagious or possible contagious disease and who do not show signs or symptoms of a contagious

quarantine is authorized when individuals refuse to submit to an examination, treatment or vaccination as discussed above, as well as when they are "the least restrictive means necessary to prevent the spread of a contagious or possibly contagious disease to others."[45] Again the Model Act does not require that the "contagious disease" which is the object of the isolation or quarantine be the illness that triggered the public health emergency in the first place. Thus the appearance of anthrax, a non-contagious bioterrorist agent, could theoretically trigger isolation for HIV or hepatitis if the public health authority believed that it was the "least restrictive means necessary to spread" the infection.

The Model Act relies heavily upon judicial procedures to oversee and legitimate the use of isolation and quarantine. Within ten days of subjecting an individual to isolation or quarantine, the public health authority is required to file a petition to a court stating the reasons for the order.[46] Within five days of receiving the petition, a hearing must be held, although "[i]n extraordinary circumstances and for good cause" it may be postponed for up to 10 days, meaning that the individual can be held for up to 20 days before any judicial review may occur.[47] At the hearing, the court may grant the petition if "by a preponderance of the evidence, isolation or quarantine is shown to be reasonably necessary to prevent or limit the transmission of a contagious or possibly contagious disease to others."[48] An order approving the isolation or quarantine may extend for thirty days, although the court, upon motion, may extend it for another thirty days.[49] An individual may also be released upon successfully petitioning the court for an order to show cause why the individual should not be released.[50] For all hearings regarding an individual's isolation and quarantine, the court must appoint counsel for the individual.[51] In appropriate circumstances, cases may be consolidated.[52]

Concerned about the human rights and dignity of those subject to these orders, the Model Act requires the state to provide for the

---

> disease, from non-quarantined individuals, to prevent or limit the transmission of the disease to non-quarantined individuals.

Id. at § 104(o).

[45] MODEL ACT, *supra* note 3, at § 604(b)(1).

[46] *Id.* at §§ 605(a)(4), (b)(2).

[47] *Id.* at § 605(b)(4).

[48] *Id.* at § 605(b)(5).

[49] *Id.* at §§ 605(b)(5)(1), (b)(6).

[50] MODEL ACT, *supra* note 3, at § 605(c)(1).

[51] *Id.* at § 605(e)(1).

[52] *See id.* at § 605(e)(2) (listing the circumstances when consolidation is proper).

"needs" of individuals subject to the order, by providing them with at least "adequate food, clothing, shelter, means of communication . . . medication, and competent medical care."[53] Interestingly, the Act does not explicitly require the state to provide for the economic consequences, such as loss of wages or unemployment, that an individual may face due to an isolation or quarantine order, although this may perhaps be included as part of an individual's "needs." Likewise, the Act does not explicitly obligate the state to care for an affected individual's dependants. Moreover, the stringent immunity provisions of the Model Act would appear to foreclose the possibility of any damage remedy for the state's failure to abide by some of those provisions, as well as any compensation for any economic or other injuries that may result from inappropriate or unnecessary isolation.[54]

II. "AIDS EXCEPTIONALISM"

It is not surprising that the advent of a frightening, seemingly new public health menace has prompted consideration of coercive measures. Throughout history, new plagues have been met with restrictions upon individual liberties. Sometimes this has been because such restrictions are the only or most effective way to preserve the community given the circumstances. Too often, however, the reliance on coercion has been unnecessary and ineffective and in hindsight can be recognized as nothing more noble than the scapegoating, if not vilification of marginalized groups.[55] So it was with AIDS.

The arrival of a deadly and terrifying new disease, transmitted sexually, and associated in the public's mind with homosexuals elicited cries to remove, isolate, and even brand those who were infected.[56] Today we may forget that in the 1980s HIV positive school children were commonly cast out of their classroom, but such was the state of fear when Ryan White became a well-recognized name.[57] Indeed, surveying the state of public opinion in 1987, Professor Gostin along with his co-author Andrew Ziegler wrote that

---

[53] *Id.* at § 604(b)(6).

[54] *Id.* at § 804(a).

[55] Wendy E. Parmet, *AIDS and Quarantine: The Revival of an Archaic Doctrine*, 14 HOFSTRA L. REV. 53, 55-58 (1985); Guenter B. Risse, *Epidemics and History: Ecological Perspectives and Social Responses*, *in* AIDS: THE BURDENS OF HISTORY 33 (Elizabeth Fee and Daniel M. Fox eds., 1988).

[56] Parmet, *supra* note 55, at 53-54.

[57] *See* Wendy E. Parmet & Daniel J. Jackson, *No Longer Disabled: The Legal Impact of the New Social Construction of HIV*, 23 AM. J.L. & MED.7, 10 (1997) (discussing Ryan White's plight against discrimination based on his HIV positive status).

> There is some public support for restricting the liberty and autonomy of HIV-infected people. In five national public opinion polls conducted between September 1985 and November 1986, 28 to 54 percent of the respondents favored 'quarantine' of people with AIDS in 'special places to keep them away from the general public.'[58]

They then went on to discuss the various proposals taken up by state legislatures to increase state authority to confine HIV positive individuals.[59]

Perhaps the most serious and difficult debate about the use of coercive powers and HIV concerned the use of wide-scale mandatory testing.[60] For many reasons, this was never implemented. No doubt, the timing of the HIV epidemic played some role in the initial rejection of mandatory testing. Arriving after the Civil Rights movements, Watergate, the birth of the gay rights movement and even the revelations about the Tuskegee experiments, HIV made its appearance at a time when the public was especially sensitive to claims of individual rights and particularly skeptical of government authority. But even more important than the zeitgeist, perhaps, was the reality that given the fact that HIV was transmitted by private behaviors, and that an individual remained infectious throughout his or her life, it was difficult to see how mandatory testing could aid efforts to thwart the disease's spread. Rather, by the late 1980s most public health officials had come to believe that the trust of those infected and the cooperation of communities at risk was key to protecting the public against HIV, and both of these could and would be undermined by the imposition of coercive measures. As Professor Samuel Bagenstos has written,

> when public health officials forewent coercive measures in their responses to AIDS, their position reflected less a capture by an important interest group than a hardhearted calculation that an epidemic spread by the intimate conduct of particular segments of the community simply could not be brought un-

---

[58] Larry Gostin & Andrew Ziegler, *A Review of AIDS-Related Legislative and Regulatory Policy in the United States*, 15 LAW, MED. & HEALTH CARE 5, 11 (1987).

[59] *See id.* (noting that at the time some states had already enacted HIV isolation policies, while others were still considering it).

[60] For an early discussion of the issue, see Michael L. Closen et. al, *AIDS: Testing Democracy – Irrational Responses to the Public Health Crises and the Need for Privacy in Serologic Testing*, 19 J. MARSHALL L. REV. 836 (1986).

> der control by measures that failed to pay attention to the interests of those segments of the community.[61]

Although by the late 1980s, a broad consensus had rejected the use of broad-scale mandatory testing and a variety of other coercive measures (such as the exclusion of children from schools), the debate continued about the more limited application of coercive powers.[62] For example, in 1991 Dr. Marcia Angell editorialized in the *New England Journal of Medicine* for the mandatory screening of pregnant women and infants.[63] Writing in the same issue, Ronald Bayer, also counseled for the reconsideration of more "traditional" public health powers.[64] Arguing that HIV had been treated "exceptionally," Bayer wrote:

> In the first years of the AIDS epidemic, U.S. officials had no alternative but to negotiate the course of AIDS policy with representatives of a well-organized gay community and their allies in the medical and political establishments. In this process, many of the traditional practices of public health that might have been brought to bear were dismissed as inappropriate. As the first decade of the epidemic came to an end, public health officials began to reassert their professional dominance over the policy-making process and in so doing began to rediscover the relevance of their own professional traditions to the control of AIDS.[65]

---

[61] Samuel R. Bagenstos, *The Americans with Disabilities Act as Risk Regulation,* 101 COLUM. L. REV. 1479, 1503 (2001).

[62] The debate has also never ended as to whether HIV status alone should be a reportable disease. For a discussion of this issue, see Lawrence O. Gostin & James G. Hodge, Jr., *The "Names Debate": The Case for National HIV Reporting in the United States*, 61 ALB. L. REV. 679 (1998).

[63] Marcia Angell, *A Dual Approach to the AIDS Epidemic,* 324 NEW ENG. J. MED. 1498, 1499-1500 (1991). The question of whether pregnant women or newborns should be subject to mandatory testing has never gone away. Although the CDC formulated a policy calling for routine counseling and voluntary testing of all pregnant women, FY 1995 Epidemiologic Research Studies of Acquired Immunodeficiency Syndrome (AIDS) and Human Immunodeficiency Virus (HIV) Infection, 60 Fed. Reg. 35405, 35406 (July 7, 1995), New York State passed the nation's only law requiring testing of newborns. N.Y. PUBLIC HEALTH LAW § 2500-f (McKinney 2002). For more on the current debate, see Leslie Ayers, Note,-*Is Mama a Criminal?—An Analysis of Potential Criminal Liability of HIV-Infected Pregnant Women in the Context of Mandated Drug Therapy,* 50 DRAKE L. REV. 293, 297-98 (2002).

[64] Bayer, *supra* note 7, at 1502-04.

[65] *Id.* at 1502-04. The claim that political necessity led to the rejection of traditional public health approaches in the early years of the HIV epidemic also ap-

Bayer and Angell were not alone. Lee Reichman, director of the National Tuberculosis Center, stated "[t]raditional public health is absolutely effective at controlling infectious disease. It should have been applied to AIDS from the start, and it wasn't. Long before there was AIDS, there were other sexually transmitted diseases, and you had partner notification and testing and reporting. This was routine public health at its finest."[66]

Although some commentators at the time questioned the "AIDS exceptionalism" thesis,[67] by the mid-to-late 1990s many scholars and public health officials had begun to question the rejection of coercive measures vis-a -vis HIV.[68] Thus when multi-drug resistant tuberculosis appeared in New York in the early 1990s, many experts concurred on the need to institute mandatory treatment and isolation (as well as directly observed therapy).[69] The efficacy of those methods in the "war" against MDR-TB seemed to vindicate the exceptionalist thesis which premised the importance of restricting individual liberties in the name of public health.[70]

The legal corollary to the exceptionalism thesis was that the police power provided states with the authority to restrict individual liberty in the name of public health. Just as the HIV exceptionalists believed that restrictions on individual liberty were key to public health's ability to control communicable diseases, public health scholars viewed liberty-restraining regulations as the sine qua non of public health law. In 1999 Professor Gostin along with his colleagues Professors Burris and Lazzarini wrote: "A reliance on coercive reactive

---

pears in Bayer, *supra* note 1, at 21.

[66] Chandler Burr, *The AIDS Exception: Privacy v. Public Health*, THE ATLANTIC MONTHLY, June 1997, at 57, 66.

[67] *See* Burris, *supra* note 8, at 252 (noting that AIDS exceptionalism "never quite existed").

[68] *See* Burr, *supra* note 66 (providing examples of advocates for traditional, coercive measures).

[69] *See* Teri Flowers, *Quarantining the Noncompliant TB Patient: Catching the "Red Snapper,"* 28 J. HEALTH & HOSP. L. 95 (1995) (advocating quarantining of tuberculosis patients); Patricia C. Kuszler, *Balancing the Barriers: Exploiting and Creating Incentives to Promote Development of a New Tuberculosis Treatment*, 71 WASH. L. REV. 919, 930-37 (1996); Karen H. Rothenberg & Elizabeth C. Lovoy, *Something Old, Something New: The Challenge of Tuberculosis Control in the Age of AIDS*, 42 BUFF. L. REV. 715, 729-31 (1994) (discussing tuberculosis treatment and experts' desire to institute mandatory isolation and treatment as done in the 19th and early 20th centuries).

[70] *See* Thomas R. Frieden et al., *Tuberculosis in New York City – Turning The Tide*, 333 NEW ENG. J. MED. 229, 229-31 (1995) (illustrating the great success of using directly observed therapy and treatment completion in controlling the spread of tuberculosis).

control methods – particularly nuisance abatement, quarantine, and isolation – can be said to form the deepest layer of American disease control law, a layer that is often invisible, but that still shapes the structure of the statutory landscape."[71] Likewise in his 2000 opus, Public Health Law: Power, Duty and Restraint, Professor Gostin again noted the central role that coercion of individuals plays in public health promotion, stating that "[t]he study of the coercive powers of the state is a staple of what we call public health law."[72]

Professor Gostin's appreciation of the states' coercive powers has never been uncritical. Indeed, as far back as 1986 he criticized the antiquated nature of many state laws, noting that they often fail to reflect contemporary understandings of both epidemiology and constitutional law.[73] In 1999 he, along with Professors Lazzarini and Burris wrote:

> The most striking characteristic of state disease control law, and the one that underlies most of its defects, is its overall antiquity . . .
>
> Certainly, old laws are not necessarily bad laws. A well-written statute may remain useful, efficacious, and constitutional for many decades. Nevertheless, old public health statutes that have not been substantially altered since their enactment are often outmoded in ways that directly reduce both their efficacy and their conformity with modern standards. These laws often do not reflect contemporary scientific understandings of disease, current treatments of choice, or constitutional limits on states' authority to restrict individual liberties.[74]

Thus long before the terrible events of the fall 2001, Professor Gostin and many others had come to believe that despite prevailing HIV-policies, the core to public health law was the states' coercive powers. These powers, however, were seen as in serious need of up-

---

[71] Lawrence O. Gostin et al., *The Law and the Public's Health: A Study of Infectious Disease Law in the United States*, 99 COLUM. L. REV. 59, 102 (1999).

[72] LAWRENCE O. GOSTIN, PUBLIC HEALTH LAW: POWER, DUTY, RESTRAINT 19 (2000).

[73] Lawrence O. Gostin, *The Future of Public Health Law*, 12 AM. J.L. & MED. 462, 463-71 (1986). *See also* William J. Curran, Mary E. Clarke & Larry Gostin, *AIDS: Legal and Policy Implications of the Application of Traditional Disease Control Measures*, 15 LAW MED. & HEALTH CARE 27 (1987) (stating concerns about traditional ways of handling diseases as applied to the AIDS epidemic).

[74] Gostin et al., *supra* note 71, at 102-06 (citations omitted).

dating.[75] But by revising them to reflect "modern" understandings of disease and law, these scholars believed that states could more effectively protect public health by restraining individuals while respecting their legal rights. These three axioms that public health law is most fundamentally about the restraint of individual liberties, that it requires modernization, and that modernization can ensure the protection of individual rights while restraining those rights – animate the Model Act. The question remains: how valid are these premises?

III. THE ROLE OF COERCIVE POWERS IN PUBLIC HEALTH PROTECTION

There can be no doubt that the restraint of individuals, especially via quarantine and isolation, has long played an important role in public health law. During the middle ages, lepers were subject to isolation throughout Europe.[76] On these shores, quarantines against smallpox were instituted as far back as 1622.[77]

There can also be little doubt that courts have generally upheld the use of isolation and quarantine for public health goals.[78] When communities were threatened by devastating epidemics, judges were loathe to question actions that were taken in the name of public health.[79] Thus in the famous case of *Jacobson v. Massachusetts*, which upheld a law requiring vaccination against smallpox, the Supreme Court of the United States said:

> Upon the principle of self-defense, of paramount necessity, a community has the right to protect itself against an epidemic of disease which threatens the safety of its members . . . [I]t is equally true that in every well-ordered society charged with the duty of conserving the safety of its members the rights of the individual in respect of his liberty may at times, under the pressure of great dangers, be subjected to such restraint, to be

---

[75] *See* Gostin et al., *supra* note 25, at 623. The drafters of the Model Act repeated that point in 2002. Echoing the 1999 article by Gostin, Lazzarini and Burris, they wrote, "[S]tate public health statutes frequently are outdated and were built up in layers during the 20th century in response to each new disease threat. Consequently, these laws often do not reflect contemporary scientific understandings of disease (e.g., surveillance, prevention, and response) or legal norms for protection of individual rights."

[76] Parmet, *supra* note 55, at 55.

[77] *Id.* at 56.

[78] *Id.* at 59-66.

[79] *Id.* at 64-69. However, U.S. judges often did engage in a limited form of review, determining whether public health authorities had exceeded the scope of their authority and had not acted arbitrarily and without reason. *See id.*

enforced by reasonable regulations, as the safety of the general public may demand.[80]

The ubiquity and legality of quarantine and isolation, however, do not in themselves establish that they have been or ought to be seen as the core to public health law in general or central to our efforts to confront bioterrorism or many emerging threats.[81] With respect to history, the focus on isolation and quarantine of individuals overlooks the fact that historically quarantines were probably more often instituted against cargo vessels than against individuals.[82] Indeed, in U.S. constitutional law, the police power doctrine developed significantly in contests over the government's ability to regulate commerce.[83] In the 19th century it was often business interests, not advocates for individual rights, who challenged the authority of public health boards.[84]

These points are salient not because they question the ability of government to restrain the liberty of individuals, but because they should remind us that public health, in practice and in law, generally has had as much or more to do with regulatory efforts to shape the market than to restrain individuals. In the 19th century, after all, the great early steps taken by public health focused on the supply of clean water and wholesome foods.[85] In these instances government restrained liberty, but it was not the personal liberty of individuals to

[80] Jacobson v. Massachusetts, 197 U.S. 11, 27, 29 (1905).

[81] For arguments that quarantine and isolation would likely be fairly useless under most bioterrorism scenarios, see Joseph Barbera et al., *Large-Scale Quarantine Following Biological Terrorism in the United States, Scientific Examination, Logistic and Legal Limits, and Possible Consequences*, 286 JAMA 2711 (Dec. 2001).

[82] *See* WILLIAM J. NOVAK, THE PEOPLE'S WELFARE: LAW AND REGULATION IN NINETEENTH-CENTURY AMERICA 204-05 (1996) (explaining the frequent use of maritime quarantines on vessels arriving on American shores). *See also* Sylvia N. Tesh, *Miasma and "Social Factors" in Disease Causality: Lessons from the Nineteenth Century*, 20 J. HEALTH POL. POL'Y & L. 1001, 1005 (1995) (discussing how quarantines not only interfered with commerce but he interest of the people).

[83] Wendy E. Parmet, *After September 11, Rethinking Public Health Federalism* 30 J.L. MED. & ETHICS 201, 202-03 (2002).

[84] NOVAK, *supra* note 82, at 209. On the other hand, business interests also sometimes favored public health regulations, for example a historian of food inspection laws claims that the livestock and packing industries pressed for regulations so that European countries would open their markets to American meat. VIVIAN WISER, U.S. DEP'T OF AGRIC, MEAT AND POULTRY INSPECTION IN THE UNITED STATES DEPARTMENT OF AGRICULTURE.

[85] *See* GEORGE ROSEN, A HISTORY OF PUBLIC HEALTH 216-16 (expanded ed., The Johns Hopkins Univ. Press 1993) (1958) (discussing the causes of public health reform in the 19th century). *See also* Wendy E. Parmet, *From Slaughter-House to Lochner: The Rise and Fall of the Constitutionalization of Public Health,* 40 AM. J. LEGAL HIST. 476, 489 (1996) (stating the importance of clean water and pure food).

control their movement or make decisions about their own health care and bodily integrity; rather it was the liberty of businesses to sell unpasteurized milk or the liberty of taxpayers to avoid supporting a public water supply.

Certainly as the germ theory and contagionism took hold and the massive epidemics of the 19th century faded from memory, public health practitioners were more apt to see an individual who carried an infectious agent rather than filth or miasma as the source of danger. Likewise, as clinical medicine became more efficacious and more dominant, public health increasingly adopted its individualistic orientation and came to believe that identifying patients and getting them to treatment was central to its mission.[86] As a result, public health advocates began to stress the virtue of contact tracing and isolation.[87] But this vision of public health was never uncontested.[88] Even in the heyday of the public health movement, some adherents stressed education over coercion, arguing for the need to obtain a patient's cooperation.[89] Other public health notables argued that public health had to focus less on identifying and treating individuals and more on what we today would call the social conditions for health. In 1904, for example, Herman Biggs claimed that the time had come for public health to emphasize the occupational conditions that give rise to morbidity.[90] Less than two decades later, C.E.A. Winslow, noted that while "[s]anitation, isolation, vaccine and serum therapy, provided the complete machinery necessary for controlling many of the acute communicable diseases; . . . it became clear that the major problem of tuberculosis required other methods for its solution."[91] He described these

---

[86] Parmet, *supra* note 85, at 491. Scott Burris has noted that the so-called traditional public health powers have been used only infrequently and have "deep roots in a medicalized approach to public health." Burris, *supra* note 8, at 257.

[87] *E.g.*, George H. Rohe, *Recent Advances in Preventive Medicine*, 9 JAMA 1, 10-11 (1887) (arguing that the first requirement for dealing with an infectious disease from a "State Medicine Point of View" is notification and the second is segregation. The third requirement according to Rohe was disinfection).

[88] Burris, *supra* note 8, at 256 (noting that the process of identifying and treating at-risk individuals had the effect of separating social reform from medical treatment in the field of public health). *See also*, Barbara Gutmann Rosenkrantz, *Cart Before Horse: Theory, Practice and Professional Image in American Public Health*, 1870-1920, J. HIST. MED. & ALLIED SCI. 55, 66-68 (1974) (discussing problems associated with registration and tracing of tuberculosis patients as prevention of spreading the disease).

[89] *See* Rosenkrantz, *supra* note 88, at 63-64 (emphasizing the importance of educating the public to increase health improvements and battle diseases).

[90] Herman M. Biggs, *Preventive Medicine: Its Achievements, Scope, and Possibilities*, 65 MED. RED, 956 (1904).

[91] C.E.A. Winslow, *The Evolution and Significance of the Modern Public*

methods as including the organization of sanatoriums and dispensaries, the development of ambulatory care and home visits, and most especially a campaign of public education.[92] It might also include, he suggested, the establishment of some system of health care financing to permit the poor to pay for the kind of medical care that public health advocated.[93]

In the twentieth century, the jurisdiction of public health fragmented. Many of the problems, and legal controls, that were once within the purview of public health boards fell to other governmental bodies, such as the Environmental Protection Agency, the Food and Drug Administration and state agencies.[94] Often, these agencies focus on regulating large actors in the marketplace, not individuals. But that does not mean that such agencies do not "do" public health. They do. As a result, the claim that coercion of individuals is core to public health is in part an artifact of the divestment of many public health functions to other agencies.

All of this is not to deny a role, even a vital one, for the restriction of individual liberty in times of public health crisis. But it is to question the claims of the AIDS exceptionalists that such restraints are core to public health powers. Rather, other forms of government activity, including especially the regulation of goods and services and the formation of government services, such as the provision of clean water and the inspection of food supplies, are far more apt candidates for the title of core public health powers (even if some of these activities are no longer carried out by boards of health).

This suggests that the assumption of the drafters of the Model Act that updating and expanding the government's ability to coerce individuals is central to confronting bioterrorism may well be misplaced. There is no evidence to conclude that public health in the past has been most successful when it has relied primarily upon individual coercion and there is little reason to believe that such a policy would be the most effective approach were we faced with another bioterrorist incident.[95] Indeed, if history teaches us anything about the use of such

Health Campaign, J. PUB. HEALTH POL'Y, at 50 (3d printing 1984).

[92] *Id.* at 52.

[93] *Id.* at 61-62.

[94] 21 U.S.C. § 393 (2002); Reorg. Plan No. 3 of 1970, 35 Fed. Reg. 15623 (1970), *reprinted in* 5 U.S.C. app. 1 at 389 (1996). *See* ROSEN, *supra* note 85, at 215-16 (discussing the establishment of voluntary health association to improve public health); James G. Hodge, Jr. *Implementing Modern Public Health Goals Through Government: An Examination of New Federalism and Public Health Law*, 14 J. CONTEMP. HEALTH L. & POL'Y 93, 101-03 (1997).

[95] Barbera et al., *supra* note 81, at 2713-14. This is not to question the appropriateness of applying the coercive authority of the criminal law to the perpetrators

"traditional powers" it is that they are often, especially in crises, misused, sacrificing the rights of especially vulnerable individuals often for little or no public health benefit.[96] Whether that might happen under the Model Act depends, in large part, upon whether the drafters are correct in assuming that a modern statute, incorporating contemporary legal standards, can prevent the abuses of public health authority so common in history. It is to this question that I now turn.

IV. THE ROLE OF LAW IN PROTECTING INDIVIDUAL RIGHTS

A central tenet of the Model Act is that a modern, carefully drafted statute, providing for current standards of due process can help avoid the abuses of public health authority that have occurred in prior epidemics. Two premises are implicit in this tenet. First, that a modern statute will clarify ambiguity and prevent misuses of legal authority.[97] Second, that contemporary legal standards provide meaningful protections against abuses of authority. Each deserves brief discussion.

Responding to Professor Gostin's long-articulated belief that public health statutes are in a shambles and badly in need of updating, the Model Act seeks to resolve issues of authority and rights by providing clear and contemporary language. But while Professor Gostin and others have demonstrated by their review of state statutes that many state public health laws are old and confusing, there is little evidence to conclude that they have impeded public health protection.[98] Moreover, it is by no means clear that *any* new code could provide greater clarity and legal certainty than do current statutes. Indeed, there are many reasons to doubt that it could.

---

of bioterrorism. My focus here is on the application of coercion to *victims* of bioterrorism.

[96] For a discussion of how public health officials in San Francisco in the early 1900s came to equate bubonic plague with race and as a result imposed a quarantine on Chinatown, see NAYAN SHAH, CONTAGIOUS DIVIDES: EPIDEMICS AND RACE IN SAN FRANCISCO'S CHINATOWN 120-57 (2001).

[97] *See* Gostin et al., *supra* note 25, at 623-24. The drafters also hope that a modern statute will clarify the vigorous nature of authority, when it is needed.

[98] For example, in a recent article on New York's initial response to the West Nile Virus, Wilfredo Lopez, counsel for the Department of Health noted that "the existing authority of the Board of Health, which in the abstract may seem vague or ambiguous, is still sufficiently flexible, effective, and amazingly powerful when appropriately applied to a particular situation." Wilfredo Lopez, *West Nile Virus in New York City* 92 AMER. J. PUB. HEALTH 1218, 1221 (2002). According to Lopez, the West Nile experience teaches the need for greater understanding of existing laws and greater cooperation among agencies and professionals. *Id.*

First, although the Model Act was drafted by luminaries in the field, it has its own ambiguities. For example, as was noted above, the Act is quite unclear about what treatments and tests may be required once a public health emergency is declared.[99] The Act's treatment of individuals who refuse forced vaccinations for reasons other than those provided for in the Act is also uncertain.[100] Nor are the mandatory reporting requirements applicable to pharmacists crystal clear in their meaning.[101]

These uncertainties are not pointed out as criticism of the drafters' work. Instead, there is a significant reason to wonder whether *any* new code can possibly foresee and resolve all of the issues that may emerge if and when there is a major bioterrorist incident. Indeed, precisely because the drafters are writing for the unthinkable, we may well wonder whether they really can make it all that clear and certain.

To be sure, existing state public health laws do not deserve any Strunk and White awards for clarity of prose. However, when we ask "what is the law" we generally do not ask only what the statute says, but also what the courts and administrative agencies have said about it. Old laws therefore, have at least one virtue lacking in any new law: there are often judicial and administrative interpretations (not to mention shared practices and understandings that have guided agencies) that resolve some of the ambiguities and fill in some of the drafters' holes. Any new statute, precisely because it is new, lacks that annotation and thus, in some significant sense, may be more prone to ambiguity than its predecessor. The Model Act's drafters have tried to mitigate this problem by basing their language on some pre-existing state laws and providing a legislative history to each section which cites to those laws. Nevertheless, the lack of interpretative gloss may be especially problematic because doctrines precluding advisory opinions will make it difficult in many states to know precisely how states will actually interpret specific provisions new to their states until an emergency declaration is made, but that, of course, is precisely the time for which the drafters hoped to provide certainty.[102]

---

[99] *See* MODEL ACT, *supra* note 3, at § 602 (noting that the Act only instructs that the tests "must not be such as are reasonably likely to lead to serious harm to the affected individual").

[100] *See id.* at § 603(b)(3) (listing only three reasons why individuals may not be willing to submit to vaccination).

[101] *See id.* at § 301(b) (listing when a pharmacist needs to report).

[102] Some states do permit their courts to offer advisory opinions. This would be especially useful, especially in states where there may be colorable claims that the Model Act violates provisions of the state constitution. *See* PAUL M. BATOR ET AL., HART & WECHSLER'S THE FEDERAL COURTS AND THE FEDERAL PROCESS 70 (3d ed. 1988).

Even if clarity can be obtained, however, the ability of any emergency statute to prevent abuses is worth pondering. As Professor Gostin and his colleagues have aptly stated:

> The greatest risk to liberties may be that safeguards that are adequate in principle will not be practically sufficient in the face of the terror of an attack, that government officials may use a false emergency as a pretext for oppressive acts, or that social factors like race, religion, or class will influence decision makers. Racial, religious, and class bias have influence public health responses to epidemics in many instances in our past. We also must be concerned that the breakdown of civil order may include a break-down of administration in many social institutions, including the court system. The right to challenge a quarantine in court cannot be exercised if there are no court clerks or judges to accept writs or hear cases.[103]

The response of the Model Act's drafters to these problems is that states ought to develop contingency plans and conduct training to prepare for such emergencies. They write: "[i]n this sense, the Model Act also attempts to promote the protection of civil liberties by requiring planning and training for a public health emergency."[104] However, the Act itself does not actually mandate any training; it simply requires the preparation of an emergency plan which may or may not deal with the problem adequately and may or may not ever be given vitality through training and the deployment of adequate resources.[105] But even if the Act does spur training and planning aimed at ensuring the implementation of the legal procedures and guarantees the Act provides, and even if the courts were to stay open in the event of a declaration of a public health emergency, the question remains whether the Act's legal procedures can play the role the Model Act envisions for them.

The reliance upon courts to mediate the tensions between public health and individual rights also derives in part from the AIDS epidemic. Although courts reviewed public health actions prior to HIV, the AIDS epidemic was certainly the first fully litigated public health crisis. Space here precludes a full discussion of the important role that courts played in the HIV epidemic, but there can be no doubt that they played a critical role in signaling the inappropriateness of dis-

---

[103] Gostin et al., *supra* note 25, at 627.

[104] *Id.*

[105] *See* MODEL ACT, *supra* note 3, at §§ 202(a)(1)-(15) (listing the components of such an emergency plan).

crimination against people who are HIV positive.[106] Indeed, looking at the role that courts played during the HIV epidemic, Professor Gostin was able to write confidently about the courts' insistence that infringements on civil liberties can be undertaken only after careful consideration and when no less restrictive alternative is available.[107] This substantive standard has been incorporated, with modification, into the Model Act.[108]

Without denying the critical role legal standards and judicial process played with respect to HIV, there are serious reasons to examine whether they can be expected to play as constructive a role in the event of a bioterrorist event. Indeed, it may be that the judiciary's initial response to HIV, not public health's rejection of coercion, is what made AIDS policy truly exceptional. In other times, judges have been far less apt to protect the rights of individuals subject to public health orders.[109]

Generally limitations on individual liberty made in the name of public health are imposed by public health officials. In the case of HIV, in contrast, limitations upon an individual's freedom, or discrimination, usually came not from a public health official, but from a private citizen or another governmental agency not charged with or particularly expert in public health.[110] In those cases, more often than not, public health officials sided with the individual and argued that the restriction upon the individual's rights would not advance any public health goal.[111] Thus when the courts in those cases safe-

---

[106] *See, e.g.*, Bragdon v. Abbott, 524 U.S. 624, 641 (1998) (ruling in favor of a plaintiff seeking anti-discrimination protection on the basis of disability under the ADA due to her HIV infection).

[107] Lawrence O. Gostin, *Public Health Theory and Practice in the Constitutional Design*, 11 HEALTH MATRIX 265, 306-08 (2001).

[108] More specifically the Model Act uses the language of "least restrictive means" to limit the methods of isolation employed, not the actually determination of whether or not isolation or quarantine is required. Sec. 604(b)(1) states:

> Isolation and quarantine must be by the least restrictive means necessary to prevent the spread of a contagious or possibly contagious disease to others and may include, but are not limited to, confinement to private homes or other private and public premises.

When reviewing whether to grant a petition to isolate or quarantine an individual, the Model Act requires that the court determine whether the isolation or quarantine is "reasonably necessary" to prevent or limit the transmission of a contagious disease. *Id.* at § 605(b)(5).

[109] Gostin, *supra* note 107, at 295.

[110] Thus several school boards voted to exclude children who were HIV positive. *See* Parmet & Jackson, *supra* note 57, at 16-20 (discussing various courts' treatment of school boards' discrimination against HIV positive students).

[111] *See* Wendy E. Parmet, *The Supreme Court Confronts HIV: Reflections on Bragdon v. Abbott*, 26 J.L. MED. & ETHICS, 225, 226 (1998) (changing the role of

guarded individual rights, they did it in a context in which public health authorities supported those rights. We cannot derive from those cases the lesson that courts can be trusted to engage in a meaningful review of public health powers, especially when those powers are exercised during an emergency.

Reliance on the HIV cases for faith in the ability of courts to serve as a check on misuse of authority may be misplaced for another reason. Times have changed. In the early years of the HIV epidemic, plaintiffs were almost always successful when they used disability discrimination laws to challenge discrimination based upon HIV status. This trend reached its zenith in 1998 in *Bragdon v. Abbott*, in which the Supreme Court held that the Americans with Disabilities Act may be used by a woman who was HIV positive but not overtly symptomatic with the disease.[112] Since then, however, the Supreme Court has consistently narrowed its interpretation of the definition of disability under the ADA, making it ever harder for plaintiffs to demonstrate that they are "in the protected class."[113] Perhaps even more relevant is the fact that the Court has shown an increasing willingness to defer to the decisions of regulators and even employers who have concluded that individuals with disabilities pose a health threat to themselves or others.[114] While these cases would not be directly relevant to the question of how courts would review any exercise of coercive powers under the Model Act (although they would be relevant if an individual challenged the Model Act for its failure to adhere to the ADA)[115] they should provide reason to question whether courts can be

public health from restricting to protecting individual rights).

[112] 524 U.S. at 641.

[113] *See also* Matthew Diller, *Judicial Backlash, the ADA, and the Civil Rights Model*, 21 BERKELEY J. EMP. & LAB. L. 19, 22 (2000) (noting recent decisions that narrow the approach to interpreting the ADA). *E.g.*, Toyota Motor Mfg., KY., Inc. v. Williams, 534 U.S. 184, 198 (2002) (holding that to "be substantially limited in performing manual tasks, an individual must have an impairment that prevents or severely restricts the individual from doing activities that are of central importance to most people's daily lives. The impairment's impact must also be permanent or long term"); Sutton v. United Air Lines, Inc., 527 U.S. 471 (1999).

[114] *See* Chevron U.S.A., Inc., v. Echazabal, __ U.S. ___, 122 S. Ct. 2045, 2047 (2002) (supporting the idea that the ADA allows employers not to hire disabled individuals if the employer believes the individual will be harmed); Albertson's Inc. v. Kirkinburg, 527 U.S. 555, 558 (1999); Bagenstos, *supra* note 61, at 1479-80 (describing the latitude given to employers and professionals by the Court when they believe disabled individuals pose safety risks).

[115] An individual's ability to do so may be thwarted by the Supreme Court's ruling in Bd. of Trustees v. Garret, 531 U.S. 356 (2001) (holding that sovereign immunity bars claims against state entities under Title I of the ADA).

relied upon to engage in a meaningful assessment of risk during the due process proceedings called for under the Model Act.[116]

The Act's faith in procedural due process hearings should be questioned for another reason. In recent years, the federal courts have imposed numerous procedural hurdles that make it very difficult for individuals to bring due process or constitutional claims, especially against states, who now enjoy broad sovereign immunity from federal constitutional claims.[117] Moreover, while the federal courts have not disclaimed key earlier precedents establishing the right to a hearing before civil commitment,[118] recent cases have demonstrated a willingness to limit to some extent the sweep of procedural protections,[119]

---

[116] *See* Lawrence O. Gostin, *Impact of the ADA on the Health Care System, in* IMPLEMENTING THE AMERICANS WITH DISABILITIES ACT 175, 183-84 (Lawrence O. Gostin & Henry A. Beyer eds., 1993) (indeed, Professor Gostin has longed looked to disability law and the courts' jurisprudence there as to when individuals with disabilities create a "direct threat" to the health or safety of others as a model to be applied in public health law generally). There is little doubt that this jurisprudence has influenced the Model Act and is, to some extent, part of the "modern" legal standards imported into the Act. Recent case law under the ADA, however, should give pause as to whether these standards are as protective of individual interests as was once thought, and whether judges acting under the hurried procedures called for under the Model Act are more likely to engage in a dispassionate review than are federal judges presented with the luxury of full and unhurried review in ADA cases. Of course, isolation orders and quarantines under the Model Act will be reviewed by state as opposed to federal judges, and it may well be that they will be less deferential to those seeking to limit the rights of people who are claimed to be a threat to others than has been true in federal, ADA cases.

[117] This is not relevant to the question of whether a due process hearing would be available under the Model Act, but it does suggest that the judiciary in general is less amenable to due process type claims today than it was twenty years ago. Moreover, sovereign immunity would present a problem if an individual sought to challenge the Model Act in federal court. *See* Erwin Chemerinsky, *Against Sovereign Immunity,* 53 STAN. L. REV. 1201, 1202-03, 1215-16 (2001) (noting that the Court has not indicated a willingness to relax to relax federal sovereign immunity). And the Model Act itself imposes its own brand of sovereign immunity. MODEL ACT, *supra* note 3, at § 804.

[118] For a list of critical early cases *see* Vitek v. Jones, 445 U.S. 480, 491 (1980) (holding that transfer of a prisoner to a mental hospital requires a hearing before an independent decision maker); Addington v. Texas, 411 U.S. 418, 425 (1979) (discussing the need for due process protection in civil commitments); and Mathews v. Eldridge, 424 U.S. 319, 333 (1976) (emphasizing the idea that due process requires the right to be heard).

[119] *See* Heller v. Doe, 509 U.S. 312, 322 (1993) (analyzed under the Equal Protection Clause, permitting a lesser standard of proof for the commitment of mentally retarded individuals than is applied to cases involving the commitment of mentally ill individuals); United States v. Sahhar, 917 F.2d 1197, 1205-06 (9th Cir. 1990) (holding that a jury is not required for civil commitment under 18 U.S.C. 4246); United States v. Baker, 45 F.3d 837 (4th Cir. 1995) (use of video conferencing does not violate procedural due process rights of an inmate subject to civil commitment).

and some Supreme Court justices have even questioned whether a constitutional claim may be brought when an individual was denied a hearing prior to a civil commitment.[120] To the extent that these cases limit an individual's right to due process, the Model Act should be credited with possibly granting individuals even more procedural protections than they are ensured under the Constitution. However, the courts' attitude toward recent procedural due process cases should again raise qualms about the usefulness and impact of such hearings. Courts that are so confident that public officials will "do the right thing" that they do not believe it is necessary to provide a strong degree of procedural protections are not likely to engage in a very rigorous review when hearings actually occur.[121]

This is not to say that access to the courts is not crucial. It remains the indelible core of the rule of law. But we should question whether the due process/anti-discrimination model of legal rights, that relies so heavily upon individual hearings and individual claims before courts, that emerged from the HIV epidemic, can be counted on in the future to play the critical role that it played with respect to HIV.

V. RETHINKING THE ROLE OF QUARANTINE AND ISOLATION

There is no magic bullet for bioterrorism, just as there isn't one for most public health threats. Unfortunately, protection of the public health usually requires a complex array of strategies, from public education to surveillance, from vaccine development to market controls. Most or all of them will involve law. Only a few of them will require the curtailment of individual liberties.

The sponsors and drafters of the Model Act are acutely aware of the need for a sophisticated, multi-prong approach to bioterrorism. They have never advocated that restrictions on individual rights should play the sole or even leading role in that struggle. Instead they rightly see the Model Act and the coercive powers it would provide as but a single element in a multi-tiered process. And, they have attempted to construct that process while providing for significant judicial protections for individual rights.

---

[120] *E.g.,* Zinermon v. Burch, 494 U.S. 113 (1990) (O'Connor, J. dissenting joined by Rehnquist, C.J., Scalia, J., and Kennedy, J.) (arguing that the state's failure to follow own procedures and permit an involuntary commitment to a mental hospital without a hearing is not unconstitutional).

[121] Of course, again, the hearings under the Model Act will occur in state not federal court. On the other hand, they will occur in an emergency, which is not generally the case in the procedural due process context.

Nevertheless, there is a danger that the dissemination of the Model Act may be construed by political leaders and others as "solving" the problem of legal preparedness. Today when our public health infrastructure is sorely tattered,[122] and when "solutions" seem hard to envision, the clarification of coercive powers may provide an easy and relatively inexpensive fix.[123]

The danger brought by such a balm is not merely the illusion of false comfort. It is the potential for distraction and misdirection of priorities. By focusing on how we can update the law to do a better job of isolating and quarantining individuals, or vaccinating them without their consent, we risk overlooking the other ways that we can and should use law proactively to help prevent and prepare for bioterrorism.

One obvious candidate for legal attention is the international development and transport of dangerous pathogens and other ingredients of biological weapons. Last year, a few weeks after the unveiling of the Model Act, the Bush administration announced its rejection of international talks aimed at strengthening the 1972 Biological Weapons Convention.[124] More recently, the Administration has stated that it is abandoning efforts to strengthen the Convention.[125] While a full analysis of that particular international effort is beyond the purview of this paper, the point remains that there is a critical need for legal efforts to curtail the creation and shipment of biological weapons. Emergency powers designed to contain a bioterrorist outbreak by isolating individuals can never be a substitute for legal efforts designed to prevent one in the first place.

Domestically, last spring's Public Health Security and Bioterrorism Preparedness and Response Act ("PHSBPRA") undertook many important steps, greatly increasing federal funding for state and local preparedness and tightening the regulation of laboratories that use

---

122 COMMITTEE FOR THE STUDY OF THE FUTURE OF PUBLIC HEALTH, THE FUTURE OF PUBLIC HEALTH 73-106 (1988).

123 For example, last fall Governor Jane Swift of Massachusetts supported the Model Act and promised to push for its passage in her state. Justin Gills, *States Weighing Laws to Fight Bioterrorism*, THE WASH. POST, November 19, 2001, at A01. Only a few days later the state passed a budget that slashed public health programs and the Governor vetoed part of that program, imposing further cuts on public health. *See* Rick Klein, *Legislators are Likely to Restore Social Funding*, BOSTON GLOBE, Dec. 5, 2001, at B-4.

124 Steven Erlanger, *Bush's Move on ABM Pact Gives Pause to Europeans*, N.Y. TIMES, Dec. 13, 2001, at A-19.

125 Peter Slevin, *U.S. Drops Bid to Strengthen Germ Warfare Accord*, WASH. POST, Sept. 19, 2002, at A01.

dangerous pathogens.[126] Nevertheless, if we focus upon law's ability to regulate and structure markets, as opposed to its ability to restrain individuals, gaps appear. For example, although the PHSBPRA gives the Secretary of Agriculture authority to expand the capacity of the Food Inspection Service to protect against bioterrorism, the Act does not provide anything close to a comprehensive approach for inspection and protection of the food supply. In a recent report,[127] the National Academy of Science warned that inadequate attention has been given to this issue and the nation remains vulnerable to a bioterrorist attack on the food supply.[128] Likewise, the PHSBPRA does not require states to rebuild their broken public health systems to ensure the "dual-use' capacity that is so clearly needed.[129] While the PHSBPRA authorizes grants to help states address bioterrorism,[130] the danger remains that states will remain unprepared as their public health systems as a whole remain unsupported.[131]

At the state level, once we move away from thinking about law as coercion, other significant issues appear. Once again, the most obvious issue concerns resources. Laws allocate resources – and they can also create entitlements to them. Yet, we have not considered in our legal preparation for bioterrorism the creation of any entitlement to the resources necessary to confront bioterrorism. Indeed, while the Model Act would grant governors the authority to exercise emergency powers, there is nothing in the Act to commit states to undertake the deployment of resources that is crucial to preparing for bioterrorism.

Theoretically, a state law aiming at bioterrorism could focus not on the state's power to mandate vaccines, but on ensuring that vaccines will be available and administered smoothly, when needed. Indeed, guidelines recently released by the CDC for states to use in preparing a response to a potential outbreak of smallpox raise a host

---

[126] Pub. L. No. 107-188, §§ 131 et seq; 201 et seq; 301, 116 Stat. 594 (2002) (codified at 42 U.S.C. §§ 243; 262 et seq.)

[127] 21 U.S.C. § 679(c) (2000).

[128] National Academies, *Better Plan Needed to Protect U.S. Agriculture from Bioterror Attack*, *at* http://www4.nationalacademies.org (Sept. 19, 2002).

[129] Experts agree that preparation for bioterrorism requires an overall enhancement of the public health infrastructure, which should be built upon and would expand public health's capacity to respond to naturally occurring disease outbreaks. *See* GENERAL ACCOUNTING OFFICE, BIOTERRORISM-FEDERAL RESEARCH AND PREPAREDNESS ACTIVITIES, GAO-01-915 (September 2001), at 6. A pressing problem today is that investments made for bioterrorism preparedness activities will not offset cuts made elsewhere in public health budgets, thereby weakening the overall public health infrastructure. *See* note 124, *supra*.

[130] 42 U.S.C. § 247d-3(a).

[131] *See* Gostin et al., *supra* note 71, at 95-97 (discussing the decline in funding and support for state public health systems).

of important legal questions for Congress and the states to address, many of which are unanswered by the Model Act.[132] Although the original CDC guidelines cited to and recommended the Model Act,[133] and the recent additions continue to rely in part upon quarantine,[134] their primary focus is upon the implementation of a massive, population-wide campaign of voluntary vaccination.[135] If such an effort is to be carried out successfully, it will undoubtedly require a great deal of trust and confidence on the part of the public and this may well require new and creative legal approaches. For example, the CDC's mass vaccination program depends upon individuals revealing whether they are immune suppressed, something that experience with HIV suggests individuals may be far more likely to do if they feel comfortable knowing that the information will be kept confidential and not be used against them.[136] As a result, states interested in facilitating a massive vaccination program may want to consider taking additional steps to ensure that information conveyed in a vaccination clinic would not be further disseminated and could not be used against an individual (indeed, the possibility that this information might be used to mandate isolation apart from one's family may lead people to not be forthright at the clinics). Likewise, since a mass effort will inevitably lead to long lines and confusion, states may want to consider ensuring that individuals are protected against adverse employment (or welfare) impacts for the time lost at the clinic. States may also want to give thought on ways to guarantee that individuals who lack health insurance can be confident in receiving prompt care for vaccine-related injuries. And states may want to reassure health care workers that they will not be liable for the injuries that will inevitably result from a massive vaccination program.[137] Given the complexities

---

[132] Centers for Disease Control and Prevention, *Smallpox Response Plan and Guidelines, Guide C: Isolation and Quarantine Guidelines* C-14 to C-17, *at* http://www.bt.cdc.gov/agent/smallpox/response-plan/files/guide-c-pages1-18only.pdf (last modified Sept. 23, 2002).

[133] *Id.* at C-14 to C-15.

[134] *See* Centers for Disease Control and Prevention, *Smallpox Response Plan and Guidelines; Annex 3: Smallpox Vaccination Clinic Guide,* A3-31, 37, *at* http://www.bt.cdc.gov/agent/smallpox/response-plan/files/annex-3.pdf (last modified Sept. 23, 2002) (providing guidelines for isolating patients).

[135] *Id.* at A3-3, *at* http://www.bt.cdc.gov/agent/smallpox/response-plan/files/annex-3.pdf (last modified Sept. 23, 2002).

[136] The guidelines call for different treatment for individuals depending upon their immune status. *Id.* at A3-29.

[137] *See* Katharine C. Rathbun & Edward P. Richards, *Federal Smallpox Immunization Policy-A Short Critique, available at* http://biotech.law.lsu.edu/blaw/bt/smallpox/Critique01.htm (Sept. 26, 2002) (noting that, "[g]iven the probable level of vaccine complications, litigation would cripple the

and challenges of such a massive program, there is more than enough legal work to be done without thinking about the powers to coerce individuals. Indeed, in such circumstances, a focus upon coercion may well serve to undermine the trust of the public.

Likewise, in developing quarantine strategies, a state may want to go beyond enhancing its powers to impose detention orders and providing legal process for those who are detained involuntarily. Instead, a state may want to give thought to how *voluntary* quarantine and/or isolation recommendations may be more tolerable and acceptable to the population. In other words, the state may want to think about how it can promote voluntary compliance. After all, the state will never have sufficient resources to "round up" and involuntarily detail large numbers of people. But in order to obtain voluntary compliance, states may need to move beyond a police power model, and think not only about how they can enforce laws and protect legal rights of those detained, but also how they can make quarantine less frightening and more palatable. The Model Act moves in that direction by requiring that states provide for the needs of those involuntarily detained, but as noted above, it does not specifically address the economic consequences of quarantine, nor does it ensure that dependents will be care for.[138] In addition, the Model Act does not provide for the care or compensation of individuals who stay put without the imposition of a public health order. But, if quarantine is critical to the public good, then perhaps like jury duty or reserve duty, those who serve (voluntarily or involuntarily) should be provided with job protection and compensation.

In preparing for bioterrorism, a state may also want to consider ways that law can be used to ensure that health care facilities will have the needed surge capacity. While the Model Act gives the states power to impound facilities during an emergency,[139] it does not consider the complex and difficult issue of how state health care licensing and financing regulations affect the number of beds and personnel on hand in the state. Yet, if law is to be used to prepare for and against bioterrorism, these issues must be part of the preparation.

Finally, once we turn our eyes to structural approaches we may discover that they also offer some promise not only for protection against bioterrorism but for the protection of individual rights and liberties in the event an emergency occurs. The Model Act relies heavily upon the courts and the protections offered by individual hear-

---

public health system").

[138] MODEL ACT, *supra* note 3, at § 604(b)(6).

[139] *Id* at § 502(b).

ings. But in times of crisis, this approach has seldom proven successful.

The political theory of our founding fathers offered a different, structural approach. The Constitution relies primarily not upon judicial review or due process hearings, but the division of power and checks and balances in order to thwart tyranny. As James Madison famously said, "ambition must be made to counteract ambition."[140]

So, too, as we prepare for bioterrorism, we need to think long and hard about the structures of government, and how they can be most effectively utilized both to invigorate the public sector to prevent and respond to bioterrorism and to prevent the misuse of such powers. That may mean rethinking the boundaries of federalism and developing legal theories to provide the federal government with the power it may need to address problems national in scope as well as limits upon it to prevent an erosion of legitimate state interests.[141] At the state level, it may mean thinking carefully about the relationship between governors, state health departments, local health departments, and legislators. To give one example, while it seems obvious that governors may need the power to act quickly in the event of a catastrophe, the Model Act's decision to prevent state legislatures from repealing any declaration of an emergency for thirty days may unnecessarily remove a structural and political check upon the misuse of authority, a check that might well do more to curtail unnecessary limitations upon individual rights than would due process hearings. Likewise, the Act's reliance on the governor alone, without the necessity of consultation by the public health department, or municipal leaders, again appears to vest authority in a single source, negating the possibility that multiple centers of power (what we use to call "checks and balances"), may offer the best opportunity to define and preserve the common good, without unduly disadvantaging minority groups.

When health threats appear, as in times of war, there is an inevitable tendency to focus on the need for efficient power and the virtues of a powerful executive. But just as our framers taught us that the preservation of peace requires a far more complex and less tidy political state than is needed to win a war, so too, we may recall that the protection of public health whether from bioterrorism or natural causes ultimately requires complex and multifaceted laws. There is a lot of work for lawyers yet to do.

---

[140] THE FEDERALIST PAPERS NO. 51, at 319 (James Madison) (Isaac Kramnick ed., 1987).

[141] *See* Annas, *supra* note 25 at 1337, 1341; Parmet, *supra* note 83, at 207-08.

[10]

Bioethics and the National Security State

Jonathan D. Moreno

"...it is mandatory that in building up our strength, we enlarge upon our technical superiority by an accelerated exploitation of the scientific potential of the United States and our allies."

National Security Council, NSC-68: United States Objectives and Programs for National Security, April 14, 1950[1]

"Innovation within the armed forces will rest on experimentation with new approaches to warfare, strengthening joint operations, exploiting U.S. intelligence advantages, and taking full advantage of science and technology."

George W. Bush, The National Security Strategy of the United States of America, September 17, 2002[2]

I.

During the years 1946 and 1947, U.S. policymakers were preoccupied with the reconstruction of Europe and Japan, the emerging challenge of Soviet power, and the basic revision of America's position in the world. Also in those years a few officials and medical researchers within the United States' new civilian atomic energy agency engaged in a tense debate about human research rules that culminated in what they called "informed consent." What was the relationship between the massive global post-war effort to confront the Communist threat on one hand and this seemingly improbable and highly specialized human research policy debate on the other? And how can this experience be instructive for the bioethical issues that are now emerging in the war on terror?

In a series of publications I have described the post-World War II debate within the national security establishment concerning the use of human subjects in experiments related to national defense, and the subsequent emergence of the first federal policies in this area.[3] I have argued that these developments were precursors of the discussions that began in the late 1960s in the world of civilian medicine, culminating in the work of the National Commission for the Protection of Human Subjects of Biomedical and Behavioral Research (1974-78), and the current federal regulations on human research protections. In many ways, the often secret national security discourse about appropriate human research policies during the cold war laid the groundwork for the framework with which we have become so familiar.

In another series of writings I have considered the bioethical issues raised by the events of September 11, 2001 and their aftermath.[4] Some of these issues are a continuation of evolving policies from previous years, such as the conditions that should accompany classified human studies. Others are relatively novel, including the potential for application of developments in emerging fields like genetics and neuroscience to national security arrangements. Still others are both old and new, such as the appropriate powers of public health officials in the event of an epidemic, but with the twist of a terrorist attack, either radiological, biological or chemical, as the incident that engenders the health emergency.

The burden of my argument has been that bioethics (including especially human research standards and the modern informed consent doctrine) should be conceptualized as inextricably associated with national security issues, both in its origins and in its attention to contemporary problems, rather than limited to the standard story of the birth of bioethics in scholarly circles in the late 1960s. To so reform the predominant understanding of the history of the field through a focus on pertinent national security issues is also to reconsider the relevance of bioethical discourse to the role of biology and medicine in the new national security environment.

This paper is an attempt to bring my two previous lines of work together under the rubric of the "national security state," a concept familiar to Cold War historians and political scientists. The national security state was established in the wake of World War II, was called into question with the collapse of communism, and has been newly fortified by the war on terror. The founding of the national security state was associated with the first articulations of informed consent requirements by national security agencies. My analysis indicates that strengthened consent standards, though conventionally thought to be antithetical to state interests during an international crisis, can be seen as an attempt by the postwar national security state to protect itself from critics of expanded governmental power. During the coming years the renewed mission of the national security state in the war on terror should impel students of bioethics to consider its implications for future discourse in the field.

This paper is therefore both a revised account of the origins of bioethics and an effort to alert scholars to bioethical issues concerning the national security state. In developing this account I use the phrase "national security state" as a shorthand for a particular conceptual framework that has driven U.S. policy since the end of World War II. As such, the term is undoubtedly too truncated to reflect the many voices and tensions within the policy community, yet if we can resist the temptation to reify the concept I think it serves to identify in broad terms the approach that has been presupposed by every presidential administration since that of Franklin D. Roosevelt.

I may be criticized for taking an excessively American view of the nature and origins of bioethics. Surely international bioethics has flourished and many of the issues discussed in this article are universal. Yet particularly in the area of human research ethics and related problems, such as genetics, American bioethics has set the agenda and, in the main, the predominant philosophical approaches and premises. It is therefore important for bioethicists working in other countries as well as those in the U.S. to appreciate the limitations of the standard origin story.

In this paper I do not consider in detail certain insightful cultural interpretations of national security that further illuminate these matters, such as the social construction of security crises.[5] It is worth noting, however, that although my presentation seems to suggest a contrast between static "military" and "civilian" sectors, the national security state in its historic and current manifestations gains its power precisely from the way it engages the resources of society as a whole. In this sense, it is instructive to recall Daniel Yergin's 1977 observations about the concept of national security as it functioned during the cold war:

> We must remember that "national security" is not a given, not a fact, but a perception, a state of mind....
>
> The doctrine is characterized by expansiveness, a tendency to push the subjective boundaries of security outward to more and more areas, to encompass more and more geography and more problems. It demands that the country assume a posture of military preparedness; the whole nation must be on permanent alert. There was new emphasis on technology and armed force. Consequent institutional changes occurred. All this leads to a paradox: the growth of American power did not lead to a greater sense of assuredness, but rather to an enlargement of the range of perceived threats that must urgently be confronted."[6]

II.

To place bioethics in the national security framework it is necessary to rehearse the history of the concept of the national security state, especially in connection with the role of science.[7] The year 1947 marked an historic turn in the thinking of America's foreign policy establishment, a culmination of discussions that led to a new vision of the nation's place in the world. Even before the end of World War II it was clear that the United States would emerge as a dominant power, a position for which its economic trajectory had been leading it since at least 1900 but one that the country had been unwilling fully to embrace in foreign affairs prior to the war. The isolationism that dominated pre-war policy, and which was taken as virtually a national legacy from the administration of George Washington, was no longer viewed as a viable guiding principle by the small group of major policymakers in President's Truman's executive branch.

These men (they included George Kennan, Charles Bohlen, Vannevar Bush, James B. Conan, W. Averell Harriman, Robert S. Lovett, John J. McCloy and James V. Forrestal) were academicians, scientists and corporate and financial leaders. They executed a rapid and vast expansion of federal powers, especially in the area of national defense, the goal of which was to confront an unprecedented threat in the form of the Soviet Union. To do so, they reorganized the military and intelligence establishments and, central to our discussion, sought to integrate science with military aims.

In fact, hardly a sector of American life was unaffected by the need to harness public energies to the task of protecting the American nation in a dangerous new world. No longer could national defense rely on a mere "expedition" as was the case in World War I, and then retire to a demilitarized state on the old comfortable assumption that it was protected by a (largely) non-interference foreign policy and two oceans. Rather, the country would have to gird itself for a chronic war-footing. Just as the Civil War transformed America's domestic character, so World War II transformed the face America showed to the rest of the world.

In 1947, the critical philosophical themes that guided the country's transformation were heralded in two statements. The first was the anonymous publication in *Foreign Affairs* of George Kennan's famous thousand-word "long telegram" to the State Department from Moscow in February 1946. Kennan described a Soviet state that was oppressive at home and expansionist abroad, advocating a policy of containment that was to dominate America's approach through the Reagan administration and the destruction of the Berlin Wall. The second relevant event of 1947 was a speech to Congress in which President Harry Truman asked for funding to provide aid to Greece and Turkey, which were both being threatened by Soviet demands. The Truman Doctrine established containment of the Soviet Union as national policy. A corollary was that a threat to freedom anywhere was a threat to freedom everywhere, for other countries would take the "loss" of a non-Communist state to the Soviet orbit as a sign of laxity in American resolve. And further, America's manifest destiny, its God-given opportunity to occupy a blessed land in freedom, was now extended to the defense of freedom for all who might be threatened with its loss.

Before the war, the Yale political scientist Harold Lasswell coined the term "garrison state" to describe a thoroughly militarized nation in a state of continuous war. Conservatives feared that the resulting expansion of state power justified by a chronic wartime-footing would threaten individual liberty and fundamentally alter the underlying values of the American experiment. Even some leading liberals like Columbia's John Dewey were ambivalent about American involvement in World War II due to fears about the long-term consequences of militarization in American life. These fears continued after the war in the form of congressional opposition to Truman's proposals to reorganize the national security establishment and change budget priories, initiatives that were ultimately successful.

Science played a critical role in the envisioned national security establishment. The First World War had already produced the National Research Council to bring civilian science into military preparation and the war itself. The importance of the wartime alliance between science and the military for the World War II Allied victory was beyond dispute, not only in the most obvious examples of war-fighting technologies like sonar and improved armaments, and especially the atomic bomb itself, but also in less obvious ways through military medicine. A thick two-volume report called ***Advances in Military Medicine*** published after the war attested to the many areas in which medical science enlisted for the war effort had achieved breakthroughs in basic understanding of medical sciences and in improved therapies, particularly those associated with the infectious diseases and bacterial disorders that plagued soldiers. The most impressive example of the benefits of government support of medical research was the rapid advancement in the development of penicillin, the "wonder drug" whose refinement came too late to be of much use during the war but proved to be a great boon in the post-war era.

At first academic institutions feared the intrusion of the national government in its research priorities. This attitude changed drastically in the 1930s as new academic leaders welcomed government support but tried to minimize interference in scientific work, with mixed success. No institution exemplified this new cooperative spirit between government and the academy more than MIT, which under Karl Compton devoted itself the application of physical theory to solving a host of engineering challenges. Harvard president James B. Conant, a chemist by training, and MIT's Vannevar Bush, an early computer scientist who became president of Washington's Carnegie Institution, led the Roosevelt administration's crash program to realize the benefits of scientific research for the war.

Bush led the Office of Scientific Research and Development (OSRD), which infused millions of dollars into scientific research during the war, mainly through the Committee on Medical Research (CMR). The CMR's projects included several that involved human experiments with conscientious objectors, prisoners, and the mentally retarded.[8] The OSRD was also a crucial player in the contentious wartime discussions about whether the nation's atomic energy resources would eventually be under civilian or military control or some combination. During the war that had been the province of the Manhattan Engineer District (the official name of the Manhattan Project), under General Leslie Groves. The civilians wanted to make sure that the medical and industrial potential of atomic energy was not neglected by military leadership.[9] Although the civilian control of the new Atomic Energy Commission (AEC) was finally settled by President Truman in 1948, the agency had already gone through a tense first 18 months as, under presidential order, the army reluctantly transferred the Manhattan Engineer District properties to the AEC beginning on January 1, 1947.[10]

III.

Almost soon as the new AEC went into business it was confronted with an awkward example of the simmering conflict between military and civilian concerns when the

Manhattan Project's deputy medical director proposed that a report about the secret plutonium injections be declassified. These injections had taken place at several major research hospitals in 1945 in order to learn about human excretion rates of plutonium for the sake of radiation worker safety. The scientific considerations that favored sharing data were met with a skeptical reception by an AEC declassification officer, who wrote on February 28, 1947 that this particular report, among others being reviewed, "appears to be the most dangerous since it describes experiments performed on human subjects, including the actual injection of the metal plutonium into the human body....Unless, of course, the legal aspects were covered by the necessary documents [perhaps a reference to patient consent forms], the experimenters and the employing agencies, including the U.S., have been laid open to a devastating lawsuit which would, through its attendant publicity, have far-reaching results." In addition, "the coldly scientific manner in which the results are tabulated and discussed would have a very poor effect upon the public."[11] A few weeks later, on March 19, the AEC's medical chief signaled his agreement.

Thus the outcome of this early contest between scientific openness and the secrecy needs of national security was determined by the needs for the emerging national security state to be spared of the public embarrassment that would come with lawsuits and scandal.

As the implications of this incident became apparent the AEC's non-physician officials sought to protect the government from the risk of subsequent embarrassment about human experiments by requiring what they called "informed consent" of any subjects of future agency-sponsored radiation experiments, the first known use of this expression. However, some specific provisions of their proposal proved unacceptable to the AEC's medical scientists, particularly a requirement that the subjects sign a form signaling their willingness to volunteer. Following some tense sessions in which the AEC backed off from its original position, the agency's general manager remarked wryly, "Indeed, from the discussion at the meetings of April 3-5, it seems evident to me that doctors would not allow their judgment on this matter to be influenced by anyone." The state's requirements for self-protection were one thing, the medical profession's autonomy quite another. Surely doctors could be trusted to do the right thing.[12]

Thus various interests competed for attention in this episode: the state's interest in avoiding liability and damaging publicity and medical scientists' interest in protecting their professional autonomy and authority. Recall, too, the pre-war concerns among academic leaders that the universities stood to lose their independence in setting the rules and goals of their research mission once they accepted government largesse. The resistance of medical scientists to the AEC's proposed restrictive policy on human experiments can be seen as a manifestation of these federal contractors' determination to resume their roles as civilian university professors and insist on the self-direction of the academy, free of government control, even though it was government that was to provide both the funding and the radioisotopes for their research.

IV.

There was an event besides the plutonium injections themselves that worried AEC officials and motivated them to advance informed consent as a protection of state interests. The officials were aware of the trial of Nazi doctors taking place at Nuremberg, West Germany at exactly the same time they were dealing with the plutonium experiments declassification issue. Later in the 1940s, when the AEC and the Pentagon were jointly considering the development of nuclear-powered aircraft, questions were raised about how to determine that the power source would not impair the crew. Human experiments were desirable but the most likely population, long-term prisoners, invited disconcerting comparisons to the Nazi crimes.[13]

The immediate influence on American medicine of the Nuremberg Code developed by the Nazi doctors' judges was, to put it mildly, minimal, but government officials were sensitive to both its legal and political implications. The code surfaced in military medical planning as a direct result of President Truman's creation of a single Department of Defense from the departments of the Navy and War. Undertaken in 1949, this massive bureaucratic overhaul predictably left numerous gaps in the new department's policy framework, including the field of human experimentation. There were fears that the Soviets were outstripping U.S. military scientists in the development of unconventional weapons, and in the defense against them, including the conduct of human experiments. From 1950 to 1953 several internal Pentagon advisory committees deliberated on the matter of suitable guidance. In the end both the military and medical members of all these panels largely agreed that a written policy was a bad idea, preferring instead to rely on an unwritten code of ethics and the virtues of those in charge rather opening the matter up to legal scrutiny. Once again, the traditional independence of medical scientists was cited.[14]

At first, like the AEC leadership, the Pentagon's civilian leadership was reluctant to assert itself in what was turning out to be a controversial area. Truman's Secretary of Defense, Robert Lovett, had his people working the problem on a track parallel to the military medical advisory process. The job of finding an acceptable policy was handed over to defense department legal counsel, which identified the Nuremberg Code (incorrectly) as prevailing international law. A key player in the decision to adopt the code was Lovett's deputy, Anna Rosenberg, who was assistant defense secretary in charge of manpower. She took the proposed use of the Nuremberg principles a step further by adding a written consent requirement, a consequence perhaps of her experience as a leading labor-management specialist in New York: contracts are only concluded when they are reduced to writing.

In spite of Rosenberg's advocacy and Lovett's sympathy for the proposal, internal opposition to any written policy at all was so strong that the civilians in Truman's defense department decided it would be best to refer to the matter to the incoming Eisenhower administration, as the new defense officials would have to live with the consequences of imposing an unpopular policy on the military medical bureaucracy. The matter was still urgent, the outgoing officials explained to their successors, because there was still no departmental rule that would allow important human experiments on the human effects of atomic, biological and chemical weapons. There is reason to believe that Lovett himself briefed Wilson on the issue as one among many then facing the department. Lovett believed that the 1949 reorganization of the defense establishment needed more work, so he was involved in the transition to an exceptional degree.[15] So it was that the new defense secretary, Charles E. Wilson, finally signed off on a top secret memorandum to army, navy and air force secretaries on February 26, 1953, making the Nuremberg Code the Pentagon's policy.

Secretary Wilson had been chief executive officer of General Electric and, at the time he took office, General Motors. Like Anna Rosenberg, he was experienced in labor negotiations and might well have approached the human experiments issue in a matter-of-fact manner as a contract problem, a deal between the department and the experimenter on the one hand and the human volunteer on the other. This would have been consistent with the management style he and Eisenhower agreed he should bring to the job, running the Department of Defense like an industrial corporation Wilson also intended to implement Eisenhower's "New Look" defense strategy, which included greater reliance on nuclear weapons.[16] Any help the medical experts could give on human factors in atomic warfare would clearly be welcome.

V.

In 1953, with conservative skepticism about the national security state still recent, medical and military reservations about subject consent were of less concern to policy makers than the need for legitimizing the new order. What the AEC's leadership could not accomplish in 1947 the new Eisenhower defense department, with a formidable ex-general in the White House, could. It may be that an incident in New York brought home the need for a settled policy more than ever. At the same time that Lovett's staff was communicating with the new defense officials about the need for a written subject consent policy, in January 1953, a depressed psychiatric patient died of an overdose of a mescaline derivative in a secret experiment at New York's Psychiatric Institute. The sponsor was the Army Chemical Corps, which engineered a cover-up with the state government. It is not known whether this incident further impelled Secretary Wilson to sign off on the policy without delay, but he would surely have been informed that the army had sponsored research in which a death had occurred. Only three months before, in October 1952, the Chemical Corps raised questions with Department of Defense (DoD) legal counsel about release forms for "human guinea pigs" at the same time another prisoner died in an Armed Forces Epidemiological Board-sponsored hepatitis study.[17]

That defense officials would want to introduce a clear policy to protect the government from human experiment scandals may surprise some who suppose that expanded state power led to Cold War practices that were antithetical to the high ethical principles of the Nuremberg Code, such as the CIA and army's experiments with hallucinogenic substances. To some it will be ironic that the state sought to protect itself from scandal by advancing subject consent, rather than imposing its will on innocent human beings. But seen through the lens of the garrison state a more complex analysis is required.

In fact both scenarios played out at different times and in different circumstances during the Cold War. Each was justifiable according to the needs of the national security state, which at some times was concerned about its perceived legitimacy at home, at other times concerned more with containing aggressive Soviet intentions. Thus it is noteworthy that during the middle and later 1950s the most egregious abuses of human beings in psychoactive drug studies occurred not in the Department of Defense but in the Central Intelligence Agency, an entity that was a direct result of the national security reorganization and less subject to layers of scrutiny than the military.

In the later 1950s the Nuremberg Code-based policy withered as it was variously interpreted and sporadically applied. Functionally, the national security state had less need to protect itself from the criticism that it put traditional American individualism and anti-state sentiment at risk. The old pre-World War II conservatives and isolationists lost their clout as that generation faded and as the Korean War abroad and Communist scares at home rattled Americans about their safety from alien threats. As embodied in the 1960 presidential candidacy of Richard Nixon (and his Democratic rival John F. Kennedy ran hard to Nixon's right on this point), enhanced state power was no longer seen as antithetical to American values but was considered to be central to their survival.

VI.

In the early 1960s the uniformed services created written policies on human experiments, beginning with the army's regulation 70-25, which contained vestiges of the Nuremberg Code's language. At this time the uniformed services were engaged in more regular publication of all policies. By then the vigorous internal Pentagon debates about standards for human experiments of the late 1940s and early 1950s were all but forgotten. The only significant opposition seemed to come from academic scientists whose institutions contracted with the Pentagon and who objected to being brought under an external set of rules, especially one that had been devised in light of the Nazi atrocities.

One institution that protested loudly was Harvard, which was given the opportunity to write its own ethics rules. Among those at Harvard who joined the successful opposition to the army regulations was a future icon of bioethics, Henry Beecher. His landmark 1966 paper in the *New England Journal of Medicine* on human research ethics perhaps did more to advance the issue in the United States than the trial of the Nazi doctors. But Beecher was no admirer of ethics rules laid down outside the medical profession. He preferred to rely on the virtuous medical investigator, who is in any case the ultimate guarantor of ethical science, hence his opposition to the army's Nuremberg Code-based policy being imposed on academia.

Beecher's reflections on this topic began in the 1950s, including a 1959 paper that is not nearly as well known as his NEJM publication. What was the source of Beecher's strong commitment to the ethics of human research? One element was his Christian religious commitment. Another was likely his own army-sponsored research in the early 1950s, in which he directed projects that exposed healthy subjects to hallucinogens without their consent. As Beecher himself never discussed this experience it was left to his former research fellow to describe the work in an interview with the Advisory Committee on Human Radiation Experiments. Thus it was that research sponsored by the national security state inspired one of its own investigators to take on the task of reforming the system of human experimentation.

Apart from the Harvard protest, how can we account for the apparent lack of opposition within the defense establishment when the research rules were published, as compared to a decade before? A set of exemptions in the 1962 rules may be the explanation. These exemptions stated that the written consent requirement did not apply if the intent was to benefit patients, when the studies are "training exercises," and when deception is involved and consent would compromise the value of the data.[18]

The second exemption, on training exercises, institutionalized what had been a problem with the Wilson policy throughout the 1950s. As I have elaborated in *Undue Risk*, and as the army inspector general concluded in 1975, the rules were applied quite haphazardly. In particular, even activities that involved medical monitoring, such as the deployment of over 200,000 men to atomic text shots from 1953 to 1962, were often not called human experiments but training exercises. Virtually any activity related to readiness would qualify under that rubric, which gives the military wide discretion over potential harms to personnel. When the case of a solider who had been in LSD experiments reached the U.S. Supreme Court in 1987, a 5-4 majority ruled that the veteran could not sue for injuries alleged to have been incurred in the service because to do so would bring the courts into military matters and compromise discipline, overcoming minority that cited the Nuremberg Code.[19]

As a result, the Wilson policy only applied in effect on those occasions in which the medical research aim was determined by relevant decision makers to be the central rationale for the activity. As neither the military nor medical establishments of the 1950s were familiar with the concept of written subject consent there was much inertia in this regard, and little incentive for those in the command structure to impose consent requirements in specific cases.

VII.

For roughly 20 years after the Wilson memorandum, the more the activities in question were considered to be training exercises, and the less they resembled a clinical intervention, the more likely it was that consent would not be sought. There were some significant exceptions, such as the "panic" studies of a few participants in the atomic test shots (mainly officers who did give written consent), and the defense department-sponsored total body irradiation studies at the University of Cincinnati (where researchers seem not to have been told about the written consent requirements), but the generalization holds. An interesting example that was not widely known even following the massive declassification associated with the work of the Advisory Committee on Human Radiation Experiments in 1994-95 is Project SHAD, or "Shipboard Hazard and Defense." These 1960s exercises were revealed following persistent complaints by veterans in the late 1990s. A preliminary investigation by the Pentagon in 2002 confirmed that dozens of these tests took place.

Although it has long been known that environmental tests of biological and chemical stimulants took place during the cold war in the airspace above major cities and in the New York City subway system, the Project SHAD revelations pointed to exercises on the oceans. Sailors were exposed to aerosols from tugboats mounted with biological disseminators, from spray tanks mounted on attack aircraft, towers, and other means. The purpose was to assess the vulnerability of naval ships to chemical and biological agents. It was at first thought that the substances to which sailors were exposed were inert simulates, but the DoD found that sometimes actual agents were used. On these occasions, such as a 1964 Pacific Ocean test called Flower Drum, the DoD found that extensive protective measures were used, including masks.[20]

In the SHAD tests there was some level of knowledge among the men that they were part of an experiment, but there was no consent process of any kind, written or otherwise.[21] In June 2003 the Pentagon released what it considered to be a final set of reports on exercises that might have exposed 5,842 people to chemical or biological weapons, while members of congress insisted that further investigation is warranted.[22] The DoD investigation has not reported any adverse medical findings, though an Institute of Medicine panel is engaged in a review of SHAD's long-term health effects.[23]

One of the SHAD tests, called Autumn Gold, took place in the Pacific Ocean in May 1963. A fact sheet released as part of the Pentagon investigation reported that, "According to the Autumn Gold test plan and final report, the crews who participated in the tests were not test subjects, but test conductors." Again, rules concerning consent to medical research participation would not apply under that classification. Nonetheless, the Pentagon states that "participants should have been fully informed of the details of each test." The fact sheet went on to state that the training the men received in preparation for the test should have reinforced their understanding.[24]

There is a tension within the SHAD fact sheets the Pentagon has released. On one hand the participants are described as conductors of the tests rather than subjects, on the other the DoD expresses regret at the lack of informed consent. This inconsistency can perhaps be explained by the fact that the SHAD tests would not today be readily granted an exemption as a training exercise not subject to informed consent. Looking back at Project SHAD through the prism of 40 years of scandal and regulation, the Pentagon itself seems to be unaware of the anachronistic emphasis on consent in its recent explanations of the circumstances of the SHAD tests.

VIII.

Therefore, although the military's discourse on issues of human experimentation was far in advance of any in place in the civilian world, the national security state that encouraged this discourse was largely unencumbered by the rules that resulted until 1975, when revelations of the CIA and army experiments, following media reports of the syphilis study in Tuskegee, Alabama, compelled both congressional and intra-agency investigations. In the wake of these scandals, as well as Watergate and the national reaction to the chaotic conclusion to the Vietnam War, public mistrust in government reached historic proportions. Human research protections, both in the civilian and military sectors, became far more restrictive and accountable. International conventions against chemical and biological and toxin weapons development, into which the United States entered in the early 1970s, also militated against offensive research.

Accordingly, human experiments for national security purposes appear to have been severely limited for about 25 years,[25] with the exception of defensively-oriented studies at facilities such as the U.S. Army Research Institute of Infectious Diseases (USAMRIID) at Fort Detrick, Maryland. Far from being uncharacteristic of American society, in this period traditional American skepticism about state power enjoyed something of a resurgence, as compared to the 1950s and early 1960s.

With the conclusion of the cold war a fitful debate took place in the 1990s concerning the role of the United States as the world's only superpower. As the pressure of confrontation with the Soviet Union lapsed into memory there was rising interest in learning about cold war secrets. These circumstances contributed to the creation of the President's Advisory Committee on Human Radiation Experiments in 1994-95, on which I served as a staff member. Government openness, including the declassification of thousands of documents, gained a modest foothold as the rationale for the national security state appeared implicitly to be facing its greatest challenge in 50 years.

In the months following the terrorist attacks of September 11, 2001, and the anthrax attack of October 2001, the George W. Bush administration assessed the new circumstances of a war on terror that would rival the cold war in the national will required to be victorious. But the administration's top security officials found important disanalogies to the confrontation with a distinct nation that characterized the cold war. Instead of dealing with nation-states the United States would be at war with shadowy groups, often fluid in nature, motivated by a distorted Islamist ideology and only sometimes in association with established governments. Their methods would be unconventional terror devices intended to disrupt civil society rather than to conquer it with large-scale military means. The new national security policy announced in September 2002 put unprecedented emphasis on pre-emptive military engagement as a necessary tactic to root out terrorism before it can strike.

IX.

In October 2001 I suggested that various public attitudes shaped by the 1960s may be in for further change following the terrorist attacks, including the risk-benefit balance of human experiments regarded to be in the national interest.[26] Government critics reacted with predictable concern when, on September 4, 2001, the Defense Intelligence

Agency (DIA) of the U.S. Department of Defense (DoD) acknowledged that it planned to reproduce a strain of anthrax virus suspected of still being held by Russia, one that may have been developed during the waning days of the cold war. The same report indicated that the Central Intelligence Agency (CIA), as part of a project called "Clear Vision," was building replicas of bomblets also believed developed by the former Soviet Union. The bomblets, about the size of a grapefruit, were designed to disperse biological agents, including anthrax, without destroying the microbes in the process.[27] Advocates wondered whether these activities could be considered violations of the Biological and Toxin Weapons Convention of 1973. But government attorneys were confident that, because these projects were designed to develop defensive measures, they were not in violation of any treaties. Nonetheless, advocates expressed concern and, had it not been for the terror attacks a week later, some form of protest was sure to follow.

Then, on November 13, 2001, St. Louis University published a news release concerning its NIH-sponsored trial of dilute smallpox vaccine. The statement that the trial was proceeding but that recruitment in the desired age range, 18 to 25, was the major delay.[28] St. Louis was only one of several academic centers that participated in the study. It seems that following publicity there was no difficulty recruiting numbers of anxious volunteers.[29] Ultimately the trial was successfully completed, indicating that immunity was achieved in dilutions of the original vaccine up to ten times.

Less than a year later, federal officials confirmed plans to test the smallpox vaccine with children at Cincinnati's Children's Hospital Medical Center and at Harbor-UCLA Medical Center. The stated goal was to ascertain the optimal dosage in children in the event a massive inoculation is needed following a bioterrorist attack.[30] The trial was never carried out.

The smallpox dilution trials in adults actually began with a small study involving 60 subjects before 2001, but only attracted national attention after the anthrax attacks of the autumn of 2001.[31] In spite of the inherent risks associated with the smallpox vaccine and the willingness of many critics of science to raise questions about other studies, no concerns were expressed in the scientific community or in the media about the trials in the wake of the September 11 and anthrax attacks. Clearly our thinking about risks and benefits has not been unaffected by the recent events.

As fears of terror attacks and a desire for scientific responses increase, commitments to human research protections can seem less important. Earlier I noted that the Defense Department cold war rules on human experiments, though advanced, were at best unevenly applied. The fact that the rules that governed human subject protections could be so easily avoided, often depending on whether military exercises were defined as *medical* experiments or not, is instructive in the new national security environment. Today's regulations governing human research conducted or sponsored by the U.S. military are at least as stringent as those that apply to civilian research. However, certain exemptions still apply that speak to national security issues. For example, Appendix F, item 'f' exempts "Individual or group training of military personnel such as combat readiness, effectiveness, proficiency, or fitness exercise (for example, Army Training and Evaluation Program (ARTEP), Skill Qualification Test [SQT]). Evaluation of the training's effect on individual participants may or may not be exempt depending on how the evaluation is made (for example, drawing of blood is not exempt.)" Activities that involve no more than "minimal risk" that are related to the development and testing of weapons systems, vehicles, aircraft, etc., are also exempt.[32]

These exemptions are far more nuanced than those in the 1962 army rules. In particular, they do not appear to apply to more clinically oriented research that involves interventions with discrete individuals. Therefore informed consent and prior IRB review (known in the U.S. Army as a Human Use Committee) would be required under these rules for any non-exempt research of this sort.

There are additional issues related to research involving human subjects that is classified. Currently the federal government reports that there is no classified human research taking place, but it is not difficult to imagine circumstances in which such activities would be thought important so that terrorist groups would be denied information about American capabilities. In order to satisfy the standard criteria of valid informed consent, such protocols would require security clearances for all parties, including the IRB members and the human volunteers themselves. Because there would be no publicity with regard to IRB decisions, the standard check of public scrutiny would not be available.

To compensate for the lack of public scrutiny, at least one member of the classified IRB should not be a federal employee and there should be a method of appeal of an IRB decision by any member to a superior authority. These essential elements were included in a presidential letter signed by President Clinton in 1996, which still technically applies to all 17 federal agencies that conduct or sponsor human experiments, including those with classification authority. The presidential letter was stimulated by recommendations of the Advisory Committee on Human Radiation Experiments in its 1995 final report, and was to have been transformed into a common rule amendment. This complicated amendment process which involved all 17 common rule agencies was not completed by the time President Bush took office. Currently the White House Office of Science and Technology Policy is considering amending the Department of Health and Human Services (DHHS) regulations to take classified research into account, apparently on the theory that DHHS would be a participant in classified medical research with human subjects.

These IRB-oriented measures may not be enough. Deviations from protocol are a familiar problem in the unclassified research world and have been implicated in the deaths of research subjects. Some equivalent to the function of data safety monitoring boards or committees (DSMBs or DSMC's), normally appointed to oversee double-blinded efficacy trials, should be part of any comprehensive plan to protect individuals who agree to participate in classified research studies. Members of these boards should also be given suitable security clearances and include non-government employees.

X.

If the national security state as evolved from its cold war version continues to operate for the indefinite future in the war on terror, and if a continually advancing medical science will continue to be enlisted in fighting this war, then one can anticipate that a wide range of bioethical issues will ensue. Military preparedness and medical advances have long had an intimate relationship, one that will be even more complex as the understanding of basic biological processes continues its rapid advance with prospects for practical application. In this concluding section I offer several examples of the way future ethical problems are likely to emerge from emerging research efforts. These examples are only illustrative and hardly exhaust the possibilities.

Military planners have long been interested in the development of non-lethal weapons that disorient enemy forces and render them at least temporarily dysfunctional. This was the purpose of the army LSD experiments in the 1960s. Although the theory is benign relative to violent measures, in practice the results are not at all assured. A recent example of the use of supposedly non-lethal anesthetic gases took place in the 2002 Moscow theater hostage crisis, in which Chechen rebels were dislodged when an opiate-based agent was pumped into the ducts, killing 120 hostages. The United States has acknowledged renewed interest in such weapons as useful devices in the event of such terrorist actions, although a stumbling block is the 1993 Chemical Weapons Convention, which prohibits the use of incapacitating substances.[33] The United States Marine Corps has since 1996 been responsible for the Joint Non-lethal Weapons Program, which has as its mission "to provide warfighters a family of Non-Lethal Weapon (NLW) systems with a range of optional non-lethal capabilities across the full spectrum of threats and crisis."[34] In 2002 A National Academy of Sciences panel on the United States' non-lethal weapons program neither rejected these weapons nor advocated their use, but recommended improved processes for research and development and for integrating them into weapons command structures. The social and ethical implications of these weapons are not addressed in the panel's report.[35]

Neuroscience research presents a variety of opportunities for still more futuristic military applications. Neural receptors responsible for brain development have already been enhanced in mice, with evidence that learning is significantly improved. In the heat of battle complex instructions must be recalled under highly stressful conditions, such as target orders for fighter pilots. Substances that achieved memory enhancement prior to a mission would be a very attractive under these conditions. For homeland defense, the clumsy and non-selective screening procedures now used in airports and other sensitive public places could be complemented or replaced by remote functional Magnetic Resonance Imaging (fMRI) that identified individuals with high levels of neural activity in systems associated with violence or other forms of excitability.[36] Although such applications may seem like science fiction, we have seen that the national security state leaves no stone unturned if some tactical advantage might be lurking beneath it.

There is, as well, a remarkable convergence of regulation and funding that promises to stimulate research on vaccines and antibiotics that could be used to respond to biological or chemical attacks. Under the 2002 Bioterrorism Act the standard regimen for licensing of drugs for human use has been modified to permit F.DA. approval for medications to protect against biological and chemical attacks but that cannot ethically be tested in human beings. What has become know as the "animal rule" permits licensure based on efficacy testing in animals alone, the rationale being that human challenge studies for, say, new anthrax medications would be inherently unethical. In addition to this noteworthy modification of the rules, President Bush has succeeded in securing initial funding for Project BioShield, intended to support efforts to develop new antibiotics and vaccines for the war on terror. BioShield is expected to yield billions of new research dollars for this purpose. This combination of regulation and funding promises to propel a great deal of science in the coming years; whether it will distort research priorities or complement new approaches to naturally occurring disease remains to be seen.[37]

XI.

As indicated in the epigraphs to this paper, twice in the past 50 years, U.S. national security policy has been significantly revised, once to deal with Communism, then again with terrorism. The president's 2002 policy statement on national security expressed the chief difference between the two circumstances, "America is now threatened less by conquering states than we are by failing ones. We are menaced less by fleets and armies than by catastrophic technologies in the hands of the embittered few. We must defeat these threats to our Nation, allies, and friends."[38]

Dissimilar as the circumstances are in geopolitical terms, in the adjustment to the cold war and the war on terror there are striking similarities as well. During both periods national security institutions were modified and given new powers, the military establishment's mission was reviewed and altered, and science was recognized as potentially playing a central role in providing an advantage to the U.S. and its allies. The net result is a significant expansion of state power.

But expanded state power does not automatically transfer into societal acquiescence, especially in matters affecting the public health. The clinical trials of smallpox vaccine were supposed to lead to an immunization program for emergency responders. According to the Bush administration's plans, by July 2003 500,000 health care workers were to have been immunized, but instead only ten percent of that number had received the vaccine. Nearly 50,000 doses of vaccine had to be destroyed because the contents of opened vials had expired.[39]

This result is in some ways reminiscent of the public reaction to another emergency response plan during the cold war. Initial enthusiasm for a fallout shelter program during the Kennedy administration was represented by a several hundred million dollar civil defense appropriation request from Congress. In spite of an intense campaign to convince the American people that their survival could depend on a shelter in their homes, the effort quickly faltered amid confusion about the true benefits of a shelter in the event of thermonuclear war. The administration permitted the initiative to fade away.[40]

The scientific establishment may be more or less cooperative with the national security state. Here one finds a significant contrast between the cold war experience, when physical scientists accepted secrecy arrangements, and the war on terror, when biologists and chemists are far less comfortable with restrictions on their research and publication. The difference is partly rooted in the fact that the close relationship between physicists and the federal government began during a full-scale war. Denial of atomic bomb information to America's enemies was a high priority that continued after the war. The Manhattan Project itself took place under extraordinary secrecy, and the physics community largely accepted and supported tight security arrangements. Those who were persecuted for suspicions about their "loyalty," such as Charles U. Condon, were not enthusiastically supported by the science establishment.

By contrast, current efforts to restrict access to laboratories, materials, and scientific information, and to manage the visa status of laboratory researchers, have been met with skepticism and even alarm on the part of the scientific establishment. In December 2002 the National Academies expressed concern that constraints on foreign visitors has had "serious unintended consequences for American science, engineering and medicine."[41] Products of the era of Vietnam and Watergate, many in the contemporary generation of life scientists are perhaps more critical of state power than those who came to maturity during World War II. As important, their scientific activity was not nourished by a highly secretive program with government-imposed security conditions. And the basis for suspicion in the era of the war on terror is often ethnicity or nationality rather than possession of a Communist Party card.

The issues raised for the life sciences by the reinvigorated national security state thus extend well beyond those of bioethics, but I believe the bioethical issues are emblematic of the larger agenda. It will be hard to overlook these issues if the roots of human research ethics in national security policy are understood. The failure to appreciate these origins perhaps lies in the fact that few bioethicists are familiar with military culture or national security affairs. Another factor was the failure of the individual most responsible for enlivening interest in human research ethics in the 1960s, Henry Beecher, to connect his interest in these problems with his own Army-sponsored experimental work on hallucinogens, conducted without the subjects' full knowledge or consent.[42] For the sake of a vigorous future, the time has surely come for bioethics to embrace this complex and unsettling aspect of its origins.

References

1. *Naval War College Review*, Vol. XXVII (1975): 51-108.

2. At <http://www.whitehouse.gov/nsc/nss9.html> (last visited March 14, 2004).

3. J. D. Moreno, *Undue Risk: Secret State Experiments on Humans* (New York: W.H. Freeman, 1999); J.D. Moreno, "'The Only Feasible Means': The Pentagon's Ambivalent Relationship with the Nuremberg Code," in *Bioethics, Justice, and Health Care*, W. Teays and L.M. Purdy, eds., (California: Wadsworth, 2000); J.D. Moreno, "Reassessing the Influence of the Nuremberg Code in American Medical Ethics," *Journal of Contemporary Health Law and Policy* 12 (1997):347-360; R. Faden et al., "United States Researchers, The Nazi Doctors' Trial, and the Nuremberg Code: A Review of the Findings of the Advisory Committee on Human Radiation Experiments," *JAMA* 276, no. 20 (1996):1667-1671; J.D. Moreno and S.E. Lederer, "Revising the History of Cold War Research Ethics," *Kennedy Institute of Ethics Journal* 6, no. 3 (1996): 223-238.

4. J.D. Moreno, ed., *In the Wake of Terror: Medicine and Morality in a Time of Crisis* (Cambridge, Ma.: MIT Press, 2003); J.D. Moreno, "Remember Saddam's Human Guinea Pigs," *The American Journal of Bioethics* 3, no.2 (2003): W53; J.D. Moreno, "Human Experiments and National Security: The Need to Clarify Policy," *Cambridge Quarterly of Research Ethics* 12, no. 2 (2003): 192-195; J.D. Moreno, "A New World Order for Human Experiments," *Accountability in Research* 10 (2003):47-56.

5. J. Weldes, et al., eds., *Cultures of Insecurity: States, Communities and the Production of Danger* (Minneapolis: Borderlines, 1999).

6. D. Yergin, *Shattered Peace: The Origins of the Cold War* (New York: Penguin, 1977): 196.

7. The ensuing account is especially indebted to M. J. Hogan, *A Cross of Iron: Harry Truman and the Origins of the*

National Security State, 1945-1954 (Cambridge: Cambridge University Press, 1998).

8. Moreno, *supra* note 3, at 35-36.

9. Hogan, *supra* note 7, at 235.

10. *Id.* at 241.

11. Moreno, *supra* note 3, at 136.

12. *Id.* at 137-138.

13. *Id.* at 149.

14. Id. at 162.

15. See <http://www.defenselink.mil/specials/secdef_histories/bios/lovett.htm> (last visited March 9, 2004).

16. See <http://www.defenselink.mil/specials/secdef_histories/bios/wilson.htm> (last visited March 9, 2004).

17. Advisory Committee on Human Radiation Experiments, *The Human Radiation Experiments* (New York: Oxford University Press, 1996): 56.

18. Army Regulation 70-25: *Use of Volunteers as Subjects of Research*, 28 March 1962. I am grateful to Art Anderson for calling my attention to this regulation.

19. *United States v. Stanley*, 483 U.S. 669 (1987).

20. See <http://deploymentlink.osd.mil/current_issues/shad/shad_tests.shtml>, (last visited March 14, 2003).

21. See <http://deploymentlink.osd.mil/news/jan02/news_10402_001.shtml>, (last visited March 9, 2004).

22. T. Shanker, "Reports Detail Tests of Troops For Exposures," *New York Times*, July 1, 2003: 21A.

23. See <http://www.iom.edu/project.asp?ID=4909> (last visited March 9, 2004).

24. See <http://deploymentlink.osd.mil/current_issues/shad/shad_tests.shtml> (last visited March 14, 2004).

25. Although this impression is hard to quantify, it is a conclusion reached based on my work for the Advisory Committee on Human Radiation Experiments and many conversations with agency officials.

26. J.D. Moreno, "Bioethics After the Terror," *American Journal of Bioethics* 2 (2002): 60-64.

27. "Pentagon Plans to Proceed with Development of Anthrax Strain," *New York Times*, September 4, 2001.

28. Press release, St. Louis University, "Volunteers are Still Needed for Smallpox Study," November 13, 2001.

29. "Volunteers Line Up to Test Smallpox Protection," *New York Times*, November 3, 2001.

30. "Small Number of Children to be Inoculated, Officials Say," *Newsday*, September 25, 2002.

31. S.E. Frey, et al. "Dose-Related Effects of Smallpox Vaccine," *New Eng. J. of Med.* 346, no. 17 (2002):1275-1280.

32. See <http://mrmc-www.army.mil/docs/rcq/ar70-25.pdf> (last visited March 9, 2004).

33. See <http://www.csmonitor.com/2003/0214/p02s01-usmi.html> (last visited March 9, 2004).

34. See <http://www.jnlwd.usmc.mil/mission.asp> (last visited March 9, 2004).

35. Naval Studies Board, National Research Council, *An Assessment of Non-Lethal Weapons Science and Technology* (Washington, D.C.: National Academies Press, 2003).

36. J.D. Moreno, "Neuroethics: An Agenda for Neuroscience and Society," *Nature Neuroscience* 4, no. 2 (2003):149-153.

37. J.D. Moreno, "The BioShield Bonanza and Human Experimentation," *Research USA* 1, no. 2 (2003): 29.

38. <http://www.whitehouse.gov/nsc/nss1.html> (last visited March 14, 2004).

39. "Focus on Smallpox Threat Revived," *Washington Post*, July 17, 2003: A3.

40. R. Dallek, *An Unfinished Life: John F. Kennedy, 1917-1963* (New York: Little, Brown, 2003): 464-466.

41. D. Kevles, "A Security Clampdown on Biotechnology Research," *Technology Review* 106, no. 6 (2003): 40-48.

42. Advisory Committee on Human Radiation Experiments, *supra* note 17: 79.

[11]

Public health: a neglected counterterrorist measure

Richard Horton

The war against terrorism, announced by President Bush and endorsed by western political leaders in the immediate aftermath of the Sept 11 assault on America, will fail. No matter how much international collaboration is achieved between governments, intelligence services, and police networks, terrorists will never be wholly eradicated from society. Such is the nature of terrorism.[1] A declaration of war, deemed necessary to reassure an anxious public, has raised false expectations of victory. The western response will not only come to be discredited but also may foster the very terrorist activity it is designed to prevent.

Paul Pillar, a former counterterrorism policymaker at the US Central Intelligence Agency, has studied American covert and foreign-policy approaches to terrorist threats. In his recently published analysis,[2] he argues that war metaphors are common in political circles. They drive "a tendency toward absolute solutions and a rejection of accommodation and finesse". He views traditional counterterrorist policies —diplomatic, legal, military, and economic—as ineffective and counterproductive. The best hope we have, he concludes, is not triumph but containment. Terrorism is a problem managed, never solved.

In response to the present crisis, there has been a curious failure to discuss the root causes of terrorism, except for some rather blunt criticism of America itself. Action so far has been confined to three fronts. First, the capabilities of terrorist groups have been targeted. Their organisation is being disrupted, their members sought. Second, the intentions of terrorists have been scrutinised. A capability to attack might well be available, but what makes the terrorist decide to act? Encouraging terrorists not to attack involves deterrence and diplomacy. The third front is occupying most political airtime right now—namely, defence. Airport and aircraft security, homeland protection, and military force are all important defensive instruments. None of these efforts gets close to the cause of the problem.

Terrorism is a consequence of wider political and social change. Terrorism thrives especially in countries enduring state failure. Afghanistan, Colombia, Northern Ireland, Sudan, the Palestinian territories, Iraq, and Algeria all harbour terrorist groups. All have varying degrees of state failure, where states exist. The current US response to Afghanistan fails to recognise this reality. Military escalation, the language of retaliation, and possibly even covert strikes have been the main elements of American foreign policy. Bush has also asked for "the cooperation of citizens within Afghanistan who may be tired of having the Taliban in place".[3] This incitement to overthrow the existing government is a disappointingly crude attempt at nation-building, especially given the humanitarian disaster facing Afghanistan. What is missing? Medicine and public health have important if indirect parts to play in securing peace and stability for countries in collapse. Health could be the most valuable counterterrorist measure yet to be deployed.

Afghanistan's peoples are not homogenous. Pushtuns (38%), Tajiks (25%), Hazaras (19%), and Uzbeks (6%) make up most of the country's 22 million population. Each of these groups is further subdivided into tribes and clans. The Northern Alliance, the government's principal opposition, is also a mix of peoples, but Tajiks dominate. The Taliban government is drawn mainly from Pushtuns south of the Hindu Kush mountains. If a US attack were to draw on the Northern Alliance alone for support there would be a geographical and ethnic divide that would be hard to bridge.

The recent history of Afghanistan reveals how a sink for terrorists has been created. For two centuries, the country was a strategic target for empires either in expansion or decline. Afghanistan became a place for US-Soviet conflict in the 1970s. The communist-backed King Zahir Shah was overthrown in 1973. A communist coup in 1978 led to mass killings. A reign of terror was quashed in 1979 by a Soviet invasion that backfired when Afghans launched a jihad against their invaders. Pakistan, supported by the USA, sided with Afghan resistance forces. This chronic war of attrition did much to weaken the Soviet state, and President Gorbachev eventually ended the war in 1989. The conflict went almost unnoticed by the western media. Only much later was its full horror chronicled.[4] The country was left in ruins. 1·5 million civilians died and 6 million refugees fled to Iran and Pakistan. A violent civil war filled the vacuum left by the earlier Soviet-US struggle. In 1995, the Taliban, supported by Pakistan, took over and replaced communism with Wahhabism, an extreme but widely endorsed version of Islam. Allegiances switched once again. The USA now supported a Russian-Iranian axis against the Taliban. There is talk now of the US backing a return of the 86-year-old deposed King Zahir Shah. It would not be surprising if Afghans were a little cynical of western politicians who pledge peace to the people of Afghanistan.

Indeed, because of the cruel terrorist murders in America, Afghanistan now faces accelerating destitution added to destruction. According to WHO, the quality of the country's health system ranks 173 out of 191 nations.[5] Afghanistan and Pakistan are the only two countries ranked lowest on child-health equality which are not in sub-Saharan Africa. The fertility rate (1999) is 6·7; life-expectancy at birth (1999) for men is 45·3 and for women 47·2. The United Nations Development Programme's latest report[6] paints an even bleaker picture. What follows are indicators of development in Afghanistan that can be reasonably verified (figures in brackets refer to comparable US data): infant mortality

Displacement of people from Aghanistan

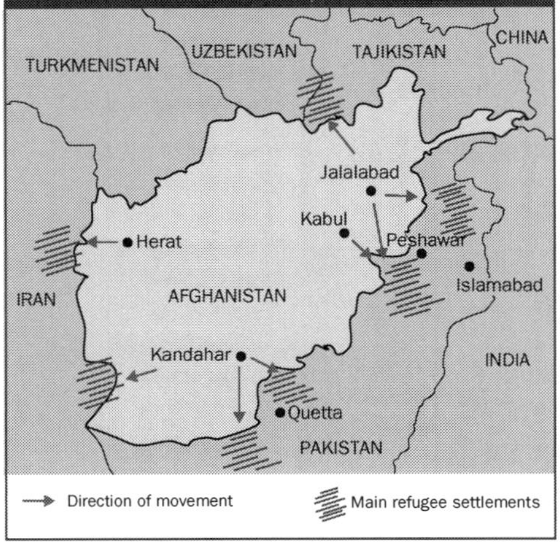

rate per 1000 live births, 165 (7); under-5 mortality rate per 1000 live births, 257 (8); adult literacy rate for people aged 15 and above, 36% (99%); undernourished people as a percentage of total population, 70 (0); population using improved water services, 13% (100%).[6]

Khabir Ahmad, *The Lancet*'s correspondent in the region, has followed persistently the impact of human-rights abuses, UN sanctions, epidemics, and the collapse of the public-health infrastructure in Afghanistan during the past 2 years.[7] Personal testimonies confirm the appalling living conditions of the Afghan people.[8] The refugee crisis (figure) is an additional burden, driven by a mix of war and drought. By 2000, 2 million Afghan refugees were in Pakistan and 1·4 million in Iran. Since the attacks on America, thousands more refugees have left for these same neighbouring countries, with the threat of up to 8 million more if armed conflict begins. Famine is already present. The UK government has spoken of a "humanitarian coalition" to soften the impact of a war. However, the challenges of refugee health are formidable and go well beyond money.[9]

Here lies an opening for a new type of counterterrorism policy. No single counterterrorist measure will succeed alone. But the existing narrow range of options could be broadened to find ways of engaging and helping rather than punishing populations at risk. The intention must be to stop recruitment to terrorist groups. Lateef Afridi, a tribal chief near the Khyber Pass and a member of Pakistan's National Assembly, noted that those wishing to reverse the Taliban's policies "must offer to build the schools and the hospitals that are so desperately needed. Otherwise, they [the Taliban sympathisers] will take their weapons and all be joining the jihad". Afghanistan has been the victim of two decades of savage exploitation by several of those countries now urging a war against terrorism. The hypocrisy of these governments is breathtaking, the consequences predictable and tragic.

In addition to the welcome promises of aid by western powers, there must be three longer-term revisions of policy. First, foreign-policy goals should incorporate health, development, and human rights as key strategic objectives.[10,11] Too often, foreign policy is reduced to little more than short-term alliances for political or military advantage. These limited goals sow the seeds for later terrorist—and humanitarian—crises.

Second, the application of sanctions must be judged more wisely. In Afghanistan, UN sanctions were aimed at forcing the Taliban government to hand over Osama bin Laden.[12] The health effects have been crushing,[13,14] while the political objective has failed entirely. Third, western powers must recommit themselves to international agencies, such as the UN, and to international treaties, such as those on criminal justice and the environment. Encouragingly, the US last week agreed to pay $582 million in back dues to the UN and, as part of its annual $99 million food aid to the country, is sending through the UN 10 000 tons of wheat to feed refugees fleeing Afghanistan.

The discipline of public health therefore adds fresh perspectives on foreign policy and counterterrorism measures. Principles of harm reduction are more realistic and practicable than false notions of a war on terrorism. Attacking hunger, disease, poverty, and social exclusion might do more good than air marshals, asylum restrictions, and identity cards. Global security will be achieved only by building stable and strong societies. Health is an undervalued measure of our global security.

Richard Horton
The Lancet, London WC1X 8RR, UK

1 Editorial. A world war against terrorism. *Lancet* 2001; **358:** 937–38.
2 Pillar PR. Terrorism and US foreign policy. Washington: Brookings Institution, 2001.
3 Bumiller E, Shanker T. Bush steps up appeal to Afghans to rid their country of Taliban. *New York Times* Sept 26, 2001, p1.
4 Borovik A. The hidden war. New York: Grove Press, 1990.
5 The World Health Report, 2000. Geneva: WHO, 2000.
6 Human Development Report, 2001. New York: UNDP, 2001.
7 Ahmad K. UN report highlights health effects of sanctions on Afghanistan. *Lancet* 2000; **356:** 839.
8 Singh M. Health care for children in Afghanistan. *Pediatrics* 2000; **105:** 160.
9 Rowland M. Malaria control in Afghan refugee camps. *Trans R Soc Trop Med Hyg* 2001; **95:** 125–26.
10 MacQueen G, Santa-Barbara J, Neufeld V, Yusuf S, Horton R. Health and peace: time for a new discipline. *Lancet* 2001; **357:** 1460–61.
11 Horton R. Croatia and Bosnia: the imprints of war— II. Restoration. *Lancet* 1999; **353:** 2223–28.
12 Ahmad K. UN sanctions on Afghanistan prompt widespread concern. *Lancet* 1999; **354:** 1536.
13 Ahmad K. UN report highlights health effects of sanctions on Afghanistan. *Lancet* 2000; **356:** 839.
14 Ahmad K. UN sanctions imposed against Afghanistan while thousands flee. *Lancet* 2001; **357:** 207.

Part IV
Avian Flu

[12]

Pandemic Influenza: Public Health Preparedness for the Next Global Health Emergency

Lawrence O. Gostin

The threat posed by avian influenza appears to be rising, yet global and national health programs are preparing only fitfully. A lethal form of avian flu has rooted itself deeply into the poultry flocks of poor Asian countries that will have a hard time eradicating it. Every so often a sick bird infects a human, who usually dies from the encounter, and on rare occasions the virus seems to have spread from one person to another before the chain of infection dies out. All it would take to set off a raging global pandemic would be for the virus to mutate into a form that is readily transmissible among humans.[1]

Severe Acute Respiratory Syndrome (SARS) garnered a great deal of public attention because it was novel and its potential for spread was unknown. However, the SARS corona virus is significantly less virulent than pandemic influenza viral infections. The annual number of deaths for seasonal influenza is 36,000 people in the United States and 250,000-500,000 worldwide. However, highly pathogenic influenza pandemics have occurred roughly 2-3 times per century, causing untold morbidity and mortality.[2] The Spanish influenza pandemic of 1918 was believed to have caused over 20 million deaths in a world less than one-third the size of the current global population;[3] modern epidemiologists now estimate that over 50 million people died. Moreover, these deaths did not occur primarily among infants and old people, as suggested by conventional wisdom. Approximately half the deaths were among people in the prime of their lives. As John Barry explains in his recent book, "One cannot know with certainty, but if the upper estimate of the death toll is true as many as 8 to 10 percent of all young adults then living may have been killed by the virus. And they died with extraordinary ferocity and speed."[4]

There are three essential prerequisites for an influenza pandemic: (1) the identification of a novel viral subtype in animal populations such as swine or poultry, (2) viral replication causing disease in humans, and (3) efficient human-to-human transmission.[5] The species "jump" from animals to humans could occur through a process known as "reassortment." If a person is exposed to both animal and human viral infections, the "genetic mixing" could lead to a strain that is transmissible human-to-human, sometimes in ways that are highly resistant to vaccination or antiviral treatment. In-

Lawrence Gostin, JD, LL.D. (Hon.) *is the John Carroll Research Professor of Law, Georgetown University; Professor of Public Health, the Johns Hopkins University; and Director, Center for Law & the Public's Health (CDC Collaborating Center Promoting Health Through Law). He is a lifetime elected member of the Institute of Medicine and serves on the IOM Board on Health Promotion and Disease Protection.*

fluenza A (H5N1), the viral strain responsible for the ongoing avian influenza outbreaks, has a worrying capacity to jump species, infecting cats and pigs, as well as, in the laboratory, ferrets and mice.[6]

Since 1997, the first two prerequisites - a novel viral strain in animals and transmission from animals to humans - have been met on numerous occasions. Although probable human-to-human transmission of a virulent strain of avian influenza has occurred, it has not yet been shown to be highly efficient.

From late 2003 through October 2004, outbreaks of highly pathogenic influenza A (H5N1) occurred among poultry throughout Asia[7] and parts of North America.[8] More than 200 million birds and other domesticated fowl have been culled or have died from the infection, including farms in the United States.[9] The severe economic and trade impacts are illustrated by CDC and USDA orders for a ban on the import of all birds (Class: Aves) from affected areas in Southeast Asia.[10] Similar restrictions were placed by countries in Europe and Asia on imports of U.S. poultry. During the A (H5N1) outbreaks of 2004 alone, there were 43 human cases, with extraordinarily high mortality rates; 31 of these individuals died.[11] The avian influenza outbreaks have provoked fears of an influenza pandemic reminiscent of the great plagues in world history.[12]

The lack of reliable vaccine production, even for "routine" seasonal epidemics, has increased fears of lethal forms of influenza. The United States, for example, is experiencing extreme shortage of influenza vaccine for the 2004-05 season. Chiron Corporation - one of two manufacturers working on a vaccine for human bird flu - had its license to make conventional flu vaccine temporarily suspended by the British government in early October 2004. Chiron had been expected to provide 46-48 million doses of the vaccine, about half of the nation's supply. Chiron is currently the subject of a criminal investigation and is facing a shareholder derivative lawsuit relating to the vaccine shortage.[13] Responses to the shortage within the United States are varied, including the promulgation of emergency orders making it a misdemeanor to administer a flu shot to an individual not in an identified risk category, imposing penalties for price gouging, and the decision of various health insurers to cover an alternate (FluMist) vaccine.[14] This is not the first time that the availability of influenza vaccines has been delayed, and, for decades, health experts have been issuing warnings concerning the fragility of the nation's vaccine supply and precarious dependence on a very low number of vaccine producers.[15]

There is now intense interest in influenza preparedness, with major planning initiatives being undertaken by the World Health Organization (WHO) and Institute of Medicine (IOM).[16] The potential for pandemic spread of a "fit" influenza strain leads to intriguing ethical and legal questions about public health interventions that could severely disrupt trade, economics, travel, and personal liberty. National and global public health agencies have mooted a wide range of interventions, asking such penetrating questions as: Should intrusive powers be exercised? At what stage in the outbreak should interventions commence and with what safeguards? How can vaccines and antiviral medications be produced reliably and delivered efficiently and fairly to large populations? Planning for the next pandemic includes not simply influenza but other novel infections, both naturally occurring and intentionally created.[17]

This article examines the principal therapeutic and non-therapeutic public health interventions for preventing or ameliorating pandemic influenza. (See Table). In each case, the hard, yet inevitable, legal and ethical questions are explored. Thereafter, the article provides several ethical values that can help evaluate public health interventions in anticipation of the next global health emergency.

Public Health Interventions to Prevent or Ameliorate Pandemic Influenza

Animal/Human Interchange

Scientists consider live bird markets, traveling poultry workers, and the movement of domestic poultry and fighting cocks to be the most likely vectors for spreading A (H5N1) from farm to farm and country to country.[18] Consequently, a critical early preventive strategy is to control animal populations and prevent the species jump from animals to humans. Humans are highly vulnerable to animal infections due to the close proximity of animal and human populations in farming and distribution of poultry and meat.[19] Strategies to diminish the risk include separation of animal and human populations; occupational health and safety in animal work (e.g., infection control and disinfection); and control of diseased or exposed animal populations (e.g., culling).

The international community faces daunting problems in implementing these strategies. International food safety law does not emphasize animal/human interchange. The Codex Alimentarius Commission, administered by the WHO and the Food and Agricultural Organization (FAO), regulates food hygiene and labeling. Codex's main concern is with the safety of the food supply and fair standards for international trade in food.[20] Occupational health and safety rules are primarily found at the national level, and country safeguards are highly variable. Countries may have a selfish interest in continuing intensive farming and food distribution. These methods are cost-effective from an

Table
Public Health Interventions: Purposes and Values

Public Health Intervention	**Purposes and Objectives**	**Strategies to Achieve Public Health Purpose**	**Ethical Issues and Recommendations**
Animal/Human Interchange	Prevent "species jump" by reducing proximity of animals and humans	Separation of animals and humans; occupational health and safety; control of diseased animals	Safeguard economic interests in farming while protecting the public's health
Global Surveillance	Timely and systematic monitoring of health threats	Cover all threats of global importance; prompt country reporting; use "small-world networks"	Ensure privacy safeguards for individuals and protection of groups
Case Contact Investigations	Prevent spread of infection to contacts of infected or exposed persons	Offer counseling, vaccination, and/or treatment to infected or exposed persons	Conduct investigations with sensitivity and respect for individuals and their contacts
Stable Vaccine Supply	Assure stable vaccine supplies for endemic and pandemic influenza	Create incentives for private industry through public/private partnerships	Balance public/private interests in intellectual property, liability, and economic investment
Vaccination and Medical Treatment	Prophylaxis, amelioration of symptoms, and/or reduced infectiousness	Offer or require vaccination or antiviral therapy to at-risk or infected persons	Balance bodily integrity with common good; ensure fair allocation of scarce resources; make therapeutics available to developing countries
Community Hygiene	Promote safer behaviors among the population	Health education and hand washing, disinfection, masks, ventilation, and avoidance of contacts	Balance health benefits with costs and cultural sensitivities; ensure equitable access
Travel and Border Controls	Prevent cross-border spread of infectious disease	Travel advisories; border restrictions; regulation of conveyances; stop lists	Health is salient; avoid unnecessary restriction of trade; safeguard against discrimination
Decreased Social Mixing/ Increased Social Distance	Increase social distance to avoid rapid spread of infection in public settings	Close civic activities, meeting places, and transportation systems	Avoid heavy costs and diminished freedoms; deliver services to the vulnerable
Civil Confinement	Separate the infected or exposed from the healthy	Isolation, quarantine, *cordon sanitaire*	Provide due precess; ensure safe and humane setting; consider compansation; gain public's trust

economic perspective but do not necessarily result in safe practices to prevent animal-to-human transmission of disease.

Even if strong international health standards did exist, public health authorities would continue to face the problem of when to implement aggressive strategies such as culling. Premature interventions have profound economic implications affecting livelihoods and trade. However, weak or tardy interventions risk devastation to animal and human populations.

Global Surveillance

Surveillance of novel infections in humans offers early warning and provides an opportunity for a timely response. Experts recommend various surveillance activities, many of which were used in the 2003 SARS outbreaks: testing and screening; health questionnaires, notices, and declarations; fever monitoring (self-monitoring, thermal scanning); and reporting and monitoring trends.[21]

Despite its importance, many countries do not conduct effective and timely surveillance. Prompt notification of an infectious disease threat can affect a country's tourism, trade, and prestige. Consequently, some governments do not respond promptly to WHO requests for information. Many countries, moreover, lack the infrastructure and resources to conduct surveillance. As a result, national surveillance activities are highly variable.

The International Health Regulations (IHR) are the principal rules covering the international spread of infectious diseases. The IHR, however, do not apply to influenza, but cover only three diseases: cholera, plague, and yellow fever. Instead, the WHO Influenza Surveillance Network was established in 1952 to identify viral strains to develop the next season's vaccinations.

The WHO is currently involved in intergovernmental negotiations to revise the IHR. The draft revised IHR, if adopted, would significantly strengthen international rules for surveillance. The rules would apply to all health threats of international importance; mandate country notifications; gather reports from unofficial sources; and provide for real-time event management.[22] Global surveillance could further benefit from "small-world networks" consisting of health professionals, scientists, and non-governmental organizations continuously monitoring disease threats.[23] It should be possible to supplement the surveillance provided by official sources with multiple public/private sources through the internet and other modern communication facilities.

Although surveillance is an essential public health strategy, even routine activities, such as reporting, affect privacy because government collects sensitive health information. Acute outbreaks can trigger more extreme measures such as continuous monitoring of certain populations such as health care workers, immigrants, and travelers. An outbreak of a novel influenza strain will inevitably raise questions about the appropriate scope of government surveillance and its affects on privacy. Surveillance needs to take place, therefore, with privacy safeguards in place.

Case Contact Investigations

Case contact investigation is a classical form of surveillance. It involves identifying infected or exposed persons and following their recent contacts. This provides an opportunity to interrupt the spread of infection. Persons exposed or infected can be offered antiviral therapy as a prophylaxis or treatment. Those who are infectious or potentially infectious can be separated from the healthy population.

Case contract investigation is ostensibly voluntary because the "index case" is under no formal obligation to reveal his or her contacts. Nevertheless, its use in sexually transmitted infections, including HIV/AIDS, has proved highly controversial.[24] The index case may feel coerced into giving information, investigations pose privacy risks, and individuals may experience stigma and discrimination. These investigations, therefore, need to be conducted with sensitivity and respect for individuals and their family, friends, and associates.

Vaccination: Scientific Innovation in a Market Economy

The dominant strategy for seasonal influenza is to use vaccinations for susceptible groups. Recommended vaccination of high-risk populations (e.g., children and the elderly) has become standard in developed countries, and mass vaccination could be recommended in the event of a more severe outbreak.

An influenza pandemic would necessitate "surge capacity" in the development and delivery of vaccines, yet the prospects for assuring large-scale access appear dim. Manufacturing capacity is sufficient to cover less that 5% of the world's population. Even highly industrialized countries such as the United States have difficulty assuring a stable vaccine supply. Evidence for the inability of the private sector to meet America's needs for vaccines has mounted, as demonstrated by sequential IOM reports.[25] A handful of major vaccine manufacturers exist in the world today; there were four times that number only 20 years ago. The problem is compounded with A (H5N1) virus because standard methods for making influenza vaccines are ineffective for highly pathogenic strains.

Unreliability in the industry is fueled by a thicket of patent, liability, and financial concerns. Developing effective vaccines requires stable markets, venture capital, and economic incentives. Manufacturer investment costs may not be recouped if a pandemic does not occur or if intellectual property rights are in dispute. The industry could also be exposed to liability for adverse effects, even if lengthy clinical trials are undertaken (which would not be feasible in an emergency situation).[26] The unreliability of vaccine supply is problematic not only for civilian but also for military purposes.[27] What is urgently needed is an effective public/private partnership to stimulate vaccine production. The IOM Council recommends the establishment of a National Vaccine Authority (NVA) to advance the development, production, and procurement of new and improved vaccines of limited commercial potential but of global public health need.[28]

Therapeutic Interventions: Public Acceptance and Rationing a Scarce Public Good

When vaccination is unavailable, public health authorities may use an antiviral medication such as Tamiflu. Antiviral therapy can be used for prophylaxis, alleviation of symptoms, and reduction of infectiousness.[29] Antivirals, however, are costly, in short supply, and may be effective only if administered during the first two days following the onset of symptoms.

Therapeutic interventions raise distinct ethical and legal concerns. Requiring competent adults to be vaccinated or treated for their own protection is an unpopular notion. Nevertheless, the law permits a reasonable interference with bodily integrity to prevent harm to the community.[30]

Although officials have the legal authority to compel vaccination or treatment to protect the public, the political and ethical dimensions underpinning such a decision are complex. There is a long history of opposition to vaccinations among certain sections of the population.[31] Anti-vaccination sentiments are not always irrational because immunizations can pose risks, as well as confer benefits. Mass vaccination to avert an influenza epidemic can go horribly wrong, as occurred with swine flu in 1976. The CDC campaign to immunize the American population cost $134 million and caused Guillain-Barre Syndrome in some vaccine recipients.[32]

Vaccination or treatment can confer considerable benefit to the individual and, ultimately, to a population. Pandemic influenza would likely result in a paucity of vaccines and antiviral medications, raising the hard problem of fair allocation of scarce resources. Which ethical values should guide rationing decisions: private need (treatment of the sick); public need (prevention among vulnerable populations); maintenance of essential services (health care workers and "first responders"); or political influence (priority for those with political connections)? Justice may require that therapeutic interventions be used to benefit the most people possible, irrespective of their power or influence. This would militate toward the use of "public need" as the guiding ethical value. Therapeutics, therefore, would be used primarily for prevention and targeted to those who pose the greatest risk of transmission. The ethical value of "public need" might also require use of therapeutics for emergency workers to ensure maintenance of essential services and ongoing assistance to the public. This would place private need and political influence lower on the priority scale.

The global reality is that rich countries will have much less scarcity than poor countries. For example, Europe and the North America have over 90% of the world's vaccine production capacity, but less than 10% of the global population. Countries with manufacturing capacities can be expected to reserve scarce supplies for their own populations, leaving poorer countries with the most acute vaccine shortages. The ethical question then arises as to whether developed countries would be expected to forego some of their precious stockpile of vaccines and antiviral medications for the sake of poorer countries experiencing a higher burden of morbidity and mortality from influenza? One might argue that it is in the richer country's self interest to do so since infectious disease can travel across the globe. Ethical analysis would prove difficult – do developed countries have an obligation to reduce the burden of disease in developing countries? If all human life has the same worth, then it may be ethically desirable to devote therapeutic resources to poor regions experiencing higher burdens of disease. This allocation of resources is likely to have the maximum beneficial effect on morbidity and premature mortality.

Community Hygiene

One of the most valuable means of infection control is also the least intrusive. Health education to promote safer behaviors such as hand washing, disinfection, masks, ventilation, and avoidance of contacts can be highly effective. Community hygiene, although largely uncontroversial, can impose costs (e.g., purchasing and distributing equipment) and cause social unrest (e.g., exaggerated concerns about health risks). Hygiene measures are also culturally sensitive – notice the difference in mask-wearing habits in Asia compared with North America and Europe.

Under what circumstances should public health authorities issue a national recommendation for aggressive hygiene measures given the costs and cultural expectations? Probably the most important concern would be the cost effectiveness of the hygiene measure. If a hygiene measure is clearly cost effective, then the public has the right to know how to adopt that measure in a safe way. Vulnerable members of the community may also need economic and technical assistance to ensure equitable access to essential hygiene measures. If a measure is not cost effective, then public health authorities have an obligation to inform the public about the lack of effectiveness and the risks. In some cases, such as the use of masks, the evidence for, or against, effectiveness may be unclear. In such instances, the principle of transparency may suggest that public health officials state honestly the lack of conclusive evidence, leaving the judgment to the individual.

Travel and Border Controls

One of the first instincts in the face of infectious disease threats is to protect national borders. Consequently, international or national health agencies may issue travel advisories, establish border restrictions, or regulate conveyances such as airplanes, ships, and trains. They might similarly use "stop-lists" to prevent specified individuals or groups from traveling. The draft revised IHR afford WHO considerable authority to regulate international travel and control borders.

Travelers legitimately claim the right to know health risks, but travel restrictions significantly affect tourism and trade. Consequently, travel advisories can be politically charged, as were WHO advisories concerning SARS in Ontario, Canada.[33] A delicate balance exists between trade and health. Indeed, the draft revised IHR direct WHO to "provide security against the international spread of disease while avoiding unnecessary interference with international traffic."[34]

When faced with the hard tradeoff between maximization of health or of trade, which should prevail and why? Arguably, health should take precedence over trade because of the fundamental value of human functioning and life itself. Despite the effects on tourism and trade, the public has a legitimate interest in knowing if there are health hazards in regions where they intend to travel. National and international public health agencies have an obligation to take steps that are necessary to prevent the spread of infection across borders. Thus, it would be legitimate to prevent travel of a person who poses a significant risk of transmission. What public health authorities may not do is use infectious disease control as a pretext for discrimination by targeting individuals based on their nationality, race, religion, or other status.

Decreased Social Mixing/Increased Social Distance

Most Americans take for granted their freedom to associate with others in a variety of social settings. Yet, public health authorities could restrict social mixing and increase social distance to avert a serious infectious disease threat. This might involve closures of civic activities (e.g., schools, workplaces), meeting places or large gatherings (e.g., sports events, theatres, and business meetings), and transportation systems (e.g., mass transit and airlines). The purpose behind restrictions on mixing is to prevent rapid spread of infection in settings where multiple people congregate.

The United States Constitution affords individuals the freedom to associate, but courts would likely defer to reasonable regulation of congregate settings to prevent transmission of infection.[35] As with other interventions, closures entail heavy costs in lost revenue as well as in diminished freedoms. When an infectious disease outbreak deeply affects a society's everyday activities, public health authorities will have to cogently explain the need for such intrusive interventions and gain the public's confidence before implementing them. Critical legal and logistical questions loom: which authority has the power to close a venue; what criteria should be used to trigger a closure and when should the restriction be lifted; and how will services be delivered to vulnerable populations who may be at risk in an isolated residence or shelter?

Civil Confinement

The potential for a mass outbreak raises the specter of civil confinement to separate the infected or exposed from healthy individuals. This might entail isolation of infected persons, quarantine of exposed persons, or quarantine of a geographic area (*cordon sanitaire*). Civil confinements may take place in hospitals or other institutions, or in a person's home. New conceptions to separate the healthy from the infectious include "sheltering in place," which public health authorities analogize to a "snow day."

Many states modernized their public health statutes in the aftermath of the terrorist attacks on September 11th, 2001.[36] Public health law reform is necessary to ensure that states and localities have the legal authority for isolation and quarantine.[37] In order to meet constitutional standards, state law must have clear criteria for the use of civil confinement and must offer procedural due process.[38]

Civil confinement, of course, raises powerful civil liberties concerns. Not only is isolation or quarantine a deprivation of liberty, but enforcement can sometimes be intrusive. For example, during the SARS outbreaks, some countries used electronic bracelets, web cameras, and police to monitor and, at times, restrict the movement of individuals. It will also be important to ensure that judicial hearings are available, particularly in a mass outbreak. Isolation or quarantine will have to take place in a humane and habitable environment. Vulnerable persons need to be protected against re-exposure to infection, offered care and treatment, and guaranteed the necessities of life such as safe food and water.[39] There may also be the need to consider compensation for lost work. Individuals are confined for the good of the community and have to forego their livelihood and other essential activities. Above all, public health authorities need to maintain the public's trust. To what extent would orders for civil confinement dissipate trust and reduce cooperation?

Acting Under Conditions of Uncertainty: The Key Scientific and Social Questions

Influenza pandemic preparedness requires careful consideration of the public health strategy as well as the legal and ethical implications. Several key scientific questions loom: Are specific interventions cost effective? What combination of measures is most cost effective? During what phase of the pandemic should interventions be implemented? When should public health measures be discontinued?

Although many of the foregoing interventions have been widely used, many still lack adequate evidence of cost effectiveness. Even if individual interventions are known to be cost-effective, public health authorities will have to form a judgment as to the combination of measures that will be maximally effective. They will need to decide when to initiate and when to end an intervention.

The decision to intervene is difficult because public health authorities may be acting under conditions of scientific uncertainty. It may be unclear whether serologic tests are reliable, vaccines or treatment are safe and effective, and coercive interventions are acceptable to the population. To be effective, agencies may have to intervene at the earliest stages, before the threat level is clear. If interventions are well targeted and timed, then public health officials may prevent untold economic and human harm. However, if the interventions over-reach, officials will be accused of disregarding essential economic interests and fundamental human rights.

These scientific questions are important because public health interventions do not take place in a vacuum. They raise fundamental economic, political, and legal questions that need to be considered:

Economics
As mentioned earlier, public health interventions can have dire effects on the economy. They impede individual economic freedoms to travel and pursue a business or livelihood. They also affect local, national, and regional economies by impacting trade, travel, tourism, and agriculture. Countries may have built-in disincentives to conduct surveillance and response in an energetic and public way.

Political
Infectious disease outbreaks can have intense sociopolitical ramifications. Diseases affect a country's prestige as well as its economy, and the electorate may hold politicians accountable. As a result, political leaders may try to de-emphasize the threat or delay taking definitive action as occurred in numerous epidemics ranging from HIV/AIDS to SARS.

Legal and Constitutional
Infectious disease outbreaks take place in countries with vastly different legal and constitutional traditions. Public health planning may be undertaken within liberal democracies with full protection of human rights or they may take place in less democratic, perhaps more authoritarian, societies. During the SARS outbreaks, for example, countries behaved very differently in their response and protection of civil liberties.[40] Infectious diseases tend to bring out the best and worst in societies. History demonstrates the potential for over-reaction, stigma, and discrimination in the face of a severe epidemic.[41] Consequently, the legal and constitutional dimensions will be important in confronting a severe epidemic.[42]

Ethical Values Underpinning Public Health Preparedness: The Cross-Cutting Issues

Public health authorities have a mandate to protect the population's health. It is crucial, however, that they act ethically. Ethical values are usually too broad to precisely determine whether an activity is morally appropriate. Nevertheless, it ought to be possible to enunciate several ethical values that can inform public health practice, particularly in an emergency.

Transparency
The ethical value of transparency requires officials to make decisions in an open and fully accountable manner. Government officials must be willing to make clear the basis for public health measures. They should honestly and openly inform the public of what is known and not known; openly acknowledge when new evidence warrants reconsideration of policies; and educate the public about the goals of intervention and the steps taken to safeguard individual rights.

Protection of Vulnerable Populations
Diseases that may differentially affect segments of the population have usually imposed the additional burden of social opprobrium. Public health officials may inadvertently amplify the process as they conduct their surveillance activities. While they may not be able to prevent stigmatization, officials have an obligation to take steps to mitigate the suffering that may attend their efforts by underscoring the irrationality and inequity of ethnic stereotyping. Consultation with representatives of the communities most at risk will be important for instrumental reasons and as an expression of social solidarity. Individuals should feel a sense of participation in crucial decisions affecting their lives and communities. People place their trust in political leaders and, in return, they deserve due consideration and respect for their health and human rights.

Fair Treatment and Social Justice
Justice requires that the benefits and burdens of public health action be fairly distributed, thus precluding the unjustified targeting of already socially vulnerable populations. Equitable public health action is based on science and assures reasoned population-based policies. Procedural justice requires a fair and independent hearing for individuals who are subjected to burdensome public health action. Due process requirements are inherently important because fair hearings affirm the dignity of the person. Furthermore, due process is instrumentally important because it best assures accurate decision-making.

SYMPOSIUM

The Least Restrictive Alternative

International human rights law is guided by the principle of proportionality: i.e., interventions should be necessary and proportional to the risk posed.[43] Interventions should be the least restrictive alternative necessary to prevent or ameliorate the health threat. Requiring the least restrictive/intrusive alternative represents a means to impose limits on state interventions consistent with the traditions of privacy, freedom of association, and individual liberties. The standard does not require officials to utilize less-than-optimal interventions. However, they must choose the least intrusive alternative that can best achieve the health objective.

The Public Health Paradox

There is no way to avoid the dilemmas posed by acting without full scientific knowledge. Failure to move aggressively in the early stages of pandemic influenza can have catastrophic consequences. Actions that prove to have been unnecessary will be viewed as draconian and based on hysteria. The only safeguard is the adoption of ethical values in formulating and implementing public health decisions. Public health policy will reflect in a profound way the manner in which humane societies both implicitly and explicitly balance the common good with respect for personal rights.

Disclaimer

Professor Gostin was a member of WHO's consultation on influenza preparedness and is working with WHO on the revision of the International Health Regulations. He also participated in the IOM Workshop on preparing for the next pandemic. The views in this article do not necessarily reflect those of WHO or IOM. A shorter version of this article appears in the *Hastings Center Report 34* (2004): 10-11.

References

1. Editorial, "The Menace From Avian Flu," *New York Times*, October 12, 2004, at A-30.
2. G. Kolata, "Genetic Material of Virus from 1918 Flu is Found," *New York Times*, March 21, 1997, at A-2.
3. J. Stevens, A.L. Corper, C.F. Basler, J.K. Taubenberger, P. Palese, and I.A. Wilson, "Structure of the Uncleaved Human H1 Hemagglutinin from the Extinct 1918 Influenza Virus," *Science* 303 (2004): 1866-70.
4. J.M. Barry, *The Great Influenza: The Epic Story of the Deadliest Plague in History* (New York: Viking, 2004).
5. Board on Global Health, Institute of Medicine, *Learning from SARS: Preparing for the Next Disease Outbreak* (Washington, DC: National Academies Press, 2004).
6. K. Bradshere, L.K. Altman, "A War and a Mystery: Confronting Avian Flu," *New York Times*, October 12, 2004, at D-1.
7. Affected countries include Cambodia, China, Indonesia, Malaysia, Japan, Hong Kong, Laos, South Korea, Thailand, and Vietnam.
8. Centers for Disease Control and Prevention, "Outbreaks of Avian Influenza A (H5N1) in Asia and Interim Recommendations for Evaluation and Reporting of Suspected Cases--United States," *Morbidity and Mortality Weekly Report* 53 (2004): 97-100.
9. J. Dao, "Bird Flu Outbreak has Farmers Jittery," *New York Times*, February 16, 2004, at A-12.
10. Orders pursuant to 42 CFR 71.32b dated Feb. 4, March 10, and Sept. 28, 2004.
11. WHO, "Cumulative Number of Confirmed Human Cases of Avian Influenza A(H5N1) since 28 January 2004," *at* <http://www.who.int/csr/disease/avian_influenza/country/cases_table_2004_10_04/en/> (last visited October 18, 2004).
12. CDC, "Outbreaks in Asia," *at* <http://www.cdc.gov/flu/avian/outbreaks/asia.htm> (last visited October 18, 2004); see H. Markel, *When Germs Travel: Six Major Epidemics that Have Invaded America Since 1900 and the Fears They Have Unleashed* (New York: Pantheon Books, 2004).
13. Pui-Wing Tam, "Chiron Receives U.S. Subpoena Over Flu Vaccine," *The Wall Street Journal*, October 13, 2004; Jerry Abejo, "Chiron Target of Shareholder Lawsuit," *The Wall Street Journal*, October 14, 2004.
14. Levine, "District to Issue Emergency Order Limiting Flu Shots," *Washington Post*, October 15, 2004, at B1; Haigh, "Bluementhal Wants Rell to Call Flu Vaccine Emergency," Associated Press, October 14, 2004; Mulder, "Some Insurers Will Pay for FluMist," *The Post-Standard*, October 14, 2004.
15. Grady, "With Few Suppliers of Flu Shots, Shortage Was Long in Making," *New York Times*, October 17, 2004.
16. R.J. Webby and R.G. Webster, "Are We Ready for Pandemic Influenza?" *Science* 302 (2003): 1519-22; World Health Organization, *WHO Consultation on Priority Public Health Interventions Before and During an Influenza Pandemic* (Geneva, Switzerland: WHO, 2004); *see* Board on Global Health, Institute of Medicine, *supra* note 5.
17. R.A. Weinstein, "Planning for Epidemics: The Lessons of SARS," *N. Engl. J. Med.* 350 (2004): 2332-34.
18. D.G. McNeil Jr., "Experts Call Wild Birds Victims, Not Vectors," *New York Times*, October 12, 2004, at D-6.
19. E.J. Emanuel, "Preventing the Next SARS" *New York Times*, May 12, 2003, at A-25.
20. The Sanitary and Phytosanitary Measures Agreement is designed to promote free trade by ensuring that national measures to protect human, animal, or plant life are scientifically-based and not pretexts to protect domestic markets from international competition. See A.L. Taylor, D.W. Bettcher, S.S. Fluss, K. DeLand, and D. Yach, "International Health Instruments: An Overview," in R. Detels, J. McEwen, R. Beaglehole, and H. Tanaka, eds., *Oxford Textbook of Public Health*, 4th ed. (Oxford: Oxford University Press, 2002): at 359-86.
21. L.O. Gostin, R. Bayer and A.L. Fairchild, "Ethical and Legal Challenges Posed by Severe Acute Respiratory Syndrome: Implications for the Control of Severe Infectious Disease Threats," *JAMA* 290 (2003): 3229-37.
22. WHO Secretariat, *Revision of the International Health Regulations*, Geneva, Switzerland: World Health Organization, January 15, 2004, Publication EB113/3 Rev.1; see L.O. Gostin, "The International Health Regulations and Beyond," *The Lancet: Infectious Diseases* 4 (2004): 606-607.
23. L.O. Gostin, "International Infectious Disease Law: Revision of the World Health Organization's International Health Regulations," *JAMA* 291 (2004): 2623-27.
24. R. Bayer, K.E. Toomey, "HIV Prevention and the Two Faces of Partner Notification," *American Journal of Public Health* 82 (1992): 1158-64.
25. V.S. Mitchell, N.M. Philipose, and J.P. Sanford, eds., *The Children's Vaccine Initiative: Achieving the Vision* (Washington, D.C.: National Academy Press, 1993); G.W. Pearson, ed., *The Children's Vaccine Initiative: Continuing Activities* (Washington, D.C.: National Academy Press, 1995).
26. K. Bradshere and L.K. Altman, "Experts Confront Major Obstacles in Containing Virulent Bird Flu," *New York Times*, September 30, 2004, at A-1.
27. Committee on a Strategy for Minimizing the Impact of Naturally Occurring Infectious Diseases of Military Importance, *Protecting Our Forces: Improving Vaccine Acquisition and Availability in the U.S. Military* (National Academy Press, 2002).
28. Statement from the IOM Council on Vaccine Development, November 5, 2001, *available at* <http://www.iom.edu/report.asp?id=5487> (last visited October 18, 2004).
29. I.M. Longini Jr, M.E. Halloran, A. Nizam, and Y. Yang, "Con-

taining Pandemic Influenza with Antiviral Agents," *American Journal of Epidemiology* 159 (2004): 623-33.
30. *Jacobson v. Massachusetts*, 197 U.S. 11 (1905); see L.O. Gostin, "Jacobson v. Massachusetts at 100: The Police Power and Civil Liberties in Tension," *American Journal of Public Health* (Forthcoming 2005).
31. S.E. Spier, "Perception of Risk of Vaccine Adverse Events: A Historical Perspective," *Vaccine* 20, suppl. 1 (2001): S78-84.
32. R. Neustadt, H.V. Fineberg, *The Epidemic That Never Was: Policy Making in the Swine Flu Scare* (New York: Vintage Books, 1983).
33. C. Krauss, "The SARS Epidemic: Toronto; Canada Increases Pressure on World Health Organization to Lift Travel Advisory," *New York Times*, April 26, 2003, at A-8.
34. Intergovernmental Working Group on the Revision of the International Health Regulations, World Health Organization, Working paper for regional consultations, Geneva (Switzerland): 2004.
35. New York v. New St. Mark's Baths, 497 N.Y.S.2d 979 (1986).
36. L.O. Gostin, J.W. Sapsin, S.P. Teret, S. Burris, J.S. Mair, J.G. Hodge, Jr., and J. S. Vernick, "The Model State Emergency Health Powers Act: Planning and Response to Bioterrorism and Naturally Occurring Infectious Diseases," *JAMA* 288 (2002): 622-628.
37. L.O. Gostin, "Public Health Law in an Age of Terrorism: Rethinking Individual Rights and Common Goods," *Health Affairs* 21 (2002): 79-93.
38. *Greene v. Edwards*, 263 S.E.2d 661 (W.Va. 1980).
39. J. Barbera, A. Macintyre, L.O. Gostin, T. Inglesby, T. O'Toole, C. DeAtley, et al., "Large-Scale Quarantine Following Biological Terrorism in the United States: Scientific Examination, Logistic and Legal Limits, and Possible Consequences," *JAMA* 286 (2001): 2711-17.
40. J.W. Sapsin, T.M. Thompson, L. Stone, K.E. DeLand, "International Trade, Law, and Public Health Advocacy," *Journal of Law, Medicine & Ethics* 31 (2003): 546-56.
41. S.L. Gilman, "Disease and Stigma," *Lancet* 354, suppl. (1999): SIV15.
42. L.O. Gostin, *Public Health Law: Power, Duty, Restraint* (Berkeley and New York: University of California Press and Milbank Memorial Fund, 2000).
43. "The Siracusa Principles on the Limitation and Derogation Provisions in the International Covenant on Civil and Political Rights," *Human Rights Quarterly* 7 (1985): 3-14.

[13]

PREPARING FOR AN INFLUENZA PANDEMIC: ETHICAL ISSUES

JARO KOTALIK

ABSTRACT

In the near future, experts predict, an influenza pandemic will likely spread throughout the world. Many countries have been creating a contingency plan in order to mitigate the severe health and social consequences of such an event. Examination of the pandemic plans of Canada, the United Kingdom and the United States, from an ethical perspective, raises several concerns. One: scarcity of human and material resources is assumed to be severe. Plans focus on prioritization but do not identify resources that would be optimally required to reduce deaths and other serious consequences. Hence, these plans do not facilitate a truly informed choice at the political level where decisions have to be made on how much to invest now in order to reduce scarcity when a pandemic occurs. Two: mass vaccination is considered to be the most important instrument for reducing the impact of infection, yet pandemic plans do not provide concrete estimates of the benefits and burdens of vaccination to assure everyone that the balance is highly favorable. Three: pandemic plans make extraordinary demands on health care workers, yet professional organizations and unions may not have been involved in the plans' formulation and they have not been assured that authorities will aim to protect and support health care workers in a way that corresponds to the demands made on them. Four: all sectors of society and all individuals will be affected by a pandemic and everyone's collaboration will be required. Yet, it appears that the various populations have been inadequately informed by occasional media reports. Hence, it is essential that plans are developed and communication programs implemented that will not only inform but also create an atmosphere of mutual trust and solidarity; qualities that at the time of a pandemic will be much needed.

INTRODUCTION

The influenza 'A' virus that causes seasonal flu outbreaks is also responsible for the occurrence of periodic world-wide epidemics or pandemics. During the last century, the world's population experienced a devastating pandemic in 1918 and two less severe global outbreaks in 1957 and 1968. Experts agree that future pandemics are highly likely and perhaps inevitable, but they are unable to predict the severity and timing of the next pandemic.[1] Given that the last three pandemics have occurred within intervals of 11 to 39 years, and that it has been 37 years since the last occurrence, the next pandemic may not be far off. A pandemic's capacity to cause illnesses and deaths as well as social and economic disruption is unique. A model created for the US demonstrates that in the US alone, 300,000 to 800,000 people may need hospitalization and 80,000 to 300,000 may die during the next influenza pandemic, while the economic losses are estimated to range from 71 to 166 billion dollars.[2]

The challenges of a future pandemic are being addressed by public health officials and expert groups in various countries of the world with the encouragement and assistance of WHO.[3] Many countries, as well as individual states, provinces and communities now have (or are in the process of creating) elaborate plans to minimize the impact of a pandemic. Among those national plans available in electronic form are the plans of Canada,[4] the United Kingdom[5] and the United States of America.[6] In the last four years, the importance of these plans has become even more apparent because some sections of the plans can be applied to other situations such as the emergence of new infectious diseases like SARS, or to outbreaks that may result from bioterrorism.

[1] C. Potter. 1998. Chronicle of Influenza Pandemics. In *Textbook of Influenza*. K. Nicholson, R. Webster & A. Hay, eds. New York. Blackwell Science Inc: 3–18.

[2] United States Department of Health and Human Services, NVPO. 2004. Washington, DC. Available at: http://www.hhs.gov/nvpo/pandemicplan/index.html (accessed 16 September 2004).

[3] R. Snacken. Pandemic Planning. *Vaccine* 2002; 20(Supplement 2): S88–S90.

[4] Health Canada. Canadian Pandemic Influenza Plan 2004. Available at http://www.hc-sc.gc.ca/pphb-dgspsp/cpip-pclcpi/ (accessed 16 September 2004).

[5] UK Health Department's influenza pandemic contingency plan. Available at http://www.dh.gov.uk/PublicationsAndStatistics/Publications/PublicationsPolicyAndGuidance (accessed 12 May 2005)

[6] US Department of Health and Human Services, *op. cit.* note 2; R. Strikas, G. Wallace & M. Myers. Influenza Pandemic Preparedness Action Plan for the United States: 2002 update. *Clinical Infectious Diseases* 2002; 35(5): 590–596.

There is no doubt that the aim of the authors of these national pandemic plans (many of them foremost experts in the field) was to base their product on the best available science. However, because every discourse about health care has not only a scientific but also a moral dimension, these plans also presuppose certain ethical values, principles, norms, interests and preferences. Yet, for whatever reason (partly, the difficulty in explicit articulation of ethical elements; partly, because bioethics scholarship has focused on other areas, and it has been only during the past few years that the discipline of bioethics has been developing a methodology for the ethical assessment of public health programs that can be applied to pandemic influenza plans),[7] the plans rarely discuss the relevant ethical elements. Among many issues that call for ethical analysis are the development of pandemic plans as a public policy exercise; prioritization schemes for vaccination and antiviral therapy; rationing of resources for intensive care and acute care; the role of personal initiatives in the stockpiling of drugs and personal protection devices; the role for markets and governments in the production and distribution of vaccine; remedies for persons harmed by preventive and responsive measures; the obligation of health care workers to serve under stressful and risky conditions; and the standard of care in temporary care facilities.

I have selected for discussion a few ethical issues that seem particularly pressing and which are germane to all three national plans listed above, and to their implementation.

ETHICAL ISSUE: SCARCITY

The pandemic, if severe, will lead to an extraordinarily high number of sick people over a large geographic area, all requiring care at the same time. As a result, the human and material resources of health care (available in ordinary times) will be rapidly overwhelmed. Many of the sick will no doubt recover with minimal assistance, but others will be seriously ill and require prolonged hospitalization, diagnostic facilities, multiple drugs, and well-trained staff if they are to have a chance to survive. A

[7] J.M. Last, ed. 1986. Ethics and Public Health Policy. In *Maxcy-Rosenau Public Health and Preventive Medicine.* Norwalk, Conn. Appleton-Century Crofts; J.F. Childress, R.R. Faden, R.D. Gaare et al. Public Health Ethics: Mapping the Terrain. *Journal of Law, Medicine & Ethics* 2002; 30: 170–178; N. Kass. An Ethics Framework for Public Health. *American Journal of Public Health* 2001; 91(11): 1176–1182; R. Bayer & A.L. Fairchild. The Genesis of Public Health Ethics. *Bioethics* 2004; 18(6): 473.

statement contained within the scenario of a future pandemic created by the US National Vaccine Program Office illustrates one aspect of scarcity: 'Intensive care units at local hospitals become overwhelmed, and soon there are widespread shortages of mechanical ventilators for treatment of patients with pneumonia.'[8]

The national influenza pandemic plans frequently allude to scarcity of resources and when they do, there often seems to be an explicit or implicit assumption that the scarcity is unavoidable and that the planning for a full complement of all resource needs during a pandemic would be impossible. For example, the Preparedness Section of the Canadian plan states: 'Advanced consideration should be given to management of adult and pediatric patients with respiratory distress when oximeters, ventilators and other respiratory support equipment must be rationed.'[9] The synopsis of the US plan suggests that 'In addition to a limited number of hospital beds and staff shortages, equipment and supplies may be in short supply.'[10] When these plans do recommend an augmentation of resources (as opposed to rationing of resources likely to take place at the time of a pandemic) there is rarely any indication of how much such a national resource – be it ventilators or hospital beds – should or could be augmented. Also, the logic of accepting the necessity for the rationing of one resource and calling for an expansion of another resource is not provided. Granted, these national plans have to deal with the 'big picture' of an anticipated health emergency and cannot provide a detailed analysis of all resources, but they do set the tone and they do offer a methodology for the planning process that should take place in all lower jurisdictions; therefore, the principles that are applied and the reasoning that is used in those national plans need to be known and deserve a critical look.

There are several concerns with this approach to contingency planning. Firstly, the assumption that scarcity of a particular resource is unavoidable is (with the exception of a shortage of flu vaccine and antivirals) an assumption that is usually not

[8] US Department of Health and Human Services, *op.cit.* note 2.

[9] Health Canada. 2004. *Canadian Pandemic Influenza Plan.* Ottawa, ON. Health Canada. Population and Public Health Branch. Available at http//:www.hc-sc.gc.ca/pphb-dgspsp/cpip-pclcpi/ (accessed 16 September 2004). Section Three: Preparedness, p.39.

[10] United States Department of Health and Human Services. 26 August 2004. *Pandemic Influenza Response and Preparedness Plan.* Executive Summary – Draft, Executive Summary, Synopsis, p. 11. Available at: http://www.hhs.gov/nvpo/pandemicplan/index.html (accessed 16 September 2004).

scrutinized. Indeed, some resources may be practically impossible to augment, but perhaps, after detailed examination, steps could be taken to have a sufficient supply of other resources – such as hospital supplies – available at the time of a pandemic, albeit at a cost.

The concern about financing of preparedness measures seems to permeate many sections of these plans. A US document frankly states that: 'Because State and local officials will likely face considerable difficulties in justifying the development of a sophisticated communication system for a problem which may or may not occur in the near term – i.e., pandemic influenza – justification and "marketing" of such a system to policy makers and legislators should be based on a more generic approach such as responding to chem/bioterrorism events . . .'[11] The concern in the mind of planners about financing of planning and preparedness measures is unavoidable, but, it should not interfere with careful determination of all measures and all resources that likely would be required for the optimal response to this health threat and maximal achievable reduction of serious illnesses and overall deaths.

It needs to be acknowledged that these pandemic plans involve not only scientific facts and forecasts, but also many value judgments, particularly judgments about the acceptability of certain human costs during a pandemic. In other words, the development of plans is not strictly a scientific and administrative task.

Every recommendation to ration an existing resource or only to augment it partially without attempting to achieve the most desirable resource configuration will clearly have a certain cost attached to it – the cost of human suffering or loss of life. The decision about providing finances for a certain resource can therefore only be made properly when that cost (and the economical and social cost) is estimated and considered. Should it not be made clear to what degree and how many people will be affected by the scarcity of resources, such as ventilators, before adopting a plan that incorporates scarcity?

An inescapable conclusion is that this balancing act cannot be the task of experts only. In open democratic societies, those who will be affected ought to have a say in the decision making process.

It is my view that such a protracted emergency situation, one that will affect virtually every citizen, calls for a more complex

[11] United States Department of Health and Human Services NVPO. 2004. *Influenza Pandemic Interim Guide* Version 2.1, p. 21. Available at http://www.hhs.gov/nvpo/pubs/pandemicflu.htm (accessed 4 April 2004).

planning process so that there can be a distinction between the contributions to planning which are appropriate for experts and the contributions that are appropriate for the society or community involved. Tentatively, I suggest that the role of experts be discharged in several discreet steps:

1. Development of several likely pandemic scenarios[12] and for each, an estimation of all resources that would ideally be required for optimal health interventions for all the affected population;
2. Determination of the gap between existing resources and those resources that would ideally be required in response to the above scenarios;
3. Description of the consequences (in terms of mortality, morbidity, human suffering, economic losses, etc.) corresponding to the degree to which the resource needs are satisfied (partially, mostly, completely);
4. Submission of these estimates to an appropriate political decision-making body which represents the population that will be affected;
5. Contribution to the public consultation process by responding to queries and clarifying the submitted estimates. At this stage, experts may advocate the resource allocation which they consider most appropriate.
6. Acceptance of the resource allocation that was made by the properly informed responsible political body on behalf of the informed population.
7. Development of plans for efficient and fair use of the resources that were allocated in this way, including the creation of plans for necessary rationing.

ETHICAL ISSUE: VACCINES AND ANTIVIRALS

The three pandemic plans under review make the assumption that an effective vaccine is the best way to reduce the impact of the new virus. Its production, however, cannot be started until the new virus strain is isolated, so no stockpiling is possible. Once the production is under way, batches of vaccine can become available in a gradual fashion. Administering the prioritization of the vaccine will therefore be necessary even if the goal is to produce

[12] M. van Genukten, M. Heijnen & J. Jager. Pandemic Influenza and Health Care Demand in the Netherlands: scenario analysis. *Emergent Infectious Diseases* 2003; 9(5): 531–538.

enough vaccine for the whole population. Pandemic planners did recognize this prioritization as an ethical issue and considerable attention was given to developing a rationale for the creation of various priority groups so that all three national plans contain well-reasoned and similar guidelines on vaccine prioritization.

The administration of antiviral drugs during a pandemic is recognized in all contingency plans as a useful way of both protecting those who cannot be vaccinated and reducing the severity of illness in others. In contrast to vaccines, antivirals can be stockpiled. Earlier versions of the plans accepted that during a pandemic there would be a great discrepancy between availability and demand for these drugs. The most current versions of the three national plans either recommend or report on the implementation of some degree of stockpiling. I suggest that the answer to the ethically charged question of 'How much vaccine or antiviral drugs should be made available?' can be arrived at by using a similar process as is outlined above for dealing with scarcity of resources – combining expert and public input. But there are other concerns with the section of the plans that deal with the administration of vaccines or antiviral drugs.

Firstly, given that these agents may be rapidly administered to thousands and later to millions of people, attention must be given to the bioethical issues of mass vaccination programs[13] and particularly to the need for careful, explicit and publicly transparent balancing of risks and burdens of these interventions. Pandemic plans (and other documents these plans refer to) seem to take the position that the advantage of these interventions is obvious and so do not provide any estimate of the magnitude of benefits that vaccination and antiviral drugs could provide, nor do they provide estimates of burdens such as adverse events and implementation costs. The current existence of active anti-vaccination lobbies and memories of the aborted 'swine flu' vaccination program of 1976, with millions of dollars paid out in US and Canada as compensation for damages,[14] suggests that a more convincing presentation in favor of these massive public health measures would be wise. A strong evidence-based argument supporting vaccination and antiviral drugs proposals would also set the stage for a more successful voluntary vaccination program, thus avoiding the need for an ethically problematic mandatory program.

[13] T. Dare. Mass Immunization Programmes: some philosophical issues. *Bioethics* 1998; 12(2): 125–149.

[14] R. Neustadt & H. Fineberg. 1982. *The Epidemic That Never Was.* New York. Random House.

ETHICAL ISSUE: HEALTH CARE WORKERS

A successful response to an influenza pandemic will depend greatly on the attitudes, skills and efforts of health care workers. Pandemic plans outline tremendous demands that will be made on health care workers during a pandemic. They will be expected to work outside their normal scope of practice, put in extra hours, cover for workers who are ill, accept the risk of infection, and be prepared to move where their services are most needed, including temporary facilities.

The good-will and cooperation of health care workers will be tested in many ways. For example, vaccination of all front-line care workers could become high priority in order to reduce staff absenteeism and to prevent them from becoming vectors of infection transfer. Some pandemic planners are looking at the possibility of compulsory measures. For example, the federal US plan asks officials of states to investigate whether mandatory vaccination could be legally implemented in their jurisdictions if it is considered 'essential' for public safety.[15] Yet, the new pandemic vaccine will be only briefly tested and health care workers will be the first population group expected to accept it. Considering then, how much will be required of health care workers, it is disquieting to note that, as yet, very few of them are familiar with pandemic plans. Therefore, if one is to hope for a strong moral commitment to the preparatory measures of the plan and an all-out effort during a pandemic, it is important to brief them rapidly about expectations and to encourage them to formulate their responses. Professional associations, colleges of health professions and relevant trade unions, can likely provide the forums for information-dissemination and discussions.

Bioethicists will likely agree that health care professionals have a strong ethical obligation to serve and accept the hardships arising out of such an extraordinary situation and that other workers in that sector will also have a moral obligation to serve, but its strength will vary from situation to situation, depending on a number of factors. But bioethicists will also insist that there are equally strong, reciprocal obligations of health care organizations to protect and support their workers.[16] This is where current pandemic plans fall somewhat short. There are a number of tasks to be completed in the pre-pandemic phase, in which we are now living, to ensure that these obligations to health sector workers

[15] US Department of Health and Human Services, *op. cit.* note 2.

[16] P. Singer, S.R. Benatar, M. Bernstein et al. Ethics and SARS: Lessons from Toronto. *British Medical Journal* 2003; 327: 1342–1344.

can be met. Health care planners and administrators will need to recruit sufficient numbers of contingency workers and volunteers, train them in the skills that will be required, stockpile protective gear and antiviral drugs, and make plans for supporting the personal and family needs of their workers. These measures would seem to warrant separate sections in the pandemic plans.

ETHICAL ISSUE: COMMUNICATIONS

Influenza pandemic plans pay considerable attention to communication needs among various levels of government and related institutions for the purposes of pandemic planning, and to those communications that will be required during an actual pandemic. But they do not include proposals for the dissemination of the plans as such. It is true that British and American plans have been on designated websites for some time and even the Canadian plan, which started as an internal document of governmental bodies, was recently deemed suitable for release to the public.

However, from a bioethics perspective, this is not sufficient. The current content of pandemic plans needs to be effectively communicated to each nation for which it was prepared. These plans foresee the need for major public health interventions, interventions that could be as severe as if the nation were engaged in war, and which would affect directly or indirectly many aspects of the personal, social and economic life of individuals. Also, all plans require further refinement and elaboration; therefore, it is important that these plans be based on 'transparent decisions within a social consensus'.[17] Principles of transparency and accountability require that those who are going to be affected, be informed. A concern that public discussion of a probable flu pandemic will cause alarm among the public is not sufficient justification for non-communication, just as a concern for a patient's anxiety would not justify not warning him of an impending stroke. Further, an optimal response to a pandemic will require the collaboration of not only all levels of government but also of public, private and voluntary sectors as well as every citizen. Launching a public education campaign now can help to build mutual trust and assist in the successful implementation of plans when a pandemic occurs.

[17] R. Fock, H. Bergman, H. Bussman et al. Conceptional Considerations for a German Influenza Pandemic Preparedness Plan. *Medical Microbiology and Immunology* (Berl) 2002; 191(3–4): 191–195.

CONCLUSION

Pandemic influenza plans represent a major, historically unique public health initiative. The quiet dedication of public health employees, experts, and administrators to developing these plans over the last two decades, away from the spotlights of public attention, is something to be lauded, and the contributors deserve recognition and gratitude. However, the ethical aspect of these public health documents and their implementation has so far been given little attention. The reading of national level pandemic plans for Canada, the United Kingdom and the United States raises several issues concerning the approach to scarcity of human and material resources; the justification of proposals for a vaccination and antiviral drug program; the care for and protection of health care workers during a pandemic; and finally, the communication of these contingency plans to the public. The purpose of this discussion is to refine these plans not only as effective road maps for the pandemic territory, but also as instruments for building mutual trust and solidarity at such time that will likely present a major challenge to our societies.

Dr. J. Kotalik
Centre for Health Care Ethics
Lakehead University
Thunder Bay, ON
Canada P7B 5E1
jkotalik@lakeheadu.ca

Part V
Climate Change

[14]

HEALTH REGULATION AND GOVERNANCE

Climate Change, Human Health, and the Post-Cautionary Principle

LISA HEINZERLING*

In this Essay, I suggest two different but related ways of reframing the public discourse on climate change. First, I propose that we move further in the direction of characterizing climate change as a public health threat and not only as an environmental threat. Second, I argue that we should stop thinking of responses to climate change in terms of the precautionary principle, which counsels action even in the absence of scientific consensus about a threat. We should speak instead in terms of a "post-cautionary" principle for a post-cautionary world, in which some very bad effects of climate change are unavoidable and others are avoidable only if we take dramatic steps, and soon. These points are related insofar as they together create a moral imperative both to adapt to the changes we cannot prevent and to mitigate those we can. Without these efforts, people will fall ill and many will die, and we know now that this will occur. No fancy moral theory is required to condemn, and to make every attempt to avert, this large-scale knowing killing.

TABLE OF CONTENTS

INTRODUCTION

In the summer of 2003, at least 20,000 people died in a heat wave that spanned Western Europe.[1] France lost the most: 14,802 lives, according to a government report produced in the aftermath of the tragedy.[2] Thousands of people also died in Great Britain, Spain, Portugal, Germany, Italy, Belgium, and the Netherlands.[3] The death toll mounted so stealthily, however, that news accounts written fully two weeks into the four-week heat wave focused more on the inconveniences and even economic advantages of the record-setting temperatures than on their lethal consequences.[4] Eventually the disaster was undeniable: heat-related deaths so overwhelmed French mortuaries, for example, that bodies were stored in refrigerated trucks and warehouses while awaiting burial or cremation.[5]

A study published in the prestigious scientific journal *Nature* in 2004 deemed it "likely" that human-induced increases in atmospheric concentrations of greenhouse gases had "more than doubled the risk of European mean summer temperatures as hot as 2003."[6] The same study found, based on scenarios assuming unmitigated future greenhouse gas emissions, that every other year would be as warm as 2003 in Europe by the 2040s, and that by 2100, a summer like 2003 "would be classed as an anomalously cold summer relative to the new climate."[7]

The European heat wave is a dramatic illustration of the two central factual premises of this Essay: climate change harms human health, and we know that climate change is happening. These facts justify reframing the public debate on climate change in two ways. First, we should do more to highlight the conse-

1. *See, e.g.*, Elisabetta Povoledo, *Heat in Europe May Have Killed 20,000*, INT'L HERALD TRIB. (Paris), Aug. 29, 2003, at 1, *available at* http://www.iht.com/articles/2003/08/29/heat_0.php. Some accounts place the death toll as high as 35,000. *See* Janet Larsen, *Record Heat Wave in Europe Takes 35,000 Lives*, EARTH POL'Y INST., Oct. 9, 2003, http://www.earth-policy.org/Updates/Update29.htm.

2. *France Heat Wave Death Toll Set at 14,802*, USATODAY.COM, Sept. 25, 2003, http://www.usatoday.com/weather/news/2003-09-25-france-heat_x.htm (last visited Oct. 16, 2007).

3. *See* J. P. Sardon, Letter to the Editor, *The 2003 Heat Wave*, EUROSURVEILLANCE, Mar. 2007, http://www.eurosurveillance.org/em/v12n03/1203-226.asp (last visited Oct. 16, 2007).

4. *See, e.g.*, Angelique Chrisafis, *The Height of Summer: Heatwave Edges Close to Record*, THE GUARDIAN (London), Aug. 5, 2003, at 3 (reporting that the heatwave boosted domestic tourism and ice cream sales); Martin Wainwright, *Heatwave: Sun Shines on Retailers as Weather Experts Get It Right*, THE GUARDIAN (London), Aug. 8, 2003, at 7 (attributing "sale increases of 365% for home barbecues, 250% for suntan cream, 80% and growing for beer, and 62% for paddling pools" to the heatwave).

5. *See* Philip Delves Broughton, *Hundreds of Heatwave Bodies Unclaimed as Paris Struggles To Clear Backlog*, THE DAILY TELEGRAPH (London), Aug. 24, 2003, at 11; *see also 'Over 11,000' Dead in French Heat*, BBC NEWS, Aug. 29, 2003, http://news.bbc.co.uk/1/hi/world/europe/3190585.stm (last visited Oct. 16, 2007).

6. Peter A. Stott et al., *Human Contribution to the European Heatwave of 2003*, 432 NATURE 610, 613 (2004).

7. *Id.* at 612–13. For a more recent account, see Catherine Brahic, *Med To Get Five Times as Many Dangerously Hot Days*, NEWSCIENTIST.COM, June 18, 2007, *available at* http://environment.newscientist.com/article/dn12086-med-to-get-five-times-as-many-dangerously-hot-days.html ("[R]esearchers say governments should brace themselves for summer heatwaves like the one that struck Europe in 2005 to become commonplace, even if they adopt climate-friendly practices.").

quences of climate change for human health. Second, we should recognize that the precautionary moment for action on climate change—the period in which we might have acted based on something less than a scientific consensus on the causes and consequences of climate change—has passed. We are in a post-cautionary world now. Together, the effects of climate change on human health and the undeniable fact that climate change is upon us have several implications for public policy. Perhaps most important, they create a moral imperative for action—dramatic action, now—on this problem.

I. CLIMATE CHANGE AND HUMAN HEALTH

There has long been discussion of the implications of climate change for human health,[8] and the link between climate change and human health has been drawn ever more clearly in recent years.[9] But it is also true that widely circulated images of current harms from climate change—melting glaciers, collapsing ice shelves, drowning polar bears—do not have a human face. And it takes some reflection to see the connection between human health and, say, higher water temperatures—reflection that is not always encouraged in our busy world. Thus, although my suggestion that we frame the debate over responses to climate change in terms of effects on human health is by no means original, it is worthwhile to draw, directly and emphatically, the link between climate change and human health, and to think about the consequences of this linkage for policies addressing climate change.

A. HEALTH CONSEQUENCES OF CLIMATE CHANGE

"The weakest are dropping like flies."[10]

More frequent and intense heat waves are only one item on the long list of the consequences of climate change that will harm human health. According to the latest scientific research, we can expect the following in our warming world: disease-carrying insects will alter their ranges, appearing in places they have not been before and where humans have not developed immunities, causing more widespread incidence of vector-borne diseases such as malaria and dengue;[11] after a slight uptick, crop productivity will decline, causing a concomitant

8. *See, e.g.*, REID A. BRYSON & THOMAS J. MURRAY, CLIMATES OF HUNGER: MANKIND AND THE WORLD'S CHANGING WEATHER (1977).

9. *See, e.g.*, WORLD HEALTH ORG. [WHO], CLIMATE CHANGE AND HUMAN HEALTH: RISKS AND RESPONSES 20 (2003) (linking ozone depletion to higher rates of skin cancer).

10. Alex Duvall Smith, *France Accused of Complacency as 50 Die in Heatwave*, THE INDEPENDENT (London), Aug. 12, 2003, at 9 (quoting Patrick Pelloux, president of an association of French accident and emergency doctors).

11. *See* INTERGOVERNMENTAL PANEL ON CLIMATE CHANGE, CLIMATE CHANGE 2007: IMPACTS, ADAPTATION, AND VULNERABILITY: WORKING GROUP II CONTRIBUTION TO THE INTERGOVERNMENTAL PANEL ON CLIMATE CHANGE 408 (2007), *available at* http://www.ipcc-wg2.org/ (follow "The Full Working Group II Contribution . . . Available Here" hyperlink) [hereinafter IPCC].

increase in the risk of malnutrition;[12] fish stocks will deteriorate, to the same effect;[13] ground-level ozone will worsen, causing adverse pulmonary and cardiovascular events;[14] water supplies will decrease due to reduced snowpack and increased drought;[15] storms will become more frequent and severe,[16] threatening Katrina-like consequences for human health and welfare; flooding will grow more frequent and severe due to storms and sea level rise;[17] diarrhoeal disease will increase due to floods and drought;[18] cholera will become more frequent and toxic due to higher water temperatures;[19] sanitation facilities will fail more often due to more frequent extreme weather events, leading to increased spread of infectious diseases;[20] ozone depletion will worsen with a changing climate,[21] leading to increased incidence of skin cancer, cataracts, and immune deficiency;[22] increased pollen production will exacerbate allergies;[23] hunger and malnutrition will rise due to drought and extreme weather events.[24]

Reviewing this list, it appears that there is almost no component of human health that will be untouched by climate change. And the list does not end here. The shrinking resource base of a warming world will also increase the likelihood of refugee crises, violent conflicts, and even wars. In this regard, it is notable that the U.S. Department of Defense appears to have cottoned on to the potentially catastrophic effects of climate change even while the Environmental Protection Agency was fighting hard not to do anything about them. A 2003 report commissioned by the Pentagon—dated a month after the EPA itself declined to regulate greenhouse gases under the Clean Air Act[25]—"imagine[s] the unthinkable" by describing the consequences of an abrupt shift in climate due to slowing of the ocean's thermohaline circulation.[26] The report predicts that shortages in the basic necessities of life—food, water, and energy resources—

---

12. *See id.* at 11.
13. *See id.* at 12.
14. *See id.* at 12, 401–02.
15. *See id.* at 11.
16. *See id.* at 12.
17. *See id.*
18. *See id.* at 418.
19. *See id.*
20. *See* Roger Few, *Health and Climatic Hazards: Framing Social Research on Vulnerability, Response and Adaptation*, 17 GLOBAL ENVTL. CHANGE 281, 281–83 (2007).
21. *See* Philip Ball, *Climate Change Set To Poke Holes in Ozone*, NATURE NEWS, Mar. 3, 2004, http://www.nature.com/news/2004/040301/full/news040301-5.html (last visited Oct. 9, 2007).
22. For the EPA's description of the health effects of the increased exposure to ultraviolet radiation that comes from ozone depletion, *see* ENVTL. PROT. AGENCY, HEALTH EFFECTS OF OVEREXPOSURE TO THE SUN, http://www.epa.gov/sunwise/uvandhealth.html (last visited Oct. 9, 2007).
23. *See* IPCC, *supra* note 11, at 9, 82.
24. *See id.* at 18.
25. *See* Control of Emissions from New Highway Vehicles and Engines, 68 Fed. Reg. 52,922, 52,922 (Sept. 8, 2003).
26. PETER SCHWARTZ & DOUG RANDALL, AN ABRUPT CLIMATE CHANGE SCENARIO AND ITS IMPLICATIONS FOR UNITED STATES NATIONAL SECURITY 1 (2003); *see also* Peter Schwartz & Doug Randall, *Future Global Warming Scenarios, Take 2*, Letter to the Editor, SCIENCE, Sept. 24, 2004. The thermohaline circulation is the "conveyor belt" that moves warm water "from the tropics toward the poles," warming

would result from abrupt climate change,[27] and that these shortages would in turn either cause or exacerbate global conflict.[28] In the event of abrupt climate change drastically lowering the Earth's carrying capacity, the report bluntly states, "Humanity would revert to its norm of constant battles for diminishing resources, which the battles themselves would further reduce even beyond the climatic effects. Once again warfare would define human life."[29]

The Pentagon report deliberately looked at extreme possibilities, noting that "it is [the Department of Defense's] job to consider such scenarios."[30] But the report's dire predictions do not seem so extreme anymore. In April 2007, eleven retired U.S. generals and admirals acting as the "Military Advisory Board" to the largely federally funded CNA Corporation, signed a study describing the national security consequences of climate change.[31] Calling climate change a "threat multiplier for instability in some of the most volatile regions of the world," the study details the ways in which climate change may push already fragile nations over the brink and put strain on even the most developed nations.[32] "To live in stability," the study observes, "human societies need access to certain fundamental resources, the most important of which are water and food."[33] Yet, as the study makes clear, these basic resources—and thus the stability on which national security depends—are threatened by climate change.[34] Armed conflict,[35] mass migration,[36] and even terrorism[37] are among the national security consequences the study associates with climate change. The seriousness of these consequences, and their link to climate change, were highlighted just one day after this study was published when the United Nations Security Council met for the very first time to discuss climate change as a security issue.[38]

The human health consequences of climate change are not just worries for the remote future; they are happening here and now. In addition to the research on the relationship between Europe's disastrous heat wave and climate change, other studies have also suggested a connection between current adverse health

Europe. ELIZABETH KOLBERT, FIELD NOTES FROM A CATASTROPHE: MAN, NATURE, AND CLIMATE CHANGE 56–57 (2006).

27. *See* SCHWARTZ & RANDALL, *supra* note 26, at 14–15.

28. *See id.* at 14, 16–18.

29. *Id.* at 16–17.

30. *Id.* at 8.

31. *See* CNA CORP., NATIONAL SECURITY AND THE THREAT OF CLIMATE CHANGE (Apr. 2007).

32. *Id.* at 44–45.

33. *Id.* at 18.

34. *See id.* at 13, 15, 20, 24, 27, 30, 32.

35. *See id.* at 15, 18, 20.

36. *See id.* at 29, 34; *see also* CHRISTIAN AID, HUMAN TIDE: THE REAL MIGRATION CRISIS 1 (2007).

37. *See* CNA CORP., *supra* note 31, at 20, 22.

38. *See* Press Release, U.N. Security Council, Security Council Holds First-Ever Debate of Impact of Climate Change on Peace, Security, Hearing Over 50 Speakers, U.N. Doc. SC/9000 (Apr. 17, 2007), *available at* http://www.un.org/News/Press/docs/2007/sc9000.doc.htm; *see also* Ctr. for Naval Analysis, Climate Change Poses Serious Threat to U.S. National Security (Apr. 16, 2007), http://www.energybulletin.net/28733.html.

consequences and climate change.[39] For example, researchers have already found that the changing climate has likely influenced the geographic range of disease-carrying insects.[40] Perhaps more remarkably, climate change has also been cited as an underlying cause of current armed conflict. The genocide in Darfur, for example, is now regarded as having arisen at least in part from territorial disputes caused by persistent drought conditions associated with a warming world.[41]

As if all of this were not bad enough, the health consequences I have described will almost certainly be worst for the poorest among us, who are least able to fend off or bounce back from such stressors.[42] The world's poorest nations already suffer from the kinds of food and water shortages that will only worsen in the coming years; their capacity to handle further scarcity is limited.[43] They also lack the resources—such as funds for relocation necessitated by rising sea levels—and services—such as health care—that will be necessary in any effort to mitigate the effects of climate change.[44] Adding insult to injury, the poorest countries have contributed the least to the present problem.[45] This inequity might itself lead to a further downward spiral in human welfare by fueling conflicts, perhaps even armed conflicts, between the climate haves and have-nots.[46]

B. POLICY CONSEQUENCES OF HEALTH CONSEQUENCES OF CLIMATE CHANGE

> "We have to give climate change a human face—it is not all about 'sinks,' 'emission trading schemes' and technology. Climate change is about people, children, families and . . . our relationship with the world around us."[47]

What are the consequences, for public debate and public policy, of framing the problem of climate change in terms of human health? I believe framing the problem this way has at least three implications: motivating political action,

39. *See, e.g.*, WHO, THE WORLD HEALTH REPORT 2002, 72 (2002), *available at* http://www.who.int/whr/2002/en/whr02_en.pdf.

40. *See* ROSS GELBSPAN, BOILING POINT 119–23 (2005); Stephen Y. Liang et al., *Climate Change and the Monitoring of Vector-borne Disease*, 287 JAMA 2286, 2286 (2002).

41. *See* CNA CORP., *supra* note 31, at 15 ("Darfur provides a case study of how existing marginal situations can be exacerbated beyond the tipping point by climate-related factors."); Stephan Faris, *The Real Roots of Darfur*, ATLANTIC MONTHLY, Apr. 2007, at 67.

42. *See* Andrew C. Revkin, *The Climate Divide: Rich Nations Find It Easier To Adapt*, INT'L HERALD TRIB. (Paris), Apr. 2, 2007.

43. *See* HM TREASURY, STERN REVIEW ON THE ECONOMICS OF CLIMATE CHANGE 92 (2006), *available at* http://www.hm-treasury.gov.uk/independent_reviews/stern_review_economics_climate_change/stern_review_report.cfm.

44. *See id.* at 99.

45. *See id.* at 29.

46. *See* SCHWARTZ & RANDALL, *supra* note 26, at 16.

47. *Human Face of Climate Change: Weather out of Its Mind*, CBC NEWS, Mar. 24, 2005, *available at* http://www.cbc.ca/news/background/climatechange/weather.html (quoting Sheila Watt-Cloutier, Chair, Inuit Circumpolar Conference, Nov. 2004).

enlarging the number and kinds of governmental institutions involved in the problem, and creating a strong moral case for action.

First, and most pragmatically, "environmental" threats rarely capture the attention of the public and policymakers unless and until they are linked to human health. People are worried about the polar bear, to be sure, but it is doubtful that the polar bear's plight alone—or even the added plight of the many other species threatened by climate change—will prompt the kinds of large changes necessary to address climate change. To take an example from early in the environmental era, many studies connected the pesticide DDT with harm to wildlife,[48] even to harm to the beloved bald eagle,[49] but it was not until DDT was tied to cancer risk in humans that the federal government decided to ban the substance.[50] The same basic story holds for the regulation of many other pollutants.[51] Speaking in purely practical terms, therefore, it makes a great deal of sense to highlight the consequences of climate change for human health.

Second, emphasizing the consequences of climate change for human health will affect the way we think about responses to this problem. If we think of climate change as purely an "environmental" problem, we will likely turn, in the United States, to the EPA for an answer. But as important as the EPA is domestically, with respect to this problem, I believe it is equally vital that we turn to other non-environmental institutions for assistance. Framing climate change as a human health threat naturally encourages resort to agencies charged with a traditional public health mission, such as the Centers for Disease Control and the National Institutes of Health. It also prompts attention to even less obvious institutions, like the United Nations Security Council. We will think differently about solutions to climate change as an institutional matter if we frame the problem of climate change as a human health problem.

Finally, recognizing the current and future consequences of climate change for human health makes the moral case for aggressive action on climate change unimpeachable. If we were simply talking about a more uncomfortable climate, or even the destruction of other species, it might be easier to dismiss the moral imperative of action on climate change. But humans are dying and falling ill due to our collective actions, and will continue to do so in even larger numbers if we do nothing. Emphasizing the human dimension of climate change brings a moral clarity to the problem that is not matched by worries about the polar bear.

---

48. *See* Stefan Böschen, *DDT and the Dynamics of Risk Knowledge Production*, 8 INT'L J. FOR PHIL. CHEMISTRY 79, 87–89 (2002), *available at* http://www.hyle.org/journal/issues/8-2/boeschen.html.

49. *See* David A. Fahrenthold, *U.S. Declares Bald Eagles No Longer Threatened*, WASH. POST, June 29, 2007, at A3.

50. *See* Böschen, *supra* note 48, at 94–95.

51. Frequently, when the government regulates pollutants that have adverse effects on both humans and other species, it highlights the former in justifying the rules. *See* Lisa Heinzerling, *Regulatory Costs of Mythic Proportions*, 107 YALE L.J. 1981, 2060–64 (1998).

II. THE POST-CAUTIONARY PRINCIPLE

The recognition that climate change is upon us and harming us now leads me to suggest one other way to reframe public discourse on this issue. We should cease discussing responses to climate change in terms of the "precautionary principle" and should begin to think instead in terms of a "post-cautionary" approach.

For a long time, climate change has been the exemplar for application of the precautionary principle.[52] This principle has taken many forms over the years, but in its simplest and perhaps most common formulation, it stands for the idea that we should not wait for scientific certainty before acting on a threat.[53] The underlying principle is that we are better off being safe than being sorry.[54]

At this moment in history, discussing climate change in terms of the precautionary principle is a serious mistake. As I discuss below, we probably blew past our precautionary opportunity sometime in the 1980s. We are now, and have been for some time, in a post-cautionary world. The scientific debate over whether climate change is happening, and whether it will hurt us, is over; the important questions are when it will get worse and by how much. I suggest, therefore, that we begin to discuss climate change in terms of a "post-cautionary principle." Recognizing that we have hurtled past precaution into a post-cautionary world has several important implications for public policies concerning climate change.

A. CLIMATE CHANGE'S PRECAUTIONARY PERIOD

> "To do nothing when the situation is changing very rapidly is not a conservative thing to do."[55]

In this section, I ask two famous questions, but about climate change rather than cover-ups: what did we know and when did we know it? My aim here is not to identify a single precautionary moment for climate change. My aim, instead, is to argue that climate change had not just a precautionary moment but a precautionary period, in which the evidence of an impending catastrophe was

52. *See, e.g.*, Douglas A. Kysar, *Climate Change, Cultural Transformation, and Comprehensive Rationality*, 31 B.C. ENVTL. AFF. L. REV. 555, 565 (2004) (advocating "the *precautionary principle* as an appropriate response to climate change, particularly with respect to its potentially catastrophic but currently inestimable risks").

53. *See, e.g.*, John S. Applegate, *The Taming of the Precautionary Principle*, 27 WM. & MARY ENVTL. L. & POL'Y REV. 13, 13 (2002) ("Where there are threats of serious or irreversible damage, lack of full scientific certainty shall not be used as a reason for postponing cost-effective measures to prevent environmental degradation.") (quoting the 1992 Rio Declaration of the UN Conference on Environment and Development).

54. Frank B. Cross, *Paradoxical Perils of the Precautionary Principle*, 53 WASH. & LEE L. REV. 851, 851 (1996).

55. SPENCER R. WEART, THE DISCOVERY OF GLOBAL WARMING 90 (2003) (quoting an unnamed scientist at the 1972 symposium on rising level of CO_2).

strong enough—and the signs of even greater future calamity clear enough—that the precautionary principle, properly applied, should have inspired us to take aggressive action. I believe that period passed in the late 1980s.

To early climate scientists, the idea of significant "climate change" was something of an oxymoron. Climate was "stable *by definition*."[56] Indeed, one of the great puzzles for early climate scientists was the cause and course of the ice ages: how could such a dramatic change in climate have happened, and how long did it take?[57] Perhaps ironically, scientists' search for the answer to the mystery of the long-ago ice ages helped spur the research that led to the "discovery" of climate change in our own time.[58]

Scientific understanding of the past and present climate proceeded fitfully at best during the nineteenth and early twentieth centuries, yet several discoveries from the nineteenth century were seminal in the study of climate. In the early 1800s, Joseph Fourier, likening the Earth's atmosphere to a "hothouse," speculated that the gases in the atmosphere prevented the sun's radiation from escaping entirely back into space.[59] In 1859, John Tyndall found that carbon dioxide was opaque to infrared radiation, and thus trapped some of the Earth's infrared radiation in the atmosphere.[60] In 1896, the Swedish scientist Svante Arrhenius undertook a computational project fit for a modern computer when he calculated the potential effect on average global temperature of changing the level of carbon dioxide (CO_2) in the atmosphere.[61] His calculations were based, of necessity, on a highly simplistic view of the drivers of climate.[62] Remarkably, however, his estimate of the effect of a doubling of CO_2 in the atmosphere—an increase in average global temperature of between nine and eleven degrees Fahrenheit—was not far off from today's estimates.[63] Nevertheless, Arhennius's work slipped into obscurity, picked up here and there by other climate scientists in the first half of the twentieth century, but not seriously pursued.[64]

Scientific findings that would lead to the discovery of climate change in our time began to steadily appear in the mid-twentieth century. In 1957, Roger Revelle and Hans Suess published a paper concluding that the then-widely accepted view that the oceans could be counted upon to absorb any amount of CO_2 we belched into the atmosphere was mistaken; most of the CO_2 that ended

56. *Id.* at 10.

57. *See id.* at 9–11.

58. *See generally id.* "It was not the vague possibility of global warming that intrigued the few people who thought about climate change, but the stupendous advance and retreat of continental ice sheets." *Id.* at 11.

59. *Id.* at 2–3.

60. *See id.* at 3–4.

61. *See id.* at 5–6.

62. *See id.* at 6.

63. *See* KOLBERT, *supra* note 26, at 41.

64. *See* WEART, *supra* note 55, at 5–11 (tracing development of Arhennius's calculations); David M. Hart & David G. Victor, *Scientific Elites and the Making of US Policy for Climate Change Research 1957-74*, 23 SOC. STUD. SCI. 643, 647 (1993) (noting scientific community's lack of interest in Arhennius's work).

up in the oceans "would promptly be evaporated."[65] At about the same time, another turning point in the development of climate science occurred when Charles David Keeling received funding to measure atmospheric concentrations of CO_2 at the Mauna Loa Observatory in Hawaii and in Antarctica.[66] With the exception of a brief hiatus in these studies as a result of a funding cutoff in the early 1960s, Keeling's measurements provided us with the first careful and consistent record of actual, year-by-year CO_2 concentrations in the atmosphere at a specific location.[67] What they showed proved indispensable to the development of modern climate science: CO_2 concentrations were on a steady upward path.[68]

Climate scientists also began to apprehend how quickly climate could change. Early climate scientists were loathe to admit that the climate could change significantly over a short period of time; they thought in terms of geological time, with changes occurring over tens of thousands of years.[69] Ice core samples from Greenland tested and eventually debunked this long-held assumption of stability.[70] A study published in 1972, for example, reported that a cold spell that happened some 12,000 years ago—dubbed the Younger Dryas—had happened in as little as one or two centuries.[71] Ice core samples also bore evidence of rapid warming and cooling periods.[72] Studies such as these upended the comfortable assumption of climate scientists (and perhaps the rest of us) of a stable climate, changeable only over many millennia.

Another venerable assumption of climate scientists was that of a balance of nature, which would lead the climate to take self-correcting actions tending in the direction of stability rather than instability.[73] Scientists in the second half of the twentieth century began serious study of the possibility of bad as well as good feedbacks. Climate models indicated that a rise in temperature could, for example, cause melting of ice which would increase the albedo effect of the oceans, which in turn would lead to further warming, and so on.[74] The models suggested that spiraling bad effects, rather than self-correcting reactions tending toward stability, would make a bad situation even worse.

By the late 1980s, then, this much was clear: the greenhouse effect was a plausible scientific theory. Manmade greenhouse gas emissions were increasing.

---

65. WEART, *supra* note 55, at 27–29; *see also* Roger Revelle & Hans E. Suess, *Carbon Dioxide Exchange Between Atmosphere and Ocean and the Question of an Increase of Atmospheric CO_2 During the Past Decades*, 9 TELLUS 18 (1957).

66. *See* WEART, *supra* note 55, at 36.

67. *See id.* at 38; Hart & Victor, *supra* note 64, at 651.

68. *See* JAMES RODGER FLEMING, HISTORICAL PERSPECTIVES ON CLIMATE CHANGE 126–28 (1998); WEART, *supra* note 55, at 38.

69. *See generally* WEART, *supra* note 55, at ch.1.

70. *See, e.g.*, *id.* at 78.

71. *See id.*; *see also* TIM FLANNERY, THE WEATHER MAKERS: HOW MAN IS CHANGING THE CLIMATE AND WHAT IT MEANS FOR LIFE ON EARTH 61 (2005).

72. *See* WEART, *supra* note 55, at 74, 80.

73. *See id.* at 8–9.

74. *See id.* at 85–86.

Atmospheric concentrations of greenhouse gases were increasing. The world was getting warmer. Climate could change abruptly. Once the climate started to change, it might deteriorate rapidly due to positive feedback effects.

Other important points were less clear. Was the world's present warming a result, at least in part, of human greenhouse gas emissions? What did the future hold? Answers to these questions were complicated by scientists' growing recognition that we might not discern the effects of climate change until they were upon us and more drastic future effects had become inevitable.[75]

In discussing scientific research spanning a century or more, involving many thousands of researchers and untold numbers of studies, it is risky to pinpoint any one moment of clarity.[76] But in a scientific field as fraught with political meaning as climate science is, one can perhaps identify moments when existing scientific research made its way into the public consciousness in such a way that public policy might have reacted to the emerging understanding. I believe such a moment happened, among other times, in the summer of 1988. That summer, which saw terrible droughts in the U.S. Midwest and unprecedentedly hot weather in the Northeast,[77] veteran NASA scientist James Hansen came before Congress and announced that global warming was upon us and that the greenhouse effect was likely the cause.[78] It was time to "stop waffling so much," he said in an interview after his testimony, and to "say that the evidence is pretty strong that the greenhouse effect is here."[79]

Congress did not act on Hansen's advice. It passed laws authorizing more research on climate change,[80] but did nothing to regulate the causes of climate change. Indeed, instead of bringing aggressive action on climate change, the years following Hansen's testimony witnessed what I regard as a retrenchment in climate policy. Scientists retreated to the newly formed Intergovernmental Panel on Climate Change (IPCC)[81] to develop careful consensus statements on

75. *See id.* at 120–22, 137–38; KOLBERT, *supra* note 26, at 11.

76. *See* WEART, *supra* note 55, at 196 ("The discovery of global warming was patently a social product, a consensus of judgments arising in countless discussions among thousands of experts.").

77. *See, e.g., id.* at 155; *see also* Peter Kerr, *The Great Flood of Heat: 42 Days and 42 Nights and Life Is Altered*, N.Y. TIMES, Aug. 14, 1988, Metropolitan at 1; Thomas W. Schierholz, *Heat Wave, Drought Put Double Squeeze on Utilities*, CHRISTIAN SCI. MONITOR (Boston), Aug. 18, 1988, at 3.

78. *See The Greenhouse Effect: Impacts on Current Global Temperature and Regional Heat Waves: Hearing Before S. Comm. on Energy and Natural Resources*, 100th Cong. 43 (1988) (statement of James E. Hansen, NASA); *see also id.* at 2 (statement of Hon. J. Bennett Johnston, S. Comm. on Energy and Natural Resources) ("The greenhouse effect has ripened beyond theory now. We know it is fact.").

79. Philip Shabecoff, *Global Warming Has Begun, Expert Tells Senate*, N.Y. TIMES, June 23, 1988, at A1.

80. *See, e.g.*, Global Change Research Act of 1990, Pub. L. No. 101-606, 104 Stat. 3096; Food, Agriculture, Conservation and Trade Act of 1990, Pub. L. No. 101-624, 104 Stat. 3359; Energy Policy Act of 1992, Pub. L. No. 102-486, 106 Stat. 2776.

81. The IPCC was formed in 1988. Background information on the IPCC is available at http://www.ipcc.ch/about/about.htm.

climate change and its effects.[82] The fossil fuel industry began to wage a years-long, multi-million dollar effort to persuade the public of the shakiness of climate science.[83] Scientific ignorance became official government policy.[84]

Into this stew of an emerging scientific consensus and a growing political backlash stepped the international environmental community. In 1992, at the "Earth Summit" in Rio, nations agreed to the United Nations Framework Convention on Climate Change, which for the first time officially linked responses to climate change to the precautionary principle. Article 3 of the Convention, setting forth the "principles" of the document, stated:

> The Parties should take precautionary measures to anticipate, prevent or minimize the causes of climate change and mitigate its adverse effects. Where there are threats of serious or irreversible damage, lack of full scientific certainty should not be used as a reason for postponing such measures, taking into account that policies and measures to deal with climate change should be cost-effective so as to ensure global benefits at the lowest possible cost.[85]

Similarly, the Rio Declaration, agreed to at the same time, stated that "in order to protect the environment, the precautionary approach shall be widely applied by States according to their capabilities. Where there are threats of serious or irreversible damage, lack of full scientific certainty shall not be used as a reason for postponing cost-effective measures to prevent environmental degradation."[86] In the years following the Earth Summit, public discourse on climate change and public discourse on the precautionary principle almost inevitably merged: in a typical formulation, the Canadian government recently stated that climate change policy should be developed with the precautionary

82. *See* WEART, *supra* note 55, at 161–62 ("Under pressure from the industrial interests, as well as from the mandate to make only statements that virtually every knowledgeable scientist would endorse, the IPCC's consensus statements were highly qualified and cautious.").

83. *See* ROSS GELBSPAN, THE HEAT IS ON 33–61 (1997) ("In their efforts to challenge the consensus scientific view about the escalating turmoil of the global atmosphere, the public relations apparatus of the oil and coal industries has publicized weather reports, and funded and distributed books and videos and self-proclaimed journals of science that are dismissed by the vast majority of scientists."); WEART, *supra* note 55, at 168.

84. *See* GELBSPAN, *supra* note 40, at 37–61 (documenting the continuing denial of climate change and continuing assertion of scientific uncertainty by the Republican Party); CHRIS MOONEY, THE REPUBLICAN WAR ON SCIENCE 78–101 (2005) (documenting the Bush Administration's policy of stressing scientific uncertainty and denying climate change); WEART, *supra* note 55, at 168 ("A White House memorandum, inadvertently released in 1990, proposed that the best way to deal with concern about global warming would be 'to raise the many uncertainties.'").

85. United Nations Framework Convention on Climate Change, art. 3, ¶ 3, May 9, 1992, S. TREATY DOC. No. 102-38, 1771 U.N.T.S. 170.

86. U.N. Conference on Environment and Development, June 3–14, 1992, *Rio Declaration on Environment and Development*, U.N. Doc. A/CONF.151/26 (Vol. I) (Annex 1, princ. 15) (June 14, 1992), 31 I.L.M. 874, 879.

principle as a guiding framework.[87]

The irony—even tragedy—in this is that the precautionary principle swept onto the climate change scene almost at the same moment it could have, and should have, departed the field. Before the Earth Summit, the IPCC—the largest peer-reviewed scientific collaboration in the history of the world—had already declared that the world was warming and that it was likely that additional warming of several degrees would occur by 2050.[88] This statement that the world was indeed warming was exactly the kind of scientific consensus the precautionary principle declared unnecessary to justify action on an impending threat of potentially grave proportions.[89] By 1995, of course, the IPCC had gone further and identified a "discernible human influence" on the climate,[90] and the long battle over the basic outlines of climate change science could have been declared over.

Yet things only got worse from there. The Senate in 1998 announced its intention to reject any international agreement on climate change that did not include binding requirements for developing nations,[91] and in 2001 the Bush Administration withdrew from the Kyoto Protocol entirely.[92] President Bush dismissed a 2002 report conducted by his own agencies linking anthropogenic greenhouse gas emissions and climate change as a "report put out by the bureaucracy."[93] In 2003 the White House edited out five of the six paragraphs referring to climate change in what was billed as a comprehensive report on the environment.[94] At the same time, critics of government regulation seized on the precautionary principle as a misguided, even dangerous, idea.[95] Thus, the battlefield over climate policy moved from the scientific arena, where all but a few, mostly industry-funded,[96] skeptics accepted the ever-more dire predictions of a coming climate catastrophe to the abstract realm of organizing principles for public policy. Perhaps, the critics hinted between the lines, one could reject

87. *See* REPORT OF THE COMMISSIONER OF THE ENVIRONMENT AND SUSTAINABLE DEVELOPMENT TO THE HOUSE OF COMMONS 26 (2006), *available at* http://www.oag-bvg.gc.ca/domino/reports.nsf/html/c20060900se01.html/$file/c20060900se01.PDF.

88. *See* WEART, *supra* note 55, at 162 (referring to the report the IPCC issued in 1990).

89. Applegate, *supra* note 53, at 27 (noting that precautionary principle is not "relevant" once "science reveals a well characterized risk").

90. Intergovernmental Panel on Climate Change, IPCC Second Assessment: Climate Change 1995, 5 ¶ 2.5 (1995), *available at* http://www.ipcc.ch/pub/sa(E).pdf.

91. *See* Byrd-Hagel Resolution, S. Res. 98, 105th Cong., S. REP. No. 105–54, at 3 (1997).

92. *See, e.g.*, Edmund L. Andrews, *Bush Angers Europe by Eroding Pact on Warming*, N.Y. TIMES, Apr. 1, 2001, at 1.

93. Katherine Q. Seelye, *President Distances Himself from Global Warming Report*, N.Y. TIMES, June 5, 2002, at A23.

94. *See* GELBSPAN, *supra* note 40, at 42.

95. One of the most prominent critics of the precautionary principle has been Cass Sunstein. *See, e.g.*, Cass R. Sunstein, *Beyond the Precautionary Principle*, 151 U. PA. L. REV. 1003, 1003 (2003) ("[T]he precautionary principle should be rejected, not because it leads in bad directions, but because it leads in no direction at all.").

96. *See, e.g.*, Chris Mooney, *Some Like It Hot*, MOTHER JONES, May–June 2005, at 36 (tracing funding of many anti-global-warming scientists and think tanks to Exxon-Mobil).

action on climate change by rejecting the precautionary principle—without ever taking a close look at the scary scientific consensus on the subject.

If my account is correct, then the precautionary principle as applied to climate change was, at best, an anachronism as soon as it was adopted. At worst, it inadvertently played into the hands of critics of swift and aggressive action on climate change, feeding the industry-funded view that the science of climate change was too uncertain to justify such action.

Subsequent reports of the IPCC, and subsequent events in the world, including the collapse of Antarctic ice sheets, melting of glaciers, and thawing of Arctic permafrost,[97] have only deepened the case for my argument that we have moved from a precautionary to a post-cautionary period. I close with a brief discussion of several implications of this development for public policy.

B. PUBLIC POLICY AND PRIVATE CONDUCT FOR A POST-CAUTIONARY WORLD

"It may be time to act up."[98]

Acknowledging that we have passed the precautionary moment with respect to climate change has several implications for public policy.

First, stressing the now-inevitable human health consequences of climate change makes untenable certain arguments that have been raised against doing much of anything at all to address this problem. All around us appear scare stories about what will happen to our economy, and even to our way of life, if we act aggressively against climate change.[99] But, as we have seen, the consequences of not acting are terrible indeed. As the renowned climate researcher James Hansen has put it, if we continue on our present course with respect to greenhouse gas emissions, we will soon, quite simply, live on "a different planet."[100] Focusing on the human consequences of climate change reveals the dangerous ludicrousness of industry's calls for "business as usual"[101]—as well as the frequent suggestion that this scenario bears zero costs. Climate change is having and will have profound effects on the economy, with enormous costs. It is a lie to pretend that inaction on climate change is a "no-cost" scenario—for anyone.

---

97. *See generally* KOLBERT, *supra* note 26 (documenting the impact of global warming on the natural world).

98. James E. Hansen, The Threat to the Planet: How Can We Avoid Dangerous Man-Made Climate Change?, Remarks on Acceptance of WWF Duke of Edinburgh Conservation Medal at St. James Palace, London (Nov. 21, 2006), *available at* http://www.columbia.edu/jeh1/.

99. For recent examples, see BJØRN LOMBORG, COOL IT: THE SKEPTICAL ENVIRONMENTALIST'S GUIDE TO GLOBAL WARMING (2007); Eric Peters, *Seppuku for the U.S. Auto Industry*, AM. SPECTATOR, July 6, 2007, http://www.spectator.org/dsp_article.asp?art_id=11687 (arguing that government-mandated carbon dioxide output reductions would require the manufacture of smaller cars, causing an industry change that would put domestic auto manufacturers at a disadvantage as compared to their Japanese competitors).

100. Andrew C. Revkin, *Climate Expert Says NASA Tried To Silence Him*, N.Y. TIMES, Jan. 29, 2006, at A1 (quoting Dr. James Hansen).

101. *See, e.g.*, Peters, *supra* note 99.

Second, acknowledging our post-cautionary status means that we cannot hope that reduction of greenhouse gas emissions alone will avert the harmful consequences of climate change. We must also adapt to the consequences that we cannot now avoid. Some environmentalists have eschewed the idea of adapting to climate change, preferring instead to talk only in terms of mitigating the problem through the reduction of greenhouse gases.[102] They worry, apparently, that if we talk about adapting to climate change, we will have less motivation to address the problem in a more preventive and fundamental way. But the problem is upon us, causing harm now. We no longer have the luxury of choosing between adaptation and mitigation; we must do both.

Third, acknowledging our post-cautionary status means that we cannot afford to discard any of the actions we are already taking to reduce greenhouse gases. In the United States, in the absence of any federal action on the matter, states and local governments have adopted numerous laws and policies aimed at reducing greenhouse gases.[103] As Congress debates its own potential responses to the issue of climate change, it must be careful not to undo any of the steps states and local governments have already taken. It would be easy enough, in a period when the Supreme Court has expanded its preemption jurisprudence,[104] for Congress—even inadvertently—to displace state and local laws on climate change. I would go so far as to say that unless Congress is willing to pass a very aggressive law or laws on greenhouse gases, it should simply stay out unless it also enacts language unmistakably disclaiming any preemptive intent. If Congress were to pass a weak law that at the same time is held by the current conservative Court to preempt state and local efforts on climate change, it would be worse than not acting at all.

Fourth, in making public policy on climate change, especially in a post-cautionary world, we must not make the best the enemy of the good. Many academics have devoted loving attention to exactly which kind of regime—international or domestic, market-based or technology-based, and so on—is ideal for the problem of climate change. We do not have the luxury of waiting for the ideal solution now, especially when the likely favorite among theoreticians—an international trading regime with participation by the United States and developing countries such as China—would entail a significant lead time. In this setting, we may do well to use non-obvious second-best solutions, including state and local actions to reduce greenhouse gases. Indeed, time appears to be so short for effective action on climate change that I believe we

---

102. *See* Bret Schulte, *Temperature Rising*, U.S. NEWS & WORLD REP., June 5, 2006, at 36–40 (noting that some environmentalists have long been reluctant to talk about adaptation "for fear it would pull the focus away from fixing the problem").

103. For discussion, see Kirsten H. Engel & Scott R. Saleska, *Subglobal Regulation of the Global Commons: The Case of Climate Change*, 32 ECOLOGY L.Q. 183, 213–14 (2005).

104. *See, e.g.*, David C. Vladeck, *Preemption and Regulatory Failure*, 33 PEPP. L. REV. 95, 105–07 (2005) (noting that the Court's decision in *Cipollone v. Liggett Group, Inc.*, 505 U.S. 504 (1992), significantly expanded the extent to which federal legislation can preempt state and local laws).

should stop waiting around for the government to act on this issue and take the matter into our own hands. We are all implicated in climate change. We drive cars, switch on the lights, turn up the AC, boot up our computers, and so on. We don't have to wait for action on climate change; we can use our own inaction—less driving, less electricity use, and so on—to start tackling the problem.

Finally, and most importantly, passing from a precautionary to a post-cautionary world has serious consequences for the moral status of the debate over climate change. In the first part of this Essay, I described how gravely human life and health are now and will continue to be affected by climate change. In this second part of the Essay, I have explained that we now know that humans will die and fall ill as a result of this problem. The first describes a consequence; the second describes our knowledge of its occurrence. Knowledge that death and suffering will result from our actions leads uncontroversially to a moral obligation to change our behavior. In the United States, knowing killing is condemned in the criminal laws of all fifty states, in modern regulatory laws at the federal level, and in civil jury awards in tort cases.[105] These laws embody a moral commitment against knowing killing that, in traditional criminal contexts, is uncontroversial. It should be no more controversial when it occurs on a global scale.

CONCLUSION

Climate change is a public health threat of the highest order. Almost every facet of human health is being or will be affected by this phenomenon. Unfortunately, we long ago frittered away climate change's precautionary period. We are at a stage now when we can expect large-scale human health consequences from a warming world. Perhaps the worst of these consequences can be avoided. We have a moral imperative to try.

105. *See* Lisa Heinzerling, *Knowing Killing and Environmental Law*, 14 N.Y.U. ENVTL. L.J. 521, 521–26 (2006).

Part VI
Tobacco Control

[15]

The Ethics of Smoking*

Robert E. Goodin

Philosophically, smoking has long been regarded as a paradigmatically private-regarding vice, best treated as such. It is a vice, to be sure: a dirty, disgusting habit, in the view of nineteenth-century moralists, best confined to smoke rooms and male company (Day 1836/1947, pp. 27–29; Schlesinger 1946, pp. 23, 38–39; Martin 1983, p. 637). But it is a private vice harming only smokers themselves;[1] and it is therefore best left to their personal discretion and moderation. Smoking has thus long been regarded as something best controlled through codes of etiquette and social pressure, and completely unsuited to any very much more serious social sanctions.

On the broad outlines of that analysis, Mill (1859/1975, chaps. 4, 5), Spencer (1893, pt. 3, secs. 214–15), and Sidgwick (1907, bk. 3, chap. 9, sec. 2) all seem agreed. That received wisdom continues to hold sway, in our own day, among the lay moralists of the medical profession, who editorialize in the *Journal of the American Medical Association* for "tobacco for consenting adults in private only" (Lundberg and Knoll 1986). Among professional philosophers, too, smoking has until recently been an area where traditional Millean precepts have been thought largely to rule (Feinberg 1971/1983, p. 11; Dworkin 1972/1983, pp. 32–33; Wikler 1978/1983, 1987; Daniels 1985, pp. 150–64).

In current controversies, that conventional wisdom is being questioned in both its parts. That smoking is a merely private-regarding vice, harming only smokers themselves, is challenged by evidence of the harmful effects of "passive smoking" (i.e., nonsmokers' inhalation of smoke given off by others smoking around them). That smoking is best treated as we would an ordinary private-regarding vice—by informal social pressure, rather than by formal legal sanctions—is also being challenged by evidence of the addictive nature of the habit, making it difficult for smokers to start and stop at will.

* I had much assistance in the preparation of this article. First I should thank Margo Goodin, whose files and continuing arguments have proven so helpful. I also received valuable assistance from Brian Barry, Richard Daynard, John Dryzek, Debbie Fitzmaurice, Mark Flanagan, Robert Fullinwider, Alvin Goldman, Steven Hetcher, Martin Hollis, Sheldon Leader, Judith Lichtenberg, Claudia Mills, Dorothy Rice, Mark Sagoff, Thomas Schelling, Robert Sugden, Robert Tollison, Robert Wachbroit, Kenneth Warner, and Albert Weale. An expanded version of this article will appear shortly from the University of Chicago Press, in the form of a book designed for classroom use.

1. And perhaps their families—though given traditional legal doctrines of privity within the family, that comes to one and the same thing.

These new developments make smoking a paradigm of another kind: an issue concerning the quality of social life, requiring codes that are formal rather than informal and enforceable rather than merely hortatory. Here, morally worthy goals cannot be achieved if backed by morals alone. Legislation is not only permissible but also, in some ways, morally mandated.

HARM TO SELF

What Are the Risks?

Folk wisdom has long held tobacco smoking to be unhealthy. During the first outbreak of the smoking epidemic in the seventeenth century, most of the crowned heads of Europe tried to prohibit it, on grounds of public health. In England, James I not only levied an excise tax on tobacco but also went to the extraordinary lengths of penning a pamphlet to warn of its dangers (Harrison 1986, p. 555). From the earliest days of our own century, cigarettes have been popularly known as "coffin nails," everyone's grandmother warned that they would stunt your growth, and so on.

Proper medical evidence scientifically supporting such suspicions began mushrooming in the 1950s and culminated in the justly famous reports of the Royal College of Physicians of 1962 and of the U.S. surgeon general two years later. The subsequent scientific literature on smoking and health—now numbering over 50,000 studies (U.S. DHHS 1986, p. vii)—has merely served to reinforce those earlier fears.[2]

The basic findings are familiar enough. Smoking leads to cancer (especially of the lung and respiratory tract, but also of the pancreas and bladder) and to cardiovascular disease (particularly coronary heart disease, but also peripheral vascular disease) and is the major cause of chronic obstructive lung disease.

If the basic findings are familiar, the magnitude of the effects can still shock. To say that smoking is responsible for more than 300,000 deaths per year in the United States is to say that about 15 percent of all deaths in the United States are smoking-related (U.S. DHHS 1986, pp. vii, 5–6). Put in more personal terms, "about a quarter of the young men who smoke a pack a day or so of cigarettes are killed before their time by smoking"; and "on average . . . [they] have lost ten to fifteen years of life" (Peto 1980, p. 45). Age-adjusted mortality rates are 68 percent higher for moderate smokers than for nonsmokers—and about double that for heavy smokers. A moderate smoker's chances of dying from lung cancer are 10.8 times greater than a nonsmoker's; of bronchitis or emphysema, 6.1 times greater; of cancer of the larynx, 5.4 times greater; of oral cancer, 4.1 times greater; of cancer of the esophagus, 3.4 times greater; of coronary artery disease or other heart diseases, 1.7 times greater; and so on (U.S. DHEW 1964, p. 29).

2. The easiest way into this vast technical literature is through the surgeon general's reports: *Smoking and Health* (U.S. DHEW 1964); the series on *The Health Consequences of Smoking,* published almost annually since 1967 and focusing on a different hazard each year; and the consolidation volume in the latter series, published in 1976 (U.S. DHEW 1976). These reports contain both nontechnical summaries for the general reader and fuller summaries of technical literature for anyone wanting to follow up some detail; to follow them up further, see the U.S. DHHS annotated bibliography, *Smoking and Health Bulletin,* published six times a year and collected annually as the *Bibliography on Smoking and Health.* The Royal College of Physicians reports (1962, 1971, 1983) are more sporadic but aimed more at a mass audience. The best single brief article is Fielding (1985).

Such findings have been confirmed time and again in subsequent reports of the surgeon general (see especially the consolidation volume, U.S. DHEW 1976). The surgeon general has, accordingly, concluded repeatedly that "cigarette smoking is the largest single preventable cause of death and disability for the US population" (U.S. DHHS 1986, pp. 5–6).[3]

(In what follows, as a kind of shorthand I shall often talk just of "cigarette smoking" and "cancer." But that is just a shorthand. All modes of consuming tobacco cause significant—if not quite so dramatic—increases in the risk of contracting cancer somewhere or another in the body [U.S. DHEW 1976, chap. 10]. And cancer, clearly, is not the only thing that smokers have to fear.)

The evidence underlying these medical conclusions is largely epidemiological in character. In the population as a whole, smokers contract those various diseases many times more often than nonsmokers; and heavy smokers contract them much more often than light smokers. These differential rates of illness are much too large to be put down to mere chance. They seem to vary, in lagged fashion, with changes in the aggregate consumption of tobacco over time. And so on.

Strictly speaking, all that that proves is that smoking correlates with those diseases. As any first course in statistics teaches, correlation is not causation. The 1964 surgeon general's report addresses this question of causation at length, arguing, inter alia, that just as cause precedes consequence, smoking precedes cancer; just as causes are spatially contiguous to consequences, smoke touches the lung where cancer later develops; there is properly controlled experimental evidence that tars from cigarette smoke cause skin cancer in other animals; and the increases over the past century in smoking correspond, in lagged fashion, so closely to increases over the same period in lung cancers that it is simply not credible that that increase in cancer could have been caused by any other factor so far suggested (U.S. DHEW 1964, pp. 19–21, 175–96; Bradford Hill 1965). None of that yet proves causation, and the last point, in particular, is still sometimes challenged (Brownlee 1965; Burch 1978; Eysenck 1986, pp. 32–43). Still, the essence of scientific explanation lies in telling "plausible stories," and all of that goes a substantial way toward underwriting the plausibility of the tale.

Statistical purists and tobacco apologists, of course, nonetheless insist that the case is "not proven" because the findings are "merely statistical" (R. J. Reynolds 1986; Burch 1978; Eysenck 1980, 1986). It pays to consider carefully what other causal paths are being contemplated when they say that. In an early letter to the *British Medical Journal,* the distinguished statistician and geneticist, Sir Ronald Fisher (1957), identified two alternative possibilities. One is that we have the causal arrow backward and that incipient cancer is what causes people to smoke rather than vice versa. So far as I can tell, nobody has taken this possibility sufficiently seriously to investigate it properly.

The other, more worrying possibility is multicolinearity. All that fancy term means is that there might be some common cause that leads both to smoking and to cancer, thus rendering any apparent connection between the two wholly spurious. Some of these confounding factors (social class, workplace exposure to carcinogens, e.g.) can be controlled statistically; when they are, the relationship between smoking and cancer still remains significant. The most worrying possibility

3. Low tar and nicotine cigarettes are less of a boon than they might seem: the evidence is that people smoke more of them, and smoke them more intensively, so as to sustain their nicotine intake (U.S. DHHS 1981, sec. 7).

is one that is hard to control statistically, however. Perhaps an individual's genetic constitution causes both his smoking and his cancer, either directly (Fisher 1957; Fisher 1958; Fisher 1959; Fisher 1974, vol. 5, pp. 377–80, 385–432; Burch 1978) or indirectly, through its influence on personality (Eysenck 1980). The best test of this hypothesis would come through a comparison of monozygotic twins (who share the same genetic constitution) and dizygotic twins (who do not, but on whom various other environmental effects are presumably much the same). Early studies suggested that the former were indeed significantly more alike, both in their smoking behavior and in their cancer history, thus lending credence to the "genetic constitution" hypothesis. Those early studies were beset by a number of problems, however (U.S. DHEW 1964, p. 190; Slade et al. 1986–87). In the latest and most thorough analysis of the most comprehensive collection of twin data, the Swedish Twin Register, the findings "speak strongly against this [genetic] constitutional hypothesis" (Cederlof, Friburg, and Lundman 1977, p. 115).[4] Furthermore, that model is implausible given what we know about the mechanisms governing genetic transmission of personality characteristics and of susceptibility to cancer.[5] So again, the case is not quite proven, but the alternative hypotheses seem substantially less credible.

Certainly carcinogens merely "trigger" tumors in those who are genetically predisposed, so not everyone is necessarily at equal risk from smoking. There may even be "genetic constitutional" as well as genuinely "causal" factors linking smoking and cancer (Burch 1978). Advocates of curbs on smoking can concede all that without cost. Their case goes through perfectly well, just so long as: a sufficiently large proportion of the population is genetically vulnerable; among them, smoking makes a sufficiently large contribution in causing their cancers; and there is no way, technically or politically, to target truly effective antismoking policies only at those who are genetically at risk. Given the likelihood of each (indeed, of all) of these conditions being satisfied, antismoking policies can nonetheless be defended as important contributions to public health.[6]

Were we to regard the case against a suspected carcinogen as "not proven" for purposes of public policymaking until we identified the precise mechanism by which it caused cancer, we would have to wait until we found the cause of cancer itself before we could regulate carcinogens at all, however strong the statistical evidence linking the substances in question to cancer might be. By that standard, wildly carcinogenic substances like plutonium could be sold over the counter. By similar standards, thalidomide could still be marketed: we know it causes birth defects, but not exactly how or why. Or, again, by similar standards we might be obliged to ban apparently safe and effective drugs from the market

4. Eysenck (1980, p. 157) dismisses those findings as "too slight to be convincing either way" but is forced to concede that the conclusions from his own twin studies are still merely "speculative" (1986, p. 49).

5. Although very occasionally a single gene causes some particular form of cancer, more typically human cancers are caused by interactions between multiple genes. So too, typically, are human personality traits. Thus, "the linkage (in a genetic sense) between multiple genes related to a habit (smoking) and a disease (lung cancer) in a heterogeneous population" is simply implausible: it "would require numerous coincidences with small probabilities" (U.S. DHEW 1964, p. 191; cf. Eysenck 1986, pp. 52–53).

6. Strides are being made in identification of those at especially high risk of lung cancer and cardiac disease in consequence of smoking (Russell 1974, p. 257), but that, in itself, is not enough to undercut this case for a general antismoking campaign.

until we knew precisely how they worked to effect their cures. In all those cases, such a standard of proof would be unreasonably high to require (Bradford Hill 1965; Armitage 1978, p. 460).

Those who argue against policies to curb smoking on the grounds that the case against it is still "not proven" are implicitly asking us to presume a product safe until proven otherwise.[7] In practice, U.S. regulatory policy characteristically employs almost exactly the opposite presumption. Under the Food, Drug, and Cosmetic Act, as amended in 1958, it is the manufacturer of a new drug or food additive that must bear the burden of demonstrating that the product is safe and effective, which in practice means "producing at least four and possibly more than ten valid studies involving rodent and nonrodent toxicity, cancer, and other tests. Moreover, no additive can be approved as safe 'if it is found . . . to induce cancer in man or animal' " at all (Breyer 1982, p. 134).[8]

For those things which we are 95 percent certain cause cancer or 95 percent certain do not, it makes no difference to our final decision which way we set the presumption. For those cases in which neither is true, however, the presumption will alone dictate the decision. There, it is absolutely crucial which way that presumption is set—if indeed we want to operate with a presumption at all in these areas. A more sensible approach might be to judge substances carcinogenic if, on the balance of available evidence, they seem more likely than not to cause cancer; such a rule would avoid unreasonably banning substances on such slight evidence as now used under the Delaney Amendment, without going so far as to allow substances to continue being marketed as presumptively safe on equally slight evidence (Page 1978; see further Morrison and Henkel 1970; Atkins and Jarrett 1979). Either way, however, surely tobacco has to be treated as if it caused cancer. It stands indicted, whether by presumption or by the balance of evidence. Indeed, on the above evidence, it would stand indicted at the 0.05 confidence level even if the presumption were set in favor of its safety: question as they might whether correlation proves causation, even friends of tobacco concede that, statistically (for what that is worth), there is much less than a 5 percent chance that the observed relationship between smoking and cancer would have occurred randomly.

7. If we see ourselves as interfering with the liberty of manufacturers, we might be more inclined to suppose that the burden of proof should lie with them to prove their product safe. If we see ourselves as interfering with the liberty of consumers, it would be a case of paternalism, and we would be more inclined to suppose that the burden lies with the government to prove products unsafe before prohibiting people from using them (Dworkin 1972/1983, pp. 33–34). Any manufactured good, cigarettes included, could equally legitimately be viewed under either description, of course; so, useful though that general principle might be in explicating the phenomenology of the situation, it is useless in providing any real policy guidance.

8. Being neither a food nor a drug, cigarettes are outside the FDA's jurisdiction. Furthermore, under this legislation, the FDA's prior approval is not required to market various categories of items: "natural constituents of food"; substances "generally recognized among experts as safe"; and products already on the market before the 1958 enactment. Note, however, that "the FDA can proceed against" the latter products "by showing in court that they are 'injurious to health' " (Breyer 1982, p. 134). Thus, such products are not necessarily exempted from regulation altogether—the burden of proof has merely shifted to the government.

Do Smokers Voluntarily Accept the Risks?

Given what we know of the health risks from smoking, we may well be tempted to "ban cigarette manufacturers from continuing to manufacture their product on the grounds that we are preventing them from causing illness to others in the same way that we prevent other manufacturers from releasing pollutants into the atmosphere, thereby causing danger to members of the community." That would be to move too quickly. As Dworkin (1972/1983, p. 22) continues, "The difference is . . . that in the former but not the latter case the harm is of such a nature that it could be avoided by those individuals affected, if they so chose. The incurring of the harm requires the active cooperation of the victim. It would be a mistake in theory and hypocritical in practice to assert that our interference in such cases is just like our interference in standard cases of protecting others from harm." Courts have been as sensitive to this distinction as moral philosophers, appealing to the venerable legal maxim, *volenti non fit injuria,* to hold that through their voluntary assumption of the risk smokers have waived any claims against cigarette manufacturers. In perhaps one of the most dramatic cases (given the well-established synergism between smoking and asbestos inhalation) the Fifth Circuit refused to enjoin cigarette manufacturers as codefendants in a suit against Johns-Manville, saying that "the danger is to the smoker who willingly courts it."[9]

Certainly there is, morally speaking, a world of difference between the harms that others inflict upon you and the harms that you inflict upon yourself. The question is simply whether, in the case of smoking, the active cooperation of the smoker really is such as to constitute voluntary acceptance of the consequent risks of illness and death. This question is decomposable into two further ones. The first concerns the question of whether smokers knew the risks. The second concerns the question of whether, even if smoking in full knowledge of the risks, they could be said to have "accepted" the risks in a sense that was fully voluntary.

The first is essentially a question of "informed consent." People can be held to have consented only if they knew to what they were supposedly consenting. In the personalized context of medical encounters, this means that each and every person being treated is told, in terms he or she understands, by the attending physician what the risks of the treatment might be (Gorovitz 1982, chap. 3). For largely anonymous transactions in the market, such personalized standards are inappropriate. Instead, we are forced to infer consent from what people know or should have known (in the standard legal construct, what a "reasonable" person should have been expected to know) about the product. And in the anonymous world of the market, printed warnings necessarily take the place of face-to-face admonitions.

Cigarette manufacturers, in defending against product liability suits, have claimed on both these grounds that smokers should be construed as having consented to the risks that they have run (Edell and Gisser 1985; AMA 1986; "Plaintiffs' Conduct as a Defense to Claims against Cigarette Manufacturers" 1986). They claim, first, that any "reasonable" person should have known, and the "ordinary consumer" did indeed know, that smoking was an "inherently

9. Johns-Manville Sales Corp. v. International Association of Machinists, Machinists Local 1609, 621 F.2d 756 at 759 (5th Cir. 1980). See further Daniels 1985, p. 155, n. 8; cf. "Plaintiffs' Conduct" 1986.

dangerous" activity.[10] Their interrogatories constantly seek to establish that plaintiffs had, in their youth, consorted with people calling cigarettes "coffin nails," and so on.[11] Manufacturers claim, second, that printing of government-mandated health warnings on cigarette packets from 1966 onward has constituted further, explicit warning to users.[12]

Now, of course, there are some risks (e.g., Buerger's disease, a circulatory condition induced, often in quite young people, by smoking that can result in amputation of limbs) of which smokers were never warned, by grandmother or government health warnings either.[13] Indeed, the warnings of both folk wisdom and cigarette packets in the 1960s and 1970s at least were desperately nonspecific; and there is a more general question whether an all-purpose warning that "*X* may be hazardous to your health," without specifying just how likely *X* is to cause just what sorts of harms, is adequate warning to secure people's informed consent at all.[14]

10. Recent tort law revisions in California and New Jersey bar product liability actions altogether against manufacturers of "products that are inherently dangerous and are known to be unsafe by the ordinary consumer" (Cohen 1987, p. 8). To avail themselves of this protection, however, manufacturers will have to prove that their products are inherently dangerous. That would compromise their defenses against liability claims in other jurisdictions and would undermine their public standing more generally, so on balance they may well prefer to shun this option.

11. See, e.g., interrogatories reprinted in the *Tobacco Products Litigation Reporter,* vol. 2, no. 7 (July/August 1987), 3.365–400 and 3.441–46. Of course, such claims sit uneasily with the same corporations' claims in the same litigation that there is no evidence that smoking causes cancer (etc.), either in general or in the plaintiffs' particular cases ("Plaintiffs' Conduct" 1986, p. 817). Caught in this inconsistency, one tobacco company recently withdrew any claims as to the plaintiff's negligence, lest it be required to answer interrogatories stating exactly what any "reasonable person" should have known about the dangers of its products (Mintz 1987).

12. Tobacco company lawyers, defending against product liability suits, have even tried to use behavior subsequent to those warnings to infer hypothetical consent to the risks before the warnings were given. As one attorney argued, "because [the plaintiff] continued to smoke for at least 15 years while warnings were on every pack she bought, she would have smoked before January 1, 1966, even if the defendants had voluntarily warned her about possible health consequences" (quoted in Mintz 1988a). American constitutional law poses the further question of "preemption." Where state statutory or common law is in conflict with federal legislation, under art. 6, sec. 2 of the U.S. Constitution the lower law is preempted by the higher. Thus, if the U.S. Congress, in mandating the warnings, had explicitly exempted cigarette manufacturers from any further liability for failure to warn of risks, then it is clear that tort claims under state common law would be constitutionally precluded. The legislative history suggests that, while Congress intended to prohibit states from requiring any further warnings, it did not prohibit companies from printing them voluntarily—nor did it intend to relieve them of ordinary tort liability if they did not when reasonable people would have (Garner 1980, pp. 1453–54; Edell and Gisser 1985; Tribe 1986). Latest court opinions seem to be tending toward accepting the preemption argument, though (Palmer v. Liggett Group, Inc., 825 F.2d 620 [1st Cir. 1987]).

13. Neither do cigarette packets warn, as some drug containers do, that the product is addictive (Garner 1980). But if tobacco is truly addictive, then it is that addictiveness rather than the failure to warn of addictiveness that blocks consent-based defenses, as argued below (cf. Wikler 1978/1983, p. 39).

14. Certainly psychological evidence suggests that an explicit, concrete message is a better spur to action than a vague, abstract one (Borgida and Nisbett 1977). Nonspecific

Furthermore, cigarette manufacturers take back through their advertising what is given by way of warnings.[15] The problem is not so much one of literally deceptive advertising—though there is evidence of that, too (U.S. FTC 1981, 1984, 1985)—as it is one of the widespread use of deceptively healthy imagery (U.S. FTC 1981, pp. 428a, 491a). The printed warnings may say "smoking kills," but the advertising images are the very picture of robust good health. Cowboys, sports, and the great outdoors figure centrally in the ads. The U.S. Federal Trade Commission has continually warned Congress that "current practices and methods of cigarette advertising" have the effect of "reducing anxieties about the health risks posed by cigarette smoking" (U.S. FTC 1984, p. 5), "negat[ing] the effect of health warnings because they imply that smoking is a habit which is compatible with performing various outdoor activities and having a strong healthy body" (U.S. FTC 1985, p. 5).[16] The point is not that advertising bypasses consumers' capacity to reason and somehow renders them unfree to choose intelligently whether or not to consume the product. The point is, rather, that tobacco companies in effect are giving out—and, more important, consumers are receiving—conflicting information. The implicit health claims of the advertising imagery conflict with the explicit health warnings and thus undercut any *volenti* or informed-consent defense companies might try to mount on the basis of those warnings (Edell and Gisser 1985).

Despite tobacco companies' best efforts, however, nearly everyone—smokers included—knows, in broad outline, the health risks that smoking entails. In a 1978 Gallup poll, only 24 percent of heavy smokers claimed they were unaware of or did not believe the evidence that smoking is hazardous ("Plaintiffs' Conduct" 1986, p. 814, n. 26; U.S. FTC 1981, p. 433a). How that recalcitrant residual should be handled is a hard question. Having smoked thousands of packets containing increasingly stern warnings, and having been exposed to hundreds of column inches of newspaper reporting and several hours of broadcasting about smoking's hazards, they are presumably incorrigible in their false beliefs in this

---

warnings might, in principle, be as much a problem with lawnmowers and insecticides as with cigarettes, of course; but in practice warnings there tend to be stated more strongly (saying that bad things will happen if the product is misused, not just that they may; mentioning death explicitly; suggesting antidotes; etc.).

15. Warnings that "smoking may be dangerous," when conjoined with pictures of people enjoying dangerous sports (white-water rafting, etc.), perversely serve to make smoking more attractive; warnings that "smoking may complicate pregnancy," when conjoined with sexually provocative photos in a magzaine devoted to casual sex without procreation, again perversely undercut the health warnings. Arguments that smokers were better informed in the past, when unregulated advertisers employed "knocking copy" to point out health risks of other brands of cigarettes (Calfee 1986), are highly suspect—the central claim of such advertisements, after all, was that an advertiser's own brand was free from those defects.

16. Literally, of course, it is—at least broadly speaking and in the short run. But in the medium to long term, participation even in purely recreational sport (not to mention serious sport, where peak performance is required) is impaired by the consequences of smoking. Insofar as young smokers are encouraged in the belief that they can always quit, should smoking become a problem later, that is a false belief (as shown by the addiction evidence, discussed below); and advertisements carrying any such implications once again would count as clearly deceptive advertising.

regard. Providing them with still more information is likely to prove pointless (cf. Feinberg 1971/1983, p. 11).

Ordinarily it is not the business of public policy to prevent people from relying on false inferences from full information which would harm only themselves. Sometimes, however, it is. One such case comes when the false beliefs would lead to decisions that are "far-reaching, potentially dangerous, and irreversible"—as, for example, with people who believe that when they jump out of a tenth-story window they will float upward (Dworkin 1972/1983, p. 31; see also Feinberg 1971/1983, p. 7).

We are particularly inclined toward intervention when false beliefs with such disastrous results are traceable to familiar, well-understood forms of cognitive defect. One is "wishful thinking": smokers believing the practice is safe because they smoke rather than smoking because they believe it to be safe (Pears 1984). There is substantial evidence that smokers believe, groundlessly, that they are less vulnerable to smoking-related diseases; there is also evidence that they came to acquire those beliefs, and to "forget" what they previously knew about the dangers of smoking, after they took up the habit (Leventhal, Glynn, and Fleming 1987). Another cognitive defect is the "anchoring" fallacy (Kahneman, Slovic, and Tversky 1982): people smoke many times without any (immediately perceptible) bad effects; and as intuitive Bayesians extrapolating from their own experience, they therefore quite reasonably but quite wrongly conclude that smoking is safe for them. Yet another phenomenon, sometimes regarded as a cognitive defect, is "time-discounting": since young smokers will not suffer the full effects of smoking-related diseases for some years to come, they may puff away happily now with little regard for the consequences, if they attach relatively little importance to future pains relative to present pleasures in their utility functions (Fuchs 1982).[17] All of these cognitive defects point to relatively weak forms of irrationality.[18] In and of themselves, they would not be enough to justify interference with

17. Sometimes that explanation is implausible: when the ill consequences would be felt tomorrow (e.g., a hangover), to ignore them on these grounds would imply a time discount of 100 percent per hour, "compounding to an annual rate too large for my calculator," as Schelling (1980, p. 99) sneers. But since the really serious consequences of smoking are some decades away for most of us, that reductio does not work there. Where genuinely "pure time preferences" are involved, the irrationality of discounting might be debatable. Economists regard time preferences as preferences like any other, neither rational nor irrational. Daniels (1985, p. 99) argues in terms of what would be prudent for a "hypothetical agent, . . . abstract[ing] from certain features of individuals" as we find them, to show that they should save for their own futures; but all that such quasi-Rawlsian appeals demonstrate is the injustice of discounting, not strictly speaking its imprudence or irrationality. My preferred argument is this. Suppose—as certainly seems plausible, in most cases—that the later person will prefer that his or her earlier self had taken his or her later interests more seriously. Then want-regarding moralities would put this later claim fully on a par with that of the earlier self (Goodin 1982, chap. 3). So long as earlier and later selves are instantiations of one and the same person, we can say that the earlier one is therefore "irrational" not to take properly into account his or her later interests. (If they are not the "same person," it is indeed appropriate to appeal to norms of justice: it is unjust for one person to take advantage of another in this way, whether or not they share the same body at different moments.)

18. The addiction evidence surveyed below is evidence of genuine, full-blown irrationality; and it might explain why people are so prone to these more modest cognitive errors, when it comes to smoking, as well.

people's liberty, perhaps. But when they lead people to take decisions that are far-reaching, potentially dangerous, and irreversible, perhaps intervention would be justified.

Interfering with people's choices in such cases is paternalistic, admittedly. But there are many different layers of paternalism (Sartorius 1983; Feinberg 1986). What is involved here is a relatively weak form of paternalism, working within the individual's own theory of the good and merely imposing upon him better means of achieving his own ends.[19] It is one thing to stop people who want to commit suicide from doing so, but quite another to stop people who want to live from acting in a way that they falsely believe to be safe (Feinberg 1971/1983, p. 10; Dworkin 1972/1983, pp. 23, 33). Smokers who deny the health risks fall into that latter, easier category.

The larger and harder question is how to deal with the great majority of smokers who, knowing the risks, continue smoking anyway. Of course, it might be said that they do not really know the risks. Although most acknowledge that smoking is "unhealthy," in some vague sense, few know exactly what chances they run of exactly what diseases. In one poll, 49 percent of smokers did not know that smoking causes most cases of lung cancer, 63 percent that it causes most cases of bronchitis, and 85 percent that it causes most cases of emphysema (U.S. FTC 1981, pp. 345a–364a). Overestimating badly the risks of dying in other more dramatic ways (car crashes, etc.), people badly underestimate the relative risks of dying in the more mundane ways associated with smoking—thus allowing them to rationalize further their smoking behavior as being "not all that dangerous," compared to other things that they are also doing.[20] Besides all that, there is the distinction between "knowing intellectually" some statistic and "feeling in your guts" its full implications. Consent counts—morally, as well as legally—only if it is truly informed consent, only if people know what it is to which they are consenting. That, in turn, requires not only that we can state the probabilities but also that we "appreciate them in an emotionally genuine manner" (Dworkin 1972/1983, p. 30). There is reason to believe that smokers do not (U.S.FTC 1981, p. 428a).

It may still be argued that, as long as people had the facts, they can and should be held responsible if they chose not to act upon them when they could

19. One of a person's ends—continued life—at least. Perhaps the person has other ends ("relaxation," or whatever) that are well served by smoking, and insofar as "people taking risks actually value the direct consequences associated with them . . . it is more difficult to intrude paternalistically" (Daniels 1985, pp. 158, 163). But assuming that smoking is not the only means to the other ends—not the only way to relax, etc.—the intrusion is only minimally difficult to justify.

20. Logically, it would be perfectly possible for people both to underestimate the extent of the risk and simultaneously to overreact to it. People might suppose the chances of snakebite are slight but live in mortal fear of it nonetheless. Psychologically, however, the reverse seems to happen. People's subjective probability estimates of an event's likelihood increase the more they dread it and the more "psychologically available" the event therefore is to them (Kahneman, Slovic, and Tversky 1982). Smoking-related diseases, in contrast, tend to be "quiet killers" of which people have little direct or indirect experience, which tend to be underreported in newspapers and which act on people one at a time rather than catastrophically killing many people at once (Lichtenstein et al. 1978, p. 567). Smoking-related diseases being psychologically less available to people in these ways, they underestimate their frequency dramatically—by a factor of eight, in the case of lung cancer, according to one study (Slovic, Fischhoff, and Lichtenstein 1982, p. 469).

have done so. It may be folly for utilitarian policymakers to rely upon people's such imperfect responses to facts for purposes of constructing social welfare functions, and framing public policies around them. But there is the separate matter of who ought to be blamed when some self-inflicted harm befalls people. There, arguably, responsibility ought to be on people's own shoulders (Knowles 1977; Wikler 1987). Arguably, we ought to stick to that judgment, even if people were "pressured" into smoking by the bullying of aggressive advertising or peer pressure (cf. Gewirth 1980, pp. 124–25; Daniels 1985, p. 159).

What crucially transforms the "voluntary acceptance" argument is evidence of the addictive nature of cigarette smoking. Of course, saying that smoking is addictive is not to say that no one can ever give it up. Many have done so. By the same token, though, more than 70 percent of American servicemen addicted to heroin in Vietnam gave it up when returning to the United States (Robins 1973, quoted in Pollin 1984; see also Fingarette 1975, pp. 429–31); yet we still rightly regard heroin as an addictive drug. The test of addictiveness is not impossibility but rather difficulty of withdrawal.

There is a tendency, in discussing *volenti* or informed-consent arguments, to draw too sharp a distinction between "voluntary" and "involuntary acts" and to put the dividing line at the wrong place, at that. The tendency seems to be to assume that any act that is in the least voluntary—that is in any respect at all, to any extent at all, within the control of the agents themselves—is to be considered fully voluntary for the purposes. If we want to claim that some sort of act was involuntary, we are standardly advised to look for evidence of "somnambulism" or "automatism" or such like (Prevezer 1958; Fox 1963). Thus, U.S. Supreme Court justices wanting to argue for more humane treatment of addicts felt obliged to assert that "once [the defendant] had become an addict he was utterly powerless" to refrain from continuing to service his addiction (Abe Fortas, dissenting opinion, *Powell v. Texas*, 392 U.S. 514, 567 [1968]). That is an implausibly strong claim, given the above evidence.

There is no need to make such a strong claim, though, to vitiate arguments that the conduct was "voluntary" and the harm thus self-incurred. For purposes of excusing criminal conduct, we are prepared to count forms of "duress" that stop well short of rendering all alternative actions literally impossible. It is perfectly possible for bank tellers to let a robber break their arms instead of handing over the money, but no one expects them to do so. A credible threat of serious pain, or perhaps even very gross discomfort, is ordinarily regarded as more than sufficient to constitute duress of the sort that excuses responsibility for otherwise impermissible behavior. So, too, with addiction-induced behavior, I would argue. The issue is not whether it is impossible, but merely whether it is unreasonably costly, for addicts to resist their compulsive desires. If that desire is so strong that even someone with " 'normal and reasonable' self-control" (Watson 1977, p. 331) would succumb to it, we have little compunction in saying that the addict's free will was sufficiently impaired that his apparent consent counts for naught.[21]

21. Fingarette (1975, p. 437; see also Fingarette 1970) questions whether drug-withdrawal symptoms in general really are so severe as to justify the claims of involuntariness by reason of "pharmacological coercion." The effects may well all be in the addict's mind and may well be feared to be worse in prospect than they would turn out to be in actuality. But the agent's beliefs are indeed the key to coercion: if the bank tellers believed the robber's gun was loaded, they handed over the money under duress and are excused for that reason, even if it turns out that the gun's chambers were empty.

This is arguably the case with nicotine addiction. To establish a substance as addictive, we require evidence of "physical need" for the substance among its users. That evidence is necessary to prove smoking is an addiction rather than just a "habit" (U.S. DHEW 1964, chaps. 13–14), a psychological dependence, or a matter of mere sociological pressure (Daniels 1985, p. 159)—none of which would undercut, in a way that addictiveness does, claims that the risks of smoking are voluntarily incurred. That physical link has now been established, though. Particular receptors for the active ingredients of tobacco smoke have been discovered in the brain; the physiological sites and mechanisms by which nicotine acts on the brain have now been well mapped, and its tendency to generate compulsive, repetitive behavior in consequence has been well established. Such evidence—summarized in the surgeon general's 1988 report (U.S. DHHS 1988, chaps. 3 and 4; see also Leventhal and Cleary 1980 and Winsten 1986)—has been one of the crucial factors leading the World Health Organization (1978) and the American Psychiatric Association (1987, sec. 305.1) to classify "nicotine dependence" as an addiction.

None of that evidence proves that it would be literally impossible for smokers to resist the impulse to smoke. Through extraordinary acts of will, they might. Nor does any of that evidence prove that it is literally impossible for them to break their dependence altogether. Many have. Recall, however, that the issue is not one of impossibility but rather of how hard people should have to try before their will is said to be sufficiently impaired that their agreement does not count as genuine consent.

The evidence suggests that nicotine addicts have to try very hard indeed. This is the second crucial fact to establish in proving a substance addictive.[22] Central among the WHO/APA criteria for diagnosing nicotine dependence is the requirement of evidence of "continuous use of tobacco for at least one month with . . . unsuccessful attempts to stop or significantly reduce the amount of tobacco use on a permanent basis" (APA 1987, sec. 305.1). A vast majority of smokers do indeed find themselves in this position. The surgeon general reports that 90 percent of regular smokers have tried to quit (U.S. DHHS 1979, quoted in Pollin 1984). Another 1975 survey found that 84 percent of smokers had attempted to stop, but that only 36 percent of them had succeeded in maintaining their changed behavior for a whole year (Benfari, Ockene, and McIntyre 1982; see further Leventhal and Cleary 1980).[23]

22. There are other physical needs that we would have trouble renouncing—such as our need for food—that we would be loath to call "addictions." Be that as it may, we would also be loath, for precisely those reasons, to say that we eat "of our own free will" (we would have no hesitation that someone who makes a credible threat of preventing us from eating has "coerced" us, etc.). Since involuntariness and impairment of free will are what is really at issue here, those thus do seem to be the aspects of addictiveness that matter in the present context.

23. The graphs mapping the relapse rate after a given period of time are almost identical for nicotine and for heroin (Winsten 1986; see more generally U.S. DHHS 1988, chap. 5), although it might be wrong to make too much of that fact. (Perhaps heroin addicts find both that it is harder to give up and that they have more reason to do so: then relapse rates would appear the same, even though heroin is more addictive in the sense of being harder to give up.) Pointing to the addiction evidence, U.S. federal courts have decided that "smoking can be an involuntary act for some persons" and that social security disability benefits may not therefore be routinely withheld from victims of smoking-related diseases

Such evidence of smokers trying and failing to stop is rightly regarded as central to the issue of addiction, philosophically as well as diagnostically. Some describe free will in terms of "second-order volitions"—desires about desires—controlling "first-order" ones (Frankfurt 1971). Others talk of one's "evaluational structure" controlling one's "motivational structure," so one strives to obtain something if and only if one thinks it of value (Watson 1975, 1977). Addiction—the absence of free will—is thus a matter of first-order volitions winning out over second-order ones, and surface desires prevailing over the agent's own deeper values. In the case of smoking, trying to stop can be seen as a manifestation of one's second-order volitions or one's deeper values, and failing to stop as evidence of the triumph of first-order surface desires over them. The same criteria the WHO/APA use to diagnose nicotine dependence also establish the impairment of the smoker's free will, philosophically.

Various policy implications follow from evidence of addictiveness. One might be that over-the-counter sales of cigarettes should be banned. If the product is truly addictive, then we have no more reason to respect a person's voluntary choice (however well informed) to abandon his future volition to an addiction than we have for respecting a person's voluntary choice (however well informed) to sell himself into slavery (Mill 1859/1975, pp. 126–27). I am unsure how far to press this argument. After all, we do permit people to bind their future selves (through contracts, e.g.). But if it is the size of the stakes or the difficulty of breaking out of the bonds that makes the crucial difference, then acquiring a lethal and hard-to-break addiction is much more like a slavery contract than it is like an ordinary commercial commitment.

In any case, addictiveness thus defined makes it far easier to justify interventions that on their face appear paternalistic. In some sense, they would then be not paternalistic at all. Where people "wish to stop smoking, but do not have the requisite willpower . . . we are not imposing a good on someone who rejects it. We are simply using coercion to enable people to carry out their own goals" (Dworkin 1972/1983, p. 32).[24] It is, of course, genuinely difficult to decide which is the "authentic" self: with whom should we side, when the person who asks us to help him "enforce rules on himself" repudiates the rules at the time they need to be enforced? (Schelling 1980, 1983, 1984a, 1984b, 1985).[25] But at least we have more of a warrant for interference in such cases than if we were never asked for assistance at all. Much of the assistance we render in such situations will necessarily be of a very personal nature and outside the scope of public policy. There is nonetheless a substantial role for public policy in these realms.

on the grounds that they are suffering from voluntarily self-inflicted injuries (Gordon v. Schweiker, 725 F.2d 231, 236 [1984]).

24. That is one way of explaining an apparent paradox surrounding "sin" taxes in general: "items such as alcohol [and cigarettes] are so commonly consumed, and so little complaint is made about large excise taxes" on them, that microeconomists are led to conclude that it simply must be in the individual's own perceived interest, somehow, to be so taxed (Crain et al. 1977).

25. It begs this question to say that the one reflects an "evaluational" and the other merely a "motivational" judgment (Watson 1975, 1977) or even to say that the one reflects a "second-order preference" and the other merely a "first-order" one (Frankfurt 1971). In the intrapersonal bargaining game that Schelling envisages, each side typically claims the superior status for its own preference ranking. From the wanton self's point of view, wanton preferences enjoy evaluational rather than merely motivational status.

Banning or restricting smoking in public places (especially the workplace) can contribute crucially to an individual's own efforts at smoking cessation, for example (Etzioni 1978, pp. 67–68; Leventhal and Cleary 1980; U.S. DHHS 1986, chap. 6).

The force of the addiction findings, in the context of *volenti* or informed-consent arguments, is to undercut the claim that there is any continuing consent to the risks involved in smoking. There might have been consent in the very first instance—in smoking your first cigarette. But once you were hooked, you lost the capacity to consent in any meaningful sense on a continuing basis. As Hume (1760) says, to consent implies the possibility of doing otherwise; and addiction substantially deprives you of the capacity to do other than continue smoking. So once you have become addicted to nicotine, your subsequent smoking cannot be taken as indicating your consent to the risks.

If there is to be consent at all, then, it can only be consent in the very first instance, that is, when you first began to smoke. That, in turn, seriously undercuts the extent to which cigarette manufacturers can rely upon *volenti* or informed-consent defenses in product liability litigation and its moral analogues. Many of those now dying from tobacco-induced diseases started smoking well before warnings began appearing on packets in 1966; their consent to the risks of smoking could only have been based on "common knowledge" and "folk wisdom."

That is a short-term problem, though, since that cohort of smokers will eventually die off. The more serious, continuing problem is this. A vast majority of smokers began smoking in their early to middle teens. Evidence suggests that "of those teenagers who smoke more than a single cigarette only 15 percent avoid becoming regular dependent smokers" (Russell 1974, p. 255); and a great majority, perhaps up to 95 percent, of regular adult smokers are thought to have been addicted before they were twenty-one years of age (Califano 1981, p. 183; Lewit, Coate, and Grossman 1981, p. 547, n. 8; Pollin 1984; Leventhal, Glynn, and Fleming 1987, p. 3373). Being below the age of consent, they were incapable of consenting in the first instance;[26] and being addicted by the time they reached the age of consent they were incapable of consenting later, either.

Do the Benefits Outweigh the Costs?

In addition to Kantian-style questions about informed consent, there are utilitarian-style questions of overall social welfare to be considered in this connection. Presumably it is in these latter terms that public health measures are ordinarily justified. We do not leave it to the discretion of consumers, however well informed, whether or not to drink grossly polluted water, ingest grossly contaminated foods, or inject grossly dangerous drugs. We simply prohibit such things, on grounds of public health, by appeal to utilitarian calculations of one sort or another.

To some extent, the same considerations that lead us to believe such measures are justified on grounds of social utility might also give us grounds for presuming people's (at least hypothetical) consent to them, also. To some extent, we can appeal to externality arguments to justify the measures: contagious diseases and

26. Strictly speaking, ability to consent is not predicated—legally or morally—upon attaining some arbitrary age but, rather, upon having attained the capacity to make reasoned choices in the matter at hand ("Plaintiffs' Conduct" 1986, pp. 812–13). The level of understanding manifested by teenagers about smoking clearly suggests that their decision to start smoking cannot be deemed an informed choice, however (Leventhal, Glynn, and Fleming 1987).

costly cures affect the community as a whole. But to some extent, the justification of public health measures must be baldly paternalistic, turning on the benefits accruing to the person himself from avoiding diseases that he might otherwise cavalierly court.

All those considerations are in play in the case of smoking. Paternalistic elements have been canvassed above. There are contagion effects, too (Preston 1971; Schelling 1986b, pp. 161–62): being among smokers exerts strong social pressure upon people to start smoking and makes it difficult for people to stop; and these contagion effects are particularly pronounced among young people, whose smoking behavior is strongly affected by that of parents and peers (Leventhal and Cleary 1980). As regards externalities, smoking is believed to cause at least half of residential fires, harming family and neighbors as well as the smokers themselves (Schelling 1986a, p. 550); treating smoking-induced illnesses is costly, and even in the United States some 40 percent of those costs are borne by the public (Breslow 1982, pp. 146–48; U.S. OTA 1985); premature deaths cost the economy productive members and entail pain and suffering for family and friends; and so on (Atkinson and Meade 1974; Schelling 1986a; cf. Littlechild 1986).

Dealing just in those nonquantified terms of human costs, smoking must surely stand indicted. The U.S. surgeon general says it is "the chief, single, avoidable cause of death in our society and the most important public health problem of our time" (U.S. DHHS 1982, preface). Cigarettes kill 25 percent of their users, even when used as their manufacturers intended they be used. Suppose a toaster or lawnmower had a similar record. It would be whipped off the market forthwith. On utilitarian grounds, there would seem to be no reason why cigarettes should be treated any differently.

For those preferring hard, solid numbers, economists (focusing principally upon medical costs and lost productivity) calculate that smoking costs the American economy on net $52–$62 billion per year (Luce and Schweitzer 1978; U.S. OTA 1985; Rice et al. 1986). By that reckoning, too, there is clearly a case to answer against smoking, on grounds of social utility.

There are, in fact, rejoinders available on two levels. One is a micro-level argument couched in terms of benefits to smokers themselves from the practice. The other is a macro-level argument, querying the real costs to society from the practice.

The first style of argument operates in standard microeconomic terms of consumer theory and welfare economics. Essentially, it amounts to a repudiation of "human capital" calculations of costs and benefits in favor of a "willingness to pay" approach (Schelling 1968; Schelling 1986a, pp. 500–502; Robinson 1986). The rights-based way of putting this point is to ask, Whose human capital is it, anyway? Unless we believe in forced labor, we must accept that even a highly productive member of the work force is entitled to quit her job and go live on a desert island; the rights theorist would say that we must accept, with the same equanimity, the productivity loss entailed in a person's (voluntary, fully informed) decision to smoke herself to death. The utilitarian way of putting this point is that cost-benefit calculations should take into account whatever subjective pleasures smokers derive from the practice (Atkinson 1974; Wikler 1978/1983, p. 42; Woodfield 1984, p. 118).[27] In the boldest statement of this very standard micro-

27. Even in tort law, "risk-utility" analysis is applied in such cases, in the form of an updated Learned Hand sort of test: the benefits have to exceed the anticipatable losses for the activity to be deemed nonnegligent. See Edell and Gisser 1985, for a discussion of the application of this more general doctrine to the case of smoking.

economic proposition, Buchanan (1970) argues that, if fully informed people would be willing to buy the product in preference to all others on the market, then we would be making them worse off (in preference—which for him equates to welfare—terms) by banning that product from the market.

One quick way around this argument is to reject "willingness to pay"—and preference-based standards, more generally—as a true measure of welfare or utility. It might be argued that, in reckoning costs and benefits, we should deal in terms of interests, not wants. Sometimes, as with cigarettes, people subjectively want what will objectively harm them. To pander to their wants in such cases would compromise their welfare and undermine their utility.

Certainly there would be little difficulty in establishing health (or life, anyway) as a Rawlsian "primary good," a necessary means that is a prerequisite for accomplishing any more particular ends that people might have. In that sense, health is indeed an "interest" that people have, whether they know it or not; and their welfare (or, anyway, their stock of resources for obtaining welfare) is indeed increased by any measures protecting their health.

Having established that health is among a person's interests, though, that argument fails to establish how we should trade off that interest for others on their behalf. Indeed, the method by which that argument established health as among one's interests (rationalizing it as a necessary means to one's other ends) inevitably legitimizes one in overriding one's health interests in pursuit of those other goals. It would be obviously absurd to let pursuit of a goal valued merely as a means get in the way of pursuit of the ends it is valued as a means toward. Thus, we may have grounds for paternalistically overriding the judgments of people who irrationally profess no interest at all in their health. We have none for overriding the judgment of people who suppose that there are pleasures (mountain climbing, racing, smoking, or whatever) that they think worth risking their health to pursue (Dworkin 1972/1983, p. 33; Wikler 1978/1983, p. 41).

The short way around the microeconomic argument being blocked, we are obliged to take a longer path. One starts from the observation that cigarette sales are substantially price inelastic. Estimates of just how inelastic vary.[28] But much evidence suggests that even rather large increases in the price of the product (induced, e.g., by increased excise taxes) result in only slight decreases in sales to adult consumers. We might infer either of two conclusions from that fact. One would be that there is an enormous "consumer's surplus" (subjective benefit, net of subjective cost) that smokers enjoy, which even large taxes would not extinguish. Price inelasticity would then be taken as evidence that there are substantial subjective gains to consumers from smoking, which ought to be set off against the calculated social costs in any utilitarian decision procedure. Which would predominate we cannot say in advance. But other things being equal, utilitarians ought be more inclined to allow smoking the more satisfaction consumers derive from it.

Alternatively, we might infer from price inelasticity that people are indeed addicted to the product (Atkinson 1974; Wikler 1978/1983, p. 48; Woodfield 1984, p. 120). Present users will pay any price for cigarettes for the same reason they will pay any price for heroin: they cannot help themselves. Most of them

28. In Maynard and Kennan's (1981, p. 39) survey, they vary from zero to −1.8919 with the majority of estimates falling in the −0.35 to −0.80 range. Lewit, Coate, and Grossman (1981) find price elasticities vary dramatically by age, being high among younger smokers (−1.40 for twelve- to seventeen-year-olds, and −0.89 for twenty- to twenty-five-year-olds) but low among older, more established smokers (−0.45 to −0.47 for the rest).

would rather not, according to surveys. Most wish they were not hooked but backslide every time they try to get unhooked.

There is, admittedly, a bit of a problem in determining what should count as a "benefit" to addicts. In one sense, they benefit from having their habits serviced—certainly they would suffer in some obvious sense otherwise. So in a way, the implication of the addiction interpretation would be much the same as that of the consumer surplus interpretation, that is, present users benefit, as indicated by their willingness to pay, from smoking. In another way, however, they would benefit—even in terms of subjective preferences—if they were to stop. In the same terms, others would benefit if they were never to start.

Addictive substances are not ordinary economic goods. Ordinarily, cultivating new tastes (acquiring a taste for fine foods, e.g.) is thought to make you better off—able to derive more pleasure—than before. With addictions, however, you are worse off, even in your own eyes, than before (Stigler and Becker 1977); whatever momentary pleasures you derive from servicing the addiction, you would prefer to stop but find that you cannot. Thus, we should do whatever we can to prevent new addicts, who would be subjectively worse off once addicted than they were before. As regards existing addicts, there may be a utilitarian case for continuing to service their habits (Oken 1985; Lundberg and Knoll 1986), though even they would be subjectively better off in the long run if they could be helped to break the habit (Schelling 1986a, p. 552).

Whereas the first rejoinder to the utilitarian argument for curbing smoking alleges an underestimate of consumer benefits from smoking, a second rejoinder alleges an overestimate of net social costs. The less interesting versions of this argument point to the tobacco industry's contribution to the aggregate economy—but a contribution of $3.3 billion to the Gross National Product, set off against the $52–$62 billion cost estimates described above, leave the industry's account well in the red (cf. Gray and Walter 1986, p. 254).

A more interesting version of this argument alleges that the above procedures overstate true social costs. As regards the narrow question of health care costs, everyone dies of something sooner or later. For an accurate assessment of the medical costs of smoking-related diseases, then, we must deduct the costs that would have been incurred had the people killed by smoking died of something else later (Wikler 1978/1983, p. 46). In terms of hospital bed days and overall medical expenditure, over the course of their lives as a whole, there is some evidence to suggest that there may be no significant difference between smokers and nonsmokers (Leu and Schaub 1983; Weinkam, Rosenbaum, and Sterling 1987; cf. Rice et al. 1986, pp. 502–4).

Similarly, perhaps we need not worry too much about externalities, in the sense of the unfair imposition of burdens on others. Smokers could be refused treatment in public hospital beds and made to pay their own way. They could be required to carry complete insurance against smoking-related diseases; and to avoid unfairness to coinsureds, we could further require that risks to smokers be pooled only with those of other smokers (Wikler 1978/1983, p. 49), as is increasingly done by insurance companies for purely commercial reasons, anyway. Alternatively, and perhaps more practically, "users of cigarettes and alcohol . . . could be made to pay an excise tax, the proceeds of which would cover the costs of treatment for lung cancer and other resulting illnesses" (Wikler 1978/1983, p. 49; see also Garner 1977 and Gewirth 1980, p. 125).

In those narrow terms, at least, smokers already more than pay their own way. In the United Kingdom, the cigarette tax accounts for over 8 percent of total government revenue (Preston 1971; Wilkinson 1986, chap. 8). It has been estimated that in Ontario it takes only 8 percent of tobacco tax revenues to pay for all public health care expenditure on smoking-related disease (Stoddart et al. 1986). Even in the United States, if we count only the share of health care costs borne by the federal government, that is almost exactly counterbalanced by the federal excise tax on cigarettes (U.S. OTA 1985)—although there, as in those other cases as well, matters would look very different if we were to count total costs to the economy and society (e.g., lost productivity) as well as just medical costs borne by the government.

In other ways, too, smokers save us money by dying early. Just think: "Smoking tends to cause few problems during a person's productive years and then to kill the individual before the need to provide years of social security and pension payments. From this perspective, the truly burdensome individual may be the unreasonably fit senior citizen who lives on for thirty years after retirement, contributing to the bankruptcy of the social security system, and using up savings that would have reverted to the public purse via inheritance taxes, had an immoderate life-style brought an early death" (Wikler 1978/1983, p. 46; see also Warner 1987b; cf. Schelling 1986a, pp. 556–57).

In the eyes of many, this will appear to be a reductio ad absurdum. What it seems to suggest is nothing less than a thinly veiled form of not-altogether-voluntary euthanasia. Many suppose it is unjust, if not necessarily uneconomic, to encourage people to die off promptly upon their ceasing to be productive members of the work force (cf. Battin 1987).

What this is a reductio of, however, is not the utilitarian calculus but, rather, an economic calculus that serves as such a poor proxy for it. Most people who are already retired would wish to enjoy a long and happy retirement; most people still in the work force would wish the same for themselves and, indeed, for their elders. Those preferences, too, must be factored into any proper calculus of social utility.[29] Once they are, early deaths induced by smoking are almost certain to turn out to be costs rather than benefits in the broader social scale of values.

Policy Options

Insofar as we are impressed with the case against smoking, in terms of harms to smokers themselves, we have six broad policy options available to us.

1. *Self-regulation.*—Tobacco companies could voluntarily restrict their own activities, refraining from advertising in certain ways and from selling to certain people (e.g., children). This, of course, is the companies' preferred option; and it is one that is still relied upon, albeit decreasingly (or as a precursor to legislation), in over a third of the OECD and in many other countries around the world (Cox and Smith 1984; Roemer 1986). Self-regulation is elevated to an art form in Britain and Australia, particularly, where most advertising and promotion of

29. Indeed, in light of those preferences, perhaps what we should regard as an external social cost is not being able to pay pensions to the prematurely deceased rather than having to pay pensions to those who live to a ripe old age. In the slightly purple prose of Schelling (1986a, p. 557), "We do not hope that 60-year-old fishermen die at sea, that 60-year-olds neglect seat belts and die in their automobiles, or that 60-year-old marital difficulties lead to suicide or homicide. . . . That people who die at retirement age bequeath more than they cost" is irrelevant to our assessment of their deaths as tragedies, and so too with smokers. "We would not be true to our own values if we . . . excused them from smoking and let them die to our benefit. That is simply not the attitude that we take toward untimely death."

tobacco products is restricted by no more than a set of "voluntary agreements" between the industry and the government. In Britain, even warning labels are the subject of mere voluntary agreements (Taylor 1985, chap. 5; Baggot 1986).

These strategies are doubly flawed. First, it is unclear in what sense the agreements are fully voluntary, since they typically are (and apparently can only be) extracted from the industry under threat of legislation if agreement is not forthcoming. Agreements extracted under duress are not voluntary in any sense that contributes to the moral legitimacy of their enforcement. That is not to say that governments have no authority to enforce such codes. It is merely to say that if the government has moral authority to extract agreements in this way, then it has the moral authority to impose the regulations without the industry's agreement (Goodin 1986).

Second, self-regulation is to a large extent tantamount to no regulation. There is anecdotal evidence aplenty for this conclusion. Frequent and flagrant violations of voluntary agreements are reported, with little apparent effect, in both Britain (Taylor 1985, chaps. 6–8; Roberts 1986; Wilkinson 1986, chap. 10) and Australia (Coleman 1985; Grabosky and Braithwaite 1986). A more systematic comparison of fifteen OECD countries' experience confirms that countries with legislation have reduced tobacco consumption by almost consistently twice as much as those relying upon self-regulation and voluntary agreements alone (Cox and Smith 1984, p. 578).

2. *Torts.*—Tobacco companies, like all other members of the community, are responsible at common law for any damage they do to others. Tort suits against manufacturers for wrongful death and injury are now increasingly common. It has long been thought that they were on solid legal ground and that it was only a matter of time before one succeeded (Garner 1980; Edell and Gisser 1985; AMA 1986; Daynard, Popper, and Gruzalski 1986). Now that one trial jury has found for the plaintiff, awarding $400,000 in damages, other plaintiff victories will no doubt follow.[30] But the problems plaintiffs have heretofore experienced nonetheless indicate the limits to this as an overall strategy for dealing with the problem (Garner 1980; Daynard 1988).

Central to a tort claim is proof of causation. Even under the sternest rules of liability, plaintiffs can recover against someone only if they can prove that that agent caused the harm that they suffered. Typically, cancers admit of multiple causes and arise only after long latency periods. Any given person's lung cancer might have been caused by smoking, by workplace contaminants, by genetic endowment, or by some combination of all of those. In tort law, of course, the standard of proof is merely "more probable than not"; so plaintiffs do not have to prove "beyond a reasonable doubt" that cigarettes caused their cancer. But proving that they are twice as likely as anything else to have caused it (which is what the 50 percent rule often comes down to) might be almost as arduous.

What we should be doing, of course, is apportioning blame among all causal factors, and assessing fractional liability to each. If there are four things that

30. The landmark case was Cipollone v. Liggett Group, Inc., decided in the U.S. District Court for New Jersey (see Janson 1988). One measure of the widely perceived likelihood of large numbers of successful tort suits, even prior to that victory, is the discount that financial markets have been applying to tobacco company stocks: in 1987, they were valued over 35 percent less than they should have been worth on the basis of their profit/earnings ratio alone (Cohen 1987, p. 5).

contributed 25 percent each to a plaintiff's cancer, each defendant should be required to pay 25 percent of the award that the plaintiff would have secured had there been but a single cause. Similarly, if it is 25 percent likely that smoking caused a plaintiff's cancer, the plaintiff should recover 25 percent of damages from the tobacco company regardless of the relative probabilities of other causes (Rosenberg 1984; Thomson 1986, chap. 12).

Moves toward some such model of "attributable risk" and "assigned share" are now afoot. But as a strategy for recovery by individual plaintiffs, it may founder on problems of inferring from aggregate data to facts about particular cases (Thomson 1986, chaps. 12 and 13). "Sure," defendants' counsel will say, "in general the statistics are as the plaintiff says; but we are not being sued by a statistical artifact but rather by a particular person. How are we to know that what is true in general is true of this person in particular?" Plaintiffs can go some way toward meeting demands for particularized evidence by factoring into the equation all their personal case histories (family background, work history, etc.). But this still falls somewhat short of ideally individualized evidence of person-to-person harm, of the sort paradigmatic in torts (e.g., in an auto crash). Some juries, rightly or wrongly, will no doubt balk at such evidence, refusing to compensate some people whom statistically they should.

There are two good ways around such problems (Garner 1977). One is to use aggregate-level statistical evidence to generate a "rebuttable presumption" that smokers' cancer is caused by their smoking, unless defendants can prove otherwise in any given case. (The Black Lung Benefits Act of 1972 imposed a similar rebuttable presumption against mine owners.) A second alternative is to have victims of smoking-related diseases transfer their tort claims to welfare agencies bearing the costs (medical care, disability/survivors' benefits, etc.) of their illnesses; welfare agencies can then mount tort suits against manufacturers for the total aggregate harm done by smoking, and in such suits aggregate-level statistical proof is obviously relevant in a way it might not be in case-by-case adjudication. (The Social Security Amendments of 1974 similarly require deserted mothers receiving AFDC to transfer their claims to child support to welfare agencies, who are then responsible for recovering payments from delinquent fathers.) How far either strategy can or will be applied against cigarette manufacturers remains to be seen, though.

Then there is the further matter of "negligence." Of course, we might argue that tobacco companies should be held strictly liable for anything that happens when people consume their products. They had the capacity to test them in the laboratory, in a way that consumers could not have done. If using the product as intended kills 25 percent of its users then there is a case for considering it an "ultra-hazardous product" and for imposing strict liability in consequence (AMA 1986; cf. "Plaintiffs' Conduct" 1986).[31]

Failing that, victims will be able to claim compensation only if they can prove that manufacturers were somehow negligent.[32] For that, plaintiffs will have to

31. Paradoxically, strict liability is imposed for "design defects" (failing to manufacture a product according to specifications) but not for defective designs.

32. Under the old-fashioned rule of "contributory negligence," plaintiffs would have also to prove that they were not themselves negligent in any way. That rule has now been supplanted by rules of "comparative negligence," allowing the Cipollone family to recover 20 percent of damages against Liggett, even though Rose Cipollone was deemed 80 percent

prove that there was information about health hazards of smoking that tobacco companies knew or should have known that would have led a reasonable man to take precautions in the manufacture and sale of the product (including, ultimately, withdrawing the product from the market).[33] Such arguments might go a long way, just on the basis of what tobacco companies should have known about the hazards of smoking from the published scientific literature. Even more compelling, though, are arguments based on companies' own early in-house research showing the carcinogenic properties of tobacco smoke: it is very difficult for companies to claim that they did not know of the evidence, or that they gave it no credence, when it came from their own scientific officers. Just such evidence emerged in the course of recent litigation of *Cipollone v. Liggett* and is now in the public domain and available for use by subsequent litigants (Bremner 1988; Gray 1988; Mintz 1988a, 1988b). Should that prove insufficient to secure judgment, however, it is bound to be even more difficult to secure the production of yet more such damaging documents.

In short, the products liability approach to remedying smoking harms through the tort law is perfectly laudable. But it is only a very imperfect solution to the overall problem.

3. *Taxation.*—Taxing cigarettes is a particularly popular way of controlling smoking overall, in the United States, Britain, and elsewhere. Judging from the evidence summarized above about the price inelasticity of cigarettes, tax-induced price rises alone may do little to curb smoking among existing adult users. The order of magnitude of probable effects is effectively indicated by British calculations that, assuming an elasticity of −0.5, it would take more than a 50 percent increase in cigarette prices to reduce cigarette sales by even 20 percent (Atkinson and Townsend 1977, p. 492).[34]

What tax-induced price rises might do is make the habit substantially less attractive to teenagers not yet addicted to the drug. Precisely the same people

---

responsible for her own death. But in half the states, these rules are written in such a way that if the plaintiff is more negligent than the defendant he cannot recover anything at all (rather than merely limiting him to recovery of less than half his total losses, as the logic of the rule surely suggests); see Cohen 1987, p. 9.

33. Indeed, if the evidence shows "reckless disregard" for customer safety in the face of compelling evidence of probable harm, there might be grounds for an "intentional tort" action and punitive damages—or perhaps even criminal proceedings for manslaughter. That day might not be far off. In Cipollone v. Liggett, federal judge Lee Sarokin refused the defendant's plea to quash the plaintiff's claim for punitive damages, saying that more than enough evidence had been produced from the company's own files to show a "callous, wanton, willful and reckless disregard" for the health of consumers; he went on to say that tobacco companies had "entered into a sophisticated conspiracy . . . to refute, undermine and neutralize information coming from the scientific and medical community and to confuse and mislead the consuming public. . . . It is difficult to envision a more compelling case for an award of punitive damages" (Bremner 1988).

34. Cox and Smith's (1984, p. 578) fifteen-nation study of income and price elasticities concludes that "a 'pricing-out' strategy towards smoking control will meet with increasing resistance amongst established smokers." Of course, publicity attendant upon increases in tax levies might indirectly remind people of health risks, and in that way reduce smoking; that is how Leu (1984) explains his interesting finding that smokers' behavior reacts strongly to nominal increases in Swiss cigarette prices induced by tax hikes, even if in inflation-adjusted terms they meant little or no real increase in prices.

whom we most want, on grounds of "informed consent," to prevent from starting to smoke are those who are least able to afford more expensive cigarettes. This a priori expectation is borne out by evidence that demand for cigarettes among teenagers is more than three times as elastic as among adults, on average; and any given price increase is almost six times more likely to make teenagers stop or never start smoking than it would adults (Lewit, Coate, and Grossman 1981).

Morally, the issue is presumably whether it is permissible to use the instrument of taxation for purposes of reducing consumption of a good in such ways. After all, the purpose of taxation is to raise revenue. Some would say that using the instrument for any other purpose is simply inappropriate. At most, it might be a happy coincidence if as a by-product of raising revenue by taxing drugs their consumption falls (Mill 1859/1975, pp. 123–24; Wikler 1987, p. 335).

Certainly it is true that taxation always needs to be justified. After all, the power to tax is the power to destroy. It is also true that the state's need for revenue to pursue its legitimate purposes provides one such justification. It is not the only possible justification, though. Mill (1859/1975, p. 123) says that "to tax stimulants for the sole purpose of making them more difficult to be obtained, is a measure differing only in degree from their entire prohibition; and would be justifiable only if that were justifiable."[35] But sometimes we are justified in destroying, in whole or in part, some sort of product or activity. The above arguments suggest that this is the case with smoking, for example. The same arguments that justify us in restricting the activity in general justify us in doing so through swingeing taxes, in particular.

The problems with the taxation strategy are political, not moral. Through it, we give one powerful bureaucratic actor—the Treasury—a substantial interest in continuingly large volumes of cigarette sales. There is a risk, which has become a reality intermittently from the time of King James I onward (Harrison 1986), of financial considerations dominating health ones in the counsels of state (Breslow 1982, pp. 130–31; Taylor 1985, chap. 8; Wilkinson 1986, chap. 8).[36]

4. *Publicity.*—Mandatory health warnings on cigarette packages and advertisements, and public health campaigns more generally, are another popular government response to smoking. Some thirty-eight countries now require such warnings (Roemer 1986, pp. 7–8). Among the more important reasons for the popularity of this strategy is that health warnings and public information campaigns are seen as the least paternalistic forms of government intervention.[37] Mill (1859/1975, p. 118) himself holds that "labelling [a] drug with some word expressive of its dangerous character, may be enforced without violation of liberty," since presumably "the buyer cannot wish not to know that the thing he possesses has poisonous qualities." In this judgment, Mill has been followed by a host of more

35. Strictly speaking, that must be untrue. The difference of degree might matter: we might be morally justified in partly destroying something, without being morally justified in destroying it completely.

36. More precisely, this gives the Treasury an incentive to oppose reductions in tobacco consumption accomplished through any means other than increased taxation. "As long as the price elasticity is less than one, the revenue will certainly increase when the tax goes up—since the fall in consumption is more than offset by the extra tax paid by those who continue to smoke" (Atkinson and Townsend 1977, p. 492).

37. Even there, though, some protest the paternalistic bossiness of public health campaigns run by medics, who are in the habit of issuing orders and prescriptions and expecting them to be carried out to the letter (Meenan 1976).

recent commentators (Feinberg 1971/1983, p. 11; Wikler 1978/1983, pp. 52–53; Littlechild and Wiseman 1984, p. 66; Buchanan 1970, p. 72; Daniels 1985, p. 158; Littlechild 1986, pp. 275–76).

No doubt publicizing health risks reduces smoking. Publication of the two great official reports—by the Royal College of Physicians in 1962 and the surgeon general in 1964—produced long-term drops in cigarette consumption by between 7 percent and 14 percent (Atkinson and Skegg 1973; Leventhal and Cleary 1980, p. 381; Warner 1981). The antismoking television advertisements, allowed under the Fairness Doctrine in the United States until the 1970 legislation banning television advertising of cigarettes altogether, seemed to have an effect almost twice as strong (Hamilton 1972, p. 406).[38]

There are reasons to believe that health campaigns cannot work in isolation from other policy initiatives, though. Specifically, allowing cigarette advertising undercuts health messages by inducing newspapers and magazines to engage in self-censorship of health reports that might offend their tobacco sponsors (Smith 1978; Warner 1985; Warner et al. 1986). Thus, a publicity campaign might not really succeed unless coupled with something stronger: an advertising ban. Otherwise the message simply might not get carried effectively.

5. *Bans.*—There are, in fact, various regulatory options under this general heading. Most modestly, we might ban cigarette advertising, either in particular settings (e.g., on television) or in general. More dramatically, we might ban sales of cigarettes, either to a certain group (e.g., children) or in general. Most dramatically, we might ban use of tobacco, either in particular settings (e.g., where there is a particular fire hazard, as in elevators, theaters, and subways, or where there are synergistic effects with other substances in the immediate vicinity, such as asbestos) or in general.

These are separable policy options, any one of which can be pursued independently of any other. From 1975, Norway has banned advertising but not sale of cigarettes. Similarly, we can ban sale without banning consumption. (Most states allow you to eat game birds and fish you shoot or catch yourself but not to sell them.) Though there is no modern experience of a general ban on sale or use of tobacco, advertising bans are reasonably common: fifteen countries have total bans, and another twelve have strong partial bans (Roemer 1986, pp. 7–8).

Advertising bans can be particularly helpful in reducing cigarette consumption among adolescents, with whom we should be especially concerned on grounds of "informed consent." There is good evidence that cigarette advertising in general, and sport sponsorship in particular, appeals to children (Aitken, Leather, and O'Hagan 1985; Aitken, Leather, O'Hagan, and Squair 1987; Chapman and Fitzgerald 1982; Ledwith 1984; Warner et al. 1986). Conversely, banning advertising of cigarettes in Norway in 1975 led to a sharp decline in the percentage of teenagers who subsequently became daily smokers (Chapman 1985, pp. 16–18; BMA 1986; Warner et al. 1986, p. 372).

38. Schneider, Klein, and Murphy (1981) argue that models used to generate those results are misspecified; on their revised estimates, the cumulative effects of the 1953 American Cancer Society and 1964 surgeon general reports were to reduce tobacco consumption by 25 percent and antismoking commercials by another 5 percent. Note that their dependent variable—tobacco consumption—can be reduced by shifts to filter cigarettes (as happened especially in the post-1953 period) as well as by reductions in cigarette consumption per se.

Against bans on the use or sale of tobacco, the Prohibition analogy is standardly urged.[39] Already we have evidence of substantial "bootlegging" (or "buttlegging") of cigarettes between states with low cigarette taxes and those with high ones (Manchester 1976; U.S. ACIR 1977). Any more serious ban on sale or use of tobacco would no doubt lead to even more illicit activity of this sort. Even accepting such slippage, however, this strategy is still bound to reduce smoking substantially. Whether more would be lost in terms of respect for the law than would be gained in terms of public health remains an open question.

6. *Medicalization.*—If smoking tobacco is addictive, then perhaps a medical rather than legal or economic response is indicated. The idea here would be to make tobacco a prescription drug, available to registered users only.[40] The model would be methadone maintenance programs for heroin addicts, perhaps. The aim in making tobacco a prescription drug would be to respond humanely to the needs of present addicts, while discouraging new users. Again, it would be impossible to stop all new users—they can always smoke the cigarettes of registered users illicitly, unless we require registered users to smoke only in the clinics. But again, such a policy would have a strong tendency in the desired direction.

HARM TO OTHERS

The Nature of the Risks

Broadly speaking, there are three classes of negative effects on others arising from a person's smoking. Two are clearly harms. The third is of only a slightly different character.

First, there is the well-established harm to the fetus inflicted by the mother's smoking (Cushner 1981; U.S. DHEW 1976, chap. 5; U.S. DHHS 1980, pp. 189–250). The extent of the effects, and the mechanism by which they are produced, is obvious. The only real question, perhaps, is whether mother and fetus really are two separate people yet, especially in the first trimester that is so crucial for the fetus's development.

Second, there is the harm to others arising from "passive smoking," that is, the inhalation of "sidestream" smoke from the burning tip of a lit cigarette and of smoke exhaled by a nearby smoker. The technical literature on this subject, though less overwhelming in sheer bulk weight than that on the direct effects of smoking on smokers, is nonetheless voluminous and increasingly compelling in its conclusions.[41] Again, the best guides to the settled scientific view are official

39. Mill 1859/1975, pp. 108–10; Schelling 1980, p. 110; Breslow 1982, p. 140; Littlechild and Wiseman 1984, p. 64; Lundberg and Knoll 1986. The analogy has more historical warrant than those employing it realize. The same moralizing fervor that led to the prohibition of the sale of alcohol also led to bans on the sale of cigarettes. At their peak, such bans were found in twelve states, but by 1927 they were all swept away, largely in reaction to Prohibition (U.S. DHHS 1986, p. 267).

40. Ironically, nicotine-containing chewing gum is a controlled prescription drug in the United States, United Kingdom, Sweden, and Canada, whereas wet snuff (whose risks are, if anything, greater) is freely available over the counter to adult purchasers (Kozlowski et al. 1982). Czechoslovakia now requires consumers of twenty or more cigarettes per day to register with the medical service that monitors respiratory diseases, perhaps as a first step in this "medicalization" direction (*Daily Express*, London, February 17, 1986).

41. Again, statistical purists might question causal claims based merely on epidemiological evidence (Burch 1986). Here, however, there is no possible source of multicolinearity nearly so plausible as genotype in the case of direct smoking. Repace and Lowrey (1986) rightly

reports, dated 1986, from both the National Academy of Sciences and the U.S. surgeon general.[42] They report that chemical analysis shows sidestream smoke to be richer in known carcinogens than the smoke actually inhaled by smokers themselves (U.S. DHHS 1986, pp. 134–37). Furthermore, evidence (from, e.g., studies of nonsmoking wives living with smoking husbands) shows that passive smokers run a 34 percent greater risk of lung cancer (U.S. NAS 1986b, p. 231; U.S. DHHS 1986, chap. 2).[43] That is a large increase in a tiny initial probability, of course, so the absolute number of people thus reckoned to die annually from passive smoking is rather small: anything from several hundred to a few thousand, depending upon how many nonsmokers actually are exposed regularly to smoke-filled environments. Those numbers are "small but not negligible" (Froggatt 1988, par. 69). Even by that modest count, passive smoking would still constitute a greater risk to life than that posed by all airborne pollutants regulated by the Environmental Protection Agency, asbestos excepted (Repace and Lowrey 1985, p. 12). Passive smoking also aggravates a number of other conditions (among them bronchitis, asthma, emphysema, angina, and allergies), and it causes irritation of the eyes, nose, and throat that can be especially severe in particularly sensitive individuals (U.S. NAS 1986b pp. 176, 214; U.S. DHHS 1986, chap. 2).

All of those are "real harms"—real health hazards imposed on one person by another's smoking nearby. Third, there are the mere disamenities that nonsmokers experience when breathing others' smoke. As the Royal College of Physicians (1983, p. 79) argues, whether or not passive smoking damages health, "there is already sufficient evidence as to the discomfort and annoyance that breathing other people's smoke can cause. Non-smokers at work and play, in transport and in public places, should have the right not to be so exposed."

Emitting offensive odors, when done by a factory, is subject to public regulation. In Malaysia, it is illegal to carry the evil-smelling durian fruit on public transportation. Many nonsmokers (especially ex-smokers) find the smell of burning tobacco similarly offensive, and it might therefore be banned on similar grounds. Here, even Mill (1859/1975, p. 120) can be enlisted in support: "There are many acts which, being directly injurious only to the agents themselves, ought not to be legally interdicted, but which, if done publicly, are a violation of good manners, and coming thus within the category of offences against others, may rightfully be prohibited." Primary among the examples Mill has in mind here are "offences against decency"—sin, blasphemy, and such like. But he goes on to say that the

---

scoff at the utter absurdity of any suggestion that the apparent link between passive smoking and lung cancer might arise because nonsmokers who are prone to lung cancer are biologically driven to marry smokers, while nonsmokers who are resistant to cancer are led to marry nonsmokers. Or, again, self-reports of smoking behavior might be unreliable; but there is no reason to suppose that spouses of smokers would be differentially prone to underreport or deny their smoking, as compared to spouses of nonsmokers (if anything, the reverse seems more likely, leading to an underestimate rather than an overestimate of the true effects of passive smoking).

42. For a gloss on these results written by one of the pioneers of this line of research expressly for philosophers, see Repace 1985.

43. Though settling on the 34 percent figure, the NAS reports that respectable studies have estimated the risk as ranging between 14 percent and 66 percent (U.S. NAS 1986b, p. 47). That leads the surgeon general to say that the question is not whether passive smoking causes cancer—on that, the evidence is clear—but merely how much cancer it causes (U.S. DHHS 1986, p. 10; see similarly Froggatt 1988, par. 68).

moral case against offensive behavior in public is "equally strong" even where (as is presumably the case with smoking) the "actions [are] not in themselves condemnable, nor supposed to be so."

"Offense," of course, is not quite harm, though it may be the first cousin to it. That makes it a notoriously tricky notion to fit into the essentially harm-based rationales central to standard moral and legal justifications for social regulation (Feinberg 1985). In such schemes, "harmless immoralities" are ordinarily deemed permissible—especially when they touch upon values of free speech and expression—whether or not others are offended by them. Certainly we have grievous qualms about letting the notion of "offense" range so widely as to ban sexually explicit plays, politically pointed protest, or interracial marriage in the deep South. We are nonetheless comfortable in regulating, as "offensive nuisances," smelly or noisy factories. They may be "mere nuisances," posing no real harms to health, but showing that they are a nuisance is more than enough to justify us in restricting what they may do and where they may do it, according to some larger calculation of social utility.

So too, perhaps, with smoking. After all, nonsmokers are in an increasingly large majority among the population, outnumbering smokers three to one (Helyar 1987). Insofar as they find smoking similarly a public nuisance, we might appeal to similar standards to justify its regulation as we do to justify regulation of smelly factories. Showing "real harm" to health is always a stronger argument for regulation, of course; and there is evidence of that, too, as shown above. The point here is just that that might not be strictly necessary. The nuisance argument might in itself suffice.

The Right to Smoke and the Right to Breathe

The argument for restricting smoking in enclosed public spaces is characteristically couched in deontological terms of the rights of nonsmokers to clean air (WHO 1986). The issue has been joined on this high deontological plane from the other side, too. The tobacco industry's UK pressure group, the Tobacco Advisory Council, maintains that smokers also enjoy a right to smoke, and that "neither group [smokers or nonsmokers] has any absolute right to dictate to the other" (TAC 1987; cf. Wikler 1987, p. 354.)

I take it that the rights-based argument can be settled, presumptively at least, in favor of the nonsmoker. In the old adage, your freedom stops at the end of my nose; and in the case of environmental tobacco smoke, your smoke obviously transgresses the privacy of my nasal passages. "Just as my bodily integrity is violated by a punch in the nose, so too is it threatened by toxins and carcinogens others place in the environment. . . . Just as I have a rights claim against those who would punch me in the nose, so too I have one against those who would batter my lungs" (Daniels 1985, p. 151; see also Gibson 1985). The surgeon general has rightly concluded, "The right of smokers to smoke ends where their behavior affects the health and well-being of others; . . . the choice to smoke cannot interfere with the non-smoker's right to breathe air free of tobacco smoke" (U.S. DHHS 1986, p. xii).

In this way, we can break down the apparent symmetry between the loss that would be suffered by the smoker, denied the pleasures of tobacco to spare the nonsmoker, and those that would be suffered by the nonsmoker, denied the pleasures of clean air to indulge the smoker. "Each interferes with the other," it is true. But the nonsmoker "merely wishes to breathe unpolluted air and, in the pursuit thereof, and unlike the smoker, does not reduce the amenity of others" in so doing. "The conflict of interest does not arise from *reciprocal* effects and does not imply equal culpability. The conflict arises from the damage inflicted by one of the parties on the other" (Mishan 1967, p. 280). The symmetry suggested by the "right to smoke versus the right to clean air" formulation is thus illusory. The crucial asymmetry is that the smoker would be neither better nor worse off if the nonsmoker did not exist, whereas the nonsmoker would be better off if the smoker (qua smoker) did not exist.[44]

At root, the grounds for assigning priority to the right to breathe clean air are simply that everyone—smoker and nonsmoker alike—needs this right in order to flourish. The point is effectively evoked by a fanciful example offered by James Repace (1985, p. 27): "Suppose that individual nonsmokers, in defense of their asserted right to breathe tobacco-smoke-free indoor air, were to release a gas into indoor spaces where they were forced to breathe tobacco smoke. Suppose further that when sucked through the burning cone of a cigarette, pipe, or cigar this gas decomposed into irritating byproducts which cause moderate to intense discomfort to the smoker, much the way ambient tobacco smoke affects the nonsmoker. Would smokers feel that they had the inalienable right to gas-free air?" If so, they must concede that nonsmokers have a right to smoke-free air, a right which takes priority over their right to smoke.

Some might say that the analogy is not a perfect one. For example, it might be argued that, unlike the antismoker gas bomber, the smoker is not intentionally harming anyone. The gas bomber actually intends to discomfort anyone who lights up a cigarette in the room. The discomfort caused to others by smokers' smoking is regarded, even by smokers themselves, as an unfortunate by-product of their smoking; they would happily remove that side effect if they could do so, without undue cost or discomfort to themselves.

To this claim, the antismoker gas bomber might reply that he does not intend to harm anyone, either. Smokers will be discomforted by his gas only if they smoke. If they refrain from smoking, they will not be harmed in the slightest. Furthermore, the gas bomber might continue, if they do smoke then nonsmokers would have been analogously discomforted. The gas bomb can thus be construed as an act of self-defense which, though preemptive, has the endearing property of harming potential aggressors only if and when they turn into actual ones.

Some such argument might establish a presumptive priority of the right to clean air over the right to smoke. Like all presumptions, however, this one can always be overcome—in this case, in either of two ways.[45] One is to show that

44. The more familiar case—equally ill formulated as a conflict of rights—of the mugger and his victim is just a more extreme case of this pattern. Not only would the victim be better off if the mugger (qua mugger) did not exist, but the mugger would actually be worse off if his victim did not exist to be robbed (cf. Kelman 1979, p. 791).

45. Both are in play in the contrasting case of the automobile driver. Nondrivers in a congested city are forced to breathe noxious fumes emitted as the by-products of others' driving, just as nonsmokers in an enclosed space are forced to breathe noxious fumes emitted as the by-products of others' smoking. In both cases, the by-products are unintended and undesired by the perpetrators; in both cases, they would happily remove them if they could do so costlessly. Yet we are not nearly so tempted to ban or restrict driving as we are to ban or restrict smoking. The reason is that cars are a necessary part of commerce which is necessary, in turn, for the well-being of all; cigarettes are not. In the first instance, that argument works in cost-benefit terms. But since people might reasonably be presumed to consent to arrangements that are so clearly beneficial to them, it might also serve to ground a consent-based argument, as well.

nonsmokers have voluntarily consented to others' smoking. The other is to show, through a calculation of costs and benefits, that the losses to smokers who are stopped from smoking would far exceed the losses to nonsmokers who are exposed to environmental tobacco smoke. Each of these possibilities will be considered, and rejected, in turn.

The Voluntariness of Passive Smoking

In the case of the smoker, it could (wrongly, as we have seen) be argued that the risks were somehow voluntarily incurred. In the case of the passive smoker, that argument would be far harder to sustain. Passive smokers do not themselves light up. They merely breathe. You can voluntarily choose to do something only if you can, realistically, choose not to do it; and no one can choose not to breathe. Since passive smoking—or, more technically, "exposure to environmental tobacco smoke"—"generally occurs as an unavoidable consequence of being in proximity to smokers, particularly in enclosed indoor environments," the surgeon general prefers simply to define passive smoking as "involuntary smoking" (U.S. DHHS 1986, p. 6).

Smokers might sometimes have sought and been granted the permission of all nonsmokers in the vicinity for them to light up. Assuming that that consent was given freely (i.e., that it was not a tyrannical boss 'asking' permission of a secretary) and that it was based on full information about the hazards of passive smoking, nonsmokers' exposure to environmental tobacco smoke would indeed then be voluntary. Given the dangers of duress and of fraudulent claims that rights have been waived, we may prefer to treat the right to clean air as if it were as inalienable as the right to life itself. But in any case, this whole voluntary waiver scenario is plausible only among moderately small groups of people.

Among larger and more anonymous groups, the only sense in which passive smoking might be thought to be voluntary would be insofar as people voluntarily enter environments they knew were or would become smoky. Thus, it might be argued that if people do not want to breathe other people's smoke, they should not go into notoriously smoky places like English pubs.

There is, of course, the question of why nonsmokers should banish themselves rather than smokers controlling themselves. In any case, there is a range of places it is unreasonable to expect people to avoid going (Gibson 1985, pp. 156–57). One is to work. Another is onto public transportation. Another is into public buildings. Another, perhaps, is to public entertainments (restaurants, theaters, and such like).[46] If people cannot reasonably be expected to avoid going to work, and getting there by public transportation, then the Humean doctrine ("no consent without the possibility of withholding consent") would imply that they have not voluntarily consented to the risks of passive smoking in those places, either.

46. There is indeed a place for the public/private distinction here. If people who have chartered an aircraft privately want to allow smoking, that is rightly regarded as their prerogative under the new U.S. regulations. Similarly, the government ought to hesitate to apply smoking restrictions to genuinely private clubs, even if they provide their members with entertainment facilities (restaurants, theaters, etc.) that would otherwise fall under such restrictions. The difference, in both cases, lies in what it is to participate fully in the life of the community. It would be unreasonable—it would unduly restrict people in their participation in social life—to tell people who do not like others' smoking that they should refrain from riding city buses, or going into the city hall, or going to the public cinema. Private activities are truly optional, by contrast. No one needs to ride a chartered airplane or to dine in a private club to participate fully as a member of our society.

Costs and Benefits

Even if we suppose that the issue is properly couched in terms of rights—and especially if we do not—a calculation of the costs and benefits to all interested parties under all policy options is nonetheless relevant. Some rights violations matter more than others, after all. It would be a violation of bodily integrity for someone else to force smoke into your lungs. It would equally be a violation of bodily integrity for someone else to brush against your arm, yet few courts would take cognizance of that invasion. Technically, it might count as a case of assault, but the law does not deal in trifles, as the saying goes. Neither should public policy.

When deciding which rights violations matter most, we tend to employ a rough-and-ready utilitarian calculus of a sort, taking into account both costs to the violated and benefits to the violator. In that calculus, the former weighs particularly heavily. If rights holders have suffered serious harm, then rights violators have wronged them, almost regardless of whatever benefits the rights violators themselves stood to gain (or losses to avert). Thus, insofar as the case against passive smoking can be made in terms of increased lung cancer and other potentially grave illnesses, the deontological case is once again quickly closed. But insofar as the stakes are more modest—offensive odors and watery eyes—we would have to take seriously into account costs and benefits to both parties, on the model of nuisance law, for example (Feinberg 1985, chap. 8).

Dealing in straight utilitarian terms, the case against passive smoking is necessarily less strong than that against direct smoking. That is simply because the passive smoker gets only a small fraction of the dose of poisonous substances that is received by the active smoker. A smoker's chances of lung cancer are increased by 980 percent, a passive smoker's by only 34 percent; and so on. Since the costs of passive smoking are necessarily lower than those of active smoking, there is more of a chance that the benefits there might outweigh the costs, in a utilitarian calculus.

As before, one easy way to meet this challenge is to conceptualize "benefits" in terms of interests rather than of preferences. However much smokers might want to smoke, it is not in their interests to do so. We are doing them a favor—conferring upon them an objective health benefit—by stopping them from smoking, even for a little while (Repace 1985, p. 27). But such arguments are subject, once again, to the rejoinders found devastating in the section, "Do the Benefits Outweigh the Costs?" in my discussion of "Harm to Self" above.

If dealing in preference-based terms, we must take account of the severity of the characteristic reactions involved: of smokers forced to suffer withdrawal for the period of time they would be constrained from smoking, on the one hand; of nonsmokers forced to suffer environmental tobacco smoke for the period of time they would be closeted with it, on the other. Of course, variable physiology on both sides means that some people will suffer more than others. Not all smokers would suffer withdrawal during a two-hour flight; not all nonsmokers would mind the smoke all that much. But most smokers would probably suffer some withdrawal symptoms over the course of a whole day at work, and surveys show that most nonsmokers suffer at least eye, nose, and throat irritation from being subjected to day-long smoking in an enclosed office. Fine-grained interpersonal utility comparisons are notoriously difficult, but it would seem that those two are roughly on a par. Smokers might usually be bothered marginally more, but probably only marginally more, at least once they have had a chance to adjust as fully as they can to the new nonsmoking regime.[47]

What is not on a par, and what decisively favors regulation of smoking in enclosed spaces, is the magnitude of the possible suffering by each party.[48] At worst, the smoker prevented from smoking suffers discomfort. The nonsmoker exposed to environmental tobacco smoke for a prolonged period might, at worst, suffer lung cancer or other debilitating diseases (Gibson 1985, p. 155; U.S. NAS 1986a, pp. 151–52). That is not the most common outcome, by a long stretch. But in light of other less risky airborne contaminants that the Environmental Protection Agency does regulate, it certainly is a common enough outcome to take seriously in framing policies.[49]

The second crucial element in a Benthamite calculus is the number of people affected, on both sides. Nonsmokers now outnumber smokers in the United States by a ratio of almost three to one (Helyar 1987). That is not a big enough differential to decide matters all by itself, perhaps. But conjoined with the above argument—that smokers will lose something less than three times what nonsmokers will gain from a ban—this fact does prove decisive. Numbers conspire with intensity in arguing for restricting passive smoking (U.S. NAS 1986a, pp. 151–52).[50]

Policy Options

There are, again, several possible policy responses to the problem of passive smoking. Among them are these.

1. *Reduce smoking.*—First and foremost, notice that anything done to reduce smoking will also, simultaneously, reduce passive smoking. Hence, all the policy options outlined under "Harm to Self" above have some relevance here, too.

2. *Self-restraint/courtesy.*—Self-regulation, at the personal level, would amount to self-restraint among smokers to curb the passive smoking they inflict upon

47. In the transition, the smoker may experience much more discomfort than nonsmokers did in the old equilibrium. Transition costs are not be be discounted. But since transitions are short-lived, their costs are at least contained. For that reason, they ought not be exaggerated, either.

48. Another thing, perhaps, is the relative voluntariness of the harms. The risks to the nonsmoker are almost wholly involuntary; the risks to the smoker are, or are widely seen to be, voluntarily incurred. (Doubt has been cast on this perception above, however.) This distinction is principally of deontological force. But it may have utilitarian bearing, as well, given that the social-acceptability-of-risk studies show that people are prepared to accept voluntary risks one thousand times greater than involuntary ones (Starr 1969).

49. In other words, perhaps we should weight the interests of hypersensitive individuals particularly heavily here. The "egg shell skull" rule operates similarly in tort law (Feinberg 1970, pp. 213–14). Or, again, in democratic theory, we might be happy to let smoking policies be set by majority vote of those concerned in ordinary circumstances, but if one among them were asthmatic we think he ought be given veto rights (Barry 1979, pp. 170–71).

50. Benham (1981, pp. 572–73) thus reports that "when faced with the prospect of actually paying (or being paid) for the property rights to the air during classroom lectures over a semester, nonsmoker students in my classes at Washington University have always placed a larger aggregate value on the air rights than smokers. Nonsmokers in these classes have generally been willing to pay from ten to 100 times as much as the smokers for air rights."

those around them. Ideally, "common sense and natural courtesy" should solve the problem (Littlechild and Wiseman 1984, pp. 60, 66; Littlechild 1986, p. 283); that has "long been the best approach to solving the occasional difference of opinion between smoking and non-smoking employees," as the tobacco industry's pamphlet on workplace smoking policies says (TAC 1987). Ideally, smokers should ask others for permission before lighting up in confined quarters. Ideally, a polite request for them to cease should suffice. As Miss Manners instructs, "If you wish to smoke in the presence of clean people, you must ask their permission and be prepared to accept their refusal to grant it" (Martin 1983, p. 637).

For those smokers who are considerate in such ways, self-restraint is indeed ideal. Not all are, however.[51] Given the nature of addictions, internal sanctions of shame at discourtesy will often be overcome by internal compulsions of nicotine cravings; and, as an example of the theory of cognitive dissonance in action, surveys show that smokers when asked grossly underestimate the extent to which they think nonsmokers find their smoking behavior discourteous (Bleda and Sandman 1977). In any case, the strategy of "polite requests" is more plausible in intimate company than in larger groups. No one presumes that one-to-one requests would be the appropriate way to regulate behavior in large, open-plan offices, on airplanes, or in restaurants.

Another form of self-restraint would be for smokers to shift over to using "smokeless" forms of tobacco: snuff, chewing tobacco, tobacco pouches, and so forth. (The recently announced "smokeless cigarette" may or may not be another example; there is some thought that it may just emit smaller particles of smoke that are harder to see, but contain much the same carcinogens [Helyar 1987].) There is no reason to suppose that any of these products pose fewer health hazards to smokers themselves, of course. But they do at least avoid inflicting similar hazards on others around them.[52]

3. *Improved ventilation/air filters.*—Passive smoking is a problem arising principally in confined spaces. If windows can be opened without problems (of undue heat gain/loss, etc.), then that is one easy solution. But there are some places—airplanes, increasingly trains, and modern office blocks—where the windows do not open. In such places, we must rely instead upon technological fixes: air filters, and such like. In practice, those presently available are both costly and inadequate. They are incapable of removing small particles and gases contained in cigarette smoke; typically, they serve merely to recirculate smoky air (Repace and Lowrey 1980; U.S. DHHS 1986, p. 11). Even air systems on aircraft—presumably the most controlled environments most of us regularly experience—fail to eliminate cigarette smoke from the air adequately, and increasing ventilation so that it is adequate to do so "is not technically feasible on existing aircraft" (U.S. NAS 1986a, p. 151). The next generation of aircraft is expected to be worse, if anything, in this respect. Of course, we should not rule out the possibility

51. Similarly, perhaps, with "children's rights": ideally, children (or social workers, on their behalf) would never have to claim such rights; but in the nonideal world in which rights need to be pressed, it is indisputably a good thing that they are there.

52. Disposal of chewing tobacco or tobacco pouches might pose public health problems of other sorts, of course. There is also some doubt that tobacco pouches are a lifelong substitute for smoking: once youngsters have become addicted to nicotine through using them, they will shift over to smoking as a way of servicing that habit whenever their personal circumstances change (through marriage, employment, etc.) in such a way as to make the use of tobacco pouches inconvenient or socially unacceptable.

of some technological breakthrough that would clean the air of tobacco smoke perfectly. Neither, however, should we count on one.

4. *Market forces.*—To some extent, ordinary market forces might take care of the passive smoking problem. If people want nonsmoking provision, then they should be willing to pay for it; they should patronize establishments offering it, in preference to ones that do not; and so on. Airlines will win more flyers, restaurants more diners, and businesses more employees and customers if they cater to such demand. Insofar as this happens naturally, no government intervention would be required (Littlechild and Wiseman 1984, pp. 60, 66; Littlechild 1986, pp. 281–82; Shughart and Tollison 1986; Buchanan 1986; Tollison and Wagner 1988).

Certainly much of this is already under way. But there are also familiar limits to market strategies. They presuppose, first, that people are perfectly informed of the costs of passive smoking. They presuppose that bargaining and other such transactions are costless (Coase 1960). They presuppose no economies of scale in provision. And so on. None of this is universally guaranteed, so there might always be some scope for public regulation.

Furthermore, there is something ironic in people who see the political world as a market, much like any other, refusing to respect the outcomes of the market in political pressure. It is an article of faith in the "public choice" school that economic and political markets differ, fundamentally, only in the currencies that they use—money in the former, votes in the latter. Assuming votes can be traded just like anything else, those currencies in turn differ fundamentally only in their distribution—money being unequal, votes being (much more nearly) equal. Thus, though the standard objection to political intervention in markets is that it is motivated by dishonorable "distributional" rather than honorable "efficiency" considerations (Shughart and Tollison 1986; Buchanan 1986), the same may be true of that objection, as well. Minimally, advocates of markets over politics must explain what makes money, and "efficiency" defined in terms of it, so decisively superior to the currency of votes and efficiency defined in terms of them.[53]

5. *Bans/restrictions on smoking in public places.*—The best way to prevent people from being subjected to environmental tobacco smoke in confined public places is to ban (or, anyway, to restrict) smoking in those places, as a matter of public policy backed, ultimately, by the force of law. On the basis of the evidence and arguments above, it seems that smoking should be curtailed especially in certain sorts of places: (*a*) Confined quarters generally. Enclosed spaces, if poorly ventilated, magnify the effects of tobacco smoke, both on the health and comfort of nonsmokers in the vicinity. (*b*) Places where a special "duty of care" is owed to others who might be harmed. Under common law, such duties traditionally fall upon: (i) public transport operators; (ii) inn keepers; (iii) employers, at least where it is impossible for workers to protect themselves from the hazards; (iv) jailers; and (v) heads of households.[54] (*c*) Places where people cannot reasonably be expected

53. Their reply dare not appeal to the universal fungibility of money, for that would invite the rejoinder that we should completely politicize everything in society so everything and anything could be bought through votes. Similarly, they dare not appeal to the economic market's requiring unanimous consent for changes to a status quo that does not itself enjoy unanimous consent.

54. Bohlen (1908) and Kirchheimer (1942) elaborate this list. Restrictions on smoking on public transport, in restaurants, and at work are now common. Suits have recently been brought to require provision of smoking and nonsmoking cells in jail (Ellis v. Director,

to avoid going. If self-contained spaces are available, designating them as "smoking rooms" and restricting smoking to them might suffice to accomplish these goals. But "the simple separation of smokers and non-smokers within the same air space"—an open-plan office, for example—"does not eliminate the exposure of non-smokers to environmental tobacco smoke" (U.S. DHHS 1986, p. 13). So if no self-contained quarters are available for designation as smoking rooms, a total ban on smoking in the whole area might be required. Such bans or restrictions on smoking in public places are now in force in four-fifths of the American states and in forty-seven countries of the world (Roemer 1986, p. 17; U.S. DHHS 1986, p. 267).

ISSUES ARISING

Fairness to People and Fairness to Products

Tobacco companies still refuse to accept that their product kills 25 percent of its users, arguing that all that has been shown is a "merely statistical" connection. This echoes, in some ways, lawyers' worries about "trial by mathematics" (Tribe 1971; see also Thomson 1986, chaps. 12 and 13; Schoeman 1987). The sort of scenario they fear goes something like this. Suppose a black man and white woman held up a store, driving away in a 1954 Buick with Idaho plates; suppose that, though no one can identify the criminals (they wore masks), a couple exactly fitting this description has been apprehended for speeding nearby; and suppose that, statistically, the chance of this particular combination of characteristics in that town were 1 in 1,000,000. Is that statistical evidence enough to convict? If "beyond a reasonable doubt" means 95 percent certainty of guilt, it seems so. Yet we have a lingering sense of unfairness here—of "trial by mathematics" rather than of trial by evidence directly pertaining to those particular individuals.

Of course, in a sense, all evidence is essentially probabilistic. Suppose an eyewitness identifies the couple in court as being, without doubt, the pair that perpetrated the crime. The jury is still left with the question of how much credence to give to that identification, which comes down to a question about their view of the probability that the eyewitness has made an accurate identification. But that probabilistic judgment feels importantly different from the other one. Judging the probable validity of evidence definitely connecting the couple to the crime is somehow different from judging on the basis of evidence probably connecting them to the crime—even if the probability number in both cases is the same. The sense of unfairness in the latter case still lingers.

Can cigarette manufacturers claim regulatory relief on the basis of this same notion of unfairness? I think not, on several grounds. First and most obviously, a different standard of proof is (and should be) required for regulatory and criminal proceedings. Before we incarcerate people, we want evidence that they are guilty beyond a reasonable doubt. That is in part because of the "expressive" function criminal trials serve (Tribe 1971). Regulatory policy, in contrast, is

---

Texas Department of Corrections, USDC TX) and by a wife with respiratory disease to enjoin her husband not to smoke in her presence (Reade v. Reade, Ontario Dist. Ct.); both are reported in the *Tobacco Products Litigation Reporter,* vol. 2, no. 7 (July/August 1987). In a similar case in New York, state Supreme Court Justice Ralph Diamond ordered Elizabeth Roofeh not to smoke in front of her estranged husband, who is particularly sensitive to tobacco smoke, or their children; she was further ordered to confine her smoking to one room of their house (*New York Times* [February 24, 1988], p. B3).

purely instrumental. There, we are perfectly prepared to keep products off the market if it is merely "more likely than not" (or maybe even if there is just "some reason to believe") that they cause serious harms. It is not just a different probability that is involved here, either. With this less demanding standard of proof, we are also intuitively more inclined to accept probability numbers and statistical evidence. The standard of evidence required is different in kind. In criminal proceedings, we may need particularized evidence. In regulatory proceedings, it is not clear that we do.[55]

Second, regulation designed to prevent harm ex ante is importantly different from ex post actions (be they punitive or merely compensatory) for remedying harms once they have happened. When making people pay for what they have done, we may need particularized evidence that they really were the ones who did it (cf. the section on tort options above). When trying to prevent harms through regulatory policy, we do not. Even in the case of crime prevention, it seems permissible to patrol some areas more intensively than others on the basis of statistical evidence about the relative frequency of crimes in those areas. For purposes of cancer prevention, it seems permissible to regulate certain classes of chemicals more closely than others on the basis of merely statistical evidence, likewise.

Third, and perhaps most tellingly, statistical evidence is more directly relevant where products than where petty thieves are concerned. With the case of the thieving couple, we are forced to talk in terms of probabilities because we are uncertain which of the few dozen couples in the country meeting that description actually perpetrated the robbery. Our fear of unfairness, in using statistical evidence to indict one of those couples, is that we may thereby be blaming one couple for the crime of another in that larger group. With the case of cigarettes, in contrast, we are forced to talk in terms of probabilities merely because we do not know which 25 percent of users they will kill. In short, with the thieving couple we are uncertain of the culprits, whereas with tobacco we are uncertain only of the victims.[56] For purposes of justifying regulatory policies, that makes all the difference.

The evidence against smoking is indeed direct, particularized evidence in the sense that matters for regulatory policies. Tobacco kills 25 percent of its users: they smoked, they died. All we do not know is, ex ante, which 25 percent it will be who die. But why should that matter? A gunman who fired a shotgun into a crowd, killing only 25 percent of its members, would not be exonerated. Why should we seriously consider a similar claim on behalf of tobacco?

Note, further, that evidence can be both "direct" and "particularized" without involving a detailed tracing of causal connections (cf. Thomson 1986, pp. 222–23, 230 ff.). Suppose we were dealing with a murderer who gassed his victims rather than shooting them. Suppose the defendant's attorney, quizzing the coroner, asked, "But how, *exactly,* does this gas kill the 25 percent of those whom you say

55. As a partial explanation of why this different standard of proof might be acceptable in regulatory circumstances, consider the very different implications of convicting people and of convicting products: capital punishment simply means something very different in the two cases.

56. Of course, it is also true that there are many carcinogens besides tobacco smoke, many of which any given individual might also have experienced. But by controlling those other factors statistically, we can say with confidence how much of a contribution tobacco makes to the causation of any given disease in general (though not, of course, in that particular individual's case).

will invariably die if exposed to it?" Suppose that with this gas, as with so much else, our knowledge is somewhat incomplete. (At some level, we do not know *exactly* how many of even the most familiar poisons work.) So under such scrutiny, a coroner simply has to throw up his or her hands and say, "Look, I have long experience in these matters, and we have a vast literature on the effects of this poison; believe me, in those doses it is somehow or another fatal in a quarter of cases." Surely that is an adequate answer in ordinary poisoning cases. Surely the same sort of answer should be adequate in the case of tobacco.

Concepts of Causation for Policymaking

Both philosophers and lawyers have come to see increasingly vast difficulties with the concept of causation (Hart and Honoré 1985). To a large extent, what you should regard as "the" cause of something is now seen to depend upon the reasons you have for asking the question about causation in the first place.

In tort litigation, we are in the business of assigning liability for harm that has already been done. There, we might want to pick out, among those multiple factors whose causal contributions cannot be easily disentangled, as "the" cause the actions of whoever can bear the cost most easily or of whoever had the last or cheapest opportunity to avert the harm (Calabresi 1970; Hart and Honore 1985; "Plaintiffs' Conduct" 1986, pp. 818–26). But the crucial thing about those judgments is that they are necessarily retrospective, coming after all is said and done.

In making public policy generally (and regulatory policy particularly) our focus is prospective. Our aim is to choose policies that will shape the future in desired ways, rather than just allocating blame for what is past. Given that aim, we ought adopt Collingwood's doctrine of looking for "causal conditions which have a handle on them which we can grasp and manipulate" and regard "causal generalizations . . . as 'recipes' for cooking up desired effects" (Feinberg 1970, p. 144). That is to say, we should isolate for policy purposes those causes that are within the policymakers' capacity to control.

For an application of this principle, consider education policy. Genes and early childhood experiences might, in some sense, make more of a contribution than school facilities or curricula to a child's ultimate educational attainment. But the latter factors are within the control of educational policymakers in a way that the former (in our society, at least) are not. The latter, therefore, ought be regarded for policy purposes as the causes of educational accomplishment among children (Cain and Watts 1970, p. 230; Hanushek and Kain 1972).

Similarly with smoking, many factors may contribute to lung cancer and so forth. Many of them are environmental contaminants, like asbestos, which are also controllable by policymakers. But many of them—for example, genetic or fundamental personality factors—are not, in a way that smoking is. For that reason, smoking ought be regarded for purposes of public policymaking as a predominant cause of cancer.[57] The words of the surgeon general are apt when

57. Were the connection between smoking and cancer wholly an artifact of a connection both have to genotype, there would be nothing that policymakers could do to reduce cancer short of genetic engineering. That is not what the evidence seems to suggest, though: even archadvocates of the "genetic constitution" model concede that there is also an independent causal path running from smoking to cancer (Burch 1978), and that path can be cut by antismoking policies. Furthermore, studies purporting to show that both smoking and

he calls smoking the largest preventable and the chief single avoidable cause of cancer death in our society (U.S. DHHS 1982, preface; 1986, pp. 5–6). It is precisely that avoidability and preventability that makes it, for policy purposes at least, causally preeminent.

Bad Habits and Addictions

Many who oppose government regulation of smoking designed to protect smokers from themselves implicitly or explicitly treat it as nothing more than a bad habit (Littlechild and Wiseman 1984, p. 65). "Assumption of individual responsibility for one's own health" is, in these terms, far preferable to treating "sloth, gluttony, alcoholic overuse, reckless driving, sexual intemperance, and smoking" as "a national, not an individual responsibility" (Knowles 1977, p. 59; see similarly Wildavsky 1977, pp. 105, 122–23; and Wikler 1987).

In many ways, these writers have a point. Presumably it is perfectly true that we expect people to alter their own bad habits—or anyway not to complain when harms befall them in consequence. After all, they could have altered their ways. Addictions, however, are otherwise. They may, in the first instance, have been self-induced. Once induced, however, they are not (easily) remediable thereafter through any simple act of will; indeed, that is one of the primary criteria used to distinguish "drug dependence from habitual behaviors" diagnostically (U.S. DHHS 1988, pp. 7–8). At root, the habit versus addiction issue really is a problem about responsibility. People may bear responsibility for their bad habits and whatever follows from them. They might even bear responsibility for having become addicted to drugs. Once addicted, though, they ought no longer be considered responsible for their addiction-driven actions.[58] For that reason, the

---

cancer are linked to genetic constitution, either directly or indirectly (through personality), fail to map conclusively the path of causation. Which way the arrows run matters. The correlation would be wholly spurious—and wholly outside the control of social policy-makers—only if the arrows ran one from genes/personality to smoking and the other from genes/personality to cancer. But the evidence is usually equally consistent with the hypothesis that, at least to a large extent, the arrows run one from genes/personality to smoking and another from smoking to cancer. Insofar as that is true, the cancer can be prevented by breaking that last link, through antismoking policies, for example. Notably, Eysenck's (1986, p. 52) twin studies conclude that genes are important in maintenance but not the origin of smoking habits; the implication is that, if smoking policies can curb the sociological influences (peer pressure, etc.) that initiate smokers into the habit, the causal chain can be broken even if it has an unbreakable genetic element elsewhere.

58. The law, presumably in a desperate effort to deter, tends to take a harder line on this matter. The Model Penal Code, e.g., suggests that (with very few exceptions indeed) people should be held fully responsible for actions committed while intoxicated (ALI 1974, sec. 2.08). But that rule sits uneasily with the basic logic of the criminal code. Insofar as those acting under the influence of a drug are in some deep sense no longer "in control" of themselves, their actions do not manifest the sort of mens rea or evil intent that we ordinarily regard as the defining feature of criminality. Such logic has led a variety of legal philosophers to conclude that those acting "under the influence," and no longer capable of distinguishing right from wrong for that reason, ought not be responsible for their actions as such; what they should be responsible for, instead, is putting themselves in such a position that they might lose control of themselves in a way that would involve the "reckless endangering" of others (Hall 1944; Fitzgerald 1961; Fletcher 1978, pp. 846–52; Brandt 1985, pp. 190–92).

addiction evidence is crucial in making the case for governmental action on smoking in several respects.[59]

Still, the distinction between addictions and mere bad habits is a hard one to draw, especially in the view of economists.[60] The central point in their argument is that all temptations are resistible, and all addictions are curable—at a cost.[61] Doing without heroin, nicotine, or whatever is certainly no fun for someone used to consuming it regularly, but it is not impossible. To the economist, the pain of withdrawal is just the cost that an addict has to pay for the good of a "clean" life. In that respect, it is formally analogous to the cost that anyone pays (also in terms of pain, or anyway discomfort) in breaking a bad habit.[62] So if we hold people responsible for the one, why not for the other as well?

Of course, it is highly desirable that people should take charge of their own lives in both respects, breaking bad habits and addictions alike. Of necessity, that must be primarily a task for individuals themselves. But there are some things that governments can do to help—such as making practices people wish to abandon more expensive (through excise taxes) or restricting the number of hours or number of places in which they can engage in them. Such assistance can be justified on the grounds that, far from imposing paternalist policies on people, we are merely helping them enforce rules of their own choosing upon themselves (Schelling 1980, 1983, 1984b, 1985; Crain et al. 1977). That rationale works equally well, whether it is a mere bad habit or an actual addiction that is involved.

Where an actual addiction is concerned, however, there is another even stronger rationale for public policy. It has not so much to do with protecting present addicts from themselves as it has to do with preventing future ones. There is nothing wrong with habituation per se. Some habits are bad; others are good, in the sense that you are better off objectively as well as subjectively for having cultivated them (Stigler and Becker 1977; Littlechild and Wiseman 1984, p. 65). Addictions are unambiguously bad, in contrast.[63] Being defined in terms of a desire to quit coupled with an inability to quit, addictions necessarily make the addict worse-off.[64] And on the evidence of the section, "Do Smokers Voluntarily Accept the Risks?" above, a vast majority of smokers are addicted in this way.

59. Ranging from publicly sponsored smoking-cessation programs to restricting or banning the sale of tobacco (see, generally, U.S. DHHS 1988, esp. chap. 7).

60. Kelman 1979. Stigler and Becker (1977) might emphasize increasing tolerance over time, which is a characteristic that nicotine dependence shares with all other addictions (Winsten 1986; U.S. DHHS 1988). That this increase "tops out" sooner (at around twenty—or, given 50 percent underreporting of smoking behavior, perhaps thirty—cigarettes a day for most addicts) rather than later (as with heroin) is surely irrelevant for purposes of defining a substance as addictive.

61. As Feinberg (1970, p. 282) puts it, "No impulse is irresistible; for every case of giving in to a desire, I would argue, it would be true that, if the person had tried harder he would have resisted it successfully."

62. Compare Kelman 1979, pp. 783–84. Neither is there any reason to suppose that the cost of the one (breaking a weak addiction, e.g.) would necessarily always exceed that of the other (breaking a long-standing, well-entrenched bad habit, e.g.). See further Tollison and Wagner (1988, p. 39).

63. Stigler and Becker (1977) talk, unhelpfully, in terms of "beneficial addiction" in cases of good habits. Here I use the term "addiction" to refer to "bad addictions" only; this is implicit in the WHO/APA criteria set out above.

64. One useful way to cast questions about welfare is this: would the people involved have chosen otherwise, if they had it to do over again (Kelman 1979)? If not, then their

The policy implications of that distinction are clear. Since habits are not necessarily bad, public policies discouraging them are not necessarily desirable. Addictions being necessarily bad, policies discouraging them are always desirable. We might wish to show compassion toward present addicts, but clearly we should do what we can to prevent new addicts.

"Grandfathering" Health Hazards

All sorts of laws regulating conduct do not apply to those engaged in such conduct at the time of enactment of the legislation. Exemptions for "preexisting" conditions, practices, or usages are often written into a law, which explicitly regulates only "new" ones arising subsequent to its enactment. Such "grandfather clauses" are most common in zoning ordinances, perhaps. But they also find some application in public health contexts. The Food, Drug and Cosmetic Act Amendments of 1958 required all new drugs to be subjected to careful screening, for example, but presumed all existing products to be safe. It is often (and rightly) said that if aspirin were invented today, it would not get past FDA testing on any plausible risk/benefit calculation. Yet because it has long been sold, we allow it to continue being sold. Perhaps tobacco might claim some regulatory relief under similar principles. Cigarettes, too, are a long-established product on the market.

What precise arguments can be offered for "grandfathering" public health hazards in such ways? I can imagine three.[65]

1. Maybe substances with which we have long experience should be subject to different and less demanding safety standards either (*a*) because that experience establishes, in Bayesian fashion, an indication of innocence, or (*b*) because the risks from that substance form part of the background risk by now.

Tobacco can claim no exemption under principle 1*a*, however. We do have long experience of tobacco use. We also have long experience of cancer, increasing (in lagged fashion, as is the way with diseases with long latency periods) with increases in smoking. Bayes's rule works, if anything, to damn smoking.

Principle 1*b* is patently absurd. Surely we should reduce natural background risks of death if we can—by removing naturally occurring carcinogens from drinking water or building materials, for example. Surely we should be no more relaxed about socially created contributions to the "normal" risk of death. If they can be removed cheaply and easily from our lives, surely they should be.

---

initial choice can unambiguously be said to have promoted their welfare; if so, it can unambiguously be said to have ill-served it. Where people merely "regret" previous choices, and would choose differently next time, that is clear enough. In cases of addiction, matters are only a little more complicated. Once addicted, people would choose the same addictive good next time as last; but if given a chance to choose over whether or not to begin consuming the addictive substance in the first place, they would choose not to do so. (That is how "addiction" is here defined and how it is operationalized in the studies demonstrating the addictiveness of nicotine.) Stopping people from becoming addicts by stopping them from beginning to consume tobacco in the first place would thus be justified in terms of their own self-assessed welfare, defined in terms of their own (hypothetical) choices. The standard is paternalistic insofar as the choices in view are hypothetical and not real, and the test counterfactual rather than actual. But the same is presumably true of the vast majority of welfare judgments policymakers are required to impute to people, inferring from the choices they make in one set of circumstances what they would prefer in other circumstances which by their nature cannot be brought into existence without relying upon those very welfare judgments at issue.

65. Building on brief remarks in Breyer (1982, p. 154).

2. Maybe substances with which we have long experience have, by virtue of that experience, greater benefits (albeit no fewer risks).

All arguments for respecting long-standing traditions turn on some such point, and sometimes those arguments for respecting traditions might entail permitting continued use of dangerous products. Consider the case of lead additives in gasoline. No doubt they do great harm, but it is argued that since most of the tractors presently in use on family farms would not run without them we cannot eliminate leaded gas (in the short term, at least) without endangering that whole way of life (Owen 1987, p. 56). Similarly, perhaps, with tobacco. Farmers growing it are dependent upon the crop; at least in the short term and for a few people, radical changes in their lives would be necessitated by any great change in tobacco consumption.[66] More important, because potentially more widespread, the "smoking ritual" might play an important role in the way of life of several broad classes of people. Insofar as we find those ways of life valuable, and insofar as they truly cannot be sustained without the smoking ritual, perhaps we ought not discourage smoking (among those groups, at least). But both those provisos are likely not to be satisfied. Central though smoking may be, few whole ways of life would disappear without it. And since it is principally those with very boring or very stressful life-styles who get hooked into these patterns of repetitive behavior (Leventhal and Cleary 1980; Spielberger 1986), these are unlikely to be ways of life we would care to see perpetuated.

3. Producers of well-established products might have a legitimate expectation, growing out of long tradition, of continuing in business.

The analogy here would be to Hume's theory of property rights, wherein rights grow out of expectations legitimated by long usage. Squatters, even though they originally have no right (and, indeed, originally may have been wronging someone) to squat, come to acquire rights if they carry on squatting long enough. Tobacco, being a long-established product, might give its producers similarly legitimate expectations of continued access to markets.[67]

What counts as "legitimate expectations" has always been the tough question for this line of analysis, though. The best Humean defenders of property can do is to cash out "legitimate" in terms of "well-founded," and to point to the benefits the public at large derives from the increased productivity generated by secure expectations. In the tobacco case, such defenses would be unavailable. It is clear, from the evidence above, that the continued marketing of the product is counterproductive of public health. It has always been clear, with tobacco as with all other consumer products, that the product's continued access to markets was predicated on the assumption that it was "safe" for consumers to use as directed.[68] Cigarettes palpably are not.

66. However, it is worth recalling, with Schelling (1986a, p. 650), that "the number of people who earn most of their living from growing tobacco is smaller than the number of people who are estimated to die annually as a result of the tobacco they smoke. One premature death per year is a pretty high social cost for keeping a tobacco [farmer and his] children from having to shift to another crop or another occupation."

67. Though not, of course, necessarily continuing high profits. Furthermore, all that those legitimate expectations would strictly speaking give rise to is a right to compensation should the state, in exercise of its police powers, upset such expectations. By analogy, when the opium trade is prohibited, we might be similarly obliged to give transitional support to traditional poppy growers to help them retool—but that is not to say we cannot prohibit the opium trade.

68. Compare the prospective ban on cigarette manufacturing and sale to that imposed on distillers and brewers by Prohibition: they were not compensated for the fact that their

The Ethics of Advertising and the Ethics of Selling

One of the currently favored strategies for preventing children from becoming addicted to tobacco is to ban advertising on television and in magazines targeted at children and young adults. There are pressures to extend those bans to all cigarette advertising.[69] Against such bans, tobacco spokesmen urge the inconsistency of banning advertising but allowing sale of the product. Their position is that, if it is legal to sell a product, then it should be legal to advertise it (Boddewyn 1986; cf. Chapman 1985, pp. 7–8; and Warner 1987a).[70]

How, exactly, that entailment is meant to work remains something of a mystery. Perhaps the idea is that there can no more be "private trade" than a "private language"—trade, by its very nature, must be interpersonal. True enough. There can, however, be such a thing as a "private sale," where the seller makes an offer to the particular buyer that has not been made to the public at large. There is nothing incoherent about the notion of such a sale, private though it may have been.

Those who say "if it is legal to sell, it must be legal to advertise" must presumably be arguing that, if it is permissible to engage in practices which are by their nature public (i.e., interpersonal), then it must be permissible to publicize those practices. But that cannot be right. Just as it is permissible for us to talk about doing all sorts of things it would not be permissible for us actually to do, it is permissible for us to keep people from talking openly about all sorts of things it would be perfectly permissible for them actually to do quietly. Surely it is legitimate for us to permit various practices between consenting adults in private, while prohibiting (in the name of public decency) their being publicly flaunted. Maybe smoking, like sexual perversions, should be among them (Lundberg and Knoll 1986).

More plausibly, the argument might turn on the justifications for having markets at all, and on the presuppositions built into them. Markets can be shown to maximize social welfare, under certain ideal conditions. One of them is that consumers have perfect information. Insofar as information is what advertising provides, its justification is thus implicit in the justification for permitting a market

---

machinery was turned into useless junk by prohibition laws, and the U.S. Supreme Court held in Mugler v. Kansas, 123 US 623, 669 (1887) that there was no need for them to be; Ackerman (1977, p. 153) suggests an explicit extension of that rule to the case of a cigarette ban.

69. "Advertising" embraces both conventional commercial advertising and "promotions" (sports sponsorships, etc.) which are designed to evade advertising bans but which are in principle indistinguishable from advertising of the ordinary sort.

70. They have even elevated the issue to a matter of high Constitutional principle, claiming that a ban on advertising violates their "right to free speech" under the First Amendment. Such a claim is tenuous, even setting aside larger questions of whether corporations really should enjoy the same constitutional protections as natural persons (Berle 1952). Commercial speech traditionally did not enjoy any protection at all under the First Amendment, and it is still very much a live issue whether such as it now enjoys can be fully justified (Jackson and Jeffries 1979). In any case, it has always been clear that any protection due commercial speech was much more highly qualified than that due other forms of speech (Blasi and Monaghan 1986). The most famous philosophical champion of free speech, Mill (1859/1975, p. 121), himself concedes that, although the general rule should be "whatever it is permitted to do, it must be permitted to advise to do," the appropriateness of that rule "is doubtful . . . when the instigator derives a personal benefit [e.g., profits] from his advice."

in the product at all. If what we have is simply an argument for the pure provision of information, however, what it would justify is no more than "tombstone advertising"—"no models, slogans, scenes or colors," just a picture of the unadorned cigarette packet with information on price and tar, nicotine, and carbon monoxide content printed in plain lettering (Warner et al. 1986, pp. 383–84). Thus, it is far from clear that anything like advertising as we know it is implicit in the logic of permitting sale of the product.

There are, of course, various other more direct responses to the argument that, if it is legal to sell cigarettes, then it should be legal to advertise them. One would be to grasp the nettle and ban cigarette sales altogether.[71] Another would be to point out that cigarette sales to minors are already banned; and judging from past experience, tobacco companies are unwilling or unable to frame advertisements in such a way that they appeal to legal (adult) consumers without also appealing to illegal (child) consumers (Warner 1987a).

Another response, yet again, would be to turn the slogan, "if it is legal to sell, it is legal to advertise" on its head. If it is morally and legally legitimate for us to ban sale of a product, then it is permissible for us to ban advertising of it. As the U.S. Supreme Court has recently held, "the greater power to completely ban" a product or activity from the market "necessarily includes the lesser power to ban advertising of it" (William Rehnquist, *Posadas de Puerto Rico Assoc. v. Tourism Co. of Puerto Rico,* 92 LEd2d 266, 283 [1986]).[72]

Furthermore, what sort of advertising we should permit depends upon what sort of argument we have for allowing continued sale of the product. If the argument is that people are better off using the product than they were before ever using it, then advertising designed to attract new customers is permissible on welfarist grounds. If the rationale is instead "servicing an addiction" of people who would have been better off never to have used the product (but who would suffer withdrawal if they discontinued using it now) then advertising that attracts new users, by design or otherwise, is definitely contraindicated on welfarist grounds. Methods of advertising that could be guaranteed to reach only existing addicts might still be permissible.[73] (Perhaps the best strategy here might be to oblige manufacturers to allow other companies to buy advertising space on the back of their own products' packets.) But insofar as cigarette advertising necessarily appeals to nonusers (children especially, though for the sake of this argument

71. Over-the-counter sales, anyway. Even if cigarettes were available as a prescription drug, the only advertising that that would justify would be in medical journals, addressed to doctors responsible for writing out the prescriptions rather than to their patients.

72. The issue in *Posadas* was casino advertising, but in passing Rehnquist's majority opinion offered, as obiter dictum, the view that cigarette advertising could be similarly restricted without infringing First Amendment rights (William Rehnquist, Posadas de Puerto Rico Assoc. v. Tourism Co. of Puerto Rico, 92, LEd2d 274, 284 [1986]). The issue continues to be queried, though, even by lawyers from the Justice Department (Kmiec 1986).

73. Insofar as cigarette advertising encourages brand switching among existing users, there are the (probably marginal) welfare gains to smokers from switching to a preferred brand that must be figured into the calculus. Manufacturers also claim that advertising is needed to communicate important product information, especially about tar and nicotine levels, to smokers. It seems likely that advertising has played a role in encouraging the shift to low tar and nicotine brands (Hamilton 1972; Boddewyn 1986). But given the evidence cited in n. 3 above about the way these cigarettes are smoked, the health consequences of this shift are less than they might appear to be.

it need not be them exclusively) as well as existing users—as the above evidence suggests that it does—then to that extent we have a welfarist case for banning advertising of the product altogether.[74]

Discrimination

One way of discouraging smoking is to put an extra tax on tobacco products. One popular way of avoiding passive smoking is to segregate smokers physically in some self-contained compartment; a variation on that latter strategy is for firms to hire only nonsmokers.

All such policies are sometimes said to involve discrimination, most directly against smokers themselves but also (since smoking correlates strongly with race and class) indirectly against lower classes and certain racial minorities. A tax that falls disproportionately upon the poor is regressive and undesirable on that account.[75] A policy of segregation, especially when its effects fall disproportionately upon historically discriminated-against racial minorities, is uncomfortably reminiscent of southern lunch counters in the age of Jim Crow (Victor 1987; Rothstein 1983). As one California assemblyman put the point in protesting against a ban on smoking on public transportation there, "This is really a civil rights issue. First you say 'smokers get to the back of the bus,' and now you're telling smokers to get off the bus" altogether (quoted in Will 1987).

One way around allegations of unacceptable discrimination would be to argue that the discrimination is against the behavior (smoking), not the person (the smoker).[76] How powerful a move this is depends upon how much of a wedge can be driven between the behavior and the person. If smoking were no more than an annoying personal habit like chewing gum or whistling off-key, then discriminating against the behavior would not be discriminating against the person, necessarily, because the person could presumably always renounce the behavior and thus avoid the sanction. If smoking were regarded as an addiction that is to

74. The evidence that is standardly offered for supposing that cigarette advertising merely encourages brand switching rather than recruiting new smokers is the weak relationship between advertising and overall volume of tobacco sales (Hamilton 1972; Fujii 1980). Although that is true for the short run, there is evidence that the relationship might be much stronger (0.2 or so) in the long run, which is where the effect of advertising in attracting new customers would really be felt, of course (McGuinness and Cowling 1975). In any case, given the rate at which smokers die and quit smoking, even a constant volume of cigarette sales would represent significant numbers of new smokers being recruited each year.

75. Tobacco taxes certainly are regressive (Savarese and Shughart 1986). Indeed, that was precisely King James I's intention in introducing the 1604 tax: "To price tobacco out of the reach of the lower classes, while leaving sufficient supplies for those of the 'better sort,' who would smoke in moderation" (Harrison 1986, p. 555). Atkinson and Townsend (1977, p. 493) suggest that "the Government could partly mitigate the effects [of an increased tobacco tax] by simultaneous support for low-income households," most likely in the form of income supplements (since it is inconceivable that any government would allow rations of patently unhealthy products on food stamps).

76. Similarly, it is one thing to punish an alcoholic for being an alcoholic, quite another to punish an alcoholic for drinking in public (Thurgood Marshall, Powell v. Texas, 392 U.S. 514 [1968]). Policies of preferential hiring might be unable to appeal to this distinction: they discriminate precisely against the person who smokes, no matter where or when. But segregating and taxing smoking are both policies arguably directed at the behavior rather than the person.

some extent beyond a person's power to alter, however, then to that extent the distinction between the person and the behavior is a distinction without a difference. It is precisely this inability of people to alter a discriminated-against characteristic that has come to define "suspect classes" in recent U.S. court cases arising under the Fourteenth Amendment ("Quasi-suspect Classes and Proof of Discriminatory Intent: A New Model" 1981; Daniels 1985, pp. 201–3).[77] It is precisely the fact that drug addicts are incapable of altering their status as addicts that has led the U.S. Supreme Court to strike down penalties for being an addict per se as involving unconstitutionally "cruel and unusual punishment" (Potter Stewart, *Robinson v. California*, 370 U.S. 660 [1962]; cf. Fingarette 1975).

Even those who are addicted, and who cannot (easily) alter whether or not they smoke, can nonetheless control where they smoke, however. Thus, insofar as the policy is merely one requiring smokers to step into another room to smoke and then return to their desks, it is a policy with which smokers can indeed comply without changing themselves in some almost impossible way. Insofar as it requires segregation of the smoker from nonsmoking workmates, the separation is brief and presumably inconsequential. There are all sorts of activities that we ask people to step out of the room to perform. Prostitution, where legalized, is characteristically confined to certain zones within the city (Yondorf 1979). No one protests that either form of segregation is unacceptably discriminatory.

Sometimes, as with preferential hiring policies favoring nonsmokers, genuine discrimination might be involved. Notice, however, that neither laws nor morals prohibit discrimination per se. All that is prohibited is arbitrary discrimination. If we are distinguishing between prospective employees on grounds clearly relevant to the task to be performed, then that is permissible; and it would remain so, even if at the end of the day more white men are hired than black women as a result. Smoking clearly is detrimental to the performance of some tasks (damaging equipment, slowing workers' reaction times); and insofar as it harms co-workers as well as smokers themselves, employers can hardly be held culpable if they display the same concern for workers' health as for their own machinery.[78] To a large extent, these problems can be solved simply by prohibiting smoking on the job. But insofar as there are significant spillovers from off-duty smoking to on-the-job performance, a policy of restrictive hiring might be justified in terms of "business necessity" (Daniels 1985, pp. 212–13).

CONCLUSION

Forty-two states have now enacted restrictions—in at least nine cases extensive ones—on smoking in public places. Smoking is now banned or restricted in over a third of private-sector business establishments (U.S. DHHS 1986, pp. 267, 285). Those responsible for governing our society have increasingly concluded

77. Presumably, the specific claim smokers would make is that they are "handicapped" by their nicotine addiction and thus deserving of whatever protections we offer other handicapped individuals.

78. It is also true that smokers cost employers more (in terms of lost productivity, higher health insurance rates, etc.) than nonsmokers (Kristein 1983). That gives employers an incentive for hiring only nonsmokers, to be sure. But if nicotine addiction is classed as a handicap, then it is unclear whether merely marginally greater costs can count as a relevant reason for discriminating against smokers. After all, the U.S. Rehabilitation Act of 1973 requires employers to make "reasonable accommodation" for employees' handicaps, including moderately costly steps like building wheelchair ramps.

that clean indoor air is a quality-of-life issue that is a fitting concern for socially enforced sanctions.

The evidence in this essay shows that there are more than adequate grounds for that conclusion. It also suggests that there are grounds, of an inoffensively weak-paternalistic sort, for going even further—curbing the advertising, and perhaps even over-the-counter selling, of cigarettes. Smoking has long ago ceased to be a private-regarding vice best treated as such. It is high time that philosophers stopped talking as if it were.

REFERENCES

Scholars and students wishing to pursue these issues further should turn first to the asterisked, and especially the double-asterisked, items.

Ackerman, Bruce A. 1977. *Private Property and the Constitution.* New Haven, Conn.: Yale University Press.

Aitken, P. P.; Leather, D. S.; and O'Hagan, F. J. 1985. Children's Perceptions of Advertisements for Cigarettes. *Social Science and Medicine* 21:785–97.

Aitken, P. P.; Leather, D.S.; O'Hagan, F. J.; and Squair, S. I. 1987. Children's Awareness of Cigarette Advertisements and Brand Imagery. *British Journal of Addiction* 82:615–22.

American Law Institute (ALI). 1974. Model Penal Code. In *Uniform Laws Annotated,* vol. 10, pp. 433–746. St. Paul, Minn.: West.

* American Medical Association (AMA). Office of the General Counsel. 1986. Tobacco Product Liability. *Journal of the American Medical Association* 255:1034–37.

American Psychiatric Association (APA). 1987. *Diagnostic and Statistical Manual of Mental Disorders.* 3d ed. Washington, D.C.: APA.

Armitage, P. 1978. Discussion of Burch 1978. *Journal of the Royal Statistical Society,* ser. A, 141:458–60.

Atkins, Liz, and Jarrett, David. 1979. The Significance of "Significance" Tests. In *Demystifying Social Statistics,* ed. Ian Miles and Jeff Evans, pp. 87–109. London: Pluto Press.

* Atkinson, A. B. 1974. Smoking and the Economics of Government Intervention. In *The Economics of Health and Medical Care,* ed. Mark Perlman, pp. 428–41. London: Macmillan.

Atkinson, A. B., and Meade, T. W. 1974. Methods and Preliminary Findings in Assessing the Economic and Health Services Consequences of Smoking, with Particular Reference to Lung Cancer. *Journal of the Royal Statistical Society,* ser. A, 137:297–312.

Atkinson, A. B., and Skegg, J. L. 1973. Antismoking Publicity and the Demand for Tobacco in the UK. *Manchester School of Economic and Social Studies* 41:265–82.

Atkinson, A. B., and Townsend, J. L. 1977. Economic Aspects of Reduced Smoking. *Lancet* 8036:492–94.

Baggott, Rob. 1986. By Voluntary Agreement: The Politics of Instrument Selection. *Public Administration* (London) 64:51–67.

Barry, Brian. 1979. Is Democracy Special? In *Philosophy, Politics and Society,* 5th ser., ed. Peter Laslett and James S. Fishkin, pp. 155–96. Oxford: Blackwell.

Battin, Margaret P. 1987. Age Rationing and the Just Distribution of Health Care: Is There a Duty to Die? *Ethics* 97:317–40.

Benfari, Robert C.; Ockene, Judith K.; and McIntyre, Kevin M. 1982. Control of Cigarette-Smoking from a Psychological Perspective. *Annual Review of Public Health* 3:101–28.

Benham, Lee. 1981. Comments on Lewit, Coate and Grossman (1981). *Journal of Law and Economics* 24:571–73.

Berle, A. A., Jr. 1952. Constitutional Limitations on Corporate Activity—Protection of Personal Rights from Invasion through Economic Power. *University of Pennsylvania Law Review* 100:933–55.

Blasi, Vincent, and Monaghan, Henry Paul. 1986. The First Amendment and Cigarette Advertising. *Journal of the American Medical Association* 256:502–9.

Bleda, P. R., and Sandman, P. H. 1977. In Smoke's Way: Socioemotional Reactions to Another's Smoking. *Journal of Applied Psychology* 62:452–58.

Boddewyn, J. J. 1986. Tobacco Advertising in a Free Society. In Tollison, ed., 1986, pp. 309–32.

Bohlen, F. H. 1908. The Moral Duty to Aid Others as a Basis of Tort Liability. *University of Pennsylvania Law Review* 56:217–44, 316–38.

Borgida, E., and Nisbett, R. E. 1977. The Differential Impact of Abstract vs. Concrete Information on Decisions. *Journal of Applied Social Psychology* 7:258–71.

Bradford Hill, Austin. 1965. The Environment and Disease: Association or Causation? *Proceedings of the Royal Society of Medicine* 58, no. 5:7–12.

Brandt, R. B. 1985. A Motivational Theory of Excuses in the Criminal Law. In *Nomos XXVII: Criminal Justice,* ed. J. R. Pennock and J. W. Chapman, pp. 165–98. New York: New York University Press.

Bremner, C. 1988. US Tobacco Giants "Plotted to Mislead Smokers." *Times* (London), April 23. p. x.

Breslow, Lester. 1982. Control of Cigarette Smoking from a Public Policy Perspective. *Annual Review of Public Health* 3:129–52.

Breyer, Stephen. 1982. *Regulation and Its Reform.* Cambridge, Mass.: Harvard University Press.

British Medical Association (BMA). Public Affairs Division. 1986. *Smoking Out the Barons: The Campaign against the Tobacco Industry.* Chichester: Wiley for the BMA.

Brownlee, K. A. 1965. A Review of "Smoking and Health" (US DHEW 1964). *Journal of the American Statistical Association* 60:722–39.

* Buchanan, James M. 1970. In Defense of *Caveat Emptor. University of Chicago Law Review* 38:64–73.

Buchanan, James M. 1986. Politics and Meddlesome Preferences. In Tollison, ed., 1986, pp. 335–42.

* Burch, P. R. J. 1978. Smoking and Lung Cancer: The Problem of Inferring Cause. *Journal of the Royal Statistical Society,* ser. A, 141:437–58.

Burch, P. R. J. 1986. Health Risks of Passive Smoking: Problems of Interpretation. *Environment International* 12:23–28.

Cain, Glen G., and Watts, Harold W. 1970. Problems in Making Policy Inferences from the Coleman Report. *American Sociological Review* 35:228–42.

Calabresi, Guido. 1970. *The Costs of Accidents.* New Haven, Conn.: Yale University Press.

Calfee, John E. 1986. The Ghost of Cigarette Advertising Past. *Regulation* 10, no. 6: 35–45.

Califano, Joseph A., Jr. 1981. *Governing America.* New York: Simon & Schuster.

Cederlof, R.; Friberg, L.; and Lundman, T. 1977. The Interactions of Smoking, Environment and Heredity and Their Implications for Disease Etiology. *Acta Medica Scandinavica,* vol. 612 (suppl. 1).

Chapman, Simon. 1985. *Cigarette Advertising and Smoking: A Review of the Evidence.* London: British Medical Association. Reprinted in BMA 1986, pp. 79–98.

Chapman, Simon, and Fitzgerald, Bill. 1982. Brand Preferences and Advertisement Recall in Adolescent Smokers: Some Implications for Health Promotion. *American Journal of Public Health* 72:491–94.

Coase, R. H. 1960. The Problem of Social Cost. *Journal of Law and Economics* 3:1–44.

Cohen, Marc I. 1987. *Cigarette Product Liability Litigation.* New York: Bernstein/James Capel.

Coleman, Geoff. 1985. The Great Ad Wars. *Australian Society* 4, no. 10:11–14.

Cox, Howard, and Smith, Ron. 1984. Political Approaches to Smoking Control: A Comparative Analysis. *Applied Economics* 16:569–82.

Crain, W. M.; Deaton, T.; Holcombe, R.; and Tollison, R. 1977. Rational Choice and the Taxation of Sin. *Journal of Public Economics* 8:239–45.

Cushner, I. M. 1981. Maternal Behavior and Perinatal Risks: Alcohol, Smoking and Drugs. *Annual Review of Public Health* 2:201–18.

Daniels, Norman. 1985. *Just Health Care.* Princeton, N.J.: Princeton University Press.

Day, Charles W. 1836. *Hints on Etiquette and the Usages of Society, with a Glance at Bad Habits.* 3d ed. London: Turnstile, 1947.

* Daynard, Richard A. 1988. Tobacco Liability Litigation as a Cancer Control Strategy. *Journal of the National Cancer Institute* 80, no. 1:9–13.

* Daynard, Richard A.; Popper, Edward T.; and Gruzalski, Bart K. 1986. *Selling Death: Individual and Organizational Responsibility and the Tobacco Industry.* A faculty colloquium, Northeastern University. Boston, Mass.: Northeastern University, Office of the Provost. Video.

* Dworkin, Gerald. 1972. Paternalism. *Monist* 56, no. 1:64–84. Reprinted in Sartorius, ed., 1983, pp. 19–34.

Edell, Marc Z., and Gisser, Stewart M. 1985. *Cipollone v. Liggett Group, Inc.:* The Application of Theories of Liability in Current Cigarette Litigation. *New York State Journal of Medicine* 85, no. 7:318–21.

Etzioni, Amitai. 1978. Individual Will and Social Conditions: Toward an Effective Health Maintenance Policy. *Annals of the American Academy of Political and Social Science* 437:62–73.

Eysenck, H. J. 1980. *The Causes and Effects of Smoking.* London: Maurice Temple Smith.

* Eysenck, H. J. 1986. Smoking and Health. In Tollison, ed., 1986, pp. 17–88.

Feinberg, Joel. 1970. *Doing and Deserving.* Princeton, N.J.: Princeton University Press.

Feinberg, Joel. 1971. Legal Paternalism. *Canadian Journal of Philosophy* 1:106–24. Reprinted in Sartorius, ed., 1983, pp. 3–18.

Feinberg, Joel. 1985. *Offense to Others.* Oxford: Oxford University Press.

Feinberg, Joel. 1986. *Harm to Self.* Oxford: Oxford University Press.

** Fielding, Jonathan E. 1985. Smoking: Health Effects and Control. *New England Journal of Medicine* 313:491–98, 555–61.

Fingarette, Herbert. 1970. The Perils of *Powell:* In Search of a Factual Foundation for the "Disease" Concept of Alcoholism. *Harvard Law Review* 83:793–812.

Fingarette, Herbert. 1975. Addiction and Criminal Responsibility. *Yale Law Journal* 84:413–44.

Fisher, Ronald A. 1957. Letter to the Editor: Dangers of Cigarette Smoking. *British Journal of Medicine* 2:297–98. Reprinted in Fisher 1959 and Fisher 1974, vol. 5, pp. 378–79.

Fisher, Ronald A. 1958. Cigarettes, Cancer and Statistics. *Centennial Review* 2:151–66. Reprinted in Fisher 1959 and Fisher 1974, vol. 5, pp. 407–22.

Fisher, Ronald A. 1959. *Smoking: The Cancer Controversy: Some Attempts to Assess the Evidence.* Edinburgh: Oliver & Boyd. Reprinted in Fisher 1974, vol. 5, pp. 377–80, 385–432.

Fisher, Ronald A. 1974. *Collected Papers.* Ed. J. H. Bennett. Adelaide: University of Adelaide.

Fitzgerald, P. J. 1961. Voluntary and Involuntary Acts. In *Oxford Essays in Jurisprudence,* 1st ser., ed. A. G. Guest, pp. 1–28. Oxford: Clarendon.

Fletcher, George P. 1978. *Rethinking Criminal Law.* Boston: Little, Brown.

Fox, S. J. 1963. Physical Disorder, Consciousness and Criminal Liability. *Columbia Law Review* 63:645–68.

Frankfurt, Harry G. 1971. Freedom of the Will and the Concept of a Person. *Journal of Philosophy* 68:5–20.

Froggatt, P., chairman. 1988. *Smoking and Health.* Fourth Report of the Independent Scientific Committee, UK Department of Health and Social Security. London: Her Majesty's Stationery Office.

Fuchs, Victor R. 1982. Time Preference and Health: An Exploratory Study. In *Economic Aspects of Health,* ed. Victor R. Fuchs, pp. 93–120. Chicago: University of Chicago Press.

Fujii, E. T. 1980. The Demand for Cigarettes: Further Empirical Evidence and Its Implications for Public Policy. *Applied Economics* 12:479–89.
Garner, Donald W. 1977. Cigarettes and Welfare Reform. *Emory Law Journal* 26:269–335.
Garner, Donald W. 1980. Cigarette Dependency and Civil Liability: A Modest Proposal. *Southern California Law Review* 53:1371–1465.
Gewirth, Alan. 1980. Health Rights and the Prevention of Cancer. *American Philosophical Quarterly* 17:117–25.
Gibson, Mary. 1985. Consent and Autonomy. In *To Breathe Freely*, ed. Mary Gibson, pp. 141–68. Totowa, N.J.: Rowman & Allanheld.
Goodin, Robert E. 1982. *Political Theory and Public Policy*. Chicago: University of Chicago Press.
Goodin, Robert E. 1986. The Principle of Voluntary Agreement. *Public Administration* (London) 64:435–44.
Gorovitz, Samuel. 1982. *Doctors' Dilemmas*. New York: Oxford University Press.
Grabosky, Peter, and Braithwaite, John. 1986. *Of Manners Gentle: Enforcement Strategies of Australian Business Regulatory Agencies*. Melbourne: Oxford University Press.
Gray, H. P., and Walter, I. 1986. The Economic Contribution of the Tobacco Industry to the Aggregate Economy. In Tollison, ed., 1986, pp. 271–84.
Gray, P. B. 1988. Smoking Foes Cite New Evidence Emerging in Tobacco Liability Suit. *Wall Street Journal*, April 4.
Hall, Jerome. 1944. Intoxication and Criminal Liability. *Harvard Law Review* 57:1045–84.
Hamilton, James L. 1972. The Demand for Cigarettes: Advertising, the Health Scare, and the Cigarette Advertising Ban. *Review of Economics and Statistics* 54:401–11.
Hanushek, Eric A., and Kain, John F. 1972. On the Value of *Equality of Educational Opportunity* as a Guide to Public Policy. In *On Equality of Educational Opportunity*, ed. Frederick Mosteller and D. P. Moynihan, pp. 116–45. New York: Random House.
Harrison, Larry. 1986. Tobacco Battered and the Pipes Shattered: A Note on the Fate of the First British Campaign against Tobacco Smoking. *British Journal of Addiction* 81:553–58.
Hart, H. L. A., and Honoré, Tony. 1985. *Causation in the Law*. 2d ed. Oxford: Clarendon.
Helyar, John. 1987. RJR Is Expected to Unveil "Smokeless" Cigarette Today. *Wall Street Journal* (European ed.), September 14.
Hume, David. 1760. Of the Original Contract. In *Essays, Literary, Moral and Political*. London: A. Millar.
Jackson, Thomas H., and Jeffries, John Calvin, Jr. 1979. Commercial Speech: Economic Due Process and the First Amendment. *Virginia Law Review* 65:1–41.
Janson, Donald. 1988. Cigarette Maker Assessed Damages in Smoker's Death. *New York Times*, June 14, pp. A1, B4.
Kahneman, D.; Slovic, P.; and Tversky, A., eds. 1982. *Judgment under Uncertainty*. Cambridge: Cambridge University Press.
Kelman, Mark. 1979. Choice and Utility. *Wisconsin Law Review* 1979:769–97.
Kirchheimer, Otto. 1942. Criminal Omissions. *Harvard Law Review* 55:615–42.
Kmiec, Douglas. 1986. Should Tobacco Advertising Be Banned? The Wrong Solution. *American Bar Association Journal* 72, no. 12:39.
Knowles, John H. 1977. The Responsibility of the Individual. *Daedalus* 106, no. 1:57–80.
Kozlowski, Lynn T.; Appel, C.-P.; Frecker, Richard C.; and Khouw, Virginia. 1982. Nicotine, a Prescription Drug Available without Prescription. *Lancet* 8267:334.
Kristein, M. M. 1983. How Much Can Business Expect to Profit from Smoking Cessation? *Preventive Medicine* 12:358–81.
Ledwith, Frank. 1984. Does Tobacco Sports Sponsorship on Television Act as Advertising to Children? *Health Education Journal* 43:85–88. Reprinted in BMA 1986, pp. 173–85.
Leu, Robert E. 1984. Anti-smoking Publicity, Taxation and the Demand for Cigarettes.

Journal of Health Economics 3:101–16.

Leu, Robert E., and Schaub, Thomas. 1983. Does Smoking Increase Medical Care Expenditures? *Social Science and Medicine* 17:1907–14.

* Leventhal, Howard, and Cleary, Paul D. 1980. The Smoking Problem: A Review of the Research and Theory in Behavioral Risk Modification. *Psychological Bulletin* 88:370–405.

** Leventhal, Howard; Glynn, Kathleen; and Fleming, Raymond. 1987. Is the Smoking Decision an "Informed Choice"? *Journal of the American Medical Association* 257:3373–76.

* Lewit, E. M.; Coate, D.; and Grossman, M. 1981. The Effects of Government Regulation on Teenage Smoking. *Journal of Law and Economics* 24:545–69.

Lichtenstein, S.; Slovic, P.; Fischhoff, B.; Layman, M.; and Combs, B. 1978. Judged Frequency of Lethal Events. *Journal of Experimental Psychology (Human Learning and Memory)* 4:551–78.

Littlechild, S. C. 1986. Smoking and Market Failure. In Tollison, ed., 1986, pp. 271–84.

* Littlechild, S. C., and Wiseman, J. 1984. Principles of Public Policy Relevant to Smoking. *Policy Studies* 4, no. 3:54–67.

Luce, B. R., and Schweitzer, S. O. 1978. Smoking and Alcohol Abuse: A Comparison of Their Economic Consequences. *New England Journal of Medicine* 298:569–71.

Lundberg, George D., and Knoll, Elizabeth. 1986. Editorial: Tobacco for Consenting Adults in Private Only. *Journal of the American Medical Association* 255:1051–53.

McGuinness, Tony, and Cowling, Keith. 1975. Advertising and the Aggregate Demand for Cigarettes. *European Economic Review* 6:311–28.

Manchester, P. B. 1976. Interstate Cigarette Smuggling. *Public Finance Quarterly* 4:225–37.

Martin, Judith. 1983. *Miss Manners' Guide to Excruciatingly Correct Behavior.* New York: Warner Books.

Maynard, Alan, and Kennan, Patricia. 1981. *The Economics of Addiction: A Survey of the Literature and a Proposed Research Strategy.* Report to the SSRC Panel on Addiction Research. York: University of York, Institute of Social and Economic Research.

Meenan, Robert F. 1976. Improving the Public's Health—Some Further Reflections. *New England Journal of Medicine* 294:45–47.

Mill, John Stuart. 1859. *On Liberty.* In *Three Essays.* Ed. Richard Wollheim, pp. 1–141. Oxford: Oxford University Press, 1975.

Mintz, Morton. 1987. A Pack of Whys: A Tobacco Company Faces a Trial in the Death of a Smoker. *Washington Post National Weekly Edition,* February 9, pp. 21–22.

Mintz, Morton. 1988a. Cigarette Trial Breaks New Ground. *Washington Post,* March 27, pp. H1 and H8.

Mintz, Morton. 1988b. Foes of Smoking Call for Congressional Probe: Tobacco Industry Lawyer Decries "Media Circus." *Washington Post,* March 27, p. A6.

Mishan, E. J. 1967. Pareto Optimality and the Law. *Oxford Economic Papers* 19:255–87.

Morrison, Denton E., and Henkel, Ramon E., eds. 1970. *The Significance Test Controversy.* London: Butterworths.

Oken, Donald. 1985. Tobacco Addiction and Compassion. *Journal of the American Medical Association* 253:2958.

Owen, David. 1987. Octane and Knock. *Atlantic Monthly* 260, no. 2:53–60.

Page, Talbot. 1978. A Generic View of Toxic Chemicals and Similar Risks. *Ecology Law Quarterly* 7:207–44.

Pears, David. 1984. *Motivated Irrationality.* Oxford: Clarendon.

Peto, Richard. 1980. Possible Ways of Explaining to Ordinary People the Quantitative Dangers of Smoking. *Health Education Journal* 39:45–46.

* Plaintiffs' Conduct as a Defense to Claims against Cigarette Manufacturers. 1986. *Harvard Law Review* 99:809–27.

* Pollin, William. 1984. The Role of the Addictive Process as a Key Step in Causation of All Tobacco-related Diseases. *Journal of the American Medical Association* 252:2874.

Preston, M. H. 1971. Economics of Cigarette Smoking. In *Proceedings of the Second World Conference on Smoking and Health,* ed. Robert G. Richardson, pp. 100–110. London: Pittman Medical.

Prevezer, S. 1958. Automatism and Involuntary Conduct. *Criminal Law Review* 1958: 361–67, 440–52.

Quasi-suspect Classes and Proof of Discriminatory Intent: A New Model. 1981. *Yale Law Journal* 90:912–31.

** Repace, James L. 1985. Risks of Passive Smoking. In *To Breathe Freely,* ed. Mary Gibson, pp. 3–30. Totowa, N.J.: Rowman & Allanheld.

Repace, James L., and Lowrey, A. H. 1980. Indoor Air Pollution, Tobacco Smoke and Public Health. *Science* 208:464–72.

Repace, James L., and Lowrey, A. H. 1985. A Quantitative Assessment of Nonsmokers' Lung Cancer Risk from Passive Smoking. *Environment International* 11:3–22.

Repace, James L., and Lowrey, A. H. 1986. A Rebuttal to Criticism of Repace and Lowrey (1985). *Environment International* 12:33–38.

Rice, Dorothy P.; Hodgson, Thomas A.; Sinsheimer, Peter H.; Browner, Warren; and Kopstein, Andrea N. 1986. The Economic Costs of the Health Effects of Smoking, 1984. *Milbank Quarterly* 64:489–547.

R. J. Reynolds Tobacco Co. 1986. The Health Effects of Smoking. A Submission in the Case of *Browner v. R.J. Reynolds* (California Superior Court, County of Contra Costa). Reprinted in *Tobacco Products Litigation Reporter* 1, no. 4:5.45–56.

Roberts, John L. 1986. *Code Busting by Tobacco Companies.* A Report for the Health Education Council from the North Western Regional Health Authority. Manchester: Project Smoke Free.

Robins, L. 1973. *A Follow-up of Vietnam Drug Users.* Interim Final Report, Special Actions Office for Drug Abuse Prevention. Washington, D.C.: Executive Office of the President.

Robinson, James C. 1986. Philosophical Origins of the Economic Valuation of Life. *Milbank Quarterly* 64:133–55.

Roemer, Ruth. 1986. *Recent Developments in Legislation to Combat the World Smoking Epidemic.* Division of Non-communicable Diseases, Smoking and Health Program. WHO/ SMO/HLE/86.1. Geneva: World Health Organization.

Rosenberg, David. 1984. The Causal Connection in Mass Exposure Cases: A "Public Law" Vision of the Tort System. *Harvard Law Review* 97:849–929.

Rothstein, M. 1983. Employee Selection Based on Susceptibility to Occupational Illness. *Michigan Law Review* 81:1379–1496.

Royal College of Physicians. 1962. *Smoking and Health.* London: Pittman Medical.

Royal College of Physicians. 1971. *Smoking and Health Now.* London: Pittman Medical.

Royal College of Physicians. 1983. *Health or Smoking?* London: Pittman Medical.

Russell, M. A. H. 1974. Realistic Goals for Smoking and Health. *Lancet* 7851:254–58.

* Sartorius, Rolf, ed. 1983. *Paternalism.* Minneapolis: University of Minnesota Press.

Savarese, J. M., and Shughart, W. F. II. 1986. The Incidence of Taxes on Tobacco. In Tollison, ed., 1986, pp. 285–308.

Schelling, Thomas C. 1968. The Life You Save May Be Your Own. In *Problems in Public Expenditure Analysis,* ed. Samuel B. Chase. Washington, D.C.: Brookings Institution. Reprinted in Schelling 1984a, pp. 113–46.

Schelling, Thomas C. 1980. The Intimate Contest for Self-Command. *Public Interest* 60:94–118. Reprinted in Schelling 1984a, pp. 57–82.

* Schelling, Thomas C. 1983. Ethics, Law and the Exercise of Self-Command. *Tanner Lectures on Human Values* 4:44–79. Reprinted in Schelling 1984a, pp. 83–113.

Schelling, Thomas C. 1984a. *Choice and Consequence.* Cambridge, Mass.: Harvard University Press.

Schelling, Thomas C. 1984b. Self-Command in Practice, in Policy, and in a Theory of Rational Choice. *American Economic Review (Papers and Proceedings)* 74:1–11.

Schelling, Thomas C. 1985. Enforcing Rules on Oneself. *Journal of Law, Economics and Organization* 1:357–74.

* Schelling, Thomas C. 1986a. Economics and Cigarettes. *Preventive Medicine* 15:549–60.

* Schelling, Thomas C. 1986b. Whose Business Is Good Behavior? In *American Society: Public and Private Responsibilities*, ed. Winthrop Knowlton and Richard Zeckhauser, pp. 153–80. Cambridge, Mass.: Ballinger.

Schlesinger, A. M. 1946. *Learning How to Behave.* New York: Macmillan.

Schneider, L.; Klein, B.; and Murphy, K. M. 1981. Governmental Regulation of Cigarette Health Information. *Journal of Law and Economics* 24:575–612.

Schoeman, Ferdinand. 1987. Statistical vs. Direct Evidence. *Noûs* 21:179–98.

Shughart, W. F. II, and Tollison, R. D. 1986. Smokers vs. Nonsmokers. In Tollison, ed., 1986, pp. 217–24.

Sidgwick, Henry. 1907. *The Methods of Ethics.* 7th ed. London: Macmillan.

Slade, J.; Kopelowicz, A.; Hahn, A.; Gill, J.; Kabis, S.; and Vasen, A. 1986–87. An Analysis of R. J. Reynolds' Position Paper on the Health Effects of Smoking. *Tobacco Products Litigation Reporter* 1, no. 8:5.97–105; 1, no. 10:5.115–21; 2, no. 2:5.11–21.

Slovic, P.; Fischhoff, B.; and Lichtenstein, S. 1982. Fact vs. Fears: Understanding Perceived Risks. In Kahneman, Slovic, and Tversky, eds., 1982, pp. 463–89.

Smith, R. C. 1978. The Magazines' Smoking Habit. *Columbia Journalism Review* 15, no. 5:29–31.

Spencer, Herbert. 1893. *The Principles of Ethics.* London: Williams & Norgate.

Spielberger, C. D. 1986. Psychological Determinants of Smoking Behavior. In Tollison, ed., 1986, pp. 89–134.

Starr, Chauncey. 1969. Social Benefits vs. Technological Risks. *Science* 165:1232–38.

Stigler, George J., and Becker, Gary S. 1977. De Gustibus Non Est Disputandum. *American Economic Review* 67:76–90.

Stoddart, Greg L.; Labelle, Roberta J.; Barer, Morris L.; and Evals, Robert G. 1986. Tobacco Sales and Health Care Costs: Do Canadian Smokers Pay Their Way? *Journal of Health Economics* 5:63–80.

Taylor, Peter. 1985. *The Smoke Ring.* London: Sphere Books.

Thomson, Judith Jarvis. 1986. *Rights, Restitution and Risk.* Cambridge, Mass.: Harvard University Press.

Tobacco Advisory Council (TAC). 1987. *Smoking at Work.* London: TAC.

* Tollison, Robert D., ed. 1986. *Smoking and Society.* Lexington, Mass.: Lexington Books, D. C. Heath.

** Tollison, Robert D., and Wagner, Richard E. 1988. *Smoking and the State.* Lexington, Mass.: Lexington Books, D. C. Heath.

Tribe, Laurence H. 1971. Trial by Mathematics. *Harvard Law Review* 84:1329–93.

Tribe, Laurence H. 1986. Federalism with Smoke and Mirrors. *Nation* 242:788–90.

United States. Advisory Commission on Intergovernmental Relations (U.S. ACIR). 1977. *Cigarette Bootlegging: A State and Federal Responsibility.* Washington, D.C.: ACIR.

United States. Congress. Office of Technology Assessment (U.S. OTA). 1985. *Smoking-related Deaths and Financial Costs.* OTA Staff Memorandum, Health Program, OTA, U.S. Congress. Washington, D.C.: OTA.

United States. Department of Health, Education and Welfare (U.S. DHEW). 1964. *Smoking and Health.* Report of the Advisory Committee to the Surgeon General of the Public Health Service. Washington, D.C.: Government Printing Office.

U.S. DHEW. Surgeon General. 1976. *The Health Consequences of Smoking: A Reference Edition.* Washington, D.C.: Government Printing Office.

United States. Department of Health and Human Services (U.S. DHHS). Various years. *Bibliography on Smoking and Health.* Washington, D.C.: Government Printing Office.

U.S. DHHS. Surgeon General. 1979. *Smoking and Health.* Washington, D.C.: Government Printing Office.

U.S. DHHS. Surgeon General. 1980. *The Health Consequences of Smoking for Women.* Washington, D.C.: Government Printing Office.

U.S. DHHS. Surgeon General. 1981. *The Health Consequences of Smoking: The Changing Cigarette.* Washington, D.C.: Government Printing Office.

U.S. DHHS. Surgeon General. 1982. *The Health Consequences of Smoking: Cancer.* Washington,

D.C.: Government Printing Office.

U.S. DHHS. Surgeon General. 1986. *The Health Consequences of Involuntary Smoking.* Washington, D.C.: Government Printing Office.

U.S. DHHS. Surgeon General. 1988. *The Health Consequences of Smoking: Nicotine Addiction.* Washington, D.C.: Government Printing Office.

United States. Federal Trade Commission (U.S. FTC). 1981. *Staff Report on the Cigarette Advertising Investigation,* Matthew L. Meyers, chairman. Public version. Washington, D.C.: FTC.

U.S. FTC. 1984. *A Report to the Congress Pursuant to the Federal Cigarette Labelling and Advertising Act.* Washington, D.C.: Government Printing Office.

U.S. FTC. 1985. *A Report to the Congress Pursuant to the Federal Cigarette Labelling and Advertising Act.* Washington, D.C.: Government Printing Office.

United States. National Academy of Sciences (U.S. NAS). National Research Council. Committee on Airliner Cabin Air Quality. 1986a. *The Airliner Cabin Environment: Air Quality and Safety.* Washington, D.C.: National Academy Press.

U.S. NAS. National Research Council. Committee on Passive Smoking. 1986b. *Environmental Tobacco Smoke: Measuring Exposures and Assessing Health Effects.* Washington, D.C.: National Academy Press.

Victor, Kirk. 1987. Strange Alliances. *National Journal* 19:2076–81.

Warner, Kenneth E. 1981. Cigarette Smoking in the 1970s: The Impact of the Antismoking Campaign on Consumption. *Science* 211:729–31.

Warner, Kenneth E. 1985. Cigarette Advertising and Media Coverage of Smoking and Health. *New England Journal of Medicine* 312:384–88.

Warner, Kenneth E. 1987a. A Ban on the Promotion of Tobacco Products. *New England Journal of Medicine* 316:745–47.

Warner, Kenneth E. 1987b. Health and Economic Implications of a Tobacco-free Society. *Journal of the American Medical Association* 258:2080–86.

** Warner, K. E.; Ernster, V. L.; Holbrook, J. H.; Lewit, E. M.; Pertschuk, M.; Steinfeld, J. L.; Tye, J. B.; and Whelan, E. M. 1986. Promotion of Tobacco Products: Issues and Policy Options. *Journal of Health Politics, Policy and Law* 11:367–92.

Watson, Gary. 1975. Free Agency. *Journal of Philosophy* 72:205–20.

Watson, Gary. 1977. Skepticism about Weakness of Will. *Philosophical Review* 86:316–39.

Weinkam, J. J.; Rosenbaum, W.; and Sterling, T. D. 1987. Smoking and Hospital Utilization. *Social Science and Medicine* 24:983–86.

** Wikler, Daniel. 1978. Persuasion and Coercion for Health: Ethical Issues in Government Efforts to Change Life-styles. *Health and Society* (now *Milbank Quarterly*) 56:303–38. Reprinted in Sartorius, ed., 1983, pp. 35–59.

Wikler, Daniel. 1987. Personal Responsibility for Illness. In *Health Care Ethics,* ed. D. van de Veer and T. Regan, pp. 326–58. Philadelphia: Temple University Press.

Wildavsky, Aaron. 1977. Doing Better and Feeling Worse: The Political Pathology of Health Policy. *Daedalus* 106, no. 1:105–23.

Wilkinson, James. 1986. *Tobacco.* Harmondsworth: Penguin.

Will, George F. 1987. Foes of Smoking on Airliners Are Right. *International Herald Tribune,* September 10.

Winsten, Jay A., director. 1986. *Nicotine Dependency and Compulsive Tobacco Use.* A Research Status Report, Center for Health Communication, Harvard School of Public Health. Reprinted in *Tobacco Product Liability Reporter* 1, no. 7.

Woodfield, Alan E. 1984. Costs and "Benefits" of Cigarette Smoking in Canada: A Comment. *Canadian Medical Association Journal* 130:118–20.

World Health Organization (WHO). 1978. *International Classification of Diseases.* 9th ed. Geneva: WHO.

WHO. 1986. *In Point of Fact,* no. 36. Geneva: WHO.

Yondorf, Barbara. 1979. Prostitution as a Legal Activity: The West German Experience. *Policy Analysis* 5:417–33.

[16]

Smokers' Rights to Health Care: Why the 'Restoration Argument' is a Moralising Wolf in a Liberal Sheep's Clothing

STEPHEN WILKINSON

ABSTRACT *Do people who cause themselves to be ill (e.g. by smoking) forfeit some of their rights to healthcare? This paper examines one argument for the view that they do,* the restoration argument.

It goes as follows. Smokers need more health-resources than non-smokers. Given limited budgets, we must choose between treating everyone equally (according to need) or *reducing smokers' entitlements. If we choose the former, non-smokers will be harmed by others' smoking, because there will be less resources available for them than if no-one smoked. This is unfair: why should non-smokers suffer because of others' unhealthy lifestyle choices? We should therefore choose the latter and reduce smokers' entitlements.*

This paper criticises the restoration argument on the following grounds. In order to avoid generating unpalatable conclusions elsewhere, it must be combined with a principle according to which activities which are sufficiently 'socially valuable' (e.g. parenting) are immune from restoration claims. This however means that what was supposed *to be one of the argument's most attractive features, its compatibility with 'liberal neutrality' with respect to the value of different lifestyles, doesn't really exist. Hence, the restoration argument is nowhere near as attractive as it at first appears to be.*

I. Introduction

Several writers have claimed that, when making decisions about the allocation of health care resources, one important consideration is whether the patient's illness has been caused by her 'lifestyle' [1]. It is argued, for example, that smokers and heavy drinkers should have their entitlements to health service resources reduced because they are less deserving than people who become ill 'through no fault of their own', the implication being that smokers and heavy drinkers are at least partly to blame for their own ill-health [2]. The *General Medical Council* recently made a strong statement against this view [3], but it is nevertheless one which enjoys substantial public support [4].

It should be stressed from the outset that there is no reason in principle why this position could not be extended to cover *any* group of risk-takers. It is normally however applied just to activities such as smoking and drinking, perhaps because such behaviours (especially smoking) are easily identifiable, relatively common and widely regarded as 'vices' [5]. I shall therefore focus just on smoking, but it should be noted that the arguments under discussion are in principle applicable to all voluntary [6] actions (or omissions) which pose a risk to health [7].

II. The Restoration Argument

Several arguments [8] have been advanced in favour of the view that smokers' entitlements to health care should be reduced provided that certain conditions are met — e.g. the smoker in question must have had (actual or constructive) knowledge of the risks involved and must be suffering from a condition which was caused by her having smoked. The most persuasive and widely accepted of these arguments is the restoration argument and this particular argument is the sole concern of this paper; it goes as follows [9].

(1) We can divide health service users into two groups: smokers and non-smokers [10].
(2) Smokers are more likely to suffer from certain diseases than non-smokers.
(3) This fact — (2) — is widely known and information about the risks associated with smoking is widely disseminated.
(4) *Therefore* (from (2) and (3)) smokers either know or ought to know about the risks to which they're exposing themselves by smoking; they *knowingly* and *voluntarily* subject themselves to additional risk [11].
(5) Because of (2), smokers are more likely to make demands on the health services than non-smokers — to consume more health service resources. Like (2), this fact is widely known.
(6) *Therefore* smokers (from (2), (3), (4) & (5)) *knowingly* increase their own likely health care needs.
(7) Health care resources are limited and, in particular, there are no additional 'ring-fenced' funds available to meet the special needs of smokers[12].
(8) Given (7) if we *don't* reduce the health care entitlements of smokers, then the non-smokers will be harmed by the smokers — because, by smoking, the smokers cause an increase in the overall demand for health care and so, for the average non-smoker, decrease the chances of her needs being met.
(9) To allow non-smokers to be harmed by smokers would be unfair. Why should non-smokers 'pay the price' for smokers' behaviour?
(10) In order to avoid this unfairness, smokers' entitlements to health care should be reduced.

In practice, what this might mean is that smokers would have to wait longer for treatment than non-smokers and/or that admission and treatment criteria would be made 'tougher' for smokers. Smokers' entitlements would be reduced to the level (no more, no less) at which it would be true that no non-smoker was made worse off (in terms of access to health care resources) than they would have been if no-one smoked. This gives us the key to the argument's name, the idea being that the quantity of health resources for non-smokers is 'restored' to the level it would have been at if the smokers had not generated extra demand [13]. So, to sum up, what the *restoration argument* says is that we ought to reduce smokers' entitlements to health care because *not* to do so would mean unfairly making non-smokers 'pay the price' for smokers' unhealthy lifestyles [14].

There are two main reasons for this argument's intuitive appeal. Firstly, and most importantly, it seems not (as do some other arguments) to advocate using health care rationing as a way of punishing people for their lifestyles, or of (coercively) deterring people from smoking, or of enforcing moral standards. Indeed, its proponents are often at pains to point out that it is not about punishing smokers [15]:

> . . . the justification, if there is one, for discriminating against a smoker when only one spare set of heart and lungs is available must be *non-punitive*. And that justification lies in *restitution* [16].

So as Smart (above) makes clear, the argument's sole concern is with (hypothetically) *restoring* the distribution of resources to the position which would have existed if it weren't for the extra demands created by smokers — *not* with punishment. This feature makes the argument palatable even for those liberals who are opposed to using the health care system punitively and/or as a means of coercively influencing individuals' lifestyle choices.

The second reason for the argument's appeal is that it seems to focus not on preventing harm to smokers but just on preventing harm to third parties, the non-smokers [17]. This saves it from accusations of paternalism and again allows it to be attractive even to liberals, since the aim of the proposed policy is not forcibly to save the smokers from themselves, but to prevent them from harming others. In these respects, the role of the restoration argument in the debate about health care rationing is similar to the role of passive smoking arguments in the debate about the permissibility of smoking in public. In the absence of passive smoking arguments, prohibiting smoking in public would strike many as unjustifiably illiberal. But the existence of such arguments, grounded in thoughts about third-party harm, makes anti-smoking (in public) policies seem acceptable even to many liberals. The same goes for the rationing debate. In the absence of the restoration argument, reducing smokers' entitlements to health care would to many seem unduly punitive (or perhaps paternalistic, if the main aims were coercion and deterrence). But the restoration argument allows even liberals to accept this policy, because it is justified purely in terms of protecting innocent third-parties.

III. An Empirical Objection to the Restoration Argument: Smoking *Saves* Money for the Health Service.

Most critics of the restoration argument do not question its logical validity, but instead criticise it either by arguing against its premises or by arguing that, although it does indeed provide a *prima facie* case for reducing smokers' entitlements to health care, this case is outweighed by other considerations such as the likely negative side-effects of the policy. My concern here is with an objection of the first kind, one attacking the argument's premises.

The objection is, quite simply, that smokers cost the health service (and/or, more generally, the taxpayer) less than non-smokers because, as Persaud puts it:

> Smokers . . . save the state money by dying early. Smoking tends to cause few problems during a person's productive years, and then kills them before social security and pensions payments are made [18].

Her 'common sense' account of the reasons why smokers are likely to be 'cheaper' seems convincing[19] and is further supported by Barendregt, Bonneux and Van Der Maas's recent work[20]. According to their study:

> Health care costs for smokers [per year] at a given age are as much as 40% higher than those of non-smokers . . . [21]

But because smokers are less likely to live into old age, smokers' lifetime health care costs are normally less than those of non-smokers:

> The . . . nonsmoking population lives longer and therefore incurs more costs . . . particularly in old age, when the costs are highest. On balance, the total costs for male and female nonsmokers are 7% and 4% higher, respectively, than for a mixed [smoking and nonsmoking] population, whereas for smokers the total costs are 7% and 11% lower [22].

> [Overall costs] if all smokers stopped smoking . . . would initially be lower . . . (by up to 2.5%) . . . With time, however, the benefit reverses itself to become a cost. The reason is that . . . smoking-related mortality declines and the population starts to age. Growing numbers of people in the older age groups mean higher costs for health care. By year 5, the benefit derived from the presence of the new nonsmokers starts to shrink, and by year 15 these former smokers are producing excess cost. Eventually a new steady stage is reached in which costs are about 7% higher . . . [23]

So assuming that they are correct, the restoration argument fails since, regardless of any philosophical merits that it might have, it is based on a false empirical assumption. Smokers do not cost the health service more than non-smokers; on the contrary, they cost less. And so the restoration argument fails just because there is in fact nothing to restore [24].

IV. Can the Restoration Argument be Run in Reverse?

If we accept that smoking saves taxpayers' money, then the view that smokers' entitlements should be reduced in order to compensate non-smokers is undoubtedly a non-starter. What I want to explore now, though, is something rather different: might the 'cheapness' of smokers provide not only a reason for not reducing their entitlements, but also a reason for giving their needs a higher priority than those of other people? The idea here is that anyone who supports the principles behind the restoration argument (in particular, anyone who thinks that *if* smokers had turned out to be more expensive, *then* their entitlements should have been reduced) ought (if they are consistent, fair, rational etc) to believe that it 'cuts both ways'. They should accept that if it turns out that the non-smokers are causing the smokers to have less health care resources available to them than they otherwise would have (if it weren't for the non-smokers' not smoking) then the *non*-smokers ought to compensate the smokers by having *their* entitlements reduced.

More specifically, the idea is that we can construct what I shall call the *reverse restoration argument*:

[1*] We can divide health service users into two groups: smokers and non-smokers.
[2*] Non-smokers are less likely to suffer from certain life-shortening diseases.
[3*] [2*] is widely known.
[4*] Therefore (from [2*] and [3*]) non-smokers either know or ought to know about the health benefits which they're accruing by not smoking; they knowingly and voluntarily increase the probability of their not acquiring various life-shortening illnesses.
[5*] Because of [2*], non-smokers are likely (in the long term) to make additional demands on the health service. Like [2*], this fact is widely known [25].
[6*] *Therefore* non-smokers (from [2*], [3*], [4*] & [5*]) knowingly increase their own likely health care needs.
[7*] Health care resources are limited and, in particular, there are no additional 'ring-fenced' funds available to meet the special needs of non-smokers.
[8*] Given [7*] if we *don't* reduce the health care entitlements of non-smokers, then the smokers will be harmed by the non-smokers. The reason for this is that, by *not* smoking, the non-smokers cause an increase in the overall demand for health care and so, for the average smoker, decrease the chances of her needs being met.
[9*] To allow smokers to be made worse-off by the non-smokers' not smoking would be unfair. Why should smokers pay the price for the non-smokers' behaviour and lifestyle choices?
[10*] In order to avoid the unfairness cited in [9*] smokers' health care needs should be prioritised (i.e. given a higher priority than those of non-smokers).

The reverse restoration argument generates a problem for proponents of the (conventional) restoration argument. If they believe that the latter is valid, then they either [a] must provide some account of why the former is unsound — either by showing that there is some relevant logical difference between the two arguments or by showing that the former contains an addtional false premise, or [b] must accept that smokers' needs should be prioritised. Clearly, [b] will be unappealing to many proponents of the restoration argument, so they must attempt [a]. The question addressed by the rest of this paper is whether and how this might be done.

V. Some Preliminary Points about Relevance

It is important first to rule two obvious objections to the reverse restoration argument out of court, namely:

[a] that it would be wrong to prioritise smokers' needs because to do so would amount to *punishing* people for pursuing a healthy lifestyle and *rewarding* people for pursuing an unhealthy one; and,
[b] that it would be wrong to prioritise smokers' needs because to do so would *deter* people from pursuing a healthy lifestyle and *encourage* them to pursue an unhealthy one.

Perhaps both [a] and [b] should be taken extremely seriously in general but their relevance to the present debate is very limited, perhaps even non-existent. First, neither [a] nor [b] are objections to the argument *per se*. Rather, both are independent arguments against its conclusion. So one could consistently accept *both* that the reverse restoration argument offers a good *prima facie* case for prioritising smokers' needs, *and* that [a] and [b] are true (and perhaps also that [a] and [b] outweigh the *prima facie* case for prioritising smokers). Second, we should take care to remember that the restoration argument is supposed not to be saying anything about punishing and rewarding or about deterring and encouraging. Indeed, as was noted earlier, one of its supposed attractions is that it involves neither taking up a punitive stance towards smokers, nor attempting to coerce smokers into stopping smoking by threatening to remove or reduce their entitlements to health care. One may, of course, seek independently to justify reducing smokers' entitlements in either or both of these ways, but such considerations are not part of the restoration argument and so are irrelevant to the present discussion.

VI. Principles of Application

One way of taking the reverse restoration argument is as a *reductio ad absurdum* of the restoration argument. For those who oppose the view that smokers' entitlements should be reduced, this is likely to be their preferred understanding, since it means that what seemed to be the best argument for reducing smokers' entitlements has been discredited. Others however may wish to defend the restoration argument by attempting to show that, in the reverse version, it has somehow been misapplied. The most promising way of doing this is to provide a principle of application which would tell us when it is legitimate to use such arguments. And so my aim in what follows is to answer the following: can a principle of application be found which [a] entails that the (conventional) restoration argument is legitimate, [b] entails that the reverse restoration argument is illegitimate, and [c] is independently justifiable and plausible? I shall consider three possibilities: the acts/omissions criterion, the self-harm criterion and the social value criterion.

VII. The Acts/Omissions Criterion

The most obvious difference between the two restoration arguments is that whereas one concerns an action (smoking) the other concerns an omission (not smoking). Perhaps then the (original) restoration argument can be defended by reference to an acts/omissions criterion, according to which people should be required to compensate others (e.g. by having their entitlements to health care reduced) if their actions deplete health care resources, but not if their omissions similarly deplete those resources. This principle certainly does the work required of it by excluding the reverse restoration argument while allowing the original version to stand. But is it independently justifiable and plausible?

We can show that it is not just by thinking about possible applications. Imagine for example a world in which not eating carrots has the same deleterious effects on health as smoking and in which not eating carrots and smoking both generate the same additional health care costs. In this world we can rank groups as follows, with the non-smoking carrot-eaters being the 'cheapest' and healthiest people and the smoking non-carrot-eaters being the most 'expensive' and least healthy.

[1] Non-smoking carrot-eaters (cheap/healthy)
[2A] Smoking carrot-eaters
[2B] Non-smoking non-carrot-eaters
[3] Smoking non-carrot-eaters (most expensive/unhealthy)

What is interesting about this scenario is that [2A] and [2B] both generate the same additional costs (compared to [1]) which raises the question of whether [2A] and [2B] should each be subject to the same restoration claims with respect to [1]. If we adopted the acts/omissions criterion, the [2A] and [2B] would be treated differently. Smoking is an action and so [2A] must compensate [1] because they have actively generated extra costs. [2B] though are not required to compensate [1] because not eating carrots is merely an omission and therefore the non-carrot-eaters are 'immune' from restoration claims (at least as far as the non-carrot-eating is concerned). But is this the correct result?

It seems to me that it would be quite unfair to subject [2A] to 'tougher' treatment than [2B] since surely what really matters here is not whether the extra costs were generateed actively or passively but that the individuals concerned *freely* and *knowingly* chose a more 'expensive' lifestyle (and let's assume that they did). Other real-life cases count against the acts/omissions criterion too. Consider for example people who don't wear seat-belts in cars, or crash-helmets on motorcycles, or 'couch potatoes' who take no exercise. It may, for a variety of reasons, be wrong to reduce such people's entitlements to health care. But should they really be completely immune from restoration claims *just* because their 'costly' lifestyle choices involve omissions rather than actions? It seems clear that the answer is 'no' and therefore that the acts/omissions criterion should be rejected.

VIII. The Self-Harm Criterion

The self-harm criterion says that restoration arguments may be used only against groups which consume additional resources by harming themselves. If we adopt this, then the *reverse* restoration argument will be ruled out, since the 'activity' in question (non-smoking) is not self-harmful. The (original) restoration argument, though, will be allowed to stand, since smoking is self-harmful. So the self-harm criterion seems to do the work required of it by allowing one argument to stand but not the other.

There remains though a question about why (and, more pressingly, whether) the distinction between depleting resources through self-harm and doing so in other ways has any moral significance. The driving thought behind the restitution argument was simply that it would be wrong to allow one group to deprive another of resources by voluntarily increasing its own needs. So why should it matter by what methods (self-harm or otherwise) a group causes an increase in its consumption? Why should harming others by benefiting oneself be treated more 'leniently' than harming others by harming oneself? I shall argue that it should not and that the self-harm criterion is unjustified; the bare difference between self-harming behaviours and others is strictly irrelevant.

The main problems with the self-harm criterion can be revealed by looking at two counter-examples: one real, the other fictitious. The first is provided by Smart:

> A miner or fireman chooses freely to subject himself to greater risk of harm or disease than is met with in most occupations. And, on the special assumpton that

> if he were not to make that choice nobody would fill his place, it may be true that he causes a shortfall [in health resources] [26].

The problem here is that, if the self-harm criterion were accepted, then restoration arguments could still be used against people with dangerous but socially necessary or useful occupations (such as fire-fighters) because they (like smokers) voluntarily create health costs by exposing themselves to danger. Clearly this is implausible and so, at best, the self-harm criterion as it stands is inadequate and needs to be supplemented by some further principle — one which distinguishes dangerous activities like fire-fighting from those like smoking.

The second counter-example is more fanciful. Imagine that just 5% of the population (call them *group P*) are so constituted that they can benefit from a drug, called *Agedelay*. If members of *P* take *Agedelay* regularly (and let's assume they all do) then they are likely to live for an extra 30 years. However, *Agedelay* doesn't significantly benefit members of *P* in any other way and so, at any given age, members of *P* taking *Agedelay* are likely to need almost the same level of health and social welfare resources as anyone else; *Agedelay* makes them live longer, but doesn't stop them from suffering various non-lethal diseases. (Perhaps this fact would make *Agedelay* undesirable to many of us.)

Clearly, members of *P* are going to be much more expensive than others, especially if we include not only health care costs, but social welfare and pension costs too, and this raises the following question. *Do the rest of us have a legitimate restoration claim against P*? Intuitions will almost certainly vary on this point but there do seem to be some reasons to answer *yes* (on the assumption for the present that there are no *general* reasons to reject restoration arguments).

One reason arises from what we might say about taxation. It could plausibly be argued that *Agedelay* should be heavily taxed in order to pay for the additional costs that its use will generate. Now provided that this claim about the legitimacy of special taxation is accepted, something very much like a restoration claim has already been implicitly accepted. For surely, if members of *P need* to pay additional tax in order to generate an entitlement to equal treatment, then if they *don't* pay additional tax, their entitlements may permissibly be reduced. Or, to look at it in a slightly different way, *P*'s additional tax burden in effect *is* a form of restoration — they are compensating (albeit in advance) the rest of us for the fact that they are going to consume more later and, in so doing, are preventing their *Agedelay* consumption from harming third-parties. So if we accept, as seems fair, that taxing *Agedelay* to pay for any extra health/welfare costs would be legitimate, then we should also accept that, *in the absence of special taxation*, reducing *P*'s entitlements would be similarly legitimate.

A second reason for reducing *P*'s entitlements arises from what we might reasonably say if we had to choose between these two candidates for a transplant organ. (Here, it is assumed that *Agedelay* is not taxed.) Smith, not a member of *P*, is aged 55. Jones, an *Agedelay*-consuming member of *P*, is aged 85. The two candidates are equal in all respects except age. But even age might not be relevant *in the standard way* because (given *Agedelay*'s effects) we should expect each of them to have the same remaining life-years, provided that they get the transplant organ. The question is: *should Jones' needs be given a lower priority than Smith's?*

A powerful reason for answering *yes* is this. Faced with the above scenario, Smith can reasonably claim that unless his needs are given priority then he is being (unfairly) harmed by Jones' lifestyle choice. If Jones hadn't (selfishly) decided to lengthen his life by taking *Agedelay* then he would be dead by now and Smith would have a 100% chance of getting the organ, rather than a 50% chance. And surely it would be wrong for Smith to have his life shortened because of Jones' use of *Agedelay*. Interestingly, this is exactly what Smart says about smokers and non-smokers:

> . . . if there is no forfeiture of equality then, the one non-smoker in need of a transplant has a 1/2 chance of acquiring the spare set rather than a 1/1 chance. Without differential treatment according to fault the non-smoker would be denied his rightful opportunity. By forfeiting his own right to equality the smoker restores the *status quo* [27].

And if this goes for users of tobacco — why not users of *Agedelay*?

These considerations are sufficient to show that (in the absence of special taxation) it would be legitimate to reduce the entitlements of *Agedelay* users (at least once they got to an age at which their continuing need was caused by their *Agedelay* consumption). If this is accepted, then we have another powerful objection to the self-harm criterion, since *Agedelay* users can quite properly have restoration arguments used against them, even though *Agedelay*-use is not self-harmful.

I want to discuss briefly one further illuminating case before moving on. Assume that parents cost taxpayers more than non-parents. Could non-parents (in principle) legitimately use a restoration argument to justify giving parents' needs a lower priority? I imagine that most of us would want to answer this question with a decisive 'no'. But if we apply the self-harm criterion to this case, we get the bizarre conclusion that non-parents may have (in principle) a legitimate restoration claim against parents, but *only if being a parent is (on average) self-harmful.* Now, non-parents may or may not have a legitimate claim. But to make the legitimacy of that claim contingent on whether or not parents happen also to be harmed by parenting seems totally unjustified. Why should the parents' suffering make any difference to a claim for *restoration*? The question of self-harm seems utterly irrelevant.

I hope that enough has now been said to show that the self-harm criterion is inadequate and that if the two restoration arguments are importantly different, that difference does not lie merely in the fact that smoking is self-harmful, whilst non-smoking is not.

IX. The Social Value Criterion

Although Smart does not explicitly discuss it in these terms, his paper gives rise to an alternative proposal: the social value criterion [28]. According to this principle, restoration arguments can be legitimately applied only if the practice [29] in question does not have sufficient social value; conversely, if a practice is sufficiently socially valuable, it acquires a kind of immunity from restoration claims, even if it depletes health and welfare resources. Of course, some idea of proportionality is built into the criterion (hence the use of 'sufficient') such that the level of resource depletion must not be so high that it outweighs whatever social value the practice has. So a practice which was *extremely* dangerous (and costly to the health service) would need to be extremely socially valuable in order to be immune from restoration claims.

The social value criterion deals well with the 'tricky' cases discussed earlier. It is able to justify differentially treating fire-fighting (which has significant social value) and smoking (which, arguably, has none). It can also explain the intuition that restoration claims should not be directed against parenting, when combined with the (common) assumption that parenting is a significant social good. It remains unclear what the social value criterion would lead us to say about the *Agedelay* users, but that is just because it is hard to say what general social value *Agedelay* would have. It seems then that the social value criterion can do the work required of it, by enabling those who advocate reducing smokers' entitlements to health care to restrict, in a 'common sense' way, the range of activities to which restoration arguments can be applied. There still though remains the question of what (if anything) justifies the moral claim that restoration arguments may be used against certain activities (those which are insufficiently socially valuable) but not against others (the socially valuable ones).

The most promising way of justifying the social value criterion is to argue that (when considering restoration claims) any social benefits generated by a particular practice should be weighed against the disbenefits which accrue in the form of increased health care costs. This is in effect just a way of broadening our perspective so that we take into account not just health costs, but other factors as well. So in each case the key question will be: does society benefit — all things considered (and in particular after having taken into account any resultant increase in health care costs) — from this kind of practice? If the answer is *yes* then the practice is immune from restoration claims, since it causes more good than harm and so there is (all things considered) nothing to restore. But if the answer is *no*, there may be a case for reducing the health care entitlements of those in question, since they have, one might say, *done more harm than good.*

An attraction of this line of reasoning is that harm to third-parties is once again given centre-stage. If one's lifestyle doesn't harm society (all things considered including health care costs) then there is no possibility of a restoration claim arising. But if it does, then one's health care entitlements may be reduced. Therefore, the social value criterion can be portrayed as a plausible and relatively 'innocent' application of the principle that third-parties should not be allowed to suffer harms as a result of others' lifestyle choices.

There are however two related problems with using 'social value' in this way. The first concerns the standard distinction between *valuable* and *valued*. Should the social value criterion appeal to what people in fact *value* (prefer, desire etc) or to what is ('objectively') *valuable*? Whichever one we choose, there are difficulties.

If we opted for the first then we would be faced with a 'majority tyranny' situation, since whether or not one was the 'victim' of a 'reduced entitlement' policy would depend largely on whether the rest of society happened to approve of one's lifestyle. And this would surely be (at least potentially) arbitrary, discriminatory and unfair. Take smoking as an example. Maybe smokers' entitlements should be reduced; maybe they shouldn't. But surely whether they are reduced or not should not depend on the extent to which society in general approves of or detests smoking.

Consider also two further examples: child-bearing and male homosexuality. Assume that both generate similar additional health care costs and that therefore there is a *prima facie* case for reducing the relevant entitlements [30]. Should we really allow (as this version of the social value criterion dictates) that *if* the majority value child-bearing highly and *if* it has very negative attitudes towards homosexuality, then this provides a moral reason for reducing male homosexuals' entitlements, while leaving mothers' entitlements untouched? Conversely, should we allow that *if* the majority valued male homosexual practices highly and *if* it had very negative attitudes towards child-bearing, then that would provide a moral reason for reducing mothers' entitlements, while leaving those of male homosexuals untouched? It seems to me that the answer to both questions must clearly be *no*.

The social value criterion, then, cannot (if it is to be ethically defensible) be based just on those values and preferences which the majority happen to have. However, attempting to base it on 'objective' value may turn out to be equally problematic. For who is to decide which activities are valuable and how are they to do so? Certainly, it seems both practically dangerous and politically unacceptable to allow health service managers or politicians to withdraw health care from certain groups because they deem that their lifestyle does not generate sufficient social value. Furthermore, to allow the State to allocate health care resources based on substantive judgements about the value (or otherwise) of individuals' lifestyles seems not to be compatible with even a modest liberal commitment to State-neutrality in such matters. Of course, these considerations do not (and are not meant to) show that social value has no moral relevance whatever. But what they do go some way towards demonstrating is that *even if* social value is morally relevant, there are serious objections to *implementing a policy* which is based on *governments' judgements* about social value — not least because of the possibility of unfair bias and discrimination.

Whichever way it is interpreted, then, the social value criterion seems problematic.

X. Why the Restoration Argument is a 'Moralising Wolf in a Liberal Sheep's Clothing'

I want now to review briefly the main findings of the paper so far. The reverse restoration argument appears to threaten the credibility of the restoration argument. Supporters of the latter therefore need to show that there is a relevant difference between smoking and non-smoking such that the restoration argument is legitimate, whilst the *reverse* restoration argument is not. The best way of doing this seems to be the idea that activities which have sufficient social value should be immune from restoration claims. If we accept this (and the assumption that non-smoking has social value, whilst smoking does not) then a difference between the arguments has been found; the *reverse* restoration argument is illegitimate because it is directed against a practice (non-smoking) which is socially valuable, whereas the restoration argument is (in principle) legitimate, because smoking is (at best) not socially valuable.

The most interesting lesson to be learnt from this is that the restoration argument is a 'moralising wolf in a liberal sheep's clothing'. Consider for a moment John Harris's persuasive argument against the view that rationing decisions should be based on moral judgements about the behaviour or character of the patients in question:

> We all . . . have a duty to encourage and promote morality, but to do so by choosing between candidates for treatment on moral grounds is to arrogate to ourselves not simply the promotion of morality but the punishment of immorality. And to choose to let one person rather than another die on the grounds of some moral defect in their behaviour or character is to take upon ourselves the right not simply to punish, but capitally to punish, offenders against morality [31].

One of the main supposed advantages of the restoration argument is that it is not vulnerable to Harris's objection, since restoration is not about punishing people or about enforcing moral standards, but merely about preventing one group from unjustly harming another. The restoration argument is normally presented as an argument which although *moral* (insofar as it is about justice) is not about what we might call *moralising*, or, to put it another way, it is normally presented as being compatible with liberal neutrality with respect to people's lifestyle choices. But this claim is, as we have seen, implausible and those who originally supported the restoration argument are faced with an uncomfortable choice between the following three options.

The first is just to accept the *reverse* restoration argument, which amounts to accepting that there is a good *prima facie* case for giving smokers' needs higher priority than those of non-smokers. While taking this line would be admirably consistent, I doubt that it is something that many would be willing to accept.

The second is to regard the *reverse* restoration argument as a decisive objection to the restoration argument — i.e. to regard it as revealing some general flaw in this style of argument. For those who originally supported the view that smokers' entitlements to health care should be reduced, this will probably be less unpalatable than the first option. But now this view faces a serious problem since what was widely regarded as the best argument for it will have to be abandoned.

The final option is to argue that the restoration argument and the *reverse* restoration argument are importantly different by adopting the social value criterion [32]. In section [IX] I suggested some independent reasons for rejecting this. But even if these are put aside or rejected, there is still a problem for the restoration argument. For, when combined with the social value criterion, it is no longer immune to Harris's objection and this, in turn, means that it has lost one of its most attractive features. It was supposed *not* to involve evaluating lifestyles or taking a punitive stance but now, with the social value criterion in place, we do after all need to make substantive judgements about the value of particular lifestyles in order to decide whether or not those who pursue them should have their entitlements reduced. That is why I earlier described the restoration argument as a 'moralising wolf in a liberal sheep's clothing'. It is *presented* as non-punitive and non-moralising with respect to people's lifestyle choices but in fact needs (in order to deal with the problem posed by the *reverse* restoration argument) to make value judgements about people's lifestyles and to treat differently those lifestyles which are valued positively from those that are not. Perhaps this does not strictly speaking amount to punishing those who have lifestyles to which we attach little (or negative) value, since those who rationed health care in this way may not have a punitive intent. But the effects of pursuing the sort of policy under consideration may turn out to be indistinguishable from a punishment policy, since people will be made to suffer (and, as Harris points out, die in some cases) because their lifestyle is not approved of by those who ration health care.

In conclusion, this paper has not provided any *decisive* objections to the view that smokers' entitlements to health care should be reduced. This view has, however, been significantly weakened, since its proponents are compelled to admit that the restoration argument is nothing like as 'neutral' (with respect to evaluating lifestyles) as it might at first sight appear. This, in turn, will make both the argument and the policy that it is supposed to support much less attractive to anyone who takes seriously Harris's objection to rationing according to 'moral worth'. [33]

Stephen Wilkinson, Department of Philosophy, Keele University, Staffordshire, ST5 5BG, UK

NOTES

[1] For interesting defences of this position see: W. GLANNON (1998) Responsibility, alcoholism and liver transplantation, *Journal of Philosophy and Medicine 23*; B. SMART (1994) Fault and the allocation of spare organs, *Journal of Medical Ethics* 20.

Further discussion can be found in: A. CAPLIN et al (1994) *Sinners, Saints and Health Care: individual responsibility for health — ethical, legal and economic questions* (Minneapolis, University of Minnesota Center for Biomedical Ethics); R. CRISP (1993) Refusing treatment to smokers, *Oxford Medical School Gazette* XLIII; M. DEAN (1993) London perspective: self-inflicted rationing *The Lancet* 341; M. KHALID (1993) Denying treatment is indefensible, *British Medical Journal*; N. MAMODE (1993) Denying access is more costly, *British Medical Journal* 306; H. MCLACHAN (1995) Smokers, virgins and health care costs, *Journal of Medical Ethics* 21; E. MORREIM (1995) Lifestyles of the risky and infamous, *Hastings Center Report* 25; A. MOSS M. SIEGLER (1991) Should alcoholics compete equally for liver transplantation?, *Journal of the American Medical Association* 265; R. PERSAUD (1995) Smoker's rights to health care, *Journal of Medical Ethics* 21; M. UNDERWOOD & J. BAILEY (1993) Should smokers be offered coronary bypass surgery?, *British Medical Journal* 306.

[2] As Glannon puts it — 'Intuitively, entitlements to health care for a diseased condition are inversely proportional to control and responsibility. The more control one has over one's health, and thus the more responsible one is for it, the weaker is one's claim to receive treatment for one's condition from the health care system. Conversely, the less control one has over one's health and thus the less responsible one is for it, the stronger is one's claim for treatment'. Glannon op. cit., 35.

[3] See the General Medial Council's pamphlet, *Duties of A Doctor* (1995), which states (e.g.) that 'you must not refuse or delay treatment because you believe the patient's actions have contributed to their condition'.

Note also the following comments in *The Guardian* (12 October 1995): 'Sir Donald [Irvine, president of the GMC] said that doctors could explain to patients the dangers of their actions, for instance that smoking might decrease the chances of a successful heart operation, but they could not sit in judgment and withhold treatment.'

[4] Williams, for example, reports: '[a] survey has been carried out in Cardiff on just over 700 people selected randomly from the electoral register. They were asked to choose between people with different characteristics when treatment could only be given to one of them. The results indicated a strong preference for the young over the old, except for the very young, where an eight-year-old-would be given preference over a two-year old . . . In addition, married people were preferred to single people, non-smokers to smokers, and light to heavy drinkers . . . I later did a similar survey on the senior members of an English health authority with strikingly similar results. Again the young were to be given precedence over the old, non-smokers over smokers and light drinkers over heavy drinkers' (11). A. WILLIAMS (1992) Cost-effectiveness analysis: is it ethical?, *Journal of Medical Ethics* 18.

Against this, Kneeshaw tells us that 'in the June 1994 Gallup poll, only 25% of the respondents favoured pushing smokers to the back of the queue' (71); the figure for 'heavy drinkers' was slightly higher at 32%. J. KNEESHAW (1997) What does the public think about rationing? A review of the evidence in B. New (ed.) *Rationing: talk and action in health care* (London, BMJ Publishing Group, 1997).

[5] Crisp, correctly in my view, claims that 'a certain moralism regarding smoking [is] developing among the middle class in Britain. Some kind of moral censure is often thought to be appropriately directed at smokers, even those who do not inflict their habit on others. Such censure would be thought odd if applied, say, to those who eat fatty foods'. Crisp, op. cit., 9.

[6] For the sake of argument, I shall assume throughout that smoking is a *voluntary* activity, although this is of course questionable given that it is addictive.

[7] This point is noted by many writers but is made most forcefully in McLachan, op. cit.

[8] These arguments can be divided into two categories: those which are 'backward-looking' and based on considerations of justice, and those which are 'forward-looking' and based on broadly utilitarian considerations. The former category contains the 'restoration argument' and the (much less plausible) 'punishment argument' according to which smokers deserve to be punished for having abused their own bodies. The latter category contains the 'deterrence argument' which says that we should give the health care needs of smokers a lower priority in order to discourage smoking; and the 'best outcome argument' which says that, since continuing to smoke makes treatments less likely to succeed, we ought not to treat smokers, because to do so would be incompatible with a commitment to maximising the 'health gain' generated by the health service.

The 'best outcome argument' is probably the one which enjoys most public exposure. However, it is relatively uninteresting because its main preoccupation is not with people's past lifestyle-choices or with the fact that they have caused their own illnesses, but rather with their *present non-compliance* — i.e. with the fact that they are presently and actively doing something which makes their physician's intervention less likely to succeed (and which their physician has no doubt advised them not to do).

[9] Probably the best exposition of this kind of argument is Smart op. cit.

[10] This is in fact too crude because the level of smoking (and associated risk) may vary considerably from one 'smoker' to another. However, for the purposes of keeping the exposition brief, I shall assume (for the sake of argument) that a reasonably 'neat' distinction between smokers and non-smokers is possible.

[11] Although this may not be true of people who became addicted to smoking, say, 50 years ago and so the restoration argument may not apply to them. Furthermore, it might be argued that (even now) people who become addicted to smoking when they are children are similarly exempt because they may not have been able fully to appreciate the risks when they started. Similar points have been made in the debate about alcoholics and liver transplantation. For example, Moss & Siegler (op. cit.) argue against reducing the entitlements of alcoholics on the grounds that alcoholism is itself a disease and not merely a preference or lifestyle choice. Similarly, Glannon (while ultimating favouring reducing entitlements in some cases) notes that 'one might object that when persons currently in need of liver transplants began to drink, say fifteen or twenty years ago, the idea that drinking could cause liver failure would not have occurred to them. Nor did medicine [at that time] have a priority system in place which might have been based on people's responsibility for their health care needs'. Glannon op. cit,. 35.

Against this, however, it may be argued that, even if drinking and smoking are addictive, they are addictions that can be broken, and so even long-standing drinkers/smokers and people who became addicted as children are (at least partially) responsible for exposing themselves to the risks involved.

See also Persaud op. cit., 282; Smart op. cit., 128.

[12] In the UK at least, this is a highly questionable assumption, given the vast amounts of additional taxation paid by tobacco consumers. It is a more plausible assumption, though, if we turn our attention instead to non-monetary goods such as organs for transplantation.

The fact that smokers *already* pay for their own (supposed) additional health care requirements through the heavy taxes on cigarettes provides, of course, an independent argument against reducing their entitlements (one which won't be considered in this paper).

See, for example, a leading article in *The Independent* ('Yes, smoking kills, but litigation is ruinous', 23 June 1997) which tells us — 'it should . . . fall to smokers to pay the cost of treating smoking-related illnesses. In America, they now will. Here, they already do . . . In Britain, four-fifths of the price of cigarettes goes in tax. In America, the average is around one-third. In this country, the £10 billion annual revenue from tobacco taxes easily covers the cost to the health service of treating tobacco-related illnesses, which is usually put at under £1 billion a year.'

[13] As Smart puts it, considerations of 'rectificatory but non-punitive justice' [30] would be used to *supplement* whatever 'distributive justice criterion' [26] is deemed to be fair. Smart, op. cit.

[14] Glannon attributes a *restoration principle* of this sort to a number of well-known philosophers including Arneson, Dworkin, Rawls and Roemer. These philosophers, he says, propound the '"social cost" argument, which says that it is unfair and unreasonable to demand sacrifice from some who do exercise control over their health in order to treat others for diseases or disabilities that result from having but failing to exercise this control'. Glannon op. cit., 35.

[15] Glannon makes a similar point — 'The policy I have proposed should not be understood as implying that the alcoholic did something wrong and is denied a liver transplantation as punishment for this wrong. Instead, it should be understood in the following way. If a person acts on autonomously formed preferences and choices, and if he is capable of knowing what the probable consequences of his behaviour will be, then he weakens his entitlement to receive treatment for a diseased condition he has brought upon himself. The weakening of the entitlement is not a form of punishment imposed on him externally, but something that he brings upon himself as the consequence of his *own* preferences, choices and actions over time'. Glannon op. cit., 44.

[16] Smart op. cit., 27 (my emphasis).

[17] See Persaud op. cit., 283.

[18] Persaud op. cit., 284.

[19] Although some figures in the UK government are clearly not convinced. See J. Lawrence (1997) Lung cancer toll worsened by attitudes *The Independent* [18/11/97]: 'the Government announced [that] the cost

of smoking to the NHS was between £1.4 billion and £1.7 billion a year — more than twice previous estimates. Tessa Jowell, the public health minister, said: "This is an appalling drain on the NHS"'.

[20] J. Barendregt, L. Bonneux & R. Van Der Maas (1997) The health care costs of smoking, *New England Journal of Medicine*, 15.

[21] Barendregt *et al.* op. cit., 1052.

[22] Barendregt *et al.* op. cit., 1055.

[23] Barendregt *et al.* op. cit., 1056.

[24] This particular empirical objection may not be applicable if we consider not *money*, but *transplant organs* — since whether or not smokers 'consume' more organs than non-smokers is a separate empirical question.

[25] For the sake of argument, I shall assume that this is widely known. The fact that it is not widely known seems not to be significant given that it *could* easily be widely publicised.

[26] Smart op. cit. 29.

[27] Smart op. cit. 28.

[28] Smart op. cit. 29.

[29] I use 'practice' in a broad sense and intend it to cover both acts and omissions.

[30] We will of course need some further assumptions here too — e.g. that both are voluntary and done in full knowledge of the consequences.

[31] J. Harris (1985) *The Value of Life* (London, Routledge), 108.

[32] Of course it will always be open to defenders of the restoration argument to provide a further candidate principle of application.

[33] I would like to thank the following peopole (listed in alphabetical order) for their helpful comments; Stephen Clark, Angus Dawson, Charles Erin, André Gallois, Eve Garrard, John Harris, David McNaughton, Alison Pettigrew, Sally Sheldon and an anonymous reader for this Journal.

[17]

Using Litigation to Make Public Health Policy: Theoretical and Empirical Challenges in Assessing Product Liability, Tobacco, and Gun Litigation

Timothy D. Lytton

In recent years, a number of prominent scholars have touted the use of litigation as an effective tool for making public health policy. For example, Stephen Teret and Michael Jacobs have asserted that product liability claims against car makers have played a significant role in reducing automobile-related injuries, Peter Jacobson and Kenneth Warner have argued that litigation against cigarette manufacturers has advanced the cause of tobacco control, and Phil Cook and Jens Ludwig have suggested that lawsuits against the firearms industry can reduce gun violence.[1] Critics have attacked this use of litigation as doing more harm than good to public health and as a misuse of the courts.[2] This debate involves two distinct controversies: one over whether the public health benefits of litigation outweigh its costs and the other over the proper role of courts within our system of government.

The first controversy remains unresolved due to insufficient empirical evidence. At this point, very little is known about the extent to which product liability litigation has improved product safety and reduced injury, or whether tobacco and gun litigation have lead to decreases in tobacco-related illness and gun violence.[3] Furthermore, any comprehensive assessment requires offsetting against these benefits the costs of litigation. With regard to product liability litigation, the costs include price increases on some products–what critics have termed the "liability tax"– the elimination of some products altogether, and less experimentation with product safety innovation for fear of litigation.[4] In commenting on tobacco litigation, critics have alleged that the master settlement agreement between state attorneys general and tobacco companies may, in the end, strengthen the industry.[5] Unfortunately, the empirical evidence concerning these matters remains largely anecdotal. Gun litigation critics have suggested that lawsuits against gun makers may decrease the availability of firearms for self-defense and crime deterrence, resulting in more, not less, gun violence.[6] This last claim is based on a number of empirical studies, which have themselves become the subject of heated controversy among social science scholars.[7] More comprehensive and less controversial data is needed to advance this part of the debate over using litigation to make public health policy.

In addition to debating the public health benefits and costs of litigation, the two sides disagree about the proper role of courts in policy making. Proponents of using litigation as a public health strategy assert that courts have an essential role to play alongside legisla-

Timothy D. Lytton *is Professor of Law at Albany Law School where he teaches torts, legislation, constitutional law, alternative dispute resolution, and jurisprudence. He holds B.A. (1987) and J.D. (1991) degrees from Yale University.*

tures and administrative agencies in making public policy. They point to the failure of legislatures and agencies to regulate product safety, tobacco, and guns more aggressively as justification for a policy-making role for courts.[8] Critics insist that the job of courts is to resolve private disputes and to enforce legislative mandates, not to make public policy. Judges, they argue, make poor policy makers because they lack both the necessary tools and the democratic credentials of legislatures and agencies.[9] Using the courts to make public policy will, in the end, critics suggest, politicize the judiciary, undermine the integrity of the litigation process, and erode public confidence in the courts.[10]

These competing views of the proper role of courts offered by both sides share one thing in common: they both derive from constitutional law. Proponents of using litigation to make public health policy invoke the leading role played by lawsuits in the civil rights revolution. Critics, for their part, cite Article I of the U.S. Constitution which vests "[a]ll legislative [p]owers" in Congress, and Article III, which describes the role of courts as limited to resolving "cases" and "controversies." In the absence of better empirical analysis about the public health benefits and costs of litigation, the cultural resonance and rhetorical power of these two constitutional ideals–civil rights reform litigation and the founders' vision of limited government–appear to be driving the debate over using litigation to make public health policy.

Proponents of using litigation as a public health strategy assert that courts have an essential role to play alongside legislatures and administrative agencies in making public policy.

This article examines arguments about the proper role of courts - which I shall refer to as institutional arguments - offered by each side and asserts two claims. First, I argue that reliance on constitutional ideals when analyzing the proper role of civil litigation in the policy-making process is misplaced. Neither of the ideals relied upon by each side accurately describes the traditional policy-making role of courts in civil litigation, which is smaller than that suggested by the comparison to civil rights litigation and greater than that suggested by citations to Articles I and III. On the one hand, whereas constitutional litigation involves judicial review of policy choices made by legislatures and agencies, in civil litigation based on common law and statutory claims like those in product liability, tobacco, and gun litigation, courts have traditionally deferred to legislative and agency policy choices under the principle of legislative superiority. On the other hand, there are many areas of life that have traditionally been and remain unregulated by statute, where, in the course of adjudicating private disputes, courts have laid down common law rules with far reaching regulatory implications. Even in areas of life regulated by statutes, ambiguities in statutory language often require courts to make policy choices.

Second, I contend that the institutional arguments of both sides require further development, on both a theoretical and an empirical level. In terms of theory, proponents of using litigation to make public health policy need to explain why the failure of legislatures and agencies to regulate industry more aggressively is a sign of dysfunction for which litigation provides a solution, rather than merely lack of adequate support for greater regulation. For their part, critics must explain why they believe it inappropriate for courts to be involved in the policy-making process when this is a role that they have traditionally played. In terms of empirical evidence, assertions by proponents about regulatory failure and by critics about politicization of the judiciary, integrity of the litigation process, and weakened public confidence in the courts are supported primarily by anecdotal evidence. More comprehensive empirical data concerning these issues is necessary to evaluate the arguments on each side.

Before proceeding further, it may be helpful to mention the difficulty of trying to analyze product liability, tobacco litigation, and gun litigation together. While they do have features in common, each involves a complex constellation of parties and doctrines that often makes it difficult to generalize about any one of them, much less all three together.[11] Nevertheless, I have chosen to do so because proponents of using civil litigation as a tool for making public health policy have offered them as case studies, and they have attracted similarly close scrutiny from critics. Many of the arguments on both sides that I analyze apply more to one or two than to all three. For stylistic convenience, I shall, on occasion, refer to them collectively as "public health litigation." Where differences are important, I will distinguish between them. In the end, I am interested in illuminating the controversy over the use of litigation to make public health policy, not making any strong claims about whether these three prominent examples represent a single phenomenon.

My discussion proceeds as follows. Part I outlines the

institutional arguments in favor of and against public health litigation. Part II analyzes how these arguments arise out of competing ideals of constitutional law and argues against reliance on any such constitutional law ideal in addressing the policy-making role of courts in the context of civil litigation. Part III suggests that the institutional arguments of both sides require further theoretical development and better empirical support. Finally, I conclude with some thoughts about the increasingly prominent role that institutional arguments have played in the debate.

Arguments For and Against Public Health Litigation

Proponents argue that litigation can influence the policy-making process in a number of ways. First, filing a lawsuit can highlight specific public health issues, placing them on the policy agendas of legislators, agency officials, and the public. Litigation is at least partly responsible for putting highway fatalities, tobacco-related illness, and gun violence at the top of the nation's domestic policy agenda. Second, lawsuits can frame the way these issues are perceived, making some policy alternatives appear more attractive than others. Litigation has presented highway fatalities as owing to unsafe automobile design, tobacco-related illness as caused by industry-induced addiction, and gun violence as a result of irresponsible marketing practices. Thus framed, industry regulation becomes a salient option in addressing these problems. Third, litigation can mobilize support for particular public health policies by generating media coverage, encouraging more lawsuits, energizing otherwise diffuse and unorganized constituencies, and serving as a basis for fundraising. Fourth, litigation can strengthen the bargaining power of public health advocates within legislative and agency policy making. The threat of liability, or even just defense costs, can extract concessions from political opponents or agency officials. Fifth, the discovery process can expose information hidden by an industry that is essential to effective regulation. One recent example of this is the discovery in tobacco litigation that manufacturers were secretly manipulating nicotine levels in the cigarettes that they sold.[12]

Aside from these ways in which litigation can affect the policy-making process – by agenda setting, issue framing, mobilizing resources, strengthening bargaining power, and uncovering information – litigation can also enact particular policies. Litigation costs or a crippling damage award can put a corporate defendant out of business or weaken an entire industry. Punitive damages punish misconduct. Liability can serve as a tax on industry that gets passed on to consumers and reduces consumption of an industry's product. It can also internalize the costs of injuries associated with a product, creating incentives for making the product safer or reducing production.[13]

Finally, litigation can complement existing policies created by legislatures or agencies. The threat of liability can enhance the enforcement of existing policies when agency resources are scarce. For example, while the Bureau of Alcohol, Tobacco, Firearms, and Explosives, which is responsible for regulating gun sales, has only enough resources to inspect one in ten gun retailers each year, the threat of tort liability created by gun litigation provides an incentive for voluntary compliance. Litigation also fills gaps in legislation and regulations. Legislative and agency regulations inevitably contain gaps where lawmakers do not anticipate ways in which industry can evade regulation within the letter of the law. The threat of litigation can fill these gaps. For example, the practice of evading federal restrictions on interstate gun sales by selling guns in the form of complete parts kits–the sale of gun parts is unregulated–has been reduced by the threat of liability created by gun litigation.[14]

In response, critics assert that courts are less well equipped than legislatures or administrative agencies to develop and implement public policy. Critics argue that judges lack the technical expertise, investigative powers, bureaucratic capacity for implementation and oversight, and enforcement options available to legislative committees and administrative agencies. Equally important, judges lack the democratic legitimacy attributed to legislators and agency officials with short-term appointments.[15]

Proponents counter that while this is true in theory, the political realities of the legislative process and agency regulation are often such that courts may be the best choice among imperfect institutional alternatives. Legislatures may fail to enact popular policy proposals due to domination of the legislative process by special interests, and agencies may fail to promulgate or enforce their regulations when they are captured by the very industries that they are supposed to regulate. Litigation, according to proponents, is an effective way to overcome domination of the legislative process and agency capture. To a significant degree, they explain, courts are insulated from the political influence that powerful industries and interests exert in legislative politics and agency rule making. By litigating, public health advocates can advance their policy agendas in a forum that eliminates much of the advantage that their political opponents have over them in the legislative and agency arenas. Litigation, by this account, offers a way to overcome the shortcomings of legislative and agency regulation.[16]

Moreover, proponents point out, the limitations of

judges as policy makers are mitigated by the fact that the regulatory effects of litigation may not require much, if any, judicial involvement. Most litigation never reaches trial, resulting instead in settlement between the parties. Plaintiffs seeking regulatory outcomes often negotiate settlements with regulatory terms. For example, the settlement between state attorneys general and the tobacco industry included restrictions on advertising and funding for smoking-reduction programs.[17] Similarly, a number of municipal gun litigation plaintiffs negotiated a settlement with gun maker Smith & Wesson requiring voluntary marketing restrictions and dealer training programs to reduce illegal retail sales.[18] More remarkable still, litigation can be an effective policy-making tool even without a settlement. The litigation process itself – filing claims, discovering facts, and generating litigation costs–independent of the final outcome in terms of a judgment or settlement, can affect the policy-making process, enact particular policies, or complement existing policies in the ways outlined above.[19]

Critics have denounced this use of the litigation process to produce regulatory outcomes as a misuse of the courts. The litigation process, they argue, is a public resource for resolving disputes, not a lobbying tool for advancing an otherwise unsuccessful legislative agenda or a means of circumventing the legislative process altogether. It is, according to critics, a misuse of the court system to employ the rules of pleading and discovery, which are enforced by the state and paid for by the public, as a way to generate press coverage, mobilize support, enact de-facto regulation, or wreak financial ruin on an industry. The purpose of these rules, and the justification for their costly imposition on parties to litigation, is to generate the information necessary to resolve claims before the court, not to promote public policy.[20]

Furthermore, critics argue that viewing litigation as a continuation of legislative politics by other means, or as a way to circumvent them altogether, threatens to politicize the judiciary. Treating the courts as merely a second front in legislative battles against the tobacco or gun industries subjects judges to political pressure. Since most state court judges are elected, judges hoping to get reelected will be more likely to decide cases in favor of their political supporters. This tendency will be exacerbated as parties increasingly employ the types of lobbying activities – in particular, making significant contributions to reelection campaigns – that characterize the legislative process.[21]

Finally, and perhaps most importantly, critics assert that using the litigation process to produce regulatory outcomes erodes public respect for the court system and, ultimately, the rule of law. For one thing, the judicial process appears to lack integrity when judicial enforcement of pleading requirements and discovery requests are justified as necessary for resolution of the plaintiff's claims before the court, but their primary function is, instead, to advance the plaintiff's policy agenda irregardless of the merits of its claims or the outcome of the litigation. For another, when judges are subjected to lobbying efforts, this undermines public confidence in their impartiality. These perceptions of lack of integrity and partiality are likely to damage public respect for the courts and their rulings.[22]

Critics assert that using the litigation process to produce regulatory outcomes erodes public respect for the court system and, ultimately, the rule of law.

Misplaced Reliance on Constitutional Ideals

The competing views on the proper role of courts presented by proponents and critics of public health litigation both rely on ideals from constitutional law. These two constitutional ideals – one rooted in the civil rights revolution and the other in the founding era – have deep cultural resonance and carry great rhetorical force. They are, however, inapposite to public health litigation. The role of courts in adjudicating the state common law and statutory claims involved in public health litigation differs significantly from that of courts when considering federal constitutional claims.

Proponents of public health litigation view it as a tool for social change in the tradition of the lawsuits that fueled the civil rights revolution. As Wendell Gauthier, the lead plaintiff's attorney in the City of New Orleans's suit against the gun industry, put it, comparing the city's suit to the most celebrated civil rights litigation, "[w]e are taking the gun dealers to court because the political process has failed us...If lawyers hadn't launched *Brown v. Board of Education*, you would never have had school integration because it was so unpopular with lawmakers."[23] Many scholarly proponents of public health tort litigation see themselves in dialogue with skeptics of constitutional reform litigation, such as Gerald Rosenberg, rather than critics of civil litigation, such as Peter Huber or Walter Olson.[24]

Critics of public health litigation also rely on a constitutional ideal. They regularly cite Article I of the U.S. Constitution, which states that "[a]ll legislative powers herein granted shall be vested in a Congress of the United States, which shall consist of a Senate and

House of Representatives," and Article III, which describes the role of courts as limited to resolving "cases" and "controversies." Critics interpret these provisions to mean that courts should refrain from playing any role in making public policy. Public health litigation, they assert, is a violation of the principle of legislative supremacy and the limited role of courts enshrined in the U.S. Constitution.[25]

Both of these constitutional ideals are inapposite to public health litigation. Unlike constitutional reform litigation, public health litigation involves the civil law function, not the constitutional law function of courts. In adjudicating constitutional claims, court's exercise oversight of legislatures. They judge the legal validity of legislative policy. By contrast, in adjudicating common law and statutory claims, courts have traditionally deferred to legislatures. In making common law rulings, they feel constrained by any relevant statutes, and in interpreting statutes, they seek guidance from legislative language, intent, and purpose. In the civil rights movement, courts often worked against legislatures because that was their constitutionally mandated role. In public health litigation, however, courts have been careful to respect legislative superiority. They have consistently refused to rule in ways that contradict relevant legislation and have generally played a secondary, supportive role in policy making, complementing rather than competing with the regulatory efforts of legislatures.

If invocations of civil rights litigation by proponents of public health tort litigation are misplaced, so too are critics' citation of eighteenth century views on the role of courts. Notwithstanding Blackstone's famous insistence that courts never make law but only apply it, the ideal of courts as entirely uninvolved in policy making is demonstrably false even with regard to the eighteenth century.[26] When adjudicating common law claims, courts have always had to grapple with doctrinal ambiguity, and they have often resolved it on the basis of public policy considerations.[27] Indeed, in many areas of life unregulated by statute, adjudication of common law claims has been the primary, or even sole, source of regulatory policies.[28] If the history of U.S. common law teaches us anything, it is that nineteenth century common law played a central role in shaping the market economy, just as twentieth century common law sought to tame it.[29] Thus, while common law courts do resolve cases and controversies, the ways in which they do so not only have often far reaching public policy implications, they often involve self-conscious judicial policy choices.[30] Even in statutory interpretation, courts must make policy choices given the inevitable ambiguities of statutory language, legislative intent, and the statute's underlying purpose.[31] Finally, it is unclear why critics think that the U.S. Constitution's view of the role of federal courts is even relevant, since most products liability, tobacco, and gun claims are either brought in state courts or involve matters of state law, or both.[32]

In the context of civil litigation today, the policy making role of courts lies somewhere in between the extreme constitutional ideals of courts as an independent policy making branch of government and courts as entirely uninvolved in the policy-making process. Traditionally, public policy has been made by all three branches of government. In areas of life where legislatures have remained silent, common law has been the primary source of public policy. Increasingly, legislatures and agencies have become involved in these areas, for the most part seeking to complement, rather than replace, common law policy making.[33] A good example of this is product liability litigation, wherein common law rules promulgated and enforced by courts provided the earliest and, arguably still, the primary mechanism for regulating product safety, complemented by the efforts of administrative agencies such as the National Highway Transportation Safety Administration (NHTSA) in the case of automobiles, the Federal Food and Drug Administration (FDA) in the case of food and pharmaceuticals, and the Consumer Product Safety Administration (CPSA) in the case of most other products. Where legislatures and agencies are more active, courts have played a more secondary policy-making role. For example, in gun litigation, courts have for the most part been careful not to make common law rulings or interpret statutes in ways that contradict the gun-control regime established by the federal and state governments. Courts have regularly refused to rule in ways that would, in effect, ban Saturday Night Specials or impose one-gun-per-month purchase restrictions where the state legislature has refused to do so.[34]

Because the constitutional ideals offered by each side are inapposite to civil litigation, the arguments presented by each side about the proper role of courts in policy making must rest upon their claims about legislative and agency regulatory failure, politicization of the judiciary, damage to the integrity of the litigation process, and erosion of public confidence in the courts. Let us now examine these claims more closely.

Theoretical and Empirical Challenges

In the last section, I argued that neither of the competing constitutional ideals relied upon by proponents and critics of public health litigation conforms to the role that courts have traditionally played in policy making. In this section, leaving aside these inapposite constitutional ideals, I evaluate proponents' claims about legislative and agency regulatory failure and critics' claims about increased politicization of the judiciary, damage to the integrity of the litigation process, and erosion of public confidence in the courts. I argue that each of these claims needs further theoretical development and better empirical support.

As we have seen, the case for public health litigation rests upon a claim that litigation is an appropriate means of making public health policy where the legislative process is dominated by special interests or the relevant agencies have been captured by regulated industries. Proponents of public health litigation have in some cases been too quick to denounce their opponents as special interests, characterizing their legislative victories as regulatory failures and their influence on agencies as capture. To be sure, powerful industry groups do at times succeed in protecting their interests by cultivating key legislators and placing industry insiders into agency positions. It is hardly the case, however, that successful lobbying alone is sufficient evidence of institutional dysfunction. For one thing, lobbying is a normal part of the legislative process. For another, recent empirical studies testing capture theory have observed vigorous agency oversight of even well organized and powerful industries.[35]

Lawsuits against the gun industry provide a case in point. Proponents of gun litigation argue that gun control policy should be made in the courts since the NRA and other elements of the gun lobby constitute a special interest that has dominated the legislative process. There is reason to be skeptical, however, of attempts to characterize the NRA as a special interest group. The NRA boasts a membership of 4.3 million members, which compares favorably with figures for the Sierra Club (700,000 members), the American Civil Liberties Union (400,000 members), and, perhaps most significantly, the NRA's counterpart, the Brady Campaign to End Gun Violence (500,000 members).[36] Given the size and complexity of our political system, such relatively small interest group organizations are a vital means of promoting and sustaining political participation. They provide information and offer individuals a way to exert meaningful influence on policy making. Characterizations of such groups as special rather than public interest groups often rests on little more than disagreement with the policies that they advocate.[37]

There is also reason to be skeptical about claims that gun lobby legislative victories are evidence of some sort of failure in the legislative process. The NRA's political tactics – cultivating key legislators to kill gun control proposals in committee, campaigning against politicians who vote contrary to their interests, organizing letter writing campaigns and protests, and insinuating themselves into the executive branch – are the same tactics employed by gun control groups, and they are normal features of legislative politics. That the NRA and the rest of the gun lobby exert powerful influence over the legislative process is beyond doubt, but this does not mean that their influence amounts to a failure in the legislative process.[38]

Proponents of gun litigation point to the legislative defeat of gun control proposals supported by a majority of Americans as evidence of regulatory failure. But here again, the defeat of measures supported by the majority is a normal feature of legislative politics, and not necessarily a bad one. The constitutional requirements that bills be approved by both the House and Senate and signed by the Executive in order to become law are designed to make even popular legislation difficult to pass. In addition to these constitutional requirements, other informal hurdles of the legislative process, such as committee approval, scheduling, and floor-debate restrictions, regularly, in the normal course of business, thwart popular legislation.[39]

As for agency capture, while it is true that, since the 1980s, the NRA has lobbied successfully for reductions in the Bureau of Alcohol, Firearms, Tobacco, and Explosives (BATFE) budget, the agency has been far from inactive.[40] The agency's *Crime Gun Trace Reports* have been a primary source of data used by plaintiffs in attempting to establish a link between industry marketing practices and the criminal misuse of guns.[41] The agency has also launched initiatives with local law enforcement to reduce gun trafficking.[42]

My point is not that all lawsuits against the gun industry are groundless or that gun litigation has no role to play in making gun control policy. It is merely that the proponents of gun litigation have been too quick to claim regulatory failure in attempting to justify the use of litigation as a legislative strategy, and, in some cases, as a way to circumvent the legislative process altogether.[43] At the very least, those who offer regulatory failure as a justification for public health litigation need to provide a more refined account of just what constitutes regulatory failure and better empirical evidence that it is occurring.

For their part, critics need to explain more clearly why, given the traditional policy-making role of courts, public health litigation is detrimental to the courts and the rule of law. The claim that it has politicized the judiciary requires further elaboration. Walter Olson does offer specific examples of large donations by tobacco and gun litigation plaintiffs' lawyers to the election campaigns of state judges, and he implies that this influences the ways in which the judges decide cases.[44] However, as judges have rejected the overwhelming majority of claims in these cases, it is unclear on what basis Olson believes that donations by these groups have influenced judges. Indeed, it is possible that the publicity surrounding tobacco and gun litigation acts as an incentive for judges to be more impartial in these

It is my suspicion that increasing interest in institutional arguments on both sides is driven, in part, by a desire to avoid having to confront the hard – perhaps impossible – task of obtaining comprehensive empirical data about the benefits and costs of the litigation.

cases than in other types of litigation.[45] Moreover, before accepting critics' claims about politicization, we need to know more about how much corporate defendants contribute to judicial elections, and whether the donations of one side influence judges more than those of the other. The matter is complicated by the fact that many judges accept contributions from both sides. It is possible that the way judges decide cases influences contributions more than contributions influence the way they decide cases. That is, judges may receive contributions from the parties with whom they already agree, as is often the case with legislators.[46] While contributions may help reelect judges whose decisions favor the contributors, the contributions themselves may not be influencing the way that judges decide cases. Thus, while the increasing role of money in judicial elections may be a serious problem for judicial elections, it may not be affecting the adjudication of cases. And even if it does, perhaps critics of public health litigation should be calling for greater regulation of judicial elections, or a move away from elections altogether, rather than restrictions on civil litigation.

Critics' claim that using litigation to make public policy is a misuse of the courts also requires further elaboration. Plaintiffs usually have mixed motives for bringing a lawsuit, and litigation normally serves a number of functions simultaneously. Plaintiffs may seek redress in the form of money damages; they may aim to get the attention of a defendant who refuses to address their complaints; they may desire a public airing of their claims; they may wish to ensure that what happened to them never happens to anyone else; and they may want to teach the defendant a lesson. When filing a lawsuit, plaintiffs may have any one, some combination, or all of these goals in mind, and litigation has traditionally fulfilled all of these functions.[47] This is certainly the case with product liability, tobacco, and gun litigation. Critics need to explain why some of these motivations for and functions of litigation are illegitimate, and if they are, how to assess litigation that mixes allegedly legitimate and illegitimate elements. Of course, courts themselves police misuse of court resources by requiring that plaintiffs' claims meet a minimum threshold – that they have a sufficient factual and legal basis – and when they do not, courts may impose sanctions under Rule 11 of the Federal Rules of Civil Procedure and state equivalents. But Rule 11 type violations are rare in products liability, and have not been applied to plaintiffs in tobacco and gun litigation. Given that the courts have not judged these claims as unworthy of court resources, it is unclear what basis the critics of public health litigation have for doing so.

Critics' claim that public health litigation has eroded public confidence in the courts, or is likely to do so, is similarly in need of elaboration. It is unclear that the public views the function of pleading and discovery as exclusively for the clarification of claims before the court, such that their use to influence public policy represents a lack of integrity. As the above discussion of the mixed motives for bringing a lawsuit indicates, the public may have a more complex understanding of the functions of the litigation process, and, thus, may not view product liability, tobacco, or gun litigation as lacking in integrity. There is similarly little empirical support for critics' claim that public confidence in judicial impartiality has been shaken. Again, in the context of tobacco and gun litigation, judges have rejected the overwhelming majority of claims, leaving one to question on what basis the public might consider them partial to plaintiffs. At the very least, critics need to offer empirical measures of public confidence and demonstrate that it is, or is likely to, decline as a result of public health litigation.

Conclusion

Leading proponents of public health litigation Peter Jacobson and Kenneth Warner have characterized the debate over public health litigation as a contest between pragmatists and ideologues. They assert that "proponents of the litigation can appeal to compelling practical concerns to justify its role in the policy process," whereas, "it is predominantly philosophical considerations that militate against litigation as policy making."[48] This characterization seems wrong on both counts. The leading proponents of public health litigation not only lack essential empirical data concerning the practical results of the litigation, their defense of it relies heavily on theoretical analyses of legislative failure and agency capture. The most well known and strident critics – Peter Huber, Walter Olson, Philip Howard, and Catherine Crier – have all published books chock full of detailed factual accounts of what they consider to be the practical failings of public health litigation without the necessary theoretical framework to support their conclusions.[49] Indeed, if anything, the arguments of proponents are heavy on theory, while those of critics focus on anecdotal evidence of practical results.

Instead, I have argued that both sides in the debate rely on claims about the practical public health benefits and costs of litigation, as well as competing theoretical accounts of the proper role of courts in making public policy. Advancing this debate requires better empirical data on both sides about the benefits and costs of litigation, as well as further theoretical elaboration of and empirical support for each side's institutional arguments.

It is my suspicion that increasing interest in institutional arguments on both sides is driven, in part, by a desire to avoid having to confront the hard – perhaps impossible – task of obtaining comprehensive empirical data about the benefits and costs of the litigation. This is a perfectly sensible reaction. Scholarly commentators and policy makers ought to focus on the questions that they can answer rather than dwelling on those they cannot. For this focus on institutional arguments to be fruitful, however, greater theoretical sophistication and better empirical support are necessary. In the absence of these, the institutional dimension of the debate remains largely a contest of competing sensibilities – whether, in the abstract, one favors the ideals of public risk regulation and progressive government or free enterprise and institutional stability. Advancing the debate beyond this clash of abstract ideological commitments is a necessary first step in properly assessing the use of litigation as a tool for making public health policy.

This is not, however, to minimize the contributions that both sides' institutional arguments have made. Proponents' arguments encourage us to explore whether policy making is enhanced by the involvement of courts; they challenge us to consider more carefully what the "separation" of powers really means in our system of government. Critics have highlighted how impartiality, integrity, and public confidence in the courts are essential to their ability to resolve disputes peacefully, which is itself vital to public health.

Acknowledgments

I wish to thank Rachel Anisfeld, Beverly Cohen, Howard Erichson, Joel Linsider, Greg Mandel, Dale Moore, Richard Nagareda, Robert Rabin, Peter Schuck, Tony Sebok, Stephen Sugarman, Jon Vernick, and Wendy Wagner for helpful comments and suggestions, as well as Jon Vernick for inviting me to present a draft of this article at the American Society of Law, Medicine & Ethics conference on The Public's Health and the Law in the 21st Century. Alexandra Harrington and Luke Nikas provided essential research assistance. I received generous support for this project from an Albany Law School Summer Research Grant. I welcome comments at <tlytt@mail.als.edu>.

References

1. S. Teret and M. Jacobs, "Prevention and Torts: The Role of Litigation in Injury Control," *Journal of Law, Medicine & Health Care* 17 (1985): 17-22; P. D. Jacobson and K. E. Warner, "Litigation and Public Health Policy Making: The Case of Tobacco Control," *Journal of Health Politics, Policy, and Law* 24 (1999): 769-804; P. Cook and J. Ludwig, "Litigation as Regulation: Firearms," in W. K. Viscusi, ed., *Regulation as Litigation* (Washington, D.C.: AEI-Brookings, 2002): 67-92.
2. See, P. Huber, *Liability: The Legal Revolution and Its Consequences* (New York: Basic Books, 1988); M. Krauss, *Fire and Smoke: Government Lawsuits and the Rule of Law* (Oakland, CA: Independent Institute, 2000); J. Reh, "Social Issue Litigation and the Route Around Democracy," *Harvard Journal on Legislation*, 37 (2000): 515-520; W. Olson, ed., *The Rule of Lawyers: How the New Litigation Elite Threatens America's Rule of Law* (New York: St. Martin's Press, 2003); Catherine Crier, *The Case Against Lawyers* (New York: Broadway Books, 2002); J. Turley, "A Crisis of Faith: Tobacco and the Madisonian Democracy," *Harvard Journal on Legislation* 37 (2000): 433-480.
3. See J. Vernick, J. Samia Mair, S. Teret, and J. Sapsin, "The Role of Litigation in Preventing Product-Related Injuries," *Epidemiologic Reviews* 25 (2003): 90-98, at 91.
4. For a discussion of the "liability tax," see R. Litan, "The Liability Explosion and American Trade Performance: Myths and Realities," in P. Schuck, ed., *Tort Law and the Public Interest: Competition, Innovation, and Consumer Welfare* (New York: Norton, 1991): 127-150, at 132-138. For a discussion of reduction in safety innovations for fear of litigation, see Huber, *supra* note 2, at 153-171.
5. H. Dagan and J. White, "Government, Citizens, and Injurious Industries," *New York University Law Review* 75 (2000): 354-428, at 378-382.
6. H. S. Burnett, "Suing Gun Manufacturers: Hazardous to Our Health," *Texas Review of Law and Politics* 5 (2001): 433-494, at 478.
7. For an introduction to the debate about defensive gun use, see G. Kleck, *Targeting Guns: Firearms and their Control* (New York: Aldine de Gruyter, 1997): 147-190 and D. Hemenway, "Policy and Perspective: Survey Research and Self Defensive Gun Use: An Explanation of Extreme Overestimates," *Journal of Criminal Law and Criminology* 87 (1997): 1430-1444. For an introduction to the debate over gun ownership and crime deterrence, see J. Lott, *More Guns, Less Crime: Understanding Crime and Gun Control Laws* (Chicago: University of Chicago Press, 1998); I. Ayres and J. Donahue III, "Shooting Down the 'More Guns, Less Crime' Hypothesis," *Stanford Law Review* 55 (2003): 1193-1299.
8. See Vernick, *supra* note 8, at 91; Jacobson and Warner, *supra* note 1, at 784; P. Jacobson and S. Soliman, "Fields of Law: Litigation as Public Health Policy: Theory or Reality?" *Journal of Law, Medicine & Ethics* 30 (2002): 224-235, at 225.
9. See P. Schuck, "Why Regulating Guns Through Litigation Won't Work," in T. Lytton, ed., *Suing the Gun Industry: A Battle at the Crossroads Gun Control and Mass Tort* (forthcoming, Ann Arbor: University of Michigan Press, 2005): chapter 9.
10. See P. Schuck, "The New Judicial Ideology of Tort Law," in W. Olson, *supra* note 2, 4-17, at16.
11. On the complexities of tobacco litigation, see R. Rabin, "The Third Wave of Tobacco Tort Litigation," in R. Rabin and S. Sugarman, eds., *Regulating Tobacco* (Oxford and New York: Oxford University Press, 2001): 176-206; on gun litigation see, T. Lytton, "An Overview of Lawsuits Against the Gun Industry," in Lytton, *supra* note 9, "Suing the Gun Industry," introduction.
12. On these ways in which litigation can affect the policy making process, see L. Mather, "Theorizing About Trial Courts: Lawyers, Policymaking, and Tobacco Litigation," *Law and Social Inquiry* 23 (1998): 897-940, at 912-932.
13. On these ways in which litigation can create specific regulatory outcomes, see S. Sugarman, "Comparing Tobacco and Gun Litigation," in Lytton, *Suing the Gun Industry*, *supra* note 9, chapter 8.
14. On the ways in which litigation complements legislative and agency policy making, see T. Lytton, "The Complementary Role of Tort Litigation in Regulating the Gun Industry," in T. Lytton,

Suing the Gun Industry, *supra* note 9, chapter 10.
15. See Schuck, *supra* note 9, "Why Regulating Guns Through Litigation Won't Work."
16. Jacobson and Warner, *supra* note 1, at 784; P. Jacobson and S. Soliman, "Fields of Law: Litigation as Public Health Policy: Theory or Reality?" *Journal of Law, Medicine & Ethics* 30 (2002): 224-235, at 225. See generally, Neil Komesar, *Imperfect Alternatives: Choosing Institutions in Law, Economics, and Public Policy* (Chicago: University of Chicago Press, 1994).
17. E. Alden and N. Buckley, "All Cigarette Makers But One Oppose FDA Regulation Plans: Restrictions on the Market Will Just Entrench Philip Morris's Position as Number One, Say Its Rivals," *Financial Times*, July 19, 2004, at 6; D. Zak, "Teen Smokers Packing it In; Both Nationally and Locally, Rates are Down as More Students are Kicking the Habit," *Buffalo News*, July 7, 2004, at A1.
18. This settlement eventually unraveled. See, P. Brown and D. Abel, *Outgunned: Up Against the NRA* (New York: Free Press, 2003): 182-214, 298-299.
19. R. Nagareda, "Gun Litigation in the Mass Tort Context," in T. Lytton, *Suing the Gun Industry*, *supra* note 9, chapter 7.
20. Olson, *supra* note 2, at 7-8, 12-13. For an especially thoughtful account of the tort system as an institution primarily designed for the adjudication of private claims for redress, see J. C. P. Goldberg, "Tort Law for Federalists (and the Rest of Us): Private Law in Disguise," *Harvard Journal of Legislation & Public Policy* 28 (2004): forthcoming.
21. Olson, *supra* note 2, at 77-78, 226-229.
22. Catherine Crier goes so far as to call citizens to "revolt" and "break the rules!" issued by policy making courts. Crier, *supra* note 2 at 5.
23. Brown and Abel, *supra* note 18, at 10. On the invocation of civil rights litigation by plaintiffs' lawyers in high-stakes contingent fee litigation, see H. Erichson, "Doing Good, Doing Well," *Vanderbilt Law Review* 57 (forthcoming 2004), introduction. But see Mather, *supra* note 12, at 907-908.
24. See e.g. Jacobson and Warner, *supra* note 1, at 782-783; Jacobson and Soliman, *supra* note 8, at 224 fn. 1; Mather, *supra* note 12, at 899.
25. See e.g. Olson, *supra* note 2, at 94-98, 306-314; Crier, *supra* note 2, at 4. For a more thoughtful invocation of the founders' view of government, see Turley, *supra* note 2, at 463-469.
26. William Blackstone, *Commentaries on the Laws of England, A Facsimile of the First Edition of 1765-1769, Volume I: Of the Rights of Persons (1765)* (Chicago and London: University of Chicago Press, 1979): at 69.
27. On the use of public policy considerations in common law adjudication, see generally Melvin Eisenberg, *The Nature of the Common Law* (Cambridge: Harvard University Press, 1988).
28. For example, compensation for injury due to most forms of negligent conduct is regulated by common law.
29. See Horowitz, *The Transformation of American Law*, 1980-1860 (New York: Oxford University Press, 1992); Goodman, *Shifting the Blame: Literature, Law, and the Theory of Accidents in Nineteenth Century America* (Princeton: Princeton University Press, 1998); Bergstrom, *Courting Danger: Injury and Law in New York City 1870-1910* (Ithaca: Cornell University Press, 1992); G. White, *Tort Law in America: An Intellectual History* (Oxford: Oxford Press, 1980); William Nelson, "From Fairness to Efficiency: The Transformation of Tort Law in New York, 1920-1980," *Buffalo Law Review* 47 (1999): 117-226.
30. For example, determining whether the defendant owed the plaintiff a duty of care in negligence claims involves explicit judicial policy inquiries. The doctrine in New York is typical: "the definition of the existence and scope of an alleged tortfeasor's duty is usually a legal, policy-laden declaration reserved for Judges to make prior to submitting anything to fact-finding or jury consideration." *Palka v. Service Master*, 83 NY 2d 579, 585 (NY 1994). As Justice Benjamin Cardozo put it, "when the question is one of supplying the gaps in the law, it is not of logical deductions, it is rather of social needs, that we are to ask the solution." J. Cardozo, *The Nature of the Judicial Process* (New Haven: Yale University Press, 1921): at 123.
31. See generally, W. Eskridge, *Dynamic Statutory Interpretation* (Cambridge: Harvard University Press, 1994).
32. I am indebted to Peter Schuck for pointing this out.
33. I am indebted to Robert Rabin for pointing out that in many instances, legislatures, not courts, are the "gap fillers."
34. T. Lytton, "The Complementary Role of Tort Law," *supra* note 14.
35. See C. Weissert and W. Weissert, *Governing Health: The Politics of Health Policy*, 2nd ed., (Baltimore: Johns Hopkins University Press, 2002): at 173.
36. This membership figure for the NRA is from Richard Robinson, Tennessee field representative for the NRA, quoted in O. Schroeder, "Movement Afoot to Form Local NRA Committee," *The Leaf-Chronicle*, January 12, 2003, at 7B. O. G. Davidson, *Under Fire: The NRA and the Battle for Gun Control* (Iowa City: University of Iowa Press, 1998): at 306, puts the figure lower at 2.7 million members in 1998, a figure which may include deceased lifetime members. The membership figure for the Brady Campaign is from G. Overholser, "Staying on Target; With Plans for Theme Restaurant on Times Square, The NRA Continues to Lack Common Sense," *Chicago Tribune*, May 31, 2000, at 23; for the Sierra Club from Sierra Club, "Why Join the Sierra Club," *available at* <http://www.sierraclub.org/membership/why/?promocode=J04W0T0010> (Last visited Sept. 14, 2004), and for the ACLU from ACLU, "About the ALCU," *available at* <http://www.aclu.org/about/aboutmain.cfm> (Last visited on Sept. 14, 2004).
37. See P. Schuck, *The Limits of Law: Essays on Democratic Governance* (Boulder: Westview, 2000): 204-250.
38. For more on the NRA and Brady Campaign legislative tactics, see T. Lytton, "The NRA, the Brady Campaign, and the Politics of Gun Litigation," in Lytton, *Suing the Gun Industry*, *supra* note 9, chapter 6.
39. See W. Eskridge, P. Frickey, and E. Garrett, eds., *Cases and Materials on Legislation: Statutes and the Creation of Public Policy*, 3rd ed., (St. Paul: West, 2001): 66-69.
40. P. Gailey, "The Gun Lobby vs. The Government," *New York Times*, Sept. 18, 1981, at A18.
41. See, e.g. Bureau of Alcohol, Tobacco, and Firearms, Department of the Treasury, *ATF Crime Gun Trace Analysis Report* (February 1999).
42. *Ibid*, *ATF Report*, at 20-22.
43. For example, some lawsuits against the gun industry have attempted to force the gun industry to adopt one-gun-per-month purchase limits that some state legislatures have failed to pass. See Lytton, *supra* note 14, "The Complementary Role of Tort Law."
44. Olson, *supra* note 2 at 77-8, 226-9
45. I am indebted to Peter Schuck for suggesting this.
46. Eskridge, *supra* note 39, et. al at 60-62.
47. Erichson, *supra* note 23, introduction.
48. Jacobson and Warner, *supra* note 1, at 14.
49. See Huber, *supra* note 2; Olson, *supra* note 2; Crier, *supra* note 2.

Part VII
Vaccination

[18]

MASS IMMUNISATION PROGRAMMES: SOME PHILOSOPHICAL ISSUES

TIM DARE

ABSTRACT

Most countries promote mass immunisation programmes. The varying policy details raise a raft of philosophical issues. I have two broad aims in this paper. First, I hope to begin to remedy a rather curious philosophical neglect of immunisation. With this in mind, I take a broad approach to the topic hoping to introduce rather than settle a range of philosophical issues. My second aim has two aspects: I argue that the states should have pro-immunisation policies, and I advance a view on the subsequent and more specific question as to which sorts of pro-immunisation policies they should prefer. I use the immunisation policies of the United States and New Zealand to frame my discussion of these substantive questions. Immunisation is effectively compulsory in the United States. New Zealand, by contrast, requires evidence not of immunisation but of immunisation status upon school enrolment: New Zealand's policy effectively makes immunisation choice compulsory. I argue that, as between the pro-immunisation policies of the United States and New Zealand, the latter should be preferred. Though the threshold question as to whether states should have pro-immunisation policies should be answered affirmatively, the move to compulsory immunisation cannot be justified.

I. INTRODUCTION

Mass immunisation programmes attract both fulsome praise and intense opposition. On the one hand the authors of a leading text write that "[w]ith the exception of safe water, no modality, not even antibiotics, has had such a major effect on mortality reduction and population growth".[1] On the other, vaccination has always attracted

[1] Susan and Stanley Protkin 'A Short History of Vaccination', in *Vaccines* 2nd edn, eds Stanley Protkin & Edward Mortimer (WB Saunders & Co, Philadelphia, 1994) 1.

a good deal of opposition.[2] Critics question the benefits and risks of immunisation, often claiming that medical corporations and authorities either lack or withhold information which would allow policy-makers, medical practitioners and parents to make informed immunisation choices. Policy-makers have tended to side with pro-immunisation lobbies. Most countries at least promote immunisation, some going so far as to require proof of vaccination before children may be enrolled in school, effectively making immunisation compulsory. Within the varying detail of policy and response lie a raft of philosophical issues.

I have two broad aims in this paper. First, I hope to begin to remedy a rather curious philosophical neglect of immunisation. Given the rise of applied ethics in the past two decades, the scope and medical significance of mass immunisation programmes, and — as I hope to show — the philosophical fertility of the topic, it is surprising that it has been given almost no attention by philosophers.[3] Though I will not touch upon, let alone definitively address, all that might be of interest to philosophers about mass immunisation programmes, I hope nonetheless to say enough to indicate that they raise issues deserving philosophical attention. My second aim has two aspects: I wish to argue that the question of whether states should have pro-immunisation policies should be answered affirmatively, and to advance a view on the subsequent and more specific question as to which sorts of pro-immunisation policies states should prefer. I will use the immunisation policies of the United States and New Zealand to frame my discussion of these substantive questions. All of the states of the United States require vaccination for school entry and, despite a number of challenges, no court has held mandatory vaccination laws unconstitutional.[4] As a result immunisation is effectively

[2] J. Clark-Nelson and J. Rogers, 'The Right to Die? Anti-Vaccination Activity and the 1874 Smallpox Epidemic in Stockholm', in *Social History of Medicine*, 23, (1992), pp. 370–381. Emile Roux, one of Louis Pasteur's closest colleagues, resigned from Pasteur's laboratory over the first human vaccinations, of Joseph Miester and Jean Baptiste Jupille against rabies in 1885. Forty -five years earlier variolation had been made a felony in England.

[3] I know of only two explicitly philosophical treatments: Heta Hayry & Meta Hayry, 'Utilitarianism, Human Rights and the Redistribution of Health through Preventive Medical Measures', *Journal of Applied Philosophy*, 6, (1989), pp. 43–51 and Paul Menzel 'Non-Compliance: Fair or Free-Riding' *Health Care Analysis*, 3, (1995), pp. 113–115. Menzel's piece is a contribution to symposium on immunisation: 'The Pros and Cons of Immunisation' *Health Care Analysis*, 3, (1995), pp. 99–115.

[4] The leading case is *Jacobson* v *Massachusetts* 197 US 11 (1905). A recent case upholding the requirement is *Hanzel* v *Arter*, 625 F Supp. 1259 (SD Ohio 1985). Some states do not require all of the standard paediatric vaccines: twenty do not require mumps vaccination and nine do not require pertussis (whooping cough).

compulsory in the United States. New Zealand, by contrast, has recently introduced a 'national immunisation strategy', aimed at increasing immunisation coverage, which requires evidence not of immunisation but of immunisation *status* upon school enrolment, and which allows unimmunised children to be removed from school for the duration of relevant disease outbreaks.[5] New Zealand's policy effectively makes immunisation *choice* compulsory. Upon school enrolment, parents or guardians will be required to confront the immunisation options and declare their child's status. Children may remain unimmunised, but they will not do so without someone — typically a parent or guardian — making a positive choice to that effect. I shall argue that, as between the pro-immunisation policies of the United States and New Zealand, the latter should be preferred. Though the threshold question as to whether states should have pro-immunisation policies should be answered affirmatively, the move to policies which make immunisation compulsory cannot be justified.

II. EMPIRICAL UNCERTAINTY

I begin by addressing what seems to have been the most significant factor in the long and occasionally vigorous public debate about immunisation, namely stark empirical disagreement between the parties to that debate. Opponents of immunisation claim, for instance, that it is a major contributor to cot death (or Sudden Infant Death Syndrome) rates;[6] proponents that "[t]here is absolutely no connection between immunisation and cot death".[7] Proponents acknowledge records of adverse reactions but argue that even granting their incidence, it is safer to be immunised than not; opponents produce figures showing that vaccines are both much more dangerous and much less effective than proponents acknowledge. And so on. For every empirical claim one way or the other, advocates for the opposing view produce an empirical claim to the opposite effect. I do not wish to enter directly into this empirical debate. I have nothing

[5] The contrast may seem independently interesting, since the United States is in general far more individualist than New Zealand. New Zealand's immunisation programme targets nine diseases: Haemophilus influenzae type b (hib), hepatitis b, mumps, rubella, measles, pertussis (whooping cough), tetanus, polio and diphtheria.

[6] "[T]he cot death rate would be halved if vaccination were to be suspended." Sheibner and Karlsson, 'Cot Death Linked to Vaccinations', *Nexus* (Australia), October/November, 1991.

[7] From a letter by S.L. Tonkin of the New Zealand National Children's Health Research Foundation, Cot-Death Division, dated July 8 1992, responding to the Sheibner and Karlsson article quoted in the previous footnote.

to say about the empirical evidence that has not already been said by people more competent in the relevant areas. There are, however, a number of conceptual points to be made about the empirical debate that contribute to the case for certain sorts of pro-immunisation policies, if only by showing that that debate and the uncertainty it seems to evidence does not militate conclusively against pro-immunisation policies.

It seems likely that complete certainty about the effects of immunisation — about their precise effect on disease incidence and immunity levels, about the incidence and distribution of adverse reactions, and so on — will be impossible to achieve. Given problems of interpreting evidence, of isolating causal factors, of obtaining data about necessary coverage rates, of proving negatives, and the like, the best we can hope for are assessments of 'degrees of probability'. It is important, however, not to misinterpret this conclusion and its significance.

There are a number of related points to be made here.

First, it is important not to equate 'scientific' with 'actual' uncertainty. Scientific method requires that scientific claims be made and held 'conditionally': that scientists remain ready to review them in light of new evidence, that opposing views be raised and tested, that dialogue and experimentation continue. These apparent indicia of uncertainty, however, say as much about the scientific method as they do about the reliability of data or scientific claims. They do not show that scientific claims are especially doubtful, or unreliable, or actually uncertain. The mere fact that such claims have not been proved in some absolute and eternal sense or the mere possibility that new evidence might arise, does not entail that they are unreliable, and an absence of scientific (or medical) unanimity does not settle the question of the reliability of the data. In fact, many scientifically uncertain claims are no less certain than beliefs upon which we quite properly base personal decisions and public policy. Whether the degree of a scientific claim's truth is high enough to warrant reliance on that claim in the determination of political policy is itself, ultimately, a matter requiring a social or political decision. One might expect these social or political decisions to be based upon the sort of considerations raised in the substantive sections of this paper.

Second, it should not be supposed that it is unethical to make social policy, even coercive policy, where outcomes are less than absolutely certain (even where, as with immunisation, among the possible outcomes are very severe iatrogenic illnesses). This is obvious in those familiar cases, of which immunisation seems an example, where there really is no possibility of 'doing nothing': failing to immunise counts as doing something as surely as does immunising.[8] More generally, policy makers will often have to act under conditions of uncertainty since those are the inescapable conditions in which we find ourselves much of the time. It is likely to be an unethical abrogation of responsibility to refuse to act other than in conditions of certainty; in this world, little would get done. One way to put this is to say that policy-makers are likely to act improperly if they require unreasonably high degrees of probable truth or claim unwarranted precision or confidence in the scientific claims used in policy making.[9]

Third, it is important to note that ethical and policy issues will typically remain despite the settling of empirical issues. The point is worth making, since one reason to focus upon empirical disagreement to the neglect of ethical or policy issues is the belief that the latter will be settled if only the facts can be determined. But while it is certainly true that policy or ethical analysis that ignores the facts will rarely be helpful, it is a mistake to suppose empirical inquiry to be a substitute for such analysis or to avoid such analysis in the hope that empirical inquiry will render it unnecessary. Suppose, for instance, it were 'certain' that attaining a 95% immunisation coverage would eradicate Hib disease and equally certain that Hib immunisation carried some risk. Future generations would benefit from the eradication, both because they would not face the threat of the disease and because they would not need to undergo the risk of immunisation. In these circumstances, which seem close to the actual ones, the facts do not settle the ethical question about the legitimacy of requiring or encouraging me and my children to take risks for the benefit of others, in this case unborn others.

The apparent impossibility of achieving absolute certainty about immunisation, then, does not militate conclusively against pro-immunisation policies. The significance of such uncertainty is a normative matter to be considered against the background acknowledgment that scientific uncertainty is primarily a methodological assumption, that policy-makers cannot avoid making policy under conditions of uncertainty, that they must not demand or claim spurious precision in the use of probabilities or degrees of confidence, and that the ongoing and laudable search for higher degrees of certainty, however successful, will not remove the need to address ethical issues.

[8] This remark assumes a certain view about the supposed distinction between acts and omissions. I will return to the issue briefly below.

[9] The point has an august pedigree. Aristotle has it in mind when he proposes that "[i]t is the mark of an educated man to look for precision in each class of things just so far as the nature of the subject admits; it is evidently equally foolish to accept probable reasoning from a mathematician and to demand from a rhetorician scientific proofs". *Nichomachean Ethics* I.1, 1094b24–28. (trans WD Ross)

Thus far I have been concerned with the consequences empirical uncertainty *does not* have for policy-making and normative inquiry. Nothing I have said shows that uncertainty has no normative significance. Indeed, it is important to see that the features of scientific practice and policy-making sketched above, much of it a response to uncertainty, should be of considerable normative consequence. Though both scientists and policy-makers may be justified in regarding such uncertainty as attaches to a claim as primarily a methodological assumption, and in making decisions and policy in the face of the uncertainty they do face, they have responsibilities to ensure that their conduct is based upon the best possible information, especially where important consequences — both beneficial and threatening — are at stake. Very briefly, in science this responsibility will normally require adherence to appropriate scientific method. For instance scientists must exercise care in systematically gathering data extensive and diverse enough to distinguish genuine from merely apparent causal relationships and to isolate the relevant factors in those relationships when they develop and check theories and explanations, and they should remain open to new information and alternative theories and explanations.

For their part, policy-makers working in areas which rely upon scientific claims must ensure that they know so far as possible the degree and cause of the uncertainty under which they act and must actively monitor and respond to relevant scientific developments. They must be especially careful, in light of an obvious temptation, not to give undue weight to the protection of 'investment' in policies based on earlier information. While investment and consistency is certainly relevant to policy-making, policy-makers must not ignore shifts in scientific consensus. Given the nature of scientific method, policy-makers must be familiar with a range of opinions, with controversies affecting their policy area, and with the degree of certainty with which opinions are offered. Though they need not replicate the work of scientists, they have a responsibility to know, at least in broad terms, what support there is for the claims upon which they rely; what supporting studies have been carried out, what quantities of evidence was surveyed, and the like. And, insofar as the force of scientific opinion depends upon adherence to appropriate methodology, the claims of lay persons must not be dismissed simply because they are lay persons. The issue is whether their claims are defensible by the same standards applied to expert opinions.[10]

[10] One specific implication of these positive duties is the obligation to consider vaccines individually. Even if, in general, it seems that immunisation is desirable, scientists and policy-makers ought not to be blind to evidence that some vaccines

III. THE PHENOMENOLOGY OF IMMUNISATION CHOICE

The last section began with the claim that there had been the stark empirical disagreement between the parties to the debate about immunisation. I suggested that such uncertainty as there is about immunisation does not itself rule out pro-immunisation policies. Indeed it seems likely that we could go further and conclude that, so far as the empirical evidence goes, we are entitled to treat certain claims about immunisation as 'practically certain' for policy purposes. I have already said that the justifiability of immunisation policies will not be settled on empirical grounds; empirical certainty, practical or otherwise, will not bring normative certainty. Before turning to the substantive normative issues, however, there is at least one further step necessary to bring into focus the policy significance of the sort of empirical disagreement one encounters in the immunisation debate. In the context of the current debate, it will be useful to approach this step by way of a discussion of the phenomenology of immunisation choice.

Immunisation choices, we have seen, involve judgments of probability under uncertainty. We know quite a bit about how people make such judgements. They tend to rely not upon complex mathematical calculations of probability but upon 'heuristics' or rules of thumb.[11] One heuristic that has special relevance to risk perception and assessment, and which seems especially applicable in immunisation choices, is 'availability': our estimations of the frequency or probability of an event are often based upon the ease with which instances of that event come to mind.[12] Because frequently occurring events are easier to imagine or recall than rare events, availability, in this technical sense, is often an appropriate cue to frequency and probability. But heuristics such as availability can lead to serious and systematic error, tending to be less than perfectly correlated with the variables that actually determine probability. Availability, for instance, is affected not only by frequency of occurrence, but also by factors such as an event's 'strikingness', salience to an assessor, or how recently or often it has been portrayed in the media. Serious iatrogenic sequelae, for instance, are striking so are likely to stand out among a comparatively bland albeit

— the pertussis vaccine for instance — seems to be less efficient and more prone to side effects than other common vaccines.

[11] See, for instance, the papers collected in *Judgment Under Uncertainty: Heuristics and Biases*, eds. Daniel Kahneman, Paul Slovic, and Amos Tversky (Cambridge University Press, Cambridge, 1982).

[12] Amos Tversky and Daniel Kahneman, 'Availability: A Heuristic for Judging Frequency and Probability', *Cognitive Psychology*, 5, (1973), pp. 207–232.

large background of unproblematic immunisations. By the same token, those who have 'experienced the horror' of vaccine preventable epidemics, such as polio, may be led by the availability heuristic to overestimate the probability of such epidemics occurring in the future.

It seems plausible, indeed, that availability may generally lead us to misrepresent the risks and benefits of preventive as compared to 'curative' medicine. It would not be surprising if immunisation, for example, attracted a level of opposition incommensurate both with its intrinsic and comparative risk-benefit ratios, because immunisation is given to people who are well where other treatments are given to people who are ill. In the latter case both the threat from illness and the benefits of treatment are likely to seem more real because we feel ill or know we have some condition which threatens our well being. The actual or intended pay-offs in such circumstances are obvious, and are, phenomenologically, more readily used to discount any risks posed by the treatment. In the case of immunisation, however, there is no guarantee that we ever would have been ill failing the intervention, there remains some chance that immunisation will not effectively protect us, and indeed there is some small chance that it will make us ill. From a purely phenomenological perspective, on the one hand the pay-offs are much less obvious, and hence less readily used to discount risk, while on the other the risks themselves are more striking against a background which does not include an existing illness.

Suppose the availability heuristic with its attendant threat of error, was a significant phenomenological characteristic of immunisation choice.[13] In that case there would be need for special care in examining our assessments of the risks and benefits of immunisation. The authors of much of the original work in heuristics seem to have this modest recommendation in mind when they conclude that their findings pose a series of challenges:

> For non-experts ... to be better informed, to rely less on unexamined or unsupported judgements, to be aware of factors that might bias risk assessments, and to be open to new evidence .... For experts and policy makers ... to recognise and admit one's own cognitive limitations, to attempt to educate without propagandising, to acknowledge the legitimacy of public concerns, and somehow to develop ways in which these concerns can find expression in societal decisions without, in the process, creating more heat than light.[14]

[13] Noting that availability is offered only as an example. Immunisation choices seem likely to be vulnerable to various other sources of cognitive dissonance.

[14] Paul Slovic, Baruch Fischhoff and Sarah Lichtenstein, 'Facts Versus Fears: Understanding Perceived Risk', in Kahneman, Slovic, and Tversky, *Judgment Under Uncertainty: Heuristics and Biases*, pp. 463–489, 488–489.

Perhaps these phenomenological characteristics will seem to support even more dramatic recommendations. If we are confident that risk assessments in these areas are likely to be defective, shouldn't we simply disregard them in policy development and enforce public policy which reflects correct assessments? We may think the challenge posed by the availability heuristic too demanding — the more so once we notice the ironic implication that discussion of an event intended to show its occurrence unlikely may increase its availability and hence perceived probability![15] Alternatively, it may be that there is an obvious reason not to take this more dramatic step of ignoring what we take to be unreliable risk assessments. Perhaps we should be reluctant to impose policy on dissenters even where we regard their views as mistaken, when we must concede that that policy, though we think it more reliable, is itself based upon assessments of probability rather than certainty — notice that Slovic *et al* offer their modest conclusion to experts as well as to non-experts. I do not think this last point is a compelling ground against compulsion. Again, the absence of certainty, compounded by the lack of a clear criteria of rationality with respect to attitude to risk averseness,[16] no doubt places obligations upon scientists and policy-makers. Within the bounds of those obligations, however, we are entitled to treat some conclusions as 'practically certain' — as literally certain for practical purposes — and will sometimes act improperly if we fail to make and impose policy on the basis of such conclusions.

But this is not the end of the issue. The exclusion or discounting of strongly held views and the implementation of policy which will lead to the coercion of proponents of those views is a serious matter that we should not countenance without strong justification. In short, to justify ignoring risk assessments we are prepared to count as unreliable, we need to show not just that an assessment is mistaken but that tolerating it has some significant cost. I will have more to say about the costs of tolerating mistaken views about immunisation later. For now I offer the preliminary conclusion that accepting the truth of some narrow range of risk assessments does not settle what we should do about immunisation. Even when the facts are in, we are left with the question as to what policies are justified by those facts. Again, that is a moral not an empirical question, and it is to this substantive question that I now turn.

[15] Ibid 465

[16] We will return to this issue in the next section.

IV. UTILITY

Utilitarianism, or its descendant cost-benefit analysis, is the most obvious theoretical model from which to begin a substantive normative analysis of mass immunisation policies. The general thrust of such approaches will be familiar: each alternative course of action is evaluated according to the ratio of its costs to its benefits. The option which 'maximises happiness', in the sense of having the highest cost-benefit ratio is recommended. Where costs and benefits are uncertain, their expected values are calculated by discounting each possible cost or benefit by the probability of its occurrence. Further wrinkles may be added to take account of varying degrees of risk averseness. Crudely speaking, as an ethical theory the approach identifies as 'right' that option which has the highest expected utility.

There are a number of reasons for starting with utilitarian strategies. They have become the orthodox approach to public policy making generally, and to public policy making under uncertainty in particular. Furthermore, since immunisation is a definable event and since the manifestations of vaccine preventable diseases and the adverse effects of vaccines are 'practically certain', immunisation has seemed an especially promising field for cost-benefit analysis.[17] The more traditional utilitarian justification of immunisation programmes will be obvious: if we accept as practically certain the standard claims for the benefits and risks of immunisation, then immunisation promises great benefits to large numbers of people, albeit at the cost of perhaps very serious harms to a small number of people. Hence John Last writes that "[t]he ethical issues that arise when we seek to protect the population by immunising *have long been clearly defined*. The risks of adverse effects to individuals have to be balanced against the benefits to the community."[18] Last gives the 1947 smallpox immunisation in New York city as an illustration: "Faced with an outbreak of smallpox ... the public health authorities ... vaccinated about 5 million people; the human costs of this were 45 known cases of post-vaccinal encephalitis with four deaths — an acceptable risk, in view of the enormous benefit, the safety of the city

[17] Consequently there have been literally hundreds of cost-benefit studies of vaccination programmes and of particular vaccines, all of which, one study concludes, "have shown that immunisation represents a remarkably efficient use of resources ....". *Alan Hinman & Walter Orenstein*, 'Public Health Considerations', in Protkin & Mortimer, *Vaccines*, pp. 903–932, 919. The authors reference some ninety-eight cost-benefit studies of immunisation programmes and specific vaccines.

[18] John M. Last, *Public Health and Human Ecology* (Appleton and Lange, Ottawa, 1987), pp. 353–354. Emphasis added.

of 8 million, but a heavy price for the victims of vaccination, and their next of kin."[19] If the public health officials had not vaccinated, the number of cases of encephalitis and deaths would have been much higher, so organising the vaccination programme was the right thing to do.[20] A crude indication of the comparative risk of immunisation and disease might be derived from a smallpox epidemic among a largely non-immunised population in India in 1974-1975. Overall the epidemic had a fatality rate of 17.4%, reaching 43.5% for children under one year old.[21] Although one obviously needs to be careful about the influence of other factors, such as hygiene, climate and living conditions, the comparative risks seem dramatically in favour of immunisation, and thus to support the initial utilitarian conclusion.

At the same time, utilitarian (or cost-benefit) approaches to social policy are subject to a long list of familiar objections. Some flow naturally from the discussion in the previous section: such approaches often rely upon individual preference. Factors which distort those preferences in a given context may result in distorted utility values: sufficiently serious, widespread and robust cognitive dissonance would significantly reduce the attraction of preference-based approaches to policy-making. Furthermore, it will not always be easy to determine what is to count as a 'distorted preference'. Parents are likely to be especially risk averse when making decisions concerning their own children, but we may be reluctant to count such risk aversion as irrational or distorted, and also reluctant to endorse an approach to social policy which called upon us to do so, even where it prompts parents to act other than as a 'disinterested' calculus would recommend. One wants to say both that such risk aversion need not be mistaken or distorted, but instead a proper response to the particular attachments and values which frame a specific parent's decision, and that it *is* mistaken or distorted to the extent that it does not track actual probabilities. The contrast can be brought into focus by imagining a discussion with a parent committed to being conservative as to which option — immunisation or non-immunisation — *counted* as the conservative path. Beyond this, such approaches must solve the 'comparability' problem. They must explain how the different benefits at issue in policy decisions — in the immunisation case benefits such as (but not only) the preservation of human health and life, the recognition of autonomy, and of course money — are to be

[19] Ibid

[20] See Hayry & Hayry 'Utilitarianism, Human Rights and the Redistribution of Health', for this very conclusion about the New York case.

[21] See Donald Henderson & Frank Fenner, 'Smallpox and Vaccinia', in Protkin & Mortimer, *Vaccines*, pp. 13–39, 19.

weighed and compared. The problem here arises from the attempt to assign the correct weights or rates of exchange among these benefits. It seems obvious that our society considers all of them valuable, but it is far from clear that there is a satisfactory metric for weighing them together and trading them off. And it may seem simply wrong to solve the comparability problem even if we could. One way to put this last point is to say that goods such as human life cannot be equated with money, or with any other resource, at any rate of exchange. To assign a monetary or resource exchange value to such goods is to treat them as commodities when they really have a different kind of value. This objection suggests that it is necessary not only to find a method for weighing different goods but also to find an appropriate way of expressing or regarding different values.

I do not wish to suggest that this brief assessment is a stake in the heart of utilitarian approaches to policy making. They have survived more vigorous attacks and various utilitarian responses are available, though commentators have concluded that "[t]aken together [familiar problems with utilitarianism and its modern instantiation] should suffice to motivate the search for alternative principles which can be used to guide decision making on environmental and analogous issues".[22] In the meantime, utilitarian analysis can advance the current discussion. Allow for the sake of the argument that utilitarian considerations favour at least *some* pro-immunisation policy. Such approaches require policy-makers to take the least expensive or harmful route to a goal. Suppose further that all, or almost all, of the benefits of a compulsory immunisation policy could be achieved by a voluntary policy. Now, if compulsion is itself a disutility, carrying with it costs associated with surveillance and enforcement, with resentment, with loss of autonomy and the like, utilitarian analysis may require political states to take the voluntary route. The overall utility of the voluntary policy may be higher than that of its compulsory alternative, once the disutility of compulsion is taken into account.

All of this seems to be true of immunisation policies. For example, various models predict that 92 to 96% of children need to be immune to measles to eradicate the disease.[23] Since no vaccines are completely effective, coverage rates need to be higher than required immunity rates: given a 95% effective vaccine, a target of 92% immunity

[22] R.E. Gooden, 'Ethical Principles for Environmental Protection' in *Environmental Philosophy* eds Robert Elliot & Arran Gare (1983), 6, pp. 3–20.

[23] See eg R.M. Anderson and R.M. May 'Vaccination against Rubella and Measles: Quantitative Investigations of Different Policies', *Journal of Hygiene*, 90, (1983), pp. 259–325, and H.W. Heathcote, 'Measles and Rubella in the United States', *American Journal of Epidemiology*, 117, (1983), pp. 2–13.

requires a coverage of 98%. The United States has attained coverage in the order of 95%, so falling marginally short of elimination rates. Though it is not entirely clear what proportion of the coverage is due to school immunisation laws[24] it will do for current purposes to simply compare this coverage figure with that attained in countries with voluntary programmes. Voluntary programmes in the Netherlands, Norway, and Sweden have attained coverage rates of 93%, 90% and 92% respectively.[25] Given that none of these countries, the United States included, have achieved the 'utility bonus' of eradication, it is unlikely that the existing difference in coverage rates contributes to significantly different utility returns. If this is right, then even if utilitarian analysis supports immunisation programmes of some sort, it may not support compulsory programmes. To justify these on utilitarian grounds, it needs to be shown that the extra benefits promised by such programmes outweigh the disutility of compulsion.

We may be able to go a little further here. What utilitarians and cost-benefit theorists seek is high benefit at low cost. There is reason to suppose, I think, that the New Zealand policy is especially well placed this regard. Surveys have suggested that a very high proportion of those who do not immunise fail to do so not because they have 'positive objections' to immunisation but because of apathy, inconvenience, ignorance or the like.[26] This suggests, I propose, that a policy such as New Zealand's, which requires parents and guardians to make immunisation choices one way or the other and which puts into place various other immunisation support mechanisms, will significantly increase coverage rates without resorting to compulsion.

[24] There have been attempts to identify this figure. One notes that voluntary immunisation has reached a coverage rate of 80% by the second birthday and suggests that the improvement of 15% to the coverage figure of 95% is therefore attributable to the school laws. This is problematic in both directions. It is surely likely that at least some of those who immunise their children before their second birthday do so in anticipation of the requirement that all immunisations be completed by school entrance age, and that at least some of those who complete immunisation programmes after their second birthday but prior to school entrance are voluntarily following a schedule to that effect. Alternatively, a 1978 study compared low and high measles incidence areas with similar demographic characteristics, vaccine uptake in children under two, and surveillance systems concluding that the only relevant difference between the two areas was the vigour with which school immunisation laws were enforced; more strictly and comprehensively in low incidence areas. Norman D. Noah reports both approaches in 'Immunisation before School Entry: Should there be a Law? *British Medical Journal*, 16 May 1987, pp. 270–271.

[25] See Noah, ibid, for details.

[26] Lester Calder, Central Auckland Community Medicine Registrar, 'What is the Best Way to Inform High risk Groups About Hepatitis B Immunisation?: A Survey by Polynesian Community Health Workers' Unpublished, 1988.

The claim is that there is little reason to suppose that most of those who fail to immunise require compulsion to do so. Given the actual grounds for non-immunisation, it seems likely that, required to choose, many will choose to immunise. If this assumption is correct about the likely effect of policies such as New Zealand's, then such policies promise high benefits (in terms of increased immunisation coverage) without the costs attendant upon compulsion borne by their United States' style counterparts.

This last conclusion depends, of course, upon certain key empirical assumptions. Perhaps the most obvious is that the immunisation patterns achieved voluntarily in countries such as New Zealand and Scandinavia would be attained under similar programmes in a country such as the United States. It may be, however, that factors such as the larger and denser populations of urban poor to be found in the United States than in New Zealand or Scandinavia, or the stronger hold of broadly libertarian views among the United States citizenry, would make voluntary programmes less effective there than in these other countries. The upshot is that some empirical care must be taken with the utilitarian conclusion.

V. INDIVIDUAL LIBERTY AND THE HARM PRINCIPLE

According to standard liberal theory, states may interfere with individual liberty only to prevent those whose liberty is interfered with harming others, and neither to prevent people harming themselves nor to compel them to benefit themselves or others. The 'harm principle' may seem to prohibit compulsory immunisation since, *prima facie*, the non-immunised do not harm others, though immunisation bestows benefits both upon the immunised and others. Any harm that results from nonimmunisation is done by the disease. At worst, those who fail to immunise omit to do something that might make it less likely that others will encounter vaccine preventable diseases.

The distinction between harms and benefits is commonly presented in terms of movements relative to a welfare baseline. On some accounts the baseline is the position of a person prior to the relevant intervention, so *A* benefits *B* when *B* is better off as a result of *A*'s intervention than he was before, and *A* harms *B* when *B* is worse off as a result of *A*'s intervention than he was before. Other accounts suggest that the baseline should be set at *B*'s 'normal' position. A familiar philosophical example illustrates the difference: *B* is drowning. *A* could save *B* with no personal risk and little inconvenience. If *B*'s baseline is his position immediately prior to *A*'s arrival, then *A* would benefit *B* were he to rescue him. *A*'s intervention would improve *B*'s interests above the position they were in when the two crossed paths. Since *A*'s intervention is (merely) a benefit, the harm principle prohibits political states imposing duties to rescue in such circumstances. If *A* walks on he fails to benefit *B* but does not harm him since he has done nothing to make *B* worse off than he was when the two met.[27] If we take the relevant baseline to be *B*'s normal position — a position, let us suppose, considerably above that he occupied as he was about to go under for the third time — then *A*'s intervention moves *B* back toward that baseline. Though the rescue obviously improves *B*'s position, it will not count as a benefit for the purposes of the harm principle and failing to effect a safe and easy rescue may count as a harm. Joel Feinberg has argued convincingly that we should favour the baseline geared to a person's normal welfare position. State coercion, he maintains, can never be used to force one person to bestow a windfall profit on another, but:

> .... easy rescue of a drowning child is not mere benefiting in this sense. It is a benefit only in the ... sense of affecting a child's interests favourably, specifically by preventing a drastic decline in his fortunes from a normal baseline. That is quite another thing than conferring a windfall profit on him.[28]

How does this bear upon immunisation? It might seem that the threat posed by vaccine preventable diseases is natural — "any harm done by nonimmunisation is done by the disease" — and therefore part of our normal baselines. Anything done to reduce that threat would be to move the beneficiaries above the baseline and so to benefit them. To fail to reduce the threat would be (merely) to fail to benefit rather than to harm. But I propose that we should not so link 'normal' to 'natural' so closely. The positioning of normal baselines should be seen in part at least as a function of community decisions and expectations which impose demands, distribute risks, and set standards. Educational requirements provide an illustration. Those who lack a minimal education — who cannot read, do basic mathematics, communicate reliably — are seriously disadvantaged in our community because of community set standards and requirements of basic literacy and numeracy. To fail to educate children to the level required for a 'normal' life, is to fail to bring them up to the normal baseline, and hence, in light of the proceeding discussion, is to harm not merely to fail to benefit them.

The discussion may already allow us one conclusion about immunisation. The drowning and education cases seem to suggest

[27] It might be argued, though, that it is worse to drown knowing someone could have rescued you if they could been bothered, than it is to drown simpliciter.

[28] Joel Feinberg, *Harm to Others: The Moral Limits of the Criminal Law*, (Oxford University Press, New York, 1984), p. 136.

that we should not put too much weight upon the apparent distinction between acts and omissions. In appropriate circumstances, it seems clear that 'failing to act' — in this case failing to rescue or educate — can count as a harm. The work is done, I suggest, not by the act/omission distinction itself, but by independent judgements about the contents of our duties to others. Sometimes those duties require positive action, sometimes omissions.

Beyond this, I suspect immunisation will often be very similar to the education case. The populations of countries such as the United States and New Zealand enjoy high levels of immunity to polio because of effective immunisation programmes. The immigration policies of both countries reflect this immunity level in taking relatively little care to prevent the import of polio; those countries do not ban travel from polio areas or rigorously check incoming travellers for polio exposure. The assumption is that only moderate care is required, since the chances of people catching the disease in New Zealand and America are small, given vaccine generated immunity rates. If the assumption were that Americans and New Zealanders were more vulnerable to polio than they are, we would expect significantly different attitudes toward immigrants from polio areas.

A similar situation is likely to obtain with other vaccine preventable diseases and the management of other sources of risk. A good deal of the public health policy of countries such as New Zealand and the United States is based upon assumptions that the welfare baseline of their citizens includes immunisation. To the extent that this is true, failing to immunise one's children may be to harm them in the same way that failing to educate them is to harm them.

In New Zealand my child's baseline is in part constituted by existing high, vaccine generated, immunity rates. It follows, I suggest, that the failure of others to contribute to those rates may count as a harm, rather than a mere failure to benefit. Many aspects of my child's life would be different if we lived in a community which did not enjoy high immunity to diseases such as polio and tuberculosis. We send our children to school confident that they are unlikely to encounter serious diseases. We do not take precautions we would take were the 'natural' baseline of vulnerability to disease the normal baseline. This immunity is part of my child's normal welfare baseline and her life is ordered, in part at least, in reliance upon it. So described, location of the baseline is affected considerably by the conduct of others. Those who fail to contribute to that baseline cause harm to others; they do not merely fail to benefit those others.

Perhaps it will seem, however, that even if the unimmunised do threaten harm to others, it will only be to those who have 'consented' to that risk by themselves choosing not to immunise. The real issue for the harm principle, that is, may seem to be the availability of a *volenti non fit injuria* defence.[29] But if we get to the point of requiring the defence (ie., if the principle seems at least *prima facie* to prohibit pro-immunisation policies), then I do not think the defence succeeds. First, note that the group who are most obviously at risk from vaccine preventable diseases are children, who will not have made a decision about immunisation at all. The point may seem to cut both ways: if children have not plausibly consented to bear the risks of nonimmunisation neither have they consented to the risks of immunisation. But for the moment I am interested in the *volenti* defence and not an attempt to justify pro-immunisation policies by appeal to consent. Second no immunisation is absolutely effective, as noted above. Some of those who choose to immunise will not gain immunity. To the extent that the decisions of non-immunisers increase the chances of these people encountering the disease, arguably non-immunisers do threaten harm to people who have not chosen that risk. Third, some of those who have not immunised will have failed to do so because they cannot. Some people, for instance, have temporary or permanent medical grounds for not having certain immunisations. In some sense and in some of these cases, such people will have chosen not to immunise, but they will not easily fit into a category of voluntary non-immunisers for the purposes of a *volenti* defence. Finally, and perhaps most significantly under this heading, the appeal to the *volenti* defence portrays a community of informed persons who have voluntarily assumed whatever risk non-immunisation carries. But, as we have seen, surveys of immunisation coverage in New Zealand suggest that this is a somewhat romantic view of the unimmunised community. The most common reasons for failing to have children immunised against Hepatitis B in South Auckland were a lack of transport or problems with the timing or location of immunisation clinics.[30] It seems likely that these results would be borne out elsewhere: that only a relatively small portion of those who do not immunise fail to do so as the result of a conscious choice to that effect. If this is right, we should not suppose that those at risk from non-immunisation are only the members (or children) of a community of informed objectors. Non-immunisation seems to be more often due to ignorance or socio-economic disadvantage than to choice.

But serious doubts may remain as to the implications of the harm principle for immunisation policies. We can bring some of these doubts into focus by noting an important difference among the

[29] The latin maxim translates roughly as 'no harm is done to one who consents'.
[30] Lester Calder, 'What is the Best Way ...'.

'vaccine preventable' diseases. Some diseases can be completely eradicated by immunisation — smallpox is the most famous example. Given sufficiently high coverage rates with sufficiently effective vaccines, immunisation can rob diseases of potential hosts, so that the diseases die out altogether. Other diseases cannot be completely eliminated, but immunisation can control disease outbreaks and provide individual protection. In some cases, such as that of tetanus, this is because the disease has non-human hosts untouched by immunisation. In others, sufficiently effective vaccines are not currently available, or required effective coverage rates are very high.[31] The harm principle may bear differently upon these two disease categories: ineradicable and eradicable. Accept for the sake of the argument that immunisation is effective but carries some risk. In the case of ineradicable diseases, the choice of those who refuse to immunise does not bear upon the need for others to carry on taking the risk of immunisation. They would need to do so in any case, since no matter what level of immunisation coverage was attained those seeking protection would need to immunise. The situation seems somewhat different in the case of eradicable diseases. Here if enough people immunise, all may be able to abandon the risks of the disease and of immunisation. The choices of those who maintain a host population through nonimmunisation preserve the threat of the disease and the need to immunise to obtain protection, along with the attendant risks of immunisation. In the case of eradicable diseases, then, the choice of the unimmunised may be regarded as posing a threat to others, so falling under the harm principle.

Note, however, that the aim of eradication goes beyond even the already stretched reading of 'welfare baselines' defended earlier. Here we do seem to be in the realm of benefit rather than harm prevention. It may be, of course, that we should simply reject the harm principle and argue that some public goods are sufficiently valuable to warrant overriding individual liberty. I would like to finish this discussion, however, by sketching a possible response to the general harm principle objection that will allow at least New Zealand-style immunisation policies.

First, as between the New Zealand and United States policy options, the harm principle most obviously challenges the latter. John Stuart Mill himself was careful to allow attempts to inform people of

[31] Of the nine diseases targeted by New Zealand's immunisation programme, Hib, hepatitis b, mumps, and rubella could be eliminated. Measles, pertussis (whooping cough), and tetanus can be controlled, but are thought unlikely to be eliminated. Polio and diphtheria have been eliminated in New Zealand but not everywhere else — immunisation for these in New Zealand is intended to protect against occasional imports and contact abroad.

the risks attendant upon proposed courses of action and to persuade people to act in ways that the harm principle prevented us from requiring them to act, and it is not hard to see why. For Mill the harm principle is motivated by a commitment to the value of autonomy. At least minimal levels of information and education seem required by meaningful understandings of autonomy, and the coercive element in the New Zealand policy requires precisely that individuals make rather than avoid choices. It should not be denied of course that the New Zealand policy is pro-immunisation. The state in New Zealand is not neutral as between immunisation options and that preference is apparent on the face of its policy. Nonetheless, the policy preserves a meaningful and not enormously expensive or punitive opportunity for people to act contrary to state preference. If our concern were just to examine the legitimacy of the New Zealand policy, we might simply stop here without further inquiry into the implication of the harm principle.

Second, suppose the harm principle allows coercive immunisation policies such as those of the United States. Even here we might think the principle favours New Zealand over United States policies. It seem uncontroversial that the New Zealand policy is *less* coercive than its United States counterpart. The harm principle is standardly taken to licence only such interference with liberty as is necessary to avert threatened harm. And now we encounter a familiar issue when comparing United States and New Zealand immunisation policies: all or almost all of the harms which are avoided under the United States policy of compulsory immunisation are also avoided under the New Zealand policy. The New Zealand approach however involves less interference with liberty than its United States counterpart. Again, from the perspective of the harm principle, it is to be preferred as between the two.

Finally, perhaps we should not be overly troubled if interference with immunisation choices does turn out to be paternalist — to involve interference not to prevent harm but to promote the good of those interfered with. The harm principle aims to protect the liberty of those in a good position to judge their own interests: "it is, perhaps, hardly necessary to say", said Mill nonetheless, "that this doctrine is meant to apply only to human beings in the maturity of their faculties. We are not speaking of children ...."[32] In discussing immunisation, of course, we *are* typically speaking of children. Appeal to the harm principle against pro-immunisation policies amounts to an attempt to use the principle to protect the liberty of parents to choose whether their children should be vaccinated. There is a difficult and distinct

[32] John Stuart Mill *On Liberty*, (1859), Introduction.

question here, about the rights of states to interfere with parents' decisions as to how their children are to be treated. In the states with which we have been concerned there is a long history of leaving parents considerable, though not absolute, discretion in these matters. For the moment it will do to suggest that immunisation is not a clear case under the harm principle: we might think that were states to compel children to receive immunisation, they would be acting in any case outside the ambit of the harm principle.

VI. FREE RIDING AND PARADOXES OF REASON

The decision whether or not to immunise (or more accurately, whether or not to have children immunised) appears to depend crucially upon what others decide to do. If there is a correlation between immunisation and the incidence of targeted diseases, then the larger the proportion of my community who decide not to immunise, the more important it is likely to be that my child does. In a community in which few have their children immunised, I should do so since there is a higher probability that my children will encounter a vaccine preventable diseases. In a community in which most immunise, however, that probability is lower, so it is less important that my children immunise.

This feature of the immunisation decision has some interesting results:

First note that it renders advice not to immunise somewhat paradoxical. Suppose I decide not to immunise my child. If it is true that the larger the proportion of my community who decide not to immunise, then the more important it is that my child does, I must now hope that most others do not share my view. The more likely I believe it to be that they will share my view, paradoxically, the more reason I will have to disregard my original assessment. On at least some constructions, the smaller the number of people who are moved by the recommendations of those opposed to immunisation, the more attractive those recommendations become.

This 'decision paradox' has familiar implications for public policy. Suppose I reason that most people will have their children immunised, and judge that, because they do, it is safe for me not to; I judge that the relatively high rate of immunisation means that the risk of contracting vaccine-preventable diseases is sufficiently low to make it safe for my children to avoid the risks of immunisation. Suppose further, that a significant proportion of my community agrees with me, and also gives up immunisation. At some point the benefits of immunisation will be lost to all. The problem for social policy is that, for *any* individual, it is best if they have the benefit of high immunisation rates without themselves bearing the risk (or paying the cost) of contributing to the attainment of that rate. But if too many people seek what is best for them, they will do worse than they would have done had they been less concerned to maximise their own benefit. The fact that the decision to immunise — in common with decisions as to whether to contribute to other public goods — has this paradoxical structure might recommend compulsion, or at least the imposition of a model which constrains the pursuit of self interest. Policy-makers recognising that every individual will be motivated by self interest to act in ways which will threaten both public and self-interest might legislate as a way of restructuring the decision for individuals.

The last paragraph sketches a standard response to familiar problems surrounding individual contributions to public goods. What drives the approach is the idea that certain acknowledged goods would be threatened if individuals were allowed unfettered appeal to self interest. The argument plainly does not warrant *any* fetter. Even if the general line is accepted, it will only justify such intervention as is necessary to secure the good. And now, again, the approach seems to favour New Zealand over United States policy options. Given the empirical assumptions I have made as to the likely effect of New Zealand style policies, it seems that requiring people to make an explicit choice about immunisation will lead to satisfactory coverage rates. The 'compulsory choice' option appears to be a sufficient restructuring of individual's decision contexts to avoid the threat posed to the public good of immunisation. On the face of it, that is, the New Zealand policy is a sufficient and hence appropriate restructuring, while the United States option imposes unnecessary, and hence unjustified compulsion.

There is a further issue here. Given the way in which the wisdom of the decision not to immunise depends upon the fact that most others do immunise, one might argue that the unimmunised are 'free-riders' in the sense that they take the benefit of high immunisation rates without exposing themselves to the risks unavoidably attendant upon attaining those rates. We need to be careful about this conclusion. Though the term free-riding may seem pejorative, not all free-riding is morally objectionable. The residents of an avenue along which I travel may bestow benefits upon me through their commitment and contributions to a street-beautification project, making my journey to work more pleasurable than it would otherwise be. Surely, however, they cannot impose contributory obligations upon me simply by putting in place a scheme from which I benefit as a commuter. Suppose the residents of my own street announce that they have entered into a similar project, with the aim of increasing the values of all of the properties in the street. The scheme can be expected to be able to tolerate a certain degree of defection. If one or two people decide not to go along with the plan, values in the street will still increase, perhaps settling only slightly below the point they would have reached had there been full participation. Under these circumstances, those who do not participate may seem to be free-riders. They will get the benefits of the scheme without paying any of the costs (and if the real-estate maxim 'buy the worst house in the best street' is good advice, they may do especially well since their unimproved houses in a now beautiful street may attract a premium). But again this free-riding does not seem morally objectionable. The mere fact somebody has come up with a scheme which will benefit others does not seem to allow them to unilaterally impose obligations upon those who stand to benefit from their efforts.[33]

Whether free-riding *is* morally objectionable in a given case is likely to depend upon a number of factors, none of which will be decisive. Relevant concerns seem to include the extent to which non-participation threatens the project as a whole, whether the project promises a benefit (as in the street beautification project) or aims to avoid a harm, whether the benefit was imposed upon the free-rider or whether they went out of their way to take it, and whether their participation in the benefit increases the costs to others. We have already addressed most of these issues. Mass immunisation programmes can tolerate small numbers of defectors without significant reductions in the benefits they provide. If the evidence I have mentioned as to the make-up of the set of non-immunisers is correct — that is, if most of them would be expected to immunise under a policy which required them to make an explicit choice whether to do so or not — then it may be that such programmes can tolerate a rump of 'voluntary non-immunisers'. Their defection or free-riding will not threaten the project as a whole. Concern with whether or not non-immunisers go out of their way to take advantage of immunisation programmes leads us into worries about the character of non-immunisers. Plainly this can be relevant to moral assessment but the necessary inquiry into individual motivation cannot be taken very much further here. A couple of points can be made given what has gone before. First, it seems unlikely that those who fail to immunise on grounds of ignorance, apathy, inconvenience, or the like will properly be counted as deliberately taking advantage of immunisation schemes, though the conduct may be morally blameworthy on other grounds. Second, we have seen that at least

[33] For a fuller discussion to similar effect see Robert Nozick *Anarchy, State and Utopia* (Basil Blackwell, Oxford, 1974) pp. 90–95.

some voluntary non-immunisers are motivated by their rejection of the orthodox account of the risks and benefits of immunisation. It seems that we should not count these people as deliberately taking advantage of immunisation schemes either. After all, their conduct is motivated by scepticism as to the existence or extent of those advantages. There seems no straightforward way in which the decisions of defectors from immunisation schemes increases the costs of such schemes to others. For the most part, the actions appropriate for those who choose to immunise will not be changed by the decisions of those who do not do so. Again, it may be that the answer here will differ as between eradicable and controllable diseases. Immunisation programmes, though efficient by comparison with the mortality and morbidity they prevent, are nonetheless expensive. In the case of eradicable diseases, it is tempting to conclude that, where the choices of non-immunisers have the effect of prolonging the need for such programmes, they do impose costs on communities. Were it the case that the effect of their choices was that the costs of immunisation against a particular disease could not be abandoned once and for all — as the costs of immunising against smallpox has been abandoned once and for all — we might wish to conclude that their non-participation does increase costs to others.

On balance it seems to me that we can properly describe at least some non-immunisers as free-riders, but that their conduct is not morally objectionable. Given what seem to be plausible assumptions about attainable coverage rates, immunisation programmes are able to tolerate a small rump of voluntary non-immunisers. Though it may be too much to ask contributors to abandon their resentment of those who free-ride upon their contributions, given that free-riders in the immunisation case do not significantly increase the costs of the scheme for others, significantly alter what contributors should do given their preference to immunise, and since the conduct of free-riders does not seem to threaten the attainment of the good of immunisation, I see little ground to justify moral criticism of non-immunisers on the ground that they are free-riders. It is perhaps worth making explicit a couple of caveats to this conclusion: first, the conclusion — and many others in this paper — depends upon the empirical assumption about the likely result of New Zealand style policies. If voluntary non-immunisation does threaten the good promised by immunisation schemes, free-riding may become morally objectionable. Second, it seems probable that moral criticism is one important way of restructuring decision contexts to avoid the public good problem sketched above. Policy makers need to be aware of the likely effect of a perception that there has been an increase in willingness to tolerate defection from immunisations schemes. If such tolerance were to threaten the attainment of the good of immunisation, most obviously by significantly increasing the number of voluntary non-immunisers, policies of toleration may have to be revised.

VII. CONCLUSION

I said at the outset that I had two broad aims in this paper. I hoped, first, to begin to remedy a rather curious philosophical neglect of immunisation and, second, to argue that immunisation programmes are typically justifiable as well as to suggest that states should prefer certain kinds of pro-immunisation policies. I began by discussing two preliminary issues. I addressed the significance of deep empirical disagreement in the debate about immunisation, arguing that it was important not to give the wrong significance to the probable impossibility of attaining complete certainty about immunisation. It was important, I claimed, to distinguish scientific from actual uncertainty, to recognise that policy-makers are often under an ethical obligation to act under uncertainty, that the fact of uncertainty raises certain specific obligations both for scientists informing policy-makers and for policy-makers themselves, and, finally, to note that ethical questions are typically not settled empirically. I then addressed the significance of a cluster of phenomenological constraints upon immunisation decisions, suggesting that while those constraints impose obligations to be especially careful in examining the risks and benefits of immunisation, they do not themselves warrant the dismissal of possibly distorted risk assessments in policy-making. How policy-makers should react to the possibility of such assessments was, I claimed, an ethical rather than an empirical question. I then turned to substantive moral analysis, arguing that although there is reason to be wary of the efficacy of utilitarian or cost benefit analysis of immunisation policy, to the extent these approaches apply, they favour policies that preserve choice over those which render immunisation compulsory. In the context of this paper, this is to say that such approaches favour New Zealand over United States policy alternatives. I came to a similar conclusion when examining immunisation policies from the perspective of the liberal harm principle. That principle did not, I argued, prohibit immunisation policies in general and, as between the New Zealand and United States alternatives, recommended the New Zealand model. Finally, I discussed a cluster of issues raised by the status of immunisation as a public good and the attendant problems attaching to individual choices about contributing to such goods. I concluded again that the New Zealand policy was an adequate and justified response to these problems. I also suggested that, while some non-immunisers might legitimately be regarded as free-riders, moral criticism of them on that score was not justified. All of this suggests that states should favour certain, New Zealand style, pro-immunisation policies.

Department of Philosophy
University of Auckland, New Zealand

[19]

PUBLIC COMMUNICATION, RISK PERCEPTION, AND THE VIABILITY OF PREVENTIVE VACCINATION AGAINST COMMUNICABLE DISEASES

THOMAS MAY

ABSTRACT

Because of the nature of preventive vaccination programs, the viability of these public health interventions is particularly susceptible to public perceptions. This is because vaccination relies on a concept of 'herd immunity', achievement of which requires rational public behavior that can only be obtained through full and accurate communication about risks and benefits. This paper describes how irrational behavior that threatens the effectiveness of vaccination programs – both in crisis and non-crisis situations – can be tied to public perceptions created by media portrayals of health risks. I concentrate on childhood vaccination as an exemplar of 'non-crisis' preventive vaccination, and on the recent flu vaccine shortage as a 'crisis' situation. The paper concludes with an examination of the steps necessary to resolve these threats through better public communication.

The shortage of flu vaccine caused by contamination at the manufacturing plant of vaccine maker Chiron has necessitated social policies that restrict access to vaccine, targeting distribution to 'high-risk' groups such as infants, pregnant women, the elderly, and the immuno-compromised. Despite attempts at public education about these restrictions, problems have arisen concerning compliance with distribution standards: while many high-risk people have had difficulty gaining access to flu vaccine, the vaccine has been available to many who are not eligible for access under CDC guidelines. For example, bioethicist Art Caplan describes not only a litany of access violations, but his own personal experience of offers of access to flu vaccine in an editorial published at the MSNBC website.[1] Lack of compliance with vaccine distribution policy, I argue below, reflects a fundamental failure of public communication that permeates our public health system. This fundamental flaw must be addressed if we hope to have the compliance with public health policies necessary to maintain the level of control over infectious disease epidemics achieved during the 20th century.

No policy for vaccine distribution is likely to succeed until public fears that motivate counter-productive behaviors are addressed. Caplan's editorial describes criminal acts of burglary to obtain flu vaccine, as well as price gauging by wholesalers offering vaccine that normally costs about $10/dose for as much as $88. Such behaviors are not resolvable through public policy alone: indeed, burglary and price gauging are already prohibited in public policy. Resolution of these behaviors must involve addressing the fears that motivate non-compliance. The behaviors described are, in most cases, irrational behaviors resulting from misperceived risks and benefits related to the flu vaccine. Although there are certainly benefits to flu vaccination for the majority of the population, for most individuals (who do not fall into 'high risk' groups), the most significant benefits of vaccination are related to protection of others. It is for this reason that CDC efforts to increase flu vaccination normally emphasize hospital and nursing home workers, and those who come into contact with 'high-risk' individuals. Although these individuals also benefit by avoiding a bout of the flu, the more significant benefit is the immunity that keeps them from spreading the flu to 'high-risk' patients that they are in contact with. In short, the direct benefits of flu vaccination for individuals not in 'high risk' groups fails to connect to the self-interest-based demand reflected in motivations that underlie the types of criminal burglary and price gauging that have occurred.

Previous flu vaccine shortages have also been tied to 'irrational' demand created by events highly visible in the media. In the fall of 2001, anthrax was mailed to political and media figures in the immediate wake of the September 11 tragedies, creating bioterror fears throughout the country. Because early symptoms of anthrax (as well as a number of other bioterror agents) mimic the flu, demand for flu vaccine skyrocketed, creating shortages in some areas. This occurred despite the fact that the flu vaccine provided no protection against anthrax, but only served to help in diagnosing the potential cause of flu-like symptoms. In each of the above

1 http://www.bioethics.net/articles.php?viewCat=2&articleId=70.

cases, the problems in question were 'created' by lack of effective public communication, resulting in a (mis)perception of risks that led to behavior which not only failed to optimize public health goals, but was actually counter-productive. Because of the nature of preventive vaccination programs, the viability of these public health interventions is particularly susceptible to public perceptions. Both the success of vaccination in non-crisis situations (especially childhood vaccination, as I discuss below), as well as the effective use of vaccination in crisis situations (such as the flu vaccine shortage described above) require rational public behavior that can only be achieved through full and accurate communication about risks and benefits. Below, I describe how irrational behavior that threatens the effectiveness of vaccination programs can be tied to public perceptions created by media portrayals of health risks; and the steps necessary to resolve these threats through better public communication.

RISK PERCEPTION AND IRRATIONAL BEHAVIOUR

Although particularly salient for vaccination programs, the problem of misperceived risk is not unique to vaccination. George Gray and David Ropeik describe fear-induced behavior following the September 11 terror attacks as resulting in actions that actually increased risk for many individuals, rather than lowering it (e.g. purchasing guns, driving instead of flying, etc.).[2] Barry Glassner argues that irrational fear is a pervasive feature of contemporary American culture.[3] In many cases, the fears motivating irrational behavior are the result of media coverage that heightens a sense of risk. As G. Ray Funkhouser and Eugene Shaw describe, there is considerable evidence that media present distorted views of the world that increase 'false expectations' and 'undesirable behaviors'.[4] Trends toward sensationalization in 'established' news sources, combined with inherent issues of unreliability in many 'new' news sources (like the internet), can exacerbate this problem.[5]

For example, one study of media communication during this anthrax scare found that coverage included alarmist crawls/

[2] G.M. Gray & D.P. Ropeik. Dealing With the Dangers of Fear: The Role of Risk Communication. *Health Affairs* 2002; 21(6): 106–116.

[3] B. Glassner. 1999. *The Culture of Fear.* NY. Basic Books.

[4] G.R. Funkhouser & E. Shaw. 2000. How Synthetic Experience Shapes Social Reality. In *Media Power in Politics.* Doris Graber, ed. Washington, DC. CQ Press.

[5] L. Downie & R. Kaiser. 2002. *The News About the News.* NY. Alfred A. Knopf.

taglines by Cable TV, and the use of large, sensational headlines such as 'Baby falls ill as scare widens across U.S.' by print media.[6] Although actual anthrax cases were limited to clusters in Boca Raton, Florida, New York City, and Washington DC (though spores were found in distant locations such as Indianapolis and Kansas City,[7] a fact not overlooked by the media), the threat was perceived to be much greater. According to an Institute of Medicine report, 'The widespread reporting of the anthrax contamination in the weeks after September 11 served to expand those events from several localized incidents into a potential generalized threat.'[8] The result was striking: according to an article published in the *Journal of the American Medical Association*,[9] more than 30,000 people are estimated to have received antibiotics related to the anthrax scare. Beyond supply issues, over-use of Cipro has threatened the effectiveness of this drug for a number of conditions. In his testimony before the US House of Representatives Subcommittee on National Security, Institute of Medicine President Kenneth Shine stated: 'In the case of anthrax, less than 20 cases resulted in thousands of people taking antibiotics that were not indicated. Perhaps 20 percent of these individuals experienced some side effects from these drugs. These antibiotics changed the bacteriological environment and may have rendered some organisms resistant to the antibiotics employed.'[10] In short, media portrayals of a threat can, as stated by the Institute of Medicine report, 'inadvertently change the basic dimensions' of a threat.

This type of influence can be seen clearly in public behaviors following the announced flu vaccine shortage. In most years, the problem faced by the public health community is one of convincing the public to accept vaccination, rather than restricting access to flu vaccine. Ironically, the shortage of flu vaccine has seemingly

[6] Kristen A. Swain. Finding Fact Before the Frenzy: Bioterrorism Communication Facts and Fiction. Presentation at the American Medical Writers Association National Convention, Miami, FL, Sept. 2003.

[7] H.C. Lane & A. Fauci. 2002. Bioterrorism on the Home Front. In *Bioterrorism: Guidelines for Medical and Public Health Management.* Donald Henderson, T. Inglesby & T. O'Toole, eds. American Medical Association Press.

[8] Institute of Medicine. 2002. *Making the Nation Safer: The Role of Science and Technology in Countering Terrorism.* Washington, DC. National Academies Press: 275.

[9] Lane & Fauci, *op. cit.* note 7, p.7.

[10] K. Shine. Testimony before the House Committee on National Security, Veteran Affairs, and International Relations, Committee on Government Reform. Cited in Institute of Medicine 2003. *The Future of the Public's Health in the 21st Century.* Washington DC. National Academies Press: 324.

increased demand, despite the lack of serious risks for many who are now seeking access to the flu vaccine. All of the above examples demonstrate the need for better public communication about health risks – communication that reflects reasoned assessments of risks and potential courses of action. This is true not only for visible 'crisis situations' (such as the anthrax scare or the flu vaccine shortage), but also for more 'mundane' public health programs like childhood vaccination. In this context, fear motivates refusal of vaccination rather than demand, but the basic problem remains the same: irrational behavior (in non-compliance with vaccination policy) motivated by misperception of risks.

Since its inception, the program of mandatory childhood vaccination for children entering the U.S. public school system has been remarkably successful – widely recognized as one of (if not *the*) most successful public health programs in history.[11] The program has resulted in the eradication of smallpox, the elimination of polio, and a radical reduction in the number of cases of diphtheria, measles, pertussis (whooping cough), rubella, mumps, and a number of other serious diseases. For example, diphtheria has dropped from a peak of 206,939 cases in 1921 to only 4 cases in 1990, and similar drops in cases have occurred for measles, mumps, pertussis, and rubella.[12] The success of the childhood vaccination program, however, faces threats from an increasingly visible anti-vaccination movement, and from visible (though extremely rare) cases of adverse reactions to vaccination. The DTP vaccine results in adverse events such as convulsions or shock for 1 in 1,750; acute encephalopathy for 0–10.5 in 1,000,000; and the MMR vaccine results in encephalitis or severe allergic reaction for 1 in 1,000,000.[13] These risks are extremely low when compared to the adverse consequences from contracting vaccine-preventable disease (for pertussis, encephalitis for 1 in 20; death for 1 in 200; for measles, encephalitis for 1 in 2,000; death for 1

[11] Centers for Disease Control and Prevention, Achievements in Public Health, 1900–1999, Control of Infectious Diseases, 48 *MMWR* 1999; 621; Centers for Disease Control and Prevention, Ten Great Public Health Achievements – United States, 1900–1999, 48 *MMWR* 1999; 241; Centers for Disease Control Prevention, Impact of Vaccines Universally Recommended for Children – United States, 1990–1999, 48 *MMWR* 1999; 243.

[12] W.A. Orenstein & A.R. Hinman. The immunization system in the United States – the role of school immunization laws. *Vaccine* 1999; 17 (supp 3) October 29.

[13] Centers for Disease Control and Prevention. Six Common Misconceptions about Vaccination. Available at: http://www.cdc.gov/nip/publications/6mishome.htm

in 3,000); however, the success of the vaccination program has made the chances of actually contracting a vaccine-preventable disease very small. In one study of the incidence of measles and pertussis in exempted children from 1987–1998, it was found that although the incidence of measles and pertussis in exempted children was 22 times greater than in vaccinated children, the annual incidence of measles was only 32.2 per 100,000, and of pertussis 80 per 100,000.[14] It is only if one is unlucky enough to contract the disease, then, that one assumes the risks associated with that disease.

Several popular books and anti-vaccination advocacy groups have touted this balance as a reason to forego vaccination, offering parents advice on how to successfully apply for exemption to vaccination on behalf of their children.[15] Media reports of a possible link between the MMR vaccine and autism (a link investigated and rejected in the medical literature and by the IOM[16]) further motivates non-compliance, as the low level of perceived risk for contracting vaccine-preventable diseases makes vaccine safety issues more weighty for parents. Importantly, however, the perceived balance of risks for individuals may not coincide with the balance of risks considered on a population-wide level: that is, the level at which is it rational for an individual to accept the risks of vaccination may not correspond to the level at which community-wide considerations make vaccination rational.[17] The dangers of refusing vaccination are often hidden by statistical risks calculated on the basis of circumstances that would not hold true if non-compliance were widespread.

No vaccine is 100% effective. The success of vaccination programs relies on a concept known as 'herd immunity,' wherein protection is achieved through attaining a high enough level of immunity to a disease so as to make exposure to the organism that causes the disease extremely unlikely. If a critical mass of people is immune, then, those who are not immune are protected

[14] D.R. Feikin, et al. Individual and community risks of measles and pertussis associated with personal exemptions to immunizations. *JAMA* 2000; 284(3145).

[15] H.L. Coulter & B.L. Fisher. 1987. *A Shot in the Dark.* Avery Press; J. Murphy. 1993. *What Every parent Should Know About Childhood Immunization.* Boston. Earth Healing Products.

[16] Institute of Medicine. *Immunization Safety Review: Measles-Mumps-Rubella Vaccine and Autism.* April 23 2001. Available at: http://www.iom.edu/report.asp?id=4715

[17] P. Fine & J. Clarkson. Individual versus Public Priorities in the Determination of Optimal Vaccination Policies. *American Journal of Epidemiology* 1986; 124 (6).

through 'herd immunity'. It is for this reason that vaccination does not require 100% compliance to be effective – a feature central to the success of most vaccination programs, and a feature that skews the level of risk for contracting vaccine-preventable disease where herd immunity exists. The actual level of vaccination necessary to maintain herd immunity is different for each potential disease (depending on the rate of effectiveness for the vaccine in question), but generally ranges from 83%–94%.[18] So long as this level of vaccination is attained, those who refuse to be vaccinated are nonetheless protected through the unlikelihood that they will ever be exposed to the disease. The problem arises from this phenomenon: individuals who seek exemption from mandatory childhood vaccination will be protected from contracting vaccine-preventable diseases through herd immunity, gaining this protection as a result of the widespread vaccination of others, while assuming no (real or perceived) risk of adverse reactions to the vaccines themselves. If exemptions to vaccination should be great enough to threaten herd immunity, however, significant harms through exposure to vaccine-preventable disease could result not only for those exempted, but for those who are excluded from vaccination for medical reasons, and for those who are vaccinated yet remain susceptible to the disease (since, again, vaccination is not 100% effective).

This sets up a classic 'free-rider' problem.[19] In his classic work *The Logic of Collective Action*, Mancur Olson states: 'In a large, latent group there will be no tendency for the group to organize to achieve its goals through the voluntary, rational action of the members of the group, even if there is perfect consensus.'[20] The reason for this is that the action of any one individual will have a nearly imperceptible effect on the achievement of a collective goal, motivating free-riding behavior that seeks to garner the collective good at no cost to the individual in question. This will be true so long as an individual cannot be excluded from the collective good (as exemptors cannot be excluded from the protection provided when herd immunity is achieved), no matter how agreed upon the desirability of the collective good. However, widespread noncompliance with behavior necessary to achieve

[18] http://www.bt.cdc.gov/agent/smallpox/overview/intro-to-smallpox.pdf

[19] See T. May & R. Silverman. Free-Riding, Fairness, and the Rights of Minority Groups in Exemption from Mandatory Childhood Vaccination. *Human Vaccines* 2005; 1(1): 12–15.

[20] M. Olson. 1971. *The Logic of Collective Action.* Cambridge, Mass. Harvard University Press: 59–60.

the collective good can result in loss of the good entirely – even for those who comply – a phenomenon often described as a 'tragedy of the commons.' This phenomenon may well be playing out at an early stage: a growing number of parents are seeking exemption to childhood vaccination on behalf of their children. In Colorado, for example, the number of children receiving exemptions on philosophical or religious grounds increased by 59% from 1987 to 1998.[21] Similar increases in exemption rates have occurred in several other states,[22] most notably in Utah, where exemptions to mandatory vaccination rose high enough to threaten herd immunity and result in a measles outbreak where half of those contracting measles had been vaccinated but had not achieved immunity (not surprising, since the rate of exemption was roughly equal to the rate of vaccine ineffectiveness).[23]

PUBLIC HEALTH AND PUBLIC COMMUNICATION

Traditionally, the type of free-rider collective action problem posed by childhood vaccination has been viewed as resolvable only through enforced compliance, because 'under the logic of collective action, voluntary cooperation cannot be assured.'[24] Given the harms that could result from lack of compliance, this approach would be justified if vaccination rates fell below certain levels. Enforced compliance, however, poses special problems that are particularly worrisome in a society that values both individual freedoms as well as respect for the rights of minority groups (as many exemptors refuse vaccination on religious grounds).[25] For this reason, it is desirable that vaccination programs remain voluntary in all but the most dire circumstances.

Because childhood vaccination does in fact provide benefits for most who are vaccinated even in the absence of herd immunity (most routine vaccination effectiveness rates – rates at which immunity is achieved – are high), and because exemptions seem tied to misperception of the balance of statistical risks skewed by the protection afforded through herd immunity (a balance that is significantly altered should herd immunity be lost), it should

[21] Feikin et al., *op. cit.* note 14.

[22] R. Silverman & T. May. Private Choice Versus Public Health: Religion, Morality and Childhood Vaccination Law. *Margins* 2001; 1(2).

[23] T. May. Vaccines as Community-Oriented Therapy. *Expert Review of Vaccines* 2003; 2(3).

[24] R. Hardin. 1982. *Collective Action.* Johns Hopkins University Press. Especially chapter 4: Types of Collective Action Problems. Quote taken from p. 52.

[25] May & Silverman. *op. cit.* note 19.

be possible to address the problems created by increasing exemptions through targeted education of the public. For this to occur, however, it is essential that strategies be developed for clear, accurate, and non-sensationalized communication between health officials and the public, and that the information conveyed be placed in appropriate context. In order to attain this type of clear, non-sensationalized coverage, efforts must be undertaken on the part of both the media and the health community to work toward responsible communication of information to the public. This, in turn, requires an understanding of the complex nature of conventions of scientific language, newsworthiness, and the characteristics of journalistic reporting that facilitate both miscommunication and sensationalism.

It is common to hear news stories justified by the idea that 'the public has a need to know', yet this basic justification ignores the fact that neither scientists nor journalists regard their role as one of educating the public in a straightforward sense.[26] Scientists are normally focused on discrete facts about a specific phenomenon, rather than the broader social relevance of this information. According to Dorothy Nelkin, the dependence of science reporters on the scientific community for information has, therefore, produced a representation of science that ignores the social and political context of scientific information.[27] In addition, differing expectations about the role of caveats and qualifications, for example, result in miscommunication about the nature of information conveyed. Most writers who study the phenomenon of sensationalism in media coverage of scientific information agree that such sensationalization is in part facilitated by the failure of both scientists and reporters to appreciate each other's conventions of professional communication,[28] resulting in each profession blaming the other for the misleading nature of sensationalized stories.[29]

Not all sensationalism, however, is due to simple misunderstanding. What is 'newsworthy' is often quite different than what is 'something the public should be educated about', and a focus

[26] J. Gregory & S. Miller. 1998. *Science in Public: Communication, Culture and Credibility*. NY. Plenum Press: 109.

[27] D. Nelkin. 1995. *Selling Science: How the Press Covers Science and Technology*. NY. W.H. Freeman.

[28] M. Shuchman & M. Wilkes. Medical Scientists and Health News Reporting: A Case of Miscommunication. *Annals of Internal Medicine* 1997; 126(12); J. Winsten. Science and the Media: The Boundaries of Truth. *Health Affairs* 1985; 4(1); Institute of Medicine, *op.cit.* note 10, chapter 7: Media.

[29] Winsten, ibid.

on the former is the leading concern of journalists. The result can be a story that is misleading. As Shuchman and Wilkes describe, 'The journalist overstates the scientific finding and, as a result, the public is misled about the implications of that finding. This sort of reporting has its roots in newsroom pressures to dramatize stories by sounding alarms or touting cures . . .'[30] Jane Gregory and Steve Miller observe: 'The shift toward . . . popularizations of science – and the sensationalism that may result – is, then, not a punishment inflicted on science stories by disdainful or malicious journalists. It arises because of the rhetorical conventions of popularization.'[31] The need to make a story 'newsworthy' results in several recognized strategies of news reporting that give news stories characteristics of 'drama' and 'personalization' that tend to distort the information conveyed.[32] These characteristics are widely recognized among media scholars. As W. Lance Bennett has observed, there is remarkable consensus on these characteristics of media stories, over a vast literature that has considerable empirical support.[33] Journalists interviewed in one study cited the competition for prominent display of their stories as a leading cause of overstating scientific claims. In the words of one reporter: 'A weak statement will go no place.'[34] The focus of stories, therefore, tends to reflect the conventions of 'newsworthiness' that are the primary concern of reporters.

What exactly are these conventions that lead to sensational stories? According to Gregory and Miller, several factors are relevant to the determination of whether a story is 'newsworthy.' First, the story must meet a 'threshold standard'. That is, the story must be perceived as 'big'. The headline 'Small Earthquake in Chile – Not Many Dead' is not newsworthy, but the headline 'Thousands escape Injury in South American Quake' is newsworthy, despite the fact that both headlines describe the same phenomenon. Second, there is a need for a clear relevance for current circumstances. Often, this is accomplished through 'personalization', emphasizing the immediate potential of the phenomenon to affect the lives of readers. Gregory and Miller offer the example that a small earthquake in Chile is not as interesting as even a

[30] Shuchman & Wilkes, *op. cit.* note 28, p. 976.

[31] Gregory & Miller, *op. cit.* note 26, pp. 116–117.

[32] W.L. Bennett. 1996. *News: The Politics of Illusion.* NY: Longman Publishers, chapter 2.

[33] Ibid. p. 47.

[34] Winsten, *op. cit.* note 28, pp. 8–9.

smaller earthquake close to home. Finally, there is a need for a clear 'good news or bad news' focus to a story. According to Gregory and Miller, bad news is often more newsworthy than good news, and of bad news, potential deadliness is the biggest (and most dramatic) danger to humans, so media emphasize deadliness. Thus, 'the mass media are interested in risk because danger is dramatic'.[35]

It is precisely these types of conventions that are apparent in reporting about the flu vaccine shortage. To the extent that this shortage poses risks to *everyone* rather than only to select high-risk groups, the story becomes more 'newsworthy'. Thus, 'personalization' leads reporters to imply the risks are more widespread than they actually are. Likewise, the need to meet a 'threshold standard' provides an incentive for reporters to emphasize the most serious risks, and downplay the more mundane health risks that contracting the flu poses for the majority of the population. Likewise, the risks posed by childhood vaccination are more newsworthy than more mundane stories that confirm vaccine safety. This problem is exacerbated by the fact that most contemporary parents have never experienced an epidemic.[36] The last widespread epidemic to occur in the United States involved polio, which (because of the success of vaccination programs) has been virtually eliminated since vaccination against this disease was introduced in the mid-1950s. At the same time, there is an increasing hesitancy to seek medical intervention unless it is perceived as necessary, due to recent reports of widespread medical errors and mistakes.[37]

One example of the experiences that have resulted in Americans' reluctance to accept vaccination is the Swine Flu Affair of 1976. That failed vaccination campaign resulted in more than 1,000 cases of Guillain-Barre syndrome (a paralytic disease) among those seeking protection against an outbreak that never materialized.[38] This history is perhaps one reason why it has been so difficult for the medical community to dissuade fears stemming from media reports about possible links between childhood

[35] Gregory & Miller, *op. cit.* note 26, pp. 112, 188–189.

[36] M.J. Rosenau. The Uses of Fear in Preventive Medicine. *Boston Medical and Surgical Journal* 1910; 162(10), March 10.

[37] L. Kohn, J. Corrigan & M. Donaldson, eds. 1999. *To Err Is Human: Building a Safer Health System.* Report of the Institute of Medicine. Washington, DC. National Academy Press.

[38] R. Neustadt & H. Fineberg. 1978. *The Swine Flu Affair: Decision-Making on a Slippery Slope.* Washington, DC. U.S. Department of Health Education and Welfare.

vaccination and autism. In short, the fact that contemporary parents have not experienced social conditions of widespread epidemic tends to weaken the perception of need for vaccination. At the same time, contemporary parents *have experienced* increasingly visible reports on medical errors and possible vaccine safety issues, resulting in a tendency to view vaccination with suspicion. These facts are particularly important because they influence public retention of health information: studies show that past experiences and the expectations created by past ('cumulative') communication are important components in the general public's processing and retention of information.[39] Thus, the public is more likely to retain a story about a possible link between vaccination and autism (which is a story that 'matches' expectations set by past experience, and both is 'personal' and meets the threshold standard for dangerous risk), than a story that discredits this (which meets none of these).

Overcoming these conventions will require conscientious effort on the part of both journalists and the medical/scientific/public health community. W. Lance Bennett identifies the need for journalists to downplay the 'personalized' and 'dramatic' characteristics of news reporting in favor of developing the historical, institutional, and social contexts of stories as his leading recommendation for better and more accurate media communication.[40] But responsibility also lies with the medical, scientific, and public health community to take steps to facilitate better reporting of the type Bennett advocates. Indeed, current public health communication strategies often exacerbate the problem by using 'shock tactics' and statistics that amplify risks as a means to gaining public attention.[41] While use of such tactics may seem effective in the narrow context of gaining public attention, in a broader context this strategy can backfire and undermine both public understanding and trust.[42] The negative consequences of overstating risk for political reasons is perhaps nowhere better illustrated than in the Swine Flu Affair,[43] where overemphasis

[39] L. Jeffres. 1997. *Mass Media Effects.* 2nd Edition. Prospect Heights, IL. Waveland Press.

[40] W. Lance Bennett. 1996. *News: The Politics of Illusion.* NY. Longman Publishers: 208.

[41] N. Guttman & C. Salmon. Guilt, Fear and Knowledge Gaps: Ethical Issues in Public Health Communication Interventions. *Bioethics* 2004; 18(6): 531–532.

[42] L. Goodman & M. Goodman. Prevention – How Misuse of a Concept Undercuts its Worth. *Hastings Center Report* 1986; 16(2): 26–38.

[43] A. Silverstein. 1981. *Pure Politics and Impure Science: The Swine Flu Affair.* Baltimore, MD. Johns Hopkins University Press.

of the risks of outbreak resulted in public mistrust that continues to this day.

Rather than adopting the tactics of sensationalization, the medical, scientific and public health community must make efforts to recognize the importance of 'packaging' information for intended audiences so as to maximize the likelihood of communicating the message intended. Here, 'packaging' information does not allude to 'spinning' or misrepresentation of the facts. Instead, it refers here to the presentation of facts in a manner that will be understood and retained by the greatest number of people. The structure and rhetoric of messages are essential in determining how the message is received and interpreted by the public.[44] In this context, public communication must account for the background schemas under which the public understands and processes information.

Packaging is particularly important for communication in matters of health policy because a significant gap may exist between communicator and audience. Studies have shown, for example, that political experts remember information that is both consistent *and* inconsistent with background schema (mental structures that organize information), while the general public remembers only information that is consistent with background schema unless particularly motivated to make sense of the message.[45] The result is that politically-oriented health policy experts may fail to recognize that an intended message might fail to resonate with an intended audience if it lacks an accompanying explanation that sufficiently relates the information to existing public perceptions. This type of 'mis-packaged' communication may be extensive: in the published proceedings of the Institute of Medicine's Mini-Symposium on 'Science and Risk Communication', Baruch Fischhoff describes the importance of recognizing cultural, economic, and experiential diversities that create communication differences: '. . . people of lower socioeconomic status tend to receive health information from a few local, community-based sources. Conversely, scientists tend to communicate in ways that provide greatest benefit to members of the highest socioeconomic

[44] N. Terkildsen, F. Schell & C. Ling. 2000. Interest Groups, The Media, and Public Debate Formation: An Analysis of Message Structure, Rhetoric and Source Cues. In *Media Power in Politics*. Doris Graber, ed. Washington, DC. CQ Press.

[45] Jeffres, *op. cit.* note 39.

groups.'[46] The result is a gap in information dissemination, both in source and interpretation.

In the same vein, we must redouble efforts to streamline communication to the general public. As anyone who has ever played the children's game 'telephone' will know, the further away from the source a message gets, the more it will differ from its original intent. Streamlining communication requires that primary, 'authoritative sources' of information be made available early in the reporting process. This need was illustrated dramatically in the recent case of Terri Shiavo, where confusion over her condition was caused by reporting that conflated comatose, brain dead, and persistent vegetative state conditions. Subsequent publications in the *New England Journal of Medicine* helped alleviate the confusion in many circles, but occurred too late in the process to help clarify public opinion. Streamlining communication, however, can only occur if efforts are first taken to resolve the 'packaging' gap between communicator and audience just described. It is reasonable to assume, for example, that one reason people of lower socio-economic status receive health information from local sources is that the poorly 'packaged' information relayed by authoritative sources simply fails to resonate. If packaging concerns are not addressed, then, streamlining will be ineffective.

With all of these efforts made, there should be optimism for the prospect of more rational public behavior related to risks. For example, in the case of childhood vaccination, while vaccine safety will continue to be a concern among some segments of the population, the vast majority can be expected to comply with vaccination requirements once the true balance of risks is understood. Perhaps most importantly, developing a sound public health 'communication infrastructure' designed to accurately convey health information can go along way in mitigating crises created through fear (in cases like that of the flu vaccine shortage). In this regard, public behavior in the immediate wake of the September 11 2001 terror attacks offers reason for optimism. The public displayed remarkable altruism in behaviors that placed community needs above personal interests.[47] If public

[46] B. Fischhoff. The Challenges of Risk Communication. In the Institute of Medicine Report: Science and Risk Communication: A Mini-Symposium Sponsored by the Roundtable on Environmental Health Sciences, Research, and Medicine, 2001. Available in CD-ROM format: Public Health Preparedness: Recent IOM Reports. Institute of Medicine.

[47] S. Brill. 2003. *After: The Rebuilding and Defending of America in the September 12 Era.* NY. Simon & Schuster.

communication can succeed in relaying the serious social risks associated with non-compliance with vaccination policies (both 'mundane' and 'crisis-oriented'), it is not unreasonable to hope for similar respect for public duties.

Thomas May, Ph.D
Center for the Study of Bioethics
Medical College of Wisconsin
8701 Watertown Plank Road
Milwaukee, WI 53226
USA
tmay@mcw.edu

[20]

THE DETERMINATION OF 'BEST INTERESTS' IN RELATION TO CHILDHOOD VACCINATIONS

ANGUS DAWSON

ABSTRACT

There are many different ethical arguments that might be advanced for and against childhood vaccinations. In this paper I will explore one particular argument that focuses on the idea that childhood vaccinations are justifiable because they are held to be in the best interests of a particular child. Two issues arise from this idea. The first issue is how best interests are to be determined in the case of childhood vaccinations. The second issue is what follows from this to justify potential interventions within the family in relation to such vaccinations. I argue that best interests must be characterised objectively in such situations and that this means that, in at least some cases, parental decision-making about vaccinating their children may be overridden.

There are many different ethical arguments that might be advanced for and against childhood vaccinations. In this paper I will explore one particular argument that focuses on the idea that childhood vaccinations are justifiable because they are held to be in the best interests of a particular child. Two issues arise from this idea. The first issue is how best interests are to be determined in the case of childhood vaccinations. The second issue is what follows from this to justify potential interventions within the family in relation to such vaccinations.

Many childhood vaccinations are given to children at a very young age, often when they are just a few months old. A key aspect of this paper is the thought that this group of children are incompetent, and therefore not able to make decisions about their own care.[1] This means that some other method of decision-making about their care needs to be in place. In such a situation one or more persons is required to make a decision on behalf of the incompetent child. The core issues are who this should be, and on what basis they should make the decision. It is generally believed that such decisions ought to be left to the parents of the child and, in most cases, I believe this is perfectly appropriate.[2] This is, at least partly, because we tend to think that parents will make health care decisions about their child on the basis of what is in that child's best interests. However, whilst we might assume that parents always act in the best interests of their child, this is a reputable presumption. I will argue that in at least some cases this presumption is misconceived and parental decision-making in relation to vaccination should sometimes be overridden. Such a situation arises where there is a substantial risk of significant harm resulting from the decision to either vaccinate or not to vaccinate. Justifiable cases of such interventions will seek to protect the child from potential harm with little or no risk of harm resulting from the intervention itself. In such a situation, I will argue, relevantly constituted third parties[3] should not merely be *able* to exercise their powers in order to protect the child by overruling the parental decision, they are *obligated* to do so. My proposed justification for this view is based upon what I will term the 'best interests argument'. This argument is intended to provide a reasoned basis for justifying the possibility of overriding a parental decision on at least some occasions and can be used to explain the nature of such justified circumstances.

It might be argued that public health issues such as childhood vaccination policies should not be discussed in terms of 'best interests' at all as such an approach focuses upon the individual child rather than the population as a collective body. However, I suggest there are three reasons why it is important to consider this argument.

[1] If we are talking about an older child then they may be competent, in which case, we should treat them in the same way as we would a competent adult (although the latter issue is not discussed in this paper).

[2] I will use the term 'parents' throughout. This term is to be read as a shorthand form to include anyone holding the appropriate legal relationship of parent or guardian. Of course 'parents', where there is more than one, can disagree amongst themselves. I will ignore this issue here, and will assume for the purposes of argument that parents agree as to what is in fact in their child's best interest in relation to vaccinations.

[3] That is justified in the appropriate sense, for example, by being bound by a relevant legal duty of care or statutory duty.

The first is that parents themselves often phrase the issue in these terms.[4] This is perfectly understandable as parents are considering, quite rightly, whether a particular vaccination at a particular time is in *their* child's best interests. A judgment about this may well take into account the prevailing facts about the rates of vaccination in the population as a whole and hence the existence or not of 'herd protection' for that disease in the population. Whilst parents might care deeply about the population's health, the central focus for any parent when faced with the prospect of a possible vaccination will surely be what they believe to be in the best interests of their own child.

Secondly, some commentators have made reference to the issue of best interests as being of central relevance to the arguments about childhood vaccination.[5] The idea behind this point is presumably that both parents and professionals can agree that decision-making about what is in the child's best interests is the central issue within the context of a clinical encounter. However, precisely how best interests are to be determined in such a context is open to dispute, and it is this issue that is discussed in this paper.

Thirdly, and finally, the courts are likely to apply a best interest test in any relevant cases involving childhood vaccinations. This is what happened in a recent legal case in the UK, where two different sets of parents were in disagreement about whether it was appropriate to vaccinate their children. The court applied a 'best interest' test in relation to each child and each vaccination.[6]

However, I do not want to suggest that the 'best interests' argument is the only argument that is relevant to the issue of childhood vaccinations or even that it is the most important one. It is only one possible argument among many. However, it is one that has not so far been explored in the literature.[7]

[4] See, for example, M. Evans, M. Stoddart, H. Condon, L.M. Grizzell, M. Mullen & R. Mullen. 2001. 'Parents' perspectives on the MMR immunisation: a focus group study' *British Journal of General Practice*. 2001; 51: 904–910.

[5] See T. Heller, D. Heller & S. Pattison. 2001. 'Ethical debate: Vaccination against mumps, measles & rubella: is there a case for deepening the debate?' *BMJ*. 323. 838–840. R. Fry. 2002. 'Debate crystallises dilemma facing many medical disciplines' *BMJ*. 324. 733; P. English. 'General practitioners' two roles are not in conflict with MMR immunisation. *BMJ*. 324. 733.

[6] See *A & D and B & E* [2003] EWHC 1376 (Fam) and the appeal of the same case *B (Child)* [2003] EWCA Civ 1148.

[7] This paper is one in a series that seeks to explore all of the different possible arguments that there might be about childhood vaccination. I will therefore not be discussing other possible arguments in favour of vaccination of children based upon such things as the good of the community or harm to others etc in this paper. However, for some discussion of these other arguments see

The structure of the paper is as follows. In section 1, I outline the 'best interests argument' itself, before considering various key components of the argument in the next three sections. I begin this task in section 2, where I discuss different possible senses of 'best interest' and argue that one particular formulation has to be adopted in this context. In section 3, I consider the nature of harm and how decisions about harm are to be made, and section 4 focuses upon who it is that should make decisions about childhood vaccinations.

1. THE 'BEST INTERESTS' ARGUMENT

In this section I outline, and briefly discuss, what I will call the 'best interests argument' for childhood vaccinations. In short the argument takes the following form:

1. Medical decisions about incompetent patients should be made on the basis of what is in their best interests (where prior wishes are unknown or non-existent).
2. Pre-school infants are incompetent (and have no prior wishes).
3. Therefore, decisions about the medical care of infants should be made on the basis of what is in their best interests.
4. Best interests in relation to infants should be determined by seeking to balance the potential harms and benefits of possible actions and inactions.
5. Where the parents make a decision about an infant's care which is likely to result in substantial risk of significant harm to that infant then third-parties (such as the state) have an obligation to intervene to protect the infant from the consequences of that decision.
6. Given 4, what is in the best interests of infants in relation to vaccinations is to be decided by seeking to balance the harms and benefits associated with vaccination versus non-vaccination.
7. Given 3, 5 and 6, where it is in an infant's best interests to be vaccinated (or not vaccinated) and the parents decide the other way then the state (or other legitimate third-parties) have an obligation to ensure that the infant is protected from the consequences of such a decision.

A. Dawson. 'Vaccination and the prevention problem', *Bioethics* 2004; 18 (6): 515–530; M. Verweij & A. Dawson. 'Ethical principles for collective immunisation programmes'. *Vaccine.* 2004; 22: 3122–3126; A. Dawson. 'Herd protection as a public good: vaccination and our obligations to others' (ms).

Conclusion: Parental decision-making about childhood vaccinations can be overruled legitimately in at least some cases.

There are, of course, a number of these premises that might be contested. Some of them turn upon the relevant empirical evidence, whereas others involve controversial normative claims. I will add a few notes to this outline in the remainder of this section to aid interpretation, and to defend the argument from possible objections. I will then discuss some of the components of the argument in more detail in the next three sections.

The first premise requires some explanation. Where individuals are incompetent there are generally three possible grounds for making decisions about their care. The first is on the basis of previously expressed wishes. This is irrelevant in the case of such young children as they have never been competent and have no such views to be taken into account. The second possibility is for some sort of substituted judgement to be made on behalf of the child. This, in turn, is open to various interpretations. If the judgment is to be on the basis of what this individual would have decided if they were competent, then this too is irrelevant for the same reason that previously expressed wishes can be discounted: that is, we have no idea what such an individual would decide. If, on the contrary, the judgment is to be made in terms of what a rational person would decide then this is likely to end up being, in effect, quite close to a decision based upon best interests, which is the third possible way of making decisions for incompetent individuals. The parents of the child might argue that they are able to make a substituted judgment on behalf of the child as they are able to predict what the individual child's views will be as it is *their* child. However, we might question what status this statement has. Is this just a prediction as to what the child's views are expected to be once competent to make such decisions for themselves or is it a statement as to what the parents would prefer the child to choose if it were competent? In either case, it is not clear that this is a sound basis for such decision-making. Given the fact that such young children are, and always have been, incompetent, the most reasonable grounds for decision making in such a context is, I would argue, to appeal to the idea of best interests. This avoids merely 'guessing' what the individual would decide if they were competent. Of course, the definition of best interests itself is a controversial issue which will be discussed in detail in section 2.

For the sake of completion we should also consider another possible option here, because we are concerned with parents making decisions on behalf of their children. This view holds that it is for parents to decide what sort of person their child will become just because this follows from the very nature of the parent-child relationship. Such a view might be based on a number of different possible justifications. For example, grounds might include the thought that parents in some sense 'own' their children and therefore have the right to decide what should happen to them; or that parents just *by virtue of being parents* decide how their child should be brought up; or perhaps, most plausibly, that the family is a private institution that is not legitimately open to outside interference in relation to the choices that will shape the child. Of course such views open up general issues about the child-parent relationship. For our purposes it is sufficient to note that we can side-step these objections because the child is an individual in their own right and parents have no absolute right to put the child at risk for the sake of their own beliefs. Whilst any of the above points might have some merits, their absolute forms are not convincing. The supporters of such views are likely to concede that there will have to be limits upon parental authority, in at least some cases, unless they want to defend a very implausible absolutist form of their argument. This means that the argument then just returns to a more specific discussion about the criteria that are appropriate for such interventions against the parental will. A key component of this will be the determination of the risk of harm relevant to the parental decision.

The second premise is important, but I hope uncontroversial. It is important because one vital aspect of my argument is that it is focused upon a particular group of individuals who cannot make decisions for themselves, that is, pre-school children.[8] Whilst some older (teenage) children may well be competent to make these judgments, I do not believe that children less than two[9] can weigh up the risks and benefits of vaccination programmes. I will therefore restrict my discussion in this paper to the latter group. The third premise follows from the first and second. The fourth premise offers a suitable basis for deciding what constitutes 'best interests' in relation to pre-school infants. It might be controversial but this is discussed and defended in detail in section 2.

[8] This should be acceptable even to the advocates of the greater participation of children within decision-making about their health care sure as P. Alderson & J. Montgomery. 1996. *Health Care Choices: Making Decisions with Children*. London. Institute for Public Policy Research.

[9] This is the standard age for many existing vaccination programmes. See, for example, the suggested ages in Health Education Authority. 1997. *A Guide to Childhood Immunisations*. London. HEA

Some people might also consider the fifth premise controversial in at least some cases, although it should be noted that this is just a general claim. Even someone willing to argue that parents do have an absolute right to decide how their children should be treated, should be able to accept it. The principle behind this premise is that incompetent individuals are generally vulnerable and need to be protected from the ill-informed, reckless or negligent decisions of others. It does not really matter who functions as such a protector in any particular society, as long as someone does. It may be a role shared by the other members of society, or it might be delegated to a particular individual or agency (e.g. social services department; courts etc).[10] This premise seeks to justify a protective role for the state or any other relevantly constituted third party in relation to such vulnerable individuals.

The sixth premise is an attempt to apply the general principle contained in the fourth premise about the nature of best interests for incompetent infants to the specific issue of vaccinations. Although this may be held by many to be deeply controversial, it should be noted that the statement in the sixth premise is a general one, and no claim is made on behalf of any *particular* vaccination programme. The premise is only suggesting that in at least some (non-specified) cases it *may* be in the child's best interests to be vaccinated (or not). This argument can only be applied once we have considered the nature of best interests and any relevant empirical issues in relation to the potential risk of a particular disease and the particular associated vaccination for that disease. This will be discussed in detail in section 3.

The seventh premise gets to the core of the argument and appeals to both empirical and normative elements. The claim is that where there is a high risk of significant harm to the child resulting from the parent's decision, and an alternative choice is in the best interests of the child, then that parental decision should be overruled. Once again this is a general claim, and any application of this argument to specific circumstances will depend upon the relevant facts in relation to a particular disease and a particular vaccine. This premise assumes that where a parent refuses (or accepts) a vaccination (of an unspecified sort for an

[10] There is here a general theory of obligation at work in the background. In short, I would argue that we all have moral obligations to each other arising from the fact we are sentient beings, but that parents are given a special set of obligations by society in relation to their children. However, these are revocable, and they should be revoked where the parents do not carry out the particular obligations (whether positive or negative) that we expect someone in a parental role to perform; for example, where a child is abused or neglected.

unspecified disease) on behalf of their child it is at least *possible* that they are not acting in that child's best interest.[11]

This first section has attempted to explain the 'best interests' argument but, as many of these premises are open to debate, the rest of this paper will seek to justify and defend the core claims of the argument. I will focus the remaining discussion upon just three essential components of this argument in the following three sections. These are:

(a) What are 'best interests'? How are they determined in this situation?
(b) How is the idea of substantial risk of significant harm to be understood?
(c) Why think that the parental decision can be legitimately overridden?

2. WHAT ARE 'BEST INTERESTS'?

It is surprising that there is so little literature about what 'best interests' might be, given the fact that they are invoked so often in discussions in health care, especially in relation to decisions about incompetent patients. However, there appears to be two recognisable sets of views as to what the term might mean. For the sake of simplicity I will call these an 'objective' and a 'subjective' account of best interests.[12]

The advocate of an 'objective' account argues that the concept of 'best interests' is to be explained in terms of maximising the individual's welfare, well-being or good. On this view, the action or inaction that brings about the maximisation of the relevant consideration in a particular situation is that which is in the individual's best interests. Buchanan and Brock have produced perhaps the clearest outline of what such a view would involve. They argue that the decision arrived at can only be judged to be 'best' if such an action would bring about the most good for the patient.[13] The idea is that this judgment about best interests can be determined independently of what the relevant individual themselves might believe or desire to be relevant to the production of their good. In addition, the true determination of best

[11] This general claim can be accepted even if we don't actually know, or cannot agree upon, what is in that child's best interests.

[12] This is, of course, a simplification of very complicated issues. I say much more about this in 'What are "best interests"?' (ms).

[13] A. Buchanan & D. Brock. 1989. *Deciding For Others: The Ethics of Surrogate Decision Making*. Cambridge. Cambridge University Press: p. 94.

interests on this view need have nothing to do with what the majority of people might choose in such a situation. The only relevant factor is which outcome will maximise the welfare of the individual.

Such 'objective' accounts are, of course, going to be controversial as it means that very different competing factors will have to be assessed and weighed against each other to reach a judgment about what will produce best interests. This means that such views are open to parallel objections to those often aimed at some forms of consequentialism, such as 'how do we do the calculations' and 'how do we weigh incommensurable goods'? This is not the place to explore all the objections and any possible responses to this view. The important point for my purpose in this paper is that on this view the judgment as to what is in an individual's best interests is to be determined by the outcome which would maximise welfare even if we are ignorant or mistaken about which outcome that might, actually, be. This means that on such a view, allowance can be made for the fact that someone either gets the calculations wrong or abuses their position in making such a decision, say, by deciding what is in their own interests, rather than genuinely in the best interests of the relevant party. However, whilst such distortions can occur, they do not take away from the fact that there is an answer as to what will maximise welfare even if we are not clear what it might be.

The advocate of the 'subjective' account of 'best interests', by contrast, holds that the concept is to be defined in terms of what the individual themselves does choose, or if they are incompetent, what they would be expected to choose if they were able to do so. This view might take two forms. It might be that a moderate form argues that where knowledge is available of an individual's views, these are taken into account when judging 'best interests' for that person in that situation. Or a more radical form might be that what an individual believes is in their best interests, where known, *is* what is in their best interests. The moderate view should perhaps be seen as a way to emphasise the role that autonomy might play in judgments about best interests. The idea here is that if I value certain types of, say, religious beliefs then actions that fail to take account of these will tend not to be in my overall best interests precisely because my beliefs have been ignored. The more radical view seems more focused on making an epistemic point rather than one about the relative priority of autonomy in an assessment of best interests. The radical view captures a certain type of scepticism about the possibility of identifying best interests independently of what the individual concerned *believes* to be in their interests. We might describe this scepticism as a variety of a more general form that argues that we have no independent access to metaphysical facts beyond what we believe about them. On this view, as the central issue is what might be in your best interests, and you have the clearest access to your experiences, you have the decisive role in determining what *is* in your interests.

However, how is this theoretical discussion about best interests relevant to the core issues of this paper? In this case, of course, someone else is making the decision on behalf of the infant because the child is incompetent. Such a decision cannot be made on a 'subjective' basis, as we have no insight into the relevant party's beliefs as they do not have any that are sophisticated enough to count. It might be made on the basis of the parental 'subjective' beliefs but it is not clear that this would reflect a 'best interests' standard at all. When making decisions on the basis of best interests relative to an always-incompetent individual, the only way to make a decision in *their* best interests is to use an *objective* test. Therefore this allows us to sidestep many of the difficulties associated with the arguments about the relative merits of subjective and objective accounts of best interests because only an objective test is available in this type of case. We will leave open for the moment what sorts of factors will play a key role in the decision about best interests in relation to childhood vaccinations and we'll come back to this after discussing the issues in relation to harm in more detail in the next section.

However, it is worth noting that an objective determination of 'best interests' for infants is likely to focus on a number of key issues. Buchanan and Brock (1989: p. 247) usefully distinguish between what they term 'current interests' and 'future-orientated interests' of the child. The reason to mark the distinction is that the two can come into conflict. Current interests are largely formulated in relation to experiential considerations, whereas future-orientated interests are focused on developmental considerations.[14] For example, the idea is that the performance of an operation may impact upon current interests (through the production of pain) but this is not enough to count against the intervention if it can be justified through the promotion of longer-term interests (perhaps by ensuring that the child can participate in a wider variety of physical and social activities as a

[14] Clearly, in relation to infants these future-orientated interests are very important. They are the type of thing Feinberg calls attention to in: J. Feinberg 'The Child's Right to an Open Future', in *Freedom & Fulfillment: Philosophical Essays*, Princeton, NJ: Princeton University Press.

result).[15] When we consider the future-orientated as well as the current interests in any assessment of best interests we will, rightly, be tempted to assign great weight to harm prevention considerations. This will be particularly true where decisions will have a likely significant impact upon the child's future development, such as when the potential harms may result in death or serious long-term or permanent injury.[16] On this view then risks of health-related harms might well play a key role in judgments about best interests although we cannot simply move from an assessment of medical best interests to best interests *per se.*[17]

3. THE ANALYSIS OF SUBSTANTIAL RISK OF SIGNIFICANT HARM

The 'best interests argument' is a *general* argument, but it will only be applicable in the real world once we consider both a particular type of disease and the relevant vaccination that is available to combat that disease. This is because the argument as a whole is dependent upon the idea of the relative risk of harm produced through two incompatible decisions (to vaccinate or not vaccinate).[18] A sound judgment cannot be made in the abstract, but only in the light of the relevant and available empirical evidence. Where we have an incompetent patient with no previously expressed wishes the only way health care decisions can be made is on the basis of what is in that individual's best interests. This, in turn, is to be decided by judging which action or inaction will bring about least harm and the greatest overall good.

This is again a controversial claim as it might be held that there is a moral difference between seeking to minimise harm, on the one hand, and promote good, on the other. The thought here is

[15] This is, of course, true of adults as well. However, the difference lies in the fact that some decisions made on behalf of children will close off various options in later life in a way not true of adults. This is because children have various non-actualised developmental interests that need to be protected.

[16] It is worth noting that in cases involving the serious risk of such harms it is no good merely to state that the child can review the situation themselves once they have obtained a suitable threshold of competence, since as a result of a parental decision the potential harm might already have occurred.

[17] I am very grateful for the comments of an anonymous referee for prompting improvements in this section.

[18] 'Harm', here, is used in Feinberg's sense of 'set back to interests'. See J. Feinberg. 1984. *Harm to Others.* Oxford University Press; chapter 1. Such an account is also employed by P. Allmark, S. Mason, A. Gill & C. Megone. Is it in a neonate's best interest to enter a randomised controlled trial? *J Med Ethics.* 2001; 27: 110–113.

that, using the language of the four principles, non-maleficence takes priority over beneficence. This might be used as an argument against third-party non-parental sponsorship of vaccinations because it is claimed that such acts are focused upon intentionally promoting the best possible good, whereas parental refusal is seeking to prevent harm, therefore the latter should take priority. Such an argument is not convincing, of course, because even leaving to one side the issue of non-maleficence supposedly taking precedence over beneficence,[19] the harm likely to arise as a result of non-vaccination may be greater than that likely to be caused by the vaccination itself. However, in this case we can avoid the debate over the strict relation between beneficence and non-maleficence because the issue can be assessed either in terms of preventing harm (this can be accepted as a fundamental value e.g. non-maleficence) or as part of promoting the good (beneficence). This means that even if someone wishes to concentrate only upon harms in relation to this issue, it is still possible to construct a strong argument in favour of vaccination in at least some cases, or so I will argue.

If we choose therefore to focus upon harms, we still need some way of weighing the relative risks of different harms against each other. How should we do this? I suggest that it is reasonable in such circumstances to weigh up objectively both the likelihood of the risks occurring and the magnitude of those risks.[20] This is in line with standard risk assessment strategies.[21] Both factors can be most clearly seen to be relevant to the issue of vaccinations if we consider some examples. These cases are intended to illustrate how the issue of risk of harms associated with vaccination or non-vaccination may be relevant to decision making about whether vaccinating a particular child for a particular disease is in their best interests or not.

[19] There is no good reason to do this, of course, because the assessment should be done in terms of both harms and benefits, not merely on harms. Personally, I see no reason to justify prioritising either harms or benefits in decision-making.

[20] It might be argued that the assessment of such risks necessarily involves some evaluative element. To some extent this is true. However, I would argue that we should not give up on the importance of the distinction between the likelihood of a harm occurring (the probability of the harm) and what such an occurrence might mean to me (the meaning of the harm). The idea, here, is that the likelihood of a risk occurring might be very low but I choose to prevent that risk occurring because the consequence would be significant to me.

[21] See, for example, T. Beauchamp & J. Childress. 2001. *Principles of Biomedical Ethics (5th edition)*. Oxford. Oxford University Press: pp. 199–200.

Consider the three following cases:

(a) *Blue Spot Disease.* This (fictitious) disease results in a mild rash of small blue spots on the skin but with no other consequences. A (fictitious) vaccination is available, but carries a high (<10%) risk of causing breathing difficulties and a lower (<1%) risk of death.

(b) *Yellow Fever.* This disease is fatal in a significant number of cases (ranging from 5% to over 50%). It is confined to just a few places in the world and an effective low risk vaccination is available.[22] However, let's pretend for the purposes of the argument in this paper that it is prevalent throughout the world.

(c) *Measles.* This is a highly contagious disease which as a result of complications can cause serious permanent medical problems and, in at least some cases, death.[23] A vaccination as part of the Measles-Mumps-Rubella (MMR) vaccine is widely available, but the relevant evidence for its effectiveness and the risk of causing harm are contested.

I suggest that if faced by the facts as outlined above in these three cases it would be clearly in the child's best interest to have the Yellow Fever vaccination, not have the Blue Spot vaccination, and the measles case will be the most difficult to decide.[24] However, it can be argued that whether or not this third possible vaccination is in the best interests of the child needs to be determined in exactly the same way as the others. In all such cases, anyone trying to decide what is in someone's best interests in relation to these possible vaccinations should ask the following questions. What is the evidence of the risk of harm resulting from the vaccination? What is the likelihood of it occurring and how significant are these potential consequences? However, such questions need to be weighed against the likelihood of contracting that infection and the potential harm caused by the relevant illness itself.[25]

[22] See D. Salisbury & N. Begg, N. (eds.). 1996. *Immunisation Against Infectious Disease.* London. HMSO, p. 263.

[23] See D. Salisbury & Begg, N. eds. 1996. *Immunisation Against Infectious Disease.* London. HMSO. Complication rates from the disease can be as high as one in fifteen cases (p. 125).

[24] Remember that for the purposes of this paper, I'm ignoring the 'harm to others' considerations.

[25] Relevant evidence in relation to MMR vaccine, *though not of equal value* might include: A. Wakefield et al. Ileal-lymphoid-nodular hyperplasia, non-specific colitis and pervasive developmental disorder in children, *Lancet* 1998; 351: 637–641. & A. Wakefield & S. Montgomery. Measles, mumps and rubella

Whilst it can be conceded that the empirical evidence in favour or against a particular medical procedure is never likely to be conclusive, this does not mean that we cannot formulate best interests judgments in relation to such issues. Indeed making such judgments in the light of provisional evidence is most likely to be the standard case. However, where the evidence is contested or unclear, it is especially important that it is judged fairly and dispassionately. There are two main potential threats to this being achieved. The first threat to a fair judgment is a lack of relevant information, and the second threat is the factors that can bias a judgment in a particular direction. The first can be dealt with by ensuring that the decision makers have all of the relevant information. The second is more difficult to counter but where potential psychologically-distorting factors are known about these can be taken into consideration when information is provided.[26] A decision that weighs the evidence of the relevant relative risks of harm, without any of the potential elements that might lead to a misjudgement, will be a vital component of any judgment as to what is in the infant's best interests. In most cases the parents' judgment as to what is in their child's best interests is likely to be accepted. However, there must always be a residual obligation of the state to review such decision-making if necessary. It is to this issue that I now turn.

4. SHOULD PARENTAL DECISIONS BE OVERRULED?

Is there a role for the state, or some other relevant third-party, to step in to protect the child from at least some parental decisions? The vast majority of people will accept that some parental decisions should be overruled but the difficulty is determining when this should be the case. In the UK such powers have been used in a number of situations, such as the overruling by the

vaccine: through a glass, darkly. *Adverse Drug React Toxicol Rev* 2000; 19: 265–283. D. Elliman & H. Bedford. MMR vaccine: the continuing saga. *BMJ* 2001; 322: 183–184; A. Patja et al. Serious adverse events after measles-mumps-rubella vaccination during a fourteen-year prospective follow-up. *Pediatr Infect Dis J* 2000; 19: 1127–1134. H. Peltola & O. Heinonen. Frequency of true adverse reactions in measles-mumps-rubella vaccine. A double-blind placebo-controlled trial in twins. *Lancet* 1986; 1: 939–942. & K. Madsen et al. A population-based study of measles, mumps and rubella vaccination and autism. *NEJM* 2002; 347: 1477–1482. L. Smeeth et al. MMR vaccination and pervasive developmental disorders: a case-control study. *Lancet* 2004; 364: 963–969.

[26] See Department of Health. 1998. *Communicating About Risks to Public Health.* London. Department of Health, for a discussion of some of these issues.

courts of parental refusal of treatment for their children on the basis of parental beliefs,[27] or the fact that education is compulsory whatever the views of the parents.[28] Of course, the mere fact that there are such cases where parents are overruled does not on its own justify such an approach. However, we can ask whether there is anything that might be considered to be more systematic behind such judgments? On what basis should such decisions be made? Can a coherent and justified basis be given for them? The relevant underlying principle is that children should be protected from significant harm, or even the risk of significant harm where there is a high risk of it occurring.[29] This principle can be seen at work in the dramatic case of child protection legislation as well as in the cases cited above. In these situations third parties will make the judgment that parents are not acting in their child's best interests. The types of considerations they will take into account are not just the scale and likelihood of the risk of harm, but also whether the parents are making a sound assessment of any relevant evidence. If there is, in turn, evidence of negligence or recklessness in the decision making process this will count against the parents. The third parties will also consider what the likely consequences of the parent decision might be. Where the decision is likely to have a detrimental impact on the child's future development or quality of life this will play a major role in the justification for overruling the parental decision.[30]

Clearly the state does play some role in protecting the child against parental decisions in such situations. Is it appropriate in the vaccination case? In at least some cases it surely is. If we are considering vaccinations, then I suggest the key relevant factor is the relative risk of harm (and any benefits) resulting from the potential vaccination or non-vaccination. Here there is a need to weigh the magnitude of the risk and the likelihood of that risk occurring in cases of actions and omissions.[31] Once again, the decisive factor is the relevant empirical evidence. For example, in

[27] See, for example, *Camden London Borough Council v A, B, C (By her Guardian ad Litem)* [2000] 2 WLR 270, and *Re A (Children)* [2001] 4 all ER 961.

[28] See Education Act 1996, s.8.

[29] See H. La Follette. Licensing parents. *Philosophy and Public Affairs* 1980: 9: 183–197.

[30] A good example of the way these considerations are weighted in a real case is provided by the previously cited *A, B, C* case [2000], which involved the risk of transmission of HIV through breast-feeding.

[31] I assume there is no relevant moral difference between the two when assessing what outcome is in the best interests of an incompetent individual.

the yellow fever case, the state might be more strongly justified in stepping in to insist the infant is vaccinated[32] than in some other cases where the balance of risk is unclear or finely balanced. Where the balance of risk is unclear or finely balanced there is a strong argument for saying that the state should not intervene given, in turn, the risk of harm to the parent–child relationship, linked to such interference by the state. This might be referred to as the 'good faith' defence. Where parents have taken a 'reasonable' decision (that is they are able to provide publicly defensible reasons for their decision) it is unlikely that the judgment will be made that interference in relation to that decision is justified on the grounds of best interests even if a different conclusion would be reached by the relevant third parties. However, where it is *clearly* the case that vaccination is in the best interests of an infant it can be argued that the state has a role to ensure that its public health policies take this child protection issue into account by legislative action such as ensuring that, if necessary, childhood vaccinations are compulsory on the grounds of the best interests of the child.[33]

In conclusion, the state should play a role in protecting children from parental decisions in at least some cases. The hard fact is determining exactly when this should occur. It is relatively easy in some cases to decide to intervene or remain detached whereas, in other cases, it is difficult to decide where the balance of best interests might lie. However, the relevant issue is what is objectively in the child's best interests, and a key component of this judgment is going to be the relevant empirical evidence.[34] When evidence is lacking as to what is in a child's best interests, there is an urgent need to seek it. Where a parent's decision in relation to a vaccination is held to be negligent or reckless, and there is a high likelihood of significant harm resulting from that choice, then the state should have a residual power to step in to secure what is in the child's best interests. In reality this is likely to be a rare event.[35]

[32] Or insist the infant is not vaccinated in such cases as blue spot disease perhaps.

[33] This point is likely to be strengthened once the 'harm to others' considerations are added in.

[34] Not just about the effectiveness of the vaccination and the risk of side effects, but also about other considerations I've chosen to ignore to simplify the argument (such as the percentage uptake for a particular vaccination within a population).

[35] However, see the legal case, mentioned earlier, in footnote 6, where this was the relevant legal test.

Moreover, it might be objected that the proposed 'best interests' argument is paternalistic. This, of course, is true. However, this on its own is not an objection, unless it can be demonstrated that it is not only paternalism, but also an unjustifiable form of paternalism, and is thereby wrong. My thought here is that even liberals and libertarians may allow that so-called 'weak paternalism' may be justified.[36] 'Weak paternalism' can be defined as being, an intervention motivated by the beneficent wish to prevent harm resulting from an individual's non-autonomous decisions. Whereas 'strong paternalism' is held to be, an intervention motivated by the beneficent wish to prevent harm resulting from decisions even when an individual is autonomous, informed and acting in a voluntary manner. In the case of an incompetent infant we are talking about weak paternalism, as a child less than two has no autonomy to overrule. The justification for such weak paternalistic intervention is largely one of appealing to the best interests of the incompetent individual. As we have seen above this is a difficult and perhaps controversial judgment, but this can be the only basis for such a decision in relation to infants. The onus is on the objector to such a policy to explain why, where the intention is to ensure that decisions about the care of children are made in their best interests, such interventions are not just paternalistic but also wrong.[37]

CONCLUSION

There are many different arguments that can be discussed in relation to childhood vaccinations. In this paper I wish to put to one-side arguments that appeal to things like harm to others or the good of the community or the common good. Is it possible to formulate and defend an argument for childhood vaccinations that rests upon an appeal to the 'best interests' of a particular child in at least some cases? I believe that it is, and have sought to argue this in this paper. If this is accepted, then intervention against parental wishes is justified in at least some possible vaccination cases, and this may form the basis for public

[36] Certainly J. Mill. 1859. *On Liberty* & J. Feinberg. 1973 *Social Philosophy* Prentice-Hall: 45–52 do so.

[37] As an anonymous referee suggested it might be possible to argue that the state is, here, acting paternalistically upon or through the parents. If this is the case the justification for the action might switch from an appeal to paternalism to a more general 'harm prevention' principle in the light of the perceived negligent decision of the parents.

health policies that enforce compulsory vaccinations for at least some diseases.

Angus Dawson
Centre for Professional Ethics
Keele Hall
Keele University
Staffs
ST5 5BG
UK
a.j.dawson@keele.ac.uk

Acknowledgments

Thanks to Eve Garrard, Mike Dawson, Richard E. Ashcroft and two anonymous referee for very helpful comments on a previous draft. An earlier version of this paper was given at the 'Human Dignity and Human Rights in Relation to Public Health and Bioethics' conference in Sheffield. July 2001. I'd like to thank Jim Childress, Darren Shickle, and Michael Joseph Smith for helpful discussion on that occasion.

[21]

Ethical issues for vaccines and immunization

Jeffrey B. Ulmer and Margaret A. Liu

Vaccination is the only type of medical intervention that has eliminated a disease successfully. However, both in countries with high immunization rates and in countries that are too impoverished to protect their citizens, many dilemmas and controversies surround immunization. This article describes some of the ethical issues involved, and presents some challenges and concepts for the global community.

Vaccines stand out as being among the most efficacious and cost-effective of global medical interventions[1] (BOX 1). Vaccines have saved millions of lives, prevented significant morbidity and suffering, and even eradicated a disease. This last accomplishment, the eradication of smallpox, highlights what can be achieved by vaccination. However, unfortunately, the inequalities in the distribution and use of vaccines are also striking. If vaccines

Box 1 | **The economic benefits and cost-effectiveness of vaccines**

The statistics for the eradication of smallpox illustrate the benefits and economics of vaccines and disease eradication. The eradication of smallpox has probably saved 40 million lives over the past two decades[6], at a cost of US $25 million per year during the eradication campaign. The equivalent of US $275 million is saved annually in terms of quarantine and treatment because of the eradication of smallpox[3].

The eradication of polio is also within reach. Between 1988 and 2000, coordinated public-health efforts, with a large contribution from Rotary International, have decreased the number of polio cases from approximately 350,000 to 3,500 per annum[6]. The potential future cost savings of polio eradication have been estimated at US $1.5 billion per year[6], although the actual savings will probably be less than this owing to the need to continue immunization after eradication.

The cost of immunizing a child with the six core vaccines that are recommended by the Expanded Program on Immunization (tuberculosis, measles, diphtheria, tetanus, pertussis and polio) is US $17 (REF. 6). Of this amount, only a few dollars are for the cost of the vaccines, with the rest paying, for example, for personnel and transportation of the vaccine (including refrigeration).

The benefits of vaccines are obvious in terms of the lives that are saved and the morbidity that is prevented or reduced, but the economic benefits extend beyond the benefits to the individuals that are protected. The economic benefits of immunization campaigns include savings in health-care costs for the treatment of illness and quarantine, the economic productivity of having a healthy workforce (or of not having parents removed from the workforce to care for an ill child) and coincident benefits that result from the immunization programme (such as an improved health-care infrastructure).

can be deployed so successfully worldwide that a disease can be eliminated, why do millions of children still die each year from other vaccine-preventable diseases? From ethical and humanitarian perspectives, this should be unacceptable. However, despite the medical evidence of the benefits of vaccines, both immunization itself as a goal, as well as the actual efforts for global immunization, are often debated and criticized. So, the ethics of whether, and how, to vaccinate all of the world's population are much more complex than it would seem at first glance. Some of these issues will be examined and a call for action raised in this article.

Current state of immunization rates

At present, in industrialized countries such as the United States, infants routinely (~80–95% coverage) receive vaccines against diphtheria, pertussis (whooping cough), tetanus, measles, mumps, rubella, polio, *Haemophilus influenzae* type b, hepatitis B, varicella, pneumococcus and, often, hepatitis A. The efficacy of these vaccines and the success of routine immunizations are such that in the United States, for example, the morbidity from previously routine childhood diseases has been reduced by 90–100% since the introduction of standard immunization[2] (TABLE 1). In developed countries, the near disappearance of these diseases from normal childhood has removed much of the fear of the illnesses that they cause. The result is that the consequences of not vaccinating against these diseases are sometimes not fully appreciated by the public.

In developing countries, one in every four children born annually will not be vaccinated[3]. In many of the impoverished countries in which these children reside, the concomitant lack of health care, inadequate nutrition[4], higher prevalence of disease, decreased hygiene and over-crowding conspire to increase the incidence of, as well as the morbidity and mortality from, both vaccine-preventable and other infectious diseases. Six children die every minute as a result of infectious diseases that could be prevented by existing vaccines, and for measles alone, nearly one million children die each year[3]. So, each day, 4,000–8,000 people[3], mainly children, die from vaccine-preventable diseases (TABLE 2).

Various efforts to increase global immunization rates have protected many children successfully. For example, in 1974, before the Expanded Program on Immunization (EPI) was established, an estimated 8 million children died each year from measles[5]. Since then, the EPI has targeted six diseases: tuberculosis, measles, diphtheria, tetanus, pertussis and polio (FIG. 1). By 1980, the incidence of measles had been reduced by ~50% (FIG. 2). In that year, the World Summit for Children set a goal of 80% coverage for these six basic immunizations to be achieved by 1990. Laudably, those efforts succeeded in raising global immunization rates from less than 10% to almost 80% in that decade[6], with a concomitant reduction in disease burden (for example, see FIG. 2). But, a combination of complacency, competition for health-care resources with other diseases (such as HIV) and other factors, such as an inadequate and ageing health-care infrastructure, resulted in a subsequent plateau[5] or decline in average immunization rates in the developing world[6]. This trend is worrying because of what it represents in terms of the commitment and sustainability of immunization programmes. Maintenance of a high level of coverage for immunization is crucial — unless a certain minimum percentage of the population is immune, the benefits of herd immunity (when sufficient people are immune such that a pathogen cannot easily persist and spread in a population) will not be achieved.

Ethics of immunization and vaccines

The economic and human benefits of vaccination are clear for many vaccines. But, economic and political realities, along with philosophical questions, raise certain ethical issues concerning the use and distribution of vaccines[7]. What are the rights of individuals in deciding about vaccination versus the rights of, and risks to, society? Should different standards for the efficacy and safety of a particular vaccine be set for different populations for which the risk:benefit ratio might be different? How should priorities be set for different areas

Table 1 | **Reduction of the number of vaccine-preventable diseases in the US**

Disease	Number of cases		
	Maximum	*1997*	*% change*
Diphtheria	206,939	4	99.99
Measles	894,134	138	99.98
Mumps	152,209	683	99.55
Pertussis (whooping cough)	265,269	6,564	97.52
Polio (paralytic)	21,269	0	100.00
Rubella	57,686	181	99.69
Congenital rubella syndrome	20,000*	5	99.98
Tetanus	1,560‡	50	96.79
Influenza (<5 years)	20,000*	165	99.18

Data taken from REF. 5. * estimated; ‡ mortality.

between and within countries? Which regulatory bodies have the right to make decisions at the individual or national level? Although few would argue against the responsibility of developed nations to help poorer countries and peoples to develop and use the necessary vaccines, what are the precise responsibilities of both developed and developing countries? Here, we examine several of these issues to highlight the complexities of the ethics of vaccine development and use.

Whose choice is it? During the period when polio epidemics struck terror into the hearts of the population, the public clamoured for, supported the development of (for example, The March of Dimes in the United States, a national public compaign to raise donations to fund the research and development of polio vaccines) and welcomed a vaccine against polio. The live attenuated vaccine made possible a global mass-immunization campaign; on a single day of the various National Immunization Days, 83–147 million children were immunized[8,6]. Now, at a time when wild-type polio has been eliminated from the Western Hemisphere and nearly eradicated globally, the only cases of polio in the Western Hemisphere are caused by reversion mutants of the live-attenuated vaccine strain of the virus. For society as a whole, the total elimination of polio seems the obvious and correct path. But, as the probability of an individual being exposed to the virus decreases, and as the devastation of the historic polio epidemics fades in our memories, the rare cases of disease due to reversion of the vaccine itself become more prominent. The benefit of immunization for any given individual decreases (due to a lower probability of contracting the disease), whereas the perception of risk might increase[9]. So, what is best for the individual might be seen as potentially different from what will benefit society as a whole. However, it has only been through the participation of hundreds of millions of individuals in vaccination programmes that unimmunized individuals have the luxury of an altered risk:benefit ratio. Interestingly, in 1980, the year that smallpox was officially declared to be eradicated, prominent individuals in the international health-planning community were critical of the smallpox campaign. They felt that the approach of 'top–down' (mandated and orchestrated by global bodies) programmes was wrong and contrary to more-localized, primary health care[10,11]. Even this pre-eminent example of the beneficial power of immunization was not without controversy.

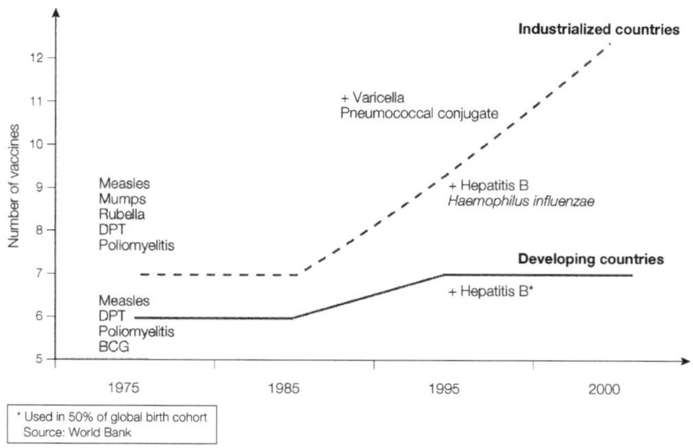

Figure 1 | **Number of children's vaccines used routinely in developing and industrialized countries.** As shown, the number of vaccines (*y* axis) that are given to children has risen steadily since 1985 in industrialized countries, but not in developing countries. DPT is a combination vaccine against three separate pathogens: diphtheria (D), pertussis (P) and tetanus (T). BCG is the *Mycobacterium bovis* bacillus Calmètte–Guerin vaccine against tuberculosis. The loss of life due to lack of infant immunization in developing countries is due to the smaller number of vaccines that are routinely used, as well as to lower immunization rates. Reproduced, with permission, from the World Health Organization[6].

In the same manner, other vaccines have become victims of their own success. As diseases disappear from the general population after successful vaccination campaigns, the real risk of an individual contracting the disease decreases and the perception of the seriousness of the disease, even if contracted, is reduced. Concomitantly, concerns about the real or imagined adverse effects of the vaccines increase. As a result, individuals might disagree with government mandates for population-wide vaccination. For example, before the introduction of a vaccine against pertussis, there were approximately 2 million cases annually in the United States. In Great Britain, in the mid-1970s, some adverse reactions to the vaccine were widely publicized, and immunization rates declined from 80–90% to 30%. As a consequence, the population was vulnerable to two subsequent severe outbreaks of whooping cough, which resulted in more than 120,000 recorded instances of disease, hundreds of cases of serious complications and 28 deaths[12]. More recently, heightened fears of the perceived adverse effects of other vaccines (such as measles and hepatitis B), even if unproven, have had an impact on immunization rates and the incidence of disease[6,13–15]. A greater awareness of the consequences of failure to vaccinate, through better education, might be the best tool to combat this problem[16].

Table 2 | **Global vaccine-preventable deaths through infant immunization**

Disease	Number of preventable annual deaths
Hepatitis B	900,000
Measles	888,000
Tetanus (including 215,000 neonatal deaths)	410,000
Haemophilus influenzae type b (Hib)	400,000
Pertussis (whooping cough)	346,000
Yellow fever	30,000
Diphtheria	5,000
Polio	720
Total	***2,979,720***

Data taken from the World Health Organization (WHO) World Health Report 1999 and the WHO Department of Vaccines and Biologicals.

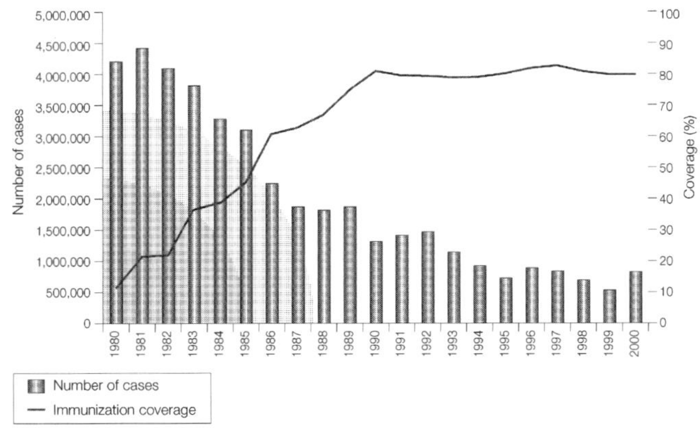

Figure 2 | **Measles global annual reported incidence and immunization coverage, 1980–2000.** The global incidence of measles has declined as immunization coverage has increased. The level of immunization coverage plateaued in the 1990s, leaving a significant number of cases of measles still occurring each year. Reproduced, with permission, from the World Health Organization[22].

Poverty and priorities. In wealthier countries, the ethical issues that surround vaccination tend to focus on the rights of individuals versus government or society. In poorer countries, the fundamental issue is the lack of access to basic necessities for health, such as adequate nutrition, clean water, medicines or vaccines. Although poverty is clearly the main cause of these deficiencies, other factors contribute, such as the low priority given to health and preventive measures, the disenfranchisement and lack of political and economic power of the people most affected (children and women), corruption and regional warfare.

In the year 2000, only 10% of global medical-research funds were directed towards the 90% of diseases that affect the world's poorest people[6]. It would seem obvious from the economic benefits that prevention of disease (and health in general) should be a priority for poor countries. It would seem equally obvious that helping to ensure such health should be a high priority for wealthy nations, even if simply to protect their own populations. Not only can newly emerging diseases spread rapidly across the globe, but pathogens eliminated from one population can be 're-imported' (or new strains introduced) by travellers or immigrants[17].

At present, only about 1% of contributions to overseas development are directed towards immunizations[6]. The hurdle is not simply the purchase price or availability of vaccines, but for many poor countries, there is a lack of infrastructure for health care in general, and vaccine delivery specifically. The needs are so great and so widespread, both geographically and technologically, that assigning priority is difficult. This prioritization is considered by some to be an ethical issue, but in reality, it might be simply that the pie is not sufficiently large, rather than that the pie should be sliced differently. The trade-off of protecting children now from disease versus an emphasis on the development of new vaccines to protect children in the future is not a debate that can be resolved even by Solomonic wisdom. Neither trade-off is ethically defensible, and the world should, instead, work constructively to increase the resources devoted to health, nutrition, prevention and specifically immunization, to make vaccines available to all people as required. But, how is this to be accomplished?

'Trickle-down' or simultaneous introduction. A marked effort is required to introduce vaccines into all necessary areas of the globe in a more timely fashion. The average time lag between licensing of a new vaccine for industrialized countries and its use in less developed countries is 10–20 years[6]. There are many reasons for this, including the lack of manufacturing capability for vaccines that require new technology in their production, return on investment and the cost of manufacturing newer technology-based vaccines. For example, when the recombinant hepatitis B virus vaccine was first introduced, there was not sufficient capacity worldwide for its production. Moreover, the cost of manufacturing such a 'high-tech' vaccine put it beyond the reach of the existing purchasing programmes at the time. Although the technology that supports recombinant protein vaccines is now available worldwide, it took time and effort to develop that capacity, even in developed countries.

People are created equal, but different

The simultaneous introduction of vaccines into developed and developing countries is an important goal. However, this is easier said than done. In addition to the issues of availability and economics, it cannot be assumed that disease burden, strain prevalence, vaccine efficacy and effectiveness (how well a vaccine works in clinical trials and real-world settings, respectively), immunization schedules or risk:benefit ratio will be standard or will justify the use of a vaccine in all areas. Differences in genotype and health status of individuals could affect how their immune system responds to a given immune stimulus. Environmental influences on the immune system (for example, indigenous parasitic infections that affect the predominant cytokine-secretion profile of helper T cells, or bacterial infections that facilitate or hinder immunity against closely related pathogens) might affect the immunological outcome of a particular type of vaccine.

Just as a vaccine that works in one population might not be as effective in another population, so might adverse effects of a vaccine be specific to one population. Hence, a vaccine company might be reluctant to simultaneously test a vaccine in two populations, for fear that an adverse effect in one population (due to genetic, nutritional or other health factors, or limitations of the infrastructure for vaccine delivery) would halt the development of a vaccine that could be both useful and commercially viable in another population. More importantly, the higher background rates of morbidity and mortality in certain developing countries might cause problems when presenting vaccines for licensure in more developed countries.

A counter-example to illustrate why vaccines might need to be tested simultaneously in developed and developing countries is provided by a rotavirus vaccine. Rotavirus is a major cause of diarrhoea in infants. In the United States, 20 children die each year from rotavirus infection, and worldwide, the virus kills 600,000 children under the age of five annually[18]. In 1998, a new rotavirus vaccine was licensed in the United States. But by 1999, reports emerged from American clinics of the occurrence, after immunization, of a small number of cases of intestinal intussusception

— a 'telescoping' of the small intestine that often requires emergency surgery[18]. The number of cases was small, and the aetiological link has been debated, but the vaccine was withdrawn from the market. Clinical trials that were testing the vaccine in developing countries were stopped. So, we do not yet know whether the vaccine would have been effective or caused side effects in children from developing countries, for whom the risk:benefit ratio might well be quite different. More than half a million children continue to die each year due to rotavirus infection (although it is hoped that other rotavirus vaccines that are under development will be approved for use). The issue of how to speed up vaccine deployment for developing countries and how to develop vaccines that specifically address the needs of those countries should not be oversimplified. Different vaccines (for example, for different virus strains) might be required to prevent the same disease in different parts of the world. The needs of people in developing countries must be specifically, rapidly and directly addressed to develop appropriate vaccines. To make this happen in a timely manner, more thought and effort is required at early stages of vaccine development. But, by whom and at whose expense?

A farewell to arms

In the face of the unacceptable and gaping inequalities in access to vaccines, the temptation has been to 'point the finger' at various countries or segments of society. A chief target for many of these denouncements has been large vaccine manufacturers, as well as the people and governments of their home countries. It has been easy to stir up indignation, although a thoughtful evaluation of the real contributions, roles and responsibilities of all parties has been more productive (BOX 2). The cries for companies to lower the prices of their vaccines has reinforced the unwarranted notion that vaccines should be inexpensive — an idea that perpetuates the vicious cycle of the low valuation of health care, prevention and children's lives. Obviously, low cost might be an important means of increasing access to vaccines, but the fundamental problem is the low priority given to children, health and prevention.

Most vaccines that are in use today were developed fully and are manufactured by industry, rather than the public sector. Commercial companies have responsibilities to their shareholders and are driven by profits. But, it is these profits that have enabled the companies to take the huge economic risks that are required for the long process of discovery, research and development of vaccines.

> Box 2 | **Potential mechanisms to achieve equity in health**
>
> The unequal access to existing vaccines and the relative lack of effort being applied to develop and produce vaccines for diseases that predominate in developing countries is part of the larger problem of extreme poverty in many nations. Although the roots and other manifestations of poverty must also be addressed, as Jorge Jiminez of the World Health Organization has said, "Health is seen more and more as preceeding development and not only as a consequence of wealth"[20]. Rather than relying on governments or international bodies as the sole means to address these problems, new models of public–private partnerships (PPPs) have arisen.
>
> The fundamental idea of a PPP is to bring together entities from both the public sector (government or intergovernmental agencies) and the private sector (for example, industries, such as vaccine companies) to address a particular need, with each partner undertaking specific activities on the basis of their particular expertise and capacity.
>
> Participation by industry might be in the form of donating a product, or applying research and development expertise to diseases (or types of health intervention) for which the market alone would not provide sufficient incentive. The motivation of the pharmaceutical industry might range from pure philanthropy (global citizenship and garnering goodwill) to economies of scale (if the product has a market elsewhere that will allow for higher prices to offset the lower prices in developing countries)[21].
>
> Recent PPPs have been established to tackle the challenges of developing and producing vaccines for diseases such as HIV and malaria. The input of effort or intellectual property from a 'for-profit' company and the potential loss due to 'opportunity costs' (that is, the possible revenue from a highly recompensed product if the effort had been directed towards that product rather than a vaccine for a developing country) can be strong disincentives for companies to participate in PPPs. Another approach that might become increasingly useful is the provision of early access to new vaccines and technologies for developing countries by the transfer of technology from a pharmaceutical company in an industrialized country to a local manufacturer in a developing country. Key roles for governmental and intergovernmental agencies include the regulation of products, and testing and manufacturing processes, and the prevention of reflow of products produced for lower pricing in developing countries into countries in which companies anticipate higher pricing to recoup the costs of development and make profits for reinvestment in future products.

If all economic incentive were removed, or made too small, even fewer companies would bother to make vaccines[19], and, instead, would concentrate solely on therapeutic agents, because people will pay more for drugs that treat, rather than prevent, disease.

So, companies should not be expected to be philanthropic, although they should be expected to be generous global citizens. Indeed, industry-driven scientific and technological advances have had an important impact on improving global health. Combination vaccines — whereby several vaccines can be given with a single injection — were developed in part for the market advantage that they would provide but have been an important tool for increasing global vaccination rates. In addition, industry and academia are both contributing to the continuing development of vaccines that do not require refrigeration or needles and can be given orally or nasally — a true 'farewell to arms'.

In most walks of life, philanthropy usually comes as a consequence of success, and the same is true for medicines. So, the profit-driven priorities of vaccine companies are not unethical *per se*; rather, they are not driven primarily by ethical concerns, and the challenge is how to increase the efforts of industry that are directed at improving health on a global basis. The fact that only 1% of pharmaceuticals that reached the market-place between 1975 and 1997 were approved specifically for diseases of the developing world[6] shows that, as a society, we need to re-evaluate our priorities and our paradigms, not that the economic model of financial incentive driving technical advances is wrong.

The challenge

We should challenge each economic sector, population and government to appropriately fulfil its responsibility to fellow humans or its own citizens; in other words, they should treat all of the world's children as their own, rather than denouncing particular groups as causing these inequities. Further support must be given rapidly to those whose efforts will result in vaccines that are better tailored for developing countries, both in terms of the disease focus and the development of technologies that will facilitate vaccine access and sustainability. New paradigms, including novel public–private partnerships (BOX 2) and alliances that are designed to engage local governments and manufacturers at early stages of research and development, are required. In this way, each group can contribute what they do best to the common goals of improving access to existing vaccines, developing new vaccines and technologies for existing diseases (such as HIV and malaria), and ensuring that increases in immunization rates are sustainable. Perhaps most difficult of all will be to change the mindset of people all over the globe. We need to place a higher priority on health and disease prevention, and above all, to value the lives of all people, no matter where they live — even if they are impoverished and powerless.

Jeffrey B. Ulmer is at Vaccines Research, Chiron Corporation, 4560 Horton Street, Emeryville, California 94608, USA.
Margaret A. Liu is at Transgene, 11 rue de Molshelm, 67082 Strasbourg Cedex, France.
Correspondence to M. A. L.
e-mail: liu@transgene.fr

DOI: 10.1038/nri780

1. Ten great public health achievements — United States, 1900–1999. *MMWR Morb. Mortal. Wkly Rep.* **48**, 241–243 (1999).
2. Impact of vaccines universally recommended for children — United States, 1990–1998. *MMWR Morb. Mortal. Wkly Rep.* **48**, 243–248 (1999).
3. Global Alliance for Vaccines and Immunizations. *Global immunization challenges* [online], <http://www.vaccinealliance.org/reference/globalimmchallenges.html>
4. Rice, A. L., Sacco, L., Hyder, A., & Black, R. E. Malnutrition as an underlying cause of childhood deaths associated with infectious diseases in developing countries. *Bull. World Health Organ.* **78**, 1207–1221 (2000).
5. Hinman, A. Eradication of vaccine-preventable diseases. *Annu. Rev. Public Health* **20**, 211–229 (1999).
6. World Health Organization. *State of the World's Vaccine and Immunizations* (in the press)
7. Feudtner, C. & Marcuse, E. K. Ethics and immunization policy: promoting dialogue to sustain consensus. *Pediatrics* **107**, 1158–1164 (2001).
8. Foege, W. in *New Generation Vaccines* (eds Levin, M., Woodrow, G., Kaper, J. & Cobon, G.) 97 (Marcel Dekker, New York, 1997).
9. Wilson, C. B. & Marcuse, E. K. Vaccine safety–vaccine benefits: science and the public's percepion. *Nature Rev. Immunol.* **1**, 160–165 (2001).
10. Henderson, D. A. Eradication: lessons from the past. *Bull. World Health Organ.* **76**,17–21 (1998).
11. Henderson, D. A. Primary health care as a practical means for measles control. *Rev. Infect. Dis.* **5**, 606–607 (1983).
12. Ada, G. in *New Generation Vaccines* 2nd edn (eds Levine, M. *et al.*) 13–24 (Marcel Dekker, New York, 1997).
13. Wakefield, A. *et al.* Ileal-lymphoid-nodular hyperplasia, non-specific colitis and pervasive developmental disorder in children. *Lancet* **351**, 637–641 (1998).
14. Birmingham, K. UK immunization highs and lows. *Nature Med.* **7**, 135 (2001).
15. Duffell, E. Attitudes of parents towards measles and immunisation after a measles outbreak in an anthroposophical community. *J. Epidemiol. Community Health* **55**, 685–686 (2001).
16. Bazin, H. The ethics of vaccine usage in society: lessons from the past. *Curr. Opin. Immunol.* **13**, 505–510 (2001).
17. Hinman, A. Eradication of vaccine-preventable diseases. *Annu. Rev. Public Health* **20**, 211–229 (1999).
18. Instussusception among recipients of rotavirus vaccine — United States, 1998–1999. *MMWR Morb. Mortal. Wkly Rep.* **48**, 577–581 (1999).
19. Wilde, H. What are today's orphaned vaccines? *Clin. Infect. Dis.* **33**, 648–650 (2001).
20. Jimenez, J. Vaccines — a wonderful tool for equity in health. *Vaccine* **19**, 2201–2205 (2001).
21. Vandermissen, W. WHO expectation and industry goals. *Vaccine* **19**, 1611–1615 (2001).
22. Department of Vaccines and Biologicals. WHO Vaccine-Preventable Diseases: Monitoring System 2001 Global Summary (World Health Organization, Geneva, 2001) <http://www.who.int/vaccines-documents/GlobalSummary/GlobalSummary.pdf>

Acknowledgements
We would like to thank C. Wiley and, in particular, R. Ingrum for their assistance.

Online links

FURTHER INFORMATION
Public–private partnerships:
Global Polio Eradication Initiative: http://www.polioeradication.org/
Global Program to Eliminate Lymphatic Filariasis: http://www.filariasis.org/index.shtml
International AIDS Vaccine Initiative: http://www.iavi.org/
Mectizan Donation Program: http://65.208.79.90/MDP/
Medicines for Malaria Venture: http://www.mmv.org/pages/page_main.htm
The Global Alliance for TB Drug Development: http://www.tballiance.org/
Governmental and professional groups:
Global Alliance for Vaccines & Immunization: http://www.vaccinealliance.org
National Network for Immunization information: http://www.immunizationinfo.org
World Health Organization: http://www.who.int/home-page/
Access to this interactive links box is free online.

Part VIII
Public Health and Genetic Health

[22]

From Genes to Public Health: The Applications of Genetic Technology in Disease Prevention

Muin J. Khoury, MD, PhD, and the Genetics Working Group

ABSTRACT

Objectives. With advances in the Human Genome Project, the implications of genetic technology in disease prevention should be assessed.

Methods. The paradigm suggested in *The Future of Public Health*—assessment, policy development, and assurance—was used to examine the continuum from genetic technology to public health practice.

Results. First, important public health functions are to (1) assess the impact of genes and their interactions with modifiable disease risk factors on the health status of the population and (2) assess the impact and safety of genetic testing on the population. Second, given the many implications of genetic testing, the public health community should participate in policy development related to the timing and use of genetic testing in disease prevention. Third, whenever appropriate, the public health community needs to ensure the development of public health genetics programs (e.g. newborn screening) and evaluate the quality and effectiveness of the use of genetic testing in disease prevention.

Conclusions. Although most current genetic tests are not ready for disease prevention, there is an important role for the public health community in translating genetic technology into disease prevention. (*Am J Public Health.* 1996;86:1717–1722)

Introduction

During the past decade, there have been tremendous advances in molecular genetic technology. These advances have led to the Human Genome Project, a long-term initiative to map and sequence the human genome. In the next decade, most if not all human genes will be mapped and sequenced.[1–3] Relatively simple technology such as the polymerase chain reaction is now available to examine genetic variation at many gene loci by using small amounts of human tissue (e.g., blood spots and cheek swabs).[4] This emergence of genetic technology is accompanied by increasing concern regarding the use and misuse of genetic information in society.[5–8]

Despite the advances in molecular genetics and their implications in disease prevention,[9,10] it is not entirely clear when and how genetics can be applied in this regard. As genetic tests are proliferating in the US population, their appropriate usage in the public health setting needs careful scrutiny. In its evaluation of the future of public health in the United States, the Institute of Medicine defined the core functions of public health agencies as assessment, policy development, and assurance[11] (Table 1). In this commentary, we discuss the potential applications of genetics in the context of these core public health functions.

From Gene Identification to Public Health Applications

The Human Genome Project is targeting our estimated 50 000 to 100 000 human genes, only a small fraction of which have been identified so far.[12,13] Many identified human genes are associated with relatively uncommon disorders, such as phenylketonuria and hemophilia. Also, there are disease genes that account for a small fraction of the more common chronic diseases, such as α_1-antitrypsin deficiency in pulmonary emphysema.[14] Furthermore, genes play important roles in the etiology of most, if not all, human diseases ranging from cancer to coronary heart disease.[15] The roles that genes play differ greatly, ranging from genes that completely determine the disease state (i.e., disease genes) to genes that interact with other genes and environmental factors in causing disease (i.e., susceptibility genes). These genetic risk factors include numerous polymorphic traits and enzyme systems involved in the metabolism of drugs and carcinogens.[16–18]

Molecular technology is allowing research applications in family studies to identify disease and susceptibility genes. These studies, which are mostly based on high-risk families with multiple affected individuals, rely on the use of genetic analysis methods such as linkage and segregation analyses.[10] A notable example is the intense search for breast cancer genes in high-risk families. Using linkage analysis[19] and, more recently, direct sequencing of the gene,[20,21] investigators have identified a gene on chromosome 17 (BRCA1). Women who inherit BRCA1 mutation(s) may have a 90% lifetime risk of developing either breast or ovarian cancer.[22] The application of the identifica-

The authors are with the Centers for Disease Control and Prevention, Atlanta, Ga. See the Acknowledgments for a complete listing of the members of the group.

Requests for reprints should be sent to Muin J. Khoury, MD, PhD, Birth Defects and Genetics Diseases Branch, National Center for Environmental Health, Centers for Disease Control and Prevention, Mailstop F45, Atlanta, GA 30341-3724.

Editor's Note. See related comment by Omenn (p 1701) in this issue.

TABLE 1—Public Health Core Functions in Applying Genetic Technology to Disease Prevention

Step	Description of Activities	Disease/Gene Examples
Assessment	Epidemiological studies (assess risks and attributable fractions; gene–environment interactions)	Rheumatoid arthritis, Alzheimer's disease, breast cancer
Policy development	When and how genetic tests are to be applied in disease prevention programs	Testing for various genes
Assurance	Development of public health genetic programs, evaluation of prevention effectiveness, quality assurance	Newborn screening for sickle cell disease, proficiency testing for newborn screening

tion of such genes has been in the context of genetic counseling and the delivery of preventive medical health care to individuals in high-risk families. However, the only available means of primary prevention thus far has been prophylactic mastectomy, which may not provide full protection against the development of breast cancer[23,24] and which raises important issues regarding widespread genetic testing for BRCA1. In addition, the contribution of the apparently numerous BRCA1 mutation(s) to the overall risk of breast and ovarian cancer in the population needs further evaluation.

Genetics and the Levels of Disease Prevention

Prevention strategies include primary, secondary, or tertiary interventions. Primary interventions seek to prevent disease before it occurs. For rare, fully penetrant, and lethal single-gene and chromosomal disorders, medical and community-based interventions thus far have focused on carrier detection and premarital counseling, as well as on prenatal diagnosis and pregnancy termination. (This last may not be considered primary prevention.) Such approaches have been applied for several single-gene conditions such as Tay-Sachs disease[25] and for chromosomal disorders such as Down's syndrome.[26,27]

Primary prevention will have an important role in genetically influenced disorders other than the rare and lethal single-gene disorders, an excellent example being neural tube defects. A promising avenue for primary prevention is the discovery that maternal periconceptional folic acid use reduces both the risk of recurrence of neural tube defects among women with a previously affected pregnancy, as well as the risk of first-time occurrence of neural tube defects in the population.[28] A recent analysis of the relationship between folate levels and neural tube defects suggests that food fortification with folic acid may be the most cost-effective way to reach women of reproductive age.[29,30]

Secondary prevention targets clinical manifestations of disease by early detection and intervention during the preclinical phase of the disease. A classic example in public health genetics is newborn screening for metabolic disorders such as phenylketonuria and galactosemia,[31] with resulting early intervention.

Tertiary intervention minimizes the effects of disease by preventing complications and deterioration. One example of a tertiary prevention effort for a genetic disease is that of antibiotic prophylaxis and immunization for individuals with sickle cell anemia to prevent life-threatening bacterial infections.[32] Another example is the identification of factor VIII gene mutations and associated HLA genotypes that predispose hemophilia A patients to develop factor VIII inhibitors.[33,34] Early identification of this propensity can provide an opportunity for intervention with an immune tolerance program to prevent life-threatening bleeding complications of hemophilia.

Nevertheless, most chronic diseases are etiologically heterogeneous; no single gene is likely to account for a significant attributable fraction of cases. Furthermore, not all persons with a susceptibility genotype will develop the disease. Since most nongenetic risk factors for chronic diseases usually have low predictive value for these diseases,[35] the use of genetic tests is likely to improve the disease predictive value of environmental risk factors.[36] Therefore, a new paradigm of the primary prevention of many chronic diseases could be the identification and interruption of environmental cofactors that lead to clinical disease among persons with susceptibility genotypes.[36] For most diseases and genetic risk factors, such cofactors are poorly understood, and much work is needed before the results of basic genetic research and findings in high-risk families can be translated into population-based interventions.[37]

Core Public Health Functions in Genetics

Assessment

The Institute of Medicine has recommended that "every public health agency regularly and systematically collect, assemble, analyze and make available information on the health of the community, including statistics on health status, community health needs, and epidemiologic and other studies of health problems."[11(p 7)] If the public health applications of the Human Genome Project are to be widespread, the impact of genes in the population at large has to be carefully evaluated through epidemiological studies. Such studies quantify the impact of susceptibility alleles on disease incidence and prevalence. Population-based cohort, cross-sectional case–control studies are needed to estimate relative and absolute risks (positive and negative predictive values) associated with each allele, as well as the population-attributable fraction for the disease of interest.[10] The case–control method, which compares the frequency of specific alleles between affected and unaffected individuals drawn from the same population, has great appeal since DNA studies provide biological markers for susceptibility that do not change over time.[38] Also, multiple genes can be assessed in case–control studies as independent factors in epidemiological analyses. Case–control approaches also provide an important way to look for effect modification and to illuminate biological interaction between genes and nongenetic risk factors (such as occupational exposures and diet and lifestyle factors).[38] The study of gene–environment interaction can provide an important basis for refining the predictive value of traditional epidemiological risk factors and for targeting intervention and prevention activities for individuals in high-risk groups.[10]

One example of a population-based study is the evaluation of the association between the HLA system and rheumatoid arthritis. The contribution of this genetic system to the genetic etiology of rheumatoid arthritis is estimated to be on the order of 30% of the total risk.[39] The immune response *HLA-DR4* allele (*DRB*0401*) is associated with up to a sixfold relative risk of disease. Among Whites, it is also associated with a more severe form of rheumatoid arthritis, in which a gene dosage effect is observed.[40] Screening for *HLA-DR4* among patients with rheumatoid arthritis may therefore be useful in disease management. Although no single environmental factor or infectious agent has been associated with rheumatoid arthritis, it is interesting that *HLA-DR4* is also associated with an increased risk of chronic Lyme arthritis (*Borrelia burgdorferi* infection).[41] Other genes, such as T-cell receptor sequences, may also be involved in rheumatoid arthritis etiology.

Another example of a population-based study is the evaluation of the association between Alzheimer's disease and the apolipoprotein E *E4* allele. Mounting evidence suggests that the apolipoprotein E *E4* allele is strongly associated with both late-onset familial Alzheimer's disease and the more common sporadic Alzheimer's disease.[42-44] Among families at high risk of late-onset Alzheimer's disease, disease risk has been shown to increase with the number of *E4* alleles; 47% of people heterozygous for the *E4* allele and 91% of people homozygous for the *E4* allele were shown to be affected.[42] Risk ratios for heterozygotes and homozygotes were 2.8 and 8.1, respectively.

Public Health Policy Development

The Institute of Medicine has recommended that public health agencies use the scientific knowledge base obtained from an assessment of the health of the population in the decision making and formulation of public health policy. In the arena of genetics, one goal is the use of genetic testing in medical practice as well as in population programs designed to reduce morbidity and mortality associated with disease and susceptibility genes. In any formulation of sound public health genetic policy, however, several issues need to be considered before genetic tests can be applied in population-based prevention programs (Table 2).

The avalanche of genomic information expected to accrue over the next decade has already led to concerns regarding the potential misuse of such information.[5-8] Holtzman[6] argues that there is a great need to "proceed with caution" in applying genetic testing in human populations because (1) society's use of genetics has, in the past, led to human rights abuses; (2) an accelerating trend toward commercialization of DNA technology and motivation for profit could lead to differential development of testing for certain diseases but not for others; (3) indiscriminate application of genetic tests could occur without an understanding of the limitations in interpreting their results; and (4) our ability to detect susceptibility genes will outpace our ability to provide effective intervention after these genes are detected. Nevertheless, the detection of disease susceptibility genes provides the exciting possibility of learning about gene functions and could open entirely new approaches for treatment as well as prevention.

One example of the ethical questions involved in genetic testing is the use of DNA testing in detecting a predisposition to cancer. Despite the recent successes in identifying breast and colon cancer genes, the National Advisory Council for Human Genome Research recently concluded that "it is premature to offer testing of either high-risk families or the general population as part of general medical practice."[45(p785)]

Another ethical issue has involved genetic testing in the workplace for use in job placement, relocation, and the targeting of medical surveillance.[47-50] The objectives of such testing could include differential diagnosis in cases with clinical symptoms, monitoring for toxic effects, and screening for susceptibility to the effects of chemicals.

Steps and safeguards have been suggested to deal with ethical issues surrounding genetic testing. These include protection of individual autonomy and the right to decide based on a proper informed-consent process, preservation of the confidentiality of results of genetic testing, limitation of genetic testing in the workplace and by insurance companies, careful scientific evaluation of the ability of genetic tests to measure the underlying susceptible genotype, and education of the medical profession and the general public.[6] There are definite concerns regarding employment discrimination against individuals with specific genotypes. At present, genetic tests are not generally recommended because of a lack of information on their predictive value. This suggests that applied epidemiological studies are necessary to evaluate genetic tests both within and outside the workplace. Increasingly, many people will belong in one or more subgroups that are genetically sensitive to the effects of exposure. There are currently no good models for dealing with genetic variation in environmental and occupational regulations.

TABLE 2—Issues to Consider in Using Genetic Testing in Disease Prevention

1. Public health impact of disease: incidence, prevalence, morbidity, mortality
2. Prevalence of genotype
3. Laboratory quality issues: analytic sensitivity, specificity, and predictive values of genetic test
4. Magnitude of association between genotype and disease: relative, absolute, and attributable risks
5. Interaction with known modifiable risk factors for the disease
6. Available intervention or prevention methods
7. Cost of test
8. Ethical, legal, and social issues

Furthermore, as the genetic basis for complex behavioral disorders continues to unravel,[51-53] ethical issues will become prominent in potential applications of genetic testing for predispositions to behavioral patterns and psychiatric disorders. Discussions about these issues should be ongoing before any genetic tests are applied in medicine and public health.

Finally, it seems prudent to enact new laws that serve as guidelines or restrictions for applying genetics in public health programs as current regulations do not adequately protect an individual's privacy regarding genetic information. Detailed discussion of these issues is beyond the scope of this article.

Assurance

Assurance can be viewed in the context of the three overlapping strategies for disease prevention: behavior prevention, environmental prevention, and clinical prevention.[54]

The behavior prevention strategy requires the ability to educate individuals regarding the risks for diseases in them, their progeny, and their relatives based on the unique combination of their genetic background and their lifetime experiences. Although human gene therapy trials are in progress for a multitude of single-gene disorders, it is unlikely that this form of intervention will be readily available for common human diseases in the near future. Thus, while genotypes of individuals remain unchanged, environments can be modified at the level of either individuals or populations, and behavior prevention efforts could be targeted toward elimination, reduction, or change of the environmental exposures to individuals. Education and behavior modification can sometimes be most effective in population groups at highest risk for the disease in question (e.g., HIV infection[55]). In genetics, the basic premise is that education and behavior modification can be targeted toward individuals with differential genetic susceptibilities to specific environmental factors in order to reduce the risks for specific diseases.

The environmental prevention strategy is oriented toward reducing exposures in the workplace and in the home, and reducing disease risks by supplementing food or water with certain essential nutrients. For example, water fluoridation programs have contributed to the tremendous decline of dental caries in many countries. Environmental strategies for intervention are geared toward the population as a whole and do not inherently address genetic differences among individuals. Sometimes, global programs such as food supplementation, while beneficial to most people, may be deleterious to a relatively small fraction of genetically susceptible individuals who could be more sensitive to adverse effects from this intervention (such as deleterious effects of iron supplementation for persons with hereditary hemochromatosis).

The clinical prevention strategy emphasizes preventive medicine in the health care setting. This is the traditional method of family-based intervention through genetic counseling. In an era of health care reform and cost control, the delivery of high-quality preventive care is essential. Although new medical technologies can be expensive, the appropriate use of molecular genetic technology is likely to improve the cost-effectiveness of screening and intervention strategies by targeting prevention strategies to persons at high risk of developing diseases. This is true for several reasons. First, procedures used to amplify DNA obtained from blood samples and to identify specific disease-related alleles are becoming increasingly automated and refined. As a result, the cost of DNA-based testing will continue to decrease dramatically. Second, many traditional methods used to identify persons at increased risk of disease, such as a family history of cancer or heart disease, analysis of blood lipids, dietary assessment, and blood pressure measurement, are often weak predictors of disease risk and frequently result in either a false-positive or a false-negative classification of an individual's risk status. Thus, the improved ability of molecular genetic techniques to classify risk factor status accurately can reduce the costs as well as increase the effectiveness of intervention strategies.

One essential public health function is to translate research into practice. Although research efforts can identify the efficacy of specific interventions, the effectiveness of such interventions needs to be carefully evaluated in population settings. Thus, an important public health application of genetics is to evaluate the effectiveness of population-based programs (e.g., follow-up after newborn screening) and to ensure the quality of genetic testing in the population.

For example, sickle cell disease is an autosomal recessive disorder affecting about 1 in 400 African-American newborns. Affected children have long been known to be at increased risk for morbidity and mortality because of complications such as septicemia, especially between the ages of 1 and 3 years.[56] Using a randomized controlled clinical trial, researchers have shown that the early institution of penicillin prophylaxis is highly effective in reducing morbidity and mortality among infants and children with sickle cell disease,[32] so penicillin prophylaxis is now used widely in the comprehensive primary care of children with this disease. This has led, in part, to the initiation of pilot newborn hemoglobinopathy screening programs in the 1970s. A National Institutes of Health Consensus Conference concluded that screening newborns for sickle cell disease could reduce morbidity and mortality.[57] By 1993, more than 40 states had responded with programs for screening at least selected newborns.[57] But despite the well-documented beneficial effects of early medical intervention for sickle cell disease, no population-based national data are yet available with which to assess and track the effectiveness of preventing morbidity and mortality among infants with sickle cell disease ascertained through newborn screening. In particular, more information is needed regarding determinants of morbidity and mortality among such infants.

Finally, an important component of assurance is the quality assurance of genetic testing. For more than 17 years, the Centers for Disease Control and Prevention has conducted research on material development and has assisted laboratories with the quality assurance for newborn dried-blood-spots screening tests. These quality assurance services primarily support newborn screening tests (e.g., for congenital hypothyroidism, phenylketonuria, and hemoglobinopathies) performed by state laboratories. The quality assurance program enables screening laboratories to achieve high levels of technical proficiency and continuity that transcend changes in commercial assay reagents. In addition, the program provides laboratories with quarterly panels of blind-coded dried blood specimens and gives them an independent external assessment of their performance.

Laboratories that perform genetic tests and report those test results back to patients must comply with the regulations put forth by the Clinical Laboratory Improvement Act of 1988.[58] Prior to reporting test results, laboratories must establish for each method the performance specifications for the accuracy, precision, analytical sensitivity and specificity, and reportable range of patient test results; the reference range of normal values; and any other applicable performance characteristics. These regulations, which ensure that genetic tests can have high sensitivity, specificity, and predictive value for the genotype they are measuring, have obvious implications not only in clinical medicine but also in public health programs (e.g., newborn screening).

Concluding Remarks

If the Human Genome Project is to have widespread applications in disease prevention, population-based epidemiological studies are needed to assess the role of genes in specific diseases, and the interaction with known and modifiable disease risk factors. Such studies provide the scientific foundation for validating genetic tests in the population. At the same time, ethical, legal, and social issues need to be carefully evaluated before any genetic tests can be used for disease prevention. Finally, it is essential that public health agencies evaluate the effectiveness of genetic testing programs and ensure the quality of genetic testing in the US population. □

Acknowledgments

Members of the Genetics Working Group, by their affiliation within the Centers for Disease Control and Prevention or elsewhere:

National Center for Environmental Health: Myron Adams, Vicki Brown, Andrew T. L. Chen, J. David Erickson, William Hannon, Joanne Mei, Cynthia Moore, Patricia Mueller, Godfrey Oakley, Richard Olney, Chin-Yih Ou, John A. Reidy, Karen Steinberg, Nedra Whitehead.

National Center for Chronic Disease Prevention and Health Promotion: Robert F. Anda, Carol Ballew, Janet B. Croft, Wayne H. Giles, Gail Janes, Juliette Kendrick, Nancy C. Lee.

National Center for Health Statistics: Mark Eberhardt, Geraldine McQuillan, Diane Wagener.

National Center for Infectious Diseases: Janet McNicholl, Frederick Rickles.

National Institute for Occupational Safety and Health: Paul Schulte.

References

1. Watson JD. The Human Genome Project: past, present and future. *Science.* 1990;248: 44–49.
2. Jordan E. The Human Genome Project: where did it come from? Where is it going? *Am J Hum Genet.* 1992;51:1–6.
3. Hoffman EP. The evolving genome project: current and future impact. *Am J Hum Genet.* 1994;54:129–136.
4. Richards B, Skoletsky J, Shuber AP, et al. Multiplex PCR amplification from the CFTR gene using DNA prepared from buccal brushes/swabs. *Hum Mol Genet.* 1993;2:159–163.
5. Suzuki D, Knudston P. *Genethics: The Clash between the New Genetics and Human Values.* Cambridge, Mass: Harvard University Press; 1989.
6. Holtzman NA. *Proceed with Caution: Predicting Genetic Risks in the Recombinant DNA Era.* Baltimore, Md: Johns Hopkins University Press; 1989.
7. Hubbard R, Wald E. *Exploding the Gene Myth.* Boston, Mass: Beacon Press; 1993.
8. Garver KL, Garver B. The Human Genome Project and eugenic concerns. *Am J Hum Genet.* 1994;54:148–158.
9. Schull WJ, Hanis CL. Genetics and public health in the 1990's. *Annu Rev Public Health.* 1990;11:105–125.
10. Khoury MJ, Beaty TH, Cohen BH. *Fundamentals of Genetic Epidemiology.* New York, NY: Oxford University Press; 1993.
11. Institute of Medicine. *The Future of Public Health.* Washington, DC: National Academy Press; 1988.
12. McKusick VA. *Mendelian Inheritance in Man: Catalogs of Autosomal Dominant, Autosomal Recessive, and X-Linked Phenotypes.* 10th ed. Baltimore, Md: Johns Hopkins University Press; 1992.
13. McKusick VA, Amberger JS. The morbid anatomy of the human genome: chromosomal location of mutations causing disease. *J Med Genet.* 1994;31:265–279.
14. Scriver CR, Beaudet AL, Sly WS, Valle D, eds. *The Metabolic Basis of Inherited Disease.* 6th ed. New York, NY: McGraw-Hill Information Services Co; 1989.
15. King RA, Rotter JI, Motulsky AG. *The Genetic Basis of Common Diseases.* New York, NY: Oxford University Press; 1992.
16. Kalow W. Pharmacogenetics: past and future. *Life Sci.* 1990;47:1385–1397.
17. Grandjean P, ed. *Ecogenetics: Genetic Predisposition to the Toxic Effects of Chemicals.* New York, NY: Chapman and Hall; 1991.
18. Moutschen J. *Introduction to Genetic Toxicology.* New York, NY: John Wiley and Sons; 1985.
19. King MC, Rowell S, Love SM. Inherited breast and ovarian cancer: what are the risks? What are the choices? *JAMA.* 1993; 269:1975–1980.
20. Miki Y, Swensen J, Shattuck-Eidens D, et al. A strong candidate for the breast and ovarian cancer susceptibility gene. *Science.* 1994;266:66–71.
21. Futreal PA, Liu Q, Shattuck-Eidens D, et al. BRCA1 mutations in primary breast and ovarian carcinomas. *Science.* 1994;266: 120–122.
22. Easton DF, Ford D, Bishop DT, et al. Breast and ovarian cancer incidence in BRCA1 mutation. *Am J Hum Genet.* 1995;56:265–271.
23. Salmon RJ, Vilcoq JR. Breast cancer after preventive subcutaneous mastectomy. *Presse Med.* 1995;24:1167–1168.
24. Decker D. Prophylactic mastectomy for familial breast cancer. *JAMA.* 1993;269: 2608–2609.
25. Kaback MM, Lim-Steele D, Dabholkar D, et al. Tay-Sachs disease-carrier screening, prenatal diagnosis and the molecular era: an international perspective, 1970 to 1993. *JAMA.* 1993;270:2307–2315.
26. Shohat M, Legum C, Romem Y, et al. Down's syndrome prevention program in a population with an older maternal age. *Obstet Gynecol.* 1995;85:368–373.
27. Wald NJ, Densem JW, Smith D, Klee GG. Four-marker screening for Down's syndrome. *Prenat Diagn.* 1994;14:707–716.
28. US Public Health Service. Recommendation for the use of folic acid to reduce the number of cases of spina bifida and other neural tube defects. *MMWR Morb Mortal Wkly Rep.* 1992;41:1–7.
29. Daly LE, Kirke PN, Molloy A, et al. Folate levels and neural tube defects: implications for prevention. *JAMA.* 1995;274:1698–1702.
30. Oakley GP, Erickson JD, Adams MJ. Urgent need to increase folic acid consumption. *JAMA.* 1995;274:1717–1718.
31. Guthrie R. Newborn screening: past, present and future. In: Carter TP, Willey AM, *Genetic Disease: Screening and Management.* New York, NY: Alan R. Liss; 1986:317–342.
32. Gaston MH, Verter JI, Woods G, et al. Prophylaxis with oral penicillin in children with sickle cell anemia: a randomized trial. *N Engl J Med.* 1986;314:1593–1599.
33. Schwaab R, Brackmann HH, Meyer C, et al. Haemophilia A: mutation type determines risk of inhibitor formation. *Thromb Haemost.* 1995;74:1402–1406.
34. Ely AM, Aledort LM, Lee TD, Hoyer LW. Histocompatibility antigen patterns in haemophiliac patients with factor VIII antibodies. *Br J Haematol.* 1990;76:238–241.
35. Khoury MJ, Newill CA, Chase GA. Epidemiologic evaluation of screening for risk factors: application to genetic screening. *Am J Public Health.* 1985;75:1204–1208.
36. Khoury MJ, Wagener DW. Epidemiologic evaluation of the use of genetics to improve the predictive value of disease risk factors. *Am J Hum Genet.* 1995;56:835–844.
37. Childs B, Motulsky AG. Recombinant DNA analysis of multifactorial disease. In: Childs B, Holtzman NA, Kazazian HH, Valle D, eds. *Molecular Genetics in Medicine.* New York, NY: Elsevier;1988:180–194.
38. Khoury MJ, Beaty TH. Applications of the case–control method in genetic epidemiology. *Epidemiol Rev.* 1994;16:134–150.
39. Wordsworth BP, Bell JI. The immunogenetics of rheumatoid arthritis. *Springer Semin Immunopathol.* 1992;14:59.
40. Weyand CM, Hicok KC, Conn DL, Goronzy JJ. The influence of HLA-DRB1 genes on disease severity in rheumatoid arthritis. *Ann Intern Med.* 1992;117:801–806.
41. Steere AC, Dwyer E, Winchester R. Association of chronic Lyme arthritis with HLA-DR4 and HLA-DR2 alleles. *N Engl J Med.* 1990;323:219.
42. Corder EH, Saunders AM, Strittmatter WJ, et al. Gene dose of apolipoprotein E type 4 allele and the risk of Alzheimer's disease in late onset families. *Science.* 1993;261:921–923.
43. Saunders AM, Strittmatter WJ, Schmechel D, et al. Association of the apolipoprotein E allele E4 with late-onset familial and sporadic Alzheimer's disease. *Neurology.* 1993;43:1467–1472.
44. Tsai MS, Tangalos EG, Petersen RC, et al. Apolipoprotein E: risk factor for Alzheimer's disease. *Am J Hum Genet.* 1994;54: 643–649.
45. National Advisory Council for Human Genome Research. Statement on use of DNA testing for presymptomatic identification of cancer risk. *JAMA.* 1994;271:785.
46. *Genetic Monitoring and Screening in the Workplace.* Washington, DC: Office of Technology Assessment; 1990. OTA-Ba-455.
47. Schulte PA, Halperin WE. Genetic screening and monitoring for workers. In: Harrington JM, ed. *Recent Advances in Occupational Health.* Edinburgh, Scotland: Churchill Livingstone;1987:35–154.
48. Vineis P, Schulte PA. Scientific and ethical aspects of genetic screening of workers for cancer risk: the case of the N-acetyltransferase phenotype. *J Clin Epidemiol.* 1995;48: 189–197.
49. Andrews LB, Jaeger AS. Confidentiality of genetic information in the workplace. *Am J Law Med.* 1991;17:75–108.
50. Billings PR, Beckwith J. Genetic testing in the workplace: a view from the USA. *Trends Genet.* 1992;8:198–202.
51. Keverne EB. Molecular genetic approaches to understanding brain development and behavior. *Psychoneuroendocrinology.* 1994; 19:407–414.
52. Plomin R, Owen MJ, McGuffin P. The genetic basis of complex human behaviors. *Science.* 1994;264:1733–1739.

53. Billings PR, Beckwith J, Alper JS. The genetic analysis of human behavior: a new era. *Soc Sci Med.* 1992;35:227–238.
54. Centers for Disease Control. A framework for assessing the effectiveness of disease and injury prevention. *MMWR Morb Mortal Wkly Rep.* 1992;41(Reports and Recommendations 3):1–13.
55. Berkelman RL, Curran JW. Epidemiology of HIV infection and AIDS. *Epidemiol Rev.* 1989;11:222–228.
56. Leikin SL, Gallagher D, Kinney TR, et al. Mortality in children and adolescents with sickle cell disease. *Pediatrics.* 1989;84:500–508.
57. Sickle Cell Guideline Panel. *Sickle Cell Disease: Screening, Diagnosis, Management and Counseling in Newborns and Infants. Clinical Practice Guideline No. 6.* Rockville, Md: Public Health Service, Agency for Health Care Policy and Research; April 1993. AHCPR publishing 93-0562.
58. Clinical Laboratory Improvement Act of 1988. 53 *Federal Register* 29590.

[23]

Public health and the 'new' genetics: balancing individual and collective outcomes

EVAN WILLIS
La Trobe University, Australia

ABSTRACT *This paper considers the consequences for public health of developments in the understanding of the genetic basis of disease associated with the Human Genome Project (HGP). It develops a sociological perspective on the main social policy issue that arises—that of maximizing any benefits that may arise and minimizing any drawbacks, especially as regards public health. Some opportunities and dangers are discussed, as are three case studies of the impact of the human genome project on specific public health issues.*

Introduction

The 'dawning' metaphor gets a lot of use these days: of a new millennium which coincided almost exactly with a much heralded new age of genetically based healthcare following the completion of the first draft of a map of the human genome about the middle of the first year. But if the 'dawning' metaphor has been a powerful one for the science of genetics, it has occurred under overcast conditions as far as the understanding of the social implications (including legal and ethical) of new and more powerful maps are concerned.

This paper considers the consequences for one particular field of healthcare of these developments: that of public health. Rather than attempting to analyse these implications in general, three specific case studies are developed in this paper. It considers the main social policy issue that arises as the project unfolds, one of maximizing any benefits that may arise and minimizing any drawbacks. If advances in the understanding of the genetic basis of disease have outpaced the related understanding of the social and societal implications, how can social scientists contribute to the evolution of policies to guide and regulate the new genetically based technologies, their development, practices and the uses to which they are put? Such policies are needed at all levels: individuals, families, societies and globally.

Correspondence to: Evan Willis, Professor of Sociology, Faculty of Humanities and Social Sciences, PO Box 821, Wodonga, Vic, 3689, Australia. Fax 61 2 6058 3811; email E.Willis@aw.latrobe.edu.au

Public health

Several caveats to the analysis should be mentioned first. While public health is conventionally defined in terms of the organized effort by society in disease prevention and health promotion, the term is commonly used in two senses: public in contrast with private health on one hand and public in contrast with clinical on the other. This paper focuses on the latter, perhaps more academically based, definition, being mainly concerned with the usage of the term public health in contrast with clinical medicine practised at the bedside. The differences between the two are ones of emphasis: on prevention rather than treatment, on providing the conditions under which disease can be minimized and health promoted through safe water, clean air, safe working conditions and so on (see Detels *et al.*, 1997). Traditionally concerned with working and living conditions, and based on the discipline of epidemiology, a 'new public health' has emerged with the Ottawa Charter and the Alma Ata declaration (see Baum, 1998).

Second, none of what is written below should be interpreted in such a way as to minimize the individual burden of genetic disease. The focus of this paper instead is about the balance between individual and collective uses of the knowledge arising from the 'new' genetics and the technologies based on that knowledge. Third, the paper should not be read as emphasizing excessively the differences between geneticists on one hand and the public health community of academics and practitioners on the other (see Cunningham-Burnley & Kerr, 1999). Both deal at the level of the population and study the interaction between genetic and environmental factors. The common ground between the two groups is substantial, in other words, with many geneticists acutely aware of the social, legal and ethical issues that flow from the project.

The opportunities

There is now a substantial literature on the opportunities that advances in genetic understanding of disease offer for the improvement of human health, and that is not in contention here (see for example Bodmer & McKie, 1997). There is also plenty written on how to maximize the benefits such advances may bring and the whole emerging discipline of public health genetics is dedicated to that end (see for example Khoury *et al.*, 2000). What there is less of is literature on how the 'new' genetics is affecting health policy (see Kaufert, 2000). This paper will focus instead on the challenges and indeed the dangers of these advances and how social scientists may contribute to the process of minimizing these.

The question is one of balance—maximizing the upside whilst acknowledging that a downside does exist and must be confronted with regulatory and other strategies. Balancing the positives with the negatives is a policy issue at a number of levels. This is especially so in the context of the health and social policy issue of the appropriate role of genetic testing; studied amongst others by the US Task Force on Genetic Testing run as part of the ELSI aspect of the HGP (Holtzman & Watson,

1997). Questions of insurance, employment, discrimination and privacy together constitute potentially the downside of developments to be guarded against, alongside the benefits (see for example Otlowski, 2001).

But it is the broader implications for public health with which this paper deals and there are a number of relevant issues to discuss. The first arises out of a classic tension between individual and collective uses of emerging genetic biotechnologies. These technologies do not occur in a vacuum but as part of a social context that must be taken into consideration. The genetic biotechnologies have both individual uses and collective uses and the potential exists for a tension to exist between the two.

Three case studies

The shape of the impact of the HGP on public health is only beginning to emerge. Furthermore, while there seem to be some common issues, it is difficult to discuss the impact in general terms. Instead three case studies will be briefly considered and then analysed.

Ozone and the melanoma gene

In 1997, the biotechnology firm Myriad genetics was awarded a patent on the MTS1 (Multiple Tumor Suppressor 1) melanoma gene, which gave it the right to develop a test for the identification of individuals who have an increased risk of developing melanoma through inherited susceptibility (http://www.myriad.com/pr/19970430.html). What public health role might such a test have?

> An MTS1 genetic test for melanoma has the important potential role of alerting individuals at high risk for skin cancer to take precautionary measures before the cancer develops and to have suspicious lesions removed, so that the risk of melanoma may be substantially reduced in these individuals. [http://www.oncolink.upenn.edu/cancernet/99/dec/712705.html#11]

So high-risk individuals can be identified, monitored and counselled on what they can do to reduce the likelihood of developing melanoma at the individual level (as well as the group level of melanoma-prone family members). Currently, management recommendations include monthly skin self-examination, clinical skin examination once or twice yearly, a low threshold for simple excision of changing pigmented lesions, moderation of sun exposure and appropriate use of sunscreens (Greene, 1999).

What relevance would such tests have for the residents of the southern Chilean city of Punta Arenas with 120 000 residents, 3500 kilometres south of the Chilean capital of Santiago, when the hole in the ozone layer over Antarctica reached a world population centre for the first time in the spring of 2000, exposing residents to the very high levels of ultraviolet radiation that can cause melanomas?

> Government authorities in Punta Arenas last week unveiled a special public education program urging citizens to take precautions from the fierce glare of ultraviolet radiation caused by the depleted ozone layer. . . . The program—'Magallanes Ozone 2000'—instructs citizens to minimize their exposure to the sun by wearing wide-brimmed hats, long pants and long sleeved shirts, and religiously apply sun screen on a daily basis. . . . Other program recommendations include keeping infants entirely out of the sun until six months of age. Older babies and children should only go in the sun for short periods of time and always with plenty of sunscreen. . . . The yellow alert does not include suspending school classes but does mean that sports practices and other activities cannot be held out of doors. [http://oc.orientation.com/en/topstories/6731404.html]

Individualizing the risk of skin cancer by allocating resources to screening does, of course, have a place in responding to the risk. But arguably, in this case (perhaps the first of many such cases), individualist solutions are less important than collective responses. Everyone needs to both follow precautionary measures at an individual level and pursue collective action. Collectivizing the risk of skin cancer would result in political agitation to encourage implementation of the 1987 Montreal Protocols to eliminate CFCs as well as the 1997 Kyoto Protocol to reduce greenhouse gas emissions that have led to ozone thinning, in the face of attempts by an American President beholden to greenhouse polluters for massive campaign contributions, to abandon them, or at least water them down.

The social context has further importance in influencing the societal response and deciding resource allocation in a developing country. On what health strategy should public health authorities spend a limited public health budget to deal with the citizens who have become the subjects of a global environmental experiment on 'what are the consequences of living under the growing ozone hole?'.

Patented gene testing technology to screen for those with heightened susceptibility does not come cheaply. Nor are city authorities keen to publicize the extent of the risk because of the threat to the city's attempts to build a tourism industry. Issuing health alerts that those with pale skin can stay in the sun for only seven minutes is hardly conducive to such an aim. Nor are the city's infamous high winds conducive to the erection of shade measures or even hats staying on. Not only that, but the means of measuring ozone thinning as a basis for the issuing of alerts may not be available. 'Officials acknowledge the critical need to address the problem —but claim they won't be able to afford $180,000 for an ozone- and radiation-measuring instrument after Punta Arenas scientists return the only one they have later this month to the institute in Brazil from which they borrowed it' (McKeen, 2000).

Bladder cancer and chemical workers

The occupational health and safety of the workforce is one potential area of application for advances in the genetic understanding of disease. Here the balance of benefits and drawbacks depends on whose point of view it is being considered from. Bladder cancer in chemical industry workers is a classic case of an occupational health hazard (akin to that affecting chimney sweeps) and has long been documented, being one of the first workplace-induced cancers to be associated with industrialization (Kantoff *et al.*, 1998). Systematic research as long ago as 1954 documented the relationship, especially with a type of chemical known as aromatic amines (see Case *et al.*, 1954).

The identification of the p53 gene associated with bladder cancer (Semenza and Weasel, 1997) has raised complex issues about the role of screening as part of pre-employment medical examinations. Should a putative test for mutations of the p53 gene be given to workers and 'carriers' denied employment in the chemical industry? At the individual level, of course, it would appear prudent for the potential worker themselves to seek employment elsewhere rather than knowingly expose themselves to higher risk (though the salutary case is perhaps the 30% of the adult population who smoke tobacco). At the collective level, however, the issues are a little different. Screening out potential compensation claimants amongst workers who subsequently develop bladder cancer is a means for chemical industry employers to use genetic biotechnologies for social control purposes to discriminate against those carrying the gene. Furthermore, the approach is compatible with the traditional method of dealing with occupational health and safety hazards summed up by the phrase 'fix the worker not the workplace'. If machinery is noisy, workers should wear hearing protection rather than quieter machinery being installed. Instead of discriminating against workers with the 'defective' gene, a more appropriate collective response (long favoured by trade unions) is to monitor the workplace to make it safer so harm to individual workers is minimized. As Draper (1996) argues:

> The important underlying question here is: Do we focus on the individual or on the environment? In fact, a certain percentage of people may develop these diseases and others may not, but in most cases the idea that a biological trait of the workers themselves causes the problem is unproven. Focusing on the individuals and their possible predispositions too often is a way of inappropriately changing the subject, away from the workplace hazards. Screening and monitoring are two major alternatives that have developed in response to the identification of genetic and biological traits and hazardous substances. Screening has developed as an alternative to monitoring, in that high-risk individuals have been identified and screened out as a favored means of reducing exposure to environmental contaminants. Employers increasingly favor a screening approach to environmental hazards. In fact, the screening approach is winning, which leads to some significant problems. The screening approach involves

> detecting individuals who then will be excluded from exposure to the toxic substance. In contrast, the declining monitoring approach involves monitoring contaminants in order to determine whether exposures are too high for those who are exposed to them—like measuring levels of air contaminants with a radiation badge.

Genetic testing for inherited susceptibility to bladder cancer, as with testing for susceptibility to skin cancer, represents the measuring of genetic risk within an individualist paradigm consistent with existing power structures of industry. In other words, the social relations of the medical technology of genetic testing give another more powerful social control tool for individualizing the risk of bladder cancer. An alternative approach, long favoured by unions, would be to work to eliminate cancer-causing agents from the workplace in general.

Hemochromatosis

There is a case in which, arguably, individual and collective benefits coincide. Hemochromatosis (HH) is an:

> . . . autosomal recessive disease of iron regulation, resulting in excessive iron absorption and ultimately in iron overload, leading to end organ disease. Complications of HH include cirrhosis, primary liver cancer, cardiomyopathy, arthritis and diabetes. Screening studies using serum iron measures suggest a prevalence of 1/200–1/400. . . . In all clinical series, males outnumber females. HH is much rarer in Asians and African-Americans than in people of European descent. A different iron overload syndrome, probably genetic, has been described in African-Americans and sub-Saharan Africans. In 1996, a candidate gene for HH was identified adjacent to the major histocompatibility locus. The gene has been designated HFE. . . . Removal of iron by phlebotomy increases survival in symptomatic patients. In a small cohort, institution of regular phlebotomy (3–4 times per year) prior to the development of cirrhosis or diabetes was associated with an apparently normal life expectancy. (Burke, 1998)

So the complications of HH can be largely avoided by individuals donating blood 3–4 times a year, making it something of a model for evaluating the public health impact of genetics! Here an individual benefit potentially coincides with a public benefit. But whether the blood removed from phlebotomies can be entered into the blood supply is more problematic (as a specific treatment for iron deficiencies in others?). The Red Cross blood service in Australia recently decided to use it but it does not yet occur in the USA although there appear to be plans to do so as the 'stigma' associated with HH blood is removed (see http://www.victorherbert.com/ash1999.htm). It has not been utilized previously seemingly because of complications about the act of donating being both a chargeable treatment (for HH) and a money-earning act in the US system. There are also complexities about ensuring the safety of the blood supply by requesting information about sexual practices and the like, which is not usually part of treatment regimes. The other model aspect of HH is its simplicity, with (at least in the Australian context) commercial interests relatively absent.

But again, as trials of workplace screening of individuals for HH are planned in the Australian context (*The Age*, 18 October 2000), the question remains: should resources be spent identifying at-risk individuals to receive treatment for HH, or for encouraging greater levels of blood donation to ensure the blood supply for treatment purposes? The latter course of action also provides opportunities for screening of persons with HH at the time of donation (see Khoury *et al.*, 2000). The question is clearly one of balance.

Individuals and the state

The tension between individual and collective interests is a common theme in the brief analyses of the case studies and can be considered more generally in the public health context. Some degree of regulation and restraint on the liberty of individuals is largely accepted in most societies in the promotion of public health although the extent varies societally. In the Australian context, quarantine, gun control, fluoridation of water supply and pasteurization of milk are examples as are car seatbelt and bicycle helmet wearing and prohibition of mobile phone use while driving. How might discoveries in genetics be translated into public health action in this context? How can public health opportunities for health promotion and disease prevention be balanced against decisions concerning the appropriate use of information and technologies based on these discoveries? In pursuing disease prevention and health promotion, balancing the rights of individuals against a state pushed by rampant biotechnology commercial interests is a difficult health policy challenge for the future.

Most of the activity thus far has been of the mapping variety and actual technological innovations have been slower to follow. If gene therapy is still largely a feature of the pre-dawn hopeful glow on the horizon of medicine then how else might these advances be translated into the full light of day? The conventional distinction between primary, secondary and tertiary prevention is useful here, although exactly how this scheme translates into the 'new' genetics is far from clear. Primary prevention focuses on stopping the illnesses, genetic or otherwise, before they occur. Secondary prevention targets clinical manifestations of the disease by early detection, and tertiary prevention minimizes the effects of the disease by preventing complications and deterioration (see Khoury, 1996).

Yet genetic testing technologies bring new questions to the issue of what it means to prevent or control disease. Applied to the field of genetic medicine, primary prevention involves prenatal testing and termination if the fetus is shown to carry the gene for particular conditions and is likely to manifest that genetic illness during his/her lifetime. Yet social relations of prenatal diagnosis are complex. They are tied up with not only the politics of abortion but the issue of the seriousness of the genetically caused disease. Clear eugenic overtones are implicit in the question of 'How perfect does a fetus, on the basis of prenatal diagnosis, have to be before the pregnancy is allowed to proceed to term?'.

Secondary prevention involves—and is being translated to mean—genetic screening, such as for HH. Yet, as the case studies illustrate, the social relations of screening technology are complex. In the recent history of medical technology, assessment resolving issues of whether population screening for non-genetic conditions is safe, effective and cost efficient has been muddied by a variety of factors not the least of which is an economic/commercial imperative that often masquerades as a technological imperative (see Willis, 1997). The squabbling over the relative roles of commercial biotechnology company Celera Genomics vis-à-vis the publicly funded effort in the human genome project (see Cook-Deegan, 1994) does not augur well for resolving the complex health policy issues of whether to embark on genetic screening for a variety of genetically caused conditions that the new knowledge about the human genome has made possible.

Then there are difficulties in defining what is 'normal' and 'abnormal', such definitions being both culturally and historically conditional. A Danish attempt to define what counts as a genetic disorder (i.e. to construct a list of diseases relevant for screening) was abandoned on the grounds that:

> . . . the question was not only medical but also social, and should be worked out in co-operation with patients. This question includes consideration of the implications of the following: degrees of severity of disorder (e.g., cleft lip vs. Huntington's disease) and variation within a disorder (e.g., mild vs. severe haemophilia), how the carrier state should be regarded, the importance of recognition of partial penetrance (the proportion of those with the genotype that manifest the phenotype), and the distinction between unifactorial and multifactorial conditions. (Chadwick *et al.*, 1993)

The dangers

But if there are opportunities provided by the increase in the understanding of the genetic basis to disease there are also many dangers, which the remainder of this paper is devoted to analysing. One is the overgeneticization of disease. With a large increase in at least theoretical knowledge about particular conditions, a perhaps understandable frustration on the part of practitioners trying to assist their patients and an aggressive biotechnology industry keen to pursue the green fields of profitability from their inventions, a tendency has arisen to overemphasize the role of genetic factors. Cancer is a good example. It is widely accepted that the causes of cancer are a combination of genetic and environmental. Advances in genetic understanding of cancer have opened up new areas of research and treatment that it is hoped will help alleviate this scourge. Yet there is a tendency to overemphasize the genetic element in the manner described by Kaplan (1964) over 30 years ago as the Law of the Instrument: 'Give a small boy a hammer, and he will find that everything he encounters needs pounding.' It echoes a Swedish saying that 'When you're holding a hammer everything looks like a nail'. In psychology, the phenomenon is called 'functional fixedness' or the Einstellung effect (Reiber, 1995).

The new tools of genetic diagnosis and screening are in danger of being overemphasized, what is a genetic nail and what is not being confused. An example is breast cancer (see Hopper, 1996). Emphasis on the 5–10% of cancers which are heritable has the potential to divert attention (and possibly research funding) from research on the 90–95% which are not, and for which ongoing research on the environmental and other non-medical determinants remains crucial. As the Council for Responsible Genetics (1997) laments:

> The overemphasis on genetic factors in cancer, when environmental carcinogens are known to make major contributions, takes attention away from environmental cleanup measures that could, in fact, reduce the incidence of cancer. Current research has identified links between cancer and a host of non-genetic factors, including organochlorides, estrogen and estrogen-like chemicals, pesticides, radiation, bovine growth hormone, diet and exercise. The 'geneticisation' of cancer creates a blame-the-victim mindset that obscures these social and environmental factors.

Another danger that relates to the above is the tendency that arises from greater genetic knowledge to individualize disease in a form of genetic reductionism; a sort of 'Genes-R-us' approach to the world. This fits neatly with an individualist paradigm of disease that views it as an individual and biological phenomenon which can be alleviated by direct procedures carried out on individuals. Public health by contrast has tended to operate with a more social and political model of disease. Health can be promoted and disease reduced by collective action to secure clean water, shorter working hours, clean air and safe working environments. The 'new' genetics has more than the potential to defuse and reduce the basis for collective action—it is already happening. Part of the attraction of the HGP has been that the better understanding of genetics fits neatly with a paradigm of economic and political orientation in which globalization and the dominance of the market have come to rule. If individuals get sick it is because of their genes rather than the environment in which they live or work. Remedial programmes can therefore be directed at those individuals rather than trying to improve the conditions of life and existence for everyone. Such a view fits well with the growing hegemony of American cultural values under globalization, where, as Nelkin & Lindee (1995 p. 194) argue, the gene has become something of a cultural icon that:

> . . . intersects with important American cultural values. Genetic explanations appear to locate social problems within the individual rather than in society, conforming to the ideology of individualism. They are thus a convenient way to address troubling social issues: the threats implied by

> the changing roles of women, the perceived decline of the family, the problems of crime, the changes in the racial and ethnic structure of American society and the failure of welfare programs.

At the same time the emerging biotechnologies also provide a powerful instrument of social control through the bio-surveillance of populations, permitting classification of individuals on the basis of genetic risk (for insurance as well as other purposes, such as in the example of the occupational health and safety field detailed earlier) as well as a narrowing of the definition of what it means to be a 'normal' human being—information of considerable actuarial relevance.

Other dangers also arise out of the globalized nature of the project. The HGP is itself a force for globalization but the danger lies in the assumption that the social relations of the biotechnologies arising out of the project will be uniform across the globe rather than reflecting particular historical and cultural contexts. Already these latter factors have been important. Germany was late to join the project, reflective of the baggage of the Nazi era together with the eugenicist overtones of the HGP (see Cook-Deegan, 1994). The first director of the HGP, James Watson, was asked how these abuses of the past could be avoided within the project in the future. His reported response was that the state should stay out of the picture because the abuses all occurred as official state policy (Wikler, 2000).

Apart from the problem that the 'state' is never conceptualized, this type of reported comment reflects a particularly North American concern, whereby the politico-economic context historically and contemporarily has been to minimize the role of the state consistent with maximizing the opportunities for capital accumulation by the private sector. With such a cultural mindset, the suggested solution to past problems is for the state to have no role in the regulation of developing genetic biotechnologies and therefore presumably to allow market forces to determine the processes of invention, innovation and diffusion. The so-called 'technological imperative' turns out on closer examination to be an economic imperative, best pursued with minimal state intervention. In the Australian context, as in many other liberal democracies, the state has a history of intervention in public health to restrain market forces in the interests of not only legitimacy generally but also policy aims of equity (of both access and resource allocation). The USA indeed is unusual amongst Western liberal democracies in persisting with individual health including genetic risk management through private health insurance rather than community risk assumption through national health insurance schemes such as Medicare in Australia or the National Health Service in Great Britain. Restrictions on what Americans call the liberty of individuals in the interest of public health have long been accepted more in Australia and other countries than in the United States. So while Americans argue about whether the compulsory wearing of seatbelts interferes with one's god-given right to kill oneself in a motor accident, this public health measure has long been accepted in many other countries. Australians have supported the restrictions of guns in the community as a public health measure, largely unencumbered by arguments about the 'right' to own and carry firearms. Similar examples are the compulsory wearing of bicycle helmets, the banning of the use of mobile phones whilst driving and many others. So the state is already heavily involved in the regulation of the knowledge arising from the improvements in the genetic understanding of disease and should continue to be so.

Another danger is the re-emergence of sociobiological explanations for human behaviour. Evolutionary psychology, as it is now called, is more sophisticated than some of the earlier controversial work (e.g. Wilson, 1980). Advances in the genetic understanding of disease have generated interest in whether some sorts of behaviour can also be explained genetically. Those mentioned include various sorts of mental illness, homosexuality, alcoholism, obesity, homelessness and the 'holy grail' of intelligence. But whereas, in its earlier outbreak several decades ago, sociobiology pitched its explanation (for male dominance for instance) in terms of crude instinct and 'innateness', now evolutionary psychologists are able to go a step further in genetic reductionist explanation to explain human behaviour in genetic terms (see Dusek, 1999). Fortunately the earlier critique of sociobiology has been expanded to include a powerful argument that individuals are not just the sum of their genes (see Rose *et al.*, 1984) and that the relationship between nature and nurture remains a complex one in which both are relevant and important in explaining human behaviour. It is quite possible to acknowledge that all human diseases of public health importance are the result of the interaction between genetic variation and the environment, without resorting automatically to a genetic reductionist position of the pre-eminence of genetic causation.

A further danger, however, is the compatibility between this view of behaviour and neo-conservative political agendas that now sweep the globe. Human societies are becoming increasingly polarized into rich and poor, both globally and also relatively speaking within countries. A form of economic apartheid is emerging such that issues of social as well as environmental sustainability loom, as social cohesion within and between countries is threatened. The dangers of explanations that locate the reasons for inequality in their crudest form in people's genetic makeup encourage and support a political programme that sees inequality therefore as somehow natural and immutable. Interpreted in this way, the HGP provides a rationale and a justification for inequality. State programmes to address the effects of inequality as a result are not necessary or effective, and cuts in government and aid spending that attempted to ameliorate this polarization are legitimized by business elites. In that sense the globalizing nature and influence of the human genome project have very much a negative aspect, especially if the social relations of the biotechnologies that flow from the project have a strong flavour of American capitalism about them.

Conclusion

This paper concentrates on the broadest level of impact of advances in the genetic understanding of disease, on public health in both its traditional and 'new' senses. The challenge, in which social scientists must be involved, is to harness the benefits of advances in the genetic understanding of disease and help ensure that these outweigh the apparent drawbacks. These drawbacks occur at several levels including those of commercial and other pressures such as the capacity for bio-surveillance and social control. This paper also points to a wider level, that of what might broadly be called the politico-economic context, to show the consequences (both intended and unintended) of the Human Genome Project for public health. Many of the policy decisions have to do with resource allocation questions of where to invest for maximum possible health gain. Crucial in this decision is the central social science issue of the relationship between the individual and society, or as expressed in health terms between individual and population health, in pursuing this aim.

Many questions remain that constitute a research agenda for social scientists. What might be the balance between individual and collective interests and how would one strike it? What might be some of the options before us and how might public debate be pursued in order to arrive at an informed community view? If gene technology were to be used expressly for public health benefit, what would be the applications and how would we know it?

To be clear, the argument here is not that amelioration in the individual manifestation of genetic disease should not be pursued but that balancing resource allocation between individual and population health is a difficult task when the whole politico-economic context in which these advances are taking place makes investment in population health issues problematic. The clear and present danger is that individual health ends are being sought at the expense of the sort of population health benefits that have always been the concern of public health.

References

Baum, F. (1998) *The New Public Health: An Australian Perspective* (South Melbourne, Oxford University Press).

Bodmer, W. & McKie, R. (1997) *The Book of Man: the Human Genome Project and the Quest to Discover Our Genetic Heritage* (New York, Oxford University Press).

Burke, W. (1998) Hemochromatosis: Public Health Implications of Screening. Abstracts From The 1st Annual Conference on Genetics and Public Health. CDC Atlanta [available at: http://www.cdc.gov/genetics/publications/abstracts.htm].

Case, R., Hosker, M. & Macdonald, D. (1954). Tumours of the urinary bladder in workmen engaged in the manufacture and use of certain dyestuff intermediaries in the British chemical industry: part I. *British Journal of industrial Medicine*, 11, pp. 75–104.

Chadwick, R., Coli, D., ten Have, H., Husted, J., Pogliano, C. & Shickle, D. (1993) A Report to the Commission of the European Communities: Ethical Implications of Human Genome Analysis for Clinical Practice in Medical Genetics with special reference to Genetic Counselling. University of Wales, Cardiff Centre for Applied Ethics [available at: http://www.uclan.ac.uk/facs/ethics/gencoun.htm].

Cook-Deegan, R. (1994) *The Gene Wars: Science, Politics, and the Human Genome* (New York, Norton).

Council for Responsible Genetics (1997) BRCA1 and breast cancer; myths and facts. Boston, CRG [available at: http:www.essential.org/crg/BRCA-1.html].

Cunningham-Burnley, S. & Kerr, A. (1999) Defining the 'social': towards an understanding of the medical and scientific discourses on the social aspects of the 'new genetics'. *Sociology of Health and Illness*, 21(5), pp. 647–668.

Detels, R., Holland, W. & Knox, G. (1997) *Oxford Textbook of Public Health*, 3rd edn (New York, Oxford University Press).

Draper, E. (1996) Social Issues of Genome Innovation and Intellectual Property. *Risk*, 7, pp. 201–230 [available at: http://www.fplc.edu/risk/vol7/summer/draper.htm].

Dusek, V. (1999) Sociobiology sanitized: the Evolutionary Psychology and Genetic Selectionism Debates. Science-as-Culture forum [available at: http://www.human-nature.com/science-as-culture/dusek.html].

Greene, M. (1999) The genetics of hereditary melanoma and nevi. *Cancer*, 86, pp. 2464–2477.

Holtzman, N. & Watson, M. (1997) *Promoting Safe and Effective Genetic Testing in the United States.* Final Report of the Task Force on Genetic Testing .National Institutes of Health-Department of Energy Working Group on Ethical, Legal, and Social Implications of Human Genome Research [available at: http://www.nhgri.nih.gov/ELSI/TFGT_final/].

Hopper, J. (1996) Some public health issues in the current state of genetic testing for breast cancer in Australia. *Australian and New Zealand Journal of Public Health*, 20(5), pp. 467–472.

Hubbard, R. & Wald, E. (1999) *Exploding the Gene Myth* (Boston, Beacon Press).

Kantoff, P., Zietman, A. & Wishnow, K. (1998) Bladder cancer. In: Holland, J., Frei, E., Bast, R. Kufe, D., Morton, D. & Weichselbaum, R. (eds) *Cancer Medicine*, 4th edn (Chicago,Williams & Wilkins), Ch. 125
[available at: http://intouch.cancernetwork.com/CanMed/Ch125/125-2.htm].

Kaplan, A. (1964) *The Conduct of Inquiry* (San Francisco, Chandler).

Kaufert, P. (2000) Health policy and the 'New Genetics'. *Social Science and Medicine*, 51(6), pp. 821–829.

Khoury, M. (1996) From genes to public health: the applications of genetic technology in disease prevention. *American Journal of Public Health*, 86(12), pp. 1717–1722.

Khoury, M., Burke, W., & Thomson, E. (2000) *Genetics and Public Health in the 21st Century: Using Genetic Information to Improve Health and Prevent Disease* (New York, Oxford University Press).

Kolberg, B. (2000) *Gene Therapy— Status and Prospects in Clinical Medicine.* SMM report 1/2000 Norwegian Center for Health Technology assessment
[available at: http://www.oslo.sintef.no/smm/News/FramesetNews.htm].

MacKeen, D. (2000) Living under the hole in the sky
[available at: http://www.salon.com/health/feature/2000/11/03/ozone/].

Nelkin, D. & Lindee, S. (1995) *The DNA Mystique: The Gene as a Cultural Icon* (New York: Freeman).

Otlowski, M. (2001) *Implications of Genetic Testing for Australian Insurance Law and Practice*, Occasional Paper No 1 (Tasmania, Centre for Law and Genetics, University of Tasmania).

Reiber, A. (1995) *The Penguin Dictionary of Psychology* (Harmondsworth, Penguin).

Rose, S., Lewontin, R. & Kamin, L. (1984) *Not in Our Genes: Biology, Ideology and Human Nature* (Harmondsworth, Penguin).

Semenza, J. & Weasel, L. (1997) Molecular epidemiology in environmental health: the potential of tumor suppressor gene p53 as a biomarker. *Environmental Health Perspectives*, 105(Suppl. 1), pp.155–163.

Wikler, D. (2000) Should the state intervene in ethical decisions in genetics. *Proceedings Third Menzies Scholars Symposium Human Genome Research: How far should we go? The post genomic world*, Melbourne, October [available at: http://home.vicnet.net.au/~menzies/].

Willis, E. (1997) The prostatic imperative and the social relations of medical technology *International Journal for Technology Assessment in Health Care.* 13(4), pp. 602–12

Wilson, E.O. (1980) *Sociobiology* (Cambridge, MA, Harvard University Press).

Wilson, J.M.G. & Jungner, G. (1968) *Principles and Practice of Screening for Disease*, Public Health paper (Geneva, WHO).

[24]

Genetic Screening from a Public Health Perspective: Some Lessons from the HIV Experience

Scott Burris and Lawrence O. Gostin

Science has produced a powerful new technology in genetic screening, and the medical and biotechnology industries have been quick to find diagnostic and therapeutic uses for it in the care of individual patients. If one assumes that medicine is the same as public health—that public health is simply the sum of millions of individual outcomes—it is natural to assume that genetic screening technology will also be useful to public health. The main questions for public health users of the technology, then, would be how effective are the individual interventions following testing and how may we overcome the various problems posed by the socially dangerous quality of genetic information. On this view, the proper topic for this chapter would be the efficacy of genetic treatment and the adequacy of privacy and antidiscrimination law.

That, however, is not to be this chapter. If we have learned one lesson from the HIV epidemic, it is that disease and our responses to it are constructed of more than microbes (or genes). Much of the discussion of the human genome has been in a scientistic, positivist mode, stitched without a seam to a construction of health and health care as a medical commodity. The discourse has focused on issues in the therapeutic relationship between physician and patient—such as reproductive counseling, informed consent to treatment, confidentiality of genomic information, and the "right to know" certain information. The literature seldom addresses the issue of the benefits of genetic screening and interventions for whole populations. What aggregate health benefits accrue to discrete populations and at what aggregate cost? From a public health perspective, emphasizing the health of a population and seeking determinants of health in the population's ecology, we are not ready to assume that genetic screening invariably has public health benefits that outweigh its costs. In spite of the enormous long-term potential of genetic research, a critical evaluation of the public health interest in genetic screening must be equally wary of the zeal of those who aspire to do good and those who wish to do well.

Putting aside the assumption that widespread collection of genetic data is both desirable and inevitable sets a very different genetic agenda for public health law. As a preliminary matter, we are required to ask, what criteria need to be satisfied to justify a particular genetic intervention in public health terms and to what extent have they been satisfied? Our experience with HIV teaches that these are not purely epidemiological questions. Any use of government authority to collect and use sensitive information reflects often controversial assumptions about whose health counts and how. It entails the potential for abuse. It requires social negotiation to ensure voluntary compliance—it must be sold, that is, both to those in society who write laws and budgets and to those in society whose information is to be sought. We consider these issues later in this chapter.

The HIV epidemic has also taught us yet again how difficult it is to do public health work and how little we know about many important questions of method. The experience of HIV testing illustrates the social and political potency of testing technology. As public health lawyers asking first and foremost about the role of law in genetic public health policy, we focus on how state authority can be wielded to promote the health of the community and to protect, or avoid harming, those whose health data will be sought in that cause. Without revisiting in detail the legal analyses of antidiscrimination and privacy law found in other chapters, we turn our gaze to the protective ambit of law in the HIV epidemic. This critical view reveals problems with the use of privacy as a proxy for discrimination and, indeed, with the antidiscrimination paradigm itself, not to mention that we know less about how to use this sort of law to influence behavior than we might at first admit.

ASSESSING THE PUBLIC HEALTH INTEREST IN GENETIC SCREENING

Genetic data are collected for discrete purposes and in different forms. A taxonomy of genetic screening provides a foundation for our subsequent assessment of the benefits and risks of genetic screening from a population-based perspective. First, we distinguish between genetic testing and screening. Testing represents a method of identifying disease or the potential for disease in an individual patient. Typically, and preferably, testing is accomplished through a careful process of discussion, nondirective counseling, and informed consent between a physician and a patient. Screening, by contrast, involves the systematic application of a testing instrument to a defined population. Its purpose is often to assess the prevalence or incidence of disease, or the potential for disease, within the population.

The objectives of testing and screening include clinical treatment, epidemiological assessment and intervention, and research. Clinical testing is often intended to prevent (e.g., reproductive counseling) or treat (e.g., somatic gene therapy) disease in the individual or his or her family. Screening, however, is usually intended to determine the prevalence or incidence in the population and, if possible, to intervene to reduce the overall burden of disease (e.g., through changes in behavior, diet, or environment).

Genomic data are collected in several forms, often in large databases held by government agencies like the Department of Defense[1] and the Centers for Disease Control and Prevention,[2] or such research institutions as the University of Utah. In addition to DNA, researchers, health care providers, and health departments frequently collect and store human tissue such as serological samples. Because human tissue is remarkably stable over a long period, stored tissue samples may be regarded as inchoate databases, given the technology to extract from the samples a vast amount of current and future genomic data. The public health and research communities have shown increasing interest in using existing tissue samples for genetic testing and for creating new genetic databases. In some cases genomic information is being extracted from large collections of tissue samples that were stored well before the advent of genetic testing; any consent that may originally have been obtained for tissue samples did not envisage future genetic applications. The most prominent example of an inchoate genetic database is the testing program for phenylketonuria (PKU, an inherited metabolic disease), whereby blood spots are taken from almost all newborns throughout the United States and stored in a dry condition on cards.[3]

For some conditions, genetic factors seem to be the sole or predominant cause of illness. In these instances, genetic testing may detect a carrier state, a current illness, or a marker indicating the likelihood of future illness. In most instances, however, genetic testing will identify only one factor among many other possible determinants of illness in the individual and his or her environment. Such information may help specify the individual's relative risk, as well as shedding light on the etiology of the condition generally. Any information from a genetic test is subject not simply to the limits of its predictive power in relation to illness but also to the reliability of the test itself. This is limited by the sensitivity and specificity of the test instrument and by the proportion of the known mutations in a target population the test is capable of detecting. For example, early screening programs could detect only about 75% of cystic fibrosis mutations in the white population of the United States.[4]

Testing for health conditions may be conducted with various degrees of coercion. Testing may be compelled by the state. For example, PKU screening is mandatory for newborns in almost every state. Testing, when not actually required, may be a condition precedent for the receipt of benefits or privileges. For example, testing requirements for a marriage license are in some sense coercive because the individual cannot obtain a state-issued license absent the test result. "Routine screening" refers to a program of systematically testing everyone who satisfies certain criteria.[5] Depending on the criteria, such screening may or may not have much to do with the subject's personal characteristics; compare, for example, PKU screening, conducted of all newborns, with amniocentesis, which is triggered by the age and health history of the mother.

Routine screening may be conducted with prior informed consent or may be done unless the patients affirmatively "opts out" of the test. Such a patient veto may have to be exercised without the information sharing that, ideally, is part of the process of informed consent, so it may be less than "voluntary." Even where informed consent is required, testing may not be completely voluntary because of the absence of adequate information and understanding. Merely signing a form does not assure genuine informed consent. HIV testing is the prime example of a form of testing generally subject to a higher level of informed consent, both in terms of the information presented and in the documentation of the patient's consent. Finally, screening may be done anonymously or with identifiers that lead more or less easily back to the subject.

THREE PRINCIPLES OF PUBLIC HEALTH SCREENING

The discourse on genetic screening in bioethics and health law has focused on the individual patient's right to information and hope of therapy. Without discounting either that debate or the value of genetic information to patients, the analysis of genetic screening is very different for public health than for health care. Indeed, the differences between the justifications for genetic testing in health care and genetic screening for public health purposes underline the importance of analyzing potential public health uses of genetic screening in public health terms. To that end, we offer the following three principles as useful in assessing the costs, benefits, and political prospects of particular screening programs to public health.[6]

Principle 1. Screening should enhance the health of the population. Much of the impetus for using genetic testing comes from the health care sector, but public health and health care aspire to complementary but meaningfully different ends. Public health aims to improve the health of the group, as measured by aggregate outcomes. Medicine aims to improve the health of the individual, as measured largely by the individual's satisfaction with his or her own outcome. Any number of differences follow from this basic distinction, among them: population health depends more on the causes of incidence of disease in populations than the causes of illness in individuals, and from the population standpoint, it is the distribution of cases rather than the accidental fate of any particular person that matters. Individual risk factors, which seem to explain why certain people get sick, do not tend to explain why certain ills are prevalent in certain populations. Thus, genetic differences may help to explain why people exposed to the same environmental co-factors differ in their health, but environmental factors provide the chief explanation of health differences between populations living in different environments. Because health risks constituted in a population are different than those expressed in individuals, even a very powerful individual risk factor may not constitute a public health priority if the prevalence of the marker is low.[7]

The breast cancer 1 gene (BRCA1) for breast cancer is an example. As Caryn Lerman and Robert Croyle observe, "Much of breast cancer is not caused by inherited susceptibility at all, but results from somatic events that produce genetic changes in a woman's breast cells during her lifetime. Moreover, the majority of women who develop breast cancer have no known major risk factors."[8] To find a genetic screening measure "ethical" in the public health sense, then, we need to determine that it has a reasonable probability of leading to information that can be used to reduce the incidence of genetic illness or mortality in the society as a whole or in a significant population facing a special threat. If it does not, the measure, however useful to individuals, may not be an important public health priority and may not be worthy of significant public sector resources.

Principle 2. The measure should be an efficient and just use of resources. Although rationing may be ethically problematic for many doctors, in public health it is a "moral imperative . . . in the face of scarce resources."[9] Ideally, each public health dollar will be spent to achieve the greatest marginal increase in the level and distribution of well-being in the population. Although the problems of comparing incommensurate values quickly burst any illusions about the objectivity or mechanical quality of this analysis, this principle is nevertheless a useful reminder to build waterpipes and sewers before cholera wards and to bear in mind the relative costs and benefits of oral rehydration kits and heart transplants. The high cost of health care accentuates the resource problem. Although doctors can often do miraculous things for individual patients, such care not only does not help the public health but has a price that may drive out nonmedical forms of prevention.[10] Even assuming that an expensive regimen of screening and treatment might be worthwhile in purely theoretical terms, there is always the problem that our current health care payment system will not provide equitable access. Even counseling, which is often the only intervention of consequence in genetic testing, depends on the deployment of thousands of well-trained counselors throughout the health care system, a cadre of professionals who exist largely in the hopes of genetic optimists.[11]

Screening programs often illustrate the significance of marginal cost in public health planning. There is an impulse in medicine to routinize the use of a test or treatment that seems to work for the individual, an impulse that is often quicker off the mark than the validation of the measure's efficacy on a large scale.[12] Making a useful test routine sometimes carries with it in turn the impulse to make it "mandatory," which the HIV experience has shown is a highly problematic move. Decreeing that an entire population shall be tested has a superficial logic when a test seems to promise health benefits to each and all, and it allows politicians to underline their concern and their toughness with one and the same vote. Yet apart from the difficulties of enforcing compliance, which we shall discuss next, the move to routine or mandatory testing makes a more fundamentally faulty assumption: that the cost-benefit ratio of reaching hard-to-find or resistant targets is comparable to that of reaching the compliant and eager. For example, the medical benefits of prenatal HIV screening of pregnant women may be great; it hardly follows, however, that the reduction of HIV transmission to newborns will be maximized by testing every pregnant woman regardless of the cost.[13] Indeed, particularly in the instance of tests that offer the patient useful information about relative risks or even therapeutic options, one might most logically start with the assumption that most people at risk will accept the test without intervention from public health authorities.

Both the efficiency and fairness of a public health intervention should be evaluated in more than just monetary terms. Indeed, in this case efficiency demands what justice requires. Genetic conditions may often be stigmatizing, leading to ostracism and discrimination. The problem tends to be greater when a particular condition is linked to other disfavored traits. Stigma is thought to increase resistance among the targets of health measures, raising their cost and reducing their effectiveness. Social dispute about the meaning of conditions is a serious and constant friction on the workings of health and prevention programs and can render utterly impractical measures that seem wonderful in theory.

The morality of public health's utilitarianism is rooted in the imperative to improve the distribution as well as the level of health. Were there truly a mechanical formula for achieving the greatest good for the greatest number, ethics would be largely self-executing, for the marginal gains of measures to help a large number of those in need would almost always be greater than the benefits of helping the fortunate few.[14] In fact, nothing could be more complicated and controversial than deciding who is needy and should get what help. In a politicized world of scarcity, there is a constant danger that health expenditures will reflect existing distributions of wealth and influence. Ill health follows and reflects social disadvantage; social differences create different health problems.[15] Spending money to address the leading killers of the population as a whole may exclude expenditures on the leading killers of subgroups in the population. Although cancer is the leading cause of death in the population as a whole, spending to find its genetic causes must be seen in light of such facts as the toll of violence and HIV on young African-American men. We believe that a just health policy requires recognition of the pernicious synergies of socioeconomic disadvantage and the problematic nature of existing social entitlements. To the extent that disease is a social product, public health ought to act as a conscience.[16]

Principle 3. The measure should be as acceptable as possible to its targets. This principle has roots in both practicality and morality. Public health depends largely on voluntary compliance with its guidelines. This is equally true of "voluntary" advice, like wearing a bike helmet in most states, and of "mandatory" rules, like wearing seat belts. Resistance can raise costs enormously, the more as prevalence of the condition rises. It has proven possible, with a fair amount of money and talent, to impose directly observed therapy on a few hundred recalcitrant tuberculosis patients in a few major cities;[17] it is unlikely ever to have been feasible to isolate and monitor the sex lives of tens of thousands of people with HIV. Even most "mandatory" measures are either largely voluntary in effect (e.g., premarital screening) or are so broadly acceptable that they are not resisted (like screening for PKU). The success of a public health intervention and its cost therefore depend significantly on the degree to which its targets perceive it to be more beneficial than costly.

Resistance to health measures is rarely as irrational as it might seem to the paternalistic professional observer. A measure that leads to immediate and short-term health benefits for targeted individuals is obviously more desirable than one that does not; there is the difference between PKU screening and HIV testing (at least before the advent of effective combination therapy). Monetary or other incentives may increase the benefits of compliance, as is sometimes done with directly observed therapy (DOT). The costs of compliance are often in something like inverse proportion to the treatability of the condition: the less we can do for a trait, the more social costs screening is likely to entail. Being marked as having a dangerous, untreatable condition may be costly in psychological terms and may expose the subject to the risk of social stigma. These sorts of costs may be addressed to some extent through counseling and the legal protection of social status, but this, as we will see, is difficult and problematic in its own way. In moral terms, this principle emphasizes the fairness of allocating both the benefits and burdens of a disease that threatens public health or the public generally rather than placing them primarily on the shoulders of those who have the illness.

In the HIV epidemic, resistance to public health rules has taken on a perhaps unprecedented but now widely followed political dimension. Legal and advocacy organizations, capable of generating grass-roots action and of effectively lobbying and litigating, have demonstrated their capacity to influence the development of public health policy.[18] In many respects this has been a boon to public health, facilitating the social negotiation necessary to design broadly acceptable measures. It has also, however, added even more complexity to the rich symbolic politics of health and disease. A final caution under the heading of the principle of acceptability thus is that measures may not always be judged for their intrinsic merits, or even their objective likelihood of causing harm to the target population. The example of HIV reporting typifies a measure that has in many states been strongly opposed by advocates, despite the excellent record of health departments in protecting the confidentiality of their records. In this instance, the fear of what government might someday do with an "AIDS list" outweighs health departments' excellent track record.[19]

GENETIC SCREENING INITIATIVES AND PUBLIC HEALTH

It is well beyond the purpose of this chapter to apply these principles to any genetic screening initiative. Nevertheless, an overview of genetic screening shows the need for caution in designing large-scale screening programs in the name of improving the public's health.

Genetic illness is an important threat to public health. Historically, genetic disease has been seen both as a major source of ill health and premature mortality and as largely intractable.[20] With its significant impact on the population as a whole as well as on distinct subpopulations, genetic illness is obviously an important challenge to public health.[21]

Some level of pure research would surely be a wise and just use of resources for population health, provided always that information about the impact of genetic factors on health is integrated into a broader examination of the determinants of health.[22] There is good historical evidence that the facts of the germ theory had a greater impact on the decline in mortality in the United States in the past century than did the medical interventions derived from them.[23] Research may help identify important co-factors for illness in the environment or help provide behavioral guidance. Likewise, epidemiological research, including formal surveillance, is justified precisely because of the difficulty of assessing the potential of genetic knowledge on public health. Some commentators have lamented the state of genetic-related data collection in public health. James Hanson argues that

> for the most part, public health officials are not well-informed on birth defects or on medical genetics in general and have tended to view birth defects surveillance as a private responsibility rather than as a part of a broader public health agenda. There is also the general perception that birth defects and genetic conditions are rare events, and not subject to prevention or intervention. Yet recent advances in genetics (through the Human Genome Project and other genetics research programs), molecular biology and teratology offer substantial evidence to the contrary, and have

extraordinary implications for preventive health care, including birth defects prevention.[24]

Public health data collection is a prerequisite for according genetic illness greater public health priority.

The value of screening individuals in medical care depends from a public health point of view on such elements as the extent and severity of the condition in the population, the cost of detecting it, and the availability of some intervention to cure or prevent the expression of the condition. In those relatively few instances in which the identification of a genetic trait leads to effective, life-sustaining therapy at a reasonable cost—PKU, for instance—screening evidently has real public health value. More controversial but comparably effective at the population level is prenatal screening to which the preventive response is contraception or abortion. Chorionic villus sampling (CVS) and amniocentesis, for instance, have led to a substantial reduction in the prevalence of Down syndrome at birth, although some racial and ethnic differences may reflect unequal access to prenatal diagnostic services.[25] As the complexity and cost of the response increases—as might happen in the area of prenatal surgery—both the public health cost-benefit ratio and the problem of access increase.

This is all fairly obvious, as is the observation that the most problematic use of genetic screening, from both the medical and the public health standpoint, is in cases when little or nothing can be done to prevent an illness or its intergenerational transmission or where the genetic factor is but one among many individual or environmental co-factors to a higher relative risk of an illness. The psychological value of knowing about something one cannot alter may be positive or negative for the individual,[26] and likewise may make for a net increase or decrease in the sum total of public well-being. Stigma and stress add to the social costs of screening for risk factors, as does an increase in the prevalence of that most modern of ills, being "at risk." In the case of illnesses with behavioral co-factors, there has been some support for the proposition that personalized relative risk information can enhance the chances of behavior change, but the impact may be slight and short-term, and in any event must be placed in the context of the overall difficulties of changing behavior.[27] In a larger sense, genetic screening threatens to be a readily commodifiable, culturally powerful approach to dealing with disease that will complicate the discovery and alteration of the pathogenic elements of the ecology. Angus Clarke argues that "the focus on genetic factors may distract attention from 'the real challenge of the future which appears to be the behavioral and social issues of risk reduction.'"[28]

Although the potential costs of genetic screening are high, they are not uniformly distributed across all uses of the technology. Genetic databases collected by the state, or under its auspices, for research purposes can be reliably protected, even in an environment consisting largely of electronic records, because there is no need to allow access for medical care or payment purposes. Such programs could move as much as possible to blinded collection or storage and can maintain rigid barriers to access without significantly burdening bona fide research.

Various populations are also likely to accept genetic screening to varying degrees, reflecting the different social and medical impacts genetic information can have and the level of access different populations have to those benefits, as well as their confidence in the legal protection of their social status. Resistance on the general ground of state intrusion into privacy is likely, including spill-over from efforts to gather and use genetic information for purposes of identification and law enforcement. Markers of serious future or inheritable diseases are likely to be stigmatizing, particularly insofar as insurers and employers use them to avoid health care costs. As genetic factors have more and more influence on individual social status, we can expect more principled resistance to screening. The popularity of prenatal screening, for example, is giving rise to concerns about the perceived value of disabled lives.[29]

The use of genetic screening for public health purposes will tend to be most effective when it serves a clear population goal, has a healthy ratio of overall economic and social benefits to costs, entails a just use of resources, and is acceptable to the populations it targets. We recognize that the public health agenda is never written by fully autonomous, fully informed rational actors on a clean slate.[30] Yet precisely because social and political factors influence public health policy so heavily, it is important to seize the opportunity for reflection before the time for action arrives and to at least aspire to rationality in the heat of action.

Given the unresolved issues of social cost and the limited promise of population health benefits, we remain skeptical that there is a clear basis for organized public health intervention on genetic matters. We are not arguing that screening is never useful, rather that the current ethical and legal implications of screening do not justify implementation of population-based screening for genetic conditions until there is for each intervention a clearer public health rationale and a strategy to win the acceptance of the targeted population.

LAW, POLITICS AND PUBLIC HEALTH: INSIGHTS FROM HIV SCREENING

The Rush to Testing and Screening

Screening tends to be powerfully attractive: the diagnostic gold standard for the physician, the key to accurate surveillance for the epidemiologist, and, for the worried citizen, the magic marker of the sick. Screening is feasible, tangible—if not the link to a cure, then the first step toward it. And there is money to be made. Commercial companies, for example, are quick to market "home tests" for BRCA1, even absent an established intervention.[31] It is precisely because testing can be so attractive, on so many levels, that there is a danger of investing in it too much, too soon. The HIV experience suggests that a major public health investment can be made under pressure, with enormous political consequences, simply because the technology exists. The adoption of counseling and testing by the Centers for Disease Control and Prevention as the centerpiece of its prevention program reflected the considerable political pressure to identify carriers, a medicalized view of public health, the control practices applied to sexually transmitted diseases and tuberculosis, even a desire to find ways to allow explicit education without offending the public or Senator Jesse Helms (R-N.C.). The strategy was chosen before basic decisions had been made about the use of the result, in reporting and partner notification, and before laws protecting testing privacy and prohibiting discrimination were solidly in place. Although the counseling and testing protocols of the CDC reflected the input of advocates, the program was launched with little data about how people would react to testing. Assessment of its probable impact on sexual or other risk behavior was almost entirely theoretical, to the degree there was a theory. A decade and several billion dollars later, there is still room to dispute its effectiveness.[32] Even the CDC's Advisory Committee on the Prevention of HIV Infection questioned the agency's excessive reliance on testing as the centerpiece of HIV prevention activities.[33]

In spite of the resources thrown into testing, its acceptance has not been overwhelming. Millions of tests have been performed, but there are still concerns that people at high risk are not taking the test as much as public health officials would like. Though screening programs and other associated measures like reporting and partner notification have been seen by some as "traditional," they have traditionally been problematic.[34] If large numbers of people are unhappy or worried and the requirement is avoidable, the HIV experience reminds us yet again that the rules can be frustrated.[35]

The experience with HIV sheds special light on the problem of using antidiscrimination and privacy law to reduce the social costs of screening and increase its acceptability. The passage of state privacy laws and, indeed, the extension of disability discrimination laws and their application to HIV were heavily influenced by the public health importance given to testing. The practical concern of encouraging compliance and avoiding stigmatization is mentioned explicitly in leading cases like School Board of Nassau County v. Arline and in statutes themselves.[36] This "antistigma project" in the law should by no means be taken to have succeeded, much less to be a model for use in the context of genetic screening.

Using Law to Reduce the Social Consequences of Screening

The most significant sociolegal experiment in HIV control has been the widespread use of privacy and confidentiality law to protect the social status of persons living with HIV and AIDS and to encourage them to comply with health advisories. When applied to genetic screening, this becomes problematic on several levels: the social construction of genetic "inferiority," the practical difficulties in extending meaningful protection to genetic status, and the lack of data on how law affects stigma-related behavior.

It is common to speak of health and illness as being socially constructed, meaning that these states depend for their definition on a web of social and cultural meanings of which we are commonly unconscious.[37] Law, too, is a social construct, but it is also a meaning-creating activity. Indeed, on some accounts, the main function of law is to normalize certain social arrangements and render others "deviant" or even unthinkable.[38] Law, on this view, both reflects and influences the social construction of those things to which it pertains.

People with HIV have been protected by privacy and disability discrimination laws, but from a critical standpoint, these laws have also contributed to the stigma associated with the disease. The price of having a refuge against discrimination has been acceptance of the label of "disabled," a source, at least, of cognitive dissonance for anyone "living with HIV." More fundamentally, as Wendy Parmet explains, there is a basic problem with the discrimination paradigm: in seeking to ensure "equal" treatment of people with HIV, it sets as the norm the status of those who do not have it, thus validating the very difference it purports to make suspect.[39] Similarly, the right to be left alone is the mirror image of the secrecy of stigma, so that, in the HIV epidemic, protection of privacy has been justified because "society's moral judgments about the high-risk activities associated with the disease, including sexual relations and drug use, make the information of the most personal kind."[40] Thus does law "protect" the silence of the love that had better not dare speak its name.

Carrying these arguments into the genetic field, Susan Wolf has argued the dangers of what she calls "geneticism":

> Like racism and sexism, it is a long-standing and deeply entrenched system for disadvantaging some and advantaging others. It can be seen in the pervasive individual and institutional use of genetic information and concepts to disadvantage people whether singly or by creating groups. It predates any accurate understanding of genetics, and now refers to social structures, practices, beliefs, and predispositions that together support disadvantaging based on a mixture of accurate and inaccurate genetic ideas.[41]

In her view, "antidiscrimination analysis cannot deal adequately with the pressing issues of genetic labeling and disadvantage. . . . [C]linging to 'genetic discrimination' . . . actually does damage by creating a false genetic 'norm,' frustrating structural reform, obscuring the deep psychological roots of genetic stereotyping and prejudice, and isolating genetic from other harms."[42] If we believe that law is supposed to influence attitudes and behaviors, we have to be worried about the content of the message, which not only supplies information but structures how we think about the issue. By "protecting" those with genetic "differences" from stigma and discrimination, we are actually reinforcing the belief in their inferiority or otherness. Although this may be a necessary evil, it ought not to be an unrecognized one.

Not that protection is easy. There are real practical problems to using the law for these purposes. The legislative response to genetic privacy concerns is following much the same track as the HIV experience: failed attempts at a national standard but widespread passage of state laws.[43] Providing for both efficient access and adequate privacy protection for health data are enormously complicated problems that we have not solved.[44] The patchwork protection of specific kinds of information, such as we have seen in both the HIV and genetic realms, is a response in avoidance of the problem. Such legislation is more politically "do-able"[45] and may have the advantage of sending a particularly strong message of the importance of privacy to the holders and users of records (though, as we discuss next, we know little about the effects of such laws), but in the end it cannot escape the larger privacy problem. A narrow definition of the protected information fails to provide adequate security, whereas broadly written provisions may impose unnecessary burdens on the proper use of data.[46]

Patchwork protection in and of itself is faulty on several grounds. Special rules require holders and transmitters of data, who seldom hold only those relating to HIV or genetic information, to apply different standards to different bytes of information in their possession. The practical burdens of segregating data or subjecting different quanta of data to different standards is probably substantial. Patchwork protection also accentuates the idiosyncratic quality of individuals' privacy concerns. Many people do indeed see secrecy as shame and are "out" about their HIV or genetic differences. For others, a diagnosis of venereal warts or genital herpes is as sensitive as one of HIV.

One of us has suggested elsewhere that "a more thoughtful solution would be to adopt a comprehensive federal statute on health information privacy, with explicit language applying privacy and security standards to genomic information. If genomic data were insufficiently protected by these legal standards, additional safeguards could be enacted."[47] Several bills providing a national privacy standard, including genetic privacy, are pending in Congress.[48] Passing individual statutes at the state or even the federal level will provide some protection, as it has for people with HIV, but even more than in the case of HIV it will leave loopholes, which will themselves reflect the political difficulties of securing protection as well as the problems inherent in protecting one kind of health data. We do not argue against privacy protection but do note the likely limits on its efficacy.

Of course, the fact that our health care and public health systems function reasonably well without strong privacy protection may suggest that privacy is more valued in theory than in practice. Americans, in spite of their strong expressions of concern to pollsters, may not frequently make health-related decisions based on privacy concerns.[49] We have already noted the corollary of this, that privacy can be a potent political issue even absent evidence of a breach. One of the conundrums of privacy law is that it may both fail to protect privacy in ways that hurt people, but of which they are unaware, and fail to reassure them in areas where it is, in fact, effective.

In both the HIV and genetic realms, privacy has been used as a proxy for antidiscrimination protection, particularly in insurance. That is, the role of the law is not to prevent the collection or proper use of the information but rather to prevent its falling into the wrong hands and being used to deprive the subject of a job, a service, or insurance. This is proving problematic. Absolute privacy cannot be guaranteed, particularly in the context of insurance. Insurers and self-insured employers, as the payers, have a claim on some information about what they are paying for that is not only reasonable but backed by considerable political clout. In both the HIV and genetic realms, it has often been difficult to place strong limits on insurers' access to records through state law. Even when limits are in place, insurers, whose business is built on discrimination, have a strong incentive to deduce information from other factors (like behavior in the case of HIV or family history in the context of genetics). As Parmet notes, "Substantive law allows—and public policies which encourage market-driven health insurance may even encourage—the precise types of discrimination that procedural privacy seeks to thwart."[50] In spite of the adage about the ounce of prevention, trying to control records in the hands of the good to forestall misbehavior by the bad could prove both burdensome for the good and ineffective against the bad.

This takes us to a final concern: the notion that public health policy makers can count on privacy and antidiscrimination law to regulate behavior and attitudes toward persons with genetic disease rests on two barely tested assumptions—that people know about the law and that it influences their behavior in desired ways. Our experience with HIV would suggest that the wish is not father to the deed. Although we rely on federal laws like the Americans with Disabilities Act and state statutes protecting confidentiality to influence the attitudes of the masses and the behavior of both those who might discriminate and those who might suffer discrimination, we have little evidence that any of these populations know about or understand the rules. Many public opinion polls have asked respondents about their views on matters such as isolation and screening and a patient's right to know his or her doctor's HIV status,[51] but they have not asked people if they are aware of or approve the legal rules relevant to these policies. Indeed, a review of 32 national opinion surveys between 1988 and 1991 reported only one asking respondents whether they supported the passage of the Americans with Disabilities Act.[52] Thus, even though we know a great deal about how the public feels about fair treatment and privacy, we do not know whether the attitudes reflect the law, the law reflects the attitudes, or the two are entirely unconnected. Without better data, we cannot begin to measure the influence of the antistigma project on public attitudes or predict with confidence the effect of genetic discrimination and privacy laws.

Similarly, studies of particular populations in a position to discriminate against people with HIV—employers, providers of public accommodations, and holders of medical information—shed little light on people's level of awareness of the law, how closely their understanding of its behavioral commands matches the prevailing views of lawyers and judges, how other attitudes influence their comprehension and interpretation of legal rules, and their attitudes toward the rules and the legal system generally. In fact, the only study we know of that probes this question, an attitude study of residents and house staff at a Pennsylvania medical center, found that most were unaware of a recently passed state HIV privacy and testing law.[53]

As for people subject to stigma and discrimination, the studies that have come closest to examining legal knowledge and attitudes have been those of people seeking the HIV test.[54] This literature supports the idea that privacy matters to people who are considering taking an HIV test but not whether they are aware of privacy and antidiscrimination laws and whether these laws influence their attitudes and behavior. Indeed, we know very little about the actual level of discrimination and breach of confidentiality. Although there are some reliable data on frequency of claims, litigation is not a good indicator of frequency of the underlying behavior.[55] "Testing" data are rare, so generally we must estimate the extent of HIV discrimination either by reference to self-reports by people with or at risk of HIV or from attitude studies of potential discriminators.[56]

Even less information is available about the relation of law to behavior of people with or at risk of the disease. The claim that legal protection against discrimination and release of private information will encourage people to be tested and, in a larger sense, provide a social context that supports positive changes in behavior, remains the most important and least studied policy argument in the HIV epidemic. It is notable that Tamara Hoxworth and colleagues found that only 1% of respondents indicated fear of reporting as their main reason for choosing anonymous testing.[57]

All this is not to suggest that the efforts to protect people with HIV have been unjustified and that no such effort should be made to protect those with disease of genetic origin. It does claim, however, that we can and should know more about both the extent of the problem and its nature in various contexts as we begin to craft sweeping policies to handle it. Above all, our claim is that the best protection against discrimination and invasions of genetic privacy lies in rigorous examination and justification for collection and use of genomic data, particularly on a population basis.

CONCLUSION

We do not oppose genetic screening and research, nor do we dispute that these pursuits hold important promise for public health; rather, we assert the critical value of the null hypothesis as a check on policy enthusiasm. We believe that much good has come from the use of law to protect people living with HIV and AIDS from the social consequences of the disease, but that is difficult to prove, and even if we could prove it, we would surely find that the blessings were not unmixed. We challenge proponents of public health interventions in genetics to address the issues we and others have identified in the hopes not of impeding technological progress but in using advancements in genetic understanding to enhance the health of the population.

NOTES

1. The Department of Defense's Registry and Specimen Repository for Remains Identification was authorized in 1991 to serve as an improved method for identifying soldiers' remains. Deputy Secretary of Defense memorandum no. 47803 (Dec. 16, 1991). See Information Management and Technology Division, General Accounting Office, CHCS Deployment Strategy, GAO/IMTEC-91-47 (1991), 1.
2. U.S. Department of Health and Human Services, *National Health and Nutrition Examination Survey III* (Washington, D.C.: Government Printing Office, 1994).
3. Jean E. McEwen and Philip R. Reilly, "Stored Guthrie Cards as DNA 'Banks,'" *American Journal of Human Genetics* 55 (1994): 196, 196–97.
4. Benjamin S. Wilfond and Norman Fost, "The Cystic Fibrosis Gene: Medical and Social Implications for Heterozygote Detection," *Journal of the American Medical Association* 263 (1990): 2777, 2779.
5. See Allan M. Brandt, Paul D. Cleary, and Lawrence O. Gostin, "Routine Hospital Testing for HIV: Health Policy Considerations," in Lawrence O. Gostin, ed., *AIDS and the Health Care System* (New Haven: Yale University Press, 1990).
6. In this we follow the model of Allan M. Brandt and colleagues.
7. For discussions of the differences between medicine and public health goals, upon which we have relied, see Geoffrey Rose, "Sick Individuals and Sick Populations," *International Journal of Epidemiology* 14 (1985): 32; Bernard Lo, "Ethical Dilemmas in HIV Infection: What Have We Learned?" *Law, Medicine, and Health Care* 20 (1992): 92; Mary Northridge, "Public Health Methods: Attributable Risk as a Link Between Causality and Public Health Action," *American Journal of Public Health* 85 (1995): 1202; and Ralph L. Keeney, "Decisions About Life-Threatening Risks," *New England Journal of Medicine* 331 (1994): 193.
8. Caryn Lerman and Robert Croyle, "Psychological Issues in Genetic Testing for Breast Cancer Susceptibility," *Archives of Internal Medicine* 154 (1994): 609.
9. Richard H. Morrow and John H. Bryant, "Health Policy Approaches to Measuring and Valuing Human Life: Conceptual and Ethical Issues," *American Journal of Public Health* 85 (1995): 1356.
10. See, e.g., Robert M. Kliegman, "Neonatal Technology, Perinatal Survival, Social Consequences, and the Perinatal Paradox," ibid., 909.

11. See Philip R. Reilly, "The Impact of the Genetic Privacy Act on Medicine," *Journal of Law, Medicine and Ethics* 23 (1995): 378, 380.
12. For a recent example, see Dermot MacDonald, "Cerebral Palsy and Intrapartum Fetal Monitoring," *New England Journal of Medicine* 334 (1996): 659; and Karin B. Nelson et al., "Uncertain Value of Electronic Fetal Monitoring in Predicting Cerebral Palsy," ibid., 613.
13. See discussion in Charles F. Clark and Michael D. Knox, "The Effectiveness of Condoms: An Individual versus a Societal Perspective," *AIDS and Public Policy Journal* 8 (1993): 193.
14. See Morrow and Bryant, "Health Policy Approaches."
15. See Paul Sorlies, Eric Backlund, and Jacob Keller, "U.S. Mortality by Economic, Demographic, and Social Characteristics: The National Longitudinal Mortality Study," *American Journal of Public Health* 85 (1995): 949; David Blane, "Editorial: Social Determinants of Health—Socioeconomic Status, Social Class, and Ethnicity," *American Journal of Public Health* 85 (1995): 903; Thomas A. LaVeist, "Segregation, Poverty, and Empowerment: Health Consequences for African Americans," *Milbank Quarterly* 71 (1993): 41; and George D. Smith and Matthias Egger, "Socioeconomic Differences in Mortality in Britain and the United States," *American Journal of Public Health* 82 (1992): 1979.
16. See Mervyn Susser, "Health as a Human Right: An Epidemiologist's Perspective on Public Health," *American Journal of Public Health* 83 (1993): 416.
17. See Thomas R. Frieden et al., "Tuberculosis in New York—Turning the Tide," *New England Journal of Medicine* 333 (1995): 229.
18. See Ronald Bayer, *Private Acts, Social Consequences: AIDS and the Politics of Public Health* (New York: Free Press, 1989); and Robert M. Wachter, *The Fragile Coalition: Scientists, Activists, and AIDS* (New York: St. Martin's Press, 1991).
19. For data on the fears of gay men with regard to data collection, see K. Siegel et al., "The Motives of Gay Men for Taking or not Taking the HIV Antibody Test," *Social Problems* 36 (1989): 368.
20. See Thomas McKeown, *The Role of Medicine: Dream, Mirage, or Nemesis* (Princeton, N.J.: Princeton University Press, 1979).
21. See Centers for Disease Control and Prevention, "Surveillance for and Comparison of Birth Defect Prevalences in Two Geographic Areas—United States, 1983–88," *Morbidity and Mortality Weekly Report* [SS–1] (1993); Centers for Disease Control and Prevention, "Surveillance for Anencephaly and Spina Bifida and the Impact of Prenatal Diagnosis—United States, 1985–1994," *Morbidity and Mortality Weekly Report* 44 [SS–4] (1995).
22. See Angus Clarke, "Population Screening for Genetic Susceptibility to Disease," *British Medical Journal*, July 1, 1995, 35.
23. See Samuel H. Preston and Michael R. Haines, *Fatal Years: Child Mortality in Late Nineteenth-Century America* (Princeton, N.J.: Princeton University Press, 1991).
24. James W. Hanson, "Birth Defects Surveillance and the Future of Public Health," *Public Health Reports* 110 (1995): 698.
25. Centers for Disease Control and Prevention, "Down Syndrome Prevalence at Birth—United States, 1983–1990," *Morbidity and Mortality Weekly Report* 43 (1994): 617.

26. See Sandi Wiggins et al., "The Psychological Consequences of Predictive Testing for Huntington's Disease," *New England Journal of Medicine* 327 (1992): 1401; Lerman and Croyle, "Psychological Issues in Genetic Testing"; and Paul R. Marantz, "Blaming the Victim: The Negative Consequence of Preventive Medicine," *American Journal of Public Health* 80 (1993): 1186.
27. See Rose, "Sick Individuals and Sick Populations."
28. Clarke, "Population Screening" (quoting Roger R. Williams, "Nature, Nurture and Family Predisposition," *New England Journal of Medicine* 318 [1988]: 769).
29. See Lois Shepherd, "Protecting Parents' Freedom to Have Children with Genetic Differences," *University of Illinois Law Review* (1995): 761.
30. Geoffrey Vickers, "What Sets the Goals of Public Health?" in Alfred H. Katz and Jean S. Felton, eds., *Health and the Community: Readings in the Philosophy and Sciences of Public Health* (New York: Free Press, 1965).
31. Tim Beardsley, "Vital Data: Trends in Human Genetics," *Scientific American* 274 (March 1996): 100.
32. For a review of the effectiveness of testing and counseling, see Jeff Stryker et al., "Prevention of HIV Infection: Looking Back, Looking Ahead," *Journal of the American Medical Association* 273 (1995): 1143. On the development of HIV testing policy, see Ronald Bayer, *Private Acts, Social Consequences;* and Scott Burris, "Testing, Disclosure, and the Right to Privacy," in Scott Burris, Harlon L. Dalton, and Judith Leonie Miller, eds., *AIDS Law Today: A New Guide for the Public* (New Haven: Yale University Press, 1993).
33. Centers for Disease Control and Prevention, Advisory Committee on the Prevention of HIV Infection, *External Review of CDC's HIV Prevention Strategies* (June 1994).
34. Scott Burris, "Public Health, 'AIDS Exceptionalism,' and the Law," *John Marshall Law Review* 27 (1994): 251.
35. Bernard J. Turnock and Chester J. Kelly, "Mandatory Premarital Testing for Human Immunodeficiency Virus: The Illinois Experience," *Journal of the American Medical Association* 261 (1989): 3415.
36. School Board of Nassau County v. Arline 480 U.S. 273 (1987); see Pa. Stat. Ann. tit. 35, § 7602 (1995).
37. See Elizabeth Fee and Nancy Krieger, "Thinking and Rethinking AIDS: Implications for Health Policy," *International Journal of Health Services* 23 (1993): 323.
38. Robert Gordon, "New Developments in Legal Theory," in David Kairys, ed., *The Politics of Law: A Progressive Critique,* 2d ed. (New York: Pantheon, 1990).
39. Wendy E. Parmet, "Discrimination and Disability: The Challenges of the ADA," *Law, Medicine and Health Care* 18 (1990): 331.
40. Doe v. Borough of Barrington, 729 F. Supp. 376, 384–85 (D.N.J. 1990).
41. Susan Wolf, "Beyond 'Genetic Discrimination': Toward the Broader Harm of Geneticism," *Journal of Law, Medicine and Ethics* 23 (1995): 345, 349–50.
42. Ibid.
43. Compare Scott Burris, "Testing, Disclosure, and the Right to Privacy," with Karen H. Rothenberg, "Genetic Information and Health Insurance: State Legislative Approaches," *Journal of Law, Medicine and Ethics* 23 (1995): 312.
44. Lawrence O. Gostin, "Health Information Privacy," *Cornell Law Review* 80 (1995): 451.

45. Usually, but not always. See Neil A. Holtzman, "The Attempt to Pass the Genetic Privacy Act in Maryland," *Journal of Law, Medicine and Ethics* 23 (1995): 367.
46. The depth of this problem is attested to by several of the contributors to a recent symposium on genetic screening and the law. See Lawrence O. Gostin, "Genetic Privacy," ibid., 320, 322; Reilly, "Impact of Genetic Privacy Act"; Rothenberg, "Genetic Information and Health Insurance"; and Wolf, "Beyond 'Genetic Discrimination.'"
47. Gostin, "Genetic Privacy"; accord Scott Burris, "Healthcare Privacy and Confidentiality: The Complete Legal Guide (Review)," *Journal of Legal Medicine* 16 (1995): 447.
48. See, e.g., S. 1360, 104th Cong., 2d Sess. (1996).
49. Gostin, "Health Information Privacy," 454.
50. Wendy E. Parmet, "Legislating Privacy: The HIV Experience," *Journal of Law, Medicine and Ethics* 23 (1995) 371, 372.
51. For example, Gregory M. Herek and John P. Capitanio, "Public Reactions to AIDS in the United States: A Second Decade of Stigma," *American Journal of Public Health* 83 (1993): 574; Robert J. Blendon, Karen Donelan, and Richard A. Knox, "Public Opinion and AIDS: Lessons for the Second Decade," *Journal of the American Medical Association* 267 (1992): 981; and Barbara Gerbert et al., "Physicians and Acquired Immunodeficiency Syndrome: What Patients Think About Human Immunodeficiency Virus in Medical Practice," *Journal of the American Medical Association* 262 (1989): 1969.
52. Blendon, Donelan, and Knox, "Public Opinion and AIDS."
53. Margaret Hoffman-Terry, Luther V. Rhodes, and James F. Reed III, "Impact of Human Immunodeficiency Virus on Medical and Surgical Residents," *Archives of Internal Medicine* 152 (1992): 1788. The literature on dental health care workers' attitudes, which one of us has recently reviewed, is more typical. Two studies of dental health care workers suggest the potential for law-related questions, but also the pitfalls for the legally unwary. See Scott Burris, "Dental Discrimination Against the HIV-Infected: Empirical Data, Law and Public Policy," *Yale Journal on Regulation* 13 (1995): 1.
54. Laura J. Fehrs et al., "Trial of Anonymous Versus Confidential Human Immunodeficiency Virus Testing," *Lancet* 1988 (2): 379; D. Hirano et al., "Anonymous HIV Testing: The Impact of Availability on Demand in Arizona," *American Journal of Public Health* 84 (1994): 2008; Tamara Hoxworth et al., "Anonymous HIV Testing: Does It Attract Clients Who Would Not Seek Confidential Testing?" *AIDS and Public Policy Journal* 9 (1994): 1982; S. M. Kegeles et al., "Many People Who Seek Anonymous HIV-Antibody Testing Would Avoid It Under Other Circumstances," *AIDS* 4 (1990): 585; Siegel et al., "Motives of Gay Men"; Pamela A. Meyer et al., "Comparison of Individuals Receiving Anonymous and Confidential Testing for HIV," *Southern Medical Journal* 87 (1994): 344.
55. Lawrence O. Gostin, "The AIDS Litigation Project: A National Review of Court and Human Rights Commission Decisions, Part I: The Social Impact of AIDS," *Journal of the American Medical Association* 263 (1990): 1961; Gostin, "The AIDS Litigation Project: A National Review of Court and Human Rights Commission Decisions, Part II: Discrimination," ibid., 2086; B. Friedland and R. Valachovic, "State Dental Boards' Policies on a Practitioner's Duty to Care for HIV Seropositive or AIDS Patients," *Journal of the American College of Dentists* 62, no. 3 (1995): 37.

56. Herbert M. Hazelkorn, "The Reaction of Dentists to Members of Groups at Risk of AIDS," *Journal of the American Dental Association* 119 (1989): 611; see Burris, "Dental Discrimination."
57. Hoxworth et al., "Anonymous HIV Testing."

[25]

Biobanking: International Norms

Bartha Maria Knoppers

While the socio-ethical and legal issues surrounding clinical genetics have long been the subject of international interest,[1] the thorny questions of genetic research and biobanking are more recent.[2] Add to this the fact that national guidelines and laws usually precede international policymaking, and the delay in international approaches is understandable. In that regard, the United Nations Educational, Scientific and Cultural Organization's 1997 Universal Declaration on the Human Genome and Human Rights[3] is unique in its prospective guidance on genetic research. Also, it is in the very nature of international normative instruments to be general, except on specific issues considered to be in the interest of humanity, such as research into human reproductive cloning[4] or access to AIDS drugs.[5]

It was, and is, the possibility of combining the power of informatics and microchip technologies with increasing knowledge of the probabilistic nature of genetic risk factors in common diseases that has propelled the debate on the ethical, social and legal questions of biobanking into the foreground. Indeed, it is the need for access to tissue (both normal and affected) for research into proteomics and pharmacogenomics as well as for the validation of an understanding of the relationship between genes and the environment, that has encouraged whole countries to undertake population biobanking projects.[6] While biobanks are attracting the interest of policymakers at the national level, there has been a corresponding debate at the international and regional (European) levels. This debate has focused on both the collection of DNA samples and access to genetic information for research.

It should be mentioned at the outset that there is considerable confusion in the terminology used to describe the identifiability of the samples deposited in biobanks. Only terms such as "identified," "nominative," or "personally identified" are understandable in the international arena. In contrast, "identifiable," "traceable," "pseudonymized," and "proportional" or "reasonable" anonymity are used interchangeably with the terms "coded" or "double-coded." The term "anonymous" (i.e., the sample never had any identifiers, such as specimens found on archeological sites), is often confused with "anonymized," the latter also called "unlinked," or "de-identified."[7]

Bartha Maria Knoppers, Ph.D., *is the Canada Research Chair in Law and Medicine and Faculty of Law at the Centre de recherche en droit public, University of Montreal. She received a B.A. from McMaster University, M.A. from the University of Alberta, LL.B. and B.C.L. from McGill University, D.L.S. from Cambridge University, and Ph.D. from the Sorbonne (Paris I).*

For the purpose of clarity, I use the following terms to describe sample identifiability: (i) anonymized (i.e., originally identified or coded/identifiable/traceable/pseudonymized that while including clinical or demographic data is now stripped of possible identifiers); and (ii) coded (i.e. single-coded or double-coded and identifiable only through breaking the unique or the two unique codes given the sample).

I will examine the varying responses in the international and regional (European) arena in the time period 1995-2004 with respect to samples already archived which were obtained during medical care, but are now to be used for research, and then the situation of samples to be obtained for research or where other research is now proposed. I conclude with a brief review of possible commercialization and patenting.

In short, the trend is moving towards permitting research on archived medical care samples without re-consent, subject to ethics approval, if such samples are either anonymized or exceptionally, if coded.

International

Medical Care Samples

Prior to the beginning of this century, with the notable exception of the Human Genome Organization's (HUGO) 1998 *Statement on DNA sampling Control and Access*,[8] international statements and guidelines on the ethics of genetic research failed to address the specific issue of archived samples originating from medical care, the context of medical care being largely left to individual countries. This was regrettable for many reasons, the major one being the extreme difficulty, if not impossibility, of fulfilling the ethical obligation of international collaboration in research due to the lack of guidance and harmonization of approaches. Acknowledging the value of such archived material and information, the impracticability in many cases of obtaining renewed consent, as well as the harm that could be caused to individuals who could be "faced with an unwarranted approach with information that they might not wish to know,"[9] international instruments are beginning to include limited exceptions to the traditional need for a renewed informed consent. At a minimum, ethics committees are beginning to relieve researchers from consent requirements for studies on anonymized samples and data.

While in its 1998 Proposed International Guidelines, the World Health Organization (WHO) did not take a position on left-over or "abandoned" medical care samples except to say that "specimens that could be useful to families in the future should be saved and should be available,"[10] it specifically addressed the issue of archived material in its 2003 report on genetic databases.[11] The latter enables the use of such material (e.g., "pre-existing health records, specific health disorder databases or physical samples that have been retained") when anonymized, and provided no future identification is possible of the "sample's source" notably through research results.[12] HUGO,[13] the Council for International Organizations of Medical Sciences (CIOMS)[14] and UNESCO[15] have adopted a less restrictive approach, enabling stored samples and data to be used not only in anonymized but potentially also in coded form without re-consent for research, provided certain conditions are met. For example, the HUGO Ethics Committee held in 1998 that:

> Routine samples, obtained during medical care and stored may be used for research if: there is a general notification of such a policy, [and] the patient has not objected, ...[in contrast] samples obtained during medical care and stored before notification of such a policy may be used for research if the sample has been anonymized prior to use.[16]

In the same way, the CIOMS, in its 2002 ethical guidelines for biomedical research, states that consent requirements can be waived provided individuals are notified and their confidentiality or anonymity is protected. However, it holds that "waiver of informed consent is to be regarded as uncommon and exceptional, and must in all cases be approved by an ethical review committee."[17] It further maintains that such an ethics committee can also waive some or all the requirements of the initial informed consent only for studies that pose minimal risks, are expected to yield significant benefits, and could not realistically or reasonably take place were consent requirements to be imposed (impracticability). The guidelines consider that prior opting out must be respected, except in situations of public emergencies, and that reluctance or refusal to participate is not sufficient to establish impracticability.[18]

Finally, UNESCO's 2003 International Declaration on Human Genetic Data leaves it to domestic legislation to implement the specific conditions pertaining to the secondary use of samples and data collected in the course of medical care.[19] Nevertheless, it holds that research can still be undertaken where data is anonymized ("irretrievably unlinked to an identifiable individual") or when consent cannot be obtained, if provided for by domestic law and with proper ethical oversight. Waiver of informed consent may also be warranted when important public interests are at stake, assuming that fundamental human rights are respected. In short, the trend is moving towards permitting research on archived medical care samples without re-consent, subject to ethics approval, if such samples are either anonymized or exceptionally, if coded, provided there are important health interests, there is notification of such a practice, and, no objection.

Research Samples

In regards to samples and data collected for a specific research project that are to be used subsequently for other research purposes, the CIOMS specifies that subsequent research be circumscribed by the original consent, and that any conditions specified in that initial consent apply equally to secondary uses.[20] It affirms the critical need for anticipation of future uses when samples and data are first collected. Thus, investigators should, during the original consent process, inform potential participants about any foreseen secondary uses, privacy protection or destruction procedures that will be implemented, and of their rights to request destruction of any material or information they deem sensitive, or to opt out in advance of such secondary research.[21] UNESCO's 2003 Declaration on Human Genetic Data holds that, health emergencies excepted, secondary uses incompatible with the conditions set out in the initial consent to research cannot proceed without a renewed consent.[22] Thus, *a contrario,* when secondary research uses involve related conditions (i.e. compatible) or, the description of the original research was for long-term biobanking and genetic epidemiology studies generally (i.e. with no specific research hypothesis), re-consent would not be necessary. HUGO's 1998 position contemplates notification of possible secondary uses and an opt-out procedure.[23]

Obviously future uses should be specifically consented to *ab initio* if foreseeable. Yet it is worthwhile mentioning the possible emergence of the notion of a well-informed generalized consent, a broad consent to future research, particularly adapted to large-scale longitudinal studies or genomic variation using human genetic research databases. Such broad consent, sometimes called "authorization,"[24] has not yet become the norm. Eventually, it may constitute an acceptable exception for certain types of biobanking research provided it is justified both scientifically and ethically and certain criteria are met.

Indeed in 1998, and in stark opposition to the more conservative positions of the time, the WHO's Proposed International Guidelines maintained that "a blanket informed consent that would allow use of a sample in future projects is the most efficient approach."[25] In its 2003 report on genetic databases, the WHO reaffirmed the possibility of a limited "blanket consent for future research" but only when data and samples are anonymized.[26] Referring to the specific topic of large-scale population human genetic databases, it insisted on the need for strong ethical justification to deviate from traditional consent requirements. In such a situation, a certain number of criteria must be satisfied with regard to the expected benefits, privacy protection, and education of the public for re-consent to be waived.[27]

The HUGO defines informed consent for research as including "notification of uses (actual or future), or opting out, or, in some cases, *blanket consent*" (emphasis added).[28] Finally, the Consortium on Pharmacogenetics is of the opinion that some flexibility should be allowed for in consent forms, consent to a "range of related studies over time" being a reasonable policy under certain circumstances.[29]

Recently, however, UNESCO's 2003 Declaration on Human Genetic Data held that "[h]uman genetic data and human proteomic data should not be kept in a form which allows the data subject to be identified for any longer than is necessary for achieving the purposes for which they were collected or subsequently processed."[30] Thus, if the purpose of the study is longitudinal in nature, double coding could be held to constitute sufficient protection. The WHO, maintaining the value of privacy, requires the anonymization process to be scrutinized by an ethics committee, a necessary intermediary to ensure its legitimacy and maintain adequate standards.[31] In contrast, the Consortium on Pharmacogenetics assesses the advantages and drawbacks of anonymization compared to coding (single or double), stating its preference for the latter.[32]

In conclusion, the international efforts undertaken to differentiate between data and samples that are anonymized, coded, or identified should be underscored and welcomed. These distinctions impact the rules which apply to secondary uses of data and samples, publication of results, transfer and trans-border exchange of information, and the right to withdraw, to name but a few. Yet, while international bodies are more explicit in their guidance on "genetic" data, confusion still reigns due to the use of different taxonomies and overall, the failure to anticipate the need for rules for population biobanks and ongoing longitudinal studies. Moreover, the terminology used to describe samples and data is still confusing and there is no clarity. This undermines possible harmonization due to the resulting complexity, especially when new concepts such as reasonable or proportional anonymity are introduced.[33] Similarly anonymization, while often ethically and legally expedient, undermines the scientific usefulness of the samples over time since no further clinical data can be added to the database because tracing the sample back is impossible. Likewise, the individual can never personally benefit from any results. International bodies have yet to support the obvious personal and scientific advantages of double-coding.

Regional (European)

Medical Care Samples

At the regional level, other than upholding the need for informed consent for all medical interventions including research, the Council of Europe's Convention on Human Rights and Biomedicine[34] provides little guidance on genetic research with regard to archived samples left over after clinical care. Article 22 maintains that: "[w]hen in the course of an intervention any part of a human body is removed, it may be stored and used for purposes other than that for which it was removed only if this is done in conformity with appropriate information and consent procedures." No definition of what is considered appropriate can be found in the Convention, as it is left to the discretion of member states.

However, guidance may be found in the European Society of Human Genetics (ESHG) 2001 Recommendations on Data Storage and DNA Banking[35] and in the Council of Europe's Draft Proposal for an Instrument on the Use of Archived Human Biological Materials in Biomedical Research.[36] These texts do not specifically refer to samples left over from clinical care but rather to archived samples or existing collections generally. The ESHG recommendations are notable in that they distinguish existing collections based on the degree of identifiability of the samples and data and the length of storage. The Society considers that consent requirements can be waived when samples are anonymized[37] and provided there is ethics committee approval, in situations where the collection can be considered as abandoned ("old collections").[38] For collections of coded information, while in principle re-consent of participants for new studies is necessary, ethics review committees can waive the requirement for such consent when recontact is impracticable and the study poses minimal risks.[39]

In contrast, the Draft Proposal of the Council of Europe would not allow re-consent to be waived when stored biological clinical material and data are to be used subsequently for research.[40] Consent can, however, be either implicit or explicit depending on the intrusiveness of the study and the previous directives of the donor.[41] Obviously, individuals enjoy the right to withhold their sample from certain future research uses of their sample and the right to consent to subsequent procedures.[42]

Research Samples

The Council of Europe's Draft Proposal and the ESHG's recommendations both insist on the need to differentiate research samples according to their degree of identifiability. On the one hand, the Council of Europe proposal holds that the decision to use coded, identified or "linked anonymized" human biological material or personal data "shall be justified by the needs of the research" without further explanation.[43] On the other hand, the European Society of Human Genetics explains that while anonymization is acceptable for "sample and information sharing for research purposes with minimum risk," maintaining identifiability as protected by coding is valuable and advisable as it "will permit more effective biomedical research and the possibility of re-contacting the subject when a therapeutic option becomes available."[44] This is a reasonable position since it is based on the fundamental principles of ethics committee oversight and informed consent for "all types of DNA banking."[45] It contemplates the possibility of obtaining consent for broad research uses, the consequence being that individuals need not be re-contacted although they are to be kept informed and are to be given the possibility to express their desire to withdraw.[46]

While international documents urge groups, communities and populations to become involved in the discussion surrounding the establishment of large-scale population human genetic research databases, the ESHG goes one step further requiring additional consent "at a group level through its cultural appropriate authorities" for population studies.[47] This latter suggestion bears examination. How it will be implemented in practice remains to be seen. Indeed, it might prove difficult to define what would amount to adequate community or group consent, what degree of opposition would result in the study not being undertaken, and the consequences as far as other rights, notably that of individual participation or withdrawal, are concerned.

At the regional level then, there seems to be a growing recognition of the shortcomings of anonymization and the therapeutic and research potential of coding as well as for a possible broad consent for secondary uses, all subject to ethics review and the right to object and to withdraw.

Commercialization

Intimately linked to the issue of ownership of samples and data and their possible commercialization is that of the legal status of human genetic material. Surprisingly, a different legal status – person or property – has not had a concomitant impact on the ultimate issue, that of control of access by the individual over its use by others. Internationally and regionally, legal and ethical instruments acknowledge the sensitivity of genetic material. This results from its individual but also familial and communal nature, as well as potential value and significance.[48] Traditional legal categories (property or person) cannot account for the alleged, unique nature of genetic information.

At the international level, there is increasing recognition and confirmation that, at the level of species, the human genome is the common heritage of humanity,[49] and that human genetic research databases are global public goods.[50] The notion of "common heritage of humanity" means that, at the collective level of the human genome, like outer space and the sea, no individual exclusive appropriation is possible by nation states. Other characteristics of this approach include peaceful and responsible international stewardship or custodianship with a view to future generations as well as equitable access by all. In the absence of a binding international treaty (UNESCO's Declaration and HUGO's positions being only proclamatory in nature), it remains to be seen if this concept will come to legally binding fruition.

Other than upholding the need for informed consent for all medical interventions including research, the Council of Europe's Convention on Human Rights and Biomedicine provides little guidance on genetic research with regard to archived samples left over after clinical care.

The position that human genetic research databases are global public goods, however, serves to place new sequences and information into the public domain. While patenting is not the subject of this article, both a personal or property approach to DNA samples would theoretically require specific individual consent to eventual patenting. Indeed, whether the DNA sample has the status of a right of personality or that of property, consent must be obtained, or at a minimum there must be notification of patenting, as mentioned under the 1998 European Directive.[51] At the international and regional levels then, this position in favor of both the common heritage level of the collective human genome, of databases being in the public domain, and that personal control over individual samples and information has slowly been consolidated.

Moreover, the last few years have seen the emergence of a new concept in the international arena, that of benefit-sharing. This approach, first proposed in the 1992 Convention on Biodiversity (Rio Convention)[52] and then for human genetic research by HUGO[53] and subsequently adopted by UNESCO[54] and WHO,[55] is gradually taking hold. It mandates recognition of the participation and contribution of participating individuals, populations and communities. Founded on notions of justice, solidarity and equity, it upholds the common heritage approach and so encourages the "giving-back" by researchers or commercial entities.[56] This return of benefit "to the society as a whole and the international community"[57] can accrue to the population to which the participants belong, as well as to infrastructures such as healthcare systems notably through the resulting availability of new prevention and diagnostic tools and treatments proceeding from research, and finally to developing countries that do not possess the means to adequately collect and process data in their own territory.[58]

Generally, the language of property is not found in international instruments, which as we have seen, emphasize the common heritage concept[59] or the notion of "general property" or "public domain,"[60] thus obviating the issue of status, excluding private ownership by the "donor" and concentrating on "shared goods." One recent exception to this trend is, however, worth mentioning, the 2003 WHO report on Genetic Databases.[61] Promoting the protection of individual interests and rights, the WHO maintains that individuals should remain the primary controllers of their genetic information if identifiable. That is to say, in the absence of identifiability, normative instruments do not apply (tissues, as such, not being persons). But, in contrast to the language of "donors" or "gift," it recommends that "[s]erious consideration should be given to recognising property rights for individuals in their own body samples and genetic information derived from those samples." It does however, adopt the benefit-sharing approach in recommending that "some kind of benefit will ultimately be returned, either to the individual from whom the materials were taken, or to the general class of person to which that individual belongs."[62]

Turning to the regional level, the "gift" language of a decade ago, was replaced with "source," and "owner," only to return again in the following years.[63] Although mentioning the traditional gift relationship as worthy of consideration, the policy of the ESHG on Data Storage and DNA Banking of Biomedical Research[64] adopts the position that ownership and access agreements should not be regulated by legislation. It upholds the principle according to which, unless anonymized and thus abandoned, samples and data should remain under the control of the individual; the investigator and processor acting as custodians. It also affirms that in determining intellectual property rights, due consideration should be paid to the notion of benefit sharing.[65]

The 1997 European Convention[66] takes no explicit position and limits itself to prohibiting financial gain by stating, "[t]he human body and its parts shall not, as such, give rise to financial gain,"[67] thus, indirectly, eschewing a property approach. This principled proscription of financial gain is reiterated specifically in the context of archived human biological material and personal data used in biomedical research in its 2002 Draft Proposal on Archived Biological Materials.[68] The Proposal further suggests that "[r]esearch on human biological materials and personal data shall be undertaken if this is done in conformity with appropriate consent procedures."[69] Consent to the further use of stored samples and data for research includes consent to eventual commercialization as the participant must be informed of "any foreseeable commercial uses of materials and data, including the research results." It remains to be seen if this proposal is adopted. The Council of Europe in its 2001, Recommendation 1512 – Protection of the Human Genome has adopted the notion of the human genome as the "common heritage of mankind" in order to limit patenting rights, urging member states to change "the basis of patent law in the international fora."[70]

Overall then, international and regional normative instruments uphold the common heritage concept, reaffirm control by individuals of the use of their samples, promote benefit-sharing, and require at a minimum, notification of possible commercialization.

Overall then, international and regional normative instruments uphold the common heritage concept, reaffirm control by individuals of the use of their samples, promote benefit-sharing, and require at a minimum, notification of possible commercialization. The result of all this debate as well as of increased commercialization of genetic research, is that most, if not all, consent forms now inform research participants of eventual commercialization and possible patents. Yet, rarely is mention made of benefit-sharing. The issue of benefit-sharing raises the possibility of balancing the legitimate return on investment (profit-making) with concerns with equity, justice and reciprocity for participating individuals, families, communities and populations. It requires further study in order to not only ensure its practicability but also avoid it becoming indirect inducement.[71]

Finally, it should be mentioned that as concerns patentability, some clarification has been forthcoming in that raw sequences with no specific or substantial utility are seen as being in the public domain and not patentable *per se*. Furthermore, on May 18, 2004, the European Patent Office revoked Harvard's European patent on the BRCA2 gene based on the fact that there were errors in the description of the sequences and that some of the information was already in the public domain at the time of filing.[72] While an appeal has been filed by Myriad (holder of the patent), the fundamental debate is continuing in Europe on the issue of commercialization of genetic discoveries.

Conclusion

Taking the issues raised above in turn, it is clear that consent is key both to the future uses of samples archived after medical care and to the possible secondary uses of research samples. We have also seen that notification of possible secondary research and commercialization uses allows for opting-out. With the gradual move towards allowing biobanks to obtain a broad consent for future secondary research using either anonymized or (preferably) coded samples and data, public notification and the safeguards of ongoing ethics review may become sufficient. Double coding with a third party being the keyholder effectively allows the researcher to use research materials and yet send information back to the clinician via the keyholder. Likewise, the clinician can download ongoing clinical data to the researcher via the keyholder thus improving the quality of the research and eventual results. Such double coding also allows withdrawal by the participant at any time. Could it be that we are finally moving away from the privatization of the sample, from persons as owners of the "property" of every cell, to citizens participating for public health, for the public good with no immediate personal benefit? Or, will paternalistic ethics committees "protect" participants from consenting "broadly?" Isn't such consent with authorization for future unknown uses an expression of their personal values and autonomy; that is, improved research outcomes?

Acknowledgements

This article is based in part on the chapter "Ethical Aspects of Genome Research and Banking" by B. M. Knoppers, and C. Sallée in *Essentials of Genomics and Bioinformatics*, ed. C. Sensen, (2005) Wiley-VCH (forthcoming). Research was funded by DOE (0009939); Genome Canada/Quebec (0009877); CIHR (FFO-62453). The author wishes to thank Madelaine Saginur for her invaluable assistance. Research completed up to: 08/04.

References

1. J. C. Fletcher and D. Wertz, eds., *Ethics and Human Genetics: A Cross-Cultural Perspective* (New York: Springer-Verlag, 1989); J. C. Fletcher and D. Wertz, eds., *Genetics and Ethics in Global Perspective* (The Hague: Kluwer Academic Publishers, 2004).
2. B. M. Knoppers, ed., *Human DNA: Law and Policy* (The Hague: Kluwer Law International, 1997); B. M. Knoppers, ed., *Populations and Genetics: Legal and Socio-Ethical Perspectives* (Leiden: Martinus Nijhoff, 2003).
3. United Nations Educational, Scientific and Cultural Organization (International Bioethics Committee), *Universal Declaration on the Human Genome and Human Rights*, Paris, November 11, 1997, Official site of the UNESCO, *at* <http://www.unesco.org/shs/human_rights/hrbc.htm> (last visited January 13, 2005).
4. United Nations - Ad Hoc Committee on an International Convention against the Reproductive Cloning of Human Beings, Report of the Ad Hoc Committee on an International Convention against the Reproductive Cloning of Human Beings, New York, March 8, 2002, *at* <http://www.un.org/law/cloning/> (last visited January 13, 2005); Council of Europe (CE), ETS No. 168, Additional Protocol to the Convention for the Protection of Human Rights and Dignity of the Human Being with Regard to the Application of Biology and Medicine, on the Prohibition of Cloning Human Beings, Paris, 1998 *at* <http://conventions.coe.int/treaty/en/Treaties/Html/168.htm> (last visited January 13, 2005).
5. World Trade Organization, DOHA WTO Ministerial Declaration, WT/MIN(01)/DEC/1, Fourth Session, *at* <http://www.wto.org/english/thewto_e/minist_e/min01_e/mindecl_e.pdf> (last visited January 13, 2005).
6. C. Sallée, *Existing Human Genetic Research Databases: Context (Consent Mechanisms and Communication Strategies)*, paper presented at the OECD Meeting, Tokyo, Japan, February 26-27, 2004.
7. B. M. Knoppers and M. Saginur, "Towards a Common Language for Biobanking" (in preparation).
8. Human Genome Organization (1998), Statement on DNA Sampling: *Control and Access* (February 1998): 6: 1; *Genome Digest* 8, *at* <http://www.gene.ucl.ac.uk/hugo/sampling.html> (last visited February 28, 2005).
9. World Health Organization (European Partnership on Patients' Rights and Citizens' Empowerment) (2003), *Genetic Databases - Assessing the Benefits and the Impact on Human Rights and Patient Rights*, Geneva, 2003, *at* <http://www.law.ed.ac.uk/ahrb/publications/online/whofinalreport.rtf> (last visited January 13, 2005), (Sect. 4.4).
10. World Health Organization (1998), *Proposed International Guidelines on Ethical Issues in Medical Genetics and Genetic Services*, Report of a WHO Meeting on Ethical Issues in Medical Genetics, Geneva, December 15 and 16, 1997, Official site of the World Health Organization, *at* <http://whqlibdoc.who.int/hq/1998/WHO_HGN_GL_ETH_98.1.pdf> (last visited January 13, 2004), (guideline 10).
11. World Health Organization, *supra* note 9.
12. World Health Organization, *supra* note 9 (rec. 10).
13. Human Genome Organization, *supra* note 8.
14. Council for International Organizations of Medical Sciences (2002), *International Ethical Guidelines for Biomedical Research Involving Human Subjects*, Geneva, November 2002, Official site of the CIOMS, *at* <http://www.cioms.ch/frame_guidelines_nov_2002.htm> (last visited January 13, 2004), (guideline 4).
15. United Nations Educational, Scientific and Cultural Organization (2003), *International Declaration on Human Genetic Data*, Geneva, October 16, 2003, Official site of UNESCO, *at* <http://portal.unesco.org/shs/en/file_download.php/6016a4bea4c293a23e913de638045ea9Declaration_en.pdf> (last visited January 13, 2004), (arts. 16 and 17).
16. Human Genome Organization, *supra* note 8 (rec. 2).
17. Council for International Organizations, *supra* note 14 (guideline 4).
18. Council for International Organizations, *supra* note 14 (commentary on guideline 4).
19. Nations Educational, Scientific and Cultural Organization, *supra* note 15 (art. 16).
20. Council for International Organizations, *supra* note 14 (commentary on guideline 4).
21. Council for International Organizations, *supra* note 14 (commentary on guideline 4); See also, e.g. for genetic databases, *supra* note 12 (rec. 6).
22. Nations Educational, Scientific and Cultural Organization, *supra* note 15 (arts. 16 and 17).
23. Human Genome Organization, *supra* note 8.
24. V. Arnason, "Coding and Consent: Moral Challenges of the Database Project in Iceland," *Bioethics* 18 (2004): 27-49.
25. World Health Organization, *supra* note 10 (Tab. 10, guideline 10).
26. World Health Organization, *supra* note 9.
27. World Health Organization, *supra* note 9 (rec. 14).
28. Human Genome Organization (2002), *Statement on Human Genomic Databases*, London, December 2002, Official site of HUGO, *at* <http://www.hugo-international.org/hugo/HEC_Dec02.html> (last visited January 13, 2005), (rec. 4).
29. Consortium on Pharmacogenetics (2002), *Pharmacogenetics: Ethical and Regulatory Issues in Research and Clinical Practice*, April 2002, *at* <http://www.firstgenetic.net/latest_news/article_16.pdf> (last visited January 13, 2005), (Research B).
30. United Nations Educational, Scientific and Cultural Organization, *supra* note 15 (article 14 [e]).
31. World Health Organization, *supra* note 9 (Sect. 4.2 and rec. 7).
32. Consortium on Pharmacogenetics, *supra* note 29 (Research F).
33. World Health Organization, *supra* note 9 (4.2).
34. Council of Europe, *Convention for the Protection of Human Rights and Dignity of the Human Being with Regard to the Application of Biology and Medicine*, Oviedo, April 4, 1997, Int. Dig. Health Leg. 48, 99, Official site of the Council of Europe, *at* <http://conventions.coe.int/treaty/en/treaties/html/164.htm> (last visited January 13, 2005).
35. European Society of Human Genetics, *Data Storage and DNA Banking for Biomedical Research: Technical, Social and Ethical Issues*, Birmingham, November 2001, official site of the ESHG, *at* <http://www.eshg.org/ESHGDNAbankingrec.pdf> (last visited January 14, 2005).
36. Council of Europe (Steering Committee on Bioethics), *Proposal for an Instrument on the Use of Archived Human Biological Materials in Biomedical Research*, Strasbourg, October 17, 2002, *at* <http://www.coe.int/T/E/Legal_affairs/Legal_co-operation/Bioethics/Activities/Biomedical_research/CDBI-INF(2002)5E.pdf> (last visited January 14, 2005).
37. European Society of Human Genetics, *supra* note 35 (rec. 9).
38. European Society of Human Genetics, *supra* note 35 (rec. 14).
39. European Society of Human Genetics, *supra* note 35 (rec. 12).
40. Council of Europe, *supra* note 36 (art. 14).
41. Council of Europe, *supra* note 36 (art. 16).
42. Council of Europe, *supra* note 36 (art. 15.1).
43. Council of Europe, *supra* note 36 (art. 9).
44. European Society of Human Genetics, *supra* note 35 (rec. 10-11).
45. European Society of Human Genetics, *supra* note 35 (rec. 3).
46. European Society of Human Genetics, *supra* note 35 (rec. 8).
47. European Society of Human Genetics, *supra* note 35 (rec. 15).
48. See e.g. Nations Educational, Scientific and Cultural Organization, *supra* note 15 (4[a]); See e.g. Council of Europe, *supra* note 34 (art. 21).
49. See e.g. United Nations Educational, Scientific and Cultural Organization, *supra* note 3 (art. 1); Human Genome Organization (1996), *Statement on the Principled Conduct of Genetic Research* (May 1996) 3: 2 Genome Digest 2, *available at* <http://www.gene.ucl.ac.uk/hugo/conduct.htm> (last visited January 14, 2005).
50. Human Genome Organization, *supra* note 28.
51. European Parliament (1998), *Directive 98/44/EC of the European Parliament and of the Council of 6 July 1999 on the Legal Protection of Biotechnological Inventions* (July 30, 1998) L 213 Official Journal of the European Communities p.13, Official site of the European Union, *at* <http://europa.eu.int/eur-lex/pri/en/oj/dat/1998/l_213/l_21319980730en00130021.pdf> (last visited January 14, 2005).
52. *Convention on Biological Diversity*, Rio de Janeiro, June 5, 1992,

at <www.biodiv.org> (last visited January 14, 2005).
53. Human Genome Organization, *Statement on Benefit-Sharing*, Vancouver, April 9, 2003, *at* <http://www.gene.ucl.ac.uk/hugo/benefit.html> (last visited January 14, 2005); Human Genome Organization, *supra* note 28.
54. United Nations Educational, Scientific and Cultural Organization, *supra* note 15.
55. World Health Organization, *supra* note 9.
56. *Convention on Biological Diversity*, *supra* note 52.
57. United Nations Educational, Scientific and Cultural Organization, *supra* note 15 (art. 19).
58. United Nations Educational, Scientific and Cultural Organization, *supra* note 15 (art. 19).
59. United Nations Educational, Scientific and Cultural Organization, *supra* note 49.
60. Human Genome Organization, *supra* note 28.
61. World Health Organization, *supra* note 9.
62. World Health Organization, *supra* note 9 (rec. 19).
63. See e.g. European Society of Human Genetics (Public and Professional Policy Committee), *Population Genetic Screening Programs: Technical, Social and Ethical Issues, Recommendations of the European Society of Human Genetics*, July 2000, Official site of the European Society of Human Genetics, *at* <http://www.eshg.org/ESHGscreeningrec.pdf> (last visited January 14, 2005).
64. European Society of Human Genetics, *supra* note 35.
65. European Society of Human Genetics, *supra* note 35 (art. 27).
66. Council of Europe, *supra* note 34.
67. Council of Europe, *supra* note 34 (art. 21).
68. Council of Europe, *supra* note 36.
69. Council of Europe, *supra* note 36 (article 14).
70. Council of Europe (Parliamentary Assembly), Recommendation 1512 (2001), Protection of the Human Genome by the Council of Europe, 2001, Official site of the European Council, *at* <http://assembly.coe.int/Documents/AdoptedText/ta01/erec1512.htm> (last visited January 14, 2005), (vi).
71. L. Sheremata and B. M. Knoppers, "Beyond the Rhetoric: Population Genetics and Benefit Sharing," *Health Law Journal* 11 (2003): 89-117.
72. European Patent Office, Press Release, *'Myriad/Breast Cancer' Patent Revoked after Public Hearing* (May 18, 2004). Online: <http://www.european-patent-office.org/news/pressrel/2004_05_18_e.htm> (last visited January 14, 2005).

[26]

Harnessing the Benefits of Biobanks

Lori B. Andrews

We have a thriving biotechnology industry in the United States. There are over 1,450 biotechnology companies developing diagnostic and treatment technologies in medicine, creating more nutritional foods, and innovating new industrial processes.[1] Yet this $28.5 billion sector of the economy is not without controversy.[2] The "bio" in biotechnology comes from living, biological entities - people, plants, animals, and even bacteria. In the realm of biobanking, people are the source of the raw material for the discovery of genes for research, diagnosis, and therapy, raising a host of issues about rights and responsibilities, fiduciary duties and societal obligations.

When I was growing up, it was said that the chemicals in the body were worth 89 cents. Today, though, like a bullish stock market, the price tags on body parts have soared. The value of a human egg can be tens of thousands of dollars. A single cadaver can be mined for medical and research uses - its skin worth $36,522, its bones $80,000, its tendons $21,400, and so forth. The value of a particularly interesting human gene - or even snippets of human genetic material - can be billions.

New uses for human tissue are constantly being discovered. Researchers funded by the biotech company Geron used leftover embryos that had been created by *in vitro* fertilization (IVF) patients to create the most coveted of human cells: embryonic stem cells, which are primitive cells that can grow into every type of body tissue, including nerves, bones, and muscles.[3] In the future, biotech companies could use stem cells to produce marketable treatments - such as new heart cells to inject into an ailing heart, which would then repair itself.

And it is not just the medical sector that finds human tissue useful. Tissue such as blood, hair, and DNA - and even human corpses - are used as a medium by artists. In the United States, artist Marc Quinn created *Self*, a sculpted model of his head using nine liters of his own frozen, congealed blood.[4] In Great Britain, Canadian artist Richard Gibson was fined for outraging public decency when he sculpted a head of a woman and then used actual aborted human fetuses as earrings.[5] German pathologist Gunther von Hagens has outraged and entertained people around the world with his controversial *Korperwelten* exhibit featuring real human corpses in artistic displays, often in familiar poses such as running, sitting, gesturing, and playing chess.[6]

Due to its multiple uses in the biotechnology age, human tissue is being gathered and stored in reposito-

Lori B. Andrews, J.D., *is Distinguished Professor of Law, Chicago-Kent College of Law, Director, Institute for Science, Law and Technology at Illinois Institute of Technology and Chairman of the Board, Institute on Biotechnology and the Human Future. She received her B.A. (1975) and J.D. (1998) from Yale.*

Biobanks can be established without oversight, even without the knowledge of people whose tissues are used. Yet the practice of biobanking raises profound ethical and legal questions about the circumstances under which such banks are established and how the benefits of the banks are harnessed.

ries known as biobanks. Some biobanks have been created indirectly, when, for example, the pathology department of a hospital stores biopsy samples from cancer patients or the criminal justice system keeps blood samples collected from felons for DNA databases. Others have been created directly, such as ones owned by entrepreneurs who solicit hospitals for access to their tissue samples or by families of patients with particular diseases who want to encourage research into their disorder.

The range of human tissue sources available to researchers and biotech companies is extraordinary. There are brain tissue banks, breast tissue banks, blood banks, umbilical cord banks, sperm banks, and tissue repositories for studying AIDS, Alzheimer's, other mental illnesses, and aging. Over 282 million archived and identifiable pathological specimens from more than 176 million individuals are being stored in United States repositories.[7] At least 20 million new specimens are added each year. Some specimens are anonymized or coded and not identified with specific individuals; others carry patient names or codes that allow personal identification.[8] Between these pathology samples, forensic samples, public health samples, and samples collected on people associated with the military, virtually everyone has his or her tissue "on file."

Expanding markets have increased the value of this tissue. Hospitals, research laboratories, and the state and federal repositories that store tissue samples find they possess a capital resource. In October 2001, I spoke to the national meeting of the College of American Pathologists and learned that health care institutions were routinely selling their patients' tissue to biotechnology companies, often without consent of the patients involved. Some pathologists in the audience said that adequate diagnosis was being impeded by these sales. Pathologists would attempt to undertake an autopsy, but find that the bones and other tissue had already been removed for sale, preventing them from correctly assessing the medical condition of the individual. One forensic coroner said that he had to put his foot down and require that sales be made after his autopsy because the practice was impeding his ability to investigate crimes. Other attendees suggested that these sales were the death knell for non-commercial research. A geneticist indicated that he had attempted to do a study on leftover placentas in his hospital, but was told that the Obstetrics and Gynecology Department had sold them all to a biotech company.

Biobanks vary in whether the biobank owner is willing to allow access by outside researchers to the tissue samples. In some instances, any researcher can order cell lines of particular types of patients through a catalogue. The entries in American Tissue Culture Catalogue[9] and its foreign counterparts,[10] for example, describe in telegraphic style the people whose tissue is for sale. CRL 5867 – a 49-year-old black female with cancer of the lymph node. JCR B0068 – a 14-week-old Japanese fetus who died of cytomegalovirus. SK-HEP-1 – a 52-year-old German man with liver cancer. Thousands of individuals are listed, but it is doubtful that more than a handful of them or their families realize that they are part of this elite market.[11]

The more recent trend, however, is for most research biobanks to hoard tissue samples, rather than to share them with other researchers. When Jonathan Shestack wanted to fund research on the genetics of autism, each university researcher he visited told him that they did not have enough tissue samples from families with autism to identify the gene responsible for the disease.[12] When Shestack asked why they did not share samples with researchers at other institutions, the researchers described their commercial motives. They each said they wanted to be the one to discover the autism gene and patent it.

Biobanks can be established without oversight, even without the knowledge of people whose tissues are used. Yet the practice of biobanking raises profound ethical and legal questions about the circumstances under which such banks are established and how the benefits of the banks are harnessed. While the concept of battery protects living people from physical interventions, and the Uniform Anatomical Gift Act gives them control over what happens to their body parts after they die, there is no overriding legal concept to govern the relationship between the tissue source and the biobank. Indeed, the principle most commonly applied seems to be that of "finders keepers" where pathologists, physicians, and researchers who have access to patient tissue feel no qualms about keeping it for their own use, beyond the purposes for which the tissue was collected.[13]

Biobanking raises a series of questions, which this issue of the journal seeks to address, such as:

What type of information, if any, should the source of the tissue be given before tissue is entered into a biobank?

What cultural and personal values might it violate for person's tissue to be used without his or her informed consent?

What should be done with genetic information gleaned from a biobank?

Under what circumstances is commercialization of biobank samples and information appropriate?

How should the fruits of biobanking be distributed?

How can people protect themselves from unauthorized and unwanted use of, or commercialization of, their tissue samples?

What new institutional policies and legal regulations might be necessary to govern the emerging biobank economy?

Informed Consent and the Sensibilities of the Tissue Source

A basic tenet of research law and ethics is that research should not be undertaken without the subject's consent.[14] The research goals of advancing scientific understanding and curing diseases are laudable, but research is not a matter of conscription. People can refuse to participate in research, even if it involves no risk to them and enormous potential benefit to the community. Thus, they could readily refuse to give blood to a biobank in the first place. With respect to federally-funded research, the protections of human subjects, including the right to refuse to participate in research, are codified in federal regulations.[15] But what about research that involves not an intervention on the person, but on a snippet of their tissue in a biobank – or in a facility that proposes to sell the tissue to the biobank?

Some researchers argue that the federal regulations requiring informed consent for human research do not apply to previously-collected tissue samples, such as those in hospital pathology labs. Indeed, 45 C.F.R. § 46.101 of the federal regulations governing human research states that:

> (b) Unless otherwise required by department or agency heads, research activities in which the only involvement of human subjects will be in one or more of the following categories are exempt from this policy:...
>
> (4) Research, involving the collection or study of existing data, documents, records, pathological specimens, or diagnostic specimens, if these sources are publicly available or if the information is recorded by the investigator in such a manner that subjects cannot be identified, directly or through identifiers linked to the subjects.

This provision was adopted long before the advent of widespread genotyping and genetic sequencing, and before the troubling commercialization that now dominates health care institutions and academic research.[16] "The thirty years since the establishment of the National Commission for the Protection of Human Subjects (NCPHS) have seen changes in the world and in research, both swift and sweeping. The moral landscape and the horizon are no longer recognizable," note Charles MacKay and Gerald S. Schatz. Among these changes are "(t)he expanded commercialization of the research enterprise."[17] Consequently, it is inappropriate to use § 46.101(b)(4) to allow research on previously-collected samples, such as those in biobanks, without the specific informed consent of the tissue source. In some instances, the regulation on its face will not apply; for example, the provision does not provide an exception to the requirements of informed consent for samples that are collected initially in situations that do not involve diagnosis or pathology. It does not cover, for example, samples collected initially for research purposes or law enforcement uses. But, more importantly, the exemption only applies to research on samples without identifiers. Now that DNA typing is available which can identify individuals, samples cannot ever be truly anonymized.

Moreover, even if a sample could be anonymized, research on it without consent may still disturb the tissue source. Such research may conflict with the personal preferences or religious beliefs of the tissue source. Albert Einstein said he wanted to be cremated, yet his brain was kept by a young pathologist after Einstein's death without his previous consent, even though the pathologist had many opportunities to talk to Einstein across the months as he drew his blood to monitor his health.[18]

Anonymous research on biobank samples might also lead to discrimination against the tissue source, not because his or her individual identity was revealed, violating traditional notions of privacy, but because of some characteristic revealed about him or her as a member of a group. If research on samples in a biobank shows that a particular ethnic group has a higher incidence of a certain illness or a genetic predisposition to a disfavored behavior, individuals from that ethnic group may face stigmatization and discrimination.

Research on tissue from people from certain ethnic or religious groups may disturb other members of that group, including relatives of the people whose tissues were used for research. In the Orthodox Jewish community, unauthorized use of body tissue violates religious beliefs because the religion requires that the body be buried whole.[19] If a person's leg is amputated during his or her life, arrangements are made to store that body part for burial with the individual after death.[20] Rabbis apparently asked the pathologist for Einstein's brain so that it could be buried, allowing the scientist to rest in peace.[21] Similar issues are raised by research on Native Americans, when graves of their ancestors were disturbed to acquire bones for research. According to James Riding In, "Many Indians assert that disinterment stops the spiritual journey of the dead, causing the affected spirits to wander aimlessly in limbo. These affected spirits can wreak havoc among the living, bringing sickness, emotional distress, and even death."[22]

Changes in the culture of research since the adoption of the federal regulations also prompt concerns that were not envisioned at the time the informed consent exemption in § 45 C.F.R. 46.101(b)(4) was enacted. The federal human research regulations were adopted at a time when pathologists used existing tissue samples for non-commercial purposes, such as to attempt to improve a test to diagnose a certain disorder. They were adopted before the enactment of the federal technology transfer laws that allowed university researchers and federal researchers using federal funds to personally benefit financially from the research, such as by patenting a gene they identified in a patient's tissue.[23]

Now, however, any tissue sample on the shelf anywhere is potentially in the pipeline toward commercial research. Yet some individuals object to their tissue being patented[24] or their body being used by a for-profit enterprise. In 1951, a 31-year-old African-American woman, Henrietta Lacks, died of ovarian cancer. Without the knowledge or consent of Lacks or her family, her tissue was taken and made into a cell line that has been extremely valuable for research and is still sold today. In an interview in 1994, her husband said, "As far as them selling my wife's cells without my knowledge and making a profit – I do not like that at all. They are exploiting both of us."[25]

For people whose tissue is used without consent, there are concerns that their doctors will view them as "treasure troves" and order unnecessary interventions. This was underscored in the case of *Moore v. Regents of the University of California*[26] when the court recognized that physician/researchers have a fiduciary duty to their patients to disclose their intent to use patient tissue samples for research or commercial purposes. The California Supreme Court pointed out, "A physician who adds his own research interest to this balance may be tempted to order a scientifically useful procedure or test that offers marginal, or no, benefits to the patient."[27]

Because of the increasing recognition that unauthorized use of previously-collected tissue samples might violate the values of the tissue source, social norms are evolving to recognize that the tissue source should have greater control over the subsequent use of his or her samples. In Florida, for example, a person's genetic material may not be tested without consent, even for important research purposes.[28] Today, various professional organizations, and even some biotechnology companies, require that, when the tissue is first extracted from people, they be given information about potential research and commercial uses on their tissue and a chance to refuse to allow the use of their tissue for such purposes.[29] The American Medical Association's Code of Ethics provides that "[p]otential commercial applications must be disclosed to the patient before a profit is realized on products developed from biological materials" and "[h]uman tissue and its products may not be used for commercial purposes without the informed consent of the patient who provided the original cellular material."[30]

Just as professional guidelines have evolved to evince concern about the wishes of the tissue sources, so have the protocols of particular projects. NUGENE, the biobank established by Northwestern University School of Medicine, has established extensive guidelines for informed consent.[31] The biotechnology company Ardais, which has deals in place with Harvard and Duke to undertake genetic research on their hospital patients' tissue, also requires informed consent.[32]

Yet none of the professional guidelines, university consent materials, or consents used by biotechnology companies establishing biobanks provide information that could be key to a true informed consent: information about how the research on the patient's tissue or its subsequent commercialization is likely to impact access to diagnostics and treatment technologies and how commercialization might influence the research enterprise overall.

Commercialization of Biobanks

Much of the current activity of biobanks focuses on the identification – and subsequent patenting – of genes and segments of DNA that might be useful in diagnostic testing, gene therapy, and drug development. With gene patents potentially worth over a billion dollars a year to the patent holder,[33] it is no wonder that companies are willing to pay sums such as $200 million for access to biobank research on particular disorders.[34] Yet gene patenting poses potential harms to the tissue

People participate in health care research to further the development of medical diagnostics and treatments. Patenting genes discovered in biobank tissues can thwart that goal, however. Some gene patent holders have used their monopoly power to actually prevent other researchers from undertaking research on the disease that their gene patent covers.

source, the health care system, and the research enterprise. These problems are sufficiently troubling that the American Society of Human Genetics and the College of American Pathologists oppose gene patents as threatening medical advances and patient care.[35] Consequently, tissue sources should be informed - in advance of any research on their tissue - about whether or not genes discovered in their tissues (or related products created based on this genetic information) will be patented, how the patent will be licensed, and what the impact of the patent is likely to be on health care and research.

This is material information because when a gene is discovered in a biobank tissue sample and patented, the gene patent holder can charge whatever it wants for a diagnostic test for mutations in that gene (or any other use of the gene). The patent holder can prohibit anyone else from performing a diagnostic test for the gene, and instead require all doctors to send the patient's sample for testing to the patent holder's own lab, which may be in another state or even another country. In fact, the tissue source whose gene was patented could find that he cannot afford the test or treatment created with his own gene or that he cannot get access to a genetic diagnostic test for family members because the gene patent holder is restricting who may perform the test.

In the future, a person might want to get a scan of his whole genome, all 30,000 genes. The technology to do so is already technically available, but cannot be implemented due to the financial and practical limitations put in place by gene patent holders. Myriad Genetics, which holds the patent on the BRCA1 gene, charges $1500 for the test.[36] Multiply that by the 30,000 genes in a person's body and it is clear that a whole genome scan would be unaffordable if every gene was patented and access to it was priced in the Myriad way. Already, one in four laboratories has stopped performing certain genetic tests because of patent restrictions or excessive royalty costs.[37] Half had not developed a test for fear of running afoul of patent law.

People participate in health care research to further the development of medical diagnostics and treatments. Patenting genes discovered in biobank tissues can thwart that goal, however. Some gene patent holders have used their monopoly power to actually prevent other researchers from undertaking research on the disease that their gene patent covers.[38] The risks of gene patents to health care are much greater than the risks of granting a patent on a drug or medical device. Other researchers can create alternatives to drugs and devices. There are no alternatives to the patented human genes in genetic diagnosis and gene therapy.

Companies now sequence disease-causing bacteria and virus genes and gain patents on the genome of the infectious disease. In fact, in one instance, a company wants to introduce inexpensive, quick public health testing for a common infectious disease - but the company holding the patent on the gene for the infectious disease has forbidden it. Similarly, genetic tests are possible to determine if a drug will be effective on a particular patient. Most drugs only work on a percentage of patients who use them. But what if the holder of the genetic segment for the test also manufactures the drug? There may be an incentive not to employ the test in order to protect the market for the drug. For example, one pharmaceutical company has filed for a patent on a genetic test to determine the effectiveness of one of its asthma drugs. But the company says it will not develop the test - or let anyone else develop it.[39] In trademark law, the holder can lose the trademark if he does not use it for three years[40] and in some European nations, a patent holder must "work" the patent.[41] But in the United States a patent holder can deny society access to a genetic sequence for the term of the patent, twenty years from the date of filing the application.

To the extent that people's tissue is used without their consent or people are asked to donate their tissue for research purposes without being told of the specific problems created by commercialization of tissue via intellectual property rights, tissue sources cannot adequately protect themselves against the harms that gene patents entail for access to health care and for appropriate medical research. For example, knowing of the potential barriers that gene patents pose for accessible health care and widespread research, an individual may wish to donate his tissue to a biobank that will not patent any gene segments discovered - or that will allow access of other researchers and health care providers to the gene.

The Moral and Legal Obligations to Tissue Sources

The people whose tissue is used by biobanks for research and commercialization provide the raw material for an important social enterprise. Usually when an entity provides raw material for any business (including health care enterprises), they are compensated. Yet this is not the case with biobanking. The sources of tissue are not only generally unable to reap commercial rewards from the use of their own tissue, they are not even allowed to limit problematic commercial uses of their tissue by others. This manifest unfairness has led professional organizations[42] and courts[43] to question how tissue sources might share in the financial benefits that accrue from discoveries made through biobank research.[44]

The Human Genome Organization (HUGO), an international organization of genetics researchers, has pioneered the discussion of benefit sharing. Yet its recommendations seem paradoxical. It recommends against undue inducement through compensation for individual participants, families, and populations. Although HUGO recommends against financial compensation, it suggests that the communities participating in research receive non-financial benefits through "agreements with individuals, families, groups, communities or populations that foresee technology transfer, local training, joint ventures, provision of health care or of information infrastructures, reimbursement of costs, or the possible use of a percentage of any royalties for humanitarian purposes."[45]

Because HUGO is an international entity which needs to be concerned about the values of many cultures, perhaps it is understandable that it wants to protect potential research participants from the dangers associated with money.[46] HUGO would not want people in certain indigenous cultures, for example, to run roughshod over their cultural values for pay, particularly when the decision to participate in such research could disturb other members of the group. This could be true, for example, of research on Native Americans or indigenous populations around the world.

In mainstream U.S. culture, however, there are already precedents for payment for tissue and no cultural ban against it. The state laws that ban payment for organs for transplant do not ban payment for replenishable tissue, such as blood, which is the main tissue collected by biobanks. In the United States the purveyors of sperm or eggs usually receive compensation, which can be quite extensive. (One man, for example, markets his sperm over the internet for $4000 a vial.) One way for the tissue source to capture some of the value of his tissue from the biobank and to control how that tissue is used is through contracts and joint ventures that recognize the contributions from the source.[47] Already, some patient groups are entering into agreements through which they receive a portion of the royalties attributable to the patent on their gene.

Even when there has not been a specific agreement establishing a joint venture between the tissue source and the biobank, one court has suggested that the individuals who provided tissue to a researcher for the discovery of a particular disease gene, as well as some funding for the research, could maintain a claim of "unjust enrichment" against the researcher and the hospital that patented the gene and charged a fee for use of the genetic sequence in testing.[48] In extreme instances, the biobank that unjustly enriched itself might be required to disgorge all of its profits to the tissue sources.[49]

There is an inherent flaw in the three ways that the problems in biobanking have been dealt with thus far – the HUGO formulation for benefit sharing, the joint venturing with patient groups, and the legal declaration of unjust enrichment. None of these approaches provide protection against commercialization per se, or the problems that can be caused by patents. In fact, the court that recognized the claim for unjust enrichment also held that the tissue sources had no right to be informed about the potential commercialization of their tissue before they provided tissue to the researcher.[50] This could lead to the anomalous situation where a person's tissue could be used for commercial purposes without his knowledge or consent in ways that violate his personal or religious beliefs, and his only legal remedy would be to get a cut of the action after the offending act takes place. Because of the limits of these three current approaches, innovative new policies may be necessary to assure that both the contributors to biobanks and society at large are sufficiently protected.

Structuring Biobanks for the Good of Society

Adequate regulation of biobanking requires a focus on the unique aspects of this business: its raw material is derived from people; its "product" is often the genetic information derived from analysis of this raw material; there are conflicts over the legal status of both the raw materials[51] and the product[52]; and the product has no ready substitutes.

For all these reasons, health care providers and researchers establishing biobanks should be viewed as having a fiduciary duty to tissue sources. If people's samples are entered into a biobank or research is undertaken on samples already in a biobank, the biobank should assure that participation by sources is informed and voluntary. A general blanket consent to all future research should not be considered sufficient to meet the standards of informed consent.[53] People whose tissue samples are solicited or used should be given adequate information upon which to base their decision, including whether the use of their present or past tissue samples will lead to patents - and, if so, it should be disclosed that such patents can lead to higher cost diagnostics and treatments. Patient tissue sources should be told that perhaps other researchers would allow them to participate in a joint venture governing the use of their tissue.

Such requirements will protect people against having tissue used in an unauthorized way or in a way that violates their personal and religious beliefs. But those requirements may not be sufficient to protect society as a whole from the effects of biobank commercialization. For that, more radical policies might be needed - such as allowing health care providers and researchers to use the genetic sequences discovered in the people's tissue in biobanks without having to pay a royalty in order to protect access to health care and to encourage research.[54]

Whatever policies we develop, we cannot lose sight of the fact that the bio in biotechnology - the genes in the gene patents - come from people. And the scientific enterprise must have the trust of those people in order to get them to give up their tissue for research into diagnostics and cures. The raw material in the biotech industry is not widgets. It is pieces of my body, and your body, and all of our bodies. The policies that are developed should assure that society harnesses the benefits of biobanks for all of us.

Acknowledgements
The research for this article was supported in part by grants from the Office of Science, U.S. Department of Energy (Grant No. DE-FG02-02ER63460) and the Robert Wood Johnson Foundation (Investigator Awards in Health Policy Research Program). The views expressed are those of the author and do not imply endorsement by the Department of Energy or the Robert Wood Johnson Foundation. The author would also like to thank Jordan Paradise, J.D., for her intellectual insights on gene patents.

References
1. Biotechnology Industry Organization, *Biotechnology Industry Facts, at* <http://www.bio.org/speeches/pubs/er/statistics.asp> (last visited December 23, 2004).
2. Biotechnology Industry Organization, *Biotechnology Industry Facts, at* <http://www.bio.org/speeches/pubs/er/statistics.asp> (last visited December 23, 2004).
3. J. A. Watson et al., "Embryonic Stem Cell Lines Derived From Human Blastocysts," *Science* 282 (1998): 1145-1147.
4. "Incarnate" exhibition in Gagosian Gallery, New York City: Catalog (New York: Gagosian, February, 1998).
5. "Fetus Earrings Made to Promote Debate Says Artist," *Daily Telegraph* (London), February 8, 1989, at 3.
6. "Korperwelten," Catalog of the exhibit at the State Museum of Technology and Labor (Mannheim, October 30, 1997, to February 1, 1998); see also, E. L. Andrews, "Anatomy on Display and It's All Too Human," *New York Times*, January 7, 1998, at A1.
7. National Bioethics Advisory Commission, *Research Involving Human Biological Materials: Ethical Issues and Policy Guidance* (Rockville, MD: National Bioethics Advisory Commission, 1999).
8. M. Wadman, "Privacy Bill Under Fire From Researchers," *Nature* 392 (1998): 6.
9. American Tissue Culture Catalogue, *at* <http://www.atcc.org> (last visited December 23, 2004).
10. See, e.g., *World Data Center for Microorganisms, at* <http: wdcm.nig.ac.jp/DOC/menu3.xml> (last visited December 23, 2004).
11. John Moore's cells are for sale as CRL-8066; a plasmid containing Moore's DNA sequence that codes for colony stimulating factor is sold as ATCC 39754.
12. E. Marshall, "Whose DNA is it anyway?" *Science* 278 (1997): 564-567.
13. L. Andrews and D. Nelkin, *Body Bazaar* (New York: Crown Publishers, 2001): at 9-11; see also S. F. Witelson, D. L. Kigar, and T. Harvey, "The Exceptional Brain of Albert Einstein," *Lancet* 353 (1999): 2149-2153, at 2150.
14. The Nuremberg Code states that "the voluntary consent of the human subject is absolutely essential."
15. See 45 C.F.R. § 46.101 et seq. (1997).
16. The Code of Federal regulations provisions governing federal research 45 CFR § 46.101 et seq. were adopted in 1974 as 45 C.F.R. 46. The provision that is the current 46.101(b)(4) was adopted in 1981.
17. C. MacKay and G. S. Schatz, "The Unfinished Research Agenda," presentation to the National Institutes of Health Inter-Institute Bioethics Internet Group, June 7, 2004. This has led the Secretary of Health and Human Services to release a new guidance, "Financial Relationships and Interest in Research Involving Human Subjects: Guidance for Human Subjects Participation."
18. Einstein's brain tissue was tested for a genetic propensity to aneurysm. S. McCartney, "Believing Einstein's Brain Matters, Doctors Keep the Remains," *Asian Wall Street Journal*, May 6, 1994. If such a propensity was found, it could have implications for his blood relatives - since their insurers might refuse to insure them based on this genetic flaw. "Einstein's Brain," *The Economist*, April 2, 1994, at 82.
19. Jewish tradition maintains that as man was created in the image of God, in death the body should retain the unity of that image. M. Lamm, *The Jewish Way in Death and Mourning* (New York: Jonathan David Publishers, 1969): at 10. If parts are removed, they must be returned and buried with the body. *Kohn v. United States*, 591 F.Supp. 568 (E.D.N.Y. 1984), citing Fred Rosner, "Autopsy in Jewish Law and the Israeli Autopsy Controversy," in F. Rosner and J. D. Bleich (eds.), *Jewish Bioethics* (New York: Hebrew Publications, 1979): at 332. Court cases have recognized that a patient's religious beliefs should be taken into consideration in determining what is proper handling of their bodies. See, e.g., *Lott v. State of New York*, 32 Misc. 2d 296, 225 N.Y.S.2d 434 (Ct. Cl. 1962).
20. In fact, when Menorah Gardens and Funeral Chapels lost an amputated leg of an Orthodox Jewish woman, it made a $1.25 million lawsuit settlement with her daughter. "Orthodox Jews believe that at the end of time, not only will a person's soul be resurrected, but the body as well....It's important that the whole body, including blood, be buried." H. Fitzgerald, Jr., "Woman Awarded $1.25 million in Suit; Funeral Home Must Compensate for Losing Mother's Amputated Legs," *Sun-Sentinel* (Fort Lauderdale), May 16, 1997, at 1B.
21. See S. LaFee, "Einstein's Mind: His Brain Sits on a Shelf, Largely Unsought by the World," *The San Diego Union-Tribune*, May 17, 1995, at E1.
22. J. Riding In, "Without Ethics and Morality: A Historical Overview of Imperial Archaeology and American Indians," *Arizona State Law Journal* 24 (1992): 11-34, at 11, 13.
23. Prior to the 1980s, if a university or federal researcher discovered or invented something using federal funds, that advance belonged to the public. The researchers could not personally profit. But with the passage of the Bayh-Dole Act, and the Stevenson-Wydler Act in 1980, and the Federal Technology Transfer Act, in 1986, the rules changed completely.
These legal measures were enacted to encourage the commercial development of government-funded research. The Bayh-Dole Act allows universities and non-profit institutions to apply for

patents on federally-funded inventions and discoveries and provides significant tax incentives to companies investing in academic research. 35 U.S.C. § 200-211 (2004). The Technology Transfer Act allows researchers in government facilities, including scientists at the National Institute of Health, to patent their inventions, and keep up to $150,000 of the yearly royalties on top of their government salaries. 15 U.S.C. § 3710c (a) (3) (2004). The law allows government researchers to enter into commercial arrangements (known as CRADAs – cooperation research and development agreements) with for profit companies. 15 U.S.C. § 3701-3714 (2004).

Overnight, behavior that would have sent federally-funded university researchers to the penitentiary in the 1960s and 1970s – personally profiting from research done on taxpayers' expense – was not only legal, but encouraged. See L. Hayflick, "Novel Techniques for Transforming the Theft of Mortal Human Cells Into Praiseworthy Federal Policy," *Experimental Gerontology* 33 (1998): 191-207, at 204. Largely as a result of these legal changes, NIH patent applications increased nearly 300 percent. See S. Krimsky, "The Profit of Scientific Discovery and its Normative Implications," *Chicago-Kent Law Review* 75 (1999): 15-39, at 22. But not all political leaders were convinced it was a wise move. Then-Congressman Al Gore argued that the arrangement was akin to "selling the tree of knowledge to Wall Street." S. Shulman, *Owning the Future* (New York: Houghton Mifflin Company, 1999): at 114.

24. P. R. Reilly, M. F. Boshar, and S. H. Holtzman, "Ethical Issues in Genetic Research: Disclosure and Informed Consent," *Nature Genetics* 15 (1997): 16-20.
25. H. A. Washington, "Henrietta Lacks – An Unsung Hero," *Emerge*, October 1994, at 29.
26. *Moore v. Regents of University of California*, 51 Cal. 3d 120, 132-133, 793 P.2d 479, 486, 271 Cal. Rptr. 146, 153 (1990) (physician/researcher had a duty of informed consent to disclose that he was undertaking research and that he was commercializing it).
27. *Id.* at 130.
28. Fla. Stat. Ann. § 760.40 (1995).
29. American Society of Human Genetics, "Statement on Informed Consent for Genetic Research," *American Journal of Human Genetics* 59 (1996): 471-474.
30. American Medical Association, *Code of Ethics*, E-2.08, *at* <http://www.ama-assn.org/ama/pub/category/2512.html> (last visited December 23, 2004).
31. See R. Chisholm, "Protocol Title: Gene-Disease Association and Treatment Outcomes," September 18, 2002 (on file with author).
32. In 2002, Ardais earned over $4 million in subscription and licensing revenue for the library, with revenue projections set at $18 million for 2004. A. Connolly, "Ardais Ambitious With Plans For Clinical Genomics," *Boston Business Journal*, November 22, 2002, *available at* <http://boston.bizjournals.com/boston/stories/2002/11/25/story2.html> (last visited December 23, 2004).
33. S. M. Thomas et al., "Ownership of the Human Genome," *Nature* 380 (1996): 387-388.
34. R. Kunzig, "Blood of the Vikings," *Discover* 19 (1998): 90-99.
35. College of American Pathologists Advocacy, *Gene Patents Detrimental to Care, Training, Research, at* <www.cap.org/apps/docs/advocacy/advocacy_issues/issue_genepat.html> (last visited December 23, 2004).
36. Phone conversation with Myriad representative (June 2, 2004).
37. R. Kotulak, "Taking License with Your Genes: Biotech Firms Say They Need Protection," *Chicago Tribune*, September 12, 1999, at 1, citing a survey of 120 labs by University of Pennsylvania bioethicist Jon Merz.
38. K. Blanton, "Corporate Takeover Exploiting the US Patent System," *Boston Globe*, February 24, 2002, at 10.
39. G. Anand, "Big Drug Makers Try to Postpone Custom Regimens," *Wall Street Journal*, June 18, 2001, at B1.
40. 15 USCS § 1127 (2004).
41. N. Macfarlane, "The Tension Between National Intellectual Property Rights and Certain Provision of EC Law," *European Intellectual Property Review* 16 (1994): 525-530, at 526. To "work" the patent means to sufficiently commercialize the invention and make it available in order to meet the needs of the particular country.
42. HUGO Ethics Committee, *Statement on Benefit-Sharing, April 9, 2000, at* <http://www.gene.ucl.ac.uk/hugo/benefit.html> (last visited December 23, 2004).
43. *Greenberg v. Miami Childrens Hospital*, 264 F. Supp. 2d 1064 (S.D. Fla. 2003).
44. The idea of benefit sharing has been addressed on numerous occasions in the international context. See, e.g., HUGO Ethics Committee, *Statement on Human Genomic Databases, December 2002, at* <http://www.gene.ucl.ac.uk/hugo/HEC_Dec02.html> (last visited December 23, 2004) (recommendation 6: "Researchers, institutions, and commercial entities have a right to a fair return for intellectual and financial contributions to databases." They recommend that there should be "reciprocity and exchange of information with fair return" with fair return mechanisms being "non-exclusive licenses, copyright, monetary, non-monetary (e.g. publication or credits), database pools, and central repositories." They also provide that "any fees should not restrict the free flow of scientific information and equitable access."); HUGO Ethics Committee, *Statement on Benefit-Sharing, April 9, 2000, at* <http://www.gene.ucl.ac.uk/hugo/benefit.html> (last visited December 23, 2004) (Recommendation 3: "...there should be prior discussion with groups or communities on the issue of benefit-sharing."); HUGO Ethical, Legal, and Social Issues Committee Report to HUGO Council, *Statement on the Principled Conduct of Genetics Research*, March 21, 1996, *at* <http://www.gene.ucl.ac.uk/hugo/conduct.htm> (last visited December 23, 2004) (Recommendation bullet 9: "That undue inducement through compensation for individual participants, families, and populations should be prohibited. This prohibition, however, does not include agreements with individuals, families, groups, communities or populations that foresee technology transfer, local training, joint ventures, provision of health care or of information infrastructures, reimbursement of costs, or the possible use of a percentage of any royalties for humanitarian purposes."); UNESCO, *International Declaration on Human Genetic Data, October 16, 2003, at* <http://portal.unesco.org/shs/en/ev.php-URL_ID=1882&URL_DO=DO_TOPIC&URL_SECTION=201.html> (last visited December 23, 2004)(Article 19: *Sharing of Benefits:* "...benefits resulting from the use of human genetic data, human proteomic data or biological samples collected for medical and scientific research should be shared with the society as a whole and the international community." These benefits include "access to medical care," "provision of new diagnostics, facilities for new treatments or drugs stemming from the research," and "support for health services."); UNESCO, *Universal Declaration on the Human Genome and Human Rights, July 17, 2002 at* <http://www1.umn.edu/humanrts/instree/Udhrhg.htm> (last visited December 23, 2004)(Article 12(a): "Benefits from advances in biology, genetics and medicine, concerning the human genome, shall be made available to all, with due regard to the dignity and human rights of each individual."); Council for International Organizations of Medical Services (CIOMS), *International Ethical Guidelines for Biomedical Research Involving Human Subjects, 2002 at* <http://www.cioms.ch/frame_guidelines_nov_2002.htm> (last visited June 4, 2004)(Geneva)(Guideline 10: *Research in populations and communities with limited resources:* "Before undertaking research in a population or community with limited resources, the sponsor and the investigator must make every effort to ensure that: the research is responsive to the health needs and the priorities of the population or community in which it is to be carried out; and any intervention or product developed, or knowledge generated, will be made reasonably available for the benefit of that population or community.")
45. HUGO Ethical, Legal, and Social Issues Committee Report to HUGO Council, *Statement on the Principled Conduct of Genetics Research, Recommendation 9, March 21, 1996, at* <http://www.gene.ucl.ac.uk/hugo/conduct.htm> (last visited December 23, 2004).

46. This is especially true since international genetics research tends to target certain isolated populations that have greater genetic homogeniety and thus disease genes can be more readily identified since they stand out. The Pima Indians in Arizona, for example, have had a very high rate of diabetes. The Bedouins in Israel include many people with a congenital form of deafness, and the Amish have a high rate of apparently inherited depression. P. M. Rowe, "Lessons About NIDDM from the Pima Indians," *Lancet* 347 (1996): 1320; P. Salopek, "Genes Offer Sampling of Hope and Fear; Cures Possible, but Groups Worry about Exploitation," *Chicago Tribune*, April 28, 1997, at 1. Other targeted populations have been chosen as research subjects because their genes seem to protect them against specific diseases. People from the village of Limone Sur Gardi in Italy were relatively isolated until the 1950s because the road system was not nearby. They are of scientific interest because of the striking absence of heart disease in the population. Blood samples from the people, taken in 1994, revealed that thirty citizens had a unique gene that protected them from arterio-sclerosis and, therefore, from heart disease. P. Salopek, "Basically, We Are All the Same; Controversial Genetic Quest is Unlocking Secrets of the Human Rainbow," *Chicago Tribune*, April 27, 1997, at 1; S. Goetnick, "Artherosclerosis Prevention a la Milanese," *Harvard Health Letter* (May 1996). The Cherokee of Oklahoma seem resistant to Alzheimers. R. C. Risser, et al., "Genetic Factors for the Development of Alzheimer's Disease in the Cherokee Indians," *Archives of Neurology* 997-1000 (1996); and the Hagahai from Papua, New Guinea are resistant to a leukemia-causing virus, HTLV. G. Taubes, "Scientists Attacked for Patenting Pacific Tribe," *Science* 270 (1995): 1112. Elderly Chinese people are genetically interesting as research subjects because of their unusual longevity. Z. Dang and X. Lei, "Chinese Center Sues over Study Coverage," *Science* 283 (1999): 1990-1992. The genes of all these groups are potentially valuable resources.
47. When Sharon Terry learned that her two young children had inherited PXE (pseudoxanthorma elasticum), a connective tissue disorder that leads to blindness and potential heart attacks, several groups of researchers called to ask for tissue samples from her children to try to find the gene. M. Fleischer, "Seeking Rights to Crucial Gene," *The National Law Journal*, June 25, 2001, at C1. She inquired as to why they did not get samples from other researchers and was told that scientists would not share the samples. Terry started a bank with tissue samples from her children and began a collaborative project with researchers. When University of Hawaii pathobiologist Charles Boyd isolated the gene, he listed Sharon Terry as a co-inventor on the patent. The PXE patients' group she formed will make the decisions about how to license the rights to the gene. Additionally, the PXE group will give 50% of the resulting royalties to the University. This way the PXE patients' group can keep the price of diagnostic tests down by licensing providers who charge a lower fee.
48. *Greenberg v. Miami Childrens Hospital*, 264 F. Supp. 2d 1064 (S.D. Fla. 2003).
49. See *University of Colo. Found. v. American Cyanamid*, 153 F. Supp. 2d 1231, 2001 U.S. Dist LEXIS 10679 (D. Colo., 2001) for disgorgement of patent royalties in an unjust enrichment context.
50. *Greenberg v. Miami Childrens Hospital*, 264 F. Supp. 2d 1064, 1070 (S.D. Fla. 2003).
51. For example, there is a question about whether a person can have a property interest in his or her tissue.
52. For example, some commentators suggest that genes should not be patented in the first place. Patents are not allowed on formulas or products of nature. *Diamond v. Chakrabarty*, 447 U.S. 303, 309 (1980). Yet genes seem to be both. Patents are central to drug development and thus appropriate in the pharmaceutical context, but discovery of genes does not require the same incentives as drug development. Molecular biologists were attempting to identify genes long before the U.S. Patent and Trademark Office made clear that genes could be patented. As opposed to the development of drugs, which is undertaken primarily with private funds (for which investors expect a commercial return), the discovery of genes has been undertaken with vast quantities of public funds. Over $1.8 billion of taxpayer money was spent by the U.S. government and non-profit institutions on genomics in the year 2000 alone. Myriad, the genetics company that first isolated and described BRCA1, utilized over $5 million from a government agency, the National Institutes of Health. B. W. Jones, "History of a Gene Patent: Tracing the Development and Application of Commercial BRCA Testing," *Health Law Journal* 10 (2002): 123-146, at 123, 131. Even the private company that made its own efforts to sequence the human genome, Celera, used sequence data from the publicly-funded project in its sequencing.

    Moreover, no expensive clinical trials are necessary for the transition from a gene discovery and knowledge to the actual use of the gene sequence in clinical diagnostics. In some cases, a disease gene has been identified one day and testing begun almost immediately. Because the Food and Drug Administration ("FDA") does not regulate the clinical services of genetic tests (as opposed to the sale of genetic diagnostic kits or gene therapies), there is no costly FDA approval process. Thus, the need to financially compensate a gene-discoverer is not as great as the need to compensate the developer of a drug that must take it through costly clinical trials, with only a small number of drugs actually becoming commercially-viable products.

    Gene patents do not seem necessary to encourage technology transfer in the move from gene discovery to the availability of a genetic diagnostic test. As soon as information about the discovery of the hemachromatosis gene was published, laboratories began testing for mutations in the gene. After a patent on the gene was granted seventeen months later, 30% of the 119 U.S. laboratories surveyed reported discontinuing or not developing a genetic test for the disease. The patent holder was asking for an up-front fee of $25,000 from academic laboratories and as much as $250,000 from commercial laboratories, plus a fee of $20 per test. J. F. Merz, A. G. Kriss, D. G. B. Leonard, and M. K. Cho, "Diagnostic Testing Fails the Test," *Nature* 415 (2002): 577-579, at 578. The patent interfered with clinical adoption of the test and potentially compromised the quality of testing by limiting the development of higher quality or lower cost alternative testing methods.
53. As a report of a committee of the National Academy of Sciences on genetic research notes, "It is not ethically or legally acceptable to ask research participants to 'consent' to future yet unknown uses of their identifiable DNA samples." *Evaluating Human Genetic Diversity* (Washington, D.C.: National Academy Press, 1997): at 65.
54. U.S. Members of Congress Lynn Rivers and David Weldon introduced such a bill covering health care providers and non-commercial researchers in 2002, the proposed Genome Research and Diagnostic Accessiblity Act. L. B. Andrews, "Genes and Patent Policy: Rethinking Intellectual Property Rights," *Nature Reviews Genetics* 3 (2002): 803-808, at 806.

[27]

Genetic Exceptionalism & Legislative Pragmatism

by MARK A. ROTHSTEIN

Can passing antidiscrimination laws ever be a bad idea? Yes, if broad policy reform is abandoned in favor of genetic-specific legislation. But in spite of its serious flaws, both in concept and in practice, genetic-specific legislation is sometimes worth passing anyway—sometimes a bad idea is reasonable.

One of the most important and contentious policy issues surrounding genetics is whether genetic information should be treated separately from other medical information. The view that genetics raises distinct issues is what Thomas Murray labeled "genetic exceptionalism," borrowing from the earlier term "HIV exceptionalism."[1] The issue of whether the use of genetic information should be addressed separately from other health information is not merely an academic concern, however. Since the Human Genome Project began in 1990, nearly every state has enacted legislation prohibiting genetic discrimination in health insurance; two-thirds of the states have enacted laws prohibiting genetic discrimination in employment, and other state laws have been enacted dealing with genetic discrimination in life insurance, genetic privacy, and genetic testing.[2] Bills in Congress also would prohibit genetic discrimination in health insurance and employment.[3]

Much has been written on the issue.[4] Most commentators have cautioned against genetic exceptionalism, but to no avail.[5] Legislators seem enamored of genetic-specific laws. Possibly, legislators actually believe that genetic-specific laws are the best way to protect privacy and combat discrimination. Or perhaps they just think such laws are better than nothing, even though they recognize that the laws are flawed conceptually and in practice. Many legislators who hold the latter view undoubtedly also have concluded that more general laws dealing with such contentious issues as access to health care and employment discrimination have little chance of passage.

In this article, after considering the arguments in favor of and opposed to genetic exceptionalism, I argue that genetic exceptionalism represents poor public policy. Because more desirable and far-reaching "generic" laws are often politically infeasible, legislators may still reasonably decide that it is better to enact a genetic-specific law than nothing. But there are only limited conditions in which that decision is reasonable.

The Policy Framework

New developments in genetic technology have increased the capacity to identify the source of biological specimens, determine familial associations, and predict the future health status of individuals. New genetic information also has raised a variety of novel issues in such diverse fields as family law, employment law, insurance law, and criminal law.[6] In deciding on the legal response to this new information, policy-makers have three main options: (1) maintain the status quo; (2) enact comprehensive, "generic" restrictions on the collection, use, and disclosure of health information; and (3) enact provisions for the special treatment of genetic information—the preferred option to date in the United States.

If genetic-specific laws are to be successful, three conditions must be met: (1) the term "genetic" must be defined clearly, logically, and with scientific precision; (2) there must be an efficient, low-cost way to separate genetic information from nongenetic information in health records; and (3) it must not only be possible to treat genetic information differently from other health information, but there must be a compelling reason to do so.

Defining "genetic." From the standpoint of genetic privacy and genetic discrimination, *genetic* refers to predictive genetics. In determining the legal rights of individuals who are already affected with a physical or mental disorder, it is generally immaterial whether the disorder was caused by a germline mutation, a somatic mutation, environmental factors, a combination of factors, or something unknown. For example, there are two key issues in employment discrimination cases brought under the Americans with Disabilities Act (ADA): (1) Does the individual have a physical or mental impairment that constitutes a substantial limitation of a major life activity? and (2) Can the individual, with or without reasonable accommodation, perform the essential functions of the job safely and efficiently?[7] The etiology of the impairment has no bearing on either determination. Thus, the issue of genetic discrimination arises when genetic factors indicate that a currently unaffected individual is at an increased risk of developing a physical or mental impairment at some time in the future.

To a large extent, the ethical and legal challenges associated with predictive genetics stem from two important time lags. One of these is the gap between the discovery of a genetic marker for an increased risk of illness and the development of therapies to prevent, treat, or cure the disorder. Thus, in the often-used example of Huntington's disease, scientists have identified the genetic mutation responsible for the condition, but there is still no medical intervention that will prevent or ameliorate it. The second time lag is the gap between a genetic test that indicates an individual has a genetic predisposition to a disease and the onset of symptoms. These time lags give rise to such ethical issues as whether children should be tested for adult-onset disorders (such as breast cancer) that cannot be prevented or treated in childhood,[8] and whether young adults should be tested for late-onset disorders (such as Alzheimer's disease) that cannot be prevented or treated in adulthood.[9] They also create economic incentives for commercial entities, such as employers and insurers, to consider the genetically increased risk that an asymptomatic individual will become symptomatic. If there were a cheap, effective intervention that would prevent or cure these conditions, many of the social issues would disappear. In other words, the availability of a medical intervention would eliminate both time lags. Unfortunately, medical genetics has not yet advanced that far.

Even without medical breakthroughs in prevention or treatment, social policies may reduce or eliminate the economic risks of predictive genetic information. For example, in the United States, most individuals with private health insurance obtain their coverage through employment-based group health insurance.[10] The Health Insurance Portability and Accountability Act (HIPAA),[11] enacted in 1996, prohibits employer-sponsored group health plans from charging individuals higher rates or excluding certain medical conditions from coverage[12] based on an individual's current health or "genetic information."[13] Thus, the only concerns about genetic discrimination in health insurance involve individual policies and nonemployer group plans to which HIPAA does not apply.

In the group health insurance market, the broad pooling of risks eliminates the issue of genetic discrimination for the vast majority of privately insured Americans, as well as all individuals covered under publicly financed health care systems such as Medicare and Medicaid. (That is why in countries with national health care systems, the issue of genetic discrimination is irrelevant to eligibility for health care.) At least at the moment, the political consensus for risk pooling does not extend beyond employment-based group health insurance to individual and nonemployer sponsored health insurance. Thus, in the absence of legislation prohibiting the practice, health insurers would be tempted to use genetic information to deny coverage to individuals who have a genetically increased risk of disease. Of equal or greater concern is the fact that many people who are at risk for genetic disorders and who might benefit medically or socially from genetic testing decline to undergo it because of concerns about the effect it might have on their insurability.

The first step in devising a "genetic" solution to this "genetic" problem is to define "genetic." Many legislative and policy meetings have agonized over the definition. The narrow issue is sometimes cast as whether "genetic" should include only the results of a DNA-based test, or also tests for RNA, proteins, or other gene products. The real issue, however, is whether the definition should include family history, and it is on this point that attempts to define "genetic" usually falter. Definitions that fail to include genetic information derived from family histories are too narrow. For example, if a law prohibiting genetic discrimination did not include family history, it would not prohibit discrimination against an individual known to have a 50 percent risk of an autosomal dominant disorder (such as Huntington's disease) that had afflicted one of the individual's parents.[14] On the other hand, definitions of genetic that include information derived from family histories are usually considered too broad.[15] Family health histories often indicate an increased risk for common chronic disorders, and that is why they are an essential element of clinical medicine. If family health history information were deemed genetic information, then much "traditional" medical underwriting by insurers would become illegal.

As a scientific matter, the distinction between genetic and nongenetic disorders has become largely meaningless. Virtually all disorders have both a genetic and an environmental component.[16] The respective influences of genes and environment may be strong or weak, but both are factors, and even when one appears to have a strong causal role in a disorder, the other may influence the disorder's effect. Thus, even in single-gene disorders such as phenylketonuria, environmental influences like diet may determine the clinical outcome. Similarly, even in presumably environmentally caused illnesses such as infection, genetic factors may determine an individual's sensitivity or resistance, as well as the effectiveness of various pharmaceutical interventions.

With "genetic" defined narrowly, so as to include only the results of a DNA-based test, and with health care providers keeping separate charts for the results of genetic tests, it might be possible to separate genetic and nongenetic medical information in a medical record. But because a narrow definition of genetic seems to leave the door open to some kinds of discrimination, it has not been widely accepted. In addition, keeping separate charts for genetic test results raises its own ethical problems. The primary reason for excluding genetic information is to deceive commercial entities that obtain the individual's medical records pursuant to a signed authorization.[17] Even though physicians are advocates of their patients, they should not misrepresent the contents of patients' medical records. Consequently, the usual scenario is a broad definition of genetic and a single medical record.

Genetic-specific laws reinforce the stigma of genetic disorders by treating them differently from nongenetic conditions. They also ignore the underlying social problems that genetic privacy and discrimination exemplify.

Separating genetic from nongenetic information. All of the state laws intended to bar genetic discrimination in employment prohibit employers from requiring that individuals take a genetic test as a condition of employment, and most of the laws prohibit employers from requiring or requesting the results of genetic tests performed in the clinical setting. Some laws prohibit employers from requiring or requesting the disclosure of genetic information as a condition of employment, and "genetic information" could include family health histories. Virtually none of these laws, however, alters the right employers already have to require that conditional offerees sign an authorization for health care providers to disclose the individuals' complete medical records, nongenetic as well as genetic, to the prospective employer or its designee.

As a practical matter, regardless of the wording of the state law, it is impractical or impossible to limit disclosure of health information to nongenetic information. If a health care provider receives a patient's authorization to release only nongenetic information to a third party, it is impossible to identify, isolate, and disclose only the nongenetic information. For example, at a hospital, health information from myriad sources and of various types is generally compiled in a single record that may reflect decades of health care rendered by dozens of health care providers. It would take a substantial amount of time and expense to identify which information in a voluminous record satisfied the statutory definition of "genetic" under a particular legislative enactment, and then to disclose only the nongenetic information. Consequently, even when such a law exists, providers faced with a request for limited but not easily segregated medical information (ability to do physical labor, for example) often simply release the entire record. Thus, even with laws prohibiting certain commercial entities from *using* genetic information, they still obtain the information. Because genetic test results are widely accessible to employers and insurers, at-risk individuals are discouraged from undergoing genetic tests, thereby undermining an essential purpose of nondiscrimination laws.[18]

New information technology may allow for more targeted disclosures at a reasonable expense. For example, with an electronic health record divided into different data fields, it might be possible to release only certain types of health information. Nevertheless, health care providers are a long way from having such capabilities, and there is little indication that in designing new electronic health record systems, much if any thought has been given to making limited disclosures possible.[19]

Treating genetic information differently. The third requirement for a successful genetic-specific law is a compelling reason to treat genetic information differently. As I have written elsewhere, there are seven main reasons cited by proponents to justify genetic-specific laws: (1) genetic information has implications not only for the individual but also for family members; (2) genetic information may have implications for reproduction and characteristics of future generations; (3) genetic information may be predictive; (4) genetic information often carries stigma, and the misuse of genetic information has led to eugenics, racism, and genocide; (5) genetic information is regarded as unique by the public; (6) there are other "special" categories of medical information for which separate protections have been adopted, including HIV/AIDS and mental illness; and (7) the political reality is that there is greater support for genetic nondiscrimination legislation than for more general and sweeping laws.[20]

Although there is something to be said for each of these reasons, on reflection they are unpersuasive. The characteristics identified in the first three reasons are not unique to genetic information. For example, numerous socioeconomic variables (such as income level and insurance coverage) and medical factors (such as a family history of tuberculosis) also serve to predict the current and future health status of an individual. The problem of stigma and misuse—the fourth reason—does not call for the legislative responses proposed; public education and broad laws protecting the privacy of health information and prohibiting health discrimination would be more effective. The fifth reason is to some degree self-fulfilling: genetic information is regarded as unique partly because genetic-specific legislation bolsters that view. And finally, genetic information is not analogous to existing "special" categories of medical information because that information—HIV/AIDS and mental illness—is much more easily isolated in a medical record. For example, HIV/AIDS is a discrete syndrome initially diagnosed by a single test, even though the manifestations vary. By contrast, genetic factors influence virtually all diseases, and genetic information may be based on family history or on the results of tests for thousands of different DNA markers.

That leaves reason number seven, the political issue. A variety of arguments have been offered against the enactment of genetic-specific nondiscrimination laws. One is simply that it is difficult to make a moral argument that discriminating against people on the basis of genetic information is impermissible, but that discriminating against them on the basis of other medical information is okay. This argument, on which a literature already exists, I set to one side in this paper.[21] Two other concerns have already been touched on above, namely, that there are intractable problems in defining "genetic" because the definitions are either too narrow or too broad, and that it is impossible to separate genetic information from other medical information in medical records. A fourth argument is that a general nondiscrimination law is easier to comply with than one restricted to genetic information. And fifth, by enacting general laws applicable to all forms of medical information, the stigma of genetic information will be diminished rather than reinforced.

It is likely that the passage of time will eliminate some of the pressure to regulate genetic information separately. Part of the stigma associated with genetic information stems from the fact that contemporary medical records (especially those maintained by primary care physicians) still rarely contain genetic information beyond family histories. As genetic test results and other genetic information become common in the medical charts of numerous patients, at least some of the fear and sense of uniqueness associated with genetic information is likely to dissipate. Consequently, genetic information will be more widely considered indistinguishable from other medical information.

The Alternative to Genetic Exceptionalism

I have argued that genetic-specific laws have limited value in preventing or redressing harms caused by the uses and disclosures of genetic information. Genetic-specific laws also reinforce the stigma of genetic disorders (by treating them differently from nongenetic conditions) and ignore the underlying social problems that genetic privacy and discrimination exemplify. The fundamental issue raised by genetic discrimination in health insurance is the fairness of our system for allocating access to health care; the fundamental issue raised by genetic discrimination in employment is how to balance the rights of employers and employees in controlling access to employee health information and in deciding what role, if any, current or predictive health status should play in employment opportunities.

General legal standards are more effective in dealing with these problems than genetic-specific laws. As mentioned, genetic discrimination is not a concern for health care finance systems that are not based on individual medical underwriting. For example, genetic discrimination is irrelevant in government-sponsored programs, such as Medicare and Medicaid, and group-based health insurance. But individual underwriting in any insurance product is synonymous with "discrimination" (that is to say, with differentiation) since eligibility and rates are determined by risk classification. Thus, it will be virtually impossible to devise any effective measures to prevent genetic discrimination in a system based on "discrimination."

The only logical conclusion is that, as a society, we need to decide if certain social opportunities raise such important social interests that universal access should be assured. If so, then a system should be devised to eliminate all risk classification. Perhaps all health insurance should be group-based, with mandatory participation and with various risk-spreading mechanisms. For other types of insurance, such as life insurance, we may decide that there is no fundamental right of access to the product and that individual underwriting is permissible, at least under some circumstances (perhaps for policies above a certain amount).

Many options have a chance of attaining one or more important social objectives in regulating genetic and other health information, but there is one option that is guaranteed to fail. We cannot hope to single out for special underwriting or access health information that is ubiquitous and impossible to define, that cannot be feasibly segregated from other health information, and that cannot *logically* be treated specially. Unfortunately, our federal and state policies have embraced this principle, thereby promoting genetic over generic approaches to issues of access to and use of information by third parties.

With regard to employment, the common law permits employers to gather any information about applicants they deem relevant and to use any selection criteria not expressly prohibited by statute. Applicants usually have no choice but to acquiesce to employer demands for health information and must cede to employers the decision of whether their current or likely future health is compatible with certain employment.

When Is Half a Loaf Better than Nothing?

Legislative champions for genetic-specific laws are easy to find, and they include sympathetic and persuasive advocates. Opponents are few, especially if the proposed legislation is narrow in scope. Only a small number of elected officials realize that genetic-specific laws are largely ineffective and may be counterproductive. To most lawmakers, it seems obvious that if there is a problem with genetic discrimination, then the solution is to enact legislation making genetic discrimination illegal.

More savvy lawmakers still may be reluctant to propose generic, rather than merely genetic, legislation, since generic legislation is extraordinarily difficult to enact.[22] Support for logical, effective, and sweeping legislation is hard to find. The underlying issues—such as the right of access to health care, the relative rights of employers and employees to decide about health hazards in the workplace, and the principles to apply in medical underwriting for life and disability insurance—are extremely contentious. To date, efforts to address these issues have often been unsuccessful.

Because of the difficulty in enacting sweeping reforms, the policy question is whether it is a good idea to enact a genetic-specific law when there is insufficient support for broader legislation. In legislative circles it is often said that the perfect is the enemy of the good. In other words, many people would argue that it is better to have limited or even flawed protection against discrimination than no protection at all. On the other hand, enacting and then touting feel-good legislation with little or no substantive protection may mislead members of the public to rely on the law to their detriment. It may also encourage people to believe in genetic exceptionalism, thereby making it a self-fulfilling prophesy, and it may erroneously convince legislators that they have resolved the underlying issues, thereby delaying enactment of meaningful legislation.

Many would argue that a limited protection against discrimination is better than no protection at all. But enacting feel-good legislation with little substantive protection may mislead the public. The self-congratulation that follows rarely allows mention of limitations.

In my view, four conditions need to be met before it is appropriate to support a genetic-specific law as a fallback position to more sweeping legislation. First, there must be some value to the law, both in the sense that there is a demonstrated need for legislative action and that the proposed legislation will help to resolve one or more aspects of the problem. Second, the law must be drafted carefully to avoid unintended consequences, such as interfering with clinical care or medical research, or unreasonably interfering with the economic interests of third parties such as insurers or employers. Third, enacting the law must not serve to delay the enactment of legislation better designed to promote public policies, such as not coercing individuals into genetic testing and not dissuading at-risk individuals from being tested for fear of the social consequences. And fourth, both legislators and the public must realize that the law is not ideal but merely the best that can be achieved at the moment.

Many genetic-specific laws have failed to meet one or more of these four criteria. For example, several states have enacted laws providing that life insurance companies may use the results of genetic tests only if there is a sound actuarial basis for the action.[23] Every state, however, already has unfair trade practice laws that are applicable to life insurance and which require that, to be lawful, underwriting based on *any* test must be actuarially justified. The new laws thus appear to address the issue of genetics and life insurance but actually afford no new protections.

State laws that prohibit genetic discrimination in employment are another example. The number of reported instances (let alone legal cases) of genetic discrimination in employment is extremely small.[24] Nonetheless, concerns about employers' access to the results of genetic tests and possible discrimination have deterred some at-risk individuals from undergoing genetic testing.[25] Over thirty states have enacted genetic nondiscrimination laws, but only two states (California and Minnesota[26]) have enacted laws that restrict employers' access to *any* non-job-related medical information.[27] Consequently, in all but two of the states that have enacted genetic nondiscrimination laws, employers may require, after a conditional offer of employment, that an individual sign a blanket authorization to release all of his or her medical records to the company. As a result, the laws permit employers to demand access to information they cannot legally use. Attempts to be more restrictive in access are impractical because, as noted earlier, there is no way as yet to separate genetic from nongenetic information, especially when "genetic" is defined broadly, so as to include complex disorders and health histories. Therefore, without any meaningful limitations on employers' access to genetic information, individuals will continue to be discouraged from undergoing genetic testing.

These are examples of laws without much value. They have accomplished very little. Some other laws exemplify the problem of unintended consequences. Oregon enacted a law in 1999 designed to protect genetic privacy.[28] The law provided, among other things, that an individual's genetic information and DNA sample are the individual's property except when the information or sample is used in anonymous research. As it turned out, the law interfered with research because it prohibited the use of banked tissue samples that had been routinely collected in medical procedures without getting additional consent. The Oregon Legislature repealed the law after only two years, replacing the "property" language with a provision stating that "an individual's genetic information and DNA sample are private and must be protected."

It is difficult to assess whether enacting a weak or ineffective law delays the enactment of more meaningful legislation. On the one hand, the initial enactment may be viewed as "a foot in the door" or the first step to stronger legislation. Since 1995, every state to enact a law establishing a DNA forensic database for use in law enforcement has amended its law to add more categories of offenders who are required to provide DNA samples.[29] This expansion reflects the continuing efforts of the law enforcement community and its legislative advocates to promote forensic DNA banks.

On the other hand, "legislative fatigue" is sometimes used to describe the notion that having enacted *something*, legislators are ready to move on to the next issue and have no interest in reconsidering a problem they thought was resolved. For example, few amendments have been made to the privacy and antidiscrimination laws enacted in the last decade, especially to extend the privacy protections for individuals. Whether genetic legislation will be a precursor to stronger legislation or give way to legislative fatigue will depend on whether powerful legislative champions are satisfied with the initial version of the law.

My fourth condition is that legislators and the public realize that a genetic-specific law is not ideal. Unfortunately, in the press conferences and self-congratulation that usually follow enactment of legislation affording protection against genetic discrimination, there is rarely any mention of the limitations of the new laws. Many people, including legislators, probably assume that the problem has been solved. Legislative sponsors and supporters would then view it as a sign of weakness or ineptitude to admit that the bill they advocated is flawed or ineffectual. If media descriptions of the new laws are based on press releases and interviews with advocates of the legislation, then the gaps in protection are unlikely to be noted.

No Shortcuts

From a policy standpoint, studying the effect of genetics is especially valuable because it forces us to return to first principles. Who should have access to health care? In a health care system that relies heavily on optional, employer-sponsored group health insurance, on what basis should individual health insurance be underwritten and priced? What is the role of private disability insurance in a system that uses both public and private sources to replace the incomes of those who are medically unable to work? What is the social purpose of life insurance and on what basis should the risk of mortality be shared by policyholders? What are the relative rights of employers and employees in making decisions about employees' fitness for duty and about the amount of employee health information that employers may reasonably obtain?

Genetic exceptionalism undercuts this essential reconsideration of the role of predictive health information in society. It allows elected officials to avoid difficult issues by enacting genetic-specific laws that seem to respond to a perceived new crisis, but in fact offer little or no protection and may even be counterproductive. It is not surprising that elected officials would want to avoid fundamental and controversial issues and focus instead on nominally protecting the public against the highly publicized evils of invidious genetic discrimination. For the time being, at least, it seems that the public is genetically predisposed to let them.

Acknowledgment

This article was originally written for the grant, "Genetics and Disability Insurance: Ethics, Law and Policy," NIH/5R01-HG02089, for which Jeffrey Kahn and Susan Wolf, at the University of Minnesota, are principal investigators.

References

1. T.H. Murray, "Genetic Exceptionalism and 'Future Diaries': Is Genetic Information Different from Other Medical Information?" in *Genetic Secrets: Protecting Privacy and Confidentiality in the Genetic Era*, ed. M.A. Rothstein (New Haven, Conn.: Yale University Press, 1997).

2. See National Conference of State Legislatures, State Genetic Discrimination in Health Insurance Laws, at http://www.ncsl.org/programs/health/genetics/ndishlth.htm, and National Conference of State Legislatures, State Genetic Discrimination in Employment Laws, available at http://www.ncsl.org/programs/health/genetics/ndiscrim.htm.

3. The Genetic Information Nondiscrimination Act of 2005, S.306, 109th Cong., 1st Sess., was passed by the Senate on February 17, 2005 by a vote of 98-0. A companion bill, H.R. 1227, 109th Cong. 1st Sess., was introduced into the House of Representatives on March 10, 2005. Given prior failed attempts, House passage of the bill remains doubtful.

4. See D. Hellman, "What Makes Genetic Discrimination Exceptional?" *American Journal of Law & Medicine* 29 (2003): 77-116.

5. See M.A. Rothstein, "Genetic Privacy and Confidentiality: Why They Are So Hard to Protect," *Journal of Law, Medicine & Ethics* 26 (1998): 198-203; M.A. Rothstein and M.R. Anderlik, "What Is Genetic Discrimination and When and How Can It Be Prevented?" *Genetics in Medicine* 3 (2001): 354-58; S.M. Suter, "The Allure and Peril of Genetic Exceptionalism: Do We Need Special Genetics Legislation?" *Washington University Law Quarterly* 79 (2001): 669-748; S.M. Wolf, "Beyond 'Genetic Discrimination': Toward the Broader Harm of Geneticism," *Journal of Law, Medicine & Ethics* 23 (1995): 345-53.

6. See L.B. Andrews, M.J. Mehlman, and M.A. Rothstein, *Genetics: Ethics, Law and Policy* (St. Paul, Minn.: West Group, 2002).

7. 42 U.S.C. Secs. 12101-12213.

8. D.E. Hoffmann and E.A. Wulfsberg, "Testing Children for Genetic Predispositions: Is It in Their Best Interest?" *Journal of Law, Medicine & Ethics* 23 (1995): 331-44.

9. Committee on Assessing Genetic Risks, Institute of Medicine, *Assessing Genetic Risks: Implications for Health and Social Policy* (Washington, D.C.: National Academy Press, 1994), 105.

10. In 1999, 174 million of 240 million nonelderly Americans had private coverage, of whom more than 160 million received it as an employee or the dependent of an employee in an employer-sponsored group health plan. U.S. Bureau of the Census, Current Population Survey (CPS): Annual Demographic Survey (March 2000 Supp.), Table HI05—Health Insurance Coverage Status and Type of Coverage by State: 1999 (2000), at http://pubdb3.census.gov/macro/032000/health/01_001.htm.

11. 42 U.S.C. Secs. 300gg-300gg-2.

12. 42 U.S.C. Secs. 300gg(b)(1)(B), 300gg-1(a)(1)(F).

13. 42 U.S.C. Secs. 300gg (b)(1)(B), 300gg-1(a)(F).

14. See Tex. Lab. Code Ann. Secs. 21.401-402 (enacted 1997) (defining genetic information as the results of a DNA-based test).

15. See N.J. Stat. Ann. Secs. 10:5-12 (enacted 1996) (defining genetic information to include "inherited characteristics that may derive from an individual or family member").

16. M.J. Khoury, W. Burke, and E.J. Thomson, "Genetics and Public Health: A Framework for the Integration of Human Genetics into Public Health Practice," in *Genetics and Public Health in the 21st Century*, ed. M.J. Khoury, W. Burke, and E.J. Thomson (New York: Oxford University Press, 2000), 7.

17. M.A. Rothstein, "Genetics, Insurance, and the Ethics of Genetic Counseling," in *Molecular Genetic Medicine* vol. 3, ed. T. Friedmann (San Diego, Calif.: Academic Press, 1993).

18. M.A. Rothstein, "Genetics Secrets: A Policy Framework," in *Genetic Secrets: Protecting Privacy and Confidentiality in the Genetic Era*, ed. M.A. Rothstein (New Haven, Conn.: Yale University Press, 1997), 475-79.

19. See National Committee on Vital and Health Statistics, Shaping a Health Statistics Vision for the 21st Century (2002); National Committee on Vital and Health Statistics, Information for Health: A Strategy for Building the National Health Information Infrastructure (2001), at www.ncvhs.hhs.gov/hsvision.

20. M.A. Rothstein, "Policy Recommendations," in *Genetics and Life Insurance: Medical Underwriting and Social Policy*, ed. M.A. Rothstein (Cambridge, Mass.: MIT Press, 2004).

21. See N. Daniels, "The Functions of Insurance and the Fairness of Genetic Underwriting," in *Genetics and Life Insurance: Medical Underwriting and Social Policy*, ed. M.A. Rothstein (Cambridge, Mass.: MIT Press, 2004); T. Lemmens, "Selective Justice, Genetic Discrimination, and Insurance: Should We Single Out Genes in Our Laws?" *McGill Law Review* 45 (2000): 347-412.

22. M.A. Rothstein, "Genetic Privacy and Confidentiality: Why They Are So Hard to Protect," *Journal of Law, Medicine and Ethics* 26 (1998): 198-203.

23. B.R. Ostrager and T.R. Newman, *Handbook on Insurance Coverage Disputes*, tenth ed. (New York: Aspen Law & Business, 2000), Sec. 12-03 [b],[c].

24. See M.A. Hall, "Legal Rules and Industry Norms: The Impact of Laws Restricting Health Insurers' Use of Genetic Information," *Jurimetrics Journal* 40 (1999): 93-125.

25. See E.V. Lapham et al., "Genetic Discrimination: Perspectives of Consumers," *Science* 274 (1996): 621-24.

26. Cal. Gov't Code Secs. 12926, 12940; Minn. Stat. Ann. Secs. 363.01-02.

27. See M.A. Rothstein et al., "Protecting Genetic Privacy by Permitting Employer Access Only to Job-Related Employee Medical Information: Analysis of a Unique Minnesota Law," *American Journal of Law & Medicine* 24 (1998): 399-417.

28. Or. Rev. Stat. Sec. 192.537 (2001).

29. See M.A. Rothstein and S. Carnahan, "Legal and Policy Issues in Expanding the Scope of Law Enforcement DNA Data Banks," *Brooklyn Law Review* 67 (2001): 127-78.

Part IX
Public Health and Equity

[28]

Ethical Issues in the Use of Cost Effectiveness Analysis for the Prioritisation of Health Care Resources

DAN W. BROCK

Resources to improve health are and always have been scarce, in the sense that health must compete with other desirable social goals like education and personal security for resources.[1] It is not possible to provide all the resources to health, including health care and health care research, that might provide some positive health benefits without great and unacceptable sacrifices in other important social goods. This should go without saying, and in other areas of social expenditures resource scarcity is not denied, but in health care many people mistakenly persist in denying this fact. It follows from resource scarcity that some form of health care rationing is unavoidable, where by rationing I mean some means of allocating health care resources that denies to some persons some potentially beneficial health care. That rationing may take many forms. In most countries with a national health system it is done through some form of global budgeting for health care. In the United States much rationing is by ability to pay, but in both public programmes like the Oregon Medicaid programme and in many private managed care plans more systematic efforts to prioritise health care resources have been carried out.

This chapter draws heavily on my 'Considerations of Equity in Relation to Prioritization and Allocation of Health Care Resources', in *Ethics, Equity and Health For All* Z. Bankowski, J. H. Bryant, and J. Gallagher (eds.), Geneva: CIOMS (1997) and 'Ethical Issues in the Development of Summary Measures of Population Health States', in *Summarizing Population Health: Directions for the Development and Application of Population Metrics*, Washington, DC: National Academy Press (1998).

[1] Interventions that would improve health should be understood broadly, and in particular extend substantially beyond health care. It is widely agreed that other factors such as improved sanitation and economic conditions have contributed more to the health gains of the past century than has health care. However, in this chapter I shall largely confine myself to health care interventions.

To many health policy analysts it is an unquestioned, and so generally undefended, assumption that in the face of limited health care resources, those resources should be allocated so as to maximise the health benefits they produce, measured by either the aggregate health status or disease burden of a population. Cost effectiveness analysis (CEA) that compares the aggregate health benefits secured from a given resource expenditure devoted to alternative health interventions is the standard analytic tool for determining how to maximise the health benefits from limited resources. Natural, even self-evident, as this maximisation standard may appear to many health policy analysts and economists, it assumes a utilitarian or consequentialist moral standard, and more specifically a standard of distributive justice, and the utilitarian account of distributive justice is widely and I believe correctly taken to be utilitarianism's most problematic feature.

Cost effectiveness analysis comparing alternative health interventions in the quality-adjusted life years (QALYs) produced from a given level of resources constitutes a quantitative method for prioritising different interventions to improve health. There are many unresolved technical and methodological issues in QALYs and CEA, none of which will be my concern here. My concern will be instead with the ethical issues in the construction and use of CEAs for the prioritisation of health care resources. The specific issues that I shall briefly discuss below all constitute potential ethical criticisms of CEA as a normative standard, specifically criticisms concerning justice or equity, and so one might hope concerns for justice or equity could be integrated into these quantitative methodologies. There are at least two reasons, however, for caution, at least in the near term, about the possibility of integrating some of these ethical concerns into cost effectiveness models and analyses. First, although a great deal of work in economics and health policy has gone into the development and validation of measures of health status and the burdens of disease, as well as of cost effectiveness methodologies, much less work has been done on how to integrate concerns of ethics and equity into cost effectiveness measures, although I shall mention one means of doing so later. The theoretical and methodological work necessary to do so remains largely undone. Second, each of the issues of ethics and equity that I take up below remain controversial. Since no clear consensus exists about how each should be treated, there is in turn no consensus about what qualifications or constraints they might justify placing on the cost effectiveness goal of maximising health.

This second difficulty is not likely to be solely a near term limitation, awaiting further work on the ethical issues that I will identify. Instead, most of these issues represent deep divisions in normative ethical theory and in the ethical beliefs of ordinary people; I believe they are likely a permanent fact of ethical life. As I understand and shall present these ethical issues, in most cases there is not a single plausible answer to them. Even from within the standpoint of a particular ethical theory or ethical view, these issues' complexity means that different answers may be appropriate for a particular issue in the different contexts in which CEAs are used. Thus, what is necessary at this point is work developing more clearly and precisely the nature of the issues at stake, the alternative plausible positions on them together with the arguments for and against those positions. Until much more of this work is done, we will not know how deep the conflicts go and the degree to which any can be resolved.

Norman Daniels and James Sabin have recently argued that because ethical theories and theories of justice are indeterminate and/or in conflict on some of these issues, we must turn to fair procedures to arrive at practical solutions to them for health policy (Daniels and Sabin 1997: 303–50). As practical policy matters that need resolution now they are no doubt correct, and a single quantitative measure or model of equity and justice for health care resource prioritisation is certainly not possible now, if it will ever be. But that is not to deny that much important work remains to be done on the substantive issues of equity in health care, and that work should inform the deliberations of those taking part in the fair procedures that we will need to reach practical resolutions and compromises on these issues in real time. What then are some of the main issues of equity raised by cost effectiveness approaches to resource allocation of health care?

10.1. FIRST ISSUE: HOW SHOULD STATES OF HEALTH AND DISABILITY BE EVALUATED?

Any CEA in health care requires some summary measure of the health benefits of interventions designed to improve the health status and reduce the burden of disease of a given population. Early summary measures of the health status of populations and of the benefits of health interventions often assessed only a single variable, such as life expectancy or infant mortality. The usefulness of life expectancy or infant mortality rates is clearly very limited, however, since they give us information about only one of the aims of health interventions, extending life or preventing premature loss of life, and they provide only limited information about that aim. They give us no information about another, at least as important, aim of health interventions, to improve or protect the quality of life by treating or preventing suffering and disability.

Multi-attribute measures like the Sickness Impact Profile (Bergner et al. 1981: 787–805) and the SF 36 (Ware and Sherbourne 1992: 473–83) provide measures of different aspects of overall health related quality of life (HRQL) on which a particular population can be mapped, and an intervention assessed for its impact on these different components of health, or HRQL. Since these measures do not assign different relative value or importance to the different aspects or attributes of HRQL, they do not provide a single overall summary measure of HRQL. Thus, if one of two populations or health interventions scores higher in some respect(s) but lower in others, no conclusion can be drawn about whether the overall HRQL of one population, or from one intervention, is better than the other. Much quantitative based resource prioritization requires a methodology that combines in a single measure the two broad kinds of benefits produced by health interventions—extension of length of life and improvements in the quality of life (Brock 1992).

Typical summary measures of the benefits over time of health interventions that combine and assign relative value to these two kinds of benefits include QALYs and disability-adjusted life years (DALYs). Measures like QALYs and DALYs require a measure of the health status of individuals and in turn of populations at different points in time, such as the health utilities index (HUI) (Torrance et al. 1992) and the quality of well-being scale (QWB) (Kaplan and Anderson, 1988: 203–35), so as to be able to measure the health benefits in terms of changes in HRQL and length of life produced by different health interventions. The construction of any measure like the HUI or QWB requires a two-step process: first, different states of disability or conditions limiting HRQL are described; second, different relative values or utilities are assigned to those different conditions.

The determination of a person's or group's different health related conditions in terms of the various areas of function on the HUI or QWB both before and after a particular health intervention is an empirical question, which should be answered by appeal to relevant data regarding the burden of a particular disease and the reduction in that burden that a particular health intervention can be expected to produce. Needless to say, often the relevant data are highly imperfect, but that is a problem to be addressed largely by generating better data, not by ethical analysis.

The second step of assigning different relative values or utilities to the different areas and levels of function described by a measure like the HUI is typically done by soliciting people's preferences for life with the various functional limitations. This raises the fundamental question of whose preferences should be used to determine the relative value of life with different limitations in function and how they should be obtained. The developers of the DALY used the preferences of expert health professionals, in part for the practical reason that they are more knowledgeable about the nature of different health states, but the degree to which various conditions reduce overall HRQL is not a matter to be settled by professional expertise. Moreover, health professionals may have systematic biases that skew their value judgements about quality of life from those of ordinary persons. Other measures like the HUI and QWB use the value judgements of a random group of ordinary citizens to evaluate different states of disability or limitations in function.

A central issue concerning whose evaluations of different states of disability or functional limitation should be used arises from the typical responses of individuals to becoming disabled: adaptation, that is improving one's functional performance through learning and skills development, coping, that is altering one's expectations for performance so as to reduce the self-perceived gap between them and one's actual performance; and adjustment, that is altering one's life plans to give greater importance to activities in which performance is not diminished by disability (Murray 1996). The result is that the disabled who have gone through these processes often report less distress and limitation of opportunity and a higher quality of life with their disability than the non-disabled in evaluating the same condition. If the evaluations of disability states by the non-disabled are used for ranking different states of health and disability, then disabilities will be ranked as more serious health needs, but these rankings are open to the charge that they are distorted by the ignorance of the evaluators of what it is like to live with the conditions in question. Moreover, those valuations will assign less value to extending the lives of persons with disabilities. If the evaluations of the disabled themselves are used, however, the rankings are open to the charge that they reflect a different distortion by unjustifiably underestimating the burden of the disability because of the process of adaptation, coping, and adjustment that the disabled person has undergone. Moreover, they will assign less value to prevention or rehabilitation for disability because of the results of this process. The problem here is to determine an appropriate evaluative standpoint for ranking the importance of different disabilities which avoids these potential distortions (Brock 1995: 159–84).

Since the preferences for different states of disability or HRQL used to determine their relative values should be informed preferences, it is natural to think that the preferences of those who actually experience the disabilities should be used. Because they should have a more informed understanding of what it is actually like to live with the particular disability in question, we can hope to avoid uninformed evaluations. But this is to miss the deeper nature of the problem caused by adaptation, coping, and adjustment to disabilities.

Fundamental to understanding the difficulty posed by adaptation, coping, and adjustment to disabilities for preference evaluation of HRQL with various disabilities is that neither the non-disabled nor the disabled need have made any mistake in their different evaluations of quality of life with that disability. They arrive at different evaluations of the quality of life with that disability because they use different evaluative standpoints as a result of the disabled person's adaptation, coping, and adjustment. Disabled persons who have undergone this process can look back and see that before they became disabled they too would have evaluated the quality of life with that disability as non-disabled people now do. But this provides no basis for concluding that their pre-disability evaluation of the quality of life with that disability was mistaken, and so in turn no basis for discounting or discarding it because mistaken. The problem that I call the perspectives problem is that the non-disabled and the disabled evaluate the quality of life with the disability from two different evaluative perspectives, neither of which is mistaken. It might seem tempting to use the non-disabled's preferences for assessing the importance of prevention or rehabilitation programmes, but the disabled's preferences for assessing the importance of life-sustaining treatments for the disabled, but this ignores the necessity of a single unified perspective in order to compare the relative benefits from, and prioritise, the full range of different health interventions.

Moreover, what weight to give to the results of coping with one's condition may depend on the causes of that condition, for example, disease or injury that are no one's fault as opposed to unjust social conditions. Most measures of HRQL include some measure of subjective satisfaction or distress, a factor that is importantly influenced by people's expectations. In a society which has long practised systematic discrimination against women, for example, women may not be dissatisfied with their unjustly disadvantaged state, including the health differences that result from that discrimination. The fact that victims are sufficiently oppressed that they accept an injustice as natural and cope with it by reducing their expectations and adjusting their life plans should not make its effects less serious, as measures of HRQL with a subjective satisfaction or distress component would imply.

When measures like the HUI or QWB are applied across different economic, ethnic, cultural, and social groups, the meaningful states of health and disability and their importance in different groups may vary greatly; for example, in a setting in which most work is manual labour limitations in physical functioning will have greater importance than it does in a setting in which most individuals are engaged in non-physical, knowledge-based occupations, where certain cognitive disabilities are of greater importance. Different evaluations of health conditions and disabilities seem to be necessary for groups with significantly different relative needs for different functional abilities, but then cross-group comparisons of health and disability, and of the relative value of health interventions, in those different groups will not be possible. The health programme benefits will have been measured on two different and apparently incommensurable valuational scales. These differences will be magnified when summary measures of population health are employed for international comparisons across very disparate countries.

Some of this variability of perspective may be avoided by a focus on the evaluation of disability instead of handicap, as these are traditionally distinguished, such as in the 1980 International Classification of Impairments, Disabilities and Handicaps (ICIDHWHO 1980). The ICIDH understands disabilities as 'any restriction or lack (resulting from an impairment) of ability to perform an activity in the manner or within the range considered normal for a human being', whereas handicap is 'a disadvantage for a given individual, resulting from an impairment or disability, that limits or prevents the fulfilment of a role that is normal (depending on age, sex, and social and cultural factors) for that individual'. There will be greater variability between individuals, groups, and cultures in the relative importance of handicaps than of disabilities since handicaps take account of differences in individuals' roles and social conditions that disabilities do not. But it is problematic whether these differences should be ignored in prioritising health resources for individuals, groups, and societies, that is, whether disabilities or handicaps are the correct focus for evaluation.

10.2. SECOND ISSUE: DO ALL QALYS COUNT EQUALLY?

QALYs standardly assume that an additional year of life has the same value regardless of the age of the person who receives it, assuming that the different life years are of comparable quality. A year of life extension for an infant, a forty-year-old, and an eighty-year-old all have the same value in QALYs produced, and in turn in a cost effectiveness analysis using QALYs, assuming no difference in the quality of the year of life extension. This is compatible, of course, with using age-based quality adjustments for interventions affecting groups of different age patients to reflect differences in the average quality of life of those different groups; for example, if average quality of life in a group of patients of average age eighty-five is less than that of patients of average age twenty-five, a year of life extension for the twenty-five-year-old would have greater value in QALYs than would a year of life extension for the eighty-five-year-old.

In the World Bank Study, *World Development Report 1993; Investing in Health* (World Bank 1993), the alternative DALY measure was developed to measure the burden of disease in reducing life expectancy and quality of life. Probably the most important ethical difference between QALYs and DALYs is that DALYs assign different value to a year of life extension of the same quality, depending on the age at which an individual receives it; specifically, life extension for individuals during their adult productive work years is assigned greater value than a similar period of life extension for infants and young children or the elderly. The principal justification offered for this feature of DALYs was the different social roles that individuals typically occupy at different ages and the typical emotional, physical, and financial dependence of the very young and the elderly on individuals in their productive work years (Murray 1994).

This justification of age-based differences in the value of life extension implicitly adopts an ethically problematic social perspective on the value of health care interventions that extend life, or maintain or restore function, that is, an evaluation of the benefits *to others* of extending an individual's life, or maintaining or restoring his or her function, in addition to the benefit to that individual of doing so. This social perspective is in conflict with the usual focus in clinical decision-making and treatment only on the benefits to the individuals who receive the health care interventions in question. Typical practice in health policy and public health contexts is more ambiguous on this point, since there benefits to others besides the direct recipient of the intervention are sometimes given substantial weight in the evaluation and justification of health programmes; for example, treatment programmes for substance abuse are argued to merit high priority because of their benefits in reductions in lost work days and in harmful effects on the substance abusers' family members. This social perspective is ethically problematic because it gives weight to differences between individuals in their social and economic value to others; in so doing, it discriminates against persons with fewer dependents and social ties, which arguably is not ethically relevant in health care resource allocation. The social perspective justifying the DALY measure is therefore ethically problematic, in a way the alternative QALY measure is not, if the value of health benefits for individuals should focus on the value to the individuals treated of the health benefits, not on the social value for others of treating those persons. The ethical difficulty here is briefly explored further in the section below on what costs and benefits should count in a CEA.

Giving different value to life extension at different ages, however, might be justified ethically if done for different reasons. For example, Norman Daniels has argued that because everyone can expect to pass through the different stages of the life span, giving different value to a year of life extension at different stages in the life span need not unjustly discriminate against individuals in the way giving different weight to life extension for members of different racial, ethnic, or gender groups would unjustly discriminate (Daniels 1988). Each individual can expect to pass through all the life stages in which life extension is given different value, but is a member of only one race, ethnic group, and gender. Thus, all persons are treated the same at comparable stages of their lives regarding the value of extending their lives, and so the use of DALYs would not constitute unjust age discrimination comparable to gender, ethnic or racial discrimination.

Moreover, individuals, and in turn their society, might choose to give lesser weight to a year of life extension beyond the normal life span than to a year of life extension before one has reached the normal life span based on a conception of what equality of opportunity requires, or on what Alan Williams calls the 'fair innings' argument (Williams 1997: 117–32). People's plans of life and central long term projects will typically be constructed to fit within the normal life span, and so the completion of these central projects will typically require reaching, but not living beyond, the normal life span (Daniels 1988; Brock 1989).

10.3. THIRD ISSUE: WHAT COSTS AND BENEFITS SHOULD COUNT IN COST EFFECTIVENESS ANALYSES OF HEALTH PROGRAMMES?

It is widely agreed that cost effectiveness analyses in health should reflect the direct health benefits for individuals of their medical treatment, such as improving renal function or reducing joint swelling, and of public health programmes, such as reducing the incidence of infectious diseases through vaccination programmes. The direct costs of medical treatment and public health programmes, such as the costs of health care professionals' time and of medical equipment and supplies, should also be reflected. But medical and public health interventions typically also have indirect non-health benefits and costs. For example, some disease and illness principally affects adults during their working years, thereby incurring significant economic costs in lost work days associated with the disease or illness, whereas other disease and illness principally affects either young children, such as some infectious diseases, or the elderly, such as

Alzheimer's dementia, who in each case are not typically employed and so do not incur lost wages or lost work time from illness. Should an indirect economic burden of disease of this sort be given weight in a cost effectiveness analysis used to prioritise between different health interventions? (Brock 2003).

From an economic perspective, as well as from a broad utilitarian moral perspective, indirect non-health benefits and costs are real benefits and costs of disease and of efforts to treat or prevent it, even if not direct health benefits and direct treatment costs; they should be reflected in the overall cost effectiveness accounting of how to use scarce health resources so as to produce the maximum aggregate benefit. A possible moral argument for ignoring these indirect non-health costs and benefits in health resource prioritisation is grounded in a conception of the moral equality of persons. Giving priority to the treatment of one group of patients over another because treating the first group would produce indirect non-health benefits for others (e.g. other family members who were dependent on these patients) or would reduce indirect economic costs to others (e.g. the employers of these patients who incur less lost work time) could be argued to fail to treat each group of patients with the equal moral concern and respect that all people deserve; in particular, doing so would fail to give equal moral concern and weight to each person's health care needs. Instead, giving lower priority to the second group of patients simply because they are not a means to the indirect non-health benefits or cost savings produced by treating the first group of patients gives the second group of patients and their health care needs lower priority simply because they are not a means to these indirect non-health benefits or cost savings to others. It would violate the Kantian moral injunction against treating people solely as means for the benefit of others.

In public policy we often use a notion of 'separate spheres', which in this case could be used to argue that the purpose of health care and of public health is health and the reduction of disease, and so only these goals and effects should guide health care and public health programmes (Walzer 1983; Kamm 1993). There are obvious practical grounds for the separate spheres view from the difficulty of fully determining and calculating indirect benefits and costs. But the Kantian moral argument could serve as a principled moral basis for ignoring indirect benefits and costs in a cost effectiveness analysis to be used to prioritise health resources and interventions that serve different individuals or groups.

10.4. FOURTH ISSUE: SHOULD DISCOUNT RATES BE APPLIED TO HEALTH CARE BENEFITS?

It is both standard and recommended practice in cost effectiveness analyses, within health care and elsewhere, to assume a time preference by applying a discount rate to both the benefits and costs of different programmes under evaluation, although the reasons for doing so and the proper rate of discount are controversial (Gold 1996: chapter 7). It is important to separate clearly the ethical issue about whether health benefits should be discounted from other economic considerations for discounting, as well as to be clear why the issue is important for health policy. It is not ethically controversial that a discount rate should be applied to economic costs and economic benefits; a dollar received today is worth more than a dollar received ten years from now because we have its use for those ten years, and there is a similar economic advantage in delaying the incurring of economic costs. The ethical issue is whether a discount rate should be applied directly to changes in life extension and well-being or health. Is an improvement in well-being, such as a specific period of life extension, a reduction in suffering, or an improvement in function, extending, say, for one year of substantially less value if it occurs twenty years from now than if it occurs next year?

Future benefits are appropriately discounted when they are more uncertain than proximate benefits. Proximate benefits, such as restoration of an individual's function, also are of more value than distant benefits if they make possible a longer period of, and thus larger, benefit by occurring sooner. But neither of these considerations require the use of a discount rate—they will be taken account of in the measurement of expected benefits of alternative interventions. The ethical question is whether an improvement in an individual's well-being is of lesser value if it occurs in the distant future than if it occurs in the immediate future, simply and only because it occurs later in time. This is a controversial issue in the literature on social discounting and my own view is that no adequate ethical justification has been offered for applying a discount rate directly to changes in health and well-being, though I cannot pursue the justifications offered by proponents of discounting here. The avoidance of paradoxes that arise when no discount rate is applied or when different discount rates are applied to costs and benefits, has influenced many economists to support use of the same discount rate for costs and benefits (Keeler and Cretin 1983: 300–6), but I believe these are properly dealt with not through discounting, but rather through directly addressing the ethical issues they raise, usually about equity between different generations.

The policy importance of this issue is relatively straightforward in the prioritization of health care interventions. Many health care and public health programmes take significantly different lengths of time to produce their benefits. Applying a discount rate to those benefits leads to an unwarranted priority to programmes producing benefits more rapidly. It results in a programme that produces benefits in health and well-being say twenty years into the future being given lower priority than an alternative health care programme that produces substantially less overall improvement in health and well-being, but produces that improvement much sooner. Many public health and preventive interventions, for example, vaccination programmes and changes in unhealthy behaviour, reap their health benefits years into the future. If those benefits are unjustifiably discounted, they will be given lower priority than alternative programmes that produce fewer aggregate benefits. The result is a health policy that produces fewer overall health benefits over time than could have been produced with the same resources.

10.5. FIFTH ISSUE: WHAT LIFE EXPECTANCIES SHOULD BE USED FOR CALCULATING THE BENEFITS OF LIFE SAVING INTERVENTIONS?

In calculating QALYs it is standard practice to take account of differences in the average ages and in turn life expectancies of patients served by different health care programmes; for example, a treatment for a life-threatening childhood disease would produce more QALYs than a comparable treatment for a life-threatening disease affecting primarily the elderly. Similarly, accurate estimates of the expected QALYs from different interventions would adjust for differences in the average life expectancies of patients caused by diseases other than those treated by the interventions; for example, an intervention that improved the quality of life of patients with cystic fibrosis, who have a much lower than average life expectancy as a result of their disease, would produce fewer QALYs than an intervention with a comparable improvement in lifetime quality of life for patients with average life expectancies undiminished by disease. This latter case raises difficult issues about discrimination against people with disabilities that I take up later. But there are other differences in the life expectancies of different groups that an accurate estimate of QALYs produced by health interventions serving those groups would seemingly have to reflect; for example, there are significant differences in the life expectancies between different genders, racial and ethnic groups, and socio-economic groups within most countries. Internationally, the differences in life expectancies between different countries are often much larger. Should these differences affect calculations of the QALYs gained by health care and public health interventions that extend life or improve quality of life? An accurate estimate of the additional life years actually produced by those interventions should not ignore differences in life expectancies that the health care interventions will not affect, but the result will be that it is less valuable to save the life of a poor person in an underdeveloped country than a rich person in a developed country.

The differences in life expectancies between different racial, ethnic, and socio-economic groups within a single country, as well as the very large differences between life expectancies in economically developed and poor countries, are often principally the result of unjust conditions and deprivations suffered by those with lower life expectancies. It would seem only to compound those injustices to give less value to interventions that save lives or improve quality of life for groups with lower life expectancies caused by the unjust conditions and deprivations from which they suffer. Differences in life expectancies between the genders, on the other hand, are believed to rest in significant part on biological differences, not on unjust social conditions. Whether the biologically based component of gender differences in life expectancies should be reflected in measures like QALYs or DALYs is more controversial. For example, on the one hand, the lower life expectancy of men does not result from any independent injustice, but, on the other hand, it is explicit public policy and required by law in the United States to ignore this gender-based difference in most calculations of pension benefits and annuity costs so as to avoid gender discrimination. The developers of the DALY explicitly chose to use a single uniform measure of life expectancy (except for the biological component of the gender difference), specifically that observed in Japan which has the highest national life expectancy, to measure gains from life saving interventions. They justified their choice in explicitly ethical terms as conforming to a principle of 'treating like events as like', although the reasoning was not pursued in any detail (Murray 1994: 7). How this issue is treated can have a substantial impact on the priorities that result from the cost effectiveness analysis, especially at the international level where country differences tend often to be greater than group differences within specific countries.

Each of the preceding five ethical issues can be considered issues in the *construction* of a cost-effectiveness analysis in health care. The other issues I want to briefly note can be considered issues in the *use* of cost effectiveness analysis in health resource prioritisation. They are each issues of distributive justice or equity raised by the fact that a cost effectiveness analysis is insensitive to the distribution of health benefits and of the costs of producing them. Yet people's beliefs about equity and justice directly affect the relative priority they assign to different health interventions. One standard response to this point is that a CEA can only be an aid to policy-making in general, and health resource prioritisation in particular, and that policy makers must take account of considerations of equity in final policy decisions and choices. But as with the ethical issues in the construction of CEAs, much work remains to be done to clarify and assess alternative positions on these issues of equity so the policy choices on them can at least be better informed, even if they remain controversial. Here, there is only space to state four of the main equity issues in the use of CEAs and some of the principal ethical considerations supporting different positions on them (Daniels 1993: 224–33). After doing that, I shall mention an alternative quantitative methodology that, unlike CEA, incorporates considerations of equity within the quantitative analysis.

10.6. SIXTH ISSUE: WHAT PRIORITY SHOULD BE GIVEN TO THE SICKEST OR WORST OFF?

It is a commonplace that most theories of distributive justice require some special concern for those who are worst off or most disadvantaged (Brock 2002); for example, it is often said that the justice of a society can be measured by how it treats its least well-off members. In the context of health care allocation and the prioritisation of health interventions, the worst off with regard to need for the good being distributed might reasonably be thought to be the sickest patients. In many cases, the sickest will be given priority by a CEA comparing treating them as opposed to less sick patients; the sickest have greater possible improvements in HRQL because they begin from a lower HRQL, and so, for example, in comparing fully effective treatments those for the sickest will produce the greater benefits. But in other cases giving priority to the sickest will require a sacrifice in aggregate health benefits. An abstract example makes the point most concisely. Suppose Group A patients have a very serious disease that leaves them with a health utility level of 0.25 as measured by the HUI, and this would be raised only to 0.45 with the best available treatment because no treatment is very effective for their disease; for example, patients with severe chronic obstructive pulmonary disease or with severe chronic schizophrenia that is largely resistant to standard pharmacological treatments. A similar number of Group B patients have a health utility level of 0.60 because they have a considerably less serious disease, but since treatment for their disease is more effective, although no more costly, it would raise their health utility level to 0.90; for example, patients with asthma, or with milder forms of pulmonary disease or schizophrenia that both leave them less disabled without treatment and are more responsive to treatment. Should we give priority to treating Group B because doing so would produce a 50 per cent greater aggregate health benefit at the same cost, as the CEA standard implies, or to treating Group A who are the sickest? In some empirical studies, both ordinary people and health professionals prefer to sacrifice some aggregate health benefits in order to treat the sickest patients, although the degree of sacrifice they are prepared to make is variable and not statistically reliable (Nord 1993: 227–38).

One difficulty raised by this issue is determining what weight to give to this particular aspect of equity—concern for the worst off. Virtually no one would prefer to treat the sickest, no matter how costly their treatment and how small the benefit to them of doing so, and no matter how beneficial and inexpensive treatment for the less sick might be. However, there seems no objective, principled basis for determining how much priority to give the sickest, that is, how much aggregate health benefits should be sacrificed in order to treat or give priority to the sickest. Instead, the most one can say is that most people and many theories of distributive justice have a concern both for maximising overall benefits with scarce health resources and for helping the worst off or sickest, but there is a large range of indeterminacy regarding the proper tradeoff between these two concerns when they are in conflict.

One issue in understanding this concern for the worst off important for health care priorities is whether it should focus on who is worst off at a point in time or instead over an extended period of time, such as a lifetime. When choosing between patients to receive a scarce resource, such as in organ transplantation, it is often plausible to focus on lifetime well-being, since otherwise we may give priority to the patient who is worst off at the time the distributive choice is made, but whose lifetime level of well-being is far higher than the other patient. Frances Kamm has defended a notion of need in this context according to which the neediest patient is the patient whose life will have gone worst if he or she does not get the scarce resource, such as an organ transplant (Kamm 1993: chapter 8). However, some justifications for giving priority to the worst off may support focusing on the sickest here and now.

What are the ethical justifications for giving priority to the worst off? I can mention only two possibilities here. One is that we must give priority to the worst off in order to avoid increasing the already unjustified disadvantage or inequality they suffer relative to those better off. But it is worth noting that a concern for the worst off is not always the same as a concern to produce equality in outcomes. In the example above of Groups A and B, equality could be achieved by what Derek Parfit has called 'levelling down', that is by bringing B's health utility level down to that of A's instead raising A's level up to that of B (Parfit 1991). If equity here is equivalent to equality in outcomes, then if it were not possible to raise A's level above 0.40 with treatment, equity would seem to support not treating Group B and letting their condition deteriorate until it reached the lower level of Group A. The fact that no one would defend doing this suggests that this aspect of our notion of equity or justice is best captured by the idea of giving priority to improving the condition of the worst off, rather than by a simple concern for equality in outcomes. A different justification for giving priority to treating the sickest, offered by some participants in Nord's research, is that it would be subjectively more important to the sickest to obtain treatment, even if the health benefits they receive from treatment are less than those that would go to the less sick; this justification might support focusing on who is worst off at the point in time at which the decision about who to treat is made, not whose lifetime well-being will be lowest (Nord 1993: 227–38).

One further issue concerning the priority to the worst off should be mentioned. In the context of health resource prioritisation in health policy it seems natural to understand the worst off as the sickest. But this may not always be correct. At the most fundamental ethical level in our general theories of equity and distributive justice, our concern should be for those who are overall or all things considered worst off, and they will not always be the sickest. It could be argued that giving priority to the worst off in health resource prioritisation sometimes requires giving priority to those with the lowest levels of overall well-being, even at some cost to aggregate health benefits produced *and* at the cost of not treating sicker persons whose overall well-being is much higher. A preference for health interventions that raise the level of well-being of those who are worst off in overall well-being, instead of giving priority to the sickest, might be justified in order not to increase the unjustified disadvantage suffered by those with the lowest overall level of well-being. If, instead, the priority to the worst off in health resource prioritisation should focus only on health states and so on the sickest, a justification of this narrowed focus is needed.

10.7. SEVENTH ISSUE: WHEN SHOULD SMALL BENEFITS TO A LARGE NUMBER OF PERSONS RECEIVE PRIORITY OVER LARGE BENEFITS TO A SMALL NUMBER OF PERSONS?

Cost effectiveness and utilitarian standards require minimising the aggregate burden of disease and maximising the aggregate health of a population without regard to the resulting distribution of disease and health, or *who* gets what benefits. The issue about priority to the worst off focuses on who gets the benefits. A different issue concerns *what* benefits different individuals get. Some would argue that health benefits are often qualitatively different and so cannot all be compared on a single scale like the HUI, or in turn by a single measure like QALYs, but that is not the issue of concern now. In its most general form the issue about aggregation concerns what ethical limits there are, if any, on aggregating together different size benefits for different persons in comparing and prioritising different health interventions; CEA accepts no such limits. There are many forms in which this issue can arise which cannot be pursued here (Kamm 1993: Part II), but the version that has received the most attention, and which Daniels has called the aggregation problem, is when, if ever, large benefits to a few individuals should take priority over greater aggregate benefits to a different and much larger group of individuals, each one of whom receives only a small benefit. This issue arises when a very serious disease or condition for those affected that is also very costly to prevent or treat is compared with a much more prevalent disease or condition that both has a very small impact on each individual affected and is very inexpensive to treat or prevent in any one individual. Applying cost effectiveness or utilitarian standards, preventing or treating the very prevalent but low impact disease or condition at a given cost will receive higher priority when doing so produces greater aggregate benefits than using the same funds to treat or prevent the disease or condition that has a very great impact on each individual affected. The example that received considerable attention in the United States arose in the Oregon Medicaid priority setting process where capping teeth for exposed pulp was ranked just above an appendectomy for acute appendicitis, a potentially life-threatening condition. Because an appendectomy was estimated to be about 150 times as expensive as capping a tooth for exposed pulp, the aggregate benefit of capping a tooth for 150 patients was judged to be greater than the benefit of an appendectomy for one patient. Since Medicaid coverage decisions were to be made according to the list of treatment/condition pairs ranked in terms of their relative cost effectiveness, it could have turned out, depending on the overall level of resources available to the Medicaid programme, that tooth capping would have been covered but appendectomies not covered.

This result, and other less extreme cases like it, was highly counterintuitive and unacceptable to most people, whose intuitive rankings of the relative importance or priority of health interventions are based on one-to-one comparisons, for example, of one tooth capped as opposed to one appendectomy performed. In the face of these results Oregon made a fundamental change in its prioritisation methodology, abandoning the cost effectiveness standard in favour of a standard that did not take account of differences in costs. This was not a minor problem requiring tinkering at the margins of the CEA standard, but a fundamental challenge to it and so required a fundamental revision in it.

Yet, it is by no means clear that no such aggregation can be ethically justified. The very case that precipitated Oregon's Medicaid revision was a twelve-year-old boy in need of a bone marrow transplant as the only effective chance to save his life. Oregon denied coverage under its Medicaid programme on the grounds that it could do greater good by using its limited resources to improve prenatal care for pregnant women, in this case giving higher priority to small benefits to many over a potentially much larger benefit to a few. Moreover, many public policy choices appear to give higher priority to small benefits to many over even life-saving benefits to a few; for example, governments in the United States support public parks used by tens or hundreds of thousands of persons, while reducing funding for public hospitals resulting in quite predictable loss of life.

The cost effectiveness or utilitarian standard that permits unlimited aggregation of benefits might be defended by distinguishing between the clinical context in which physicians treat individual patients and the public health and health policy context in which health resource allocation decisions are made that will affect different groups in the population. In the clinical context, physicians forced to prioritise between individual patients typically will first treat the patient who will suffer the more serious consequences without treatment, or who will benefit the most from treatment, even if doing so will prevent her treating a larger number of less seriously ill patients. But from a public health or health policy perspective, it could be argued that the potential overall or aggregate effects of alternative interventions on population health is the appropriate perspective. However, the Oregon experience makes clear that even when allocating public resources for interventions to improve the health of a population it is ethically controversial whether always giving priority to producing the maximum aggregate benefits, even when that is done by giving small benefits to many at the cost of forgoing large benefits to a few, is justified.

Just as with the problem of what priority to give to the worst off, part of the complexity of the aggregation problem is that for most people some, but not all, cases of aggregation are ethically acceptable and equitable. The theoretical problem then is to develop a principled account of when, and for what reasons, different forms of aggregation satisfy requirements of equity and when they do not (Kamm 1993). There is no consensus on this issue either among ordinary persons or within the literature of health policy or ethics and political philosophy. As with the problem about priority to the worst off, the complexities of this issue have received relatively little attention in bioethics and moral and political philosophy, and there is much difficult but important work to be done.

10.8. EIGHTH ISSUE: THE CONFLICT BETWEEN FAIR CHANCES AND BEST OUTCOMES

The third ethical issue in the use of CEA for health resource utilisation that I will mention here has been characterised as the conflict between fair chances and best outcomes (Daniels 1993: 224–33). The conflict is most pressing when the health intervention is life saving and not all those whose lives are threatened can be saved, but it arises as well when threats are only to individuals' health and well-being. In the context of health care, this issue first received attention in organ transplantation where there is a scarcity of life-saving organs such as hearts and lungs resulting in thousands of deaths each year of patients on waiting lists for an organ for transplant; an abstract example from transplantation can illustrate the issue most clearly and succinctly (Brock 1988).

Suppose two patients are each in need of a heart transplant to prevent imminent death, but there is only one heart available for transplant. Patient A has a life expectancy with a transplant of ten years and patient B has a life expectancy with a transplant of nine years (of course, precise estimates of this sort are not possible, but the point is that there is a small difference in the expected benefits to be gained depending on which patient gets the scarce organ), with no difference in their expected quality of life. Maximising health benefits or QALYs, as a CEA standard requires, favours giving the organ to patient A, but patient B might argue that it is unfair to give her no chance to receive the scarce heart. Just as much as A, she needs the heart transplant for life itself and will lose everything, that is her life, if she does not receive it. It is unfair, B might argue, to give the organ to A because the quite small increment in expected benefits from doing so is too small to justly determine who lives and who dies. Instead, she argues, each of them should receive a fair chance of getting the organ and having their health needs met; in this case, that might be done by giving each an equal chance of receiving the transplant through some form of random selection between them, or by a weighted lottery that gives the patient who would benefit more some greater likelihood of being selected to receive the organ, but still gives the patient who would benefit less some significant chance of getting it instead (Broome 1984: 38–55; Brock 1988; Kamm 1993: Part III).

Most prioritisation and rationing choices arise not from physical scarcity of the needed health resource, as in organ transplantation, but from economic scarcity, limits in the money society devotes to health care. Will this issue of equity arise in health resource prioritisation and allocation choices forced by economic scarcity? Two considerations will often mitigate the force of the ethical conflict between fair chances and best outcomes there. First, allocation of resources in health care is typically not an all or nothing choice, as in the case of selecting recipients for scarce organs, but is usually a matter of the relative priority for funding to be given to different health programmes or interventions.

That one health programme A promises a small gain in aggregate health benefits over a competing programme B need not entail that A is fully funded and B receives no funding, but only that A should receive higher priority for, or a higher level of, funding than B. Persons with the disease or condition that A treats will have a somewhat higher probability of being successfully treated than will those who have the disease or condition that B treats; in the case of prevention, those at risk of A will have a somewhat higher probability of successful prevention than will those at risk of B. When there is significant resource scarcity this will involve some sacrifice in aggregate health benefits that might have been produced by always preferring the more cost effective alternative. But doing so means that individuals who are served by B have no complaint that the small difference in expected benefits between programmes A and B unfairly prevents them from having their health needs met at all. Instead, the small difference in expected benefits between programmes A and B need only result in a comparably small difference in the resources devoted to A and B; it is not obvious that this is unfair to those patients served by B, whose needs are somewhat less well served than patients in programme A because of B's lower priority and level of funding.

The second consideration that may mitigate some of the conflict between fair chances and best outcomes in health resource prioritisation forced by economic scarcity is that often, probably usually, the diseases and health problems to be treated or prevented are not directly life threatening, but instead only impact on individuals' quality of life, and often for only a limited period of time. In these cases, the difference in health benefits between individuals who receive a needed health intervention that is given a higher priority and individuals who do not receive a needed health intervention because their condition is given lower priority, is much less, making the unfairness arguably less compelling.

These two considerations may mitigate, but they do not fully avoid, the conflict between fair chances and best outcomes in prioritisation decisions about health interventions forced by economic scarcity. When a more cost effective health programme is developed for one population instead of a different less cost effective health programme for a different population, individuals who would have been served by the second programme will have a complaint that they did not have a fair chance to have their needs served only because of a small gain in the benefits that are produced by the first programme. The fair chances versus best outcome conflict will arise in prioritising health interventions in health policy; how this conflict can be equitably resolved is complex, controversial, and unclear.

10.9. NINTH ISSUE: DOES USE OF CEA TO SET HEALTH CARE PRIORITIES UNJUSTLY DISCRIMINATE AGAINST THE DISABLED?

In several contexts using CEA to set health care priorities will result in assigning lower priority to both life extending and quality of life improving treatment for disabled rather than non-disabled persons with the same health care needs (Brock 1995: 159–84; 2000: 223–35). Here are five such contexts. First, since already disabled persons have a lower HRQL from their disability than non-disabled persons, treatment that extends their life for a given number of years produces fewer QALYs than the same treatment that extends the life of a non-disabled person for the same number of years. Second, if two groups of patients with the same HRQL have the same need for a life sustaining or quality of life improving treatment, but one will be restored to normal function and the other will be left with a resultant disability, more QALYs will be produced by treating the first group. Third, persons with disabilities often have a lower life expectancy because of their disability than otherwise similar non-disabled persons. As a result, treatments that prevent loss of life or produce lifetime improvements in quality of life will produce fewer QALYs when given to disabled than to non-disabled persons with the same health care needs. Fourth, disabilities often act as comorbid conditions making a treatment less beneficial in QALYs produced for disabled than for non-disabled persons with the same health care needs. Fifth, the presence of a disability can make treatment of disabled persons more difficult and so more costly than for non-disabled persons with the same health care needs; the result is a lower cost effectiveness ratio for treating the disabled persons.

In each of the five cases above, disabled persons have the same medical and health care need as non-disabled persons, and so the same claim to treatment on the basis of their needs. But treating the disabled person will produce less benefit, that is, fewer QALYs, *because of their disability* than treating the non-disabled. Thus, their disability is the reason for their receiving lower priority for treatment. This at least arguably fails to give equal moral concern to disabled persons' health care needs and is unjust discrimination against them on grounds of their disability. Indeed, United States Health and Human Services Secretary Louis Sullivan denied Oregon's initial request for a waiver of federal regulations for its proposed revisions to its Medicaid plan on the grounds that Oregon's method of prioritisation of services was in violation of the Americans with Disabilities Act (ADA).[2] Sullivan cited some of the five kinds of cases I noted above in support of that position, and Oregon in turn made essentially ad hoc revisions in its ranking to avoid the putative violation of the ADA.

Disabled persons charge that in cases like the first I cited above concerning life saving treatment, the implication of use of CEA to prioritise health care is that saving their lives, and so their lives themselves, have less value than non-disabled persons' lives. They quite plausibly find that implication of CEA threatening and unjust. There are means of avoiding these problems about discrimination against persons with disabilities, but they involve abandoning fundamental features of CEAs. For example, one response to the first case cited

[2] Unpublished letter from Secretary of Health and Human Services, Louis Sullivan, to Oregon Governor, Barbara Roberts, 3 August 1992.

above would be to give equal value to a year of life extension, whatever the quality of that life, so long as it is acceptable to the person whose life it is (Kamm 1993: Part I). But that has problematic implications too since, for example, a small percentage of persons in surveys say they would want their lives sustained even if they were in a persistent vegetative state. I cannot pursue the issues further here, but I believe the problem of whether CEA unjustly discriminates against the disabled is a deep and unresolved difficulty for use of CEA and QALYs to prioritise health care.

The sixth, seventh, and eighth issues above all raise possible criticisms of the maximisation standard embodied in CEA; in each case, the claim is that equity requires attention to the distribution of health benefits and costs to distinct individuals. Steadfast utilitarians or consequentialists will reject the criticisms and hold fast to the maximisation standard. But most people will accept some departure from the maximisation standard of CEA; there are two broad strategies for how to do so. The first and probably most common is to propose CEA as an aid to policy-makers who must make prioritisation and allocation choices in health care, but then to remind those policy-makers that they must take account of these considerations of equity as well in their decision-making; this may be, but usually is not, accompanied by some guidance about alternative substantive positions, and reasons in support of them, on the equity issues. Moreover, some use of CEA in health policy and health programme evaluation does not raise these last three issues of equity; for example, CEA of alternative treatments that each have uniform but different benefits for a group of patients with a particular medical condition. And outside of a CEA, either QALYs or DALYs can be used for evaluating alternative interventions, or for monitoring changes over time in health status or the burdens of disease, in a given group or population.

The second strategy for responding to concerns about equity seeks to develop a quantitative tool that measures the specific weight people give to different equity concerns in comparing interventions that raise issues of distributive justice because they serve different individuals or benefit individuals differently. The most prominent and promising example is the 'person trade-off' approach which explicitly asks people how many outcomes of one kind they consider equivalent in social value to *X* outcomes of another kind, where the outcomes are for different groups of individuals (Nord 1999). For example, people can be asked, as in our earlier example, to compare treatment A for very severely ill patients who are at 0.25 on the HUI without treatment and who can be raised only to 0.45 with treatment, with treatment B of less severely ill patients who are at 0.60 and can be raised to 0.90 with treatment; filled out detailed examples, of course, will make the comparisons more understandable. Respondents are then asked how many patients treated with A would be equivalent in social value to treating 100 patients with B. Answers to questions of this form will tell us in quantitative terms how much importance people give to treating the sickest when doing so conflicts with maximising aggregate health benefits.

The person tradeoff approach is designed to permit people to incorporate concerns for equity or distributive justice into their judgements about the social value of alternative health programmes. There has been relatively little exploration and use of this methodology in health care evaluation in comparison with the mass of methodological work on and studies of aggregate QALYs and CEAs, in part because many health policy analysts and health economists assume, often with little or no argument, that the social value of health programmes is the sum of the individual utilities produced by the programme. As I noted in the introduction to the chapter, the early stage we are now at in the development and use of the person tradeoff approach is a reason for caution at the present time about using it to settle issues of equity in health resource prioritisation. While the utilitarian assumption in CEA is rejected in most philosophical work on distributive justice, as well as in the preferences most ordinary people express for different health outcomes and programmes, I also noted in the introduction a second more important reason for caution about bringing considerations of equity into health policy decision-making through a quantitative methodology like the person tradeoff methodology—the issues of distributive justice that must be addressed by equitable health resource prioritisation represent deep and long-standing divisions in moral and political philosophy about which there is not now, and may never be, anything approaching consensus. There is a strong case to be made, though I cannot pursue it here, that important value conflicts about justice of this sort should be addressed in public, democratic political processes, or in fair, participatory, and accountable procedures within private institutions like managed care organisations (Daniels and Sabin 1997: 303–50). The person tradeoff method can be a useful aid to those deliberative decision-making processes in providing more structure and precision to different people's views about equity in health care resource prioritisation and tradeoffs, but it is not a substitute for that deliberation. Despite these briefly noted reservations, I do emphasise that for purposes of resource prioritisation and allocation, the person tradeoff approach is the proper perspective, in comparison with CEA, because it correctly reflects that the choices are typically about how health benefits and costs are distributed to different individuals.

10.10. CONCLUSION

I have distinguished above nine distinct issues about equity and justice that arise in the construction and use of cost effectiveness analysis to minimise the burdens of disease and to maximise health outcomes. In each case the concern for equity is in my view valid and warrants some constraints on a goal of unqualified maximisation of health outcomes. There has not been space here to pursue at all fully any of these nine issues regarding equity and justice—each is complex, controversial, and important. In each case, my point has been that there are important ethical and value choices to be made in constructing and using the measures; the choices are not merely technical, empirical, or economic, but moral and value choices as well. Each requires explicit attention by health policy-makers using CEA. In a few cases I have indicated my own view about how the potential conflict between equity and utilitarian maximisation might be resolved, but in other cases I have simply summarised briefly some arguments for giving the particular concern about equity some weight when it conflicts with maximisation of utility. For some of these issues, the literature and research is at a relatively early stage and one cannot be confident about how the issues should be resolved or even about the range of plausible positions and supporting reasons on them. However, this is not grounds for ignoring the issues, but instead for getting to work on them and for ensuring that they receive explicit attention and deliberation in decisions about health resource prioritisation and allocation.

References

Bergner, M., R. A. Bobbitt, W. B. Carter, and B. S. Gibson (1981). 'The Sickness Impact Profile: Development and Final Revision of a Health Status Measure', *Medical Care*, 19: 787–805.

Brock, D. W. (1988). 'Ethical Issues in Recipient Selection for Organ Transplantation', in D. Mathieu (ed.), *Organ Substitution Technology: Ethical, Legal, and Public Policy Issues*. Boulder and London: Westview Press.

——(1989). 'Justice, Health Care, and the Elderly', *Philosophy & Public Affairs*, 18(3): 297–312.

——(1992). 'Quality of Life Measures in Health Care and Medical Ethics', in A. Sen and M. Nussbaum (eds.), *The Quality of Life*. Oxford: Oxford University Press.

——(1995). 'Justice and ADA: Does Prioritizing and Rationing Health Care Discriminate Against the Disabled?' *Social Theory and Policy*, 12: 159–84.

——(2000). 'Health Care Resource Prioritization and Discrimination Against Persons With Disabilities', in L. Francis and A. Silvers (eds.), *Americans With Disabilities*. New York: Routledge.

——(2002). 'Priority to the Worst Off in Health Care Resource Prioritization', in M. Battin, R. Rhodes, and A. Silvers (eds.), *Medicine and Social Justice*. New York: Oxford University Press.

—— (2003). 'Separate Spheres and Indirect Benefits,' *Cost-Effectiveness and Resource Allocation* 1: 4.

Broome, J. (1984). 'Selecting People Randomly', *Ethics*, 95: 38–55.

Daniels, N. (1988). *Am I My Parents' Keeper? An Essay on Justice Between the Young and the Old*. New York: Oxford University Press.

——(1993). 'Rationing Fairly: Programmatic Considerations', *Bioethics*, 7(2–3): 224–33.

——and J. Sabin (1997). 'Limits to Health Care: Fair Procedures, Democratic Deliberation, and the Legitimacy Problem for Insurers', *Philosophy and Public Affairs*, 26(4): 303–50.

Gold, M. R. et al. (1996). *Cost-Effectiveness in Health and Medicine*. New York: Oxford University Press, chapter 7.

Kamm, F. M. (1993). *Morality/Mortality. Volume One. Death and Whom to Save From It*. Oxford: Oxford University Press.

Kaplan, R. M. and J. P. Anderson (1988). 'A General Health Policy Model: Update and Applications', *Health Services Research*, June 23: 203–35.

Keeler, E. B. and S. Cretin (1983). 'Discounting of Life-Saving and Other Non-Monetary Effects', *Management Science*, 29: 300–6.

Murray, C. J. L. (1994). 'Quantifying the Burden of Disease: The Technical Basis for Disability-Adjusted Life Years', in C. J. L. Murray and A. D. Lopez (eds.), *Global Comparative Assessments in the Health Sector: Disease Burden, Expenditures and Intervention Packages*. Geneva: World Health Organization.

Murray, C. J. L. (1996). 'Rethinking DALYs', in *The Global Burden of Disease: A Comprehensive Assessment of Mortality and Disability From Disease, Injuries, and Risk Factors in 1990 and Projected to 2020*. Geneva: World Health Organization.

Nord, E. (1993). 'The Trade-Off Between Severity of Illness and Treatment Effect in Cost-Value Analysis of Health Care', *Health Policy*, 24: 227–38.

—— (1999). *Cost-Value Analysis in Health Care: Making Sense of QALYs*. New York: Cambridge University Press.

Parfit, D. (1991). 'Equality or Priority', *The Lindley Lecture*. Copyright: Department of Philosophy, University of Kansas.

Torrance, G. W. et al. (1992). 'Multi Attribute Preference Functions for a Comprehensive Health Status Classification System', *Working Paper No. 92–18*. Hamilton, Ontario: McMaster University, Center for Health Economics and Policy Analysis.

Walzer, M. (1983). *Spheres of Justice*. New York: Basic Books.

Ware, J. E. and D. C. Sherbourne (1992). 'The MOS 36-item Short Form Health Survey', *Medical Care*, 30: 473–83.

WHO (World Health Organization) (1980). *International Classification of Impairments, Disabilities and Handicaps*. Geneva: World Health Organization.

Williams, A. (1997). 'Intergenerational Equity: An Exploration of the "Fair Innings" Argument', *Health Economics*, 6(2): 117–32.

World Bank (1993). *World Development Report 1993: Investing in Health*. New York and Oxford: Oxford University Press.

[29]

Health Equity and Social Justice

FABIENNE PETER

ABSTRACT *There is consistent and strong empirical evidence for social inequalities in health, as a vast and fast growing literature shows. In recent years, these findings have helped to move health equity high on international research and policy agendas. This paper examines how the empirical identification of social inequalities in health relates to a normative judgment about health inequities and puts forward an approach which embeds the pursuit of health equity within the general pursuit of social justice. It defends an indirect approach to health equity, which views social inequalities in health as unjust in so far as they are the result of an unjust basic structure of society in Rawls' sense.*

I. Introduction

There is consistent and strong empirical evidence for social inequalities in health, as a vast and fast-growing literature shows. Social inequalities in health are significant variations in health outcomes (as measured by life-expectancy at birth, infant mortality, morbidity, etc.) across different social groups. Typically, the lower a group's social position, the worse the average health status of its members [1]. Gender, race, social class, occupational status, and socio-geographic location are examples of social categories that define social groups. More recently, a new set of studies has emerged that focuses on the relationship between income inequality and population health. Though still contested, the findings suggest that the more unequal a society, the worse its achievements in (aggregate) health [2].

Explanations for the occurrence of social inequalities in health are manifold and often difficult to establish [3]. The principal upshot of these studies is that one explanation that seems at first plausible, namely differences in access to health care, does not get us very far. Access to health care is only one social factor among others that influences people's health. The goal of empirical studies of social inequalities in health is to understand *social determinants* of health, and, increasingly, to explain the *mechanisms* or *pathways* that lead to the observed social differences in health outcomes. The latter is accompanied by a renewed interest in the social sciences and a move towards more interdisciplinary analysis of the social processes underlying inequalities in health [4].

This development is often labelled a 'new public health', but, as for example Ann Robertson stresses, "[m]any would argue that this is not so much a new public health as a return to the historical commitments of public health to social justice." [5] In the public health field, the concern with health equity and social justice is recognized as having a normative dimension, i.e. as involving value judgements in an explicit way. According to the frequently quoted definition by Margaret Whitehead, health inequities are "differences [in health] which are unnecessary and avoidable but, in addition, are also considered unfair and unjust". [6] While it points in the right direction, this definition leaves open how we should go about making judgments of unfairness and injustice. The problem a theory of health equity faces is, therefore, how to go from the *empirical* identification of *social inequalities* in health to a *normative* judgment about *health inequities*. What is needed is a framework within which the ethical issues raised by the empirical literature can be addressed and which helps in determining which inequalities in health outcomes are unjust.

Until recently, there has been little work in ethics and political philosophy that deals with these issues. Many general theories of justice, such as John Rawls' theory of justice as fairness, do not address health specifically [7]. In bioethics, efforts have tended to concentrate on access to *health care* [8]. There are, of course, good reasons for focusing on health care. The premise for any theory of justice is that there is some good that can be (re)distributed, that something can be changed about the situation that is considered unjust. If, in the context of health, the allocation of health care is perceived to be the instrument that is best suited to correct health outcomes, then conceptions of equity will concentrate on health care — not health. Furthermore, we may regard people's access to health care as being important in and of itself, independently of its contribution to an equitable distribution of health outcomes [9]. If, however, we are concerned not just with health care but also with health outcomes, and if there are serious social inequalities in health outcomes that cannot be traced back to differential access to health care, then conceptions of health equity have to go beyond health care.

The situation has started to change and a literature on public health ethics is emerging [10]. This paper seeks to contribute to this literature by putting forward a theoretical framework for making health equity judgments.

The paper defends what I call an *indirect* approach. I call an approach *direct* if it isolates health from other social spheres and is defined with respect to particular distributions of health outcomes — most existing approaches to health equity, as I shall explain later, are direct. An indirect approach, in contrast, is based on the premise that social inequalities in health are wrong not simply because actual health outcomes deviate from some pattern of health outcomes that is considered ideal, but rather because, and insofar as, they are the expression and product of unjust economic, social, and political institutions. It thus embeds the pursuit of health equity in the pursuit of social justice in general. In addition, the approach I shall present also stresses the reverse relationship between inequalities in health and social justice: an understanding of social inequalities in health and the mechanisms by which they are produced, may reveal something important about how the institutions of society work and may hence inform our assessment of the justice of these institutions. The emphasis placed on the larger social processes that bring about social inequalities in health is in line with the development in public health research to focus more on the 'upstream' influences on people's health [11].

The approach I shall present is based on John Rawls' theory of justice as fairness, in particular as it is presented in his later book *Political Liberalism* [12]. Although Rawls has not himself addressed the topic of health, I shall argue that the conception of justice as fairness provides a useful framework for evaluating social inequalities in health.

I shall elaborate on the distinction between direct and indirect approaches to health equity in section III and will highlight some important concepts of Rawls' theory of justice as fairness in section IV. Section V synthesizes the previous two sections in a framework for health equity analysis. Before pursuing further the question of how to make judgments of health equity, it will be important to discuss the notion of health itself — this is the subject of the next section.

II. Health

What makes thinking about health equity difficult from the outset is that the concept of health itself is not easy to grasp and varies considerably across places and times. Although general observations can be made with respect to the meaningfulness of different definitions of health, it is likely that their adequacy will vary with the context in which we refer to it.

As, for example, the authors of the Black Report stress, a relationship between health and society is present not only at the level of social inequalities in health but already at the level of health itself [13]. They argue that the medical profession's approach to health is only one among others, and its partiality may impede finding solutions to pressing health problems. Instead of the "medical model", they advocate a "social model" of health — grounded in the social sciences. They suggest that the role of social studies of health problems should be "in part, to increase understanding of the social and socio-economic factors which play a part in the promotion of health and the causation of disease and in part to take the natural next step and relate these factors themselves to the broader social structure". [14]

A general criticism of the medical model is that it directs too much attention to diseases and their remedy. There is thus a danger of losing sight of such issues as why good health is important for people, what good health means to them, and what the broader social context is in which the pursuit of health and the response to disease are shaped [15].

In some sense, the WHO definition, according to which "health is a state of complete physical, mental and social well-being and not merely the absence of disease or infirmity" [16], and quality-of-life approaches to health can be read as a reaction against this paradigm [17]. A definition of health as extensive as the one by WHO runs into problems of its own, however. It is not clear in what ways health is distinct from other components of well-being. The definition thus does not allow for the possibility that (some) well-being might be achieved while health is bad, or that health might be good yet well-being low. Nor is it clear how well-being can be defined in a way that is consistent with a plurality of conceptions of the good life — a characteristic of modern democratic societies. A further objection to the WHO definition is that such a broad conception of health bears the danger of overly medicalizing social problems [18]. As Vincanne Adams writes in a related context, it may treat the social pursuit of health "as a technical problem with technical solutions, rather than a political problem with a political solution". [19]

Amartya Sen's capability approach offers a fruitful alternative for assessing health problems in society [20]. The idea underlying the capability approach is that in policy evaluation, the appropriate information is not individual utility or well-being, nor the resources people have access to (e.g. medical care), but something in between. Sen argues that what matters is what people can *do* with the resources they have access to — a notion of freedom. A person's capability tries to capture that. Capability is the set of 'functionings' — the various 'doings and beings' — that a person can achieve (but may decide not to). Examples of functionings are being adequately nourished, being able to read, or, more complex, achieving self-respect. Sen often cites good health as an example of a functioning [21]. It may, however, be more promising to see health as a capability of its own, or, more precisely, as a sub-set of a person's capability. The idea is that health itself is composed of several functionings — such as, for example, being able to move around, not being tired, etc.

Sen leaves it largely open, which functionings should be included when assessing a particular social situation. What is more, he stresses that in each case, this will require a process of selecting the relevant functionings and weighing their relative importance [22]. Seeing health as a capability (sub-set) in this way thus accommodates the insight that defining a concept of health is a process that involves value judgments and which is potentially subject to political contestation — an issue that has just recently been stressed by Robertson in her paper on the "politics of need" and its implications for public health [23]. It recognizes that defining health and determining what counts as a health problem and what as another type of social problem is not a task that can be resolved by health specialists alone, but depends on other aspects of social institutions, and may change over time. Medicine and public health can contribute to the resolution of certain social problems, but they cannot, by themselves, determine goals and priorities for individuals and for society as a whole.

III. Direct and Indirect Approaches to Health Equity

Returning to the main subject of this paper, namely to the question of how to assess the justice or injustice of social inequalities in health, let me start by discussing the distinction between direct and indirect approaches to health equity. A direct approach sees health equity as an end in itself [24]. This is to say that the goal is to achieve justice with respect to the distribution of health outcomes, independently of, but in parallel with, justice in other spheres, such as, for example, income or education.

To give an example for a direct approach, it is sometimes assumed that what is disturbing about social inequalities in health is that the health of the population *overall* is lower than it could be. The 'Black Report', for example, uses this language [25]. Such an approach is informed by the utilitarian principle of maximizing overall well-being — in our case the health of the population. Utilitarianism is, however, often criticized for being blind to distributive considerations [26]. In the case of population health, a maximizing approach implies that we are indifferent between health benefits to, say, the poor and to the rich, as long as these benefits have the same impact on overall population health.

More explicitly concerned with equity are principles of *specific egalitarianism* — another family of direct approaches to health equity [27]. Egalitarian principles recognize that equality of health outcomes is hardly obtainable, but postulate it as a goal that we should strive for insofar as possible. For the bioethicist Robert Veatch, [28] for example, egalitarianism in the context of health encompasses

> any number of closely related positions that among other things include the moral rule that justice requires that persons be given an opportunity to have equal net welfare insofar as possible and that, applied to health care, *justice requires that persons be given an opportunity to have equal health status insofar as possible* (emphasis added).

Whitehead seems to be defending an approach of that kind when she writes that health equity is "concerned with creating equal opportunities for health and with bringing health differentials down to the lowest level possible". [29]

Davidson Gwatkin, finally, articulates a third possible approach to health equity by suggesting that we should focus primarily on the health of the poor [30]. This view is akin to what is known as the "priority view" in moral philosophy. It is articulated by Derek Parfit and put forward as an alternative to egalitarianism [31]. Parfit argues that our moral concern should not be with differences in and of themselves, but rather with absolute deprivation. Improving the lot of those who suffer most will yield the greatest gain in social utility or well-being. The priority view is thus a variant of utilitarianism. Adapted to health equity — and given the premise that there is a link between health and poverty — this approach would imply giving priority to improving the health of the poor [32].

In spite of the many differences, what characterizes such direct approaches is that a situation is judged inequitable if the health status of the population differs from what is perceived to be the ideal — whether judged by a measure of aggregate population health or by a measure that is sensitive to the distribution of health outcomes (or a combined measure).

An indirect approach, in contrast, treats the pursuit of health equity as embedded in and interlinked with the pursuit of social justice. Let me explain the idea in more detail.

There are two forms of potential interlinkage between social inequalities in health and justice. First, an indirect approach sees differences in health outcomes as inequitable if they are the result of unjust social arrangements. The emphasis thus lies not on the pattern of distribution of health outcomes, but on the broader social processes underlying health inequalities. An indirect approach can thus make sense of the intuition that there is more reason to be concerned if we find that whites have significantly higher life-expectancy than blacks in similar socio-economic positions, than if we find that women have higher life-expectancy than men.

The second form of interlinkage pulls in the opposite direction. It is based on the premise that a society's achievements and failures in health may contain important information about the injustice of particular social arrangements and thus supplement our assessment of these arrangements in general. A couple of recent publications have explored this line of reasoning [33]. At this level, even in an indirect approach, there is a role for examining distributive patterns of health outcomes. They can provide a starting-point for an in-depth analysis of how social institutions work and the injustices they may embody.

One advantage of the indirect approach is that it provides a basis for selecting relevant social groups in the assessment and explanation of social inequalities in health. What the above example underlines is that even if an direct approach is adopted *prima facie*, the choice of relevant social groups is based on an implicit judgment about unjust social arrangements that disadvantage certain groups. An indirect approach makes such judgments explicit.

Moreover, by stressing interlinkages between the health sphere and other social spheres, the indirect approach avoids elevating health to an organizing principle of society, nor does it strictly privilege another social sector over health. It was argued above that health is not a static concept and that an approach to health equity should be able to accommodate this. A conception of health equity that builds exclusively on the medical model of health tends to downplay the inevitable biases and value judgments inherent in the disciplines of medicine and public health. An indirect approach to health equity is more compatible with a social model of health, which takes into account the influence of a variety of social factors on health.

It should be noted, however, that the direct and indirect approaches to health equity overlap. For it is clear that an indirect approach will need some justification for why health is considered a relevant indicator and such a justification will draw upon the nature of the good of health [34]. In other words, both need some account of why health is an important good. But they differ with respect to the context in which such an account is given and to the type of account given. While there is a tendency implicit in direct approaches to take health as an unambiguous, objective social goal, the indirect approach can better deal with the inherent complexity of health, which makes it difficult to confine health to a sphere of its own, independent of all other social spheres.

IV. A Theoretical Framework for Social Justice

Rawls' theory of justice as fairness has been the most influential theory of social justice put forward in this century [35]. As already mentioned, however, it does not specifically address the issue of health. What is more, Rawls explicitly rules out situations such as those we are interested in here. He assumes the healthy and able-bodied person as the norm and that accidents and illness are randomly distributed in society — precisely what the empirical literature on social inequalities in health shows is not the case. Rawls concedes that because accidents and illness have the potential to induce great suffering, and to hinder a person from pursuing his or her goals in life, they may require social action. But in Rawls' view, social action takes the form of restoring people to good health — of providing health care [36].

In spite of this I shall argue that the conceptions of justice as fairness and of political liberalism that Rawls has developed can provide guidelines for how to assess social inequalities in health. This section provides some necessary background.

What a theory of justice must do, according to Rawls, is provide principles for the regulation of "the inequalities in life prospects between citizens that arise from social starting positions, natural advantages, and historical contingencies". [37] A key premise of Rawls' theory of justice as fairness is that of society as a *fair system of co-operation* — to be understood in contrast with society as a loose association of individuals [38]. The idea of co-operation stresses a functional relation between the social division of labour in the production and distribution of social goods and the social roles and positions into which individuals are slotted. According to this view, the social conditions into which somebody is born have a profound impact on what she or he can achieve and aspires to achieve. From the point of view of justice, there is thus a limit on the claims people who do well have on their achievements. By the same token, people who do not do well may have a claim on social goods.

The principles of justice aim at regulating the terms of social co-operation. However, their scope is limited to what Rawls calls the *basic structure* of society — society's main political, social, and economic institutions. There are several reasons why Rawls focuses on the basic structure [39]. In *A Theory of Justice* Rawls explains it as follows [40]:

> The basic structure is the primary subject of justice because its effects are so profound and present from the start. The intuitive notion here is that this structure contains various social positions and that men [*sic!*] born into different positions have different expectations of life determined, in part, by the political system as well as by economic and social circumstances. In this way the institutions of society favor certain starting places over others. These are especially deep inequalities. Not only are they pervasive, but they affect men's initial chances in life; yet they cannot possibly be justified by an appeal to the notions of merit or desert. It is these inequalities, presumably inevitable in the basic structure of any society, to which the principles of social justice must in the first instance apply. [41]

The basic structure of society affects not only the distribution of material resources and through this people's chances to carry out different life plans, but also, as Rawls emphasizes, the talents and abilities people have [42]. Moreover, what Rawls does not mention but what the literature on social inequalities in health suggests, is how social arrangements affect people's life expectancy and general prospects of health. I shall come back to this issue in the next section.

The main idea expressed in the principles of justice as fairness is that social and economic inequalities are tolerated in the basic structure of society insofar as they do not jeopardize the fundamental equality of all members of society. More precisely, justice is seen as undermined if society's main economic, social and political institutions require sacrifices from the worse off groups purely to the benefit of the better off groups. Such a social division of labour would not be compatible with the idea of society as a "fair system of cooperation".

V. Health Equity and the Justice of Society's Basic Institutions

What does this interpretation of justice imply for an approach to health equity? I will argue that it would be incompatible with what I called a direct approach to health equity. The principal reason is related to taking as a starting-point for a theory of justice the premise that societies are characterized by a pluralism of religious, philosophical, and moral doctrines [43]. This implies that justice cannot be based on some notion of the common good, nor on some shared notion of individual well-being. Rawls explicitly rejects assessing justice on the grounds of some account of well-being [44]. In consequence, an interpretation of health that stresses well-being, such as the WHO definition, would not be compatible with Rawlsian justice. Similarly, a notion of health that claims to be objective and value-free, but that in fact is not, would not be appropriate.

Moreover — and again in respect of pluralism — justice as fairness refrains from specifying a particular distributive pattern for certain goods:

> [T]he two principles of justice do not insist that the actual distribution conform at any given time . . . to any observable pattern, say equality, or that the degree of inequality computed from the distribution fall within a certain range, say of values of the Gini coefficient [45].

For this reason, a Rawlsian approach to health equity is necessarily an indirect approach [46]. In the passage just quoted, Rawls continues: "What is enjoined is that (permissible) inequalities should make a certain functional contribution to the expectations of the least favored, where this functional contribution results form the working of the system of entitlements set up in public institutions." The idea here is that how basic social institutions work is more important than the resulting outcomes — as characterized by distributive patterns — that are observed. In Rawlsian justice, the focus is thus shifted from health outcomes to the mechanisms implicit in basic social institutions that produce social inequalities in health.

Above, I introduced two forms of interlinkage between social inequalities in health and justice. How do they relate to Rawlsian justice? On the one hand, justice as fairness offers a framework for evaluating social inequalities in health — for making health equity judgments. It points to the particular weight of inequalities that can be traced back to society's principal social and economic institutions. And it identifies as unjust those class, race, gender or socio-geographical inequalities in health that originate in the basic structure of society and are the result of a social division of labour that benefits the better off groups at the expense of the worse off. Again, the goal is not to achieve a specific pattern of health outcomes, but a just basic structure of society. If the basic structure is just, then all outcomes these institutions produce can be considered just [47].

On the other hand, research on social inequalities in health and their causes may tell us something about whether basic social arrangements have the effect of undermining the fundamental equality of all members of society — whether these arrangements do or do not constitute a "fair system of social cooperation". Because of the links the empirical literature on social inequalities in health demonstrates between cultural, social, and economic parameters and health outcomes, such information can supplement economic and sociological information about the achievements of different social arrangements in the basic structure of society and their changes over time.

At this stage, it will be important to discuss a possible objection to this approach. It may be argued that the correct way to apply Rawlsian justice is to say that since health does not enjoy special status in justice as fairness, all social inequalities in health must be regarded as just, provided that the basic structure of society is just. In other words, this argument perceives only a one-way relationship between justice as fairness and social inequalities in health and fails to recognize how information about social inequalities in health may help one in assessing the justice of the basic structure. This particular link between justice as fairness and social inequalities in health requires further justification, therefore.

In principle, justice as fairness suggests that the basic structure of society should be evaluated on the basis of 'primary goods' [48]. The list of primary goods includes basic rights and liberties, and income and wealth, among other things, but not health. The most important primary good, according to Rawls, is the social basis for self-respect [49].

This stems again from the idea of society as a fair system of co-operation, which requires that nobody is excluded a priori. If inequalities in the basic social arrangements which shape individual lives express a disvaluation of certain social positions and occupations in such a way that people cannot gain a sense of self-respect, then these structures are unjust.

The notion of 'social bases of self-respect' is of course very ambiguous and needs specification. In general, it can be said that the *implementation* of Rawlsian justice cannot avoid taking into account information that reaches beyond the primary goods framework that Rawls has laid out. Health information — in particular, research that attempts to uncover the more "upstream" causes of social inequalities in health — may play an important role in gaining understanding about how the organization of the basic structure of society affects people and groups of people. For instance, discrimination and lack of social respect seem to show in health outcomes (among other variables), as recent studies on inequalities between blacks and whites in the US demonstrate [50].

VI. Concluding Remarks

This paper has outlined an approach to health equity that proceeds indirectly and embeds health equity within the general pursuit of social justice. Building on Rawls' theory of justice as fairness, it was argued that social inequalities in health are unjust or inequitable if they result from an unjust basic structure of society — i.e. a basic structure that imposes sacrifices to the worse-off only to benefit the already better-off groups. This entails that to be able to form a judgment on social inequalities in health, we need an understanding of the underlying causes. At the same time, information about the health status of people may give us important information to assess the justice of social arrangements. Understanding the effects the basic structure has on people's prospects of health may help us decide whether or not these institutions ensure the social bases for self-respect for everybody. While justice as fairness cannot offer a complete blueprint of what a just society would look like, it certainly provides a framework for thinking about issues related to social justice.

Fabienne Peter, Department of Economics, University of Basel, Petersgraben 51, 4003 Basel, Switzerland. E-mail: fabienne.peter@unibas.ch

Acknowledgements

I have benefited from so many people, that it is impossible to acknowledge everybody. But I would like to thank those in the Global Health Equity Initiative who made me start thinking about these issues; I am particularly grateful to Ben Amick, Sudhir Anand, and Tim Evans. I would also like to thank Sissela Bok, Norman Daniels, and Dan Wikler for very helpful comments.

NOTES

[1] See M. MARMOT, G. ROSE, M. SHIPLEY, and P. HAMILTON (1978) Employment grade and coronary heart disease in British civil servants, *Journal of Epidemiology and Community Health* 32; BLACK, D.,

J. N. Morris, C. Smith, P. Townsend (1990) The Black Report in P. Townsend and N. Davidson (eds.) *Inequalities in Health* (London, Penguin).; N. Krieger, D. L. Rowley, A. A. Herman, B. Avery, and M. T. Phillips (1993) Racism, sexism, and social class: implications for studies of health, disease, and well being, *American Journal of Preventive Medicine*, 9, suppl.; D. R. Gwatkin and M. Guillot (2000) *The Burden of Disease among the Global Poor: Current situation, future trends, and implications for strategy* (Washington D.C., International Bank for Development and Reconstruction and World Bank).

[2] See R. Wilkinson (1996) *Unhealthy Societies: The afflictions of inequality* (London and New York, Routledge); I. Kawachi, B. P. Kennedy, and R. G. Wilkinson (1999) *Income Inequality and Health.* (New York, New Press).

[3] For a good review, see M. Marmot, M. Bobak, and G. D. Smith (1995) Explanations for social inequalities in health, in B. C. Amick, S. Levine, A. R. Tarlov, and D. Chapman Walsh (eds.) *Society and Health* (New York and Oxford, Oxford University Press).

[4] C.f. L. F. Berkman, T. Glass, I. Brissette, and T. E. Seeman (2000) From social integration to health: Durkheim in the new millenium, *Social Science and Medicine*, 51.

[5] A. Robertson (1998) Critical reflections on the politics of need: implications for public health, *Social Science and Medicine*, 47, 10, p. 1419. See also N. Krieger and A.-E. Birn (1998) A vision of social justice as the foundation of public health: commemorating 150 years of the spririt of 1848, *American Journal of Public Health*, 88, 11.

[6] M. Whitehead (1990) *The Concepts and Principles of Equity and Health* (Copenhagen, World Health Organization), p. 5.

[7] J. Rawls (1971) *A Theory of Justice* (Cambridge, Mass, Harvard University Press).

[8] See N. Daniels (1985) *Just Health Care* (Cambridge, Cambridge University Press).

[9] As Poland *et al.* have stressed (B. Poland, D. Coburn, A. Robertson, and J. Eakin (1998) Wealth, equity and health care: a critique of a 'population health' perspective on the determinants of health, *Social Science and Medicine*, 46, 7), the population health perspective should not be read as implying that health care is not important.

[10] J. Pereira (1993) What does equity in health mean? *Journal of Social Policy*, 22, 1; S. Marchand, D. Wikler, and B. Landesman (1998) Class, health, and justice, *The Milbank Quaterly*, 76, 3; D. E. Beauchamp and B. Steinbock (1999) *New Ethics for the Public's Health* (New York, Oxford University Press); N. Daniels, B. Kennedy, and I. Kawachi Health and inequality, or why justice is good for our health, in S. Anand, F. Peter, and A. Sen (eds.) (forthcoming) *Public Health, Ethics, and Equity* (Oxford, Clarendon Press).

[11] See for example the contributions in B. C. Amick III, S. Levine, A. R. Tarlov, and D. Chapman Walsh (eds.) (1995) *Society and Health* (New York and Oxford, Oxford University Press).

[12] J. Rawls (1993) *Political Liberalism* (New York, Columbia University Press).

[13] Black *et al.*, *op.cit.*, chapter 3.

[14] Black *et al.*, *op.cit.*, p. 36.

[15] René Lériche wrote: "in disease, when all is said and done, the least important thing is man" (quoted in Canguilhem, G. (1991) *The Normal and the Pathological* (New York, Zone Books), p. 92). Critical medical anthropology in particular examines the meaning of illness for people. See, for example, A. Kleinman (1988) *The Illness Narratives: Suffering, healing, and the human condition* (New York, Basic Books); E. Corin (1995) The cultural frame: context and meaning in the construction of health, in Amick, B. III *et al.* (eds.) *Society and Health* (New York and Oxford, Oxford University Press); A. W. Frank (1995) *The Wounded Storyteller: Body, illness, and ethics* (Chicago, University of Chicago Press). See also M. Foucault (1973) *The Birth of the Clinic* (New York, Pantheon Books) for an account of the development of the biomedical model and its political context.

[16] World Health Organization (1976) *World Health Organization: Basic documents*, 26th edition (Geneva, World Health Organization), p. 1.

[17] Brock discusses the switch that has taken place in the public policy context from the biomedical model to a quality-of-life approach for evaluating health and the implications thereof for social evaluation in general. See D. Brock (1993) Quality of life measures in health care and medical ethics in M. Nussbaum and A. Sen (eds.) *Quality of Life* (Oxford, Clarendon Press).

[18] H. T. Jr. Engelhardt (1986) writes: "Medicine medicalizes reality. It translates sets of problems into its own terms. Medicine molds the ways in which the world of experience takes shape; it conditions reality for us". (p. 157) A few pages below he adds (*ibid.* p. 163): "Seeing an element of life as a medical

problem raises more than issues of scientific medicine. The medicalization of reality raises issues of public policy and of ethics". *The Foundations of Bioethics* (Oxford and New York, Oxford University Press).

[19] V. ADAMS (1998) *Doctors for Democracy: Health professionals in the Nepal Revolution* (Cambridge, Cambridge University Press), p. 6. See also V. DAS (n.d.) What do we mean by health? (Baltimore, Johns Hopkins University, *mimeo*).

[20] In A. SEN (1993) Capability and well-being, in M. Nussbaum and A. Sen (eds.), op cit., Sen provides a good overview of the capability approach.

[21] e.g. Sen, *op.cit.*, p. 31.

[22] Nussbaum, in some contrast to Sen, argues for a specific set of capabilities. See M. C. NUSSBAUM (1992) Morality, politics, and human beings: II. Human functioning and social justice: in defense of Aristotelian essentialism, *Political Theory*, 20, 2.

[23] Robertson, *op.cit.*

[24] For a good review of such approaches, see Marchand, Wikler, and Landesman *op.cit.*

[25] Black *et al. op.cit.* I owe this point to Marchand, Wikler, and Landesman *op.cit.*

[26] A critique of utilitarianism can be found in Rawls (1971, *op.cit.*, pp. 22–33); Rawls formulated his theory of justice as fairness as an alternative to utilitarianism. See also B. WILLIAMS A critique of utilitarianism, in J. J. C. Smart and B. Williams (eds.) (1973) *Utilitarianism: For and against* (Cambridge, Cambridge University Press).

[27] I borrowed the term 'specific egalitarianism' from Marchand, Wikler, and Landesman (*op.cit.*). On various forms of specific egalitarianism in health, see, for example, B. WILLIAMS The idea of equality, in B. Williams (1973) *Problems of the Self* (Cambridge, Cambridge University Press); M. WALZER (1983) *Spheres of Justice* (Oxford, Blackwell); R. M. VEATCH (1991) Justice and the right to health care: an egalitarian account, in T. J. Bole and W. B. Bondeson (eds.) *Rights to Health Care* (Dordrecht, Kluwer); Nussbaum (1992, *op.cit.*). R. DWORKIN (1993) Justice in the distribution of health care, *McGill Law Journal*, 38, 4, in contrast, argues against what he calls the 'insulation thesis' — the tendency to single out health as a special good.

[28] Veatch, *op.cit.*, p. 83.

[29] Whitehead, *op.cit.*, p. 9.

[30] D. R. GWATKIN (2000) Health inequalities and the health of the poor: what do we know? What can we do? *Bulletin of the World Health Organization*, 78,1.

[31] D. PARFIT (1997) Equality or priority, *Ratio* 10.

[32] If there is no such empirical link, the priority view would require focusing on the sickest, independently of their social situation, and one would have to distinguish from that view one that focuses on the health of the poor. On this, see Marchand, Wikler, and Landesman *op.cit.*

[33] A. SEN (1998) Mortality as an indicator of economic success and failure, *The Economic Journal*, 108; J. Y. KIM, J. V. MILLEN, A. IRWIN, and J. GERSHMAN (2000) *Dying for Growth* (Monroe, Common Courage Press).

[34] What I am concerned with here is not so much the *empirical* correlation between health outcomes and some indicator of general performance. The issue is, rather, the *theoretical* question whether perfomance in the health space might tell us something important about social arrangements. I thank Sudhir Anand for pointing this difference out to me.

[35] See in particular Rawls (1971, *op.cit.*, and 1993, *op.cit.*).

[36] "[W]e assume that persons as citizens have all the capacities that enable them to be cooperating members of society. . . . [W]e do not mean to say, or course, that no one ever suffers from illness and accident; such misfortunes are to be expected in the ordinary course of life, and provision for these contingencies must be made" (Rawls (1993), *op.cit.*, p. 20).

[37] Rawls (1993) *op.cit.*, p. 271.

[38] See, for example, Rawls (1993, *op.cit.*, p. 15).

[38] I cannot discuss this issue in full here, but see in particular Rawls (1993) *op.cit.*, pp. 257–88.

[40] Rawls (1971), *op.cit.*, p. 7.

[41] Just to avoid confusion: when Rawls speaks of 'expectations of life', he is not alluding to mortality, but to the chances people have of carrying out different life plans.

[42] "[W]e cannot view the talents and abilities of individuals as fixed natural gifts. To be sure, even as realized there is presumably a significant genetic component. However, these abilities and talents cannot come to fruition apart form social conditions, and as realized they always take but one of many possible forms. . . . So not only our final ends and hopes for ourselves but also our realized abilities and talents

reflect, to a large degree, our personal history, opportunities, and social position" Rawls (1993), *op.cit.*, 270.

[43] Rawls (1993), *op.cit.*, p. 3f.

[44] J. RAWLS (1982) Social unity and primary goods, in A. Sen and B. Williams (eds.) *Utilitarianism and Beyond* (Cambridge, Cambridge University Press).

[45] Rawls (1993), *op.cit.*, p. 283.

[46] Justice as fairness is often called a *procedural* conception of justice — in contrast to consequentialist theories. Consequentialism requires us to assess different social arrangements with respect to the goodness of the consequences in which they result. Given that the approach to health equity sketched here builds on Rawls' theory of justice, one may call it a procedural approach to health equity. I decided against using this term, and called my approach 'indirect' instead, to underline the need to include considerations of goodness in assessing health equity.

[47] It may be added that justice as fairness does not translate into a right to health. In general, it can be said that the interpretation of justice as fairness presented here is less threatened by the 'bottomless pit' problem that is sometimes discussed in relation to the maximin principle — a reductionist version of Rawls' difference principle.

[48] For a list of primary goods, see Rawls (1993, *op.cit.*, p. 181).

[49] See Rawls (1993, *op.cit.*, p. 440).

[50] N. KRIEGER, S. SIDNEY (1996) Racial discrimination and blood pressure: the CARDIA study of young black and white women and men, *American Journal of Public Health* 86; B. P. KENNEDY, I. KAWACHI, K. LOCHNER, C. JONES, and D. PROTHROW-STITH (1997) (Dis)respect and black mortality, *Ethnicity and Disease*, 7, 3.

[30]

POINT–COUNTERPOINT

Health by association? Social capital, social theory, and the political economy of public health

Simon Szreter[1] and Michael Woolcock[2]

Accepted 6 August 2003

Three perspectives on the efficacy of social capital have been explored in the public health literature. A 'social support' perspective argues that informal networks are central to objective and subjective welfare; an 'inequality' thesis posits that widening economic disparities have eroded citizens' sense of social justice and inclusion, which in turn has led to heightened anxiety and compromised rising life expectancies; a 'political economy' approach sees the primary determinant of poor health outcomes as the socially and politically mediated exclusion from material resources. A more comprehensive but grounded theory of social capital is presented that develops a distinction between bonding, bridging, and linking social capital. It is argued that this framework helps to reconcile these three perspectives, incorporating a broader reading of history, politics, and the empirical evidence regarding the mechanisms connecting types of network structure and state—society relations to public health outcomes.

Keywords Social capital, social support, public health, political economy, inequality, the state, British 19th century history

In the ongoing quest to improve our understanding of the conditions that make for improved public health and well-being, scholars, practitioners, and policymakers have recently returned in earnest to a theme with a long and distinguished history in the social sciences—namely, following Durkheim, the importance of social circumstances in shaping the quality of life one enjoys.[1,2] This has been fuelled in part by the indifferent performance of a series of high-profile public service delivery reforms, the widening rhetorical appeal of communitarian and neo-liberal policy discourse,[3] and a growing recognition that ever more sophisticated medical interventions and media campaigns have had a disappointing impact on some of society's most persistent social ills (e.g. smoking, depression, teen pregnancy). Within the public health field, these failures of policy have increasingly focused attention on the limitations of a narrowly 'individualist' approach to population health, associated with the rise of clinical epidemiology during the post-war era.[4] The debate, reviewed below, has centred on the persistence of health inequalities in affluent societies, and the extent to which more effective research and policies should prioritize the psychological experience of individuals and their relationships to others in their community and society, or the material deprivations due to overall economic structures and national political choices.

All sides in this debate have deployed the idea of social capital in support of their particular claims, in the process encapsulating many of the (inherent) conceptual ambiguities, dilemmas, and concerns surrounding the term in general. Identifying the nature and extent of the impact of social relationships—generally referred to as 'social capital', following the influential work of Robert Putnam[5,6]—has become a veritable cottage industry across the social sciences. Scholars have documented the importance of social capital in fields ranging from economic development and government performance to criminal activity and youth behaviour,[7,8] but 'in none is the importance of social connectedness so well established as in the case of health and well-being'.[6] General guides to how the concept of social capital has been applied to various health issues can be found elsewhere.[9–18] In this paper we wish to focus instead on (a) the

[1] Faculty of History and Fellow of St John's College, University of Cambridge, Cambridge, UK.

[2] Development Research Group, The World Bank, and Kennedy School of Government, Harvard University, USA.

Correspondence: Simon Szreter, St John's College, University of Cambridge, Cambridge CB2 1TP, UK. E-mail: srss@cam.ac.uk

analytical and political controversies that surround this literature, in particular the emerging divide between those focusing on the primacy of (1) support networks, (2) economic and social inequality, and (3) access to resources for explaining health outcomes; and (b) the contemporary policy lessons for public health emerging from both historical studies of public health issues and the broader theoretical and empirical debates in the (ever-expanding) field of social capital research.

Our central thesis is that it is desirable and possible to reconcile the controversies surrounding social capital as it applies to issues in public health, but that doing so requires incorporating empirical and conceptual insights from history and the broader social capital literature. Importantly, all camps in the field of public health generally agree that social capital 'matters' in some basic sense—unlike in say, the field of economic development, where selected critics paint it as a politically vapid distraction, and argue for its abandonment.[19,20] Most participants also agree that, while imperfect, efforts should be (and indeed have been) made to resolve lingering disputes on the basis of the empirical evidence. Even so, however, with highly provocative summary claims such as those by Putnam—'[i]f you smoke and belong to no groups, it's a toss-up statistically whether you should stop smoking or start joining'[6] (drawing on James House *et al.*,[21] Lisa Berkman,[22] and Teresa Seeman.[23] But see also Lynch, Davey Smith *et al.*[24])—it is not hard to see why the idea of social capital has generated both acclaim and disdain in the field of public health.[25,26] While taking the critics seriously, we believe social capital, properly understood, can indeed make a significant contribution to public health theory, research, and policy.

The paper proceeds as follows. Section I explores the current terms of the debate between three emergent camps in the field of social capital and public health, and seeks to provide an analytical basis for discriminating between them. Section II outlines a theoretical framework for reconciling the different views. Section III provides a historical perspective on a key set of public health concerns from 19th century Britain, demonstrating both the efficacy of the theoretical framework and the more general importance of incorporating historical insights into contemporary policy debates. Section IV discusses the significance of these arguments for social capital theory and public health. Section V concludes, with a brief summary of the policy implications for public health arising from both the analysis presented and the broader social capital literature.

I Rival views of social capital and public health

In the past few years there has been an intensive exchange in the journals and at conferences among several of the leading figures in the field of public health and epidemiology over the concept of 'social capital'.[3,23,27–44] Social capital has entered these fields principally through the work of two individuals, namely Robert Putnam—whose seminal 1993 book on regional government in Italy, *Making Democracy Work,*[5] drew heavily on (and provided a new empirical base for) social capital theory (but did not itself address public health issues)—and the more directly relevant work of Richard Wilkinson, whose 1996 book, *Unhealthy Societies,*[45] first introduced Putnam's notion of social capital to the public health field. In addition, Putnam has drawn on, and indirectly contributed to, research on social capital and public health in his most recent study of social capital in the US, *Bowling Alone*, published in 2000.[6] Richard Wilkinson, by contrast, has been working for many years[46] within the field of comparative epidemiology to further our understanding of the relationship in relatively affluent societies between income inequalities and mortality patterns, and is one of the principal protagonists in the recent debates.

The debates generated by these authors have primarily treated 'social capital' as if it is a (presumably) more sophisticated formulation of the broader concepts of 'social cohesion',[44] 'social support',[47–50] 'social integration',[51] or 'civil society'.[41] Epidemiologists have noted that the term 'networks' is often used by the proponents of social capital, and this strikes a familiar note for them with a body of respected empirical literature, dating from Brown and Harris's path-breaking study, *Social Origins of Depression,*[52] and the Alameda County Study, demonstrating that individual risks from a range of chronic and degenerative conditions, such as myocardial infarctions, are improved where there are good social support networks.[51,53] For the purposes of our present discussion, we call these studies the 'social support' school. This is a view of social capital—defined simply as the nature and extent of one's social relationships and associated norms of reciprocity[54,55]—as connected to health outcomes via some variation of a direct social support mechanism.[56]

The specific research connecting social capital to health outcomes via a social support mechanism is vast. In this sense, social capital has been empirically linked to, among other things, improved child development[57] and adolescent well-being,[58] increased mental health,[59] lower violent crime rates and youth delinquency,[60,61] reduced mortality,[62] lower susceptibility to binge drinking,[63] to depression,[64,65] and to loneliness,[66] sustained participation in anti-smoking programmes,[67] and higher perceptions of well-being[68–70] and self-rated health.[71–74] Where urban neighbourhoods and rural communities (and particular sub-populations) are demonstrably low in social capital, residents report higher levels of stress[75] and isolation,[76] children's welfare decreases, and there is a reduced capacity to respond to environmental health risks[77] and to receive effective public health service interventions.[78–84]

There remain significant ongoing methodological disputes and expressions of scepticism over exactly what this work is demonstrating, particularly in the two central areas of relationships between health measures and both inequality and trust.[27–32,34–40,85,86] It can be particularly noted that the implications for health and welfare of issues such as trust and reciprocity are likely to be strongly context-dependent. It is entirely commonplace to accept, following Portes,[87] that social capital can equally function in both a socially exclusive and an inclusive way, having positive welfare effects for some and negative for others. Kunitz, for example, provides a valuable account of how social capital might be both a part of the problem and solution to local health problems.[88] For this reason, it has been argued that it is still premature (at best) to include social capital measures in official public health surveys.[89,90] Findings have to be interpreted very carefully and certainly cannot necessarily be generalized from one level of aggregation to another. More fully satisfactory evidence and methodologies—such as multilevel modelling and randomized experiments—are still rare in the literature, so that the most recent contributions of Subramanian, Kawachi, and colleagues represent an important advance in this respect.[91–93] But as a general field of research it is hard not to be impressed with the volume and diversity of the empirical evidence indicating that social capital is likely to be a significant determinant of at least some important health outcomes. Furthermore, it is not necessary for social capital to fully explain a vast range of empirical public health outcomes as a pre-condition for being taken seriously—it would be very useful if it could be carefully linked to just two or three. The issue that animates the academic debates, and which this paper seeks to reconcile, however, is whether social capital is a direct or secondary 'cause' of these outcomes—that is, whether changes in the stocks and flows of social capital *per se* are making significant independent contributions to observed health outcomes, or whether they are merely responding to the changing character of broader political and economic forces.

In the mid-1990s, Richard Wilkinson[45] led a break from the social support literature, arguing that social capital concerns were relevant to the extent that they were part of the psycho-social effects of widening levels of socioeconomic inequality. He argued that in the handful of most affluent, post epidemiological transition[94] societies (excluding Eastern Europe), where lethal diseases associated with sanitation, infection, and absolute poverty now play only a very small part in determining the overall death-rates, that significant changes in the degree of socioeconomic inequality have a particularly strong influence over the differentially evolving comparative epidemiology of these populations. He contended that among the most affluent societies those which have moved towards more uneven income distributions (most notably a number of liberal market economies such as the US and the UK over the last two decades) are characterized by individuals with increased anxiety and declining social support institutions, and by rising levels of violence and disrespect between citizens. This results in poorer population health performances, in terms of national average life expectancy figures, which fail to improve as much as those of comparable economically advanced societies, such as Canada, Japan, or Sweden, which have not experienced such a degree of widening income inequality and associated decline in civic trust and collective support for social infrastructure.[4–5,95,96]

Michael Marmot and his colleagues' long-standing research has been important in identifying a physiological mechanism to explain these results, linking social support with more tractable notions of 'stress' such as the absence or loss of autonomy over one's life-course, or over one's working or neighbourhood environment.[97,98] *Prima facie* bio-medical plausibility for this lies in research showing correlates of such perceptions of stress in states of anxiety and physiological arousal, which result in the enhanced chronic secretion of harmful levels of doses of cortisol, adrenaline, and nor-adrenaline within the body's neuro-endocrine system.[99,100] Marmot also sees widening absolute and relative inequality as the primary driver of public health outcomes in affluent societies.

Wilkinson's principal critics—John Lynch, George Davey Smith, Carl Muntaner, and their various collaborators[24,26–36,101,102]—have argued that inequalities in health are always fundamentally rooted in differences of access to material resources (including housing and relevant neighbourhood amenities), which are, in turn, ultimately the product of political and ideological decisions.[103] They are concerned that the drift of Wilkinson's analysis is to support a form of 'health transition thinking', which would deny the significance of the material and the political under advanced economic conditions of affluence. This 'transition thinking' would imply that material deprivations are only of significance to health at lower levels of economic development and that, with the withering away of 'real' (i.e. absolute, survival-threatening) poverty in higher-income societies, only the psycho-social causes remain as significant factors producing health inequalities. This could give succour to the neo-liberal position because it appears to imply that such differentials can be fixed 'on the cheap' with 'social support' and 'self-help' networks, without needing to give any serious attention to the more contentious issues of inequalities in ownership of wealth and in distribution of power.

In his most substantial response to this critique, Wilkinson[38] makes four relevant points in rapid succession:

(1) Part of the difficulty with the concept of social capital is that it was borrowed from other disciplines rather than being developed specifically for the health field.
(2) No doubt it is a popular concept because it holds out the idea that there are costless ways that poor communities can pull themselves up by their bootstraps...
(3) ... But an important part of the growing health interest in social capital comes not from ignoring income distribution, but precisely from the opposite direction: from trying to understand why income distribution is important to health.
(4) [As such,] the evidence suggests that more egalitarian societies are more cohesive, less violent, more trusting, and foster more involvement in community life.

Moreover, he subsequently added:

(5) If we fail to reduce income inequalities, societies will be more likely to show tendencies towards discrimination and victimisation of vulnerable groups. ... [T]hese dimensions of social reality may have a special salience as determinants of levels of anxiety and physiological arousal in a population. Because members of the same species have all the same needs there is a potential for continuous conflict between them. But ... human beings can also be the greatest source of [mutual] assistance, [and] support ... Similarities between some of the physiological effects of low social status produced under experimental conditions in monkeys and those associated with social status in human beings, suggests that an important part of the social gradient in human health is attributable to the direct effects of social status, rather than to other influences on health like poorer housing, diet and air pollution.

Among this sequence of points, we believe that the first is crucial, and will return to it at length later in this article. In fact, Wilkinson's critics, notably John Lynch, have repeatedly urged this and have cited the wider theoretical literature in their contributions. It is crucial because it is difficult to debate the utility of a fundamentally sociological concept substantively and productively without full reference to its original provenance and its current meaning, as developed in the sociological literature. This requires significant expository work where a concept as potentially powerful, complex, and contentious as social capital is concerned.

Wilkinson, in his second point, acknowledges the same political and policy-related dangers identified by Lynch *et al.* In his third point he comes even closer to the position of his critics, concurring that inequality, of which measures of income distribution form one important index, is highly significant for health outcomes. In his fourth point he endorses the kind of view of the virtues of social capital that Putnam[5] developed in his study of differences in institutional performance between Italian regions; this acts as the premise for the key point of difference between the two sides in the epidemiological debate, which emerges from the long, fifth quotation from Wilkinson. This difference is not over whether inequality is highly significant in accounting for class variations in health experience in economically advanced societies, but over the nature of the *principal* pathways of causation involved. The fifth extract shows that Wilkinson believes that there is something directly psycho-physiological going on, and that this is of prime importance. He believes that the concept of social capital is helpful because it is pointing us towards the source of this biological, evolutionary-programmed health effect, which flows from the relative social cohesiveness (or lack thereof) of a local or a national community.

For Wilkinson, the extent to which an affluent society is experienced as either a 'hierarchy' or, conversely, a 'community of equals' determines the overall extent to which those citizens who find themselves at the bottom of the socioeconomic pecking order will, as a characteristic response, experience states of anxiety and arousal, resulting in long-term damage to their health if this becomes a chronic situation for them. Even in more egalitarian societies, some citizens will inevitably still find themselves in this unfavourable position, possibly for long periods. But this will not necessarily produce the damaging physiological reactions if they do not perceive their predicament in the same demeaning and threatening way. It should be noted that this is not a simplistically biological determinist argument, since culturally constructed perceptions play a key role. The physiological mechanism of damage is donated by evolution, but whether or not it is invoked depends crucially on potential victims' perceptions of their predicament. This in turn depends on whether or not they see themselves as living in a cohesive, egalitarian, social-capital-rich society, or in one that is changing from being more to less egalitarian.

It is important to observe, incidentally, that the research on which Wilkinson and others and their critics have so far based most of their claims (and counter-claims) has almost exclusively consisted of statistical comparisons of income inequality measures for national and sub-national populations. However, since it is really *perceptions* of inequality (and/or lack of opportunity for social mobility) that are at issue, it is arguably a rather different kind of evidence that is truly required to assess the hypothesis. For instance, American society may be very unequal by such income measures and may be fast becoming more unequal.[104] However, its citizens'—even its poor citizens'—typical perceptions of the degree of injustice involved in this may be significantly less than that provoked by much smaller absolute increases in income inequality experienced by the inhabitants of another country, which has a strongly established self-image as an egalitarian society.[105] Clearly there must be some correlation between absolute levels or absolute changes of income inequality and perceptions of 'hierarchy', 'egalitarianism', and possibilities for 'mobility',[106] but the scope for flexibility in these assessments due to differences in national political cultures and cherished myths—i.e. prior histories and dispositions—should not be underestimated.

While Lynch and his colleagues may (or may not) agree that these physiological effects occur in societies that are perceived as unequal, they certainly do not think these effects are anything like as important as the direct health-damaging consequences of what they term the 'neo-material' realities of poverty, even in an affluent society. The range of such effects includes poor quality and even dangerous housing, the tendency to be restricted to lower quality food and clothing, greater exposure to environmental pollutants (including low air quality), higher likelihood of accidents and violence of most kinds, and less likelihood of access to effective medical care when required.

The thought naturally occurs to the observer of this debate that both sides have a point. It is certainly the case that if one or the other viewpoint could be shown empirically to be much the more substantial effect, then this would have important and rather different consequences for indicating the priorities that remedial policies should take. In the absence of such compelling evidence, however, it would seem most sensible to assume that both viewpoints could be valid. This might be conducive to the implementation of a superior, third kind of strategy for policy, which could embrace both points of view—indeed, would also embrace the older 'social support' view. This article will now attempt to arrive at the outline of such a strategy, on the basis of a review and application of social capital theory.

It is important to this line of thinking that, despite their dispute with Wilkinson, Lynch *et al.* remain relatively well disposed to the concept of social capital. They are careful to withhold their approval from many of the narrow policy formulations of social capital that abound (e.g. as being little more than volunteering and charity work); indeed, they are highly critical of it. They insist that the concept only has potential value to public health and epidemiology if properly located within a broad and comprehensive framework, embracing a role for the state and for the motivating role of political ideology. Indeed, we are encouraged that they have cited our work[7,107–109] in arguing for such a formulation. It seems to us, then, that if the concept of social capital is properly developed and carefully spelled out, it may well provide the means to mediate in this dispute. With the assistance of a more fully elaborated specification of the concept of social capital, the extent of common ground between these positions may then be clarified.

II Social capital and social theory revisited

There is a particular need for extended conceptual reflection on social capital as it relates to the public health field because none of the authors who have brought social capital to the attention of epidemiology have themselves been directly involved in developing a detailed theory to locate the concept. Neither Robert Putnam (and his Harvard colleagues) nor Richard Wilkinson—nor, for that matter, John Lynch and his various collaborators—have undertaken fundamental theoretical work on the concept. The two seminal social theorists of the late 20th century who placed social capital in a theoretical context in this way were the French sociologist Pierre Bourdieu[110] and the American sociologist James Coleman.[7,111–115] However, they produced quite distinct formulations during the 1980s, each of which has been highly influential but neither of which is now considered to be a satisfactory or full specification.[7,87,116,117]

While debate over the concept continues, it seems likely that social capital is destined to become, like 'class', 'gender', and 'race', one of the 'essentially contested concepts' of the social sciences. These are concepts that are simply too politically and ideologically important for those at any point on the political spectrum to concede to a definition of the term that they do not see as squaring with their own beliefs, assumptions, and principles. Contested concepts reflect a consensus on the broad nature of the phenomenon they refer to and its great importance, without any agreed-upon closure on the terms of its definition. It now seems likely, after almost a decade of discussion, that 'social capital' may join the ranks of the 'essentially contested concepts' category.

An obvious and enduring point of contention surrounds the very definition of social capital, and, concomitantly, the appropriate unit of analysis to which it should be applied. The narrowest definitions of social capital, not surprisingly, are those of neo-classical economists,[118] who regard it as the property of individuals (i.e. their social skills, or capacity to negotiate solutions to joint problems). At the other end of the spectrum, political scientists such as Francis Fukuyama[119] have described entire societies as having high or low social capital; empirical cross-study growth research by the economists Stephen Knack and Philip Keefer[120,121] has also been influential in this regard, using data on trust and participation from the World Values Survey to impute social capital scores for whole countries. In between are particular writers who wish to include or exclude additional features such as 'norms' and 'trust', and those such as Evans,[122] Woolcock,[7] and Szreter[108,109] who assign a prominent role to the nature and extent of state—society relations as a necessary part of the theory, if not the actual definition, of social capital.

Though contributions across this spectrum abound, the centre of gravity in the field as a whole is located far towards the more micro end. This is the realm in which James Coleman pioneered modern research on the topic, and where Putnam continues to lead today. In his most recent formulations, however, Putnam[6] has sharply distinguished his position from that of Coleman, who believed that, by definition, social capital could only yield positive outcomes. Putnam's view, consistent with our own position, and that of Portes,[87] is that the purposes to which a given resource can be put should be analytically distinct from how it is defined. Thus knowledge ('human capital') and technology ('physical capital') can be put to purposes that most people find thoroughly detestable—e.g. building chemical weapons—but this does not, in and of itself, prevent those inputs from still being unambiguously 'capital' (or assets).

Putnam leans increasingly towards a relatively restricted definition of social capital as the nature and extent of networks and associated norms of reciprocity.[6] As such, social capital enables individuals to gain access to resources—ideas, information, money, services, favours—and to have accurate expectations regarding the behaviour of others by virtue of their participation in relationships that are themselves the product of networks of association. This occurs as individuals elect to engage in various activities with others in order to pursue their leisure, familial, ethnic, local environmental, or wider political interests. Social capital is thus viewed at a relational level—it is the property of individuals, but only by virtue of their membership in a group. Aggregate measures are thus plausible to the extent that they are summations of responses drawn from an appropriate sample of individuals from a larger population, but, for Putnam, it is not only the aggregate *per se* that 'has' social capital. Network scholars[123–125] take a somewhat orthogonal approach, arguing that social capital refers to the resources (e.g. information, social control) that flow through networks, not the network structure itself. In this sense, the 'mainstream' social capital literature, represented paradigmatically by the work of Putnam, regards social capital as the 'wires' (or social infrastructure) while network theorists regard it as the 'electricity' (or social resource). We would want to add that it is crucial to know in what kind of encompassing contexts the networks of wires and their flows of electricity are embedded, particularly with respect to the vertical 'topography' of power gradients in society, across which networks may or may not provide links.

The idea of social capital has made such an enduring impact on the contemporary academic research and policy agenda largely because of the attention it has focused on the role and strength of civic associations. Putnam is particularly worried that there has been a fall-off over the last two or three decades in the propensity of American individuals to join associations and participate together in a range of activities. He attributes this to the lifestyle of the two generations raised since the Second World War, who have been socialized into suburban sprawl (driveways from the road into garages and no walkways between homes) and long commutes (less time in the neighbourhood), the advent of dual careers (and over-working at that), and over-reliance on the television as a (vastly inferior) substitute for local social interaction.[6]

Putnam is additionally concerned that the kind of social capital that may be proliferating in America today is too often the 'wrong' kind. This follows from an important conceptual revision within social capital theory, which occurred in the late 1990s, when the distinction was made between (what are now popularly called) 'bonding' and 'bridging' social capital.[126] It had become apparent that not all networks of association produced norms of trust and confidence between their members that could be said to serve the best interests of the wider community, nor sometimes the best interests of some of those within the network.[87] The mafia was an obvious example of this, which Putnam[5] had previously dealt with by distinguishing between networks based on 'horizontal' egalitarian relations and those that were more 'vertical' and hierarchical, with only the former considered to be capable of producing genuine forms of social capital. But more difficult was the case of the dangerously anti-social militia bands of contemporary US society, nominally egalitarian in their associational structure, such as the Oklahoma City bombers.

The 'bridging' and 'bonding' distinction facilitates discrimination between such different kinds of social capital. Bonding social capital refers to trusting and co-operative relations between members of a network who see themselves as being similar, in terms of their shared social identity. Bridging social capital, by contrast, comprises relations of respect and mutuality between people who know that they are not alike in some socio-demographic (or social identity) sense (differing by age, ethnic group, class, etc). The precise nature of the social identity boundaries, and the political salience of bonding and bridging groups are thus highly context specific. Within the US, at least, it then becomes clear that Putnam's particular concern is the decline of 'bridging' social capital.

In recent years a further conceptual refinement has been introduced into the social capital literature, 'linking' social capital.[107,109,127,128] We would define linking social capital as norms of respect and networks of trusting relationships between people who are interacting across explicit, formal or institutionalized power or authority gradients in society. This refinement seeks to incorporate a distinction among all those social relationships that would otherwise be grouped together in the 'bridging' social capital category, namely between those relationships that are indeed acting to 'bridge' individuals that are otherwise more or less equal in terms of their status and power ('bridging' is, after all, essentially a horizontal metaphor)—e.g. ethnic traders seeking counterparts in overseas markets, participants in artistic activities, or professionals of different nationalities exchanging business cards at international conferences—and those that connect people across explicit 'vertical' power differentials, particularly as it pertains to accessing public and private services that can only be delivered through on-going face-to-face interaction, such as classroom teaching, general practice medicine, and agricultural extension.[129] This latter distinction, called 'linking' social capital, draws empirical support from a range of studies[130–132] showing that, especially in poor communities, it is the nature and extent (or lack thereof) of respectful and trusting ties to representatives of formal institutions—e.g. bankers, law enforcement officers, social workers, health care providers—that has a major bearing on their welfare.

Linking social capital as defined here seeks to introduce a conceptual and empirical distinction as it pertains to individuals' overall portfolio of social relationships that is demonstrably central to shaping welfare and well-being (especially in poor communities). Accordingly, just as health outcomes can be improved by expanding the quality and quantity of bonding social capital (among friends, family and neighbours) and bridging social capital (trusting relations between those from different demographic and spatial groups), so, too, is it crucial to facilitate the building of linking social capital across power differentials, especially to representatives of institutions responsible for delivering those key services that *necessarily* entail on-going discretionary face-to-face interaction. Linking social capital, it should be added, like bonding and bridging, can also be put to unhappy purposes—e.g. nepotism, corruption, and suppression. To repeat, the definition of social (and any other form of) capital does not turn on the purposes, favourable or otherwise, to which it can be put.

In our view social capital must be the property of a group or a network. This is, however, far from clear if the empirical literature on social capital is scrutinized. The reason for this is that in order to study and—especially—to attempt to measure social capital,[133,134] there has been a strong tendency to develop a methodology that can capture its observable outcomes through individuals' expressions of degrees of trust in other people. The gathering of information on trusting relationships from individual interviewees has, thus, given the impression that social capital is a property of individuals. Moreover, the fact that another outcome of social capital is that it enables individuals to do things they otherwise could not do means that social capital can manifest itself as a resource that individuals can draw on in certain circumstances.

In addition to subjective questions regarding general (as popularized through the canonical World Values Survey question and other national surveys) and particular (e.g. politicians', different demographic groups', service providers') perceptions of trust, social capital has been measured through, among other things, participation rates in local organizations (including the organization's purpose, demographic composition, and rules governing entry, decision-making, and leadership selection), nature and extent of informal or everyday socializing, sources and forms of social support (both given and received), voting rates, access to sources of information and transport routes, political engagement (knowledge of politics, writing to newspapers, protesting/campaigning, running for office), personal efficacy, social cohesion/exclusion, and sources of local-level conflict. Many of the early measures of social capital were derived from secondary sources—that is, from surveys not explicitly designed to measure 'social capital'. While obviously imperfect, these attempts nonetheless provided a considerable spur for advancing the subsequent design and funding of primary survey and ethnographic work, a task now being undertaken by groups ranging from local community associations and universities to the OECD and World Bank (and many of their respective member governments). The formal definition of social capital, which we have outlined here, renders it inherently difficult as a subject for precise comparative empirical measurement.[135] However, this is to acknowledge no more than that social capital is subject to the same problems which afflict most other important concepts in the social and economic sciences, very few of which can in fact be measured directly and most of which are observed through their imputed effects and outcomes.

If social capital is not a property of individuals, *per se*, it is, however, a property of their relations with each other, occupying the abstract socio-cultural space of relationships between individuals. One way of envisioning this is as Putnam's 'wires'. However, it has to be remembered that any one of these 'wires' connecting any pair of individuals only exists, *qua* social capital, by virtue of its being part of a larger network of relationships (or wires). Otherwise, the relationship of trust between the two people concerned would be a simple interpersonal dyadic one, carrying no implications for the transitivity or 'portability' of their trust in their engagements with other parties in the network. That larger network is crucially premised on its participants having shared norms of reciprocity—and these must be a trans-individual and group property; hence Putnam's formula that social capital inheres in 'networks and norms'.

But it is important to think further about what makes those shared norms in a network possible. At one level, this can be explained simply as a form of trust built up by repeated interaction. But one must still ask: might there be crucial preconditions for such interaction to create trusting rather than distrusting relations or indifference? This requires more than just the capacity to communicate via a shared language. For trusting social norms to develop, there needs to be a minimum degree of understanding among the participants in the network in their mutual dealings with one another that they share each other's goals and purposes, and are working together towards mutually compatible ends. This, in turn, needs to be based upon a shared sense of fairness (justice in at least a relative sense) and mutual respect. That, in turn, can only be the product of a prior history of political, constitutional, and ideological work to construct the conditions for such a shared sense of fairness to be perceived by those choosing to participate in the network in question. Thus bridging social capital between people who know themselves to be unalike in terms of social identity can only occur spontaneously in a civil society where there already exists a rough and ready approximate equivalence between unalike individuals, in order that these networks, premised on shared norms (despite differences of social identity) can still form.

Where, however, there are circumstances—sustained by legal institutions (e.g. Jim Crow laws, apartheid), high economic inequality, rigid social status differentials (e.g. caste distinctions)—in which all individuals do not perceive themselves as enjoying such a rough equivalence, it is entirely unrealistic to expect spontaneous bridging social capital to form between haves and have-nots, or between officials, professionals or non-governmental organizations (NGO) (in less-developed countries) and the poor communities they work with, whose compounding disadvantages place them in a position of virtual social isolation.[136] In these circumstances, bridging social capital, if it is to exist at all, must be carefully created. The onus in these difficult circumstances is on those with the power and resources to think very carefully about how to create the shared sense of fairness, including mutual respect between all concerned, which is the necessary precondition for shared understandings and group norms of joint goals to emerge and so to create the proliferating networks of trusting relationships between different people, which are bridging social capital. Of course, the poor remain active agents, albeit heavily disadvantaged; the initiating push for linking social capital may well still come from the poor themselves, as has been documented, but such studies also show that a sympathetic, skilled response from those in power and authority will be critical, too.[137,138] Social capital that is created in this way in these difficult circumstances, rather than spontaneously emerging from the (approximately) level playing field of civil society, is a qualitatively different kind, which we would term 'linking' social capital. This reflects the explicit appreciation that it represents relationships of trust between members of a network who know themselves not only to be different in terms of social identity (bridging social capital) but also in terms of their institutionalized endowments of power and resources.

Why bother with social capital in these circumstances? Because without attention to the quality of the relationships between those with differential access to power and without paying attention to the need to build extensive transitive networks of respect and trust in such frequently met circumstances, efforts at poverty alleviation, economic development, and service provision to the poor are unlikely to succeed. In the field of health services, in both developing and developed societies alike, this is particularly relevant for the effective implementation of measures to assist the ill, poor, and the 'socially excluded'.

The three-dimensional approach to conceptualizing the forms of social capital resolves (at least partially) some of the earlier criticisms of social capital theory, especially as it has become manifest in public health and epidemiology. It does so by retaining a relatively parsimonious conceptual and empirical focus (on different types of networks) yet also enables a greater range of important social, economic, and political outcomes (both positive and negative) to be encompassed, while providing a more concrete basis for policy and project responses. We believe it can provide a basis for resolving the disputes between those in the 'social support', 'inequality', and 'political economy' camps of social capital and public health, but to do so requires addressing one final theoretical issue, namely the role of the state.

As indicated above, for some authors the state itself is part of the definition of social capital (since 'societies' are deemed to have social capital properties, and the state is a major component of 'society'). This is not our view; the definition of social capital *per se* should not encompass features of the state. Yet it is impossible to understand how particular networks and social structures are initiated and sustained without reference to the state. The state and its laws are a primary influence upon many of the patterns of association (or lack of them), which students of social capital and public health wish to examine and interpret. This means that while social capital can be empirically studied *as if* it was merely a phenomenon of civil society (in order to make the job of research manageable and tractable), as Putnam prefers to do, interpreting the findings will remain incomplete, and so can be misleading, without placing them—and the concept of social capital—in an adequate, encompassing theoretical and political context. This requires acknowledgement of the variable relationship between state and society.[139,140]

We have each separately emphasized that the nature and extent of the relationship between the state and its citizens is a critical factor in understanding how key outcomes are attained, even though it is not itself part of the formal definition of social capital.[7,107–109] This is, firstly, in the constitutional sense of the ways in which the state does or does not underwrite equally the entitlements and the capabilities of all citizens, regardless of gender, age, ethnic origins, and creed.[141] Secondly, it is in the moral sense of the historically contingent disposition, which citizens have towards the collective, of which they form a part, which motivates their actions. This can range from outright rejection and hostility or studied indifference to patriotic fervour or blind obedience. Somewhere in the large space between these extremes lies the central range of more healthy, balanced, and mature dispositions, characterized by both informed commitment to a wider society, while retaining independence and liberty, corresponding to Evans's[142] and Woolcock's[7] notion of 'embedded autonomy'.[143] Thirdly, there is the issue of the state as the appropriate public arbiter of the liberal polity's collective resources. It is an absolutely essential role of the state in a liberal democratic society with a market economy that it act as the just arbitrator among all the different interest groups and parties who stake a claim to the commonwealth's collective resources. This is quite simply because some form of redistribution of such resources is necessary to ensure that all, including the temporarily and permanently dependent, the marginal and the unfortunate, are permitted their equal chances to participate to the full in the community's life; if this is taken seriously and not performed in a merely token manner, it is an expensive collective undertaking and one that does not get any cheaper as societies become wealthier (and, usually, older).

By now it should be clear that the sense in which 'the state' is being used here is as much an idea (or set of principles) as a formal institution or agency.[144] It is certainly not intended that 'the state' be used to denote simply 'the central government', as in 'Whitehall' or 'Washington', the bureaucratic caricature beloved of those libertarians who offer the simplistic doctrinaire dichotomies of 'the state' versus 'civil society' or 'the market' in place of serious thought.[122] In those societies where 'the state' has come to mean only monolithic organs of the centre, it has not, ultimately, played a constructive role in its citizens' lives, as Soviet Moscow discovered to its cost.[145,146] Thus, genuinely devolved and vigorous, elected, local self-government and regional self-government, with these bodies not acting as mere ciphers or transmission lines for centralist policies but as independent, democratic agencies with a high degree of local participation and autonomy, should be conceptualized as a vitally important component of the more complex concept of 'the state'.[147] This is the form of the state that is found in a society well-endowed with extensive social capital of all three kinds, and (importantly) in which social relations between citizens and representatives of the state are well developed. Britain and America, but also Sweden, have been characterized by fairly well-devolved states of this kind for much of their respective histories.[148,149]

What, then, does all this mean for the debate among public health experts and comparative epidemiologists concerning the relationship of social capital to their interest in explaining and remedying inequalities of health? It means that social capital is in fact as much about highly tangible matters such as styles and forms of leadership and activism among public health workers and officials *themselves*—and structures of service delivery—as it is about the seemingly abstract properties of 'social cohesion' among communities or social collectivities of various kinds. The practical payload for practitioners and for policy design, resulting from taking linking social capital seriously, and the implied policy ideal of an autonomous but embedded and devolved state, is in fact much more immediate than might at first be appreciated. Lynch *et al.*[150] asked, 'Why do poor people behave poorly?' But what also of health professionals on the front line, and also those who set the overall tone and who design the facilities, the politicians and administrators, 'behaving poorly' with respect to their fellow citizens? The importance of linking and bridging social capital would indicate that an equally compelling question to that of material provision of adequate resources (which undoubtedly is important, as Lynch *et al.* have correctly emphasized) is to examine all the aspects of health care provision, which relate to relationships of mutual respect between citizens of different kinds and to their experience of the medical and social institutions, especially those provided by the devolved state. This inevitably relates to more general features of the national community in question, since it would be entirely unrealistic to expect such respectful relations to be observed uniquely in the health care sector, if they are not congruent with a similar pattern of behaviour in the wider society.

The nature of the general argument being put here can be verified by examining the long-term modern history of British society. The following historical account illustrates the way in which the balance between bonding, bridging, and linking social capital changed in Britain during the period 1815–1914, and the very real implications this had for the nation's population health patterns during that long period. It also demonstrates the way in which the evolution of social capital is closely related to the practices and politics of the state, both as central and as local government, and to citizens' varied relationships to this multi-faceted 'state'.

III History lessons—social capital, the state, and the resolution of public health crises in 19th century Britain

The British polity had by the beginning of the 19th century established itself as the most prosperous, socially cohesive, and socially secure in Europe, proven through the capacity of its national social security system, the Poor Law, to protect its citizens from local famines since the 17th century,[151] and its highly efficient fiscal-military regime guaranteeing external security by achieving the defeat of its principal European rival, Napoleonic France.[152] Even the momentous loss of the American colonies to the home-grown principles of liberty had not precipitated the kind of constitutional crisis which had characterized the 17th 'century of revolution'. Historians of Britain during the 18th century portray it as a 'polite', civil, commercial society, experiencing buoyant, if bumpy, economic growth, highly resilient in the face of internal stresses and external threats.[153] This was both the era of the building of country houses and of the founding of subscription hospitals by the nation's land-owning and aristocratic elite, and of the intensification of the coffee house society of the merchants of the City of London and the employing manufacturers and traders of the many fast-growing provincial towns. There was abundant and burgeoning bridging and linking social capital, particularly in the towns, in an increasingly socially mobile nation. By 1750 already almost one-fifth of the population were urban-dwellers, twice the European average.[154] For almost a century from the 1730s until the 1820s, while the population doubled in size, its average life expectancy also steadily improved, from under 35 years to reach just over 40 years.[155] But then all this changed.

For about half a century, from the 1820s until the 1870s, during the period when the British economy and national wealth was growing at unprecedented rates (historically analogous to the extremely high rates seen in East Asia during the last two decades), the health and welfare of its industrial workforce and the quality of its urban environments both became endangered in a way which had not been allowed to happen over the previous century of growth. The booming market economy was undoubtedly generating great wealth decade after decade; there was massive surplus capital initially invested in railways and later overseas; and the real wages of the workers were definitely rising (albeit not as fast as the profits and dividends of employers and rentiers). Nevertheless, the health of the industrial urban workers and their families experienced a catastrophic crisis in the second quarter of the 19th century. From the evidence of death registration it is clear that in the central parishes of cities such as Manchester, Liverpool, and Glasgow, life expectancies dropped to about 25 years, lower than had been seen at any time in those places since the Black Death in the 14th century.[156] The independent testimony of anthropometric evidence (heights) confirms such a severe urban health crisis in the second quarter of the 19th century and that it took until the generation born just before the First World War before average heights of the working classes had returned to the levels of the generation born a century earlier, immediately after the Napoleonic Wars.[157]

There is therefore a major puzzle concerning human resources and welfare during this period, when the world witnessed its first great economic success story and when British capital and trade rose to a position of global predominance. Changing patterns in the balance between bridging, bonding, and linking social capital within the domestic British polity are an important part of the explanation for this puzzle.

Two examples, each crucial for the health of the urban population, can illustrate various dimension of this: the Poor Law; and water supply and sanitation. During the era of relatively gradual but sustained economic growth, migration, and urbanization throughout the 18th century to the end of the Napoleonic Wars, the nation's social security system had been operated in an ever more generous way, with national expenditure on poor relief rising tenfold between the 1750s and 1810s.[158,159] However, with the end of the war for national survival the prescriptions of the laissez-faire, anti-welfare analysis of the new 'dismal science' of classical political economy became increasingly influential with a propertied governing elite who believed they were now paying-out far too much to the poor. A politics of distrust and suspicion towards the poor and the unemployed was replacing the more paternalistic attitudes of the past in a society increasingly composed of large urban agglomerations teeming with immigrants, recently arrived strangers from the countryside. The three consecutive decades 1811–1840 saw peak growth rates for all medium and large provincial towns (of more than 10 000 inhabitants). As a category they grew on average by 40% in each 10-year period, representing a deluge of literally hundreds of thousands of new arrivals in each decade.[160]

Class divisions of interest were rapidly opening up between capital-owning 'masters' and hired 'men', as the mechanization of successive branches of industry transformed labour relations, beginning with the mass redundancy of a quarter of a million handloom weaving families in Lancashire during the second quarter of the 19th century.[161] Such families were forced to leave their rural hamlets and head for the smoke-stacks of Manchester where the new jobs were to be found in the factories. In this context, patterns of social capital were transformed. The linking and bridging social capital of a paternalistic society and a relatively generous Poor Law was formally repudiated with the enactment of the draconian New Poor Law of 1834, which slashed social security spending in half nationally and instituted a new deterrent regime, on the premise that in order to ensure efficiency of free markets in factors of production the unemployed should be strongly encouraged to offer their labour at whatever price was available to them. No longer were there to be cash handouts to the families of the unemployed. Now they were to be segregated by sex and compelled to repay their meagre social security allowances by arduous labour inside work-houses.[162] In the name of market efficiency, the propertied classes believed themselves justified in defaulting on a previous history of more humane treatment of the poor. In this harsh climate the principal source of social security for the working classes was to be found in the growth of two types of networks, which primarily represent defensive bonding social capital. These were, firstly, workingmen's mutual insurance Friendly Societies;[163] and, secondly, denominational religious congregations and sects,[164,165] both of which proliferated in numbers and memberships greatly at this time. Meanwhile the propertied middle-classes moved out to healthier, cleaner suburbs.[166]

Thus, the towns and cities of Britain during the half-century after 1815 became both socially divided and class-segregated entities. They were culturally riven by socially exclusive and ideologically separatist sets of disparate social networks, each of them focused around a distinctive nonconformist congregation (dissenting from the Anglican Established Church), each with their own variant of Christian belief and their own pool of resources. Furthermore, there was much conflict of values and mutual political suspicion between the various factions of 'new men' on the scene. Some were rapidly becoming large employers of other men, while many were only petty capitalists of very modest and precarious means exposed to the vagaries of the free market; both of these kinds of new men were in turn quite distinct from the traditional patrician power elite, the network of mainly Anglican landowners and gentry who also continued to be a presence. Class divisions were exacerbated by the 1832 'Great Reform Act', a clever 'divide and rule' move by the landed oligarchy who still dominated the British Parliament, which split the urban industrial interest, granting the vote only to about one in seven adult males, namely those with significant property.

Britain's towns and cities therefore became socially, culturally, and politically fissured by conflicting and cross-cutting networks of power and association for a whole generation before and after 1832, such that in general all that these different fractions of property—some large, some small; some Anglican, some dissenting—could agree upon, was to disagree! The net result was administrative stalemate. There was plenty of social capital in this society. The trouble was that there was very little bridging and even less linking social capital, due to a highly negative attitude towards both the central state and local government and suspicions of all kinds between different social groups (relatively few of whom were yet full citizens with voting rights). There was an abundance only of denominational, sect-based, and trade-associated social capital of a predominantly bonding kind, with insufficient interest in bridging social capital, between congregations, between social classes, between men and women, or between different industrial regions (which virtually formed into separate linguistic groups); the heavy regional accents which developed at this time still remain a marked cultural feature of Britain today.[167]

This had profound implications for the second public health example of water and sanitation.[168] The provision of sufficient clean water and sewerage systems to preserve human health in such rapidly expanding residential centres required the effective mobilization of political will in order to solve a classic collective action problem, since the costs involved were far from trivial. Instead, the growing towns' physical environments were simply allowed to deteriorate as ever more workers crowded in to work in the money-making factories, while the voting ratepayers could not agree to tax themselves to pay for the extremely expensive municipal water supply and sanitation schemes that were needed. The central government itself was also plagued by this paralysing conflict between different ideologies and power networks of equal and opposing strength. A political ideology of laissez-faire and non-intervention by central government was most attractive to politicians and the executive in these circumstances because it legitimated the political line of least resistance in a situation where there were too many and too powerful complex, competing voices. An experiment with central fiat was tried in the late 1840s, in response to the official confirmation that death rates were unacceptably high in the big industrial cities. But the vitriolic popular reaction elicited by the nation's first general Public Health Act of 1848, threatening to compel the urban bourgeoisie to spend heavily on their health infrastructure, was so powerful that central government was forced to withdraw from such direct interference in the sacrosanct field of local self-government (local ratepayers' freedom not to tax themselves) for a further quarter century.[169] During the next two decades private interests continued to dominate the pattern of water infrastructure in British industrial cities, with the result that while water supply did increase significantly because of its value as a cheap raw material for industry (now subsidized by government because of its recognized public health virtues), there was still no matching provision of domiciliary connection or of an integrated sewers system.[170] In these circumstances urban death rates fell back from the catastrophic levels of the 1830s and 1840s but there was no absolute improvement over the unimpressive life expectancy levels of the 1820s.[156] Bridging and linking social capital, in the form of trusting relations between the central state and the local communities, or among the fractions of property holders in the cities, therefore remained a rarity in the public health and social policy field in mid-Victorian Britain.

The breakthrough did not come until the 1870s, or even later in some of the smaller towns. It was notably pioneered in the city of Birmingham through the political leadership of Joseph Chamberlain, scion of one of the city's leading screw-manufacturing dynasties, a member of the extensive and well-connected Unitarian congregation and Mayor for three consecutive years, 1873–1875.[171] After a century's rapid growth, the influence of the old landed families and their social superiority had finally all but disappeared in a city the size of Birmingham, so that by this time a man like Chamberlain, from a third-generation industrial magnate family, was indisputably part of the unchallenged natural leadership of his city. He was at the centre of a large network of families of these leading local businessmen, joined together both by their commercial interests in the prosperity of their industrial district and through their nonconformist congregations. Chamberlain simultaneously spearheaded both an ideologically transformative social and moral movement, and a practically innovative programme of political economy. Historians know the former as 'the civic gospel', which was literally preached from the pulpit of the Unitarian and Congregationalist chapels in central Birmingham by leading clerics. Chamberlain's opponents christened the latter the policy of 'gas and water socialism'. The former legitimized the moral and politically energizing imperative for the collective attack on squalor, poverty, and disease; the latter represented the fiscal magic needed to take away the financial pain from the city's ratepayers, at least for long enough that the city achieved its environmental improvements.

Some of the lessons that the British historical case may hold for relating social capital to public health practice appear to be as follows. Commercial and financial success and economic growth may not necessarily be associated with the flourishing of extensive bridging social capital or with linking social capital between agencies of the state and civil society. Instead, only socially exclusionary and sectional networks of primarily bonding social capital may proliferate in these circumstances, such as the Friendly societies and the worshipping congregations and the associated voluntary associational life of early and mid-Victorian Britain. This sectional and bonding social capital can particularly manifest itself in an incapacity or unwillingness to take expensive collective decisions on the part of the community as a whole. If the true purposes and characteristics of networks of association are not properly evaluated, there may be much confusion and conflicting results in studying the relationship between social capital, economic growth, and collective political action. Liberal, market-oriented societies may appear to be rich in voluntary associational life, a feature which has been emphasized by many leading social capital exponents, such as both Robert Putnam and Francis Fukuyama. Yet if these associations are sectional in their goals and too exclusionary in their membership, this may remain primarily bonding social capital only, and thus may impede the articulation of collective interests and the development of extensive bridging and linking social capital.

It was therefore crucial that Chamberlain's social networks were wide-ranging and multi-faceted. Within Birmingham, he benefited from a decade's patient prior work by his loyal Liberal party lieutenants, who had for the first time in British history built up a matrix of permanent party political associations right down to ward-level all across the city. This was specifically an organizational response to the Second Reform Act of 1867, which doubled the proportion of working-class men who had the vote, making their votes critical to electoral success. Chamberlain was, thus, the leader of a thoroughly 'embedded' set of networks, which crucially crossed social class and religious divides, representing a balance of bonding, bridging, and linking social capital all working together. A key element of his successful political strategy was his capacity to offer a genuine appeal to the increasingly empowered and self-organized working class. Meanwhile, his range of contacts also embraced all three key dimensions of power in his society: religion, scientific or technical knowledge, and wealth.

The British historical example also indicates that explicitly moral rhetoric and values (in the 19th century this was popularly expressed in the language of religion, applied to economic and social relationships) must be successfully harnessed for the cause in question if bridging and linking social capital is to be mobilized in order to move an entire complex community, such as a city the size of Birmingham, towards a collective goal. Science and technology, alone, is not enough. British water engineers and public health doctors technically knew how to construct a sanitary environment for a city with a domiciliary water supply and a mains sewers system since at least as early as the 1840s, but it took a religiously infused moral movement to motivate the mobilization of collective will.

Furthermore, the precise details of language, rhetoric, and policy are extremely important in accounting for the success of Chamberlain's programme; and, closely related to this question of political presentation skills, he took the fiscal sensitivities of his diverse audience extremely seriously and devoted a great deal of effective attention to those problems. He addressed directly the principal objection of small ratepayers, which had blocked collective spending throughout the mid-Victorian decades of death in British cities. He devised two extremely effective responses to the powerful objections of the petty bourgeoisie. Firstly in his political rhetoric, he ingeniously undercut and subverted the ratepayers' perennial call for 'economy' in municipal affairs by arguing that the ratepayers were mistakenly backing false economy and that '*true* economy' lay in investing in their city today so as to have healthier, more skilled, more educated, more productive, and more competitive workers and citizens tomorrow. As a practical man of business with a proven, enviable and unimpeachable track record, Chamberlain's interpretation of 'economy' commanded respect among the citizens of his town. Secondly, he used his financial genius and contacts in the City of London to innovate long-term, low-interest loans (on the security of the city's rates) to buy up productive monopoly services in the city, such as gas supply and transport, thereby raising revenue from a form of indirect taxation to fund the city's social and health services and various capital projects of improvement. Between them these novel ploys quietened the anxieties of the ratepayers for a generation—long enough to bring into being the crucial environmental improvements and a range of local preventive health and social services. By the end of the century all other cities of any size had followed the lead of Chamberlain, rebuilding and sanitizing their urban environments with the massive revenue flows generated by owning local monopoly services and utilities.[172] Central government, meanwhile, had also become integrally involved, but primarily as a facilitator of local initiatives and energies, providing loans, and inspection services, and generalizing best practices, rather than attempting to direct developments from the centre. The principal study of central-local government relations in this period has concluded that central government officials operated in a diplomatic mode in their relationships with local authorities, almost a model of linking social capital in practice, respecting the autonomy of the latter.[173]

What, then, are the valid, more general inferences of relevance to social capital and issues of health and welfare from this episode in the history of the world's first industrial society?

Firstly, British economic history indicates that a nation which places too much emphasis on the accumulation of capital in private hands as its primary objective for economic growth while abdicating responsibility towards the less fortunate in society—a direct implication of 'free market' growth models—may well be paying a high price in terms of bridging and linking social capital formation. Consequently both its environmental and its human capital may also suffer significantly (measured in the British historical case in the rather direct sense of the citizens' life expectancy and biological growth). Those studying in detail the relationship between social capital and economic success are now increasingly emphasizing the importance of 'co-production' across the false dichotomies of the 'public versus private' and 'market versus state' divides. Research by Chalmers Johnson,[174] Alice Amsden,[175] Robert Bates,[176] Robert Wade,[177] Peter Evans,[142] and Judith Tendler[178] (among others) has shown that sustainable economic success is most likely to occur through co-operative, highly negotiated engagement between 'the state' (often in the form of resource- and infrastructure-providing local government agencies), and local businesses and representative bodies of local workers and residents. The British historical case confirms this, in that Britain's industrial cities were fast becoming unworkable environments, until Chamberlain found a political means to cut the Gordian knot of social fragmentation and distrust and to implement forms of 'co-production'.

Secondly, the British case indicates that it is only when networks of association are as well-developed and as multi-faceted as Chamberlain's were, and are geared to comprehending the interests of the political majority in the community, as his were (which enabled him to *know*, understand, and respect—but also deal with—the fiscal sensitivities of the opponents to his schemes), that leaders and policy-makers will, indeed, have sufficiently detailed understanding and knowledge of the society with which they are negotiating, which will enable them to formulate effective programmes, which genuinely facilitate or persuade (rather than merely attempting to 'lead' or coerce) the wishes and interest of the majority of the citizens. This is an example of bridging and linking social capital, of Woolcock's[7] emphasis on embedded autonomy, and the importance of democratically elected local government as the responsive and accountable 'state' in action.

This leads on, naturally, to a third important issue: political participation. Chamberlain's new politics was developed directly in response to the opportunities for a more democratic and participatory urban politics opened up by the British state's belated enfranchizement between 1867 and 1884 of a large section of the working classes (two in three adult males had the vote by 1885; universal adult male franchise did not arrive until 1918 and female until 1928). Many contemporary developing societies and communities exhibit extremely poor resources in terms of civic political participation, with some important examples such as China formally channelling all political energy through the narrow nexus of the official Party apparatus, while others, such as India, too often making a mockery of their formally democratic constitutions because of the impoverished and socially excluded nature of vast tracts of their citizenry, notably rural peasants and, especially, females. Extensive bridging and linking social capital cannot possibly flourish in these circumstances, where the basic political and institutional ground-rules for citizen participation in the political processes are lacking.

The state is at its most effective in both facilitating and benefiting from social capital when it is operating in a highly devolved form, something we principally associate with the institutions of elected local government. Chamberlain showed that increasingly democratic and vigorous local government, when sufficiently politically responsive to the interests of a wide range of groups in the local community, is the most obvious and effective ally of social capital. One danger in the social capital literature has been an over-emphasis on voluntary associations, alone, as the key to healthy social capital, and a tendency to cast 'the state' only in the negative terms of an impersonal and monolithic 'big brother' figure. The British historical case indicates, however, that voluntary associations of citizens, alone, can have ambiguous consequences for a community's social capital and its public health, as in the early and mid-Victorian decades in Britain. There is a crucial facilitating role for the state, for elected, representative, and dynamic local government agencies, and for politics and ideas in the formation of the kind of balanced social capital required for promotion of population health under the dynamic conditions of continual economic growth. The recent example of the Brazilian city of Porto Alegre's 15-year experiment with participatory budget-setting confirms the continuing relevance of the historical case of Birmingham and of the bridging and linking social capital analysis presented here, which focuses on the salience of motivating moral ideals, cross-class political leadership, embedded but autonomous local government, and empowerment of inhabitants, resulting in major improvements to the city's population health.[179]

IV Discussion

The empirical base of the general social capital story—and the veritable explosion of interest accompanying it across the social and medical sciences—rests in no small part on applied research in the fields of public health and epidemiology. As such, the debates taking place within these fields deserve special attention, and are instructive for broader conceptual and policy deliberations. We have argued that while the current disagreements among the major protagonists in the field of social capital and public health manifest themselves as methodological differences regarding the efficacy of power (access to resources), inequality, or social support networks as the primary determinant of health outcomes, they are in fact better understood as products of an ill-specified (or at least less than comprehensive) theory of social capital. Indeed, closer attention to the current theoretical developments—themselves a product of close engagement with a range of empirical studies—reveals a conceptual framework that provides a basis for resolving the current debates, one that is also consistent with rich historical evidence regarding the emergence and resolution of major public health crises in 19th century Britain.

This framework centres on an analytical distinction between three kinds of social relationships in which individuals are engaged, and, crucially, the nature of the state—society relations in which these individuals and their relationships are inherently embedded. It relies on the distinction between bonding, bridging, and linking forms of social capital. Of course many other things are also required for a 'healthy society' to be capable of consistently using its material resources for the promotion of the population health of all its citizens.[180] One necessary condition, however, will be a balanced distribution of a relatively rich endowment of all three of these forms of social capital. In these circumstances the polity will be constituted by a vigorous, open and politically conscious civic society of mutually respecting and highly varied (in terms of their social identities) citizens and their many associations. In such societies, individuals and the wide range of associations that represent their interests are in active dialogue and negotiation (since there are certain to be conflicts requiring negotiation) with both their elected local governments and their central state. Without such a health-promoting, balanced development of all three forms of social capital, however, social capital, in any of its three forms, may easily be used as a resource for exclusionary and sectional interests, which may have an ambivalent or even negative consequence for the overall population health of society. It is, then, an entirely contingent question of politics, public morality, ideology, and historical events whether or not the resources of social capital, which necessarily exist in any society, will take on health-promoting or health-degrading net effects.

We would therefore wish to emphasize that this question of negotiated political and ideological contingency is crucial. Social capital is not a magic wand for improving society, nor is it a self-contained comprehensive theory. It is a useful concept, which focuses our attention on an important set of resources, inhering in relationships, networks, associations, and norms, which have previously been accorded insufficient priority in the social sciences and health literature. This is probably partly because they are not easy to categorize, study and measure in their effects. Advances are now being made, but this will continue to be a site for 'work in progress' for some time to come. It is important to remember that it recently took several decades of patient methodological work for the concept of human capital to be accepted as a tractable one by most economists, as it is today.

The theoretical formulation of social capital presented here may offer the basis for reconciling the three different positions on social capital and health outlined above. The oldest school of thought, the 'social support' view of social relationships, would tend to imply that, at least from an individual's point of view, any kind of positive social support is good for your health—the classic case is that of family and friends to get you through a critical illness. This would correspond to an undifferentiated concept of social capital as just all and any networks. Marmot and Wilkinson's inequalities approach has significantly complicated the epidemiological picture by arguing that, at least in the relatively affluent societies which they have studied, the overall patterns of individuals' social relations should be seen in a wider political and historical context, in order to be able to evaluate whether, in the aggregate, they are of net benefit to their health. In societies characterized by steep or by growing inequalities, there will be a tendency for social relationships in general to become less egalitarian and mutually respectful and instead to become more hierarchical and unsympathetic. A general disposition of goodwill towards other citizens will be replaced by one of suspicion and distrust. In turn, this has a range of negative health implications, particularly for those lower down the social status hierarchy, whose perceptions of disrespect for themselves will be harmful to their health. Although their personal friendships may still be helpful to them in fighting ill health—the 'social support' thesis—the overall pattern of the social relationships available to them in such an unequal society may be responsible for an extra burden of illness. This development in the epidemiological literature corresponds to the recognition of the importance of the distinction between bonding and bridging in the social capital literature—not all social relationships are the same and have similar supportive effects, from a health point of view.

While Wilkinson's 'political economy' critics have been content to deny the thesis that the putative socio-psychological pathways of health damage are the most important, they agree that conditions of heightened inequality are harmful to health. They would prefer, however, to emphasize the importance of the deficient material living conditions of the poor and the political and ideological factors, which result in some societies accepting conditions among some of their populace which other societies would find intolerable. This focus on the causal importance of the prior and ongoing history of the political and the ideological would correspond, in social capital theory, to the acknowledgement of the significance of questions of relationships between citizens and the state, issues which are raised through a focus on linking social capital, as an additional, distinctive category to that of bonding and bridging social capital. This would suggest that none of the three epidemiological schools of thought is wrong, in its own terms, about the relationship between social capital and health, but that, like the sequence of conceptual developments of social capital theory, they represent successively more comprehensive formulations of the scope of the causal factors involved in analysing the relationship between health, citizens, society, and, ultimately, the polity and the state.

V Policy conclusions

It was stated earlier that we would attempt to outline the policy implications which such a revised theory of social capital would have for the public health field, particularly in addressing the issues of inequality and health in relatively affluent societies, which lie at the heart of the dispute between Wilkinson, Lynch, and others. We would argue that taking seriously the concept of linking social capital problematizes in particular the quality of relationships whenever and wherever resources might flow across perceived power gradients. Potentially health-enhancing resources may be primarily material (a new hip replacement) or may be purely informational (where to go to get a hip replacement or the knowledge that one has a right to have a hip replacement), but they are most frequently an alloy of both (getting the hip replacement *and* the right advice about post-operative rehabilitation). Improving human health requires both the entitlement to appropriate 'material' needs and the capability to benefit from it, which is so often mediated through social relationships.

Lynch and the 'neo-materialists' are right to continue to emphasize that even in the most affluent societies in the world, the poor can still suffer major material deprivations that directly cause their ill health. Wilkinson and Marmot are right to stress that the perception of living in an unequal and unjust society can be so corrosive of social relationships that this can have tangible consequences on the health of the population. The concept of linking social capital makes the connection between these two through the issue of the quality of health services information and delivery influencing equality of access to health education and health knowledge. There can be little doubt that the maintenance of population health at historically high levels in affluent societies depends on a relatively high proficiency of health knowledge among citizens, both in the sense of knowing how to keep themselves healthy in the potentially highly toxic and dangerous urban environments we mostly inhabit, and having the expertise and confidence to access medical and other social services when they are needed.[181] In affluent societies that allow themselves to become particularly unequal, the underprivileged will not only suffer substantial health-compromising material deprivations, but there will also arise problems of social distance and the likelihood of deteriorating mutual respect between the haves and have-nots, if a sense of injustice arises. While Wilkinson and others have been exploring the possible direct health consequences of this, the linking social capital concept indicates that *in addition* to such physiological impacts, if relationships of trust and respect deteriorate between the poor and the range of more privileged people in their lives who are involved in delivering the essential public services of education, health, and social security, then the capacity of the poor to acquire, utilize and benefit from health-enhancing material goods will be seriously compromised.

The interaction of all these factors has, for instance, been persuasively expounded in Klinenberg's comprehensive analysis of the causes of the more than 700 fatalities due to the 1995 heat wave in Chicago.[182] These were particularly concentrated among males aged over 65. Klinenberg's comparison of two matched, poor districts showed that the disproportionately high death-rate in North Lawndale was indeed correlated with material deficits, notably such as non-ownership of air-conditioning. However, there was also a strong correlation with living alone and the strongest correlation of all was with absence of any social contacts, extending to many deceased males being found locked in their own apartments, reflecting the chronic state of fear of neighbours in this downwardly spiralling, 'abandoned', black immigrant part of town. By contrast, adjacent South Lawndale (also a poor area in which many homes lacked air conditioning) benefited from a vibrant Latino community in which people felt relatively safe in public spaces. It exhibited starkly contrasting, disproportionately low mortality during the heat wave. Thus, social capital and Wilkinson's emphasis on the social psychology of dynamic trends in inequality are clearly implicated as playing a major role, along with neo-material deficits. And finally, standing behind both of these factors, lies the causal role of the changing political economy and culture of the US. The society which only two decades earlier had responded in full to Lyndon Johnson's call for an 'unconditional war on poverty' to honour the wishes of their assassinated young President, had now, during the decades of the 1980s and 1990, acquiesced in the abandonment of whole districts like North Lawndale. Heat waves as severe as 1995 had occurred in Chicago before; in 1964, for example, a comparable heat wave generated no death peak, as many without air-conditioning had felt safe enough to sleep outside at night in the parks.

Where future policy is concerned, the social capital framework presented here indicates that in British society, which remains a strongly class-divided culture, a key problem with the universalist national health service and welfare state has been that, while it delivered a reasonable amount of 'material' inputs to the poor, this was done in the context of a relative deficit of sensitive linking social capital, whose most obvious and tangible, health-compromising results have been the profusion of poorly designed housing estates for the poor.[183,184] In the US, during the last two decades there has been a failure to deliver even half-adequate material assistance to the very poor and while the society as a whole pays lip-service to the ideals of a citizen republic of equals, its bridging and linking social capital is in tatters.[6] In Sweden, by contrast, there has been a record of adequate material assistance to the poor and much more effective linking social capital than in either of the other two cases.[148]

In view of these considerations, it is a particularly ironic misconception entertained in some quarters that the social capital approach to both the promotion of population health and also to the improvement of public services in general in a democratic society necessarily might represent a 'cheap' option and might be lacking in political radicalism. It can be seen that social capital theory, embracing not only bonding and bridging but also linking social capital, places great emphasis on both the quality and the quantity of relationships between all citizens. It also places great emphasis on whether or not these relationships are founded on mutual respect between people, differentiated either horizontally by their varying social identities or vertically by their access to different levels of power and authority. Commitment to the goal of a society of mutually respecting citizens has the potential to motivate an extremely radical political economy, carrying strong redistributionist implications.[108] The social capital perspective also informs us that if we normatively approve of the goal of enhancing population health, we cannot achieve this through material inputs alone, or simply through 'technological fixes', whether 'imposed' or magnanimously 'granted' by those with superior resources. Material assistance will almost certainly be necessary in most contexts; but equally important will be attention to the quality and quantity of relationships, which carry and make interpretable any such material or technological transfers.

In the public services and in developed societies in general it is in fact these precious resources of human relationships, effort, and care—or labour, to use an old fashioned word—that are crucial, rather than material inputs, alone. Human expertise, time, and attention are also, inevitably, increasingly expensive to deploy. Taking social capital seriously in the context of health promotion in rich or poor countries is, therefore, not in any sense a cheap option; it is an additional dimension—and one necessarily requiring additional costs—that too often has been neglected.

Acknowledgement

We are grateful to Robert Putnam for commenting on and debating the various issues this paper raises. We also wish to thank conference participants at the Institute for Public Health, University of Cambridge, the members of the Cambridge Social Capital Seminar, and attendees at the Fourth International Health Economics Association meeting (wherein earlier versions were presented). Leonardo Monasterio provided excellent research assistance, and helpful comments were received from John Lynch, John Powles, David Robinson, SV Subramanian, Richard Wilkinson, two anonymous reviewers, and the *International Journal of Epidemiology*'s editors. The views expressed in this paper are solely those of the authors, and should not be attributed to their respective organizations or executive officers. Simon Szreter held an Economic and Social Research Council Fellowship, award number R000271041, during much of his work on this article.

KEY MESSAGES

- The debate within epidemiology between proponents of a neo-materialist and a psycho-social interpretation of the relationship between health and inequality may benefit from the application of a more-developed theory of social capital.
- A new theory of social capital is put forward, distinguishing linking social capital from the more familiar bonding and bridging forms. State–society relations and considerations of power are thereby brought explicitly into the social capital framework of analysis.
- The relationship between public health, norms and networks of civic society, and the changing political economy of 'the state' may then be studied in an integrated way, as illustrated by a brief review of 19th-century British history.

References

1 Berkman L, Thomas G, Brissette I, Seeman TE. From social integration to health: Durkheim in the new millennium. *Soc Sci Med* 2000; **51**:843–57.

2 Kawachi I. Social capital for health and human development. *Development* 2001;**44**:31–35.

3 Coburn D. Income inequality, social cohesion and the health status of populations: the role of neoliberalism. *Soc Sci Med* 2000;**51**:139–50.

4 *American Journal of Public Health*. Special section on 'population health. March 2003.

5 Putnam R. *Making Democracy Work: Civic Traditions in Modern Italy*. Princeton, NJ: Princeton University Press, 1993.

6 Putnam R. *Bowling Alone: The Collapse and Revival of American Community*. New York: Simon and Schuster, 2000.

7 Woolcock M. Social capital and economic development: toward a theoretical synthesis and policy framework. *Theory and Society* 1998;**27**:151–208.

8 Woolcock M, Narayan D. Social capital: implications for development theory, research, and policy. *World Bank Research Observer* 2000; **15**:225–49.

[9] Lomas J. Social capital and health: implications for public health and epidemiology. *Soc Sci Med* 1998;**47:**1181–88.

[10] Morrow V. Conceptualising social capital in relation to the well-being of children and young people: a critical review. *Sociol Rev* 1999;**47:**744–65.

[11] Hawe P, Shiell A. Social capital and health promotion: a review. *Soc Sci Med* 2000;**51:**871–85.

[12] Veenstra G. Social capital and health. *Can J Policy Res* 2001;**2:**72–81.

[13] Macinko J, Starfield B. The utility of social capital in research on health determinants. *Milbank Q* 2001;**79:**387–427.

[14] Cattell V. Poor people, poor places, and poor health: the mediating role of social networks and social capital. *Soc Sci Med* 2001;**52:**1501–16.

[15] Cullen M, Whiteford H. The interrelations of social capital with health and mental health. Commonwealth of Australia: National Mental Health Strategy, Discussion Paper, 2001. Available at: http://www.health.gov.au/hsdd/mentalhe/pdf/inter.pdf

[16] Whitehead M, Diderichsen F. Social capital and health: tip-toeing through the minefield of evidence. *Lancet* 2001;**358:**165–66.

[17] Siegrist J. Social capital and health. *Gesundheitswesen* 2002;**64:**189–92.

[18] Leeder S, Dominello A. Social capital and its relevance to health and family policy. *Aust N Z J Public Health* 1999;**23:**424–29.

[19] Fine B. *Social Capital Versus Social Theory: Political Economy and Social Science at the Turn of the Millennium*. London: Routledge, 2000.

[20] Harriss J. *De-politicizing Development: The World Bank and Social Capital*. London: Anthem Press, 2002.

[21] House JS, Landis KR, Umberson D. Social relationships and health. *Science* 1988;**241:**540–45.

[22] Berkman L. The role of social relations in health promotion. *Psychosom Med* 1995;**57:**245–54.

[23] Seeman TE. Social ties and health: the benefits of social integration. *Annu Epidemiol* 1996;**6:**442–51.

[24] Lynch J, Davey Smith G, Kaplan G, House J. Income inequality and mortality: importance to health of individual income, psychosocial environment, or material conditions. *BMJ* 2000;**320:**1200–04.

[25] Navarro V. A critique of social capital. *Int J Health Serv* 2002;**32:**423–32.

[26] Muntaner C, Lynch JW, Hillemeier M *et al.* Economic inequality, working-class power, social capital, and cause-specific mortality in wealthy countries. *Int J Health Serv* 2002;**32:**629–56.

[27] Davey Smith G. Income inequality and mortality: why are they related? Income inequality goes hand in hand with underinvestment in human resources. *BMJ* 1996;**312:**987–88.

[28] Muntaner C, Lynch J. Income inequality and social cohesion versus class relations: a critique of Wilkinson's neo-Durkheimian research program. *Int J Health Serv* 1998;**29:**59–81.

[29] Kaplan G. Part III Summary: What is the role of the social environment in understanding inequalities in health? *Ann N Y Acad Sci* 1999;**896:**116–20.

[30] Lynch J. Income inequality and health: expanding the debate. *Soc Sci Med* 2000;**51:**1001–05.

[31] Lynch J, Due P, Muntaner C, Davey Smith G. Social capital—is it a good investment strategy for public health? *J Epidemiol Community Health* 2000;**54:**404–08.

[32] Muntaner C, Lynch J, Davey Smith G. Social capital and the third way in public health. *Crit Public Health* 2000;10:107–24.

[33] Muntaner C, Lynch J, Davey Smith G. Social capital, disorganized communities, and the third way: Understanding the retreat from structural inequalities in epidemiology and public health. *Int J Health Serv* 2001;**31:**213–37.

[34] Lynch J, Davey Smith G, Hillemeier M, Shaw M, Raghunathan T, Kaplan G. Income inequality, the psychosocial environment, and health: comparisons of wealthy nations. *Lancet* 2001;**358:**194–200.

[35] Lynch J, Davey Smith G. Commentary: Income inequality and health: The end of the story? *Int J Epidemiol* 2002;**31:**549–51.

[36] Pearce N, Davey Smith G. Is social capital the key to inequalities in health? *Am J Public Health* 2003;**93:**122–29.

[37] Wilkinson R. Income inequality, social cohesion and health: clarifying the theory. A reply to Muntaner and Lynch. *Int J Health Serv* 1999;**29:**525–43.

[38] Wilkinson R. Inequality and the social environment: a reply to Lynch *et al. J Epidemiol Community Health* 2000;**54:**411–13.

[39] Marmot M, Wilkinson RG. Psychosocial and material pathways in the relation between income and health: a response to Lynch *et al. BMJ* 2001;**322:**1233–36.

[40] Wilkinson R. Commentary: Liberty, fraternity, equality. *Int J Epidemiol* 2002;**31:**538–43.

[41] Baum F. Public health and civil society: understanding and valuing the connection. *Aust N Z J Public Health* 1997;**21:**673–75.

[42] Baum F. Social capital: is it good for your health? Issues for a public health agenda. *J Epidemiol Community Health* 2000;**53:**195–96.

[43] Wilkinson R. Deeper than 'neoliberalism': a reply to David Coburn. *Soc Sci Med* 2000;**51:**997–1000.

[44] Kawachi I, Berkman L. Social cohesion, social capital, and health. In: Berkman L, Kawachi I (eds). *Social Epidemiology*. New York: Oxford University Press, 2000, pp. 174–90.

[45] Wilkinson R. *Unhealthy Societies: The Afflictions of Inequality*. London: Routledge, 1996.

[46] Wilkinson R (ed.). *Class and Health*. London: Tavistock Publications, 1986.

[47] Berkman L. Social support, social networks, social cohesion and health. *Soc Work Health Care* 2000;**31:**3–14.

[48] Cooper H, Arber S *et al. The Influence of Social Support and Social Capital on Health*. London: Health Education Authority, 1999.

[49] Gorski PA. Caring relationships: An investment in health? *Public Health Rep* 2000;**115:**144–50.

[50] Lennartsson C. Social ties and health among the very old in Sweden. *Res Ageing* 1999;**21:**657–81.

[51] Berkman L, Glass T. Social integration, social networks, social support and health. In: Berkman L, Kawachi I (eds). *Social Epidemiology*. New York: Oxford University Press, 2000, pp. 137–73.

[52] Brown GW, Harris T. *Social Origins of Depression: A Study of Psychiatric Disorder in Women*. London: Tavistock Publications, 1978.

[53] Berkman L, Syme SL. Social networks, host resistance and mortality: a nine year follow-up study of Alameda County residents. *Am J Epidemiol* 1979;**109:**186–204.

[54] Forbes A, Wainwright SP. On the methodological, theoretical and philosophical context of health inequalities research: a critique. *Soc Sci Med* 2001;**53:**801–16.

[55] Eckersley R, Dixon J, Douglas R (eds). *The Social Origins of Health and Well-Being*. Cambridge: Cambridge University Press, 2001.

[56] Kawachi I. Social capital and community effects on population and individual health. *Socioeconomic Status and Health in Industrial Nations* 1999;**896:**120–30.

[57] Keating DP. Social capital and developmental health: Making the connection. *J Dev Behav Pediatr* 2000;**21:**50–52.

[58] Howard DE. How alienation and declines in social capital are affecting adolescent well-being. Working Paper, Department of Public and Community Health, University of Maryland, 2003.

[59] Kawachi I, Berkman L. Social ties and mental health. *J Urban Health* 2001;**78:**458–67.

[60] Hagan J, Merkens H, Boehnke K. Delinquency and disdain: social capital and the control of right-wing extremism among east and west Berlin youth. *Am J Sociol* 1995;**100:**1028–52.

[61] Sampson R, Morenhoff J, Earls F. Beyond social capital: spatial dynamics of collective efficacy for children. *Am Sociol Rev* 1999;**64**:633–60.

[62] Kawachi I, Kennedy B, Lochner K *et al.* Social capital, income inequality, and mortality. *Am J Public Health* 1997;**87**:1491–98.

[63] Weitzman ER, Kawachi I. Giving means receiving: the protective effect of social capital on binge drinking on college campuses. *Am J Public Health* 2000;**90**:1936–39.

[64] Lin N, Ye X, Ensel WM. Social support and depressed mood: a structural analysis. *J Health Soc Behav* 1999;**40**:344–59.

[65] Bullers S. The mediating role of perceived control in the relationship between social ties and depressive symptoms. *Women Health* 2000;**31**:97–116.

[66] Penninx, BWJH, van Tilburg TG, Kriegsman DMW, Boeke, AJP, Deeg DJH, van Eijk JTM. Social network, social support, and loneliness in older persons with different chronic diseases. *J Aging Health* 1999;**11**:151–68.

[67] Lindstrom M, Hanson BS, Ostergren PO, Berglund G. Socio-economic differences in smoking cessation: the role of social participation. *Scand J Public Health* 2000;**28**:200–08.

[68] Sevigny B, Belanger JP, Sullivan R. Social capital and improvement in health and wellbeing of populations. *Can J Public Health* 1999;**90**:369–71.

[69] Raphael D, Renwick R, Brown I, Steinmetz B, Sehdev H, Phillips S. Making the links between community structure and individual well-being: community quality of life in Riverdale, Toronto, Canada. *Health Place* 2001;**7**:179–96.

[70] Helliwell J. How's life? Combining individual and national variables to explain subjective well-being. *Economic Modelling* 2002;**20**:331–60.

[71] Kawachi I, Kennedy B, Glass R. Social capital and self-rated health: a contextual analysis. *Am J Public Health* 1999;**89**:1187–93.

[72] Rose R. How much does social capital add to individual health? A survey study of Russians. *Soc Sci Med* 2000;**51**:1421–35.

[73] Ellaway A, Macintyre S. Social capital and self-rated health: support for a contextual mechanism. *Am J Public Health* 2000;**90**:988.

[74] Subramanian SV, Kawachi I, Kennedy BP. Does the state you live in make a difference? Multilevel analysis of self-rated health in the US. *Soc Sci Med* 2001;**53**:9–19.

[75] Steptoe A, Feldman PJ. Neighborhood problems as sources of chronic stress: Development of a measure of neighborhood problems, and associations with socioeconomic status and health. *Ann Behav Med* 2001;**23**:177–85.

[76] Duncan C. *Worlds Apart: Why Poverty Persists in Rural America*. New Haven: Yale University Press, 1999.

[77] Wakefield SEL, Elliott SJ, Cole D, Eyles J. Environmental risk and (re)action: air quality, health, and civic involvement in an urban industrial neighbourhood. *Health Place* 2001;**7**:163–77.

[78] Rosenheck R, Morrissey J, Lam J *et al.* Service delivery and community: social capital, service systems integration, and outcomes among homeless persons with severe mental illness' *Health Serv Res* 2001;**36**:691–710.

[79] Campbell C. Social capital and health: contextualizing health promotion within local community networks. In: Baron S, Field J, Schuller T (eds). *Social Capital: Critical Perspectives*. Oxford: Oxford University Press, 2000, pp. 182–96.

[80] Ong BN. Assessing the context for partnerships between communities and the National Health Service in England. *Critical Public Health* 2000;**10**:343–51.

[81] Murray M. Social capital formation and healthy communities: insights from the Colorado Healthy Communities Initiative. *Community Development Journal* 2000;**35**:99–108

[82] Smith N, Littlejohns LB, Thomson D. Shaking out the cobwebs: insights into community capacity and its relation to health outcomes. *Community Development Journal* 2001;**36**:30–41.

[83] McCulloch A. Social environments and health: cross sectional national survey. *BMJ* 2001;**323**:208–09.

[84] Campbell C, Aggleton P. Young people's sexual health: a framework for policy debate. *Can J Hum Sex* 1999;**8**:249–62.

[85] Galea S, Karpati A, Kennedy B. Social capital and violence in the United States, 1974–1993. *Soc Sci Med* 2002;**55**:1373–83.

[86] Kawachi I, Kennedy B. Income inequality and health: pathways and mechanisms. *Health Serv Res* 1999;**34**:215–27.

[87] Portes A. Social capital: its origins and applications in modern sociology. *Annu Rev Sociol* 1998;**24**:1–24.

[88] Kunitz S. Accounts of social capital: the mixed health effects of personal communities and voluntary groups. In: Leon DA, Walt G (eds). *Poverty, Inequality and Health: An International Perspective*. New York: Oxford University Press, 2001.

[89] Pope J. Social capital should not be incorporated into surveys designed to monitor population health. *Aust N Z J Public Health* 2000;**24**:341.

[90] Harpham T, Grant E, Thomas E. Measuring social capital within health surveys: key issues. *Health Policy Plan* 2002;**17**:106–11.

[91] Subramanian SV, Kim DJ, Kawachi I. Social trust and self-rated health in US communities: a multi-level analysis. *J Urban Health* 2002;**79**:S21–S34.

[92] Subramanian SV, Blakely A, Kawachi I. Income inequality as a public health concern: where do we stand? *Health Serv Res* 2003;**38**:153–67.

[93] Subramanian SV, Lochner KA, Kawachi I. Neighborhood differences in social capital: a compositional analysis. *Health Place* 2003;**9**:33–44.

[94] Omran AR. The epidemiologic transition: a theory of the epidemiology of population change. *Milbank Mem Fund Q* 1971;**49**:509–38.

[95] Wilkinson R. Putting the picture together: prosperity, redistribution, health and welfare. In: Marmot M, Wilkinson R (eds). *Social Determinants of Health*. Oxford: Oxford University Press, 1999, pp. 256–74.

[96] Wilkinson R. *Mind the Gap: Hierarchies, Health, and Human Evolution*. New Haven: Yale University Press, 2001.

[97] Marmot M, Rose G, Shipley M, Hamilton PJ. Employment grade and coronary heart disease in British civil servants. *J Epidemiol Community Health* 1978;**32**:244–49.

[98] Marmot M, Davey Smith G, Stansfield S *et al.* Health inequalities among British civil servants: the Whitehall II study. *Lancet* 1991;**337**:1387–93.

[99] Brunner E, Marmot M. Social organization, stress, and health. In: Marmot M, Wilkinson R (eds). *Social Determinants of Health*. New York: Oxford University Press, 1999, pp. 17–43.

[100] Beaglehole R, Magnus P. The search for new risk factors for coronary heart disease: occupational therapy for epidemiologists? *Int J Epidemiol* 2002;**31**:1117–22.

[101] Ross NA, Wolfson MC, Dunn JR, Berthelot J-M, Kaplan GA, Lynch JW. Income inequality and mortality in Canada and the United States: A cross-sectional assessment using Census data and vital statistics. *BMJ* 2000;**320**:898–902.

[102] Wolfson M, Kaplan GA, Lynch JW, Ross N, Backlund E. The relationship between income inequality and mortality is not a statistical artefact. *BMJ* 1999;**319**:953–57.

[103] Navarro V, Shi L. The political context of social inequalities and health. *Int J Health Serv* 2001;**31**:1–21.

[104] Krugman P. For richer. *New York Times Magazine*, 20 October 2002.

[105] Alesina A, La Ferrara E. *Preferences for Redistribution in the Land of Opportunities*. Cambridge, MA: National Bureau of Economic Research Working Paper 8267, 2001.

[106] Dominguez S, Watkins C. Creating networks for survival and mobility: social capital among African-American and Latin-American low-income mothers. *Social Problems* 2003;**50**:111–35.

[107] Woolcock M. The place of social capital in understanding social and economic outcomes. *Can J Policy Res* 2001;**2:**11–17.

[108] Szreter S. Social capital, the economy and education in historical perspective. In: Baron S, Field J, Schuller T (eds). *Social Capital: Critical Perspectives*. Oxford: Oxford University Press, 2000, pp. 56–77.

[109] Szreter S. The state of social capital: bringing power, politics, and history back. *Theory and Society* 2002;**31:**573–621.

[110] Bourdieu P. The forms of capital. In: Richardson J (ed.). *Handbook of Theory and Research for the Sociology of Education*. Westport, CT: Greenwood Press, 1986.

[111] Coleman J. Social capital in the creation of human capital. *Am J Sociol* 1988;**94:**S95–120.

[112] Coleman J. *Foundations of Social Theory*. Cambridge, MA: Harvard University Press, 1990.

[113] Loury G. A dynamic theory of racial income differences. In: Wallace PA, LeMund A (eds). *Women, Minorities, and Employment Discrimination*. Lexington, MA: Lexington Books, 1977.

[114] Farr J. Social capital: a conceptual history. *Political Theory* 2004 (forthcoming).

[115] Jacobs J. *The Life and Death of Great American Cities*. New York: Random House, 1961.

[116] Foley M, Edwards R. Is it time to disinvest in social capital? *J Public Policy* 1999;**19:**141–73.

[117] Schuller T, Baron S, Field J. Social capital: a review and critique. In: Baron S, Field J, Schuller T (eds). *Social Capital: Critical Perspectives*. Oxford: Oxford University Press, 2001, pp. 1–38.

[118] Glaeser E, Laibson D, Sacerdote B. An economic approach to social capital. *Economic J* 2002;**112:**437–58.

[119] Fukuyama F. *Trust: The Social Virtues and the Creation of Prosperity*. New York: Free Press, 1995.

[120] Knack S, Keefer P. Institutions and economic performance: cross-country tests using alternative institutional measures. *Economics and Politics* 1995;**7:**207–27.

[121] Knack S, Keefer P. Does social capital have an economic pay off? A cross-country investigation. *Quarterly Journal of Economics* 1997; **112:**1251–88.

[122] Evans P. Government action, social capital and development: reviewing the evidence on synergy. *World Development* 1996;**24:**1119–32.

[123] Burt R. *Structural Holes*. Cambridge, MA: Harvard University Press, 1992.

[124] Burt R. The network structure of social capital. In: Sutton R, Shaw B (eds). *Research in Organizational Behavior*. Greenwich, CT: JAI Press, 2000.

[125] Lin N. *Social Capital: A Theory of Social Structure and Action*. New York: Cambridge University Press, 2001.

[126] Gitell R, Vidal AC. *Community Organizing: Building Social Capital as a Development Strategy*. Thousand Oaks, CA: Sage Publications, 1998.

[127] Woolcock M. Managing risk, change, and opportunity in developing countries: the role of social capital. In: Ranis G (ed.). *Dimensions of Development*. New Haven, CT: Yale Center for International and Area Studies, 1999.

[128] World Bank. *World Development Report 2000/01: Attacking Poverty*. New York: Oxford University Press, 2000.

[129] Pritchett L, Woolcock M. Solutions when *the* solution is the problem: arraying the disarray in development. *World Development* 2004 (forthcoming).

[130] Lipsky M. *Street-level Bureaucracy: Dilemmas of the Individual in Public Services*. New York: Russell Sage, 1980.

[131] Narayan D. *Voices of the Poor*. New York: Oxford University Press, 2000.

[132] Krishna A. *Active Social Capital: Tracing the Roots of Development and Democracy*. New York: Columbia University Press, 2002.

[133] Grootaert C, van Bastelaer T (eds). *Understanding and Measuring Social Capital*. Washington, DC: The World Bank, 2002.

[134] Grootaert C, Narayan D, Nyhan Jones V, Woolcock M. *Integrated Questionnaire for the Measurement of Social Capital*. Washington, DC: The World Bank, (forthcoming).

[135] Durlauf S. On the empirics of social capital. *Economic Journal* 2002;**112:**459–79.

[136] Wilson WJ. *When Work Disappears: The World of the New Urban Poor*. New York: Alfred A. Knopf, 1996.

[137] Gittell R, Thompson JP. Making social capital work: social capital and community Economic development. In: Saegert S, Thompson JP, Warren MR (eds). *Social Capital and Poor Communities*. New York: Russell Sage, 2001, pp. 115–35.

[138] Noguera PA. Transforming urban schools through investment in the social capital of parents. In: Saegert S, Thompson JP, Warren MR (eds). *Social Capital and Poor Communities*. New York: Russell Sage, 2001, pp. 189–212.

[139] Evans P, Rueschemeyer D, Skocpol T. *Bringing the State Back In*. New York: Cambridge University Press, 1985.

[140] Skocpol T, Fiorina MP. *Civic Engagement in American Democracy*. Washington DC: Brookings Institution Press, 1999.

[141] Sen A. *Development as Freedom*. Oxford: Oxford University Press, 1999.

[142] Evans P. *Embedded Autonomy: States and Industrial Transformation*. Princeton, NJ: Princeton University Press, 1995.

[143] Granovetter M. Economic action and social structure: the problem of embeddedness. *Am J Sociol* 1985;**91:**481–510.

[144] Dyson KHF. *The State Tradition in Western Europe: A Study of an Idea and Institution*. Oxford: Robertson, 1980.

[145] Scott J. *Seeing Like a State: Why Certain Schemes to Improve the Human Condition Have Failed*. New Haven: Yale University Press, 1998.

[146] Bunce V. *Subversive Institutions: The Design and Destruction of Socialism and State*. New York: Cambridge University Press, 1999.

[147] Mann M. *The Sources of Social Power. Vol II. The Rise of Classes and Nation-States, 1760–1914*. Cambridge: Cambridge University Press, 1993.

[148] Rothstein B. *Just Institutions Matter: The Moral and Political Logic of the Universal Welfare State*. New York: Cambridge University Press, 1998.

[149] Esping-Andersen G. *The Three Worlds of Welfare Capitalism*. Cambridge: Polity Press, 1990.

[150] Lynch JW, Kaplan GA, Salonen JT. Why do poor people behave poorly? Variation in adult health behaviours and psychosocial characteristics by stages of the socioeconomic lifecourse. *Soc Sci Med* 1997;**44:**809–19.

[151] Appleby A. *Famine in Tudor and Stuart England*. Liverpool: Liverpool University Press, 1978.

[152] Brewer J. *The Sinews of Power: War, Money and the English State, 1688–1783*. London: Unwin Hyman, 1989.

[153] Langford C. *A Polite and Commercial People: England 1727–83*. Oxford: Oxford University Press, 1989.

[154] Wrigley EA. *People, Cities and Wealth*. Oxford: Blackwell, 1987.

[155] Wrigley EA, Oeppen J, Davies R, Schofield R. *English Population History from Family Reconstitution, 1580–1830*. Cambridge: Cambridge University Press, 1997.

[156] Szreter S, Mooney G. Urbanisation, mortality and the standard of living debate: new estimates of the expectation of life at birth in nineteenth-century British cities. *Economic History Review* 1998;**50:**84–112.

[157] Floud R, Wachter K, Gregory A. *Height, Health and History: Nutritional Status in the United Kingdom, 1750–1980*. Cambridge: Cambridge University Press, 1990.

[158] Slack P. *The English Poor Law 1531–1782*. Basingstoke: Macmillan, 1990.

[159]Marshall JD. *The Old Poor Law, 1795–1834*. Basingstoke: Macmillan, 1985.

[160]Garrett E, Reid A, Schurer K, Szreter S. *Changing Family Size in England and Wales, 1891–1911: Place, Class and Demography*. Cambridge: Cambridge University Press, 2001.

[161]Bythell D. *The Handloom Weavers*. Cambridge: Cambridge University Press, 1969.

[162]Rose ME. *The Relief of Poverty, 1834–1914*. Basingstoke: Macmillan, 1986.

[163]Neave D. Friendly Societies in Great Britain. In: van der Linden M, Dreyfus M, Gibaud B, Lucassen J (eds). *Social Security Mutualism: The Comparative History of Mutual Benefit Societies*. Berne: Lang, Peter Publishing, 1996, pp. 41–64.

[164]Gilbert AD. *Religion and Society in Industrial England, 1740–1914*. London: Longman, 1976.

[165]Mason M. *The Making of Victorian Sexual Attitudes*. Oxford: Oxford University Press, 1994.

[166]Dyos HJ, Reeder DA. Slums and suburbs. In: Dyos HJ, Wolff M (eds). *The Victorian City: Images and Realities*. London: Routledge, 1973, pp. 359–86.

[167]Waller PJ. Democracy and dialect, speech and class. In: Waller PJ (ed.). *Politics and Social Change in Modern Britain*. Brighton: Harvester, 1989, pp. 1–33.

[168]Szreter S. Economic growth, disruption, deprivation, disease and death: on the importance of the politics of public health. *Popul Dev Rev* 1997;**23:**693–728.

[169]Prest J. *Liberty and Locality: Parliament, Permissive Legislation, and Ratepayers' Democracies in the Mid-Nineteenth Century*. Oxford: Clarendon Press, 1990.

[170]Hassan JA. The growth and impact of the British water industry in the nineteenth century. *Economic History Review* 1985;**38:**531–47.

[171]Hennock EP. *Fit and Proper Persons*. Montreal: McGill-Queen's University Press, 1973.

[172]Bell F, Millward R. Public health expenditures and mortality in England and Wales, 1870–1914. *Continuity and Change* 1998; **13:**221–50.

[173]Bellamy C. *Administering Local-Central Relations, 1871–1919: The Local Government Board in its Fiscal and Cultural Context*. Manchester: Manchester University Press, 1988.

[174]Johnson C. *MITI and the Japanese Miracle: The Growth of Industrial Policy, 1925–75*. Palo Alto: Stanford University Press, 1982.

[175]Amsden A. *Asia's Next Giant: South Korea and Late Industrialization*. New York: Oxford University Press, 1990.

[176]Bates RH. *Beyond the Miracle of the Market: The Political Economy of Agrarian Development in Kenya*. New York: Cambridge University Press, 1989.

[177]Wade R. *Governing the Market: Economic Theory and the Role of Government in East Asian Industrialization*. Princeton, NJ: Princeton University Press, 1990.

[178]Tendler J. *Good Governance in the Tropics*. Baltimore: Johns Hopkins University Press, 1997.

[179]Abers R. From clientalism to cooperation: local government, participatory policy, and civic organising in Porto Alegre, Brazil. *Politics and Society* 1998;**26:**511–37.

[180]Szreter S. Health and human security in an historical perspective. In: Chen L (ed.). *Health and Human Security*. Cambridge, MA: Harvard University Press, 2003 (forthcoming).

[181]Powles J. Healthier progress: historical perspectives on the social and economic determinants of health. In: Eckersley R, Dixon J (eds). *The Social Origins of Health and Well-Being: From the Planetary to the Molecular*. Melbourne: Cambridge University Press, 2001.

[182]Klinenberg E. *Heat Wave*. Chicago: Chicago University Press, 2002.

[183]Szreter S. Health, class, place, and politics: social capital and collective provision in Britain. *Contemporary British History* 2002;**16:**27–57.

[184]Power A. Area-based poverty and resident empowerment. *Urban Studies* 1996;**33:**1535–64.

Part X
Public Health and The Developing World

[31]

RETHINKING MEDICAL ETHICS: A VIEW FROM BELOW

PAUL FARMER AND NICOLE GASTINEAU CAMPOS

ABSTRACT

In this paper, we argue that lack of access to the fruits of modern medicine and the science that informs it is an important and neglected topic within bioethics and medical ethics. This is especially clear to those working in what are now termed 'resource-poor settings' – to those working, in plain language, among populations living in dire poverty. We draw on our experience with infectious diseases in some of the poorest communities in the world to interrogate the central imperatives of bioethics and medical ethics. AIDS, tuberculosis, and malaria are the three leading infectious killers of adults in the world today. Because each disease is treatable with already available therapies, the lack of access to medical care is widely perceived in heavily disease-burdened areas as constituting an ethical and moral dilemma. In settings in which research on these diseases are conducted but there is little in the way of therapy, there is much talk of first world diagnostics and third world therapeutics.

Here we call for the 'resocialising' of ethics. To resocialise medical ethics will involve using the socialising disciplines to contextualise fully ethical dilemmas in settings of poverty and, a related gambit, the systematic participation of the destitute sick. Clinical research across steep gradients also needs to be linked with the interventions that are demanded by the poor and otherwise marginalised. We conclude that medical ethics must grapple more persistently with the growing problem posed by the yawning 'outcome gap' between rich and poor.

I INTRODUCTION

Bioethics and medical ethics are necessarily a contentious enterprise. These fields have the potential to embrace not only empiric research, but also philosophical commentary, informed opinion, and essay as well. The best scholarship in these related fields often addresses 'unresolved issues' of moral conflict. Some issues are unresolved because they stem from novel developments, such as xenotransplantation or the latest in stem-cell research; other issues are unresolved because too little attention has been paid to them in recent decades, in part because the discipline of medical ethics has arisen in certain social contexts and not in others. We argue here that lack of access to the fruits of modern medicine and the science that informs it is an important and neglected topic within bioethics and medical ethics. This is especially clear to those working in what are now termed 'resource-poor settings' – to those working, in plain language, among populations living in dire poverty.

AIDS research has been a case in point. In a recent commentary on the ethics of HIV vaccine trials, physician Joia Mukherjee voiced in print what many who do not read or write are saying about the ethics of AIDS research within settings in which AIDS is now the leading infectious cause of adult death:

> When asked, 'Have you no morals?' Alfred Doolittle, in George Bernard Shaw's *Pygmalion*, answered, 'Can't afford them, governor. Neither could you if you was as poor as me.' The modern concept of human rights underpins a moral society and holds government responsible for fulfilling those rights. From informed consent to the right to privacy, civil and political rights have dominated the human rights focus of the HIV-1 epidemic. Yet, the economic and social rights of people with HIV-1 infection, in particular the rights to health care and to share in scientific advances, are glaringly disparate between rich and poor countries. This disparity has become the focus of debate in transnational HIV-1 vaccine research.[1]

Mukherjee's commentary will resonate with some and rankle others. But many of those who would find her views compelling are those who will never read a medical journal because they do not read; others read but do not have access to journals. These are the people whose views we seek to echo in offering a view of medical ethics 'from below.'

First, what is meant by 'a view from below'? What is not intended by this expression? Elsewhere, we have elaborated a critique of the scholarship of suffering from the perspective of those

[1] J.S. Mukherjee. HIV-1 Care in Resource-Poor Settings: A View from Haiti. *Lancet* 2003; 362: 994–995, at 994.

living in great poverty.[2] Here we will note in passing that dissymmetries of power are present in all medical exchanges: between well and sick, expert and non-expert, white and black – the list goes on. But these dissymmetries are often masked in the language of academic medicine and public health. In a 1992 book, Howard Brody notes that 'the word *power* is essentially absent from the vocabulary that scholars of medical ethics have constructed for their discipline and that has been accepted by almost everyone who does work in the field or tries to apply medical-ethic insights to the clinical context.'[3] This honest assessment serves as a stepping stone for our essay, which moves far beyond the boundaries of the world's most affluent nations, the birthplace of professional societies of medical ethicists and bioethicists. Since the topic of medical rationing, which implies scarcity, is a staple of the medical ethics literature,[4] we add at the outset that we refer in this essay to the world's poor, especially the poor of the poorest countries. When the question 'Who shall live?' was posed, these people were not yet in the consciousness of those building a new field.

Subaltern populations within rich and middle-income countries have long been caught up in the key dramas of medical ethics: witness the Tuskegee Syphilis Study, which followed 600 African American men in Alabama from 1932 to 1972, and continues to have its echoes even today.[5] Similar experiences have been documented in Europe, South Africa, and Brazil.[6] But, to this day, the poorest people in the poorest countries are likely to appear only in the margins of the bioethics literature if they

[2] P. Farmer. On Suffering and Structural Violence: A View from Below. *Dædalus* 1995; 125: 261–283.

[3] H. Brody. 1992. *The Healer's Power.* New Haven & London. Yale University Press: 12.

[4] V. Fuchs. 1975. *Who Shall Live? Health, Economics, and Social Choice.* New York. Basic Books.

[5] Roughly 400 of these men had syphilis, and most lived in poverty. Despite the 1947 discovery of a cure for the disease – to this day, syphilis is treated with penicillin – subjects were never offered that very inexpensive drug, even though they had joined the study assuming that they would be treated. Nor were they informed of the study's real purpose. (S.M. Reverby, ed. 2000. *Tuskegee Truths: Rethinking the Tuskegee Syphilis Study.* Chapel Hill. University of North Carolina Press. A.M. Brandt. 1987. *No Magic Bullet: A Social History of Venereal Disease in the United States Since 1880.* New York. Oxford University Press.)

[6] See, for example, commentary on Norplant trials in Brazil. A.R. Dos Reis. Norplant in Brazil: Implantation Strategy in the Guise of Scientific Research. *Issues in Reproductive & Genetic Engineering: Journal of International Feminist Analysis* 1990; 3: 111–118.

appear at all. We have seen their critiques of research ethics dismissed as confused and ill-informed commentary or as 'conspiracy theories.' But much is to be gleaned from such critiques, as more in-depth and sympathetic explorations of them suggest.[7] This paper is meant as a constructive critique of bioethics and medical ethics, not only from the point of view of those living in great poverty but from the perspectives advanced by the 'socialising disciplines.' These include anthropology, history, political economy and the sociology of knowledge; few would regard philosophy, for years the parent discipline of ethics, as a socialising discipline. It is our hope, here, to help 'resocialise' medical ethics as part of a broader intellectual and social project that is necessary as dominant cultures, academic and otherwise, increasingly favour psychological or individualist readings of social problems ranging from addiction to AIDS to 'non-compliance' with medical regimens.[8] We will draw on our experience in Haiti and the United States in order to offer an overview of what is lacking not only in ethics but also in conventional human rights discourses, which have also influenced medical ethics and bioethics.

As a physician-anthropologist and a specialist in health policy, our views may be regarded as suspect by some within the field of medical ethics. For this reason, we start our review by relying on certain voices from within the discipline of medical ethics. After pointing to deficiencies underlined from within the discipline, we turn to problems occurring right now in the course of efforts to respond to AIDS and tuberculosis, among other modern plagues.

II WHAT'S WRONG WITH MEDICAL ETHICS?

In the social field in which bioethics and medical ethics have emerged – affluent industrialised countries, by and large, and within the past few decades – practitioners of these disciplines are seen, by themselves and by others, as liberal reformers. Three major and overlapping groups may be discerned. Within clinical settings, ethicists are the guardians of morally sound practice and a safeguard against abuses. By the close of the last century, most major teaching hospitals had ethics committees; many boasted in-house ethicists active in addressing the quandary ethics of individual patients. As often as not, ethics consults in such hospitals

[7] P. Farmer. 1992. *AIDS and Accusation: Haiti and the Geography of Blame.* Berkeley & Los Angeles. University of California Press.

[8] G. Lipovetsky. 1993. *L'Ere du vide: Essais sur l'individualisme contemporain.* Paris. Gallimard.

take into consideration discord between patients' families and medical staff or withdrawal of care for those deemed unlikely to be saved by 'heroic interventions.' The salutary impact of these developments is not disputed.

A second major stream of medical ethics is constituted by the everyday practice of ethics within modern biomedical research. The research arena has been home to an explosive growth of institutional review boards (IRBs); human subjects committees abound. Disclaimers regarding potential personal gain are required in the publishing of data and it is not possible to publish even photographs or the comments of patients without 'ethical clearance.' In the university with which we are affiliated, students cannot undertake research involving human subjects without going through an ethics course and filling out an application. Again, many regard these as positive developments. But some would note that it is not easy to link the proliferation of such committees and regulations with a rise in ethical treatment of the destitute sick, especially if we take a global perspective.

It is possible to read, for example, front-page exposés of research projects conducted by first-world universities in Africa and learn that, although research subjects have signed informed-consent forms, they have no clear notion about what the research explores or about how they figure in the endeavour.[9] Other research projects, duly blessed by multiple review boards in both the research university and the host country, are so manifestly unethical in the eyes of some leaders of modern medicine that they can be termed reminiscent of Tuskegee in the world's leading medical journals. Consider studies involving what many argue are unethical placebo controls in AZT trials attempting to develop a cheaper drug regimen to prevent mother-to-child transmission of HIV.[10] Despite the fact that the US Public Health

[9] H. French. AIDS Research in Africa: Juggling Risks and Hope. *New York Times* 9 October, 1997: A1, A14.

[10] Also consider the more recent example of a randomised-control trial conducted between November 1994 and October 1998, which examined the relationship between serum viral load, concurrent sexually transmitted diseases, and other known and putative HIV risk factors. The research team screened 15127 individuals in a rural district of Uganda, of whom 415 were identified as HIV-positive with an initially HIV-negative partner. The researchers then tracked these serodiscordant couples for thirty months, following the viral load of the infected partner and the rate of seroconversion among the previously uninfected partners. The study concludes that 'viral load is the chief predictor of the risk of heterosexual transmission of HIV-1.' (T.C. Quinn, M.J. Wawer, N. Sewankambo, D. Serwadda, C. Li, F. Wabwire-Mangen, M.O. Meehan, T. Lutalo & R.H. Gray. Viral Load and Heterosexual Transmission of Human

Service began recommending the use of zidovudine to prevent MTCT in 1994, a review by Lurie and Wolfe in 1997 counted 15 studies taking place in developing countries in which some or all of participants were not receiving antiretroviral therapy to prevent MTCT.[11] Editor of the *New England Journal of Medicine* Marcia Angell explicitly compared such studies to Tuskegee, and chastised the NIH and CDC for contributing funds to several projects:

> The fact remains that many studies are done in the Third World that simply could not be done in the countries sponsoring the work. Clinical trials have become a big business, with many of the same imperatives. To survive, it is necessary to get the work done as quickly as possible, with a minimum of obstacles. When these considerations prevail, it seems as if we have not come very far from Tuskegee after all.[12]

The majority of such international biomedical research has inequality as its foundation, and ethical codes developed in affluent countries are quickly ditched as soon as affluent universities undertake research in poor countries. Then come a series of efforts to develop alternative (read, less stringent) codes 'appropriate' to settings of destitution.

A third strand of work is less closely tied to clinical care or research endeavours: teaching and scholarship on bioethics and medical ethics. Again, the explosive growth of these fields is easy

Immunodeficiency Virus Type I. *New England Journal of Medicine* 2000; 342: 921–929.) In an accompanying editorial, *New England Journal of Medicine* editor Marcia Angell voiced her hesitation about publishing the study and was quite pointed in her criticism: 'It is important to be clear about what this study meant for the participants. It meant that for up to 30 months, several hundred people with HIV infection were observed but not treated.' Furthermore, 'the very condition that justified doing the study in Uganda in the first place – the lack of availability of antiretroviral treatment – will greatly limit the relevance of the results there.' (M. Angell. Investigators' Responsibilities for Human Subjects in Developing Countries. *New England Journal of Medicine* 2000; 342: 967–969.) Explicit comparisons to Tuskegee were made in the popular press; in the electronic magazine *Slate,* one writer asked: 'The . . . volunteers in the sample were not offered treatment nor were their healthy sex partners informed that the research subjects were HIV positive. Excuse please, but why isn't this like the [*New England Journal of Medicine*] supporting the Tuskegee experiments?' (S. Shuger. Supreme Court Cover-Up. *Slate* 30 March, 2000. Available at: http://slate.msn.com/?id=1004976.)

[11] P. Lurie & S.M. Wolfe. Unethical Trials of Interventions to Reduce Perinatal Transmission of the Human Immunodeficiency Virus in Developing Countries. *New England Journal of Medicine* 1997; 337: 853–856.

[12] M. Angell. The Ethics of Clinical Research in the Third World. *New England Journal of Medicine* 1997; 337: 847–849.

to gauge simply by looking at journals, publications, and the number of faculty appointments within schools of medicine, nursing, and public health. Many of these scholars have formal training in both medicine and philosophy.

What is the primary purpose of these three overlapping strands of medical ethics and bioethics? An anthropologist might ask, what are the social fields in which they emerge? Whose interests are they intended to protect? What ends do they serve?

Such questions, which admit to multiple answers in multiple arenas, are not always welcome. None of the answers are facile ones, since even the quandary ethics of clinical practice are disputed terrain. But even more disputed are research ethics when projects span vertiginous social inequalities. The ethical dilemmas stemming from such research are almost invariably about the haves and the have-nots, and this is as true today as it was during the long decades in which the Tuskegee experiment was being conducted. But much professional commentary on medical ethics appears divorced from straightforward discussion of racism and the yawning gulf between researchers and subjects. Larry Churchill notes this at times absurd divorce between ethical dilemmas that arise in everyday life and the professional commentary they spawn:

> Bioethical disputes – as measured by the debates in journals and conferences in the United States – often seem to be remote from the values of ordinary people and largely irrelevant to the decisions they encounter in health care. In this sense, philosophical theorizing might be considered harmless entertainment, which if taken too seriously would look ridiculous, as several Monty Python skits have successfully demonstrated.[13]

Churchill's critique of philosophical theorising is even more poignant when the 'ordinary people' in question do not have access to modern healthcare. What 'decisions' are taken by the world's poorest, who are also, by any honest accounting, the globe's sickest? One of the ways to answer this question would be to spend time interviewing the destitute sick about what they regard as their ranking problems; it is also possible, we have discovered, to interview them about the ethics of research.

We draw on our experience with infectious diseases in some of the poorest communities in the world to interrogate the central imperatives of bioethics and medical ethics. AIDS, tuberculosis,

[13] L. Churchill. Are We Professionals? A Critical Look at the Social Role of Bioethicists. *Dædalus* 1999; 128: 253–274, at 255.

and malaria are the three leading infectious killers of adults in the world today. Because each disease is treatable with already available therapies, the lack of access to medical care is widely perceived in heavily disease-burdened areas as constituting an ethical and moral dilemma. In settings in which research on these diseases is conducted but there is little in the way of therapy, there is much talk of first world diagnostics and third world therapeutics.[14] To quote a woman who had returned to central Haiti, dying of AIDS, after years in the city, 'We're good enough to study but not good enough to care for.' This woman, who later received therapy for her disease and stopped dying, was nonetheless passionate about the topic well after her own lack of care was addressed and she began to respond to antiretroviral therapy. In another interview, conducted in her home, she expounded at some length:[15]

> I was diagnosed [with HIV infection] because of a research project that [a US research university] was doing. That was ten years ago. This was in [a slum in Port-au-Prince]. I went back a lot to have my blood drawn but I never got any treatment. And I knew from the radio that other people received treatment. These were people who could pay $200 a month. They were people who could go and make a deposit at a bank and then they'd get their medicines for a month . . . I came home [to central Haiti] to die, but even now that I'm better I'm still angry about it. Ten years of them sucking my blood and nothing! I was a skeleton sitting on the bench waiting for them to call my name. It's when I got to be a skeleton that the nurse told me that I didn't have to come any more. It's as if poor people were animals. But we won't serve as their guinea pigs [*Men nou p'ap sevi kom kobay yo*].[16]

Although the expression 'first-world diagnostics and third-world therapeutics' may not be the term commonly used in Haiti, the

[14] Emanuel et al. have suggested guidelines for 'what makes clinical research ethical.' Among their criteria is 'fair subject selection' – subjects should not be vulnerable individuals and must have the potential to experience the benefits of any ethical research project. (E.J. Emanuel, D. Wendler & C. Grady. What Makes Clinical Research Ethical? *Journal of the American Medical Association* 2000; 283: 2701–2711.)

[15] Several patients being treated for HIV at the Clinique Bon Sauveur in rural Haiti are quoted throughout this article. These interviews are not part of a formal ethnographic study, but rather an effort to convey patient stories in their own words.

[16] The research project mentioned has, by report, since been terminated.

idea behind the expression has wide currency among patients and non-patients there. This is because, with many infectious diseases, the research enterprise is fundamentally a transnational one. It is also a fundamentally inegalitarian exercise in the sense that medicine and science are expanding rapidly, but in a social context of growing global inequality, which ensures that the fruits of medicine and science are not available to many who need them most.[17]

Medicine, public health, and research are all caught up in a web of unequal relations. The link between research on AIDS and access to therapy for HIV has been the most scrutinised, perhaps, of this troubling aspect of modern medicine. But other startling examples abound. Organ transplantation is a disturbing case in point. This is not because the clamour for access to organs by those living with, say, renal failure and poverty has reached the ears of most who write about the ethics of the rapidly expanding practice of organ transplantation. It is rather because, globally, the poor are more likely to serve as donors, rather than recipients, of organs.

Organ transplantation is altogether unknown in countries as poor as Haiti, but is common in wealthier but inegalitarian countries and regions throughout the developing world. And almost everywhere we look, trafficking in organs occurs in predictable ways – predictable, that is, to those who look at social inequalities across borders. To quote one anthropologist who works on this topic, 'the flow of organs follows the modern routes of capital: from South to North, from Third to First World, from poor to rich, from black and brown to white, and from female to male.'[18]

The seamy underbelly of organ donation in the poor world has been noted by other anthropologists and by adventurous ethicists as well; an 'organs watch' website has even been established.[19] Although egregious violations of rights are a major problem – the literature is already rife with stories of organs, from kidneys to corneas, quite literally stolen – a far greater problem is the legal and 'ethically approved' transfer of organs across social gradients. In other words, the ethical codes currently in place have not prevented abuses grounded, however subtly, in growing inequalities.

[17] On the growth of global inequality since 1980, see: J.K. Galbraith. A Perfect Crime: Global Inequality. *Dædalus* 2002; 131: 11–25.

[18] N. Scheper-Hughes. The Global Traffic in Human Organs. *Current Anthropology* 2000; 41: 191–224, at 193.

[19] Organs Watch. University of California, Berkeley. Available at: http://sunsite.berkeley.edu/biotech/organswatch/

When someone living in destitution 'opts' to sell a kidney and signs all informed-consent forms in front of multiple witnesses, is the term 'informed consent' really meaningful? Rather, what does such informed consent really mean? That the donor is a priori informed about his or her chances of survival without the money disbursed upon donation?

So it is with much AIDS research. If individuals living in slums in African cities, unable to read and write, are to participate in clinical trials, what sort of process must they go through in order to provide informed consent? Or is there a darker possibility: that research across such deep gradients of inequality means that the research enterprise is itself fundamentally coercive unless special measures are taken?

These questions, which are not meant as rhetorical, get at one of the oldest and most fraught debates within social theory: the reticulated relationship between structure and agency. A 'view from below' would ask how poverty, racism, and gender inequality come to constrain agency, the ability to make choices. If one believes in the ability of research to lessen misery and suffering – as we do – what 'special measures' might one envision as we seek to conduct research in settings of great poverty? How might we ensure that the measures are not in and of themselves coercive, as many incentives are deemed to be?

To answer these and related questions, we note again that it is necessary to resocialise the problems at hand – the quest for vaccines, say, or novel therapeutics or organ transplantation – in order to have a broader view of the inequalities in which such endeavours are grounded, whether researchers see them or not. Efforts to resocialise problems allow all concerned to have a more meaningful understanding of what it is the research subjects (or organ donors) hope to gain from participating in what are, often enough, their only encounters with modern biomedicine. And even a preliminary attempt to consider these topics in their broader social contexts allows us to come to a preliminary conclusion: the more desperate the poverty of subaltern populations (research subjects or organ donors who live in poverty, sick prisoners), the greater the constraint on their agency. In other words, the steeper the gradient of social inequality across which such transactions occur, the greater the risk of abuse without the 'special measures' we discuss below.

One of the ways of rethinking medical ethics is to place the 'outcome gap' front and centre as an ethical issue. The term 'outcome gap' admits to many meanings, but here we follow the example of paediatrician Paul Wise, who some years ago interrogated conventional wisdom regarding low birth weights in urban United States, where race and class are strongly associated with rates of premature delivery, with weight at birth, and with rates of infant mortality. These oft-noted disparities of outcome had led, in the last quarter of the previous century, to a movement to divert money from neonatal intensive care units to social conditions for African-American women. But Wise noted that such a diversion would not get to the heart of the matter:

> Too often, those who elevate the role of social determinants indict clinical technologies as failed strategies. But devaluing clinical intervention diverts attention from the essential goal that it be provided equitably to all those in need. Belittling the role of clinical care tends to unburden policy of the requirement to provide equitable access to such care.[20]

Arguments about resource allocation – another staple, as noted, of commentary within medical ethics – are not really 'socialised' since they do not include an honest accounting of how an affluent society, or even a city, chooses to spend available resources. Resocialising the problem of low birth rate would require frank discussion of racism, subsidies for the rich and shrinking resources for the poor, military expenditures, and, again, the growing gap between the rich and the poor. It would also require careful consideration of equitable access to clinical care. These topics, like the term 'power', are rarely encountered in professional journals devoted to medical ethics.

And so it is with each of the problems mentioned in this essay: AIDS, chronic renal failure, prison-seated epidemics of tuberculosis, and racial disparities in infant mortality. Each problem has generated debates within medical ethics, and new technologies to address them may generate debates within bioethics. But it is possible to discern in scholarly discourse what might be termed a 'Luddite approach' to the problem: we should halt AIDS research in resource-poor settings, we should stop performing kidney transplants, we should focus exclusively on prison reform rather than treating epidemic tuberculosis within prisons, and we should stop building NICUs. These unwelcome conclusions are reflected not only within scholarship in medical ethics but also its pious echoes in clinical medicine, medical education, and public health.

[20] P. Wise. Confronting Racial Disparities in Infant Mortality: Reconciling Science and Politics. *American Journal of Preventive Medicine* 1993; 9: 7–16, at 9.

We are opposed to these Luddite traps. Each of the dilemmas discussed here calls for new and better technologies, whether they are for managing renal failure or for developing a vaccine for AIDS. To argue, as we do, that the primary ethical issue of modern medicine and public health is the outcome gap, itself rooted in transnational and growing social inequalities, is not to argue for merely shuffling around research and service priorities with decisions based on primitive notions of cost-effectiveness, the latest fashion in policy making. The problem is much deeper. Indeed, we have argued elsewhere that the growing outcome gap constitutes the chief human rights challenge of the 21st century.[21] This assertion will seem odd to many who term themselves experts in the field of human rights, accustomed, as they are, to exhorting governments to respect civil and political rights. But the importance of social and economic rights is paramount in settings of poverty, which are also settings of excess morbidity and mortality.

But what does it mean, for both bioethics and human rights, when a person living in poverty is able to vote, is protected from torture or from imprisonment without due process, but dies of untreated AIDS? What does it mean when a person with renal failure experiences no abuse of his or her civil and political rights, but dies without ever having been offered access to dialysis, to say nothing of transplant? What does it mean when an African-American neonate does not have ready access to the care only afforded in a NICU?

The world's poor do not live on another planet; nor do they live in countries in which such technologies are unavailable. Surveys have shown that in the world's poorest countries, the affluent have ready access to both antiretroviral agents and therapy for renal insufficiency; NICUs are close at hand for infants born to affluent families. At the same time, the world's poor, even those living in wealthy nations, do not have reliable access to good medical care or to the fruits of medical science. And if this is regarded as an ethical problem, then it is one that is growing rapidly and worsened by the development of new and more effective therapies. It is new because some of the diseases and all of the technologies are new: impossible to imagine the key philosophers of yesteryear pondering these technologies because they did not yet exist. Whenever more effective technologies are introduced there will be, in the absence of an equity plan, a

[21] P. Farmer. 2003. *Pathologies of Power: Health, Human Rights, and the New War on the Poor*. Berkeley. University of California Press.

growing outcome gap – the unmentioned elephant in the room of medical ethics.

III LINKING BIOETHICS TO SOCIAL ANALYSIS: RETHINKING THE CASE OF TUBERCULOSIS IN PRISONS

We have underlined two steps that would make medical ethics more compelling in settings of great poverty: using the socialising disciplines to contextualise fully ethical dilemmas in settings of poverty and, a related gambit, the systematic participation of the destitute sick. A third step is to link research across steep gradients with the interventions that are demanded by the poor or otherwise marginalised. Examples of the fruits of linking better analysis and better interventions have been offered elsewhere. In the cases cited above, understanding the ethics of AIDS research in Africa or Haiti would rely heavily on interviewing people living with both poverty and this disease. But what is true for AIDS is true for most other maladies afflicting the poor disproportionately.

Elsewhere, we have offered the example of prisoners in Russia who are sick with drug-resistant tuberculosis in order to underline the shortcomings of current approaches to these problems.[22] To summarise a complex biosocial process for the purposes of the current exercise, it is important to know that a doubling of incarceration rates occurred after the collapse of the Soviet Union. The infamous gulag came to be more than three times as full in 'democratic' Russia, with Siberian incarceration rates exceeding, at one point, 1000 per 100 000 population (only the United States rivals this ratio). Overcrowding, poor ventilation, interruption of medical supplies and salaries for overworked prison staff, and malnutrition led to explosive epidemics of tuberculosis within Russia's prisons. But this was not the sort of tuberculosis seen in Haiti or sub-Saharan Africa. In some senses, the Russian epidemics were more reminiscent of the prison-seated outbreaks documented in New York beginning in the late 1980s: although HIV was not a factor in the Russian epidemics, they were, as in New York, prison-based and involved strains of highly drug-resistant *Mycobacterium tuberculosis*, the organism that causes the disease.[23]

[22] P. Farmer & N. Gastineau. Rethinking Health and Human Rights: Time for a Paradigm Shift. *Journal of Law, Medicine & Ethics* 2002; 30: 655–666.

[23] For a review see: P.E. Farmer, A.S. Kononets, S.E. Borisov, A. Goldfarb, T. Healing & M. McKee. 1999. Recrudescent Tuberculosis in the Russian Federation. In *The Global Impact of Drug-Resistant Tuberculosis*. Program in Infectious

Into this dramatic and novel situation came, for the first time, non-Russian aid agencies and non-governmental organisations. To date, there have been few thorough studies of this stunning development, but such analyses are important to our understanding of what is occurring within prison walls today.[24] By the mid 1990s, such organisations were prominent players in post-Soviet states, all of which had seen catastrophic deterioration in their social safety nets and medical systems. The non-governmental organisations were mostly European and North American, and in the post-perestroika disarray they had something their Russian (and Azeri and Georgian and Kazakh, etc.) partners did not then have: money and clout. The ability of these aid organisations to shape responses to epidemic tuberculosis in Siberia was significant, and they insisted on what they termed the most 'cost-effective' approach, the one endorsed by international tuberculosis experts, including the World Health Organization: directly observed therapy with 'first-line' anti-tuberculous drugs. But some of the Russian prison physicians objected, as did members of Russia's large and crumbling tuberculosis-treatment infrastructure: the prisoner-patients had drug-resistant tuberculosis and would not be cured by standard first-line regimens; some Russian specialists made other objections. These voices were drowned in an undercurrent of censorious opinion from the international experts and the non-governmental agencies, which, flush with resources and backed by international expert opinion, insisted on giving all prisoners the same doses of the same first-line drugs.

In Siberia and in other pilot sites, treatment outcomes were nothing short of catastrophic: less than half of all patients were deemed cured (expected cure rates for supervised therapy of drug-susceptible tuberculosis exceed 95%).[25] Worse, prisoner-patients who were not cured by therapy with first-line drugs emerged from this treatment, if they survived, with 'amplified'

Disease and Social Change, ed. Boston. Program in Infectious Disease and Social Change: 39–83. See also: V. Stern & R. Jones. 1999. *Sentenced to Die? The Problem of TB in Prisons in East and Central Europe and Central Asia.* London. International Centre for Prison Studies, King's College.

[24] For one such study, see: G. Bukhman. 2001. *Reform and Resistance in Post-Soviet Tuberculosis Control.* Doctoral Dissertation, University of Arizona. Ann Arbor. University Microfilms.

[25] M.E. Kimerling, H. Kluge, N. Vezhnina, T. Iacovazzi, T. Demeulenaere, F. Portaels & F. Matthys. Inadequacy of the Current WHO Re-Treatment Regimen in a Central Siberian Prison: Treatment Failure and MDRTB. *International Journal of Tuberculosis and Lung Disease* 1999; 3: 451–453.

resistance. That is, their prognosis had worsened dramatically even if they were to be afforded care with the right drugs.[26] But the non-Russian groups, whether international tuberculosis experts or aid groups, did not concede that they had made an error. Instead, they pressed on, delivering precisely the same medications even to prisoner-patients with documented multi-drug-resistant tuberculosis.

More delegations visited Siberia in 1998. Members of at least one delegation pointed out that drug resistance was not the *likely* cause of treatment failure, it was the cause *already documented*. Somewhat discreetly, it would seem, the lead non-governmental organisation had sent sputum samples for drug-susceptibility testing to at least two reference laboratories in Western Europe. Both laboratories confirmed that patients within Siberian prisons were sick from highly resistant strains of *M. tuberculosis* – strains resistant to precisely those drugs being administered, under direct supervision, by the non-governmental organisations who had been chastising Russian experts for their lack of knowledge of modern tuberculosis control.

Well before 2000, tuberculosis had become the leading cause of death in Russian prisons. In Siberian facilities, surviving prisoners had become less and less treatable, and those with multi-drug-resistant tuberculosis were cohorted behind barbed wire and declared altogether 'untreatable.' But this was not the case: multi-drug-resistant tuberculosis is treatable with other, more expensive drugs; data from a slum in Peru and rural Haiti have made it clear that such efforts can succeed in settings far poorer than Siberia.[27] The real debate was not about the efficacy of therapy but about its costs.

By 2001, the lead non-governmental organisation appeared to yield to growing pressure from prisoners, their guards, and expert opinion: it would work with its Russian partners to treat patients with multi-drug-resistant tuberculosis with the drugs to which their strains had been shown to be susceptible. It took

[26] P. Farmer. Managerial Successes, Clinical Failures. *International Journal of Tuberculosis and Lung Disease* 1999; 3: 365–367.

[27] P. Farmer, J. Bayona, S. Shin, L. Alvarez, M. Becerra, E. Nardell, C. Nuñez, E. Sanchez, R. Timperi & J.Y. Kim. Preliminary Results of Community-Based MDRTB Treatment in Lima, Peru. *International Journal of Tuberculosis and Lung Disease* 1998; 2 (Suppl. 2): S371. C. Mitnick, J. Bayona, E. Palacios, S. Shin, J. Furin, F. Alcantara, E. Sanchez, M. Sarria, M. Becerra, M.C. Fawzi, S. Kapiga, D. Neuberg, J.H. Maguire, J.Y. Kim & P. Farmer. Community-Based Therapy for Multidrug-Resistant Tuberculosis in Lima, Peru. *New England Journal of* Medicine 2003; 348: 119–128.

the organisation well over a year to procure the drugs, but early in 2002 it announced the programme was to commence treatment right away. The need was great: in a single oblast in Western Siberia, an estimated 2000 prisoner-patients were warehoused with active multi-drug-resistant tuberculosis. But although the drugs began to arrive in Siberia, no treatment occurred in the ensuing year. In September 2003, the lead organisation issued a press release: they were pulling out of Siberia. As of today, not a single prisoner has been treated, by non-governmental organisations based in Siberia for a decade, for multi-drug-resistant tuberculosis, although thousands, perhaps more, have died of this disease. The press release blames Russian officials, particularly those in the Ministry of Health, for their intransigence, but it is likely that careful study of what occurred will come to a somewhat different conclusion.[28]

The story is a sad one, but it will become sadder: circulating strains of multi-drug-resistant *M. tuberculosis* will mean that prisoner detainees are exposed to epidemic strains of highly drug-resistant tuberculosis and then do not receive care when they need it. But that will not change the fact that the initial approach of the non-governmental organisations was incorrect: multi-drug-resistant tuberculosis cannot be cured with regimens based on the very drugs to which infecting strains are resistant, but these patients' prognosis can be worsened by such practices, even if proper therapy later becomes available. Since international authorities had endorsed these practices they should have been the first to acknowledge the error and to make pledges to help correct it. But no mea culpa has been issued from any interested party.

All interested parties, including those willing to underline the ethical lapses involved, must be part of a broader movement not merely to point to such lapses, masked or acknowledged, but also to address them. In the case of multi-drug-resistant tuberculosis in Russian prisons, that means staying and seeing these patients through treatment that is effective, not 'cost-effective.' The fact that prisoners with drug-resistant tuberculosis were given drugs that were wholly ineffective is a reminder that concepts such as 'cost-effectiveness' are in fact ideological constructs. The example is one of many and serves, too, as a reminder of the most pressing questions for modern medical ethics.

[28] MSF Ends Tuberculosis Treatment in Kemerovo Region, Russia. 30 September, 2003. Available at: http://www.msf.org/countries/page.cfm?articleid=D657393B-C8E6-4CD7-9835259FD4F8AFEF

IV ALTERNATIVE AND COMPLEMENTARY FRAMEWORKS: PRAXIS MAKES PERFECT?

The examples offered above have received scant attention in the medical ethics literature and much of that attention has been inaccurate. To blame a lack of HIV care on beleaguered and cash-poor African governments is similar to blaming tuberculosis outbreaks in Siberia on prolonged pre-trial detention or the malfeasance of local prison officials. Such observations are superficial and also convenient, since they deflect attention from the truly powerful forces and actors that, respectively, shape epidemics and declare which interventions are cost-effective and which are not. These actors are more likely to be found in New York, Washington, Geneva or London than they are to be found in Siberia, Port-au-Prince, or Pretoria. It is also superficial to spend time underlining the shortcomings of any one particular field, and we add that our goal here is not to denigrate what constitutes a robust enough intellectual enterprise, but rather to point to ways in which the medical and bioethics communities might illuminate complex and transnational ethical problems. Such analysis would prove useful across steep gradients of social inequality, the context and driving force of the world's great epidemics.[29] One cautionary lesson of Tuskegee is that it may take decades for ethics to catch up with observations that come quite naturally to those marginalised by poverty, racism, and other forces that are not often the subject of polite conversation within medical ethics.

One reason for this selective silence is that ethics in general has until recently relied heavily on philosophy, its parent discipline, and very little on the social sciences relevant to medicine. Bioethics is fundamentally socially constructed. To resocialise medical ethics – as part of a broader project, which includes critique of dominant modes of thinking in a broad variety of fields – would mean a turn towards disciplines such as anthropology, history, and political economy. But even within philosophy, John Rawls has laid out a framework that might be applied fruitfully to problems such as those now gathering force within Siberian prisons and African slums. Rawls is, of course, famous for his difference principle, which requires preferential treatment for the most disadvantaged, regardless of the social costs this principle

[29] P. Farmer. 1999. *Infections and Inequalities*. Berkeley. University of California Press.

can entail.[30] Critics have rightly noted the principle's underemphasis on health,[31] but one can read Rawls as making a broader point about how we should view social practices. For if we take Rawls seriously, we have to ask ourselves if we truly care about the most disadvantaged when we give prisoners ineffective therapy that is declared 'cost-effective.'[32]

Sociologists of knowledge will one day point to the competing paradigms that have led important ethical dilemmas to remain invisible or little noted, but in the short term much more could be said simply by restoring to these problems more of the social and historical complexities inherent in each of them. A certain humility is warranted, as philosopher Caputo wryly suggests:

> Far be it from me to make ethics tremble. I tremble even at the prospect that I will be found guilty of spreading the word that the pants of the great man are split. For that I have already prepared a defense aimed at exonerating me of all responsibility . . . The result is that it will be very hard to identify the guilty party, to find anyone who is singularly responsible, if we are all rounded up by the police and charged with inciting a riot against ethics.[33]

[30] J. Rawls. 1999. *A Theory of Justice.* Revised edition. Cambridge, MA. Harvard University Press: § 26, pp. 130–139; § 13, pp. 65–73. Rawls's more precise definition of the difference, or maximin principle, is that society must choose the scheme of institutions that most advantages the least advantaged persons in society. In practice, this emphasis on the absolute position of the most disadvantaged in society may force society to forgo schemes that produce lesser aggregate wealth or utility. Other scholars have cited the tensions between distributive 'injustice' and over-consumption by the wealthy, which may lead to such harms as environmental degradation and exploitation of the poor. See: A. Jameton & J. Pierce. Environment and Health: Sustainable Health Care and Emerging Ethical Responsibilities. *Canadian Medical Association Journal* 2001; 164: 365–369.

[31] D. Brock. Broadening the Bioethics Agenda. *Kennedy Institute of Ethics Journal* 2000; 10: 21–38. Philosopher Norman Daniels has also contributed significantly to bioethical literature by applying Rawlsian principles to justify the right to health (see, for example: N. Daniels. 2002. Justice, Health, and Health Care. In *Medicine and Social Justice.* R. Rhodes, M. Battin & A. Silvers, eds. Oxford. Oxford University Press: 6–23). Both Brock and Daniels discuss resource prioritisation for the worst off.

[32] This attitude toward prisoners is also hard to square with an equally important, though largely forgotten, aspect of Rawls's theory of justice – the inviolability of each person. As Rawls himself elegantly states, '[e]ach person possesses an inviolability founded on justice that even the welfare of society as a whole cannot override.' Rawls, *op. cit.* note 26, § 1, p. 3.

[33] J.D. Caputo. 1993. *Against Ethics: Contributions to a Poetics of Obligation with Constant Reference to Deconstruction.* Bloomington. Indiana University Press.

The sociology of knowledge is another field full of promise in the broader project to resocialise medical ethics.[34] Our understanding of science, for example, is given a significant boost when the non-rational procedures that lead to paradigm shifts come into clear relief. 'Given a paradigm, interpretation of data is central to the enterprise that explores it', writes Thomas Kuhn. 'Paradigms are not corrigible by normal science at all.'[35] Most would argue that medical ethics and philosophy are not the sorts of science that Kuhn had in mind; many practitioners of anthropology and, to a lesser extent, sociology, are willing to admit that the term 'social science' may be a bit grand. And although economists are unwilling, often, to point to the ideological frameworks that undergird their work, they are at least willing to call theirs 'the dismal science.'

In addition to the invaluable insights of sound epidemiology, which suggests the mechanisms by which social inequalities serve as the leading risk for both falling ill with infectious disease and then being denied access to adequate care, there is a special role for ethnography and for detailed case studies. If ethicists were to interview patients and sick *non*-patients – for many of the destitute sick never become patients and are never offered the chance to confront ethical dilemmas – as often as they interrogate philosophical treatises, the resocialisation of medical ethics would be well underway. Here we quote another Haitian woman, whose commentary easily spans the gulf from access to AIDS therapies to the right to employment. She made these comments in 2001 after gaining more than 20 pounds on antiretroviral medications:

> We're always sick here. If we're not dying of AIDS, we're dying of hunger, or both. Now that I am better, it's not as if my problems have disappeared. It's that I can wake up and fight them again. For two years I lay in bed, my children watching me die,

[34] Berger and Luckmann note that 'The sociology of knowledge must concern itself with whatever passes for "knowledge" in a society, regardless of the ultimate validity or invalidity (by whatever criteria) of such "knowledge". And in so far as all human "knowledge" is developed, transmitted and maintained in social situations, the sociology of knowledge must seek to understand the processes by which this is done in such a way that a taken-for-granted "reality" congeals for the man in the street. In other words, we contend that the sociology of knowledge is concerned with the analysis of the social construction of reality.' (P. Berger & T. Luckmann. 1966. *The Social Construction of Reality: A Treatise on the Sociology of Knowledge.* Garden City, NY. Anchor Books.)

[35] T. Kuhn. 1970. *The Structure of Scientific Revolutions.* Second edition. Chicago. University of Chicago Press: 122.

> bringing me sips of water . . . [Their father] is gone – my sister has seven children of her own. All I could think about was what will happen to my children when I die? My sister had already purchased my coffin but then [the clinic] gave me these [antiretroviral] medicines. Someone comes to see me everyday, to make sure I take them. The first thing that hit me was hunger. The medicines started killing the virus and then I became hungry. But we had no food in the house – how would that be possible, if [the father of her children] were gone and I was dying? Charity food does not allow you to regain your strength and to feed your children at the same time. That's why we always reach the same conclusions in our [support-group meetings]. If you want to prevent AIDS among poor women, give them jobs . . . I'm happy I'm better, and I'd rather be alive than dead. But all I do every day, still, is worry about how I'm going to feed my children. I don't want to become a thief.

In our own writing on these topics we have sought to echo and amplify such commentaries, writing about the need to re-mediate inequalities of access to healthcare as a fundamental human right. Are such calls – for the right to healthcare and to jobs – merely grandstanding when echoed by academics, broadsides dressed in scholarly guise? We would answer by insisting that both bioethics and medical ethics have a long way to go on this score before scholars in these fields can object that the views of the destitute sick receive too much emphasis in the literature.

Listening to the afflicted is not merely moral praxis, although it is that. It affords us rich insights into the sorts of problems that we have outlined in this essay. Because the poor quite literally *embody* many of the ethical dilemmas stemming from injustices within medicine and public health, they add insights that cannot be obtained through reference to philosophy. For ethical reflection is part of everyday life, and when the stakes are high – in a squatter settlement in Haiti, say, or a prison in Western Siberia – soliciting these views are central to the quest for understanding. With the exception of sociopaths, as Churchill notes, '[the capacity to think critically about moral values and direct our actions in terms of such values] is common to all of us.'[36] The same is not true of particle physics or evidence-based medicine, which do not figure prominently in everyday discourse and reasoning. But

[36] Churchill, *op. cit.* note 13, p. 259.

herein lies the great promise of a resocialised ethics: seeking the views of the destitute sick will breathe new life into medical ethics.

The call to rely more heavily on the views of the afflicted is not a call to turn our backs on philosophy but rather a call to turn our attention to those who suffer most. It is also a call to turn towards the disciplines that can illuminate the social production, and maintenance, of that suffering. Just as history and political economy can show us how science and medicine have grown but not in tandem with ethical approaches to global health equity, so too can history and political economy in turn illuminate ethnography and other 'experience-near' disciplines.

Each of the problems mentioned above is an obvious example. The distribution of HIV infection is as surely sculpted by social inequalities as is access to both HIV care and to what might be called prevention equity. To engage in ethical debate about vaccine trials or ethically sound clinical research in 'resource-poor settings', as many have done in recent years, it is necessary to understand the social inequalities that sculpt both the AIDS epidemic and social responses to it. Indeed, it is these very inequalities of risk and access that make it attractive to conduct research on diseases endemic among the world's poor. As for organ transplants, there can be no honest understanding of international movement of organs without acknowledging the steep social gradients across which they move. Such observations, even when undergirded by robust research, cause those involved in the enterprise to bristle, but that makes these observations no less true.

There are other paradigms and bodies of knowledge that can help to resocialise bioethics. Within the human rights movement is a small but growing effort to underline the importance of social and economic rights, which are the rights commonly demanded by the poorest populations. These include the right to healthcare, schooling, housing, and clean water. Some have attempted to listen to the poorest and restore these rights to their proper place in the hierarchy of rights, and also to underscore the impossibility of understanding current debates in global medical ethics without understanding the extreme disparities that underpin the 'ethical' dilemmas of the destitute sick.[37]

[37] P. Farmer. Pathologies of Power: Rethinking Health and Human Rights. *American Journal of Public Health* 1999; 89: 1486–1496.

Medical ethics also stands to gain from insights from liberation theology, as noted by Marcos Fabri dos Anjos. Although ethics and philosophy have long been entangled in religious reflection, there is thus far very little synergy between medical ethics and the one branch of theology that concerns itself chiefly with the problem of poverty in the modern world. The conclusions of dos Anjos are worth citing here:

> First, to what level of quality can medical ethics aspire, if it ignores callous discrimination in medical practice against large populations of the innocent poor? Second, how effective can such theories be in addressing the critical issues of medical and clinical ethics if they are unable to contribute to the closing of the gap of socio-medical disparity?[38]

Regardless of which or how many of the socialising disciplines are used, modern medical ethics would stand to benefit from another dramatic change. We argue here that those who study ethical dilemmas will be called increasingly to have a hand in remediating them. These calls will come from 'below', from the afflicted themselves. The concept of 'pragmatic solidarity' is instructive as medicine, science, and public health stumble and fall in the very regions most in need of them. AIDS in Africa and tuberculosis in prisons are cases in point. Pragmatic solidarity is a cumbersome term, perhaps, and one that makes many academics uncomfortable. Anthropologists, for example, have long argued that their task is to observe rather than intervene, but this claim is undermined by the arguments that anthropology's supposed neutrality was in fact perceived by others, including those studied, as a small but at times integral part of the colonial project.[39]

The social sciences, if that is what we are to term them, cannot claim neutrality. There is no social variant of Heisenberg's principle, and it is possible to argue that no field of inquiry can span such dizzying social inequalities and not influence the very topic it proposes to study. Researchers from the modern university are invariably actors in a social field and medical ethicists who work across steep gradients of inequality are, all objections to the contrary notwithstanding, powerful actors when compared to those they study.

[38] M. dos Anjos. Medical Ethics in the Developing World: A Liberation Theology Perspective. *Journal of Medicine and Philosophy* 1996; 21: 629–637.

[39] T. Asad, ed. 1975. *Anthropology and the Colonial Encounter*. London. Ithaca Press & Humanities.

Listening to the poorest will lead us back, inevitably, to the outcome gap. The 'special measures' mentioned above will vary from place to place and from problem to problem, but medical ethicists should expect to become part of teams seeking to lessen the outcome gap by remediating access to effective medical care. And once that step is taken, we will have the option of trying to ignore what we are being told by the afflicted, or to take seriously the challenge of linking the struggle for social and economic rights – the right to food, housing, clean water, education, and jobs – to scholarly inquiry that breaches the frighteningly deep gap between the haves and the have-nots.

V CONCLUSIONS OR NEW DIRECTIONS?

Like any established fields of scholarly inquiry, bioethics and medical ethics are broad and large enough to contain their own internal critics. And like many practitioners of an academic discipline, ethicists are not always eager to embrace critiques from beyond the field. But this essay is meant merely to complement ongoing research and reflection within bioethics and medical ethics.

Writing of AIDS, historian Allan Brandt astutely notes that, 'In the years ahead we will, no doubt, learn a great deal more about AIDS and how to control it. We will also learn a great deal about the nature of our society from the manner in which we address the disease. AIDS will be a standard by which we may measure not only our medical and scientific skill but also our capacity for justice and compassion.'[40] When Brandt writes of 'our society', he refers to the global village through which HIV has raced. Access to AIDS care has yet to follow. Surely this constitutes a daunting ethical problem.

Research in medical ethics has thus far been conducted largely in affluent and industrialised nations. Yet these 'resource-rich' settings are tied, and intimately so, to the poorest parts of the world. Haiti, the Western Hemisphere's most HIV-burdened nation, is the classic case in point: born of late 15th-century European expansion, Haiti was, by the 18th century, the world's most profitable slave colony. It is now commonly termed the poorest country in the Western Hemisphere. But the creation of this

[40] A. Brandt. 1988. AIDS: From Social History to Social Policy. In *AIDS: The Burdens of History*. E. Fee & D.M. Fox, eds. Berkeley. University of California Press: 147–171, at 168.

poverty over time is seen within Haiti as a result of the historical processes that created one of the most brutal slave colonies on record. The key events in Haitian history, from the slave revolt that led to the founding of Latin America's oldest republic to the 20th-century US military occupation of Haiti and subsequent generous support of military dictators, are as familiar to Haitians as they are forgotten by French and US citizens. So too was Tuskegee all but forgotten by modern medicine and yet remembered by African Americans. Indeed, historians and medical ethicists are to be thanked for having kept this issue alive until a formal presidential apology was obtained in 1997, 50 years after penicillin was found to be effective therapy for syphilis, and 25 years after the cessation of the experiment. Research in South Africa, similarly, is necessarily fraught, in part because the scars of apartheid are forgotten by newly arrived AIDS researchers but not by those who endured apartheid and now see their communities attacked by yet another foe. The Haitians have a saying, '*bay kou bilye, pote mak chonje*': he who delivers the blow forgets; he who bears the scar remembers.

Injustices of one sort or another are very often central to the modern ethical problems in medicine, public health, and science. Rawls was correct to underline the centrality of justice in considerations of ethical problems, and the process of resocialising medical ethics and bioethics is in part a process of restoring the historically deep and geographically broad analysis that comes naturally to the world's destitute sick, who bear the scars of history.

Another way of putting this is best saved for the end of this essay: medical ethics must grapple more persistently with the growing problem posed by the yawning gap between rich and poor. The central topics of bioethics and medical ethics need to be linked to questions of social justice and to consideration of how inequalities of all sorts are linked to the inequalities studied by sociologists, anthropologists, and epidemiologists. In almost all countries in which medical ethics and bioethics have taken root – which is to say in most countries, at this writing – access to care, even access to informed participation in clinical trials, is determined as much by social standing as by disease process. This basic epidemiological and social fact emboldens us to close with a warning: if social inequalities persist and grow, we will no longer be welcome to conduct research or even to comment on it. To cite Joia Mukherjee again, 'If the medical community is to use data generated in high-burden and vulnerable populations to develop an HIV-1 vaccine, we must ensure that the global community will help governments fulfill the right to health and share the fruits of research with the world's poorest communities.'[41]

Paul Farmer
Nicole Gastineau Campos
Program in Infectious Disease and Social Change
641 Huntington Avenue
Boston, MA 02115
USA
paul_farmer@hms.harvard.edu
ngastineau@pih.org

[41] Mukherjee, *op. cit.* note 1, p. 995.

[32]

LAW AND BIOETHICS

THE INJUSTICE OF UNSAFE MOTHERHOOD

REBECCA J. COOK, BERNARD M. DICKENS

ABSTRACT

This paper presents an overview of the dimensions of unsafe motherhood, contrasting data from economically developed countries with some from developing countries. It addresses many common factors that shape unsafe motherhood, identifying medical, health system and societal causes, including women's powerlessness over their reproductive lives in particular as a feature of their dependent status in general. Drawing on perceptions of Jonathan Mann, it focuses on public health dimensions of maternity risks, and equates the role of bioethics in conscientious medical care to that of human rights in public health care. The microethics of medical care translate into the macroethics of public health, but the transition compels some compromise of personal autonomy, a key feature of Western bioethics, in favour of societal analysis. Religiously-based morality is seen to have shaped laws that contribute to unsafe motherhood. Now reformed in former colonizing countries of Europe, many such laws remain in effect in countries that emerged from colonial domination. UN conferences have defined the concept of 'reproductive health' as one that supports women's reproductive self-determination, but restrictive abortion laws and practices epitomize the unjust constraints to which many women remain subject, resulting in their unsafe motherhood. Pregnant women can be legally compelled to give the resources of their bodies to the support of others, while fathers are not legally compellable to provide, for instance, bone-marrow or blood donations for their children's survival. Women's unjust legal, political, economic and social powerlessness explains much unsafe motherhood and maternal mortality and morbidity.

DIMENSIONS AND CAUSES OF UNSAFE MOTHERHOOD

The differential incidence of unsafe motherhood has been described as marking the greatest discrepancy in any health statistic between developed and developing countries of the world.[1] The most recent World Health Organization and associated agencies' estimate is that every year worldwide, about 515,000 women die of complications of pregnancy and childbirth,[2] a rate of over 1,400 maternal deaths each day. Further, at least 7 million women suffer serious health problems when they survive childbirth, and an additional estimated 50 million women suffer adverse health effects after childbirth.[3] Statistics are incomplete because many countries lack vital statistics registries and systematic examinations of causes of maternal deaths, and many women are unattended by healthcare professionals or other adequately skilled personnel during pregnancy, labour, childbirth and their resulting death or morbidity. Nevertheless, it is estimated that almost 99% of these tragic and often preventable consequences of unsafe motherhood occur in developing countries. It has been observed that 'Almost 90% of these deaths occur in sub-Saharan Africa and Asia' alone.[4]

The ends of the spectrum of maternal mortality and morbidity are not easily determined, but representative figures are that the estimated probability of pregnancy-related death faced by an average woman over her reproductive life-span is 1 in 8,700 in Canada, and 1 in 7 in Ethiopia, 1 in 6 in Rwanda and Sierra Leone.[5] Canadian statistics may conceal different rates between aboriginal and non-aboriginal women, in the same way that the United States of America's rate of 1 in 3,500 conceals differences between black, white and hispanic women and members of rural and urban populations.[6] By way of general contrast and

[1] A. Starrs. 1998. *The Safe Motherhood Action Agenda: Priorities for the Next Decade*. New York. Family Care International: 1.

[2] World Health Organization, United Nations Children's Fund and United Nations Population Fund. 2001. *Maternal Mortality in 1995. Estimates Developed by WHO, UNICEF, and UNFPA*. Geneva. World Health Organization (WHO/RHR/01.9).

[3] United Nations Population Fund. 1999. *The State of the World Population 1999, 6 Billion: A Time for Choices*. New York. UNFPA: 30.

[4] A. Starrs, *op. cit.* note 1, p. 1.

[5] See World Health Organization *op. cit.* note 2, and R.J. Cook et al. 2001. *Advancing Safe Motherhood Through Human Rights*. Geneva. World Health Organization: Appendix I, pp. 93–95.

[6] In the US the black population has a relative risk of maternal death 4.3 times higher than the nonblack population: H.K. Atrash et al. Maternal Mortality in Developed Countries: Not Just a Concern of the Past. *Obstetrics and Gynecology* 1995; 86: 700–705.

comparison, however, the average rate in sub-Saharan Africa is 1 in 14 but 1 in 70 in South Africa, the average rate in South-East Asia is 1 in 47 but 1 in 1,100 in Thailand, 1 in 60 in the Eastern Mediterranean but 1 in 430 in Tunisia and 1 in 1,300 in Europe, ranging from 1 in 4,600 in the United Kingdom to 1 in 1,000 in Romania and 1 in 450 in Kazakhstan.[7]

Causes of unsafe motherhood may in theory be separated into medical, health system, social and other causes, but in practice they often overlap. For instance, many pregnant women in developing countries suffer from anemia, which compromises their survival and health status associated with pregnancy and childbearing in general, and particularly when heavy blood loss occurs. Where food resources are inadequate due, for instance, to regional drought and famine or family poverty, the nutritional disadvantages of girl children may be aggravated by their devaluation in their homes and cultures. Food allocation practices within families that give priority to feeding husbands and sons before wives, then other family dependents such as elderly parents and lastly daughters,[8] may condemn girl children to malnutrition in the form of undernourishment, with associated anemia.

Similarly, early marriage, perhaps when adolescents are below the minimum age for marriage prescribed by law,[9] followed by premature and repeated pregnancy, create medical circumstances inimical to survival and health. These are conditioned, however, by social forces that favour or even require girls' early marriage, and fecundity. Conditioning factors include families' concerns regarding dowry payments, fears of family dishonour due to daughters' premarital loss of virginity, whether by their sexual adventure or victimization by rape, and husbands' requirement of births of sons and of evidence of their virility.

Infections such as malaria, that may be more associated with geographical rather than social considerations, pose a medical risk in pregnancy, endangering health and life itself. Equally, women with the genetic sickle-cell trait may face health hazards

[7] See World Health Organization and RJ Cook et al., *op. cit.* note 5.

[8] See e.g. J. Kabeberi-Macharia. 1998. Reconstructing the Image of the Girl-Child. In *Law, Culture, Tradition and Children's Rights in Eastern and Southern Africa*. W. Ncube, ed. Aldershot. Ashgate/Dartmouth: 47–56 at 47.

[9] For instance the Child Marriage Restraint Act in India sets the minimum age of marriage for girls at 18, but it has been recorded that about 50% of women enter their first union before their eighteenth birthday and almost 30% have their first child by age 18. See Alan Guttmacher Institute. 1998. *Into a New World: Young Women's Sexual and Reproductive Lives*. New York. AGI: 18.

due to pregnancy. However, some other medical risks aggravated by pregnancy are socially conditioned. Prominent among these is HIV/AIDS, to which women are often exposed because of their powerlessness to resist sexual intercourse with infected men or to require men to wear condoms, or their lack of access to such protection because of financial, legal, health system or other barriers. Pregnancy naturally reduces women's immunity to infection, and their vulnerability is considerably increased when HIV/AIDS has already compromised their immune systems. In some religions and cultures, female genital cutting, often described judgmentally as mutilation, also contributes to unsafe motherhood in causing medical complications antenatally, and in early labour and childbirth, including prolonged labour and, for instance, post partum hemorrhage, and death.[10]

Health system failures often add significantly to the burden of unsafe motherhood. It has been explained that in the course of pregnancy, labour and delivery, women '... in every country and every population develop complications, but women in developing countries are much less likely to get prompt adequate treatment, and are therefore more likely to die.'[11]

The scarcity of physicians, trained nurses or midwives and often of skilled birth attendants, in urban as well as rural settings, accounts for much of the incidence of maternal mortality and morbidity.[12] Social factors and customs may also be involved, however. Where prenatal and maternity care are available, for instance, women may not be allowed to travel to them alone. Further, husbands' consent or consent of unmarried adolescents' parents may be required before women can receive care, for instance because male healthcare providers are present, or pregnant women lack independent means to ensure that service fees will be paid. Cost itself is often a barrier to access to available care among impoverished families that seek it.

[10] Department of Women's Health, Family and Community Health, World Health Organization. 2000. *A Systematic Review of the Health Complications of Female Genital Mutilation, including Sequelae in Childbirth*. Geneva. World Health Organization (WHO/FCH/WMH/00.2): 48.

[11] D. Maine et al. 1997. *The Design and Evaluation of Maternal Mortality Programs*. New York. Center for Population and Family Health, School of Public Health, Columbia University: 4.

[12] W.J. Graham, J.S. Bell and C.H.W. Bullogh. 2001. Can Skilled Attendance at Delivery Reduce Maternal Mortality in Developing Countries? In *Safe Motherhood Strategies: A Review of the Evidence*. V. DeBrouwere and W. VanLerberghe, eds. Antwerp. ITG Press: 97–130.

PUBLIC HEALTH BIOETHICS AND UNSAFE MOTHERHOOD

The United Nations' International Conference on Population and Development, held in Cairo in 1994, and World Conference on Women, held in Beijing in 1995, both recognized that reproductive health failures embodied in unsafe motherhood raise concerns that transcend clinical medicine, and must be addressed in addition as public health concerns. The public health implications of developing country urbanization have come to be recognized in recent years,[13] but the public health dimensions of unsafe motherhood, and public health potential for its reduction, have escaped general attention, except for recognition that the consequences of unskilled abortion, both where abortion is legally permissible and where it is not, should be addressed less as a moral than as a public health concern.[14]

It has been conventional to observe that unsafe motherhood is strongly associated with pregnancies that come too early, too late, too often and too closely spaced in women's reproductive lives. This observation has no prognostic value in the clinical care of any individual adolescent or woman, but remains an epidemiological or public health truism. Safe motherhood depends on women's avoidance of untimely and otherwise inappropriate pregnancy, for instance by means of women's education and power to decide whether, when, with whom and in what ways to be sexually active. It also requires access to natural and assisted means of fertility control, and, for example, women's unimpaired access to medical and related care during pregnancy, labour and childbirth and the immediate and longer post-partum period. These goals are most effectively advanced through public health strategies, which may be implemented through public health law. Public health law has recently been defined as:

> [T]he study of the legal powers and duties of the state to assure the conditions for people to be healthy (e.g. to identify, prevent, and ameliorate risks to health in the population) and the limitations on the power of the state to constrain the autonomy, privacy, liberty, proprietary, or other legally

[13] See World Health Organization, Centre for Health Development, Kobe, Japan. 1996. *Urbanization: A Global Health Challenge*. Geneva. WHO (WHO/WCK/SYM/96.1).

[14] See the Programme of Action of the International Conference on Population and Development, Cairo, Egypt 5-13 September 1994, para 8.25, in Report of the International Conference on Population and Development, U.N. Doc. A/CONF.171/13/Rev.1, U.N. Sales No. 95. XIII. 18 (1995).

> protected interests of individuals for the protection or promotion of community health.[15]

In formulating this definition, Gostin, justly celebrated for his pioneering work to advance civil liberties in the UK, Europe and the US, is conscious that his acknowledgment of 'the power of the state to constrain the autonomy ... of individuals,' though limited, itself runs counter to a key ethical value in the US and beyond.[16] A prominent bioethicist, however, noting that '[a]utonomy has become a dominant bioethical value in the Western world,'[17] has pointed to instances in which individual autonomy has traditionally been subordinated to community values. An instance is social action to prevent a competent person's suicide, on the justifications that 'a person's death diminishes others as well and that therefore society is permitted to intervene.'[18] This reflects the historical observation of the English poet and cleric John Donne (1572–1631) that '[a]ny man's death diminishes me, because I am involved in mankind; and therefore never send to know for whom the [graveyard] bell tolls; it tolls for thee.'[19]

The social sense of diminution has not been raised in many countries, however, by the incidence of maternal mortality. It is observable that:

> [T]hese hundreds of thousands of avoidable deaths each year are continuing evidence and condemnation of the unstated presumption on which many societies are organized, namely that lives of mothers are expendable and that women do not matter.[20]

Making mothers and all women's lives, and health, matter, goes beyond individualistic ethics and bioethics of autonomy, to implicate macroethical and community values. These are expressed in some bioethical literature, especially by feminist writers,[21] but

[15] L.O. Gostin. 2000. *Public Health Law: Power, Duty, Restraint*. Berkeley, CA. University of California Press; New York. The Milbank Memorial Fund: 4.

[16] Ibid. Preface: xxi.

[17] S.M. Glick. Unlimited Human Autonomy A Cultural Bias? *NEJM* 1997; 336: 954–956 at 954.

[18] Ibid. at 955.

[19] J. Donne. 1624. Devotions upon Emergent Occasions-Meditation no. 17.

[20] R.J. Cook. 2001. Advancing Safe Motherhood Through Human Rights. In *Giving Meaning to Economic, Social and Cultural Rights*. I. Merali and V. Oosterveld, eds. Philadelphia. University of Pennsylvania Press: 109–123 at 109.

[21] R. Tong. 1996. Feminist Approaches to Bioethics. In *Feminism and Bioethics: Beyond Reproduction*. S.M. Wolf, ed. New York. Oxford University Press: 67–94.

particularly in human rights principles, many of which are embodied in national and international laws.

The late Jonathan Mann identified contrasts and synergies, or complementarities, between medicine and public health,[22] the former focussing on individual, clinical care and cure, the latter on population health and prevention of health hazards, but both pursuing health as defined by the World Health Organization, namely as a state of physical, mental and social well-being.[23] Similarly he proposed, in a memorable keynote address opening the International Association of Bioethics' Third World Congress of Bioethics in San Francisco in 1996, that the equivalent of the role of bioethics in medicine is the role of human rights in public health. The Summer 2001 edition of the *Cambridge Quarterly of Healthcare Ethics,* dedicated to his memory, is appropriately entitled *Keeping Human Rights on the Bioethics Agenda.*

The initial paper of this edition, an appreciation of Jonathan Mann,[24] addresses the significance of human rights in opening the public health agenda to ethical perceptions, observing that '[t]he conceptualization of the health and human rights movement resonates with ideas that the bioethics movement b[r]ought to medicine. Indeed, a conceptual parallel between this movement and bioethics is to be found in how each views the field and goals of medicine.'[25] This insight shows links between human rights and bioethics, particularly as bioethics progress beyond their contemporary US and more general Western preoccupation with individual autonomy. It constitutes a creative response to Mann's critique of the narrowness of bioethics emerging from medical or clinical experience. Writing in the US in 1997, Mann noted that:

> [T]he contribution of medicine to health, while undeniably important (and vital in certain situations) is actually quite limited. For example, it is estimated that only about one-sixth of the years of life expectancy gained in this country during this century can be attributed to the beneficial impact of medicine, medical care, and medical research. And it has been

[22] J.M. Mann. Medicine and Public Health, Ethics and Human Rights. *Hastings Center Report* 1997; 27(3): 6–13.

[23] Constitution of the World Health Organization, Preamble, para. 2.

[24] J.C. d'Oronzio. The Integration of Health and Human Rights: An Appreciation of Jonathan M. Mann. *Cambridge Q. Health Care Ethics* 2001; 10: 231–240.

[25] Ibid. at 231.

> estimated that only about 10 % of preventable premature deaths are associated with a lack of medical care.[26]

Accepting that 'none of these data . . . suggest that medical care is irrelevant; rather they suggest its limits,'[27] Mann looked beyond those limits for explanations of health differences among populations, and found explanatory materials at the public and community health levels. He concluded that the conventional understanding linking socioeconomic status to health status is inadequate, and noted that:

> Other measures, such as the extent of socioeconomic inequality within a community, the nature, level and temporal pattern of unemployment, societal connectedness and the extent of involvement in social networks, marital status, early childhood experiences, and exposure to dignity-denying situations have all been suggested as powerful potential components of a 'black box' of societal factors whose dominant role in determining levels of preventable disease, disability, and premature death is beyond dispute.[28]

It is a tragic irony that Jonathan Mann's own premature death in September 1998, while flying from New York to Geneva to attend a meeting at the World Health Organization, robbed him and us of his further exploration of how public health strategies inspired by human rights values can promote population health. A legacy, however, is his focus on how social inequality, economic powerlessness, societal exclusion and denials of human dignity condition preventable disease, disability and premature death. These factors relate directly and indirectly to women's high rates of maternal mortality and morbidity.

RELIGIOUS MORALITY AND UNSAFE MOTHERHOOD

The laws and social customs that have often conditioned unsafe motherhood and condemned generations of women to suffer pregnancy-related death and disability may have their roots in religiously-guided perceptions of morality. The demographically-driven Biblical imperative to the people of the Bible to 'be fruitful and multiply,' for instance, has cast a long moral shadow over artificial contraception. Contraceptive means frequently remain critical to women's self-defence against life- and health-

[26] J.M. Mann, *op. cit.* note 22, at p. 7.
[27] Ibid.
[28] Ibid. at p. 8.

endangering pregnancies, but until 1969, for example, the Canadian Criminal Code punished distribution of means and knowledge of contraception as a 'crime against morality.' The Roman Catholic Church maintains its prohibition of contraceptive means such as condoms, opposing distribution even in the face of the international HIV/AIDS pandemic.

This inflexible historical prohibition in fact was transformitive three decades ago in the emergence of modern, secular bioethics from traditional ethics rooted in often intransigent moral philosophy. Catholic theologians and ethicists, whose advice on contraception the Catholic Church requested in the 1960s and then discarded, became the pioneers, when their hopes and expectations to modernize religious doctrine were frustrated. An historian of that time has recorded that:

> Fertility control was the major issue that spawned bioethics, more than any other single issue – certainly more than any high-technology-related issue in medicine. It was an issue that directly affected hundreds of millions of people; it dealt with quintessentially human suffering and fulfillment ... The theologians, who were the first ethicists working in bioethics, cut their teeth on contraception/sterilization and abortion debates; and in a very real sense, much of the great energy that was turned toward bioethics around 1970/71 was energy that was diverted from the then-increasingly futile church debates on fertility control.[29]

The futility of proposing change in the moral doctrine of the Catholic Church remains, particularly since, in 1870, the Church adopted the concept of papal infallibility in pronouncements made *ex cathedra*, so that no new revelation can be accepted unless shown consistent with earlier teaching. There can be no reversal on the basis that earlier policies were erroneous.

Proponents of religiously-based morality are unpersuaded by evidence of the harmful consequences of their policies. The spread of HIV/AIDS attributable to the prohibition of condom distribution, and for instance of maternal mortality and morbidity due to Church pressure to maintain prohibitions against contraceptive methods, sterilization and abortion, are of no account to them. The deontological orientation of much religiously-based thinking rejects utilitarianism and consequen-

[29] W.T. Reich. The 'Wider View': André Helleger's Passionate, Integrating Intellect and the Creation of Bioethics. *Kennedy Institute of Ethics J* 1999; 9: 25–51 at 37.

tialism. Adherents to Church teaching feel no institutional or personal responsibility for preventable disease, disability or death that is a consequence of application of the doctrines of their faith, since such doctrines are considered to be founded on truths revealed to their divinely-appointed, infallible leader within schemes of supernatural mystery and mercy.

Many European powers of the colonial period based their laws on restrictive, ecclesiastically-derived religious morality, after as well as before the Protestant Reformation of the 16th century. It has been observed that:

> The canon law of the later Middle Ages was the first modern legal system of the West, and it prevailed in every country of Europe. The canon law governed ... a great many aspects of the lives of the laity. The new hierarchy of church courts had exclusive jurisdiction over laymen in matters of family law, inheritance, and various types of spiritual crimes.[30]

In part protective and paternalistic, but also moralistic and punitive, these laws in time became predominant in certain affairs as 'the church ... took legal jurisdiction over sins, and it influenced the secular law to conform to [its] moral principles.'[31] They applied to exclude women not only from religious ordination and authority in church life but also from political, professional, economic and scholarly life and, *inter alia*, from access to voluntary sterilization and abortion procedures.

In recent years, such European countries have largely liberalized their sterilization and abortion laws[32] in favour of accommodation of reproductive self-determination. However, the laws that they historically applied in the overseas territories they settled or conquered, by power of imperial legislative domination, have proven curiously tenacious in the post-colonial, independent countries that have re-emerged or arisen in these territories, including by successful rebellion against European

[30] H.J. Berman. 1974. *The Interaction of Law and Religion*. New York. Abingdon Press: 58.

[31] Ibid. at p. 61.

[32] See for instance the UK Abortion Act 1967, in France the 1975 Law 75–17 and 1979 Law 79–1204, in Portugal the 1984 Law 6 of 11 May, and in Spain the 1985 Organic Law 9 of 5 July; see generally R.J. Cook and B.M. Dickens. A Decade of International Change in Abortion Law: 1967–77. *Amer. J. Public Health* 1978; 68: 637–644; R.J. Cook and B.M. Dickens. International Developments in Abortion Laws: 1977–88. *Amer. J. Public Health* 1988; 78: 1305–1311; R.J. Cook, B.M. Dickens and L.E. Bliss. International Developments in Abortion Law from 1988 to 1998. *Amer. J. Public Health* 1999; 89: 579–586.

rule. Retention of these laws restrictive of women's rights in general and of their reproductive choice in particular is due in part to the remaining colonial legacy of influential European-derived religious institutions that support them. This is reflected to some extent in sometimes grossly differential rates of maternal mortality and morbidity that are not due to economic differences alone between the post-imperial European countries and those in the territories they once dominated. A recent global comparison between countries in regions with restrictive and accommodating abortion legislation has noted that 'The risk of death from unsafe abortion is about 1 in 150 procedures in Africa, and 1 in 150,000 in the USA and Europe.'[33]

A recent echo of religiously moralistic hostility to women's reproductive self-determination was heard at the two UN Conferences on Population and Development, and on Women, held respectively in Cairo in 1994 and Beijing in 1995. The Vatican employed the specious and increasingly contested statehood of the Holy See,[34] which privileges the Roman Catholic Church over other Christian denominations and different religions, to maximize its representatives' attendance, and to limit the development of legal recognition of women's human rights to fertility control. At the latter conference, the Church adopted the view that its enemies' enemies could be its friends, and sought to achieve solidarity with its historical religious adversaries, particularly the more reactionary Islamic countries, to resist 'feminist' initiatives in support of what both conferences defined as reproductive health.

REPRODUCTIVE HEALTH, ABORTION AND SAFE MOTHERHOOD

Building on the World Health Organization definition that 'health' is a state of physical, mental and social well-being, the Programme of Action developed at the Cairo conference proposed a definition of reproductive health that was endorsed at the International Conference on Women held the following year in Beijing. The definition reads:

[33] P.F. Thonneau. 2001. Maternal Mortality and Unsafe Abortion: A Heavy Burden for Developing Countries. In *Safe Motherhood Strategies: A Review of the Evidence*. V. DeBrouwere, W. VanLerberghe, eds. Antwerp. ITG Press: 151–173, at 151.

[34] See internet http://www.seechange.org.

> Reproductive health is a state of complete physical, mental and social well-being and not merely the absence of disease or infirmity, in all matters relating to the reproductive system and to its functions and processes. Reproductive health therefore implies that people are able to have a satisfying and safe sex life and that they have the capability to reproduce and the freedom to decide if, when and how often to do so. Implicit in this last condition are the right of men and women to be informed and to have access to safe, effective, affordable and acceptable methods of family planning of their choice, as well as other methods of their choice for regulation of fertility which are not against the law, and the right of access to appropriate health-care services that will enable women to go safely through pregnancy and childbirth and provide couples with the best chance of having a healthy infant.[35]

The establishment of a claim of access to methods for regulation of fertility had to be limited to methods 'which are not against the law,' since conferences that are UN initiatives cannot usually recommend illegal conduct. However, many countries maintain laws and practices that obstruct achievement of reproductive health as described in the earlier part of the definition, and the ethical status of such laws and practices is open to question on grounds of justice. Many women lack access to 'a satisfying and safe sex life,' reproductive freedom and methods of family planning, because of oppressive laws that make them dependent on the economic support of men, expose them to sexual and other violence, in their homes and outside and, for instance, leave them at risk of life- and health-endangering pregnancies.

Implicit in the above definition, because, for political reasons, it could not be stated explicitly, is the right to lawful abortion which, when available under skilled and timely medical management, is likely to be safely conducted. Religious authorities that oppose abortion in principle, such as in the Roman Catholic, Islamic and Hindu faiths, tend to allow termination of pregnancy in a clinical case when continuation of pregnancy poses an immediate threat to the survival of a particular woman. In the Catholic tradition, for instance, the doctrine of 'double effect'[36] allows the ending of an ectopic and other life-endangering pregnancy not to be characterized as abortion, in the same way that removing a man's cancerous testicles is not characterized as

[35] *Op. cit.* note 14, para 7.2.

[36] D.P. Sulmasy, E.D. Pellegrino. The Rule of Double Effect: Clearing-up the Double Talk. *Annals of Internal Medicine* 1999; 159: 545.

sterilization, notwithstanding that sterility is a secondary effect of the life-saving surgery. Laws often remain, however, that prohibit abortion where pregnancy poses an epidemiological, statistical or population-based risk to women in general but not to any one in particular. That is, even where women face a 1 in 7 or a 1 in 6 risk of maternal death in their reproductive life-span,[37] they have at least a 6 in 7 or a 5 in 6 likelihood to survive a particular pregnancy.

Unsafe or otherwise unwanted pregnancy that results in unsafe abortion, because abortion is not legally and therefore safely available, or is legally available but qualified practitioners decline to provide it,[38] raises macroethical, community-wide concerns. Governments endorsing the 1994 Cairo Programme of Action resolved: 'to strengthen their commitment to women's health to deal with the health impact of unsafe abortion as a major public health concern and to reduce the recourse to abortion through expanded and improved family planning services.'[39]

Similarly, the 1995 Beijing Conference developed a Platform for Action which recognized that: 'Unsafe abortions threaten the lives of a large number of women, representing a grave public health problem as it is primarily the poorest and the youngest who take the highest risk.'[40]

This is the case not only within countries but also among countries. That is, the highest rates of maternal mortality and morbidity due to unsafe abortion tend to be experienced in the world's poorest and younger independent countries,[41] many of which retain oppressive abortion laws inherited from colonization.

The injustice of these restrictive laws is not simply that they disrespect women as decision-makers in their own lives, but that their aim is to compel women to continue pregnancies, perhaps initiated by rape, incest or otherwise coerced sexual intercourse, to serve fetal interests or state interests in fetal life, while no other

[37] *Op. cit.* note 5.

[38] In India, abortion has been legally available through medical practitioners on liberal grounds since 1972, but subject to cumbersome conditions; of the estimated 6.7 million abortions in India each year, about 4 million are performed by non-physicians, primarily using drugs, indigenous methods and insertion of objects into the uterus. An estimated 15–20,000 abortion-related deaths occur each year. See A. Starrs, *op. cit.* note 1, p. 57.

[39] *Op. cit.* note 14, para 8.25.

[40] United Nations. 1995. Report of the Fourth World Conference on Women. New York. UN: para 97.

[41] *Op. cit.* notes 2 and 5.

persons are required to give the resources and services of their bodies to preserve the lives of others, including their own voluntarily conceived children. When children's lives are at risk due, for instance, to liver disease, leukemia or anemia, their parents and others are not compelled by law to provide liver segments for transplantation or even far less invasive bone-marrow or blood donations. The common legal requirement that parents provide their dependent children with the 'necessaries of life' is limited to financially affordable food, shelter, clothing and medical care, and has never been considered to cover even blood transfusion, which is usually a paradigm minimum-risk procedure considerably less risk-laden than continuation of routine pregnancy.

It has long been recognized that restrictive abortion laws are frequently legally avoided by women of means or influence, who receive safe, legal procedures by travelling abroad or obtaining medical explanations for local care that ends inconvenient or otherwise unwanted pregnancies,[42] but that such laws deny safe services to poor and powerless women, of all ages. Beyond resourceful avoidance, women of means may also simply evade restrictive laws. It has been observed that 'for example in Latin America, private physicians often perform safe abortions for relatively high medical fees, and the law is rarely enforced.'[43] The main effect of restrictive laws is not to reduce the numbers of abortions, but primarily to channel them into the least skilled, least safe hands, including those of desperate women who self-induce their abortion by primitive means. A leading obstetrician/gynecologist with wide-ranging international experience has observed that:

> Analysis of available data reveals that there is no direct correlation between the prevalence of induced abortion and how restrictive or liberal a country's abortion law may be ... Abortion rates seem to be more directly related to the number of unwanted pregnancies. The number of unwanted pregnancies will be greater where the desired fertility is low, and where effective methods of contraception (including emergency contraception)[44] and family-planning information

[42] A. Jenkins. 1961. *Law for the Rich: A Plea for the Reform of the Abortion Law.* London. Victor Gollancz.

[43] M.F. Fathalla. 1997. *From Obstetrics and Gynecology to Women's Health: The Road Ahead.* New York. Parthenon: 238.

[44] Post-coital contraception, within 72 hours of unprotected intercourse or of malfunction of pre-coital means.

> and education services are not available or easily accessible. In this situation, restricting access to abortion will only increase the number of illegal and unsafe abortions. The choice will not be between allowing or preventing abortion. The choice will be between decriminalizing abortion, or allowing it only to be performed as an illegal procedure.[45]

The burden of restrictive laws, which falls primarily on the poor and the powerless, can also have racial dimensions. The introductory language of South Africa's 1996 Choice on Termination of Pregnancy Act acknowledges that the country's former, restrictive law applied inequitably between women of European and African races, in stating that the new law is enacted: 'Recognizing the values of human dignity, the achievement of equality, security of the person, non-racialism and non-sexism and the advancement of human rights and freedoms which underlie a democratic South Africa.'

The denial of human dignity implicit in legally compelled involuntary continuation of pregnancy, particularly but not only when it is life- and health-endangering, was recognized in 1995, when the Beijing Platform for Action analogized it to rape in its comprehensive condemnation of 'forced pregnancy.'[46] Indeed, the International Criminal Court at The Hague, considering the denial of abortion for pregnancy following rape as included within 'forced maternity,'[47] approaches it as a war crime committed not only by rapists but also by governments and states themselves.[48] The Rome Treaty of 1998, constituting the Court and its jurisdiction, defines rape, sexual slavery, enforced prostitution, forced pregnancy and other forms of sexual violence as both war crimes and crimes against humanity,[49] equal, for instance, to torture and the most egregious international crimes against humanitarian law.

[45] M.F. Fathalla, *op. cit.* note 43, p. 239.

[46] United Nations, *op. cit.* note 40, at paras 114, 132 and 135.

[47] See Finalized Draft Text of the Elements of Crimes, Preparatory Commission for the International Criminal Court, UN Doc. PCNICC/2000/INF/3/Add.2(2000).

[48] K.D. Askin. 1997. *War Crimes Against Women: Prosecution in International War Crimes Tribunals*. The Hague, Netherlands. Kluwer Law International.

[49] Rome Statute of the International Criminal Court. 1998. U.N. Doc. A/CONF. 183/9, Articles 7 and 8.

THE MULTIPLE INJUSTICES OF UNSAFE MOTHERHOOD

Restrictive abortion laws are perhaps the most obvious, but only one of many instances of how women, particularly in developing countries, are denied safe options in their reproductive lives. They are often compelled by such abortion laws to choose between continuing a life- or health-endangering pregnancy or resorting to illegal termination, conducted by an unskilled person, frequently in unsanitary conditions. Risks to life and health are not only medical. In several countries and regions of the world, women caught in adultery[50] or found pregnant before or outside marriage face injury or death at the hands of their family members.[51] Laws against so-called 'honour killings' are not uncommonly unenforced, or applied with sentences of such leniency as to constitute them of no deterrent effect.

Injustices are aggravated when women have little or no control over their sexual availability to men. Beyond instances of pregnancy following rape, for instance in military conflicts and civil turmoil, or when women are in police or comparable custody,[52] women denied education and economic opportunities, including rights of legal inheritance, may lack any feasible options in life to early marriage and repeated childbearing. When women cannot resist their husbands' demands and have no access to contraception, for instance because it is too costly, or because their husbands refuse them access to available means or refuse themselves to use condoms, their risks of unsafe motherhood mount. Availability of contraceptive drugs in their communities is often of little avail to young girls of whose vulnerability and perhaps dependency older men take sexual advantage, even while the men are affected by sexually transmitted diseases such as HIV/AIDS. In developed as well as developing countries, high percentages of adolescent girls have been shown to become

[50] The 1960 Penal Code of Jordan, article 340, No. 16 has been translated to provide 'He who discovers his wife or one of his female unlawfuls committing adultery with another, and he kills, wounds or injures one or both of them is exempt from any penalty'; see The Center for Reproductive Law and Policy. 2000. *Reproductive Rights 2000: Moving Forward*. New York. CRLP: 47.

[51] The Penal Code of Syria, article 548, has been translated to provide 'He who catches his wife or one of his ascendants, descendants or sister committing adultery or illegitimate sexual acts with another and he killed or injured one or both of them benefits from an exemption of penalty'; ibid.

[52] See e.g. Asia Watch, Women's Rights Project. 1992. *Double Jeopardy: Police Abuse of Women in Pakistan*. New York. Human Rights Watch.

pregnant due to intercourse imposed by older men they have no social or other practical means to resist.[53]

More contentious than contraception has been sterilization. Restrictive laws and religions have generally come to allow this to women on strictly established medical grounds, but it often remains denied as a reproductive choice. Husbands and family members may also deny women that choice, even when medically indicated, particularly when the son(s) required in their culture have not yet been born. Young women's health and survival can be compromised when, instantly on marriage, they are pressured to have successive pregnancies until sons are born. The attitude of husbands and of the families into which women marry, that women's primary role is as bearers of children, especially sons, presents one of the 'dignity-denying situations' that Jonathan Mann identified as a societal factor that conditions women's 'preventable disease, disability and death.'[54] His vision of finding solutions through human rights is enlightened, but some human rights initiatives illustrate the problem as much as they may offer a solution. For instance, the International Covenant on Economic, Social and Cultural Rights provides in Article 10(2) that: 'Special protection should be accorded to mothers during a reasonable period before and after childbirth.'[55]

This provides for legal effect to be given to Article 25(2) of the 1948 Universal Declaration of Human Rights, which states that 'Motherhood and childhood are entitled to special care and assistance.'[56]

Necessary though these provisions are, they link protection of women to their pregnant status and childbearing role. This reinforces the perception that protection of women's health is an instrumental means of serving children, rather than an inherent right for women to enjoy for themselves. Valuing women as

[53] It has been estimated for instance from Peru that only 72 cases of sexual abuse are reported of the 360 that occur each day and that 60% of pregnancies among 12 to 14 year old girls result from rape by family members or persons close to the victims; S. Tuesta. 2000. *The Search for Justice*. Lima. Movimiento Manuela Ramos: 5. The US Department of Justice reported that there were 330,088 rapes and sexual assaults in 1998 on victims aged 12 and above, the 12–19 age group suffering twice as many as victims aged over 25; F. McLellan. US Paediatricians Advised to Ask About Sexual Assault. *The Lancet* 2001; 357: 1951.

[54] *Op. cit.* note 22, p. 8.

[55] See I. Brownlie, ed. 1992. *Basic Documents on Human Rights* (3rd edition). Oxford. Clarendon Press: 117. See also J. Stanchieri, I. Merali and R.J. Cook. 2000. *The Application of Human Rights to Reproductive and Sexual Health*, http://www.acpd.ca/compilation.

[56] I. Brownlie, ibid., p. 26.

mothers risks their devaluation or invisibility in other aspects of their lives as girl children, adolescents, unmarried and non-pregnant women and widows. Unsafe motherhood is gaining attention, for instance in the Safe Motherhood initiative pioneered by the World Health Organization,[57] but it remains only an epitome of the socially-constructed multiple injustices that many women suffer throughout their lives.

CONCLUSION

The over half a million maternal deaths that occur each year, in all but about five thousand cases in developing countries,[58] are more a consequence than an isolated cause or expression of gender inequity and injustice to women. These deaths have become rare in countries and communities in which women's power of self-determination approaches equality with that of men, but remain pandemic where women's equal rights are not respected in their societies. Vulnerability to social, economic, religious and related repression denies women an effective voice in the decisions that affect their initiation and continuation of pregnancy, and their access to medical and other appropriate services before and during pregnancy, and at and following childbirth. An approach to relief through improved prenatal care, birth assistance and post-partum care is necessary but not sufficient to resolve the injustice of unsafe motherhood. Attention should be directed to such conditioning factors as women's inability to regulate their conception in particular and their reproductive and sexual lives in general. Unsafe motherhood condemns political, economic, religious, judicial and comparably influential social institutions not just for their disregard for motherhood, but for their disregard for and systemic discrimination against women.

Rebecca J. Cook
Bernard M. Dickens
Faculty of Law
University of Toronto
84 Queen's Park Crescent
Toronto, Ontario
Canada M5S 2C5
bernard.dickens@utoronto.ca

[57] See World Health Organization. 1995. *Mother-Baby Package: Implementing Safe Motherhood in Countries.* Geneva. WHO (WHO/FHE/MSM/94.11).
[58] *Op. cit.* note 1.

[33]

Public health in developing countries

Sarah Macfarlane, Mary Racelis, Florence Muli-Musiime

Poverty not only excludes people from the benefits of health-care systems but also restricts them from participating in decisions that affect their health. The resulting health inequalities are well documented, and the search for greater equity attracts many concerned players and initiatives. Fundamental to the success of these efforts, however, is the need for people to be able to negotiate their own inclusion into health systems and demand adequate health care. This calls for a restatement of the centrality of people in public health and its practice. New forms of communication and cooperation are required at all levels of society, nationally, and internationally, to ensure equitable exchange of views and knowledge to formulate appropriate action to redress inequalities and improve people's health and wellbeing.

International labels such as developing, least developed, underdeveloped, demographically developing, low-income, highly indebted, and third world have long been used to describe groupings of countries in which most people are poor. Indeed, it is convenient to categorise countries whose people deserve universal support in their attempts to achieve a quality of life, health, and wellbeing that is comparable with the rest of the world. There is a danger, however, that the labels become so much associated with debt, disease, and dependence, that they disguise multitudes of differences in tradition, lifestyle, and local economy—all of which contribute to the character of people's health and public-health solutions. McKee and Jacobson[1] describe the diversity of cultures in Europe, but among countries grouped as developing, there too exist not only diversities in language and culture but also great inequalities in health determinants and outcomes (table).

Sinith Sittirak,[2] in her exploration of the meaning of development, as a Thai woman, concludes that "development is part of that 'Westernising' process of 'excluding' difference by imposing sameness...in terms of 'naming', 'studying', 'helping' and above all 'speaking' for 'others'". Our aim in this review is to remove labels and so begin to consider the people, their perspectives and assets, and the complexities of issues facing those who are responsible for the public's health in countries where good health and wellbeing are not the norm. We argue that: good public-health practice encourages people and communities to take part in decisions about their own health; countries need to recast their health systems to support people's initiatives; and new international relations are required to support countries to resolve their own public-health issues.

	Human development index[4]	Overall health system attainment WHO index (1997 estimates)[60]	Life expectancy at birth (years)[60]		Mortality rate under age 5 years (per 1000 live births)[60]	
			Male	Female	Male	Female
Western Pacific region						
Singapore*	22	88·9	75·1	80·8	4	5
Lao PDR†	140	60·1	54·0	56·6	143	126
South-East Asia region						
DPR of Korea*	30	85·7	71·3	78·2	100	99
Bangladesh†	150	67·6	57·5	58·1	113	116
African region						
South Africa*	101	61·0	47·3	49·7	85	67
Sierra Leone†	174	35·7	33·2	35·4	326	298
Region of the Americas						
Barbados*	29	84·9	72·7	77·8	11	10
Haiti†	152	62·8	50·6	55·1	120	111
Eastern Mediterranean region						
Cyprus*	26	88·6	74·8	78·8	9	8
Dijibouti†	157	69·0	45·0	45·0	169	162

Members of the Eastern Mediterranean region are all regarded as demographically developed. *Highest human development index. †Lowest human development index for this WHO region.

Vital statistics for countries classified as demographically developing[59]

Public-health realities

For many countries in Africa and Asia, the mid-20th century saw dramatic improvements in health and life expectancy brought about by technological advances, the introduction of primary health care, increased literacy, access to safe water, sanitation, and housing, and better understanding of social behaviour.[3] However, at the turn of the century, political unrest, environmental disaster, declining economic performance, the introduction of structural-adjustment programmes, unresponsive governance, weak public-health infrastructure, changing population dynamics, the advent of HIV/AIDS, and the onset of globalisation have all had great impact on the livelihoods and welfare of poor people.[4]

Some developments in the collection and analysis of comparative data worldwide have increased awareness of the complicated health scenarios that face communities and public-heath practitioners in poor countries (figure). Substantial numbers of deaths result from infectious diseases—particularly malaria, HIV/AIDS, and tuberculosis, and these—together with non-communicable diseases such as cancer and diabetes—make up the double disease burden of many developing countries.[5] To these must be added threats related to risk-taking behaviour—particularly among adolescents—violence, road traffic accidents, and psychological distress. Although in many countries the incidence of poverty has declined, the absolute numbers of poor and marginalised people have increased and disparities in their share of resources are becoming greater. There are widespread

Lancet 2000; **356:** 841–46

The Rockefeller Foundation, 420 Fifth Avenue, New York, NY 10018 USA (S Macfarlane MSc); **Institute of Philippine Culture, Atenes de Manila University, Loyloa Heights, Quezon City, Philippines** (M Racelis MA); **and The Rockefeller Foundation, International House, Nairobi, Kenya** (F Muli-Musiime PhD)

Correspondence to: Sarah Macfarlane

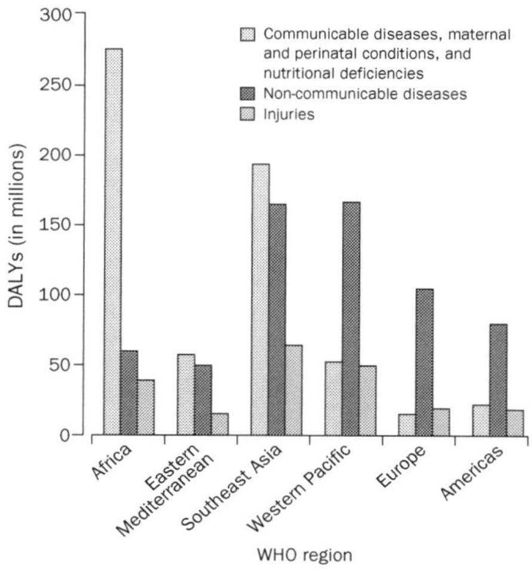

The burden of diseases by WHO region (1999 estimates)[60]

inequalities in health status, life expectancy, and in access to health care between rich and poor countries, between rich and poor people, and between poor men and women everywhere.[6-8] Women suffer disproportionately and, together with their children, have the most to gain from improved health care.[9-12]

Poor coverage and inadequacy of health facilities means that people die of disease and hunger without even being able to communicate their needs.[13] Indeed, Jeffery Sachs[14] has pointed out that "the poorest of the poor are nearly invisible...They escape our notice almost entirely, unless war or an exotic disease breaks out, or yet another programme with the International Monetary Fund is signed".

People matter

It has become customary for international agencies to advocate public-health solutions for marginalised people by describing their poverty, "1·3 billion people live on incomes of less than $1 a day",[15] by counting their diseases, "over 40 million people are disfigured and disabled by filariasis",[15] and by predicting their deaths, "deaths from non-communicable diseases are expected to climb from 28·1 million a year to 49·7 million by 2020."[16] Poor though people may be, and despite their susceptibility to all these diseases, their communities include the usual heterogeneity of sex, age, ethnicity, religion, occupation, education, and leadership ability of people in any section of society. Experience during the past few decades has shown that people can organise themselves to solve their own public-health issues and other concerns in partnership with government and non-governmental organisations (NGOs).[17,18] There are many examples of how inaccessible populations have empowered themselves, bringing about substantial changes in their own communities.

About 25 years ago, health personnel in a Mindanao municipality in the Philippines rarely ventured into the rural villages some distance away because, they said, this would not be economical in cost, time, or service provision. One community, concerned about health issues, organised its members to put pressure on the health team to visit, and the team finally agreed. When the health workers arrived they discovered, to their astonishment, that local leaders had mobilised people to come to consult with them from mountain villages as far away as 10 km over extremely rough and sloping terrain. The leaders enlisted the assistance of local teachers and better educated residents to screen and prioritise the waiting people by type of ailment and severity of their conditions. Volunteers recorded the medical team's recommendations and in forthcoming weeks undertook measures to reduce some of the diseases of public-health importance.[19]

Korogocho is an area outside Nairobi, Kenya, where non-permanent families have settled since before independence. The area, in which some 5000 families live, gained such a criminal reputation that it was subject to regular police raids. Government and other agencies would only maintain offices on the periphery of the area. In 1995, the African Network for the Protection and Prevention of Child Abuse and Neglect decided to experiment with a new approach to community organisation in this area by training local organisers to develop empowered communities. The result was that the community elected its own leadership and prioritised its own needs. Starting with the destruction of garbage mountains, the people went on to secure water drainage, build pit-latrines, target diarrhoeal disease, and organise immunisation; then they invited private health providers into the area. The choice of health and sanitation around which to start mobilisation was propitious because these were the over-riding concerns of the community, the government, and donor groups. This first experience of mobilising and empowerment gave people the confidence and expertise to handle more controversial issues. The community developed a map pin-pointing spots of criminal activity and indiscriminate police raids ceased. Finally, community leaders convinced the government to suspend further upscale land development that would displace poor residents. This action paved the way for the community to make tenure claims in the area.[20]

Such anecdotes are not designed for, and seldom reach, scientific publication. They describe community decision-making with internal subjective assessment of success, rather than scientifically designed interventions with external indicators of costeffectiveness and replicability. Since the actions described originate from within the community and from self-motivated community development, they do not require major project funding, and so they are not subjected to external pressures for scientific conformity. The advantage is that the communities get to control the situation, but the disadvantage is that success or failure may not be recognised outside the community.

In preparation for the 2000 World Development Report, the World Bank has produced "Consultations with the poor", a series of participatory studies by local organisations to listen to the voices of more than 60 000 poor women and men in 60 countries.[21,22] Overall the people's voices reflected an overwhelming feeling of powerlessness. Their experiences with governments were mostly negative, and poor quality of health and social care services were a major concern. They appreciated the work of NGOs but had mixed feelings about them, and concluded that their own local networks were the most dependable. The report ends with a strategy for change that emphasises the need to recognise the realities of poor people and to invest directly in their organisational capacities. Communities are naturally intersectoral and, with the support of civil society groups, can learn to reject inadequate services and themselves become part of the solution to their improved wellbeing.

People in public health

Although the principles of public health have been accepted for centuries, the road to public health has been chequered.[23] At the beginning of the 20th century, concern within the North American medical establishment about the need to address population-based determinants of health led to a drive to create schools of public health worldwide. By the mid-1980s there were 101 separate schools of public health in 37 countries, including 12 developing countries: Brazil, Chile, Columbia, Cuba, Egypt, India, Indonesia, Mexico, Peru, Philippines, Thailand, and Venezuela.[24] From the middle of the century, some national people-based movements began to emerge.

After its independence, India heralded the so-called golden age of public health, when the new democracy started to develop health programmes to meet the needs of the people who had supported the freedom struggle.[25] In parallel, China, still remembered for its "barefoot doctors", was making remarkable gains in life expectancy and progress with health care.[26] The 1967 Arusha Declaration of Socialism and Self-Reliance in Tanzania in 1967 focused on the achievement of equality between people, and led to exemplary practice of public health.[27] A groundswell of support for the principles of public health resulted in the Declaration of Alma-Ata in 1978—the ideal of which was that health was attainable for and by the people in a comprehensive fashion.[28]

Yet Alma-Ata was immediately followed by a series of northern-designed selective initiatives that are still being generated today (panel). In a recent article, Banerji[25] laments these international initiatives that were "let loose on poor countries" in "retribution" for the "Alma-Ata Declaration of self-reliance by peoples of the world". The economic crisis of the ensuing decade led donor governments to insert economic values—such as cost-recovery and financial sustainability—into their health assistance schemes.[29] Selective vertical programmes enabled international aid agencies to measure results and protect their financial investments from complicated, long-term, multisectoral, and interdepartmental implementation procedures. Whereas some vertical programmes have been successful in meeting their own goals (eg, child immunisation, and the Onchocerciasis Control Programme in West Africa[30]) the sum total of so many vertical initiatives makes little rational sense to the level of implementation. NGOs and religious groups have found that holistic community-based health programmes are generally undermined by narrowly selective interventions and that the sustainability of people-owned initiatives can be put in jeopardy.[31]

A contributing factor in the move away from primary health care was the difficulty in quantifying the results of integrated community-based programmes. Bilateral donors were uneasy about satisfying their taxpaying constituencies that overseas development assistance was being well spent. They became impatient at the slow pace of the processes of community participation necessary for primary health care to succeed. In addition, many of the more authoritarian governments in developing countries looked upon community empowerment, management, and demand processes as forces likely to undermine their control, not only over health but, ultimately, the entire political system; hence, they had little or no interest in fostering such

Chronology of some major international public-health initiatives initiated after the international conference on primary health care, Alma Ata, USSR, 1978

1978		International conference on primary health care, Alma Ata, USSR
1979	WHO	Health For All
	WHO	Selective primary health care
1980	World Bank	Structural adjustment/health-sector reform
1981	WHO	Guinea worm eradication
1983	UNICEF	Growth monitoring, oral rehydration, breastfeeding and immunisation (GOBI)
1985	UNICEF	Growth monitoring, oral rehydration, breastfeeding, immunisation, fertility promotion, feeding programme, and female development (GOBI-FFF)
	UNICEF	Universal programme of immunisation (UPI)
1986	WHO	Special programme on AIDS
1987	WHO, World Bank, UNFPA	Safe motherhood initiative
1988	WHO	Polio eradication initiative
	WHO	Global programme on AIDS (GPA; formerly special programme on AIDS)
1992	WHO, UNICEF	Integrated management of childhood diseases (IMCI)
1997	WHO	Lymphatic filariasis elimination
1998	WHO	Roll Back Malaria campaign
	WHO	Stop tuberculosis campaign

democratic outcomes. Nor, in another version of re-ordered power relations, were national governments willing to foster local government autonomy. Government bureaucracies—whether at national or local levels—were simply unaccustomed or unwilling to work as peers with people at the community level and therefore found it difficult to develop the needed institutional mechanisms.[32]

Some agencies with people-oriented mandates, for example the United Nations Children's Fund (UNICEF) and the United Nations Population Fund (UNFPA), have succeeded in working with governments and NGOs in support of communities mobilising for quality care. UNICEF's focus on community participation and institutional social mobilisation centered on children's rights, women's needs, family needs,[33] and UNFPA's attention to mobilising women and men around reproductive health issues are highlighted in their programmes of cooperation in the Philippines.[34]

With the Health For All campaign off the agenda and its goals deemed unrealistic,[32] events have now come full circle as advocates of health-sector reform[35] have begun to recognise the need not only for "community participation" but for "consumer responsiveness". In a recent assessment of development effectiveness in its health, nutrition, and population sector, the World Bank operations evaluation department observes that, although most projects include objectives that can only be met through client-responsive services,[36] "notably lacking in most Bank analyses is an adequate assessment of demand for health services".[37] Of 224 projects assessed, only four documented the presence of beneficiary decision-making power in the project design. The World Bank has spent millions listening to the voices of the poor[22] but if these poor women, men, and children cannot organise for their own empowerment and claim-making, little in their lives will change. Recognising the historic pitfalls of verticality, the WHO flagship programme

Roll Back Malaria describes itself as a social movement—a new challenge for an agency with a strong sectoral tradition.[38]

Concern about increasing inequalities in health and the inadequacies of national and international responses led many NGOs to hold a People's Health Assembly in Dhaka, Bangladesh, in December, 2000. With the goal of re-establishing "health and equitable development as top priorities in local, national and international policy-making", the assembly will "draw on and support people's movements in their struggles to build long-term and sustainable solutions to health problems".[39] We hope that the activities of such a movement will complement the work of health professionals and others to ensure that public health really does fulfil its definition as "the art and science of preventing disease, promoting health, and prolonging life through the organised efforts of society".[40]

The national response

The World Bank publication *Better Health for Africa* recommends the creation of an enabling environment for health through the involvement of communities, but suggests that progress in some countries has been inhibited "by a lack of government commitment to health and poor management of health services".[41] Without supportive leadership and good governance, many institutions in poor countries are ill equipped to face the fundamental changes in the pattern of need and demand for health services and the challenges of health-sector reform and health-care financing.

Rights were not granted to include this image in electronic media. Please refer to the printed journal.

A group of women discussing health issues with a community leader, Zambia

In 1988, Ghana inaugurated its health reform programme recognising the government's lack of responsiveness to the needs of consumers and its diffi-culties in coping with exter-nal pressures and demands on the use of resources from central government and donors. Accordingly, its programme Strengthening District Health Systems focused on decentralisation and empowerment of the bureaucracy at lower levels, integration of vertical and horizontal health programmes at a district level, and a participatory policy-making process that incorporated the views of health personnel closer to community levels. District level participatory planning also enabled local staff to deal with the potentially damaging effects of narrowly-conceived vertical programmes imposed on communities, and to continue protesting centralised budgeting and financial controls as destructive of local initiatives.[42] In the Navrongo district of Ghana, for example, there are now indications that during the past decade maternal and child health has improved, and malaria prevention is beginning to take effect.[43] Uganda, with its recent devolution of authority to district level and below, shows promise, in particular in preventing HIV/AIDS.[44]

In a study on Bolivia, the Central African Republic, and Tanzania that assessed health services provision capacity, researchers found that neither of the countries had achieved good capacity to deliver maternal-child health services.[45] In Bolivia, combined public and NGO programmes reached only 37% of the population, with the rural poor having the least access to public-health facilities. Medical training traditionally paid little attention to preventive medicine, poverty-related diseases, and communication and management skills. Restructuring was seriously hampered by the longstanding bias toward large hospitals and research institutes. Similarly, in the Central African Republic, maternal-child services congregated in cities and operated erratically in rural areas. People's overall distrust of government and its services further weakened health implementation. Although Tanzania's comprehensive health-care system was targeted at reaching 72% of rural people, local centres staffed by poorly trained personnel proved largely ineffective at responding to the needs of the women and children who were overwhelming their centres. Rural, preventive, and poverty-focused care could never overcome the dominant curative care based in urban hospitals.

The introduction of health-sector reform has served to accentuate many inadequacies in the health workforce which have been characterised by imbalance.[46] Numerically, some countries produce more health workers than they need whereas others do not produce enough. Qualitatively, there are often inconsistencies between the level of training and the needs of the job. In addition, there are serious problems of inequity in the distribution of health workers by geography, institution, and in the public and private mix. Most recent reports highlight the importance of better integ-ration of human resource planning within overall health-sector planning.[47] Develop-ment of human resources—the greatest asset of any health system—is fundamental to the response. Yet an under-paid, poorly motivated, poorly organised, and increasingly dissatisfied workforce also poses the greatest threat to reform.

The skills and morale of the health workforce will surely rise with improved training, better equipped and better staffed health centres, higher remuneration, greater participation in research planning, implementation, assessment, and policy-making processes, and interaction on the ground inspired by community residents whose health improves. As shown by the public-health movements leading up to Alma Ata, such changes require great political leadership. In a review of Nigeria's health programme during the past 50 years, Ransome-Kuti[48] concludes that "our work as health practitioners needs a leadership that cares for the health and well being of the people...Such leaders can be assured of the energetic, loyal and creative response of the people, and will remain forever in their memory".

The international context

At the international level, it is rational to be concerned about cross-cutting issues, recurring themes, consistent data collection, and common solutions to improve the health of the world's poor. It is also logical that this leads to the setting up of global collaborations, alliances, and partnerships to advise and support public-health practitioners, especially those in poor countries. But the bird's eye view is usually the privilege of those who can afford to fly.

International guidelines and multicountry studies are generally initiated by researchers or international agencies with access to northern donors.[49] Indicators have been developed for measuring disease burden, reproductive health, cost-efficiency, and health equity, for example, but the greatest challenge is to ensure their local relevance before incorporating their measurement into overburdened district health-information systems. Field trials of health interventions usually take place in well funded international population laboratories, but implementation is for the underfunded health practitioner. The multilateral agencies dedicated their efforts to making recommendations about how to improve health in developing countries (panel).

Those who have access to international findings, for example donors and international consultants, advise policy makers and public-health practitioners in countries with less access to information. Although exchange of information is essential to development, the nature of the communications can sometimes be counterproductive. In a study of donor behaviour in the Ugandan health sector, Okello and colleagues[50] commented that poor coordination and procedural inconsistency in the provision of technical and other assistance can "undermine the institutions which the aid program aims to support". In another study, Wolffers and colleagues[49] report African researchers' views about initiated research programmes in northern Africa: "we have to accept their priorities and interests"; "it is a kind of trade: they need the field, we are getting some funding".

Certain activities are particularly suitable for international cooperation, for example surveillance of infectious diseases, regulation and standard setting, protection of intellectual property rights, and safeguarding of vulnerable populations in conflict or disaster situations.[51] But for international cooperation for public health to succeed, it is necessary to agree on basic operating principles that include joint priority setting, mutual recognition, common values, shared goals, and above all trust.[52]

A cooperative public-health response

The principles and energy of Alma-Ata can be retrieved by providing the vehicle for people to speak for themselves and to be heard; for this to happen, there needs to be worldwide intersectoral commitment that enables people to organise freely around their interests and to support their health initiatives. These exhortations acknowledge that health is a multisectoral and political issue both in terms of resource allocation and of human rights. Accordingly, open and democratic societies are best able to generate genuine people-initiated health care. Although repressive governments have provided substantial health services to the poor, for example in the case of the regime of now ousted President Suharto of Indonesia, these services will not be sustained when the people themselves have little or no say in managing, assessing, and reformulating the process.[53]

What will also make a huge difference for quality of care is encouragement from political, public health, civil society, and business leaders for government health systems to work with and advise and support development NGOs and religious institutions that are genuinely engaged in empowering communities. This will include a wide range of concerns, of which health is but one. The examples we cite from the Philippines and Kenya, and mounting evidence from around the world, indicate that community-health processes initiated by residents and actively supported by health bureaucracies can achieve what decades of so-called top-down efforts have failed to do.[54] Some weakening of the 1980s entrenched resistance to people's initiatives is being shown by the emergence of more open and democratic governments in developing countries and widespread decentralisation of authority. Civil-society initiatives for community empowerment are beginning to take centre stage. Although more research is necessary, the important influences of aspects of local social organisation and political culture on the operations of decentralised health systems have been demonstrated, for example in a study of district health systems in Northeast Brazil.[55] National health leaders can respond by reorienting public health training and practice so that community-based, people-led health care with their support becomes the answer to sustainable wellbeing.[56,57]

Although we have focused on public health in developing countries, our message is universal. Poverty and health disparities exist and are increasing in all nations of the world. For public health to succeed, it must be re-crafted in a framework that locates organised and active communities at the centre as initiators and managers of their own health. In this paradigm, non-governmental, governmental, private sector, and international stakeholders form the periphery—listening to and learning from the people, then, discussing and making decisions jointly.

Increased opportunities for travel, communication, and information access offer hope for new forms of cooperation between organised people at all levels of society and in different sectors, including civil society, governmental and non-governmental organisations, educational institutions, and international agencies. Many forms of networks and collaborations already exist—some global, some regional (intercountry), some national (intracountry), and some community based. But it is important to take stock of existing models and explore new forms of intersectoral and multisectoral cooperation to ensure equitable exchange of views, information, and knowledge.[58]

The complex dynamics of international health inequalities call for a new form of international public-health response that recognises the interdependence of all countries, their shared resources, dependence on the natural environment, and the need for common public responsibility for the health and wellbeing of all people. Equitable international public-health cooperation involves the exchange of ideas, philosophies, expertise, and resources—to address health inequalities worldwide. In the first instance; this requires greater diversification of players—internationally and sectorally—more voice from the countries with the greatest health concerns, greater sensitivity to national public-health requirements and local solutions, and a shift in the centre of gravity of initiatives and their funding from north to south. The role of a truly international community is to provide a mutually supportive environment, and to move fast, fairly, and efficiently to lessen the pressures and harness the benefits of globalisation to ensure the health of marginalised people everywhere.

We thank the many people working in communities and in public health with whom we have given the opportunity to cooperate.

References

1 McKee M, Jacobson B. Public Health in Europe. *Lancet* 2000; **356:** 665–70.
2 Sittirak S. The daughters of development: women in a changing environment. London: Zed Books; 1998.
3 McMichael AJ, Beaglehole R. The changing global context of public health. *Lancet* 2000; **356:** 495–99.
4 United Nations Development Programme. Human development report 1999. New York: Oxford University Press, 1999.
5 Sen K, Bonita R. Global health status: two steps forward, one step back. *Lancet* 2000; **356:** 577–82.
6 Beaglehole R, Bonita R. Reinvigorating public health. *Lancet* 2000; **356:** ?????.
7 The World Bank. World Development Report 1999/2000. New York: Oxford University Press, 1999.
8 United Nations Development Programme. Human Development Report 1998. New York: Oxford University Press, 1998: 20–21.
9 Narayan D, Patel R, Schafft K, Rademacher A, Koch-Schulte S. Crumbling foundations, conflicting relations: gender, institutions, and poverty consultations with the poor; a review of World Bank Participatory Poverty Assessments. Washington, DC: World Bank, 1999.
10 Oxaal Z, Cook S. Health and poverty gender analysis. Sussex: Institute of Development Studies, 1995: 1–19.
11 Wee V, Heyzer N. The feminization of poverty: gender, poverty, and sustainable development; towards a holistic framework of understanding and action. Singapore: Singapore Centre for Environment, Gender, and Development (ENGENDER), 1995: 35–45.
12 Dube L. Nutrition and discrimination, women and kinship: comparative perspectives on gender in south and south-east Asia. New York: United Nations University, 1996: 137–45.
13 Chambers R. Poverty and livelihoods: whose reality counts? In: People: from impoverishment to empowerment, Kardar U, Sil L, eds. New York: New York University Press, 1995: 1–16.
14 Sachs J. Helping the world's poorest. *The Economist* Aug 14, 1999: 17–20.
15 WHO. WHO report on infectious diseases: removing obstacles to healthy development. Geneva: WHO, 1999.
16 Murray CJ, Lopez AD. The Global Burden of Disease: summary. Cambridge: Harvard School of Public Health, 1996.
17 Knowles JC, Pernia EM, Racelis M. Social consequences of the financial crisis in Asia: economic staff paper number 60. Manila: Asian Development Bank, 1999: 48–52.
18 Silliman GS, Garner Noble L. Citizen movements and Philippines democracy, organizing for democracy: NGOs, civil society, and the Philippines state. Honolulu: University of Hawaii Press and Ateneo de Manila University Press; 1998: 280-310.
19 Hollnsteiner R. Mobilizing the rural poor through community. *Philippine Studies* 1979; **27:** 387–416.
20 Onduu DO. Safety for children in urban areas: experiences of the community organization training programme in Korogocho. Nairobi: International Forum on Urban Poverty (IFUP), third international conference, 1999.
21 The World Bank. Consultations with the poor national synthesis reports, informal publications series prepared for Global Synthesis Workshop: consultations with the poor, poverty group. Washington, DC: The World Bank, 1999.
22 Narayan D, Patel R, Schafft K, Rademacher A, Koch-Schulte S. Voices of the poor: can anyone hear us? Oxford: Oxford University Press, 2000.
23 Sand R. The advance to social medicine. London: Staples Press, 1952: 443–57.
24 White KL. Healing the schism: epidemiology, medicine, and the public's health. New York: Springer-Verlag: 1991.
25 Banerji D. A fundamental shift in the approach to international health by WHO, UNICEF, and the World Bank: instances of the practice of "Intellectual Fascism" and totalitarianism in some Asian countries. *Int J Health Serv* 1999; **29:** 227–59.
26 Sidel VW, Sidel R. The health care delivery system in the People's Republic of China. In: Newell KN, ed. Health by the people. Geneva: WHO, 1975: 1–13.
27 Nyerere JK. On the policy of self-reliance in Tanzania. Africa Report, 1967.
28 WHO. Primary health care: report on the International Conference on primary health care, Alma-Ata, USSR. Geneva: WHO, 1978.
29 La Fond A. Sustaining primary health care. London: Save the Children, Earthscan Publication, 1995: 24–26.
30 Boussinesq M, Hougard JM. The campaign against onchocerciasis in Africa: update. *Med Trop* 1998; **58:** 285–96.
31 Canave-Anung L. Community organizing in health: the Institute of Primary Health Care experience. Palo: Third General Assembly of the Philippine Community Organizers Society (PHILCOS), 1999.
32 United Nations Children's Fund (UNICEF). Notes on CSDR/UCI and PHC: a preliminary analysis of UNICEF experience, internal working paper. New York: United Nations Children's Fund, 1988.
33 Government of the Republic of the Philippines and the United Nations Children's Fund. Communities. In: Situation of Children and Women in the Philippines, 1997. Manila: Government of the Republic of the Philippines and the United Nations Children's Fund, 1997: 21–24.
34 United Nations Population Fund (UNFPA) and the Government of the Republic of the Philippines (GOP). 1997 Country Brief. Manila: UNFPA and GOP, 1998.
35 Cassels A. Health sector reform: key issues in less developed countries. *J Intern Develop* 1995; **7:** 329–47.
36 Heaver, R. Reaching people at the periphery: can the World Bank's Population, Health, and Nutrition Operations do better? World Bank Working Paper Series 81. Washington, DC: The World Bank, 1988.
37 Johnston T, Stout S. Investing in health: development effectiveness in the health, nutrition, and population sector. Operations evaluation study. Washington DC: The World Bank, 1999.
38 WHO. Roll Back Malaria project. RBM action at country level: the inception process. Geneva: WHO, 1999.
39 People's Health Assembly. People's Health Assembly 2000. Penang: Public Health Association of Australia, 2000.
40 Acheson D. Independent inquiry into inequalities in health. London: HM Stationery Office, 1998.
41 The World Bank. Better health in Africa: experience and lessons learned. Washington, DC: The World Bank, 1999.
42 La Fond A. Government's role: the ministry of health in context. In: sustaining primary health care. London: Save the Children, Earthscan Publication, 1995: 101–15.
43 Binka FN, Nazzar A, Phillips JF. The Navrongo community health and family planning project. *Stud Fam Plann* 1995; **26:** 121–39.
44 Uganda gives lesson in stemming the AIDS epidemic. *Nat Med* 1999; **5:** 963.
45 Hilderbrand ME, Grindle MS. Building sustainable capacity: challenges for the public sector: a study for the Bureau for Policy and Programme Support, United Nations Development Programme. New York: United Nations Development Programme 1996: 27–28.
46 Adams OB, Hirschfeld M. Human resources for health-challenges for the 21st century. *World Health Stat Q* 1998; **51:** 28–32.
47 Martinez J, Martineau T. Rethinking human resources: an agenda for the millennium. *Health Pol Plan* 1998; **13:** 345–58.
48 Ransome-Kuti O. Who cares for the health of Africans: the Nigerian case. International lecture series on population issues sponsored by the Global Security and Sustainability program. Kaduna: John D and Catherine T MacArthur Foundation, 1998.
49 Wolffers I, Adjei S, van der Drift R. Health research in the tropics. *Lancet* 1998; **351:** 1652–54.
50 Okello D, Konde-Lule J, Lubanga RGN, Arube-Wani J, Lwanga JB. The role of donors in the Uganda health sector. Uganda National Council for Science and Technology, 1998.
51 Yach D, Bettcher D. The globalization of public health, II: the convergence of self-interest and altruism. *Am J Public Health* 1998; **88:** 738–41.
52 Galliard J. Les collaborations scientifiques Nord-Sud: un examen critique de huit programmes d'aide à la recherche. Les Sciences hors d'Occident au XXième siècle 7. Paris: *ORSTOM* Editions, 1996: 220–53.
53 Cholil A, Iskandar MB, Sciortino R. The life saver: the mother friendly movement in Indonesia. Jakarta: The State Ministry for the Role of Women, Republic of Indonesia, and The Ford Foundation, 1998: 104.
54 Veneracion C. Community health development: experiences from Rural Philippines. Quezon City: Ateneo de Manila University Institute of Philippine Culture; 1994: 102.
55 Atkinson S, Medeiros RL, Oliveira PH, de Almeida RD. Going down to the local: incorporating social organisation and political culture into assessments of decentralised health care. *Soc Sci Med* 2000; **51:** 619–36.
56 Racelis M. From struggle to consolidation and new visions: civil society and civil society assistance in the Philippines. In: Ottaway M, Carothers T, eds. Funding virtue: civil society and democracy promotion, Washington, DC: Carnegie Endowment for International Peace (in press).
57 Cornwall A, Lucas H, Pasteur K. IDS Bulletin: accountability through participation—developing workable partnership models in the health sector. Sussex: Institute of Development Studies, 2000.
58 Kickbusch I. The development of international health policies—accountability intact? *Soc Sci Med* 2000; **51:** 979–89.
59 WHO, The World Bank. The global burden of disease: a comprehensive assessment of mortality and disability from diseases, injuries, and risk factors in 1990 and projected to 2020. Cambridge: Harvard University Press, 1996.
60 WHO. The World Health Report 2000: health systems: improving performance. Geneva: WHO, 2000.

[34]

COMMENTARY:
JUSTICE AND MEDICAL RESEARCH: A GLOBAL PERSPECTIVE[1]

SOLOMON R BENATAR

ABSTRACT

Economic globalization has profound implications for health. The scale of injustice at a global level, reflected in inexorably widening disparities in wealth and health, also has critical implications for health related research – in particular when the opportunities for exploiting research subjects are carefully considered. The challenge of developing universal guidelines for international clinical research is addressed against the background of a polarizing, yet interdependent, world in which all are ultimately threatened by lack of social justice. It is proposed that in such a world there is a need for new ways of thinking about research and its relevance to health at a global level. Responsibility to use knowledge and power wisely requires more radical changes to guidelines for research ethics than are currently under consideration.

INTRODUCTION

When Harold Macmillan (then Prime Minister of Britain) visited Africa in 1960, he referred to the 'wind of change' that he perceived blowing through Africa – in the wake of decades of colonialism and oppression.[2] The history of sub-Saharan Africa since then has been stormy. Initial encouraging advances made by many countries in the early years of their independence have

[1] Based on the opening address given by the author at the Fogarty International Global Research Ethics Forum Bethesda, Maryland. USA, November 1999.

[2] H. Macmillan. 'The wind of change is blowing through the continent. Whether we like it or not, this growth of national consciousness is a fact.' Speech in the South African Parliament, Cape Town, February 3, 1960.

been followed by subsequent retrogression due to both external and internal influences. External factors include the adverse effects of neo-liberal economics on trade and the incurring of debts, the subsequent structural adjustment programs imposed by the IMF and World Bank, and the impact of arms trading and 'Cold War' interference in Africa. Internal factors include corruption, political patronage, power struggles and poor governance. Adverse environmental conditions and the HIV/AIDS pandemic have posed additional massive burdens to progress.[3] The 'wind of change' associated with emancipation from oppression in apartheid South Africa has culminated in a much admired peaceful transition in that country.[4] How this transition will play out in the face of the HIV/AIDS pandemic and in the context of a globalising world is of great importance.[5]

THE WORLD AT THE BEGINNING OF THE 21ST CENTURY

It is necessary to appreciate that the 'wind of change' is now being felt throughout the world, as globalising forces create ever widening disparities in wealth, with important implications for health and well being.[6] Despite great progress in science, technology and communication during the 20th century, the world at the beginning of the new millennium is characterized by chaos and despair at many levels.[7] Escalating economic disparities, especially during the past 30 years, illustrate the impact of the 'visible hand' of the market place and the 'squeezed up' effect that is, the funneling of resources upwards resulting in wider disparities in wealth and health between rich and poor than ever before – rather than the so much spoken about and praised 'invisible hand' and 'trickle down effect.' Indeed more than half the world's population lives in poverty – 25% in abject poverty.

[3] D.E. Logie, S.R. Benatar. Africa in the 21st century: can despair be turned to hope? *BMJ 1997*; 315: 1444–46. R. Sandbrook. 2000. *Closing the circle: democratization and development in Africa*. London. Zed Books.

[4] H. Adam, K. Moodley, 1993. *The negotiated revolution: society and politics in post- apartheid South Africa*. Johannesburg. Jonathan Ball Publ.

[5] K. Lee, A.B. Zwi. A global political economy approach to A1DS: ideology, interests and implications. *New Political Economy* 1996; 1: 355–73. S.R. Benatar. South Africa's transition in a globalising world: HIV/AIDS as a window and a mirror. *International Affairs* 2001; 77: 347–375.

[6] S.R. Benatar. Global disparities in health and human rights. *American Journal of Public Health* 1998; 88: 295–300. J. Frenk et al, The new world order and international health. *BMJ*, 1997; 314: 1404–7.

[7] E. Hobsbawm. 1994. *The age of extremes: a history of the world 1914–1991*. New York. Pantheon Books.

The shift in the accumulation of capital from the nation state to multinational corporations, and the creation of unpayable third world debt, have impoverished third world countries and reduced annual per capita health care expenditures to less than $10 in most poor countries – where less than 50% of the population have access to even essential drugs. Health care services are rudimentary for many in a world in which 87% of annual global expenditure on health is directed to 16% of the world's population, who only bear 7% of the global burden of disease, and in which increasingly unethical, market driven research neglects many diseases.[8] Of all US $56 billion spent annually on medical research 90% is spent on those diseases causing only 10% of the global burden of disease.[9]

Meanwhile vast expenditure continues on the military. Many small wars, fuelled by trade in weapons, have resulted in unprecedented numbers of civilian deaths and displacement of millions of people from their social roots, with profound disruption of their lives. In addition there is a world-wide movement of people, within and across national borders through urbanization, migration, tourism and illicit trading in drugs and people[10] – all favoring the rapid spread of infectious diseases. Growth of the world's population and massive increases in energy consumption (five and 30 fold increases respectively over the past 150 years) further threaten our ecology.[11]

New ecological niches created by these destructive social and environmental changes favor the emergence of many new infectious diseases, the worst being HIV/AIDS, and the recrudescence of old diseases such as tuberculosis and malaria that cause immense suffering and millions of premature deaths.[12] These and other infectious diseases that may emerge in the future challenge thinkers to better understand the world and how it could be improved.

[8] J. Iglehart. American health services: expenditure. *NEJM. 1999*; 340: 70–76.

[9] Commission on Health Research for Development. 1990. *Health Research: Essential link to equity in development.* Oxford. Oxford University Press.

[10] H.R. Friman, P. Andreas, (Eds). 1999. *Illicit global economy and state power.* New York. Rowan & Littlefield.

[11] A.J. McMichael, *Planetary Overload: global environmental change and the health of the human species.* Cambridge. Cambridge University Press.

[12] WHO. *World Health Report 1996.* Geneva. K. Lee, A.B. Zwi. A global political economy approach to AIDS.

HOW CAN THE WORLD BE EXPLAINED?

On the one hand the world can be considered as an unfortunate place in which most suffer disproportionately and unavoidably. On this account it is presumed that the manner and direction in which money flows, power is expressed, and social values develop are shaped by forces beyond the control of individuals or nations.

On the other hand an unjust world can be considered as one created by human activities, and one which can, and should be, changed. On this account the flow of money can be explained on the basis of national/international political forces and economic trends, and on such other aspects of globalization as advances in science and technology that have profoundly altered the nature of the global economy, as well as by exploitation at many levels (both overt – trade practices protecting the rich, and covert – debt trade and the arms trade as forms of enslavement). Some have used the term 'global apartheid' for the processes that have promoted (and continue to aggravate) vast disparities between rich and poor across the world.[13] Others have described third world debt, an integral component of globalization, as analogous to slavery in its impact,[14] and have called for reflection on the magnificent achievements of the 20th century, and on how the human condition and health could be improved globally.[15]

CHALLENGES FOR INTERNATIONAL RESEARCH ETHICS

This brief review of the adverse effects of progress serves to locate the context in which the controversy about research ethics has arisen and the backdrop against which the goals of change need to be considered: how to construct universally valid guidelines for collaborative international medical research with the view to enhancing sensitivity to issues of justice and our common humanity. In brief, the rationale for embarking on this endeavor now more than ever before includes:

- The scale of injustice at a global level.

[13] A. Richmond. 1994. *Global apartheid: refugees, racism and the new world order.* Oxford. Oxford University Press. T. Alexander. 1996. *Unraveling global apartheid.* Cambridge. Polity Press.

[14] A. Pettifor. 1996. Debt, the most potent form of slavery. London, *Christian Aid Society. Jubilee 2000 Coalition,* 2000. 'Kicking the habit: finding a lasting solution to addictive lending and borrowing – and its corrupting side effects." London.

[15] The Jubilee 2000 campaign. www.jubilee2000.org

- Knowledge of the history of abuse of humans in medical research and the need to protect (vulnerable) research subjects.
- The need for research on diseases that know no boundaries and potentially threaten all – e.g. HIV/AIDS, and the diseases to which antimicrobial drug resistance is developing.
- Significant growth of research to promote the use of therapeutic drugs in a lucrative market.
- The attractiveness of doing research in developing countries: easy access to patients, reduced costs, and less stringent regulations – the 'research sweat shop' equivalent.
- Understanding that researchers do not go to developing countries mainly for altruistic reasons.
- A perception by the vulnerable that they are being exploited.
- The need to balance the notion that solutions to disease and illness lie entirely in the realm of biomedicine with recognition that global forces promote emergence and resurgence of infectious diseases, and have many adverse effects on health.
- The goal of fostering empowerment through co-operation that may enhance human flourishing by making subjects essential partners in the research process.

The challenge to be faced in international research ethics is the development of universal rules for research world wide, at a time when health care is being delivered within very different health care systems (even within any single country) and in a multicultural world in which people live under radically different conditions – ranging from immense luxury to abject poverty. Variable trajectories of emancipation of individuals from communities have also given rise to a wide spectrum of how people view themselves, what it means to be ill and how health care systems should be structured.[16] With recognition of the role of social conditions in shaping the world, and how privileged people view the world and themselves, comes the realization that research cannot be considered in isolation. Medical research, health care, conditions of life around the world and how humans flourish may seem separate, but they are all interdependent. Taking such a comprehensive global perspective adds complexity to the task of crafting universal research ethics guidelines.

[16] N. Smart. 1995. *World Views: cross-cultural explorations of human beliefs*. New Jersey. Prentice Hall. R. Wilkinson. 1996. *Unhealthy societies: afflictions of inequality*. London. Routledge.

SOME SOLUTIONS TO THE CONTROVERSY ON RESEARCH ETHICS

Against this background of the context in which the controversy regarding alterations to the Helsinki Declaration and other guidelines for research ethics has arisen[17] a choice which can be made from several options. First, the status quo could be upheld in the hope that the progress of science and of economic growth will continue uninterrupted with beneficial effects for all even if disparities persist or grow. This would be the easiest choice as it presupposes no responsibility for global injustice. However, it would also be immoral as current injustices will be perpetuated and aggravated.

The second choice would be to make piecemeal changes at the margins – for example in international research by tinkering with the Helsinki Declaration and making some minor modifications. This course is also appealing to those who wish to make research easier and less accountable, but there is powerful and justified resistance to diluting protection for vulnerable research subjects and any progress made would in all probability be insufficient and temporary.[18]

Third, there could be acknowledgment of the need for a paradigm shift in thinking and action – towards reciprocal relationships between individuals, society, and the notion of rational self-interest and long term interdependence.[19] This is a more difficult decision and one that may have higher costs in the short term. It would, however, reflect recognition of the adverse impact of globalization and allow use of such desirable universal values as human rights to build a more widely achievable universalism. Such a decision could advance human relationships to the high moral ground, with the consequent best hope for long-term results. South Africa's peaceful transition through a negotiated revolution is an example. It is suggested that privileged people need to hold up a mirror to their lives, and try to see themselves from the perspective of the

[17] Revising the Declaration of Helsinki: a fresh start. *Bulletin of Medical Ethics*. 1999; 150: 3–44. Nuffield Council of Bioethics, 1999. *The ethics of clinical research in developing countries: a discussion paper*. London. D. Hellman. Trials on trial. *Report from the Institute for Philosophy and Public Policy*. 1998; 128: 142–147.

[18] The Helsinki Declaration was modified at the 52nd World Medical Association (WMA) General Assembly in October 2000, Edinburgh, Scotland.

[19] S.R. Benatar. 1997. Streams of global change. In: *Ethics, Equity and Health for all*. Z. Bankowski, J.H. Bryant, J. Gallagher (Eds). Geneva. CIOMS: 75–85. S.R. Benatar, P.A. Singer. A new look at international research ethics. *BMJ* 2000; 321: 824–26. A. Costello, A. Zumla. Moving to research partnerships in developing countries. *BMJ* 2000; 321: 827–29.

marginalised and weak in the world today and as historians in the future may see them in retrospect – as decadent and selfish.

Given the responsibility to use power and knowledge wisely, it is suggested that the deliberations at this meeting should include the possibility of introducing several new components into the Declaration of Helsinki and other international research guidelines – to extend and honor the concepts of justice and of integrity in the research endeavor:

- Vulnerable groups should be provided with increasing accessibility to research, and this should apply to the vulnerable within all countries.
- Exploitation of subjects, or their use as mere means to the ends of others, should be explicitly excluded by ensuring that the research is of relevance to the individuals participating in the research as well as their communities.
- The potential benefits of research should considerably outweigh potential risks or harms to vulnerable individuals and communities.
- Research subjects should be encouraged to participate in planning and conducting studies.
- Research in developing countries should be linked with capacity building in health care, and with economic and educational empowerment that has beneficial effects on the delivery of health care and on progress generally in the host country.

The first Global Forum on International Research, which opened discussion of all the topics listed on this agenda, was an enlightened first step forward. The second step would be to promote the addition of the newly proposed clauses to the Helsinki and other declarations. Third, there should be consideration of an expanded role for Institutional Review Boards (Research Ethics Committees) – taking them beyond mere review bodies to include duties of audit and education. Fourth, there is the need to influence mind sets – for example through societal marketing processes, rewards for compliance, wider publicity for and marginalisation of those doing unethical research, and by bringing bioethics and human rights programs closer to each other. Such actions could act as bridges, levers, and moral examples for the process of narrowing disparities. Education, the acquisition of self-knowledge coupled to activism, and moral example are all necessary for the promotion of a 'global new deal.'[20]

[20] R.J. Barnett, J. Cavanagh. 1994. A global new deal. In: *Beyond Bretton Woods: alternatives to the new world order.* J. Cavanagh, D. Wysham, M. Arruda

In summary support is provided here for the suggestion that to help the world's poorest, and indeed to foster the interests of all, the dialogue between rich and poor should be enhanced, the power of science and technology should be mobilized to address the problems of poor countries, new institutional alliances should be constructed, the concept of intellectual property rights should be re-evaluated to avoid 'ripping off the poor,' and long term financing should be planned for the international good necessary for human flourishing.[21] Herein lie the challenges to which the international research ethics endeavor could contribute.[22]

Solomon R. Benatar
Department of Medicine
University of Cape Town
Faculty of Health Sciences
Observatory 7925
Cape Town
South Africa
sbenatar@uctgsh1.uct.ac.za

(Eds). London. Pluto Press. R. Falk. 1999. *Predatory Globalization: a critique.* Cambridge. Polity Press. A.J. McMichael. 1997. *Planetary Overload.* J. Rotblat (Ed) *World citizenship: allegiance to humanity.* London. MacMillan. G. Teeple. 2000. *Globalization and the decline of social reform.* 2nd ed. Aurora, Ontario. Garamond Press.

[21] J. Sachs. Helping the world's poorest. *The Economist* 14 August, 1999: 17–20.

[22] J. Stephens et al. The body hunters. A series of six articles in the *Washington Post* 17–21 December 2000, describing some of the horrors associated with the growing commercialization of drug research in developing countries.

[35]

Education and debate

A global health fund: a leap of faith?

Ruairí Brugha, Gill Walt

See also *Editorial* by Verheul and Rowson and *Paper* p 139

Health Policy Unit, Department of Public Health and Policy, London School of Hygiene and Tropical Medicine, London WC1E 7HT
Ruairí Brugha *senior lecturer in public health*
Gill Walt *professor in international health policy*
Correspondence to: R Brugha Ruairi.Brugha@lshtm.ac.uk

BMJ 2001;323:152–4

After the 2000 G8 summit at Okinawa, the leaders of the world's richest countries announced an ambitious commitment to achieve substantial reductions in the global burden of disease and death due to HIV infection and AIDS, tuberculosis, and malaria by 2010.[1] A new global health fund, to be highlighted at the forthcoming G8 summit in Genoa, could form the cornerstone for meeting this commitment. The fund will be heavily dependent on resources from the richest countries, working in partnership with United Nations' agencies (especially the World Health Organization), the commercial sector (especially major pharmaceutical companies), other donors, non-governmental organisations, and governments of developing countries. Funds are intended to be additional to existing aid from multilateral and bilateral agencies and will be managed and disbursed by a new entity, the Global Health Fund. This is a major new form of governance (see box 1).

The Global Health Fund follows a plethora of recent global public-private partnerships to promote wider availability of existing products and stimulate product development as well as initiatives with a broader focus on health systems (see box 2).[2] Debates about these partnerships in the past year are relevant to the proposed global fund; they concern issues such as governance structures and functions, the balance of power between partners, the ability of recipient countries to determine how resources are used, and the balance between support to health systems and funding of health products. International policymakers are looking to the Global Alliance for Vaccines and Immunization (GAVI) for lessons, as this is one of the first such partnerships, with an established fund for disbursing free vaccines and funds to support health systems in some countries with a gross domestic product less than $1000 (£714).

Summary points

A new global health fund is being set up to bridge the funding gap for the control of HIV infection and AIDS, tuberculosis, and malaria

The fund is due to be established this year, but it is not yet clear exactly what it will support and how it will be run

The planning burden on developing countries could be increased by the fund if existing global health initiatives are not consolidated and simplified

Rich countries will need to make large, long term commitments to the fund if developing countries are to be successfully supported to sustain new, expensive treatment and preventive services

Governance

Concerns have been raised about the composition and governance of different global public-private partnerships, including their representative legitimacy, accountability, and competence.[2] In the case of the Global Alliance for Vaccines and Immunization, UN agencies (mainly the WHO and Unicef) have had a dominant role, while commercial representation has been less. Substantial commitments by bilateral donors such as the Netherlands ($100m) and Norway ($125m) have qualified them for seats on the board.[3] Currently, Mali and Bhutan are the developing countries represented on the board; it is unclear how they were selected and how they represent the positions of other developing countries. Only one non-governmental organisation has representation on the board, raising similar questions. While the alliance's structures are well defined and fairly transparent, the processes for selecting some of its members and for decision making are less so.

After a consultation meeting in Geneva in June 2001 there was still "no envisioned structure for the governing board" of the new Global Health Fund,[4] although working papers for the meeting had proposed an executive board of about 12-15 people. It

Box 1: What is the Global Health Fund?

- It is an alliance of partners from UN agencies, developing countries, donor governments, foundations, corporations, and non-governmental organisations
- Its purpose is to mobilise, manage, and disburse additional resources for the control, in the first instance, of HIV infection and AIDS, tuberculosis, and malaria
- It will purchase drugs and vaccines, but there is no consensus on how it will do this or whether it will also support developing countries' health systems
- Pledged contributions (as of 25 June 2001) amount to $200m from the United States, $180m from the United Kingdom, $150m from France, and $100m from the Gates Foundation. These may be one-off contributions

Box 2: Global public-private partnerships and related websites

- Global Alliance for Vaccines and Immunization (www.vaccinealliance.org)
- Stop TB (www.stoptb.org)
- Roll Back Malaria (www.RBM.who.int)
- International Partnership for AIDS in Africa (www.unaids.org/africapartnership)
- European Malaria Vaccine Initiative (www.emvi.org)
- Multilateral Initiative for Malaria (www.nih.gov/fic)
- European Commission Accelerated Action (www.europa.eu.int/comm/development)
- International AIDS Vaccine Initiative (www.iavi.org)

was proposed that this would represent all constituencies and create a governance structure with executive control over all important functions. Frequent shifts in the proposed focus of the fund suggest considerable contention behind the scenes. It may be that decisions about the governance of the fund will reflect the outcome of a struggle between the major players to determine its focus and control its development.

Regard to recipient countries' needs

Another concern is the interface between the global fund and recipient countries. The UK Cabinet Office Performance and Innovation Unit stated: "Products purchased through the fund should be in response to developing countries' requests, be suitable for delivery in developing countries and be cost-effective,"[5] reflecting a concern that national policies and priorities could be distorted rather than supported.[6]

Of the 74 countries eligible for support from the Global Alliance for Vaccines and Immunization, by mid-June 25 had successfully applied for support and 20 of these are eligible for new or underused vaccines. Seventeen are planning to introduce hepatitis B vaccine and seven intend to introduce *Haemophilus influenzae* type b (Hib) vaccine to their national programmes (GAVI Secretariat, unpublished article "Global health initiatives—lessons learned from the early days of the Global Alliance for Vaccines and Immunizations (The Alliance), 23 March 2001"). Tensions exist between a supply driven and demand driven approaches. One of the alliance's targets is that, by 2005, half of the poorest countries with a high burden of disease and adequate delivery systems will have introduced Hib vaccine; however, there is not yet adequate epidemiological evidence in many cases to justify this target. Inevitably, there is a tension between such targets for the introduction of new products and the principles of country ownership and keeping "decision making close to developing countries."[5]

Procedural costs for recipient countries

Minimising planning burdens and transaction costs for countries applying for new funds is also problematic. The Global Alliance for Vaccines and Immunization has tried to limit this "by keeping principles, policies and procedures as simple as possible" (GAVI Secretariat, unpublished article "Global health initiatives"). Nevertheless, the alliance's requirements, and those of a future Global Health Fund, are in addition to other initiatives that are time consuming for recipient countries.

One example is Sector Wide Approach programmes, which are being implemented in 19 countries of sub-Saharan Africa. The principle of these programmes is that donors, instead of funding individual projects or specific disease control programmes, pool funds to support a country's whole health sector.[7] An objective is to reduce the transaction costs for governments in managing multiple donor initiatives, with different reporting and financial management systems. Typically, senior government staff spend many weeks preparing for and participating in annual or biannual review meetings with donors and other partners. However, overstretched government staff are still too often required to manage a range of parallel and externally driven initiatives with different planning cycles and procedures and multiple inputs from local donors and external consultants.

Setting priorities

A potential benefit of the Global Health Fund is that it will focus on three major diseases (HIV infection and AIDS, malaria, and tuberculosis) that affect many poor countries. It could help to coordinate international efforts, reducing potential duplication among the different global public-private partnerships and health initiatives. At the country level, it could also reduce fragmentation by working within and supporting common frameworks and systems. However, experience has shown the difficulties of prioritising and coordinating different aid efforts. Even now, there is some uncertainty as to the fund's focus. In earlier discussions by donor organisations it was proposed to include the major diseases of childhood. More recently, Kofi Annan, the UN secretary general, called it a global AIDS and health fund (WHO, press release at World Health Assembly, Geneva, 22 May 2001), and a recent announcement has sought to clarify that a single fund was being proposed.[4] Competition between priorities, which has been a feature of international health development policies over the past half century, may well continue as other major diseases are proposed for support.

Balancing systems and product support

The need for sustainability and for strengthening health systems, especially in the poorest countries, has almost become a mantra in international policy statements. Most recognise that developing countries' health systems are fragile and yet are central to the delivery of drugs and vaccines. However, there are contested and unanswered questions about improving health systems, not least in relation to the respective roles of the private and public sectors.[8] None of these questions will be resolved in the short term—or in the initial stages of the Global Health Fund. Confusion exists as to whether the fund will support health systems: one report suggests that it should not,[5] whereas another consultation meeting envisaged support for both healthcare commodities and systems.[4]

Again the Global Alliance for Vaccines and Immunization provides useful lessons. For recipient countries that are eligible to receive new vaccines and system support, \$11.9m or 17% of funds has been allocated to strengthening health systems while the rest is targeted for providing new vaccines. The alliance's executive director is reported to have said that an opti-

IFAD/ROBERT GROSSMAN

Regina Nankabirwa, a 40 year old widow, has lost many relatives to AIDS and now cares for 18 children, 10 of whom are orphans. For the Global Health Fund to be of any help to her and thousands like her, it must be able to provide sustainable, long term aid

mum balance might be 60% of funds for new vaccines and 40% for strengthening immunisation services.[6] To encourage recipient countries to meet the targets set, additional funds for strengthening health systems will be released only once the countries have reached higher levels of immunisation coverage. Understandably, donors want to see their funding improving results. Ironically, failure to meet targets could indicate the need for greater support to weak health systems rather than withholding of funds. Governments that qualify for health systems support, have the "liberty to use the support in whatever way that leads to the planned result" (GAVI Secretariat, unpublished article "Global health initiatives"). However, the funds allotted represent only small percentages of countries' projected annual recurrent budgets for health care.

If countries receive extra funds from a global health fund they will have to decide whether to manage such funds separately, in vertical programmes with separate management and financial monitoring systems, or to submerge the additional funds within overall government health budgets. Choosing the latter would reduce transaction costs but may be less attractive to donors and might delay the achievement of targets, reducing performance based rewards. New drugs and vaccines will also place new demands on weak health systems. Seemingly minor changes, such as a change in first line antimalarial treatment from chloroquine to sulphadoxine-pyramethamine, can take years to achieve.[9] Some of the new tools, such as a vaccine to prevent HIV infection, will require new delivery systems, needing much greater levels of investment in health systems. In addition, when new products are introduced commercial companies may well want to attach additional conditions to their use, requiring parallel planning, management, and evaluation systems.[9] High value drugs in the hands of poorly paid and demoralised health workers in the public sector are also liable to leak into uncontrolled private sector channels.

Conclusions

The Global Health Fund is sending out a crucial message that rich countries have a moral and political imperative to do something about three diseases that are wreaking devastation in many poor countries. The fund may underwrite the purchase of drugs, vaccines, and other commodities where markets are too weak to respond and stimulate pharmaceutical companies to conduct research to develop new drugs and vaccines. It is only through a global fund that this kind of concerted global action between major corporate and public sector players can be achieved.

However, there are many challenges in implementing such an initiative. Firstly, the scale of the commitment will need to be sufficient to justify the level of input of international and national policymakers. Estimates of the cost of scaling up existing programmes to tackle the three diseases suggest the need for an additional $9-15bn[10] or $10-20bn[11] annually. Commitments to the fund to date have been small (see box 1). Secondly, considerably greater investment in health systems will be needed to deliver new treatment programmes, whether from the fund or from other sources. Thirdly, if there is a time limit to the international commitment, poor countries that alter their drug policies to incorporate expensive new drugs could be left with unsustainable costs at a future date. Finally, the urgency with which the global fund is now being promoted—to be operational by the end of this year[4]—suggests that the complexities of implementation have been underestimated.

Malaria, tuberculosis, and HIV infection are not new. Now they are finally receiving the degree of attention they deserve, it is important that the goodwill and commitment engendered through this initiative are not lost in failure for lack of attention to making the global fund work well. Achieving good governance for decision making will be the first step.

We thank Mary Starling for helpful comments on earlier drafts of this article.

Competing interests: None declared.

1 Ministry of Foreign Affairs of Japan. G8 communiqué Okinawa 2000. www.mofa.go.jp/policy/economy/summit/2000/communique.html
2 Buse K, Walt G. Global public-private partnerships. Part 11: What are the health issues for global governance? *Bulletin WHO* 2000;78:699-709.
3 Hardon A. Immunisation for all? A critical look at the first GAVI partners meeting. *HAI Europe* 2001;6(1). www.haiweb.org/pubs/hailights/mar2001/index.html (accessed 12 July 2001).
4 *Comprehensive summary of press briefing held at Palais des Nations on 5 June following a two-day consultation on the Global Health and AIDS Fund held in Geneva on 3 and 4 June 2001*. Geneva: United Nations Information Service, 2001.
5 Performance and Innovation Unit. *Tackling the diseases of poverty: Meeting the Okinawa/Millennium targets for HIV/AIDS, tuberculosis and malaria.* London: Performance and Innovation Unit, Cabinet Office, 2001:46-51. www.cabinet-office.gov.uk/innovation/
6 Development today. *Nordic Outlook on Development Assistance, Business & the Environment* 2001;11(8).
7 Cassels A, Janovsky K. Better health in developing countries: Are sector-wide approaches the way of the future? *Lancet* 1998;352:1777-9.
8 Smith E, Brugha R, Zwi A. *Working with private sector providers for better health care, an introductory guide.* London: Options and LSHTM, 2001.
9 Shretta R, Walt G, Brugha R, Snow R. A political analysis of corporate drug donations: the example of Malarone in Kenya. *Health Policy Planning* 2001;16(2):161-70.
10 Performance and Innovation Unit. *Tackling the diseases of poverty: Meeting the Okinawa/Millennium targets for HIV/AIDS, tuberculosis and malaria.* London: Performance and Innovation Unit, Cabinet Office, 2001:25-30. www.cabinet-office.gov.uk/innovation/
11 Sachs J. *The links of public health and economic development. Office of Health Economics 8th annual lecture.* London: Office of Health Economics, 2001. www.ohe.org/sachs%20edited%20OHE%20transcript%20final%20230501doc.pdf

[36]

The New International Health Regulations: An Historic Development for International Law and Public Health

David P. Fidler and Lawrence O. Gostin

The World Health Assembly (WHA) adopted the new International Health Regulations (IHR) on May 23, 2005.[1] The new IHR represent the culmination of a decade-long revision process and an historic development for international law and public health. The new IHR appear at a moment when public health, security, and democracy have become intertwined, addressed at the highest levels of government. The United Nations (UN) Secretary-General Kofi Annan, for example, identified IHR revision as a priority for moving humanity toward "larger freedom."[2] This article analyzes the new IHR and their implications for global health and security in the 21st century.

The IHR and the Revision Process

The WHA instructed the WHO Director-General (DG) to revise the IHR in 1995 because the Regulations did not provide an effective framework for addressing the international spread of disease.[3] Doubts about the IHR's effectiveness had, however, been present long before 1995.[4] The critiques identified the narrow scope of the regulations (applying only to a small number of infectious diseases), the lack of compliance by states, and the absence of a strategy for responding to rapid changes in public health's global economic and technological environments.

The resurgence of infectious diseases in the 1980s and 1990s highlighted the IHR's ineffectiveness. Particularly troublesome were the IHR's inapplicability to the spread of endemic diseases, such as tuberculosis and malaria, and new diseases, such as HIV/AIDS and viral hemorrhagic fevers. Concern also existed that some governments lacked the capacity or political will to report and respond to diseases of international importance. By 1995, WHO understood that the revised IHR would have to break with traditional approaches and construct a novel framework for health and security in an era of accelerating globalization. The innovative framework began to emerge with WHO's first proposal in January 1998, which had a broad scope and permitted the use of non-governmental data sources.[5]

The outbreak of Severe Acute Respiratory Syndrome (SARS) in 2003 accelerated the IHR revision process. WHO viewed its response to SARS as a "roll-out" of ideas being crafted in the IHR revision process.[6] In the wake of WHA resolutions on SARS and the IHR revision process in May 2003,[7] WHO issued a complete proposed text in January 2004, which served as the basis for WHO's regional consultations through the spring and summer of 2004.[8] These consultations led to a revised proposed text, issued in September 2004 for the first intergovernmental negotiations held in November 2004.[9] Following the first negotiating session, the Chair of the negotiations promulgated a "Chair's text" for consideration at the second negotiating session in February 2005.[10] The negotiations were completed in May 2005 prior to the WHA's annual meeting,[11] at which the Assembly adopted the new IHR.

David P. Fidler, J.D., *is Professor of Law and Harry T. Ice Faculty Fellow, Indiana University School of Law - Bloomington and Senior Scholar, Center for Law and the Public's Health, Georgetown and Johns Hopkins Universities.* **Lawrence O. Gostin, J.D., L.L.D., (Hon.),** *is Associate Dean and Professor, Georgetown University Law Center; Professor, Johns Hopkins University; and Director, World Health Organization Collaborating Center on Public Health Law and Human Rights. Dean Gostin is Adjunct Professor and Fellow at Oxford University and a lifetime Member of the Institute of Medicine.*

INDEPENDENT

The New IHR: An Important Development in Global Health Governance

The new IHR contain 66 articles organized into ten parts and include nine annexes (see Table). The purpose of the new IHR is "to prevent, protect against, control and provide a public health response to the international spread of disease in ways that are commensurate with and restricted to public health risks, and which avoid unnecessary interference with international traffic and trade" (Article 2). The IHR seek to balance the state's right to protect its people's health with obligations to take health-protecting actions in ways that do not unnecessarily interfere with international trade and travel.

The new IHR capture this balancing task by providing that "States have...the sovereign right to legislate and to implement legislation in pursuance of their health policies. In doing so they should uphold the purpose of these Regulations" (Article 3.4). By calibrating health and trade interests, the IHR resonate with international trade law under the World Trade Organization (WTO), which also recognizes the state's right to restrict trade for health purposes but limits this right to ensure that restrictions are necessary.[12] The synergies between the new IHR and international trade law emphasize that public health is embedded in an international system that facilitates economic activity through globalized markets. Finding effective ways of balancing public health and international economic activity has become critically important to the success of international trade and international health governance.

The new IHR radically depart from the traditional approach informing the old IHR. The new IHR transform the international legal context in which states will exercise their public health sovereignty in the future. As examined below, the new IHR expand the scope of the IHR's application, incorporate international human rights principles, contain more demanding obligations for states parties to conduct surveillance and response, and establish important new powers for WHO.

The transformative nature of the new IHR connects to growing consensus on the importance of public health to global governance in the 21st century. Over the decade during which the IHR revision unfolded, it became apparent that public health had emerged as critical to virtually every major global governance issue, ranging from national and international security, trade, and economic development, to environmental protection and human rights. The new IHR not only transform the traditional approach to international disease spread but they also represent a politically important opportunity for public health to engage expansively with the international community.

Table

Structure and Content of the New IHR

Part	Articles	Substance Matter
Part I	1-3	Definitions, Purpose, and Scope, Principles and Responsible Authorities
Part II	5-14	Information and Public Health Response
Part III	15-18	Recommendations
Part IV	19-22	Points of Entry
Part V	23-34	Public Health Measures
Part VI	35-39	Health Documents
Part VII	40-41	Charges
Part VIII	42-46	General Provisions
Part IX	47-53	The IHR Roster of Experts, the Emergency Committee, and the Review Committee
Part X	54-66	Final Provisions
Annex 1		Core Capacity Requirements for Surveillance and Response and for Designated Airports, Ports, and Ground Crossings
Annex 2		Decision Instrument for the Assessment and Notification of Events that May Constitute a Public Health Emergency of International Concern
Annex 3		Model Ship Sanitation Control Exemption Certificate/Ship Sanitation Control Certificate
Annex 4		Technical Requirements Pertaining to Conveyances and Conveyance Operators
Annex 5		Specific Measures for Vector-Borne Diseases
Annex 6		Vaccination, Prophylaxis, and Related Certificates
Annex 7		Requirements Concerning Vaccination or Prophylaxis for Specific Diseases
Annex 8		Model Maritime Declaration of Health
Annex 9		Health Part of the Aircraft General Declaration

Scope of the New IHR: An All-Risks Approach

As indicated above, the old IHR applied only to a short list of infectious diseases whose spread was historically associated with trade and travel (e.g., cholera, plague, and yellow fever). The Regulations now encompass public health risks whatever their origin or source (Article 1.1), including: (1) naturally occurring infectious diseases, whether of known or unknown etiological origin; (2) the potential international spread of non-communicable diseases caused by chemical or radiological agents in products moving in international commerce; and (3) suspected intentional or accidental releases of biological, chemical, or radiological substances.

This "all risks" approach embodies an important conceptual shift concerning public health's role in the IHR. Trade calculations determined the old IHR's scope, but risks to human health define the new IHR's scope. The result is a set of rules with more public health legitimacy, flexibility, and adaptability. This expanded public health approach is found throughout the new IHR. Reporting health events, handling epidemiological data, making WHO recommendations, and limiting national health measures apply across the spectrum of health events. The expanded scope creates a more demanding framework than anything that ever appeared in the traditional approach.

Incorporation of Human Rights Principles: Autonomy, Privacy, and Liberty

The traditional approach to international disease spread developed prior to the emergence of international human rights law. The new IHR incorporate human rights principles, recognizing the effects of public health interventions on civil and political rights, such as security of person and freedom of movement.[13]

The New IHR and General Human Rights Principles

The new IHR proclaim that "[t]he implementation of these Regulations shall be with full respect for the dignity, human rights and fundamental freedoms of persons" (Article 3.1). This provision raises the question whether the new IHR conform to existing international human rights principles. For a public health measure to restrict a civil and political right lawfully, the measure must (1) respond to a pressing public or social need; (2) pursue a legitimate aim; (3) be proportionate to the legitimate aim; and (4) be no more restrictive than is required to achieve the purpose sought by restricting the right.[14] The rights-restricting measure must also be implemented in a non-discriminatory manner (International Covenant on Civil and Political Rights (ICCPR), Articles 2.1 and 26). Individuals deprived of liberty must be treated with humanity and respect for the inherent dignity of the human person (ICCPR, Article 10.1).

The new IHR generally reflect the requirements in international human rights law. The Regulations require states parties to identify a public health risk that justifies imposing health measures against persons (Articles 23.2, 31.1, 31.2, and 43.1), apply an appropriate health response to such risk (Articles 23.2, 23.5, 30, 31.2, and 43.2), and implement measures that are no more intrusive or invasive of persons than reasonably available alternatives that would achieve the level of health protection desired (Articles 23.2, 31.2, and 43.1). These disciplines also apply to WHO recommendations made under the new IHR (Article 17). All health measures must be applied in a transparent and non-discriminatory way (Article 42). In addition, states parties must treat travelers with respect for their dignity, human rights and fundamental freedoms and minimize any discomfort or distress associated with health measures, including by treating them with courtesy and respect; taking into consideration their gender, socio-cultural, ethnic, or religious concerns; and providing adequate food, water, accommodation, baggage protection, medical treatment, and means of communication for quarantined or isolated travelers (Article 32).

The extent to which the new IHR incorporate human rights principles means that international human rights law is relevant to the interpretation and implementation of the new IHR.[15] The Regulation's incorporation of human rights will suffer, however, if states parties do not integrate human rights thinking into the operation of their respective public health systems. As human rights problems with HIV/AIDS and other public health concerns suggest, making the new IHR's human rights elements effective will require commitment and vigilance. WHO and states parties should have human rights principles in mind as they build the public health capacities required by the new IHR.

Informed Consent and Privacy

The new IHR also contain provisions on the important human rights areas of informed consent and privacy. States parties cannot apply health measures to travelers without their prior express informed consent, except in situations that warrant compulsory measures (Articles 23.3 and 31.2). The new IHR also reflect the right to privacy by requiring states parties to preserve the confidentiality of personally identifiable information they receive from other states parties or WHO (Article 45.1). States parties and WHO must ensure that disclosure and processing of personal information in order to address a public health risk protects individual privacy (Article 45.2). The Regulations also require WHO to respond to individuals who want to review personally identifiable data WHO possesses about them (Article 45.3).

Although an improvement over the traditional approach in terms of recognizing the importance of informed consent and privacy, problems and questions remain. For example, the new IHR fall short in terms of protecting human rights with regard to compulsory measures applied in the absence of informed consent. The rules relevant to compulsory measures only oblige states parties to apply the least intrusive and invasive measure with respect to medical examinations but not

The new IHR require WHO to share information it receives from non-governmental sources with all states parties and relevant intergovernmental organizations when necessary to enable responses to public health risks.

to vaccinations, other prophylaxis, isolation, or quarantine (Articles 23.2 and 31.2). In addition, the Regulations do not include due process protections necessary when states apply compulsory measures.

In terms of privacy, the new IHR mandate confidential treatment of personal health data by states parties "as required by national law" (Article 45.1). Similarly, the requirement of states parties to protect privacy in addressing public health risks must be fulfilled "in accordance with national law" (Article 45.2). These provisions may make privacy protections under the new IHR relative to disparate levels of national privacy protection rather than subject to internationally recognized privacy standards.

National Public Health Capacities: Surveillance and Response

The new IHR require states parties to develop, strengthen, and maintain core surveillance and response capacities (Articles 5.1 and 13.1 and Annex 1). The old IHR had requirements for public health capabilities only at points of entry and exit. The far-reaching provisions in the new IHR shore up major weaknesses in global strategies created by inadequate national surveillance and response capabilities.

The new IHR reflect, however, states' concerns about sovereignty. States parties do not have to fulfill the capacity obligations until 2012 – five years after the new IHR enter into force in 2007 (Articles 5.1 and 13.1). A state party can obtain a two-year extension by submitting a justified need and an implementation plan to WHO (Articles 5.2 and 13.2); and, in exceptional circumstances, it can request a further two-year extension that the DG has the power to grant or deny (Articles 5.2 and 13.2).

Although the new IHR's provisions on surveillance and response capacities recognize the critical need for capacity building, questions remain about the handling of this issue. The most pressing question concerns the availability of financial and technical resources needed to improve national core capacities, especially in developing and least developed countries. WHO's duties to provide surveillance and response assistance (Articles 5.3, 13.3, and 13.6) do not address its own shortage of funds and personnel. The new IHR also contain no obligations on states parties to provide financial and technical resources to support capacity-building. Although the new IHR urge states parties to provide financial and technical resources, these provisions are either non-binding (Article 13.5) or weak (Article 44.1). Given the financial demands created by other global health problems, such as increasing access to HIV/AIDS treatment[16] and meeting the health-related Millennium Development Goals,[17] the new IHR's silence on how the economic demands of the core capacity objectives will be met is a serious problem for which the new IHR provide no apparent answers or strategies.

Notification Obligations: Reporting Health Events to WHO

The new IHR require states parties to notify WHO of all events within their territories that may constitute a public health emergency of international concern (Article 6), defined as "an extraordinary event which is determined...(i) to constitute a public health risk to other States through the international spread of disease and (ii) to potentially require a coordinated international response" (Article 1.1). A "decision instrument" is used to guide states parties in determining whether a disease event may constitute a public health emergency of international concern (Annex 2) (See Figure).

In keeping with the new IHR's expanded scope, the notification obligations reflect a radically different, and more demanding, approach to addressing the international spread of disease. The notification provisions place a premium on states parties having sufficient surveillance capacities to detect disease incidents, assess them under the decision instrument, and report disease events that may constitute public health emergencies of international concern. As discussed above, whether many WHO member states have, or can develop, surveillance capacities sufficient to support these notification obligations remains a serious question.

Another problem looms for the new IHR's notification requirements. States parties often violated the old IHR by failing to report cases of diseases subject to the Regulations because they feared other countries would implement economically damaging trade or travel restrictions.[18] Will the more expansive and demanding notification requirements in the new IHR avoid the wide-spread non-compliance that undermined the old IHR? Answering this question requires considering the new IHR's approach to information supply and verification, which constitutes its strategy for countering non-compliance with notification obligations.

Figure

Decision Instrument for the Assessment and Notification of Events that May Constitute a Public Health Emergency of International Concern (New IHR, Annex 2)

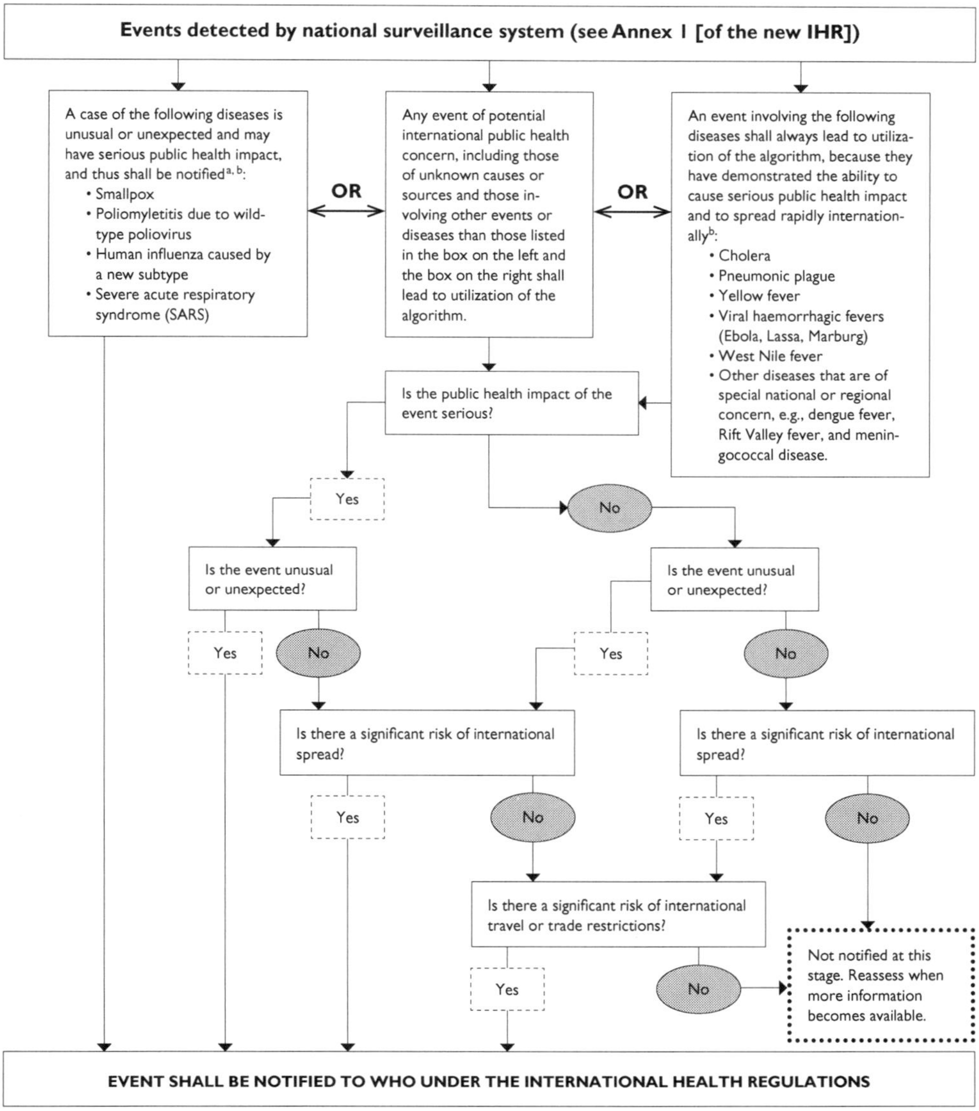

[a] As per WHO case definitions.
[b] The disease list shall be used only for purposes of these Regulations.

Data and Verification Provisions: Unofficial Sources of Information

The old IHR limited WHO to officially using information provided by states parties. This limitation handicapped WHO's ability to respond to disease events if a government refused to notify WHO of incidents, supply needed information, or otherwise cooperate. By contrast, the new IHR allow WHO to "take into account reports from sources other than notifications or consultations" from or with governments and to seek verification of such information from states parties in whose territories the events are allegedly occurring (Articles 9.1 and 10.1). States parties must respond to WHO verification requests (Article 10.2). The new IHR require WHO to share information it receives from non-governmental sources with all states parties and relevant intergovernmental organizations when necessary to enable responses to public health risks (Article 11.1).

From the beginning of the IHR revision process, WHO identified access to non-governmental sources of information as critical to constructing an effective global surveillance system.[19] Harnessing new information technologies, such as the Internet, for global surveillance has been at the heart of WHO's Global Outbreak Alert and Response Network (GOARN). GOARN - a collaborative network of institutions and experts that pools human and technical resources for rapid identification, confirmation, and response to outbreaks of international importance - is centrally important to the new IHR's functioning.[20]

WHO demonstrated the power of having access to non-governmental sources of information during the SARS outbreak.[21] Globalization has significantly decreased the state's ability to control the flow of epidemiological information into and out of its territory, and thus its prospects of keeping serious disease events hidden from international scrutiny. The avian influenza outbreaks in Asia also teach this lesson.

WHO's access to non-governmental information, its authority to request verification from states parties, and its power to share such information with the international community increase incentives for states parties to comply with the notification requirements. Further, the new IHR's information and verification provisions mitigate the consequences of non-compliance with notification obligations because WHO will, in all likelihood, learn of disease events through other sources, triggering the information verification and dissemination processes. The best chance states parties have to minimize adverse economic consequences from disease events is to be transparent and cooperate with WHO and other countries in addressing the threats. In short, the information and verification provisions privilege global health governance over state sovereignty.

The new IHR contain, however, a provision that bears watching to see how it affects the flow of non-governmental information. The Regulations require WHO to share non-governmental information with states parties "and only where it is duly justified may WHO maintain the confidentiality of the source" (Article 9.1). The general requirement on WHO to disclose the source of non-governmental information might deter non-state actors from supplying WHO with information, particularly individuals living under authoritarian regimes. In contrast to its protections for confidentiality of health-related personal information, the Regulations generally require WHO to supply information on persons who are non-official sources of information. The new IHR provide no guidance for determining under what circumstances WHO would be justified in maintaining the confidentiality of non-state sources. Such determinations might involve WHO having to assess the likelihood that governments may punish individuals in their jurisdictions for disseminating disease-related information. Thus, decisions to protect confidentiality of non-state sources will likely involve political controversy for WHO.

Declaration and Recommendation Powers

The new IHR grant two other important powers to WHO that never appeared in the old IHR. First, the new IHR accord WHO the authority to determine whether a disease event constitutes a public emergency of international concern (Article 12). States parties have to notify disease events that *may* constitute such emergencies, but the DG determines if disease events are public health emergencies of international concern. Although the DG must consult with states parties in whose territories disease events are occurring, he or she is not bound to follow their views. In other words, a state party's refusal to cooperate does not bar WHO action.

Second, if the DG determines that a public health emergency of international concern is occurring, then he or she shall issue non-binding, temporary recommendations to states parties on the most appropriate ways to respond (Article 15). The DG may also issue non-binding, standing recommendations on routine, periodic application of health measures for specific, ongoing public health risks (Article 16). The new IHR contain criteria for issuing temporary or standing recommendations (Article 17) and examples of the kinds of measures WHO could recommend (Article 18). These powers allow WHO to provide leadership on what health measures are appropriate from scientific and public health perspectives and on the proper ways to balance health protection with respect for human rights and acknowledgement of trade concerns.

Permissible Health Measures: Limits on National Public Health Interventions

States parties to the new IHR are not legally bound to follow WHO temporary or standing recommendations; but the new IHR contain binding limits on the types of health measures states parties can take against public health risks. These limits are designed to ensure adequate health protection with minimal interference with international traffic and respect for human rights. Generally, states parties cannot require an invasive medical examination, vaccination or other prophylaxis as a condition of entry for any traveler (Article 31.1); nor can a state party require any health document for travelers other than those permitted by the new IHR or recommended by WHO (Article 35). The new IHR also regulate measures states parties can apply to ships, aircraft, goods, and containers (Articles 25-29, 33-34, and 41) and harmonize the types of health documents required from ships and aircraft (Articles 37-39).

The new IHR permit states parties to apply health measures that achieve the same or greater level of health protection than WHO recommendations or that are otherwise prohibited by the IHR (Article 43.1). Such health measures must be based on scientific principles, available scientific evidence, relevant guidance or advice from WHO, and cannot be more restrictive of international traffic or more invasive or intrusive to persons than reasonably available alternatives that would achieve the level of health protection sought (Articles 43.1-43.2).

These provisions resemble the approach taken to health-protecting measures in WTO agreements, such as the Agreement on the Application of Sanitary and Phytosanitary Measures (SPS Agreement). Unlike the SPS Agreement, however, the new IHR do not have a strong enforcement mechanism if states parties fail to comply with the obligations on permissible health measures. Enforcement of the SPS Agreement benefits from the mandatory WTO dispute settlement process. Dispute settlement in the new IHR is essentially voluntary (Article 56). Failure by states to comply with the old IHR undermined their effectiveness. The lack of an enforcement mechanism in the new IHR may mean that non-compliance with rules on permissible health measures becomes a problem.

Rejections and Reservations

As a treaty, the new IHR cannot legally bind states unless they consent to be bound. Therefore, states can reject the new IHR (Article 61) or formulate reservations to provisions to which they refuse to be bound (Article 62). The changes made by, and the more demanding nature of, the new IHR may create incentives for states to reject the revised Regulations or formulate reservations. A reservation becomes effective (1) if less than one-third of relevant states object to the reservation (Article 62.5); or (2) if at least one-third of relevant states object to the reservation, and the reserving state does not withdraw the reservation, when the WHO by majority vote approves the reservation as compatible with the IHR's object and purpose (Article 62.9). Rejections and reservations have to be made within 18 months of the date of the new IHR's adoption (Article 59.1). The United States has already indicated that it will submit a "narrowly tailored" reservation providing that it will implement the IHR in a manner consistent with American federalism.[22] The process of making and reviewing reservations bears monitoring because of the potential for reservations to weaken the new IHR's universal application.

Political Controversies in the IHR Reform Process

Three political conflicts emerged during the negotiations to revise the IHR that threatened to stall or even prevent final adoption: conflicts of law with other international regimes; the role of WHO in combating biological, chemical, and nuclear terrorism; and the relationship of Taiwan to the new IHR regime.

Conflicts of International Law

WHO member states expressed concerns that the expanded scope of the new IHR would bring the Regulations into conflict with other international agencies and treaties that addressed cross-border health risks – e.g., the International Atomic Energy Agency (nuclear accidents);[23] the World Trade Organization (health measures that restrict international trade);[24] and the Codex Alimentarius Commission (food standards and guidelines to protect consumer health and promote trade in safe products). WHO addressed these concerns by demonstrating that few conflicts existed; amending the negotiating text to remove the small number of possible conflicts;[25] and adding provisions to facilitate cooperation and coordination between WHO and other international organizations (e.g., Articles 14, 17(f), 57.1).

Biological, Chemical, and Nuclear Terrorism

How the revised IHR would apply to suspected intentional releases of biological, chemical, and radiological agents proved highly controversial. Negotiating drafts required states parties to share information with WHO if they had evidence of a suspected intentional release of a biological, chemical, or radiological agent.

This proposal reflected the belief that appropriate public health responses were needed whether the risk was naturally occurring, accidental, or intentionally caused. However, the proposal was politically charged as it touched on issues of national and international security related to weapons of mass destruction. Concern was expressed that WHO's public health mission could be compromised if it had to investigate whether states had violated arms control treaties or UN Security Council resolutions.[26]

Less clear is whether the new IHR might embroil WHO in the politics of national and international security to the detriment of its core public health functions. Although it makes some experts uncomfortable, the potential for terrorism involving weapons of mass destruction connects public health to security concerns.

The new IHR handle these concerns awkwardly, reflecting difficult negotiations. The new IHR do not contain any specific requirement on information-sharing concerning suspected intentional releases. What remains is a weaker provision: "If a State Party has evidence of an unexpected or unusual public health event within its territory, irrespective of origin or source, which may constitute a public health emergency of international concern, it shall provide WHO with all relevant public health information" (Article 7). However, this article, combined with the expanded scope, makes clear that the new IHR apply to a suspected intentional release of a biological, chemical, and radiological agent. The understanding issued by the United States that the new IHR apply to all "health threats - chemical, biological, and radiological - and all causes and modes of events - regardless whether they are naturally occurring, accidental, or deliberate" is correct.[27]

Less clear is whether the new IHR might embroil WHO in the politics of national and international security to the detriment of its core public health functions. Although it makes some experts uncomfortable, the potential for terrorism involving weapons of mass destruction connects public health to security concerns. The anthrax attacks in the United States in 2001 demonstrated that public health responses to bioterrorism are critical aspects of national and homeland security. The new IHR recognize this unfortunate reality.

At the same time, the new IHR limit WHO's role to public health activities in these security-sensitive contexts. The new IHR's purpose states that the Regulations involve prevention, protection, control, and response activities concerning the international spread of disease in ways commensurate with, and restricted to, public health risks (Article 2). Provision of information under Article 7 is no different than the provision of information for any disease event or public health risk to which the new IHR apply, meaning that WHO would be focused on the health risk only. "Health measure" is defined to exclude law enforcement or security measures (Article 1.1). Although information WHO gathers and analyzes would be important in assessments of whether a state violated obligations under arms control agreements or Security Council resolutions, the new IHR do not put WHO in the position of making such assessments.

Despite these attempts to contain WHO's role in situations involving possible violations of arms control and other security obligations, the new IHR do not settle the controversies about WHO's relationship to security concerns related to weapons of mass destruction. Following recommendations made by a high-level panel of experts[28] and the UN Secretary-General,[29] the Security Council could decide to intervene in a situation involving naturally occurring diseases or a suspected intentional release of biological, chemical, or radiological agents in a way that involves WHO in politically difficult circumstances. Whether such an intervention by the Security Council would be warranted is not an issue that the new IHR could address.

The Taiwan Problem

The standoff between China and Taiwan entered the politics of the IHR revision process. Following the SARS outbreak in 2003, during which Taiwan required assistance from WHO, Taiwan advocated for being included in the new IHR regime. Taiwan argued that the new IHR should have universal geographical coverage to be effective in the era of globalized disease threats. During the negotiations, China refused to allow Taiwan to participate formally in the new IHR.

What remains of this controversy is found in the principle that "[t]he implementation of these Regulations shall be guided by the goal of their universal application for the protection of all people of the world from the international spread of disease" (Article 3.3). Taiwan interprets this provision as "a basis for Taiwan to make contact with the WHO directly without China's interference."[30] China disagrees and points to a memorandum it negotiated with WHO in May 2005 that requires China's consent before WHO has any direct contact with Taiwan.[31] In short, the new IHR do not resolve the Taiwan-China problem, nor could the IHR revision process be expected to produce *rapprochement* between Taiwan and China.

The New IHR and the Future of Global Health Governance

The new IHR contain an international legal regime unprecedented in the history of the relationship between international law and public health. The revised Regulations promise to become a centerpiece for global health governance in the 21st century. As the UN Secretary-General's support for the IHR revision illustrates,[32] the new IHR have global governance significance far beyond anything contemplated under, or achieved by, the old IHR. Whether the issue involves international security, trade, economic development, environmental degradation, UN reform, or human rights, policy makers and experts have identified public health as a central governance challenge nationally and internationally in the 21st century. The transformational nature of the new IHR create a regime that has the potential to contribute significantly to the general global governance mission of improving national and international health. The Regulations provide a framework that supports not only improved international cooperation on health but also the strengthening of national health systems, producing more robust health governance horizontally among states and vertically within them.

The new IHR's novelty should not, however, obscure hard realities facing its future. WHO was systematically using non-governmental surveillance information from GOARN's establishment in 1998, well before the IHR revision process was completed; and this strategy would have continued whether or not the new IHR had been adopted. More difficult issues arise with producing effective responses to identified public health risks. For decades, WHO has issued recommendations on many public health problems; but the mixed record of state compliance with WHO guidance should temper enthusiasm for the new IHR's recommendation provisions. The political controversies that surrounded WHO's more aggressive actions during SARS may deter WHO from taking similar actions under the new IHR. Laments about the erosion of global and local public health capabilities suggest that WHO's decades-long effort to improve health conditions in developing countries has also met with only qualified success. The new IHR will not change this dynamic overnight, particularly when the Regulations generate no fresh financial resources to support capacity-building. Compliance with international legal restrictions against the implementation of health measures that unnecessarily restrict trade or infringe on human rights has not, in the past, been stellar, as illustrated by how non-compliance helped destroy the old IHR's effectiveness. Whether the quantity and quality of compliance with the new IHR's rules on health measures are better will not depend on any improved enforcement mechanism because the Regulations do not create one.

The new IHR are no "magic bullet" for global health problems. Previous transformations in international law's relationship with public health have, over time, atrophied into insignificance. The history of the old IHR tells just such a story. Further, the new IHR's relevance to some pressing global health problems, such as increasing access to HIV/AIDS treatment in the developing world or stemming the "brain drain" of health workers from developing to developed countries,[33] is not apparent. Controversies and problems surrounding the threat of avian influenza also suggest that the new IHR do not cut through the tangled knot of very hard political, economic, scientific, and public health choices governments must make to address this public health emergency of international concern.

The new IHR are the product of a decade of work by WHO and its member states, and the revised Regulations have been designed to be a robust governance framework far into the future. Harvesting the new IHR's benefits for global health requires understanding not only the difficulties this task faces but also the potential the Regulations represent. At present, this potential exists mainly on paper, which is why the implementation phase is critical. WHO needs to approach implementation with the energy and vision it demonstrated during SARS. The seminal achievement of the new IHR constitutes only the end of the beginning. The hard work of making this transformative revision of global health governance effective for individuals, states, and the international community now begins.

References

1. World Health Assembly, *Revision of the International Health Regulations*, WHA58.3 (May 23, 2005).
2. UN Secretary-General, *In Larger Freedom: Towards Development, Security, and Human Rights for All: Report of the Secretary-General*, A/59/2005 (March 21, 2005).
3. World Health Assembly, *Revision and Updating of the International Health Regulations*, WHA48.7 (May 12, 1995).
4. P. Dorelle, "Old Plagues in the Jet Age: International Aspects of Present and Future Control of Communicable Diseases," *Chronicle of the World Health Organization* 23 (1969): 103-111; E. Roelsgaard, "Health Regulations and International Travel," *Chronicle of the World Health Organization* 28 (1974): 265-268; B. Velimirovic, "Do We Still Need International Health Regulations?" *Journal of Infectious Diseases* 133 (1976): 478-482.
5. World Health Organization, *Provisional Draft of the International Health Regulations* (Geneva, Switzerland: World Health Organization, January 1998).

INDEPENDENT

6. World Health Organization, *Severe Acute Respiratory Syndrome (SARS): Status of the Outbreak and Lessons for the Immediate Future* (Geneva, Switzerland: World Health Organization, 2003).
7. World Health Assembly, *Severe Acute Respiratory Syndrome (SARS)*, WHA56.29 (May 28, 2003); World Health Assembly, *Revision of the International Health Regulations*, WHA56.28 (May 28, 2003).
8. World Health Organization, *International Health Regulations: Working Paper for Regional Consultations*, IGWG/IHR/Working paper/12.2003 (January 12, 2004); L. O. Gostin, "International Infectious Disease Law: Revision of the World Health Organization's International Health Regulations," *JAMA* 291 (2004): 2623-2627.
9. World Health Organization, *Review and Approval of Proposed Amendments to the International Health Regulations: Draft Revision*, A/IHR/IGWG/3 (September 30, 2004).
10. World Health Organization, *Review and Approval of Proposed Amendments to the International Health Regulations: Proposal by the Chair*, A/IHR/IGWG/2/2 (January 24, 2005).
11. World Health Organization, *Revision of the International Health Regulations: Note by the Secretariat*, A58/4 (May 16, 2005).
12. World Health Organization and World Trade Organization, *WTO Agreements & Public Health: A Joint Study by the WHO and the WTO Secretariat* (Geneva, Switzerland: World Health Organization, 2002).
13. International Covenant on Civil and Political Rights, *United Nations Treaty Series* 171 (December 19, 1966): 999.
14. UN Economic and Social Council, UN Sub-Commission on Prevention of Discrimination and Protection of Minorities, *Siracusa Principles on the Limitation and Derogation of Provisions in the International Covenant on Civil and Political Rights*, UN Doc. E/CN.4/1985/4, Annex, 1985.
15. Vienna Convention on the Law of Treaties, *United Nations Treaty Series* 331 (May 23, 1969): 1155.
16. World Health Organization, The 3 by 5 Initiative, *available at* <http://www.who.int/3by5/en/> (last visited December 12, 2005).
17. World Health Organization, *Achievement of Health-Related Millennium Development Goals: Report by the Secretariat*, A58/5 (May 13, 2005).
18. D. P. Fidler, *International Law and Infectious Diseases* (Oxford, England: Clarendon Press, 1999).
19. World Health Organization, *The International Response to Epidemics and Applications of the International Health Regulations: Report of a WHO Informal Consultation*, WHO/EMC/IHR/96.1 (December 11-14, 1995).
20. World Health Organization, *Global Defense Against the Infectious Disease Threat* (Geneva, Switzerland: World Health Organization, 2002).
21. D. P. Fidler, *SARS, Governance, and the Globalization of Disease* (Basingstoke, England: Palgrave Macmillan, 2004).
22. *Statement for the Record by the Government of the United States of America Concerning the World Health Organization's Revised International Health Regulations*, May 23, 2005. Press Release, U.S. Mission to the United Nations in Geneva, *at* <http://www.us-mission.ch/Press2005/0523IHRs.htm> (last visited January 9, 2006).
23. Convention on Assistance in the Case of a Nuclear Accident or Radiological Emergency, September 26, 1986, 1457 *United Nations Treaty Series* 133; Convention on Nuclear Safety, July 5, 1994, 1963 *United Nations Treaty Series* 317.
24. General Agreement on Tariffs and Trade, April 15, 1994, in World Trade Organization, *The Legal Texts: The Results of the Uruguay Round of Multilateral Trade Negotiations* (Cambridge, England: Cambridge University Press, 1999): 424-492; Agreement on the Application of Sanitary and Phytosanitary Measures, April 15, 1994, in World Trade Organization, *The Legal Texts: The Results of the Uruguay Round of Multilateral Trade Negotiations* (Cambridge, England: Cambridge University Press, 1999): 59-72.
25. World Health Organization, *Review and Approval of Proposed Amendments to the International Health Regulations: Relations with Other International Instruments*. A/IHR/IGWG/INF. DOC./1 (September 30, 2004).
26. G. S. Pearson, *The UN Secretary-General's High Level Panel: Biological Weapons Related Issues* (Strengthening the Biological Weapons Convention, Review Conference Paper No. 14) (May 2005).
27. *Supra* note 22.
28. UN Secretary-General's High-Level Panel on Threats, Challenges, and Change, *A More Secure World: Our Shared Responsibility* (New York, New York: United Nations, 2004).
29. *Supra*, note 2.
30. J. Rickards, "Taiwan-WHO Ties Improving, Officials Say," *China Post*, May 26, 2005 *available at* <http://www.chinapost.com.tw/archive/detail.asp?cat=1&id=62934> (last visited January 9, 2006).
31. X. Yen, "Taiwan's WHO Bid Has No Legal Basis," *China Daily*, May 31, 2005, at 4.
32. See UN Secretary-General, Press Release, *World Health Assembly's Revised Regulations "Bold and Necessary Step" to Protect Global Public Health, Says Secretary-General* (May 23, 2005) SG/SM/9886, SAG/365.
33. World Health Assembly, *International Migration of Health Personnel: A Challenge for Health Systems in Developing Countries*, WHA58.17 (May 25, 2005).

Name Index